BASIC DOCUMENTS
ON
AFRICAN AFFAIRS

BASIC DOCUMENTS
ON
AFRICAN AFFAIRS

EDITED BY

IAN BROWNLIE

Fellow of Wadham College
Oxford

OXFORD
AT THE CLARENDON PRESS
1971

Oxford University Press, Ely House, London W. 1

GLASGOW NEW YORK TORONTO MELBOURNE WELLINGTON
CAPE TOWN SALISBURY IBADAN NAIROBI DAR ES SALAAM LUSAKA ADDIS ABABA
BOMBAY CALCUTTA MADRAS KARACHI LAHORE DACCA
KUALA LUMPUR SINGAPORE HONG KONG TOKYO

PRINTED IN GREAT BRITAIN
AT THE UNIVERSITY PRESS, OXFORD
BY VIVIAN RIDLER
PRINTER TO THE UNIVERSITY

PREFACE

It is believed that this collection of documents will fill a gap in the literature. The book could quite easily have been much longer but it was thought best to provide a volume which would be handy to use. Obviously, such a selection of material must rest on empirical grounds. The intention has been to include the individually important items, items which constitute a chronicle of certain developments, and items which suggest and illustrate significant themes. The emphasis has been upon international relations rather than the internal politics of individual states. However, issues concerning civil war and secession, racial discrimination in Southern Africa, and economic development necessarily impinge on both national and international affairs, not least in the African setting. A deliberate limitation has been the exclusion of material on the African involvement in the Arab-Israeli conflict and on the position of Arab North Africa in relation to Arab nationalism. The exclusion rests upon considerations of space and the opinion that a useful compendium should not try to be encyclopedic.

The policy has been to present the contemporary yet persistent issues and not to give room to the very recent but merely spasmodic happening. The raising of the question of a 'dialogue' with South Africa appears to be evidence of a desire for economic relations with South Africa on the part of certain states. Malawi is not the only African state to have entered into trade relations with South Africa recently. The Lusaka Manifesto (Appendix I) contains the considerations of principle concerning relations with South Africa. The reader should be reminded of the not insubstantial element of backsliding in the ranks of Black African states, evidence of which is not presented by the documents. Appendix III, on the Simonstown Agreement, represents a late editorial decision to provide material on a fairly specialized aspect of the arms embargo relating to South Africa.

The editor is grateful to the American Society of International Law and the editor of the Society's publication *International Legal Materials* for permission to include documents appearing in this collection at pp. 25, 30, 36, 40, 46, 196, 261, and 269.

IAN BROWNLIE

Oxford
21 *June* 1971

CONTENTS

PART THREE

NON-PROLIFERATION OF NUCLEAR WEAPONS

PART FOUR

TERRITORIAL PROBLEMS

PART FIVE

SELF-DETERMINATION AND RACIAL
DISCRIMINATION IN SOUTHERN AFRICA

PART SIX

RELATIONS WITH NON-AFRICAN POWERS

PART SEVEN
THE SITUATION IN THE CONGO
1960–1964

PART ONE

AFRICAN INTERNATIONAL ORGANIZATIONS

I. ORGANIZATION OF AFRICAN UNITY

THE system of the United Nations Charter makes provision for the existence of regional arrangements or agencies in Chapter VIII. Events concerning Guatemala in 1953 and Cuba in 1962 have highlighted the problem of defining the limits of regional action purporting to have as its purpose the maintenance of international peace and security and the relations of regional organs with the Security Council of the United Nations. Unlike the Organization of American States the O.A.U. makes no provision for regional enforcement measures comparable to those powers which the Security Council has under Articles 41 and 42 of the Charter of the United Nations. The emphasis is on co-operation and peaceful settlement of disputes within the O.A.U. There is some reference to defence, however, in Article II (1) (c) and there is provision for a Defence Commission in Article XX. In practice the militant aspect of the organization has been confined to support for liberation movements by the provision of finance: see below, p. 371.

The background to the Organization of African Unity is to be found in Legum, *Pan-Africanism*, 1962; revised edition, 1965. The Charter of the Organization was adopted by a conference of Heads of States and Governments in Addis Ababa on 25 May 1963. Thirty-two States signed the Charter: this total includes all African States with the exception of (a) States not then independent (Gambia, Malawi, Zambia); (b) the Republic of South Africa; and (c) Spain and Portugal, represented on the continent by possessions categorised as non-self-governing by resolutions of the United Nations General Assembly on the basis of the Declaration set out below, p. 366.

See further Hazlewood (ed.), *African Integration and Disintegration*, 1967. Aspects of the work of the O.A.U. are discussed by Wallerstein, *International Organization*, vol. 20 (1966), p. 774; Nora McKeon, *International Affairs*, vol. 42 (1966), p. 390; Touval, *International Organization*, vol. 21 (1967), p. 102; and Cervenka, *The Organisation of African Unity and Its Charter*, 2nd edn., 1969. The settlement of boundary and other disputes is dealt with further in Part IV. See further Padelford, *International Organization*, vol. 18 (1964), p. 521; Boutros–Ghali, *International Conciliation*, no. 546, 1964; and Elias, *American Journal of International Law*, vol. 59 (1965), p. 243.

1. *Charter of the O.A.U.*

The text is published in *United Nations Treaty Series*, vol. 479, p. 39. The Charter came into force on 13 September 1963. There are forty-one member states.

TEXT

We, the Heads of African and Malagasy States and Governments assembled in the City of Addis Ababa, Ethiopia;

CONVINCED that it is the inalienable right of all people to control their own destiny;

CONSCIOUS of the fact that freedom, equality, justice and dignity are essential objectives for the achievement of the legitimate aspirations of the African peoples;

CONSCIOUS of our responsibility to harness the natural and human resources of our continent for the total advancement of our peoples in spheres of human endeavour;

INSPIRED by a common determination to promote understanding among our peoples and co-operation among our States in response to the aspirations of our peoples for brotherhood and solidarity, in a larger unity transcending ethnic and national differences;

CONVINCED that, in order to translate this determination into a dynamic force in the cause of human progress, conditions for peace and security must be established and maintained;

DETERMINED to safeguard and consolidate the hard-won independence as well as the sovereignty and territorial integrity of our States, and to resist neo-colonialism in all its forms;

DEDICATED to the general progress of Africa;

PERSUADED that the Charter of the United Nations and the Universal Declaration of Human Rights, to the principles of which we reaffirm our adherence, provide a solid foundation for peaceful and positive co-operation among states;

DESIROUS that all African States should henceforth unite so that the welfare and well-being of their peoples can be assured;

RESOLVED to reinforce the links between our States by establishing and strengthening common institutions;

HAVE agreed to the present Charter.

Establishment

Article I

1. The High Contracting Parties do by the present Charter establish an Organization to be known as the '*Organization of African Unity*.
2. The Organization shall include the Continental African States, Madagascar and other Islands surrounding Africa.

Purposes

Article II

1. The Organization shall have the following purposes:
   (*a*) To promote the unity and solidarity of the African States;
   (*b*) To co-ordinate and intensify their collaboration and efforts to achieve a better life for the peoples of Africa;
   (*c*) To defend their sovereignty, their territorial integrity and independence;
   (*d*) To eradicate all forms of colonialism from Africa; and
   (*e*) To promote international co-operation, having due regard to the Charter of the United Nations and the Universal Declaration of Human Rights.

2. To these ends, the Member States shall co-ordinate and harmonize their general policies, especially in the following fields:
   (*a*) Political and diplomatic co-operation;
   (*b*) Economic co-operation, including transport and communications;
   (*c*) Educational and cultural co-operation;
   (*d*) Health, sanitation, and nutritional co-operation;
   (*e*) Scientific and technical co-operation; and
   (*f*) Co-operation for defence and security.

Principles

Article III

The Member States, in pursuit of the purposes stated in Article II, solemnly affirm and declare their adherence to the following principles:

1. The sovereign equality of all Member States;

2. Non-interference in the internal affairs of States;

3. Respect for the sovereignty and territorial integrity of each State and for its inalienable right to independent existence;

4. Peaceful settlement of disputes by negotiation, mediation, conciliation or arbitration;

5. Unreserved condemnation, in all its forms, of political assassination as well as of subversive activities on the part of neighbouring States or any other State;

6. Absolute dedication to the total emancipation of the African territories which are still dependent;

7. Affirmation of a policy of non-alignment with regard to all blocs.

Membership

Article IV

Each independent sovereign African State shall be entitled to become a Member of the Organization.

Rights and Duties of Member States

Article V

All Member States shall enjoy equal rights and have equal duties.

Article VI

The Member States pledge themselves to observe scrupulously the principles enumerated in Article III of the present Charter.

Institutions

Article VII

The Organization shall accomplish its purposes through the following principal institutions:

1. The Assembly of Heads of State and Government;

2. The Council of Ministers;

3. The General Secretariat;

4. The Commission of Mediation, Conciliation and Arbitration.

The Assembly of Heads of State and Government

Article VIII

The Assembly of Heads of State and Government shall be the supreme organ of the Organization. It shall, subject to the provisions of this Charter, discuss matters of common concern to Africa with a view to co-ordinating and harmonizing the general policy of the Organization. It may in addition review the structure, functions and acts of all the organs and any specialized agencies which may be created in accordance with the present Charter.

Article IX

The Assembly shall be composed of the Heads of State and Government or their duly accredited representatives and it shall meet at least once a year. At the request of any Member State and on approval by a two-thirds majority of the Member States, the Assembly shall meet in extraordinary session.

Article X

1. Each Member State shall have one vote.

2. All resolutions shall be determined by a two-thirds majority of the Members of the Organization.

3. Questions of procedure shall require a simple majority. Whether or not a question is one of procedure shall be determined by a simple majority of all Member States of the Organization.

4. Two-thirds of the total membership of the Organization shall form a quorum at any meeting of the Assembly.

Article XI

The Assembly shall have the power to determine its own rules of procedure.

The Council of Ministers

Article XII

1. The Council of Ministers shall consist of Foreign Ministers or such other ministers as are designated by the Governments of Member States. 2. The Council of Ministers shall meet at least twice a year. When requested by any Member State and approved by two-thirds of all Member States, it shall meet in extraordinary session.

Article XIII

1. The Council of Ministers shall be responsible to the Assembly of Heads of State and Government. It shall be entrusted with the responsibility of preparing conferences of the Assembly. 2. It shall take cognisance of any matter referred to it by the Assembly. It shall be entrusted with the implementation of the decisions of the Assembly of Heads of State and Government. It shall co-ordinate inter-African co-operation in accordance with the instructions of the Assembly and in conformity with Article II (2) of the present Charter.

Article XIV

1. Each Member State shall have one vote.

2. All resolutions shall be determined by a simple majority of the members of the Council of Ministers.

3. Two-thirds of the total membership of the Council of Ministers shall form a quorum for any meeting of the Council.

Article XV

The Council shall have the power to determine its own rules of procedure.

General Secretariat

Article XVI

There shall be an Administrative Secretary-General of the Organization, who shall be appointed by the Assembly of Heads of State and Government. The Administrative Secretary-General shall direct the affairs of the Secretariat.

Article XVII

There shall be one or more Assistant Secretaries-General of the Organization, who shall be appointed by the Assembly of Heads of State and Government.

Article XVIII

The functions and conditions of services of the Secretary-General, of the Assistant Secretaries-General and other employees of the Secretariat shall be governed by the provisions of this Charter and the regulations approved by the Assembly of Heads of State and Government.

1. In the performance of their duties the Administrative Secretary-General and his staff shall not seek or receive instructions from any government or from any other authority external to the Organization. They shall refrain from any action which might reflect on their position as international officials responsible only to the Organization.

2. Each member of the Organization undertakes to respect the exclusive character of the responsibilities of the Administrative Secretary-General and the Staff and not seek to influence them in the discharge of their responsibilities.

Commission of Mediation, Conciliation, and Arbitration

Article XIX

Member States pledge to settle all disputes among themselves by peaceful means and, to this end, decide to establish a Commission of Mediation, Conciliation and Arbitration, the composition of which and conditions of service shall be defined by a separate Protocol to be approved by the Assembly of Heads of State and Government. Said Protocol shall be regarded as forming an integral part of the present Charter.

Specialized Commissions

Article XX

The Assembly shall establish such Specialized Commissions as it may deem necessary, including the following:

1. Economic and Social Commission;

2. Educational and Cultural Commission;

3. Health, Sanitation, and Nutrition Commission;

4. Defence Commission;

5. Scientific, Technical and Research Commission.

Article XXI

Each Specialized Commission referred to in Article XX shall be composed of the Ministers concerned or other Ministers or Plenipotentiaries designated by the Governments of the Member States.

Article XXII

The functions of the Specialized Commissions shall be carried out in accordance with the provisions of the present Charter and of the regulations approved by the Council of Ministers.

The Budget

Article XXIII

The budget of the Organization prepared by the Administrative Secretary-General shall be approved by the Council of Ministers. The budget shall be provided by contributions from Member States in accordance with the scale of assessment of the United Nations; provided, however, that no Member State shall be assessed an amount exceeding twenty per cent of the yearly regular budget of the Organization. The Member States agree to pay their respective contributions regularly.

Signature and Ratification of Charter

Article XXIV

1. This Charter shall be open for signature to all independent sovereign African States and shall be ratified by the signatory States in accordance with their respective constitutional processes.

2. The original instrument, done if possible in African languages, in English and French, all texts being equally authentic, shall be deposited

with the Government of Ethiopia which shall transmit certified copies thereof to all independent sovereign African States.

3. Instruments of ratification shall be deposited with the Government of Ethiopia, which shall notify all signatories of each such deposit.

Entry into Force
Article XXV

This Charter shall enter into force immediately upon receipt by the Government of Ethiopia of the instruments of ratification from two-thirds of the signatory States.

Registration of the Charter
Article XXVI

This Charter shall, after due ratification, be registered with the Secretariat of the United Nations through the Government of Ethiopia in conformity with Article 102 of the Charter of the United Nations.

Interpretation of the Charter
Article XXVII

Any question which may arise concerning the interpretation of this Charter shall be decided by a vote of two-thirds of the Assembly of Heads of State and Government, of the Organization.

Adhesion and Accession
Article XXVIII

1. Any independent sovereign African State may at any time notify the Administrative Secretary-General of its intention to adhere or accede to this Charter.

2. The Administrative Secretary-General shall, on receipt of such notification, communicate a copy of it to all the Member States. Admission shall be decided by a simple majority of the Member States. The decision of each Member State shall be transmitted to the Administrative Secretary-General, who shall, upon receipt of the required number of votes, communicate the decision to the State concerned.

Miscellaneous
Article XXIX

The working languages of the Organization and all its institutions shall be, if possible African languages, English and French.

Article XXX

The Administrative Secretary-General may accept on behalf of the Organization gifts, bequests and other donations made to the Organization, provided that this is approved by the Council of Ministers.

Article XXXI

The Council of Ministers shall decide on the privileges and immunities to be accorded to the personnel of the Secretariat in the respective territories of the Member States.

Cessation of Membership

Article XXXII

Any State which desires to renounce its membership shall forward a written notification to the Administrative Secretary-General. At the end of one year from the date of such notification, if not withdrawn, the Charter shall cease to apply with respect to the renouncing State, which shall thereby cease to belong to the Organization.

Amendment to the Charter

Article XXXIII

This Charter may be amended or revised if any Member State makes a written request to the Administrative Secretary-General to that effect; provided, however, that the proposed amendment is not submitted to the Assembly for consideration until all the Member States have been duly notified of it and a period of one year has elapsed. Such an amendment shall not be effective unless approved by at least two-thirds of all the Member States.

IN FAITH WHEREOF, We, the Heads of African State and Government, have signed this Charter.

2. *Protocol of the Commission of Mediation, Conciliation and Arbitration*

This is in form a Protocol to the Charter of the O.A.U.: see Article XIX of the Charter. It was signed at Cairo on 21 July 1964 by thirty-three states and provides the background to the constructive work of the O.A.U. in the settlement or amelioration of disputes between member states, in spite of the fact that the work was done by the Council of Ministers and other bodies since the Commission did not have its first meeting until 11 December 1967: *Africa Report*, February 1968, p. 25.

The text of the Protocol appears in the O.A.U. publication entitled *Charter, Protocol of the Commission of Mediation, Conciliation and Arbitration, Functions and Regulations of the General Secretariat*, Addis Ababa, 1965.

TEXT

PART I

ESTABLISHMENT AND ORGANIZATION

Article I

The Commission of Mediation, Conciliation, and Arbitration established by Article XIX of the Charter of the Organization of African Unity shall be governed by the provisions of the present Protocol.

Article II

1. The Commission shall consist of twenty-one members elected by the Assembly of Heads of State and Government.

2. No two Members shall be nationals of the same State.

3. The Members of the Commission shall be persons with recognized professional qualifications.

4. Each Member State of the Organization of African Unity shall be entitled to nominate two candidates.

5. The Administrative Secretary-General shall prepare a list of the candidates nominated by Member States and shall submit it to the Assembly of Heads of State and Government.

Article III

1. Members of the Commission shall be elected for a term of five years and shall be eligible for re-election.

2. Members of the Commission whose terms of office have expired shall remain in office until the election of a new Commission.

3. Notwithstanding the expiry of their terms of office, Members shall complete any proceedings in which they are already engaged.

Article IV

Members of the Commission shall not be removed from office except by decision of the Assembly of Heads of State and Government, by a two-thirds majority of the total membership, on the grounds of inability to perform the functions of their office or of proved misconduct.

Article V

1. Whenever a vacancy occurs in the Commission, it shall be filled in conformity with the provisions of Article II.

2. A Member of the Commission elected to fill a vacancy shall hold office for the unexpired term of the Member he has replaced.

Article VI

1. A President and two Vice-Presidents shall be elected by the Assembly of Heads of State and Government from among the Members of the Commission who shall each hold office for five years. The President and the two Vice-Presidents shall not be eligible for re-election as such officers.

2. The President and the two Vice-Presidents shall be full-time members of the Commission, while the remaining eighteen shall be part-time Members.

Article VII

The President and the two Vice-Presidents shall constitute the Bureau of the Commission and shall have the responsibility of consulting with the parties as regards the appropriate mode of settling the dispute in accordance with this Protocol.

Article VIII

The salaries and allowances of the Members of the Bureau and the remuneration of the other Members of the Commission shall be determined in accordance with the provisions of the Charter of the Organization of African Unity.

Article IX

1. The Commission shall appoint a Registrar and may provide for such other officers as may be deemed necessary.

2. The terms and conditions of service of the Registrar and other administrative officers of the Commission shall be governed by the Commission's Staff Regulations.

Article X

The Administrative expenses of the Commission shall be borne by the Organization of African Unity. All other expenses incurred in connection with the proceedings before the Commission shall be met in accordance with the Rules of Procedure of the Commission.

Article XI

The Seat of the Commission shall be at Addis Ababa, Ethiopia.

PART II

GENERAL PROVISIONS

Article XII

The Commission shall have jurisdiction over disputes between States only.

Article XIII

1. A dispute may be referred to the Commission jointly by the parties concerned, by a party to the dispute, by the Council of Ministers or by the Assembly of Heads of State and Government.

2. Where a dispute has been referred to the Commission as provided in paragraph 1, and one or more of the parties have refused to submit to the jurisdiction of the Commission, the Bureau shall refer the matter to the Council of Ministers for consideration.

Article XIV

The consent of any party to a dispute to submit to the jurisdiction of the Commission may be evidenced by:

 (*a*) a prior written undertaking by such party that there shall be recourse to Mediation, Conciliation, or Arbitration;
 (*b*) reference of a dispute by such party to the Commission; or
 (*c*) submission by such party to the jurisdiction in respect of a dispute referred to the Commission by another State, by the Council of Ministers, or by the Assembly of Heads of State and Government.

Article XV

Member States shall refrain from any act or omission that is likely to aggravate a situation which has been referred to the Commission.

Article XVI

Subject to the provisions of this Protocol and any special agreement between the parties, the Commission shall be entitled to adopt such working methods as it deems to be necessary and expedient and shall establish appropriate rules of procedure.

Article XVII

The Members of the Commission, when engaged in the business of the Commission, shall enjoy diplomatic privileges and immunities as provided for in the Convention on Privileges and Immunities of the Organization of African Unity.

Article XVIII

Where, in the course of Mediation, Conciliation, or Arbitration, it is deemed necessary to conduct an investigation or inquiry for the purpose of elucidating facts or circumstances relating to a matter in dispute, the parties concerned and all other Member States shall extend to those engaged in any such proceedings the fullest co-operation in the conduct of such investigation or inquiry.

Article XIX

In case of a dispute between Member States, the parties may agree to resort to any one of these modes of settlement: Mediation, Conciliation, and Arbitration.

PART III

MEDIATION

Article XX

When a dispute between Member States is referred to the Commission for Mediation, the President shall, with the consent of the parties, appoint one or more members of the Commission to mediate the dispute.

Article XXI

1. The role of the mediator shall be confined to reconciling the views and claims of the parties.

2. The mediator shall make written proposals to the parties as expeditiously as possible.

3. If the means of reconciliation proposed by the mediator are accepted, they shall become the basis of a protocol of arrangement between the parties.

PART IV

CONCILIATION

Article XXII

1. A request for the settlement of a dispute by conciliation may be submitted to the Commission by means of a petition addressed to the President by one or more of the parties to the dispute.

2. If the request is made by only one of the parties, that party shall indicate that prior written notice has been given to the other party.

3. The petition shall include a summary explanation of the grounds of the dispute.

Article XXIII

1. Upon receipt of the petition, the President shall, in agreement with the parties, establish a Board of Conciliators, of whom three shall be appointed by the President from among the Members of the Commission, and one each by the parties.

2. The Chairman of the Board shall be a person designated by the President from among the three Members of the Commission.

3. In nominating persons to serve as Members of the Board, the parties to the dispute shall designate persons in such a way that no two Members of it shall be nationals of the same State.

Article XXIV

1. It shall be the duty of the Board of Conciliators to clarify the issues in dispute and to endeavour to bring about an agreement between the parties upon mutually acceptable terms.

2. The Board shall consider all questions submitted to it and may undertake any inquiry or hear any person capable of giving relevant information concerning the dispute.

3. In the absence of disagreement between the parties, the Board shall determine its own procedure.

Article XXV

The parties shall be represented by agents, whose duty shall be to act as intermediaries between them and the Board. They may moreover be assisted by counsel and experts and may request that all persons whose evidence appears to the Board to be relevant shall be heard.

Article XXVI

1. At the close of the proceedings, the Board shall draw up a report stating either:
   (a) that the parties have come to an agreement and, if the need arises, the terms of the agreement and any recommendations for settlement made by the Board; or
   (b) that it has been impossible to effect a settlement.

2. The Report of the Board of Conciliators shall be communicated to the parties and to the President of the Commission without delay and may be published only with the consent of the parties.

PART V

ARBITRATION

Article XXVII

1. Where it is agreed that arbitration should be resorted to, the Arbitral Tribunal shall be established in the following manner:

   (*a*) each party shall designate one arbitrator from among the Members of the Commission having legal qualifications;

   (*b*) the two arbitrators thus designated shall, by common agreement, designate from among the Members of the Commission a third person who shall act as Chairman of the Tribunal;

   (*c*) where the two arbitrators fail to agree, within one month of their appointment, in the choice of the person to be Chairman of the Tribunal, the Bureau shall designate the Chairman.

2. The President may, with the agreement of the parties, appoint to the Arbitral Tribunal two additional Members who need not be Members of the Commission but who shall have the same powers as the other Members of the Tribunal.

3. The arbitrators shall not be nationals of the parties, or have their domicile in the territories of the parties, or be employed in their service, or have served as mediators or conciliators in the same dispute. They shall all be of different nationalities.

Article XXVIII

Recourse to arbitration shall be regarded as submission in good faith to the award of the Arbitral Tribunal.

Article XXIX

1. The parties shall, in each case, conclude a *compromis* which shall specify:

   (*a*) the undertaking of the parties to go to arbitration, and to accept as legally binding, the decision of the Tribunal;

   (*b*) the subject matter of the controversy; and

   (*c*) the seat of the Tribunal.

2. The *compromis* may specify the law to be applied by the Tribunal and the power, if the parties so agree, to adjudicate *ex aequo et bono*, the time-limit within which the award of the arbitrators shall be given, and the appointment of agents and counsel to take part in the proceedings before the Tribunal.

Article XXX

In the absence of any provision in the *compromis* regarding the applicable law, the Arbitral Tribunal shall decide the dispute according to treaties concluded between the parties, International Law, the Charter of the Organization of African Unity, the Charter of the United Nations and, if the parties agree, *ex aequo et bono*.

Article XXXI

1. Hearings shall be held *in camera* unless the arbitrators decide otherwise.

2. The record of the proceedings signed by the arbitrators and the Registrar shall alone be authoritative.

3. The arbitral award shall be in writing and shall, in respect of every point decided, state the reasons on which it is based.

PART VI

FINAL PROVISIONS

Article XXXII

The present Protocol shall, after approval by the Assembly of Heads of State and Government, be an integral part of the Charter of the Organization of African Unity.

Article XXXIII

This Protocol may be amended or revised in accordance with the provisions of Article XXXIII of the Charter of the Organization of African Unity.

IN FAITH WHEREOF, We the Heads of African State and Government, have signed this Protocol.

DONE AT CAIRO (United Arab Republic), on the 21st day of July, 1964.

3. *Declaration on the Problem of Subversion*

This was adopted on 24 October 1965 at the Second Session of the Assembly of Heads of State and Government of the Organization of African Unity, held in Accra, 21–5 October 1965. The Declaration and the Convention which follows (below, p. 18) are concerned with a problem which has been common in Latin America and Africa. Political factions not tolerated within the national constitutional framework and also persecuted minorities (of course the two species overlap) find residence in other states. The legal status of such groups requires careful regulation and the host state is under an obligation to prevent factions carrying out subversive activities aimed at other O.A.U. members.

DECLARATION ON THE PROBLEM OF SUBVERSION

The Assembly of Heads of State and Government meeting in its Second Ordinary Session in Accra, Ghana, from 21 to 25 October 1965,
  Desirous of consolidating the fraternal links that unite us,

SOLEMNLY UNDERTAKE:

1. Not to tolerate in conformity with article 3, paragraph 5, of the Charter, any subversion originating in our countries against another Member State of the Organization of African Unity;

2. Not to tolerate the use of our territories for any subversive activity directed from outside Africa against any Member States of the Organization of African Unity;

3. To oppose collectively and firmly by every means at our disposal every form of subversion conceived, organized or financed by foreign powers against Africa, OAU or its Member States individually;

4. (*a*) To resort to bilateral or multilateral consultation to settle all differences between two or more Member States of the Organization of African Unity;
  (*b*) To refrain from conducting any press or radio campaigns against any Member States of the Organization of African Unity; and to resort instead to the procedure laid down in the Charter and the Protocol of Mediation, Conciliation, and Arbitration of the Organization of African Unity;

5. (*a*) Not to create dissension within or among Member States by fomenting or aggravating racial, religious, linguistic, ethnic, or other differences;
  (*b*) To combat all forms of activity of this kind;

6. To observe strictly the principles of international law with regard to all political refugees who are nationals of any Member States of the Organization of African Unity;

7. To endeavour to promote, through bilateral and multilateral consultation the return of refugees to their countries of origin with the consent of both the refugees concerned and their governments;

8. To continue to guarantee the safety of political refugees from non-independent African territories, and to support them in their struggle to liberate their countries.

4. *Convention on Refugee Problems in Africa*

This was signed on 10 September 1969 by twenty-four states: O.A.U. Document CM/267/Rev.1. See generally Hamrell (ed.), *Refugee Problems in Africa*, 1967.

TEXT

PREAMBLE

We, the Heads of State and Government assembled in the city of Addis Ababa, September 6–10, 1969

1. *Noting with concern* the constantly increasing numbers of refugees in Africa and desirous of finding ways and means of alleviating their misery and suffering as well as providing them with a better life and future,

2. *Recognizing* the need for an essentially humanitarian approach towards solving the problems of refugees,

3. *Aware*, however, that refugee problems are a source of friction among many Member States, and desirous of eliminating the source of such discord,

4. *Anxious* to make a distinction between a refugee who seeks a peaceful and normal life and a person fleeing his country for the sole purpose of fomenting subversion from outside,

5. *Determined* that the activities of such subversive elements should be discouraged, in accordance with the Declaration on the Problem of Subversion and Resolution on the Problem of Refugees adopted at Accra in 1965,

6. *Bearing* in mind that the Charter of the United Nations and the Universal Declaration of Human Rights have affirmed the principle that human beings shall enjoy fundamental rights and freedoms without discrimination,

7. *Recalling* Resolution 2312 (XXII) of 14 December 1967 of the United Nations General Assembly, relating to the Declaration on Territorial Asylum,

8. *Convinced* that all the problems of our continent must be solved in the spirit of the Charter of the Organization of African Unity and in the African context,

9. *Recognizing* that the United Nations Convention of 28 July 1951, as modified by the Protocol of 31 January 1967, constitutes the basic and universal instrument relating to the status of refugees and reflects the deep concern of States for refugees and their desire to establish common standards for their treatment,

10. *Recalling* Resolutions 26 and 104 of the OAU Assemblies of Heads of State and Government, calling upon Member States of the Organization who had not already done so to accede to the United Nations Convention of 1951 and to the Protocol of 1967 relating to the Status of Refugees, and meanwhile to apply their provisions to refugees in Africa,

11. *Convinced* that the efficiency of the measures recommended by the present Convention to solve the problem of refugees in Africa necessitates close and continuous collaboration between the Organization of African Unity and the Office of the United Nations High Commissioner for Refugees,

Have agreed as follows:

Article I

Definition of the term 'Refugee'

1. For the purposes of this Convention, the term 'refugee' shall mean every person who, owing to well-founded fear of being persecuted for reasons of race, religion, nationality, membership of a particular social group or political opinion, is outside the country of his nationality and is unable or, owing to such fear, is unwilling to avail himself of the protection of that country, or who, not having a nationality and being outside the country of his former habitual residence as a result of such events is unable or, owing to such fear, is unwilling to return to it.

2. The term 'refugee' shall also apply to every person who, owing to external aggression, occupation, foreign domination, or events seriously disturbing public order in either part or the whole of his country of origin or nationality, is compelled to leave his place of habitual residence in order to seek refuge in another place outside his country of origin or nationality.

3. In the case of a person who has several nationalities, the term 'a country of which he is a national' shall mean each of the countries of which he is a national, and a person shall not be deemed to be lacking the protection of the country of which he is a national if, without any valid reason based on well-founded fear, he has not availed himself of the protection of one of the countries of which he is a national.

4. This Convention shall cease to apply to any refugee if:
   (a) he has voluntarily re-availed himself of the protection of the country of his nationality, or,
   (b) having lost his nationality, he has voluntarily reacquired it, or,
   (c) he has acquired a new nationality, and enjoys the protection of the country of his new nationality, or,

(*d*) he has voluntarily re-established himself in the country which he left or outside which he remained owing to fear of persecution, or,

(*e*) he can no longer, because the circumstances in connection with which he was recognized as a refugee have ceased to exist, continue to refuse to avail himself of the protection of the country of his nationality, or,

(*f*) he has committed a serious non-political crime outside his country of refuge after his admission to that country as a refugee, or,

(*g*) he has seriously infringed the purposes and objectives of this Convention.

5. The provisions of this Convention shall not apply to any person with respect to whom the country of asylum has serious reasons for considering that:

(*a*) he has committed a crime against peace, a war crime, or a crime against humanity, as defined in the international instruments drawn up to make provision in respect of such crimes;

(*b*) he committed a serious non-political crime outside the country of refuge prior to his admission to that country as a refugee;

(*c*) he has been guilty of acts contrary to the purposes and principles of the Organization of African Unity;

(*d*) he has been guilty of acts contrary to the purposes and principles of the United Nations.

6. For the purposes of this Convention, the Contracting State of Asylum shall determine whether an applicant is a refugee.

Article II

Asylum

1. Member States of the OAU shall use their best endeavours consistent with their respective legislations to receive refugees and to secure the settlement of those refugees who, for well-founded reasons, are unable or unwilling to return to their country of origin or nationality.

2. The grant of asylum to refugees is a peaceful and humanitarian act and shall not be regarded as an unfriendly act by any Member State.

3. No person shall be subjected by a Member State to measures such as rejection at the frontier, return or expulsion, which would compel him to return to or remain in a territory where his life, physical integrity, or liberty would be threatened for the reasons set out in Article I, paragraphs 1 and 2.

4. Where a Member State finds difficulty in continuing to grant asylum to refugees, such Member State may appeal directly to other Member

States and through the OAU, and such other Member States shall in the spirit of African solidarity and international co-operation take appropriate measures to lighten the burden of the Member State granting asylum.

5. Where a refugee has not received the right to reside in any country of asylum, he may be granted temporary residence in any country of asylum in which he first presented himself as a refugee pending arrangement for his resettlement in accordance with the proceeding paragraph.

6. For reasons of security, countries of asylum shall, as far as possible, settle refugees at a reasonable distance from the frontier of their country of origin.

Article III
Prohibition of subversive activities

1. Every refugee has duties to the country in which he finds himself, which require in particular that he conforms with its laws and regulations as well as with measures taken for the maintenance of public order. He shall also abstain from any subversive activities against any Member State of the OAU.

2. Signatory States undertake to prohibit refugees residing in their respective territories from attacking any State Member of the OAU, by any activity likely to cause tension between Member States, and in particular by use of arms, through the press, or by radio.

Article IV
Non-discrimination

Member States undertake to apply the provisions of this Convention to all refugees without discrimination as to race, religion, nationality, membership of a particular social group or political opinions.

Article V
Voluntary repatriation

1. The essentially voluntary character of repatriation shall be respected in all cases and no refugee shall be repatriated against his will.

2. The country of asylum, in collaboration with the country of origin, shall make adequate arrangements for the safe return of refugees who request repatriation.

3. The country of origin, on receiving back refugees, shall facilitate their resettlement and grant them the full rights and privileges of nationals of the country, and subject them to the same obligations.

4. Refugees who voluntarily return to their country shall in no way be penalized for having left it for any of the reasons giving rise to refugee situations. Whenever necessary, an appeal shall be made through national information media and through the Administrative Secretary-General of the OAU, inviting refugees to return home and giving assurance that the new circumstances prevailing in their country of origin will enable them to return without risk and to take up a normal and peaceful life without fear of being disturbed or punished, and that the text of such appeal should be given to refugees and clearly explained to them by their country of asylum.

5. Refugees who freely decide to return to their homeland, as a result of such assurances or on their own initiative, shall be given every possible assistance by the country of asylum, the country of origin, voluntary agencies, and international and inter-governmental organizations, to facilitate their return.

Article VI

Travel documents

1. Subject to Article III, Member States shall issue to refugees lawfully staying in their territories travel documents in accordance with the United Nations Convention relating to the Status of Refugees and the Schedule and Annex thereto, for the purpose of travel outside their territory, unless compelling reasons of national security or public order otherwise require. Member States may issue such a travel document to any other refugee in their territory.

2. Where an African country of second asylum accepts a refugee from a country of first asylum, the country of first asylum may be dispensed from issuing a document with a return clause.

3. Travel documents issued to refugees under previous international agreements by States Parties thereto shall be recognized and treated by Member States in the same way as if they had been issued to refugees pursuant to this Article.

Article VII

Co-operation of the national authorities with the Organization of African Unity

In order to enable the Administrative Secretary-General of the Organization of African Unity to make reports to the competent organs of the Organization of African Unity, Member States undertake to provide the

Secretariat in the appropriate form with information and statistical data requested concerning:

(*a*) the condition of refugees;

(*b*) the implementation of this Convention, and

(*c*) laws, regulations and decrees which are, or may hereafter be, in force relating to refugees.

Article VIII

Co-operation with the Office of the United Nations High Commissioner for Refugees

1. Member States shall co-operate with the Office of the United Nations High Commissioner for Refugees.

2. The present Convention shall be the effective regional complement in Africa of the 1951 United Nations Convention on the Status of Refugees.

Article IX

Settlement of disputes

Any dispute between States signatories to this Convention relating to its interpretation or application, which cannot be settled by other means, shall be referred to the Commission for Mediation, Conciliation and Arbitration of the Organization of African Unity, at the request of any one of the Parties to the dispute.

Article X

Signature and ratification

1. This Convention is open for signature and accession by all Member States of the Organization of African Unity and shall be ratified by signatory States in accordance with their respective constitutional processes. The instruments of ratification shall be deposited with the Administrative Secretary-General of the Organization of African Unity.

2. The original instrument, done if possible in African languages, and in English and French, all texts being equally authentic, shall be deposited with the Administrative Secretary-General of the Organization of African Unity.

3. Any independent African State, Member of the Organization of African Unity, may at any time notify the Administrative Secretary-General of the Organization of African Unity of its accession to this Convention.

8760205   B

Article XI
Entry into force

This Convention shall come into force upon deposit of instruments of ratification by one-third of the Member States of the Organization of African Unity.

Article XII
Amendment

This Convention may be amended or revised if any member State makes a written request to the Administrative Secretary-General to that effect, provided however that the proposed amendment shall not be submitted to the Assembly of Heads of State and Government for consideration until all Member States have been duly notified of it and a period of one year has elapsed. Such an amendment shall not be effective unless approved by at least two-thirds of the Member States Parties to the present Convention.

Article XIII
Denunciation

1. Any Member State Party to this Convention may denounce its provisions by a written notification to the Administrative Secretary-General.

2. At the end of one year from the date of such notification, if not withdrawn, the Convention shall cease to apply with respect to the denouncing State.

Article XIV

Upon entry into force of this Convention, the Administrative Secretary-General of the OAU shall register it with the Secretary-General of the United Nations, in accordance with Article 102 of the Charter of the United Nations.

Article XV
Notifications by the Administrative Secretary-General of the Organization of African Unity

The Administrative Secretary-General of the Organization of African Unity shall inform all Members of the Organization:
   (a) of signatures, ratifications and accessions in accordance with Article X;
   (b) of entry into force, in accordance with Article XI;
   (c) of requests for amendments submitted under the terms of Article XII;
   (d) of denunciations, in accordance with Article XIII.

IN WITNESS WHEREOF WE, the Heads of African State and Government, have signed this Convention.

II. AFRO-MALAGASY COMMON ORGANIZATION, 1966

PRIOR to the formation of the O.A.U. in 1963, there was a tendency for factions to form among the newly independent states of Africa and pan-African aspirations to general regional co-operation were threatened. The 'Casablanca group' of states was faced by the 'Monrovia group', which tended to take what the western press would describe as a 'more moderate' line on major issues of regional politics and relations with the former colonial powers. The background is considered in Legum, *Pan-Africanism*, rev. ed., 1965, chapters III and IV. Nevertheless, the O.A.U. emerged as a general grouping including states of diverse political types.

In the aftermath of the Congo conflict, with its ideological implications, the more conservative Francophonic States joined together in a bloc which is bound to have an uneasy relation with the major regional body, the O.A.U. The new body, the Afro-Malagasy Common Organization (O.C.A.M.), harks back to the aims of the 'Brazzaville group' of the years 1960–1, and supersedes the Union Africaine et Malgache de co-opération économique created in 1964. On the political aspects of O.C.A.M. see *International Organization*, vol. 20 (1966), p. 857, and Nora McKeon, *International Affairs*, vol. 42 (1966), p. 390 at pp. 399–401, 406–7.

1. *Charter of the Afro-Malagasy Common Organization (O.C.A.M.) 1966*

The official name of the organization is *Organisation Commune Africaine et Malgache*, and it is commonly referred to by the initials of this title. The Charter was signed on 27 June 1966. The Organization had been founded on 12 February 1965. The French text has been published in *Afrique contemporaine, Documentation française*, 1966, no. 28. The following are members of O.C.A.M.: Cameroon, Central African Republic, Chad, Republic of the Congo (Brazzaville), Democratic Republic of the Congo (Kinshasa), Dahomey, Gabon, Ivory Coast, Malagasy Republic, Niger, Ruanda, Senegal, Togo, and Upper Volta. Mauritania, an original member, withdrew on 24 June 1965.

TEXT[1]

The African and Malagasy Chiefs of State, who met in Tananarive from June 25 to 27, 1966,
   Desiring to provide strong foundations for African unity,

[1] [Reprinted from a translation made by the Division of Language Services of the U.S. Department of State from the official French text published by the Secretariat-General of O.C.A.M., Yaoundé, Cameroon. Reproduced with permission from *International Legal Materials*, vol. 6 (1967), p. 53.]

True to the spirit, principles and objectives of the Charter of the United Nations and the Organization of African Unity,

Considering the decision of the Conference of the African and Malagasy Chiefs of State, which was held in Nouakchott in February 1965,

Considering the historic, economic, social, and cultural bonds existing between their respective countries, and

Considering the necessity of harmonizing their economic, social, and cultural policies for the purpose of maintaining conditions for progress and security:

Have agreed as follows:

Article 1. The High Contracting Parties hereby establish an organization to be called the 'Afro-Malagasy Common Organization' (OCAM). This organization shall be open to any independent and sovereign African State that requests admission and accepts the provisions of this Charter.

The admission of a new member to the OCAM shall require a unanimous decision of the members of the Organization.

Article 2. The OCAM is based on the solidarity of its members.

In the spirit of the Organization of African Unity, its purpose is to strengthen co-operation and solidarity between the African and Malagasy States in order to accelerate their economic, social, technical, and cultural development.

Article 3. For this purpose, the Organization shall seek to harmonize the action of the Member States in the economic, social, technical, and cultural fields, to co-ordinate their development programs, and to facilitate foreign-policy consultations between them, with due respect for the sovereignty and fundamental rights of each Member State.

INSTITUTIONS AND BODIES

Article 4. The institutions of the Organization shall be [as follows]:

the Conference of Chiefs of State and of Government;
the Council of Ministers;
the Administrative General Secretariat.

I. CONFERENCE OF CHIEFS OF STATE AND OF GOVERNMENT

Article 5. The Conference of Chiefs of State and of Government shall be the supreme authority of the Organization.

It shall be composed of the Chiefs of State and of Government of the Member States or their duly authorized representatives.

Article 6. The Conference shall consider questions of common interest and make its decisions in accordance with the provisions of this Charter and the internal regulations of the Conference.

Article 7. The Conference of Chiefs of State and of Government shall meet once a year in regular session.

The Conference shall meet in special session at the request of a Member State and subject to the formal approval of two-thirds of the members of the Organization.

The agenda of a special session shall contain, in principle, only the questions for which the Conference has been called.

Article 8. The Conference shall establish and adopt its own internal regulations.

Article 9. Each Member State shall have one vote.

Any Member State may be represented by another Member State; the latter shall have the right to vote at the place specified in the proxy.

A Member State may be represented by only one other Member State.

Two-thirds of the Member States of the Organization shall constitute a quorum.

Any decision taken under the conditions of a quorum or required majority shall be binding on all Member States.

II. COUNCIL OF MINISTERS

Article 10. The Council of Ministers shall be composed of the ministers of foreign affairs of the Member States, or of such other ministers as may be designated by the governments of the Member States.

It shall meet once a year in regular session.

The regular session shall be held a few days before the annual regular session of the Conference of Chiefs of State and of Government and in the same place.

Article 11. The Council shall meet in special session at the request of a Member State and subject to the formal approval of two-thirds of the members of the Organization.

The agenda of a special session of the Council shall contain only the questions for which the Council has been called.

Article 12. The Council of Ministers shall be responsible to the Conference of Chiefs of State and of Government.

It shall be responsible for preparing for that Conference, shall consider and decide any question that the Conference refers to it, and shall see that such decisions are carried out.

It shall ensure that the Member States co-operate with each other in accordance with the directives of the Conference of Chiefs of State and of Government, pursuant to this Charter.

Article 13. Each Member State shall have one vote.

Any Member State may be represented by another Member State; the latter shall have the right to vote at the place specified in the proxy.

A Member State may be represented by only one other Member State.

Two-thirds of the Member States shall constitute a quorum.

Article 14. The Council shall establish and adopt its own internal regulations.

III. ADMINISTRATIVE GENERAL SECRETARIAT

Article 15. The Afro-Malagasy Common Organization shall have an administrative general secretariat, with its headquarters in Yaoundé, Federal Republic of Cameroon.

The Administrative Secretary-General shall be appointed for two years by the Conference of the Chiefs of State and of Government on the recommendation of the Council of Ministers. His term of office may be renewed.

Article 16. Under the authority of the President of the Conference, the Administrative Secretary-General shall be responsible for the administrative functioning of the various bodies of the Organization.

The internal regulations of the Conference of Chiefs of State shall specify the conditions under which another person may serve instead of the Administrative Secretary-General if he is unable to serve, or replace him if a vacancy exists.

Article 17. The Administrative General Secretariat shall be divided into departments corresponding to the main fields of activity of the Organization.

It shall supervise the activities of joint enterprises, in particular, the multinational airline, AIR-AFRIQUE, and the Union Africaine et Malgache des Postes et Télécommunications.

Article 18. The Conference may terminate the duties of the Administrative Secretary-General in the same manner as it appoints him, when the proper functioning of the Organization warrants it.

Article 19. The conditions governing the employment of the personnel of the Administrative General Secretariat shall be prescribed by an agreement to be concluded between the Member States of the Organization.

BUDGET:

Article 20. The budget of the Organization, to be prepared by the Administrative Secretary-General, shall be approved by the Conference of Chiefs of State and of Government on the recommendation of the Council of Ministers.

It shall be maintained by the contributions of the Member States, to be fixed on the basis of the net amount of their respective operating budgets.

However, the contribution of a Member State may not exceed 20 per cent of the annual ordinary budget of the Organization.

The Member States agree to pay their respective contributions regularly within the time limits specified.

SIGNATURE AND RATIFICATION:

Article 21. This Charter shall be ratified or approved by the signatory States in accordance with their constitutional procedures.

The original instrument shall be deposited with the Government of the Federal Republic of Cameroon, which shall transmit certified copies of the document to all signatory States.

The instruments of ratification or approval shall be deposited with the Government of the Federal Republic of Cameroon, which shall notify the deposit thereof to all signatory States.

ENTRY INTO FORCE:

Article 22. This Charter shall enter into force upon receipt by the Government of the Federal Republic of Cameroon of the instruments of ratification of two-thirds of the signatory States.

REGISTRATION:

Article 23. After it has been duly ratified, this Charter shall be registered with the General Secretariat of the United Nations by the Government of the Federal Republic of Cameroon, in accordance with Article 102 of the Charter of the United Nations.

INTERPRETATION:

Article 24. Any decision concerning the interpretation of this Charter must be taken by a two-thirds majority of the Member States of the Organization.

MISCELLANEOUS PROVISIONS:

Article 25. The Administrative Secretary-General may accept, on behalf of the Organization, any gifts, contributions, or bequests to the

Organization, subject to the approval of the Council of Ministers. They shall be taken over by the budget of the Organization.

Article 26. An agreement between the Member States shall prescribe the privileges and immunities to be granted to the personnel of the Administrative General Secretariat.

WITHDRAWAL OF MEMBERSHIP:

Article 27. Any State that wishes to withdraw from the Organization shall so inform the Administrative General Secretariat in writing.

The latter shall notify the Member States.

One year after such notification, this Charter shall cease to apply to that State, which, consequently, will no longer be a member of the Organization.

AMENDMENT AND REVISION:

Article 28. This Charter may be amended or revised if a Member State sends a written request for that purpose to the Administrative General Secretariat.

The draft amendment or revision shall not be submitted to the Conference until all the Member States have been duly informed and after a period of one year from the date of submission of the amendment (or revision).

The amendment or revision shall not become effective until it has been ratified or approved by two-thirds of the Member States of the Organization.

In witness whereof, we, the African and Malagasy Chiefs of State and of Government, have signed this Charter.

DONE AT TANANARIVE on June 27, 1966.

2. *Internal Regulations of the O.C.A.M.*[1]

INTERNAL REGULATIONS OF THE CONFERENCE OF CHIEFS OF STATE AND OF GOVERNMENT OF THE AFRO-MALAGASY COMMON ORGANIZATION (OCAM)

Article 1. The Conference of Chiefs of State and of Government shall be the supreme authority of the Organization.

COMPOSITION

Article 2. The Conference shall be composed of the Chiefs of State and of Government of the Member States.

[1] Reproduced with permission from *International Legal Materials*, vol. 6 (1967), pp. 58, 62, 65.

In case of necessity, a Chief of State or of Government may be represented by a person who has been duly authorized and vested with full powers.

DUTIES

Article 3. The Conference shall, in particular:

Adopt the definitive agenda;

Admit new members;

Harmonize the action of the Member States in the economic, social, technical, and cultural fields; co-ordinate their development programmes, and facilitate foreign policy consultations between them, with due respect for the sovereignty and fundamental rights of each Member State.

Approve the budget of the Organization on the recommendation of the Council of Ministers;

Revise the structure and duties of the institutions and bodies of the Organization;

Interpret and amend the Charter;

Consider subjects that are of common interest to the Member States of the Organization.

REGULAR SESSIONS

Article 4. In accordance with the provisions of Article 7 of the Charter of the Organization, the Conference shall meet once a year in regular session.

SPECIAL SESSIONS

Article 5. At the request of a Member State and subject to the formal approval of two-thirds of the members of the Organization, the Conference shall meet in special session when called by the Administrative Secretary-General.

PLACE OF MEETING

Article 6. During a regular session, the Conference shall decide, by a simple majority of the members of the Organization, on the place where the next regular session is to be held.

All special sessions of the Conference shall be held at the headquarters of the Organization. However, the Member States may decide, by an absolute majority, to meet elsewhere.

OPEN SESSIONS AND CLOSED SESSIONS

Article 7. All sessions of the Conference shall be closed; however, the Conference may decide by a simple majority that certain sessions shall be open.

THE PRESIDENT OF THE ORGANIZATION

Article 8. At the beginning of each regular session, the Conference shall elect the President of the Organization.

In consultation with the other Chiefs of State and of Government of the OCAM, he shall perform the duty of co-ordinating and harmonizing the viewpoints of the Member States in order to give the Organization the necessary impetus toward the achievement of its aims.

Article 9. The President shall declare the opening and closing of each plenary meeting, present the minutes of meetings for approval, direct the discussion, give speakers the floor in the order in which they have requested it, submit the matters under discussion to a vote, announce the results of the voting, and rule on questions of procedure, in accordance with the provisions of the Charter of the Organization and these Internal Regulations.

THE SECRETARIAT OF THE CONFERENCE

Article 10. The secretarial services of the Conference shall be provided by the Administrative Secretary-General.

The minutes of the Conference and, on occasion, the analysis of closed discussions, shall be prepared by the Administrative Secretary-General, under the authority of the President of the Conference.

The Administrative Secretary-General shall transmit a copy thereof to the Member States as soon as possible.

Article 11. At the end of each session of the Conference, the Administrative Secretary General shall prepare a final communiqué, which he shall distribute after its approval by the President of the Organization.

AGENDA

Article 12. The provisional agenda of a regular session shall be prepared by the Council of Ministers. It shall comprise:

Items that the Conference decides to include;

Items proposed by the Council of Ministers of the Organization;

Items proposed by the Member States through the Administrative General Secretariat.

The provisional agenda shall be communicated to the Member States by the Administrative General Secretariat at least one month before the opening date of the Conference.

Article 13. The Administrative Secretary-General shall communicate the agenda of any special session to the Member States at least ten days before the opening of the session.

Article 14. The agenda of a special session shall contain, in principle, only items the consideration of which is proposed in the request for the calling of such a session.

QUORUM AND DISCUSSIONS

Article 15. For any session of the Conference, two-thirds of the Member States of the Organization shall constitute a quorum.

RESOLUTIONS

Article 16. Proposals, amendments, or draft resolutions shall be submitted in writing to the Administrative General Secretariat, which shall distribute the text thereof to the members of the Conference. However, the Conference may authorize the consideration of a proposal the text of which has not been distributed in advance.

Proposals and draft resolutions shall be considered in the chronological order of their submission.

Article 17. A proposal or a draft resolution may be withdrawn by the person who has drafted it before it is put to a vote. Any member may resubmit a proposal or a draft resolution that has been thus withdrawn.

MOTIONS ON POINTS OF ORDER

Article 18. During the discussions, any member may make a motion concerning a point of order, on which the President shall rule immediately in accordance with these Internal Regulations. If a member appeals from the decision of the President, the appeal shall be put to a vote immediately.

CLOSING THE LIST OF SPEAKERS

Article 19. During a discussion, the President may read the list of speakers and, with the Conference's consent, declare that list closed. However, the President may grant any member of the Conference the right to reply if a speech made after the list of speakers is closed justifies it.

CLOSING THE DISCUSSION

Article 20. When a question has been discussed sufficiently, any member may request that the discussion of the question under consideration be closed. No discussion of motions to close shall be permitted; they shall be put to a vote immediately.

POSTPONEMENT OF DISCUSSION

Article 21. During the discussion of any question, a member may request that the discussion of the question under consideration be postponed. In addition to the person who makes the motion, two members of the Conference may speak, one in favour of the motion and the other against it; then the motion shall be put to a vote immediately.

SUSPENSION OR ADJOURNMENT OF THE SESSION

Article 22. Subject to the terms of Article 19, during the discussion of any question, any member may request the suspension or adjournment of the session. Motions to that effect shall not be discussed; they shall be put to a vote immediately.

ORDER OF MOTIONS ON PROCEDURE

Article 23. The following motions shall take precedence, in the order indicated below, over any other proposals or motions that may be made at the session.

1. To suspend the session;
2. To adjourn the session;
3. To postpone debate on the matter under discussion;
4. To close the debate on the matter under discussion.

REQUIRED MAJORITY

Article 24. Unless otherwise provided in the Charter, in order to be carried, resolutions must be adopted by a two-thirds majority of the members of the Organization.

However, unanimity is required in the case of recommendations of a political nature.

Decisions on procedure shall be taken by a simple majority.

Two-thirds of the members present and voting shall be the majority required to decide whether or not a question is a question of procedure.

VOTING ON RESOLUTIONS

Article 25. After the discussion is closed, the President shall put the resolution, together with the pertinent amendments, to a vote immediately. The voting may not be interrupted unless a motion on a point of order is made with respect to the manner in which it is being conducted.

VOTING ON AMENDMENTS

Article 26. When a proposal forms the subject of an amendment, the amendment shall be put to a vote first. If a proposal forms the subject of several amendments, the Conference shall vote first on the one that differs most, in substance, from the original proposal.

The order of precedence of the other amendments shall then be determined in the same manner until all the amendments have been put to a vote.

If no amendment is adopted, the proposal shall be put to a vote in its original form.

A proposal shall be considered an amendment to a text if it adds to the original proposal, or eliminates or changes certain parts of it.

VOTING ON THE VARIOUS PARTS OF A PROPOSAL

Article 27. Any member may request that the various parts of a resolution or a proposal be put to a vote separately. In that event, the entire text resulting from the various votes taken shall be put to a vote.

If all parts of the body of a resolution or a proposal are rejected, the entire proposal shall be considered rejected.

VOTING AND REASON FOR VOTE CAST

Article 28. The Conference shall vote by a show of hands, but any member may request a vote by roll call; this shall be taken in the alphabetical order of the names of the member countries, beginning with the country whose name has been drawn by lot by the President.

After the voting, any member may request the floor in order to give the reason why he voted as he did.

Article 29. The voting in elections shall be secret. The same rule shall apply to any other special instance in which the Conference makes a decision by a simple majority.

ADMINISTRATIVE SECRETARY GENERAL

Article 30. The Administrative Secretary-General shall be appointed for two years by the Conference on the recommendation of the Council of Ministers of the Organization in accordance with the provisions of Article 15 of the Charter of the Organization. Pursuant to Article 16 of the Charter, he shall serve under the direct authority of the President of the Organization.

If the Administrative Secretary-General is unable to serve or that office is vacant, the highest-ranking Director with the most seniority shall serve in his stead or replace him.

AMENDMENTS

Article 31. The Conference may amend these Internal Regulations by a two-thirds majority of the members of the Organization.

DONE AT TANANARIVE on June 27, 1966

INTERNAL REGULATIONS OF THE COUNCIL OF MINISTERS OF THE OCAM

COMPOSITION

Article 1. The Council of Ministers of the Afro-Malagasy Common Organization shall be composed of the ministers of foreign affairs of the Member States of the Organization or of such other ministers or duly authorized and fully empowered persons as may be designated by their governments.

DUTIES

Article 2. The Council shall be responsible to the Conference of Chiefs of State and of Government.

Article 3. In accordance with the provisions of Article 12 of the Charter, the Council shall be responsible for preparing for the Conference, it shall consider and decide any question that the Conference refers to it and see that its decisions are carried out.

It shall ensure that the Member States co-operate with each other in accordance with the directives of the Conference of Chiefs of State and of Government.

Article 4. In accordance with Article 20 of the Charter, the Council shall submit the budget of the Organization to the Conference for approval.

SESSIONS

Article 5. The Council shall meet once a year in regular session.

That session shall immediately precede the annual regular meeting of the Conference of Chiefs of State and of Government.

Article 6. At the request of a Member State and subject to the formal approval of two-thirds of the members of the Organization, the Council shall meet in special session when called by the Administrative Secretary-General.

Article 7. At the beginning of each session, the Council shall elect, by a simple majority, a chairman and one or more vice chairmen for the duration of the session.

PLACE OF MEETING

Article 8. The annual regular session of the Council of Ministers shall be held at the same place as the Conference of Chiefs of State and of Government. Special sessions of the Council of Ministers shall be held at the headquarters of the Organization or at any other place that the Council may designate by a simple majority.

OPEN SESSIONS AND CLOSED SESSIONS

Article 9. The sessions of the Council shall be closed. However, the Council may decide by a simple majority that certain meetings shall be open.

AGENDA

Article 10. The provisional agenda of a regular session shall be prepared by the Administrative General Secretariat, which shall communicate it to the Member States at least one month before the opening of the session.

The provisional agenda shall comprise:

Report of the Administrative Secretary-General;

Items referred to the Council by the Conference of Chiefs of State and of Government;

Items that the Council has decided to include in its agenda;

Items proposed by the Member States through the Administrative General Secretariat.

Article 11. The agenda of a special session shall be communicated to the Member States at least ten days before the opening of the session.

This agenda shall contain only items the consideration of which is proposed in the request for the calling of a special session.

SECRETARIAT

Article 12. The secretarial services of the sessions of the Council shall be provided by the Administrative Secretary General.

The minutes of the Council's meetings and, on occasion, the analysis of the closed discussions, shall be prepared by the Administrative Secretary-General under the authority of the Chairman of the session.

The Administrative Secretary-General shall transmit a copy thereof to the Member States as soon as possible.

WORK GROUPS

Article 13. During each session, the Council may be divided into as many work groups as is necessary for the performance of its work.

QUORUM

Article 14. For any meeting of the Council, two-thirds of the Member States of the Organization shall constitute a quorum.

DISCUSSIONS

Article 15. The Chairman shall declare the opening and closing of each plenary meeting, present the minutes of meetings for approval, direct the discussion, give the speakers the floor in the order in which they request it, submit the matters under discussion to a vote, announce the results of the voting, and rule on questions of procedure, in accordance with the provisions of the Charter of the Organization and these Internal Regulations.

The Chairman may read the list of speakers and, with the consent of the Council, declare the list closed. However, the Chairman may grant any member of the Council the right to reply if a speech made after the list of speakers is closed justifies it.

Article 16. When a topic has been discussed sufficiently, any member may request that the discussion of the matter under consideration be closed. No discussion of motions to close shall be permitted; they shall be put to a vote immediately.

Article 17. During the discussion of any question, any member may request that the discussion of the question under consideration be postponed. In addition to the person who makes the motion, two members of the Council may speak, one in favour of the motion and the other against it; then the motion shall be put to a vote immediately.

Article 18. Subject to the terms of Article 21, during the discussion of any question, any member may request the suspension or adjournment of the meeting. Motions to that effect shall not be discussed; they shall be put to a vote immediately.

PROPOSALS AND DRAFT RESOLUTIONS

Article 19. Proposals, amendments, or draft resolutions shall be submitted in writing to the Administrative General Secretariat, which shall distribute the text thereof to the members of the Council.

However, the Council may authorize the consideration of a proposal the text of which has not been distributed in advance.

Proposals and draft resolutions shall be considered in the chronological order of their submission.

Article 20. A proposal or a draft resolution may be withdrawn by the person who has drafted it before it is put to a vote. Any member may re-submit a proposal or a draft resolution that has been so withdrawn.

MOTIONS ON POINTS OF ORDER

Article 21. During the discussion, any member may make a motion on a point of order, on which the Chairman shall rule immediately in accordance with these Internal Regulations. If a member appeals from the decision of the Chairman, that appeal shall be put to a vote immediately.

ORDER OF MOTIONS ON PROCEDURE

Article 22. The following motions shall take precedence, in the order indicated below, over any other proposals or motions that may be made at the session:

1. To suspend the session;
2. To adjourn the session;
3. To postpone debate on the matter under discussion;
4. To close the debate on the matter under discussion.

REQUIRED MAJORITIES

Article 23. In order to be considered, the recommendation of the Council to the Conference of Chiefs of State and of Government must be adopted by a two-thirds majority of the members present, or represented, and voting.

Decisions on procedure shall be taken by a majority.

Two-thirds of the members present and voting shall be the majority required to decide whether or not a question is a question of procedure.

VOTING ON DRAFT RECOMMENDATIONS AND RESOLUTIONS

Article 24. After the discussion is closed, the Chairman shall put the draft recommendation or resolution, together with the pertinent amendments, to a vote immediately.

The voting may not be interrupted unless a motion on a point of order is made with respect to the manner in which it is being conducted.

VOTING ON AMENDMENTS

Article 25. When a proposal forms the subject of an amendment, the amendment shall be put to a vote first. If a proposal forms the subject of several amendments, the Council shall vote first on the one that differs the most, in substance, from the original proposal.

The order of precedence of the other amendments shall then be determined in the same manner until the amendments have been put to a vote.

If one or more amendments are adopted, the amended proposal shall be put to a vote.

If no amendment is adopted, the proposal shall be put to a vote in its original form.

A proposal shall be considered an amendment to a text if it adds to the original proposal, or eliminates or changes certain parts of it.

VOTING ON THE VARIOUS PARTS OF A PROPOSAL

Article 26. Any member may request that the various parts of a resolution or a proposal be put to a vote separately. In that event, the entire text resulting from the various votes taken shall be put to a vote.

If all parts of the body of a resolution or a proposal are rejected, the entire proposal shall be considered rejected.

VOTING AND REASON FOR VOTE CAST

Article 27. In accordance with Article 13 of the Charter, each Member State shall have one vote.

The Council shall vote by a show of hands, but any member may request a vote by roll call; this shall be taken in the alphabetical order of the names of the member countries, beginning with the country whose name has been drawn by lot by the Chairman.

After the voting, any member may request the floor in order to give the reason why he voted as he did.

Article 28. The voting in elections shall be secret. The same rule shall apply to any other special instance in which the Council makes a decision by simple majority.

AMENDMENTS

Article 29. The Council may amend these Internal Regulations by a two-thirds majority of the members of the Organization.

DONE AT TANANARIVE on June 27th, 1966

FINANCIAL SYSTEM OF THE AFRO-MALAGASY COMMON ORGANIZATION

General Rules for the Preparation, Presentation and Execution of the Budget

1. *Preparation of the Budget*: The Secretary-General shall send his draft budget together with a statement showing the execution of the current budget, prepared as of August 1, to the Financial Controller before August 31.

The Financial Controller shall transmit the *draft budget* and his observations, opinions, and suggestions to each of the Ministers of Foreign Affairs of the States Members of the Afro-Malagasy Common Organization before September 30, a copy of that document being sent also to the Finance Ministers.

The final draft shall be prepared and presented by the General Secretariat with due regard to the observations formulated by the States.

2. *The Budget*: There shall be only one budget for the Afro-Malagasy Common Organization. It shall comprise as many chapters as there are departments.

Each chapter shall be broken down into articles, including:

> Article 1—Personnel Expenditures
> „   2—*Matériel*   „
> „   3—Transportation „
> „   4—Rental   „
> „   5—Movable Property and Vehicle Expenditures
> „   6—Expenditures relating to Closed Fiscal Years

A final chapter shall describe the annual payments for amortization of and interest on loans.

The budget *ordonnateur* (person entitled to pass on expenditures) shall be the President of the Afro-Malagasy Common Organization in office. *He may delegate his powers to the Secretary-General of the Afro-Malagasy Common Organization.*

The ordonnateur shall keep the accounting records pertaining to commitments to incur expenses and the approval of their payment and those pertaining to the issuance of receipt and payment documents, which he shall transmit to the accountant.

These accounting records shall be kept in the form that is current in the State where the Organization has its headquarters.

3. *Administration*: The Budget approved by the Conference of Chiefs of State shall be executed during the next period running from January 1 to December 31.

4. *Notification of Credits*: On January 1 and on July 1 the *ordonnateur* shall notify each Department Chief of the credits coming to him.

5. *Execution of the Budget*: Each Department Chief shall be personally responsible for incurring expenses within the strict limits of the credits made available to him.

6. *Transfer of Credits*: All transfers of credits from chapter to chapter and from article to article are forbidden.

However, transfers from article to article may be authorized once a year by the President upon the recommendation of the Secretary-General and after receiving the approving opinion of the Financial Controller.

Within an article, in case of necessity, transfers may be made from item to item *by decision of the Secretary-General upon the recommendation of the Department Chief concerned and after receiving an approving opinion supported by reasons from the Financial Controller.*

The Financial Controller may refuse to OK the proposed transfer for reasons that he shall state in his note of refusal.

He shall report immediately to the President on OK's given and on refusals to give his OK, supported by reasons.

The President shall make the final decision on any dispute in this connection referred to him by the Secretary-General or the Financial Controller.

7. *Receipts*: The receipts shall be composed of the following items:

Each State shall pay its contribution, either at one time on January 1, or in two payments, on January 1 and July 1, by transfer to the *Organization's* bank account.

The contributions to be made by each State shall be determined on the basis of the net amount of the operating (expense) budgets. Since the budgetary nomenclature may vary with the State, it is important to make the documents comparable when the given information is identical. The following items are to be excluded from the gross budget total:

—debt (with the exception of pensions and annuities)
—disbursements made in behalf of other States
—repayment in full of sums collected in behalf of the communes and the consular assemblies
—payments to the equipment budgets
—payments to the provincial budgets (Madagascar, Congo-Leopoldville, and the Federal Republic of Cameroon)
—repayment of sums improperly collected (customs duties, etc.)
—advances and loans

On the other hand, the contributions and shares of expenses paid (particularly to international organizations) shall remain in the budget total.

The quotas thus determined shall remain in effect for five years. If the number of States is increased, the new State or States shall bear a share of the common expenses starting in the year following that in which they joined.

If a State joins before the expiration of the period during which the quotas are to remain in effect, the budget total to be considered in the case of such new State shall be the one for the year in which the current contributions were fixed.

If the number of Member States declines, the new contributions shall not be computed on the basis of the budget totals for the year. The contribution of the withdrawing State shall be mathematically distributed among the other States.

Before August 31 of the fifth year, each State of the Organization shall send its operating budget for the current year to the *Secretary-General of the Afro-Malagasy Common Organization.*

The Secretary-General shall study these documents and determine the new quotas to be in effect for five years, which he shall submit to the Council at the time when the budget is studied, with the consent of the President.

8. *The Financial Controller:*

He shall report to the President of the Afro-Malagasy Common Organization, the *ordonnateur* of the budget:
—quarterly, on the status of the execution of the budget of the Afro-Malagasy Common Organization;
—whenever necessary, on his findings.

9. *The Accountant:*

The Accountant shall be appointed by the President of the Afro-Malagasy Common Organization upon the recommendation of the Council of Ministers.

The Accountant shall be put in Category I of the functions specified for the Afro-Malagasy Common Organization. The credits required for the operations of the Accounting Office shall be included in the chapter for the Administrative General Secretariat.

The Accountant, under the authority of the President of the Afro-Malagasy Common Organization, shall carry out all operations relating to receipts and expenditures.

The books of the Organization shall be kept by the Accountant in the manner and according to the regulations in effect in the State where the Afro-Malagasy Common Organization has its headquarters. The Accountant shall be required to post bond.

At the end of each fiscal period the Accountant shall submit the Organization's operating account to the Council of Ministers.

The quietus for his administration shall be given by the Council of Ministers.

Outside the Organization's headquarters, receiving and disbursing agents named by the President (after obtaining the opinion of the Accountant) may be empowered, under the conditions fixed by special regulations, to perform receiving and disbursing operations on behalf of the Accountant.

10. *Relations between* Ordonnateur, *Accountant and Financial Controller:*

The relations between the Ordonnateur and the Accountant shall be governed by the laws and regulations applicable to those holding similar positions in the State where the Organization has its headquarters.

The Secretary-General, the Accountant, and the Financial Controller may in no case be of the same nationality.

11. *The Council of Ministers:*

The Council shall examine the budget submitted to the conference of Chiefs of State and of Government for approval.

It shall examine the administrative account and the operating account for the preceding year and formulate any observations that might be called for on the occasion of that examination. After examination, *these accounts* shall be sent to the conference of Chiefs of State and of Government for approval.

12. The President shall keep in continuous touch with the Financial Controller, give him all directives of a technical nature, confirm his OK's or his refusals to give his OK, and request the submission of all information that he finds necessary in order to follow the execution of the budget of the Afro-Malagasy Common Organization.

He shall give the Secretary-General of the Organization and the Financial Controller the necessary directives for the preparation of the draft budget for the following fiscal year.

13. *Supplementary Budget:*

Since each Department Chief must execute his budget within the limits of the credits allocated to him, there can be no collective or supplementary budget during the course of a fiscal year.

14. *Definitive Account:*

Each year the definitive account for the preceding fiscal year shall be sent by the *Secretary-General* to the Financial Controller before July 31. The latter shall transmit it to the President, together with his opinions and observations, before September 1.

The President shall submit this document to the Council of Ministers for examination. After examination, the definitive account shall be sent to the conference of Chiefs of State and of Government for approval.

Organization of the Control of the Execution of the Budget by the Financial Controller

1. *Appointment*: The Financial Controller shall be appointed by the President of the Afro-Malagasy Common Organization upon the recommendation of the Council of Ministers.

2. *Headquarters*: He shall reside at the headquarters of the Organization.

3. *Administration*: From the standpoint of administration, rank, and discipline, the Financial Controller shall be directly responsible to the President of the Afro-Malagasy Common Organization, from whom he shall receive his orders and to whom he shall report.

4. *Budget Preparation*: The role of the Financial Controller in this connection shall be as defined in Article 1 of the Financial Regulations.

He shall attend the meeting of the Council of Ministers at which the budget is examined.

He shall remain in continuous touch with the President.

5. *Budget Execution*: Each month the Financial Controller shall receive a statement, *broken down by chapter and article, showing the status of the execution of the Organization's Budget, which will be sent to him by the Secretary-General.*

He shall comment upon these statements and transmit them, together with his observations and suggestions, every two months to the States (balances, indemnifications, personnel strength, expenditures for *matériel*, etc., loans, estimates, construction).

He shall ask the Department Chiefs for any information or explanations he may require regarding the execution of the budget and the keeping of accounts.

He shall transmit to the Department Chiefs his opinions, reservations, and any necessary admonitions with regard to their administration.

He shall report to the President of the Afro-Malagasy Common Organization, the *ordonnateur* of the budget:

—quarterly, on the status of the execution of the budget of the Afro-Malagasy Common Organization;

—whenever necessary, on his findings.

He shall inspect the *financial sections of each department:*

—whenever he deems it necessary;

—when instructed by the President to do so;

—at the request of one or more States sent to the President. He shall report on these inspections to the President and to the Ministers and shall suggest any measures that might remedy the difficulties, deficiencies, or irregularities noted.

6. *Rule*: Any document, no matter what it may be, that is of such nature as to tie up the financial resources of the Afro-Malagasy Common Organization must be submitted to him for an opinion before being made executory (draft texts, regulations, commitments affecting the financial resources).

Expenditures relating to equipment and investment (contracts, loans, leases, rentals of movable property, etc.) shall likewise be subject to this control.

7. *Conferences and Meetings*: He shall attend *ex officio* all conferences, meetings of commissions, and meetings of the Afro-Malagasy Common Organization in which the budget is involved.

He shall send the President and the States a concise report of the meeting together with his observations regarding the financial effects of the measures adopted.

DONE AT TANANARIVE on June 27, 1966

III. UNION OF CENTRAL AFRICAN STATES

INDEPENDENT African States with common political and economic interests have embarked upon forms of economic integration. In 1965 a treaty establishing a Central African Economic and Customs Union was concluded between Cameroon, Central African Republic, Chad, the Congo (Brazzaville), and Gabon: text in *International Legal Materials*, vol. 4 (1965), p. 699. The Charter of the Union of Central African States adopted on 2 April 1968 established a Common Market. The original participants are the Central African Republic, the Democratic Republic of the Congo (Kinshasa) and Chad, and other states may be admitted under the provisions of Article 1. The French text appears in *Afrique contemporaine*, *La Documentation française*, no. 37 (1968), p. 14. See further Borella, *Annuaire française de droit international*, 1968, p. 167. On the relation between the Customs Union (U.D.E.A.C.) and the Union created in 1968 (U.E.A.C.) see *Afrique contemporaine*, *La Documentation française*, no. 41 (1969), p. 12.

TEXT

CHARTER OF THE UNION OF CENTRAL AFRICAN STATES[1]

Pursuant to the Protocol of Agreement signed February 2, 1968 at Bangui by the Chiefs of State of the Central African Republic, the Democratic Republic of the Congo, and the Republic of Chad;

Convinced that the peoples have an inalienable right to determine their own destiny;

Knowing that it is their duty to use the natural and human resources of their countries in achieving the general progress of their peoples in all areas of human activity;

Guided by a common, sincere determination to strengthen understanding between their peoples and co-operation between their States in order to satisfy the aspirations of their peoples toward the formation of a brotherhood and solidarity within a broader Union that would transcend ethnic and national differences;

Convinced that in order to apply this firm determination in achieving the progress of their peoples, it is important to create and to maintain a climate of peace and security;

[1] [Reprinted from an unofficial translation provided by the U.S. Department of State; reproduced with permission from *International Legal Materials*, vol. 4 (1965), p. 699. The French text was supplied by the Embassy of the Democratic Republic of the Congo (Kinshasa) in Washington, D.C.]

Firmly resolved to safeguard and strengthen the hard-won independence and sovereignty and the territorial integrity of their States and to combat all forms of colonialism and neo-colonialism;

Reaffirming their adherence to the principles of the Universal Declaration of Human Rights, and the Charters of the United Nations and the Organization of African Unity;

Animated by a firm desire to strengthen the age-old bonds of brotherhood existing between their peoples;

Desiring to promote economic, commercial, cultural, and political relations between their States;

Convinced that the geographical location of their States makes it necessary for them to achieve more effective solidarity in a common transportation and telecommunications organization;

Aware of the role that the States of the Union are called upon to play among the nations of Central Africa;

Aware likewise of helping thereby to strengthen African solidarity and with due respect for the international commitments assumed by each of their States;

Resolved to promote the gradual, progressive establishment of a Central African Common market with a view to regional integration:

Persuaded that the creation of a Common Market through the elimination of the obstacles to interregional trade, the adoption of a procedure for the equitable allocation of industrialization projects, and the co-ordination of programmes for the development of the various sectors of production, will contribute greatly toward improving the standard of living of their peoples;

Desiring to strengthen their economies and to ensure their harmonious development through the adoption of provisions that will take into account the interests of each and every one and that will sufficiently alleviate, through appropriate measures, the special situation of the economically less developed countries;

Resolved to contribute, through the establishment of such a regional economic union and through co-operation on policy and on security matters, toward the attainment of the objectives of African Unity,

The President of the Central African Republic
The President of the Democratic Republic of the Congo
The President of the Republic of Chad

Hereby decide to establish the Union of Central African States (U.E.A.C.) and

Agree upon the following:

Article 1

By this Charter the High Contracting Parties establish among themselves a Union of Central African States, hereinafter called the Union.

The Union shall be open to any independent and sovereign State that requests admission; new States shall be admitted by a unanimous vote of the members of the Union.

Article 2

The High Contracting Parties hereby decide to establish a Common Market of the Central African States. To that end they hereby agree to co-ordinate their industrialization policies, their development plans, and their transportation and telecommunications policies in order to promote balanced development and the diversification of the economies of the Member States of the Union within a framework designed to make it possible to expand trade between the States and to improve the living conditions of the people.

They likewise agree upon close co-operation in the cultural field and on security matters.

Article 3

The tasks devolving upon the Union shall be carried out through: the Conference of Chiefs of State, the Council of Ministers, and the Executive Secretariat.

PART ONE. THE INSTITUTIONS

TITLE I

THE CONFERENCE OF CHIEFS OF STATE

CHAPTER I. ORGANIZATION

Article 4

The Conference of Chiefs of State shall be constituted by a meeting of the Chiefs of State or their representatives, provided with full powers. The Chiefs of State may be assisted by Ministers and Experts.

Article 5

The Conference shall meet as often as necessary, and at least once a year.

Article 6

The Chairmanship of the meetings shall rotate annually among the Chiefs of State following the alphabetical order of the names of the States, unless the Chiefs of State unanimously decide otherwise. The new Chairman shall be installed at the opening session of the first meeting of each calendar year. If additional States become members of the Union, their Chiefs of State shall act as Chairmen of the Conference after the last State in alphabetical order, of those that sign this Charter.

Article 7

If the Conference lacks a Chairman owing to a change in the regime of a member country, the Chairmanship shall be held by the next Chief of State in alphabetical order of States.

Article 8

The Chairman shall fix the date and place for the meetings and shall summon the members of the Council.

Article 9

In case of emergency, the members of the Conference may be consulted at home if the Chairman so decides.

CHAPTER II. POWERS AND DUTIES

Article 10

The Conference shall be the supreme organ of the Union for purposes of ensuring the attainment of the objectives fixed in this Charter, under the conditions specified by the latter:

1. It shall strengthen the unity and solidarity of the Member States.
2. It shall co-ordinate and intensify their co-operation and their efforts to ensure better living conditions for their peoples.
3. It shall defend their sovereignty, territorial integrity, and independence.
4. It shall guide and co-ordinate their general policies, particularly in the following fields:
   (a) Economy, Trade, Customs, Transportation, and Telecommunications;
   (b) Education and Culture;
   (c) Health, Hygiene, and Nutrition;
   (d) Science and Technology;
   (e) Defence and Security.
5. It shall have the following nonrestrictive powers:
   It shall supervise the activities of the Council of Ministers.
   It shall draw up its bylaws and shall approve the bylaws of the Council of Ministers.

It shall establish the seat of the Union.

It shall decide regarding the creation of common agencies and services.

It shall appoint the Executive Secretary and the Deputy Executive Secretary of the Union.

It shall draw up the Union's Budget and shall fix the amount of the annual contribution of each Member State upon the recommendation of the Council of Ministers.

It shall decide regarding tariff negotiations with third countries and the application of a general tariff.

It shall decide, without appeal, on all questions on which the Council of Ministers is unable to reach a unanimous decision.

It may, in addition, revise the structures, functions, and activities of all other bodies.

6. It shall arbitrate any differences that arise between the Member States regarding the implementation of this Charter.

Chapter III. Decisions, Notification, Enforcement

Article 11

Decisions of the Conference shall be unanimous. They shall be automatically enforceable in the Member States in accordance with the terms and conditions to be determined by the bylaws of the Conference.

Title II

COUNCIL OF MINISTERS

Chapter I. Organization

Article 12

The Council of Ministers shall be composed of the Ministers of Foreign Affairs or any other Ministers designated by the Governments of the Member States.

The Delegation from each State, which shall be entitled to speak and vote, must include at least one Minister.

Members of the Council of Ministers may be assisted by experts.

Article 13

The Council may summon any qualified person to act in an advisory capacity at a meeting, but he may not participate in the discussion.

The Council shall meet as often as necessary and at least twice a year.

Article 14

The Chairmanship of the meetings shall rotate annually among the Ministers of the various States following the alphabetical order of the names of the States.

The new Chairman shall be installed at the opening session of the first meeting of each calendar year.

If additional States become members of the Union, their Ministers shall act as Chairmen of the Council after the last State in alphabetical order of those that sign this Charter.

Article 15

If the Council of Ministers lacks a Chairman owing to a change in the regime of a member country, the Chairmanship shall be held by the next Minister in alphabetical order of States.

Article 16

The Chairman shall fix the date and place for the meetings and shall summon the members of the Council.

Article 17

In case of emergency, the members of the Council may be consulted at home. The Council may not hold valid sessions unless each State is represented by at least one Minister.

CHAPTER II. POWERS AND DUTIES
Article 18

The Council shall act by authorization of the Conference of Chiefs of State. Such authorization shall cover the following matters in particular:
  Tariff and statistical nomenclature;
  Common external customs tariff;
  Schedule of import duties, fees, and charges;
  Tax on Union products;
  Customs code;
  Customs legislation and regulations;
  Co-ordination of the internal taxation systems;
  Investment code;
  Allocation of industrialization projects;
  Co-ordination of development plans and the transportation and tele-
    communications policy;
  Consultation with regard to export duties, export prices of goods of
    common interest, and with regard to wage rates and social benefits;

Educational and cultural exchanges;
Defence and security.

The conditions under which the Council shall exercise these powers and duties are set forth in detail in the title below.

Chapter III. Decisions of the Council

(Notification and Enforcement)

Article 19

Decisions of the Council shall be unanimous. They shall automatically be enforceable in the Member States in accordance with the terms and conditions to be determined by the Council's bylaws.

It may likewise formulate recommendations and express its wishes.

Title III

THE EXECUTIVE SECRETARIAT

Article 20

The Executive Secretary of the Union, assisted by Deputy Executive Secretaries and an administrative staff, shall constitute the Executive Secretariat.

The Executive Secretary and the Deputy Executive Secretaries shall be appointed for a three-year term, renewable by decision of the Conference of Chiefs of State upon the recommendation of the Council of Ministers. They shall be under the direct authority of the Chairman in office of the Conference.

Article 21

In performing their duties, the Executive Secretary, the Deputy Executive Secretaries, and the staff of the Secretariat may neither request nor receive instructions from any Government, any national entity, or any international entity. They shall not hold any attitude that is incompatible with their capacity as international personnel.

The status of the personnel of the Secretariat shall be fixed by decision of the Conference of Chiefs of State upon the recommendation of the Council of Ministers.

Title IV

LEGAL STATUS

Article 22

The Union shall have legal status, particularly the power required:

(*a*) To contract;

(*b*) To acquire and to dispose of the personal and real property essential to the attainment of its objectives;

(*c*) To borrow;

(*d*) To be a party to legal proceedings;

(*e*) To accept gifts, legacies, and donations of any sort.

To that end, it shall be represented by the Chairman of the Conference of Chiefs of State, who may delegate his powers.

The power to contract, to acquire, and to transfer real and personal property, and to borrow shall be exercised by the Chairman with the prior consent of the Chiefs of all the Contracting States.

Article 23

The Conference of the Union shall decide regarding the immunities and privileges to be granted to the Union, to the representatives of the Contracting Parties, and to the personnel of the Executive Secretariat in the territories of the Member States.

TITLE V

FINANCIAL PROVISIONS

Article 24

The Budget of the organs of the Union shall be drawn up annually by the Conference of Chiefs of State. It shall be made enforceable by the Chairman of the Conference.

Article 25

The expenses of the organs of the Union shall be met out of contributions by the States, in accordance with terms and conditions to be determined by the Conference.

PART TWO. ECONOMIC AND CUSTOMS PROVISIONS

TITLE VI

ECONOMIC AND CUSTOMS CO-OPERATION

Article 26

In order to achieve the objectives set forth in Article 2 of this Charter in accordance with the schedules laid down by the Conference of Chiefs of State, the activities of the Union shall comprise:

(*a*) The adoption of a common customs tariff and schedule of charges in connection with relations with third countries;

(b) Prohibition of any import and export duties and taxes between the Member States;

(c) Elimination between the Member States of obstacles to the free movement of persons, services, and capital;

(d) The establishment of a common economic policy to ensure Member States of a continuous, well-balanced expansion, greater stability; an accelerated rise in the standard of living, through co-ordination of the internal taxation system; the adoption of an Investment Code for investments that would favour the areas far from the sea where it is more difficult to operate industries, thereby correcting the natural inequalities within the Union; and the co-ordination of development plans on the basis of the equitable, well-balanced allocation of industries, with due consideration for available resources and the development level of each of the Member States;

(e) The establishment of a common policy in the field of transportation and telecommunications in order to facilitate trade between the Member States through a reduction in the cost of transportation;

(f) The establishment of a Compensation and Investment Fund;

(g) The institution of an appropriate duty favouring growth in the consumption of the products originating in the States of the Union;

(h) The establishment of an appropriate procedure to make possible the expansion of trade between the Member States;

(i) The establishment of an Investment Bank to facilitate the economic expansion of the Union through the creation of new resources.

PART THREE

Title VII

CULTURAL CO-OPERATION

Article 27

In order to bring about closer co-operation and to develop cultural exchanges between them, the Member States consider it necessary to expand their cultural relations both in the literary and artistic field and in the scientific and technical field.

Article 28

To that end the Member States shall endeavour, in so far as their means permit:

To encourage the exchange of professors, research workers, or any other persons engaged in the various fields of culture, science, and the arts;

To promote artistic, theatrical, and sports exchanges and to encourage the exchange of students and grantees.

Article 29

To that end, the various academic establishments, institutes, and research centres new existing or to be created in each State shall be open to the nationals of the other States of the Organization.

The Union shall facilitate such exchanges, particularly by granting fellowships and training grants.

PART FOUR. SECURITY

Article 30

In order to ensure the security of their territories and to safeguard their sovereignty, the Member States hereby proclaim their solidarity and their willingness to furnish military assistance to each other in the event of foreign aggression.

Article 31

To that end, each of the Contracting States hereby promises to take all practical measures necessary to ensure the security of the borders of the Member States, particularly through a mutual exchange of information regarding anything that might constitute a threat to the internal and external security of any Member State or to the Union as a whole, through the transmission of reports or data making it possible to extradite persons sought in their countries for crimes or offences against ordinary law committed in their country of origin or in any other Member State, and all measures intended to stamp out subversion in the territory of any Member State or of the Union as a whole.

PART FIVE. TRANSITORY PROVISIONS

Article 32

Upon the entry into force of this Charter, the Contracting States shall send to the Executive Secretariat of the Union all laws, regulations, and decisions on customs and economic matters, including decisions concerning the granting of preferential treatment. The Executive Secretary shall distribute them to the Member States.

Article 33

Specialized technical commissions shall meet as soon as possible in order to submit to the Conference of Chiefs of State for decision regulations of execution on the following points:

Customs legislation and regulations;
Guidelines for the allocation of import and export duties;
The co-ordination of investment codes or the establishment of a common Investment Code;
The co-ordination of the internal taxation systems;
The procedure for the approval and allocation of industrialization projects and the industrial co-operation policy;
The system for taxation of local products;
The co-ordination of development plans, and of the transportation and telecommunications policies;
The establishment of a Compensation and Investment Fund;
The system of port, rail, river, highway, and air infrastructure services;
The free movement of persons, services, and capital, and the right of establishment.

Article 34

These regulations of execution shall form an integral part of this Charter.

PART SIX. GENERAL AND FINAL PROVISIONS

Article 35

This Charter shall enter into force upon ratification in accordance with the constitutional formalities of each of the Contracting States.

The instruments of ratification shall be deposited with the Central African Republic, designated the depositary State.

Upon receipt of the instruments of ratification, the depositary Government shall so inform all the Contracting Parties and the Executive Secretariat of the Union.

Article 36

Amendments to this Charter must be ratified by each Member State in the manner specified by its internal legislation.

Article 37

This Charter may be denounced by any Member State. The denunciation shall not enter into force, as regards the State denouncing it, until

January 1 following notification of denunciation to the Chairman of the Conference and six months after such notification at the earliest.

Denunciation by one or more Contracting States shall not entail the dissolution of the Union.

The Conference of Chiefs of State alone may decide upon such dissolution and fix the terms and conditions for distribution of the assets and liabilities.

However, the Conference shall establish the principle and the terms and conditions for indemnification if the Contracting State withdraws from the Union.

Article 38

This Charter, duly ratified, shall be registered with the Secretariat of the United Nations by the depositary Government pursuant to Article 102 of the United Nations Charter.

DONE AT FORT-LAMY, April 2, 1968

IV. ECONOMIC COMMUNITY OF WEST AFRICA

THE Articles of Association for the establishment of an Economic Community of West Africa were signed at Accra on 4 May 1967. The signatories were Dahomey, Ghana, Ivory Coast, Liberia, Mali, Mauritania, Niger, Nigeria, Senegal, Sierra Leone, Togo, and Upper Volta. The text appears in U.N. Document E/CN. 14/399 (24 May 1967), Annexe IV; and *United Nations Treaty Series*, vol. 595, p. 287. See further the Agreement on Interim Organization for West African Economic Co-operation, 28 May 1965; text in *International Legal Materials*, vol. 4, p. 916; *United Nations Treaty Series*, vol. 559, p. 273. The francophonic states have a togetherness deriving from the economic association with France and the franc zone. There is a West African Customs Union formed in 1962 and a Monetary Union formed in 1966, both related to the French Community.

On 23 May 1970 a conference of heads of state decided to establish the West African Economic Community: *Afrique contemporaine, La Documentation française*, no. 50 (1970), p. 17.

ARTICLES OF ASSOCIATION, 1967

The Contracting States of the West African Sub-Region

Desiring to establish an Economic Community of West Africa (hereinafter referred to as the 'Community') by means of a Treaty which the Contracting States undertake to negotiate and conclude at the earliest possible time;

Convinced that, pending the formal establishment of the Community, it is essential to institute a transitional arrangement for the purpose of expediting the conclusion of the said Treaty and furthering the aims of the Community;

Noting that the inter-governmental organizations for economic co-operation already existing in the West African sub-region have made a notable contribution to the attainment of the objectives of the Community;

Deeming it necessary to co-operate effectively with the afore-mentioned inter-governmental organizations;

Have agreed as follows:

Article 1

Aims of the Community

1. The aims of the Community shall be:

(*a*) to promote through the economic co-operation of the Member

States a co-ordinated and equitable development of their economies, especially in industry, agriculture, transport and communications, trade and payments, manpower, energy and natural resources;

(b) to further the maximum possible interchange of goods and services among its Member States;

(c) to contribute to the orderly expansion of trade between the Member States and the rest of the world;

(d) by all these efforts and endeavours to contribute to the economic development of the continent of Africa as a whole.

Article 2

General undertakings

1. In order to achieve the aims of the Community, the Member States shall:

(a) work in close co-operation with one another and endeavour to co-ordinate and harmonize their economic policies, both within and outside the Community;

(b) keep each other informed and furnish the Community with the information required for the achievement of its aims;

(c) within the Community, establish among themselves consultation on a continuous basis and carry out studies in order to determine the areas and lines of economic development to be undertaken jointly or in common;

(d) negotiate within the Community the progressive elimination of customs and other barriers to the expansion of trade between them as well as restrictions on current payment transactions and on capital movements;

(e) take measures which render their products relatively competitive with goods imported from outside the Community and seek to obtain more favourable conditions for their products in the world market;

(f) endeavour to formulate and adopt common policies, and negotiate and conclude Agreements among themselves or through the medium of the Community, designed to serve the achievement of its aims, including the development jointly or in common of specific branches of industry and agriculture, the joint operation of specific transport and communications services, the development and the joint use of energy, joint research, training of manpower and the implementation jointly or in common of all other projects designed to promote the objectives of the Community, as well as common trade and payments arrangements, and

(g) ensure, both within and outside the Community, that the common policies that have been adopted and the Agreements that have been concluded for the achievement of the aims of the Community are carried out.

2. Member States shall take all steps, particularly the provision of budgetary and other resources, required for the implementation of the Decisions and Recommendations of the Community, duly adopted.

Article 3

Co-operation among Member States and with other bodies

1. Individual Member States shall be entitled to take, both within and outside the Community, measures of economic co-operation without the agreement of other Member States, provided that such measures do not prejudice the aims of the Community.

2. Member States which belong to or join other systems of economic co-operation shall inform the Community of their membership and of those provisions in their constituent instruments that have a bearing on the purposes of the Community.

Article 4

Structure

1. The Community, when established shall have such principal organs and subsidiary bodies as may be required for the attainment of its objectives.

Article 5

Interim Council of Ministers—composition, powers and procedure

1. Pending the conclusion and entry into force of the Treaty an Interim Council of Ministers is hereby established.

2. Membership of the Interim Council of Ministers shall be open to all such Members of the United Nations Economic Commission for Africa as fall within the area known as the West African sub-region, comprising Dahomey, Gambia, Ghana, Guinea, the Ivory Coast, Liberia, Mali, Mauritania, the Niger, Nigeria, Senegal, Sierra Leone, Togo and the Upper Volta.

3. The Interim Council of Ministers shall have as its principal task, the drafting of the Treaty governing the Economic Community of West Africa, its submission to Member States and the initiation of action as may be deemed necessary and appropriate to facilitate the entry into force of the Treaty.

4. The Interim Council of Ministers shall have power to establish a provisional Secretariat, an Interim Economic Committee, and any other subsidiary bodies as may be appropriate.

5. The Interim Council of Ministers shall determine those areas of economic development to be undertaken jointly or in common by Member States, the manner and degree of such development and the time required therefor.

6. The Interim Council of Ministers shall establish, through its subsidiary bodies, links with existing inter-governmental organizations for economic co-operation in the sub-region, whose activities are restricted to that geographical area. In particular, these organizations shall participate, in an advisory capacity, in the work of such Committees as may be established by the Interim Council of Ministers. The Interim Council of Ministers may also establish such relations as it deems fit with any other African inter-governmental organizations such as the African Development Bank, and the Lake and River Basin Development Organizations, whose activities are in line with the objectives of the Community.

7. The Interim Council of Ministers may invite to its meetings, in an observer or consultative capacity, representatives of other African sub-regions and of any non-African donor countries or organizations in its consideration of matters in which such sub-regional representatives and those of donor countries or organizations for technical and financial assistance may be of particular assistance to the West African sub-region.

8. A quorum for the meetings of the Interim Council of Ministers shall be a simple majority of the Member States. In the event of its inability to attend, a Member State may authorize another Member State to represent it. No Member State can represent more than one other State.

Article 6

Interim Council of Ministers, decisions and recommendations

1. Each Member of the Interim Council of Ministers shall have one vote.

2. Decisions, resolutions and recommendations taken within the framework of the terms of reference of the Interim Council of Ministers as agreed by these Articles of Association shall be taken by a simple majority vote.

Article 7

Final provisions

1. The Interim Council of Ministers shall cease to exist upon the entry into force of the Treaty.

2. These Articles of Association may be signed by States of the West African sub-region and shall come into force when signed by a simple majority of these States.

3. The original of these Articles of Association, the English and French texts of which are equally authentic, shall be deposited with the Secretary-General of the United Nations who shall forward certified true copies to all the States of the sub-region.

IN WITNESS WHEREOF, the undersigned Plenipotentiaries, being duly authorized thereto by their respective Governments, have appended their signatures to these Articles of Association.

DONE IN THE CITY OF ACCRA this Fourth day of May Nineteen Hundred and Sixty-seven.

V. EAST AFRICAN COMMUNITY
AND COMMON MARKET

THE Treaty for East African Co-operation was signed at Kampala on 6 June 1967 by the Governments of Kenya, Uganda, and Tanzania. It came into force on 1 December 1967. The text reproduced here was published by the East African Common Services Organization. Functional co-operation between Kenya, Uganda, and Tanganyika existed under British administration in the form of the East Africa High Commission created in 1948. When the first of the three territories achieved independence (Tanganyika on 9 December 1961), the High Commission was replaced by the East African Common Services Organization. E.A.C.S.O. produced the functional advantages of federalism without involving commitment to federalism as a principle or programme. At the same time, there were those who regarded functional co-operation as a preparation for a higher form of political association. See generally Leys and Robson (ed.), *Federation in East Africa*, Nairobi, 1965; Green and Krishna, *Economic Co-operation in Africa*, Nairobi, 1967; Hazlewood (ed.), *African Integration and Disintegration*, London, 1967.

The East African Community and Common Market, like the European institutions of the same type, are carefully structured and combine integration for specific purposes with maintenance of political independence in general. For an account of the historical background and the institutions of the Community see Ingrid Doimi di Delupis, *The East African Community and Common Market*, London, 1970. Although the treaty does not provide in terms for admission of other states to membership, there is provision for other states to come into association with the Community and in practice 'association' may approximate to membership, at the least. Zambia, Ethiopia, and Somalia have applied for membership or association of a substantial kind. Burundi and Rwanda have applied for a limited form of association. See further Green, *Journal of Modern African Studies*, vol. 5, no. 3, Nov. 1967.

TEXT

1. *Treaty for East African Co-operation*, 1967

WHEREAS the United Republic of Tanzania, the Sovereign State of Uganda and the Republic of Kenya have enjoyed close commercial, industrial, and other ties for many years:

AND WHEREAS provision was made by the East Africa (High Commission) Orders in Council 1947 to 1961 for the control and administration of certain matters and services of common interest to the said countries and for that purpose the East Africa High Commission and the East Africa Central Legislative Assembly were thereby established:

AND WHEREAS provision was made by the East African Common Services Organization Agreements 1961 to 1966 (upon the revocation of the East Africa (High Commission) Orders in Council 1947 to 1961) for the establishment of the East African Common Services Organization with the East African Common Services Authority as its principal executive authority and the Central Legislative Assembly as its legislative body:

AND WHEREAS the East African Common Services Organization has, since its establishment, performed on behalf of the said countries common services in accordance with the wishes of the said countries and its Constitution:

AND WHEREAS the said countries, while being aware that they have reached different stages of industrial development and resolved to reduce existing industrial imbalances, are resolved and determined to foster and encourage the accelerated and sustained industrial development of all of the said countries:

AND WHEREAS the said countries, with a view to strengthening the unity of East Africa, are resolved to abolish certain quantitative restrictions which at present affect trade between them and are desirous of pursuing a policy towards the most favourable development of the freest possible international trade:

AND WHEREAS the said countries having regard to the interests of and their desire for the wider unity of Africa are resolved to co-operate with one another and with other African countries in the economic, political and cultural fields:

AND WHEREAS the said countries are resolved to act in concert for the establishment of a common market with no restrictions in the long term on trade between such countries:

NOW THEREFORE the Government of the United Republic of Tanzania, the Government of the Sovereign State of Uganda and the Government of the Republic of Kenya
Determined to strengthen their industrial, commercial, and other ties and their common services by the establishment of an East African Community and of a Common Market as an integral part thereof

AGREE AS FOLLOWS—

PART I. PRINCIPLES

CHAPTER I. THE EAST AFRICAN COMMUNITY

Article 1

Establishment and membership of the Community

1. By this Treaty the Contracting Parties establish among themselves an East African Community and, as an integral part of such Community, an East African Common Market.

2. The East African Community is in this Treaty referred to as 'the Community' and the East African Common Market is referred to as 'the Common Market'.

3. The members of the Community, in this Treaty referred to as 'the Partner States', shall be the United Republic of Tanzania, the Sovereign State of Uganda and the Republic of Kenya.

Article 2

Aims of the Community

1. It shall be the aim of the Community to strengthen and regulate the industrial, commercial, and other relations of the Partner States to the end that there shall be accelerated, harmonious and balanced development and sustained expansion of economic activities the benefits whereof shall be equitably shared.

2. For the purposes set out in paragraph 1 of this Article and as hereinafter provided in the particular provisions of this Treaty, the Community shall use its best endeavours to ensure—

   (a) the establishment and maintenance, subject to certain exceptions, of a common customs tariff and a common excise tariff;

   (b) the abolition generally of restrictions on trade between Partner States;

   (c) the inauguration, in the long term, of a common agricultural policy;

   (d) the establishment of an East African Development Bank in accordance with the Charter contained in Annex VI to this Treaty;

   (e) the retention of freedom of current account payments between the Partner States, and freedom of capital account payments necessary to further the aims of the Community;

   (f) the harmonization, required for the proper functioning of the Common Market, of the monetary policies of the Partner States and in particular consultation in case of any disequilibrium in the balances of payments of the Partner States;

(*g*) the operation of services common to the Partner States;

(*h*) the co-ordination of economic planning;

(*i*) the co-ordination of transport policy;

(*j*) the approximation of the commercial laws of the Partner States; and

(*k*) such other activities, calculated to further the aims of the Community, as the Partner States may from time to time decide to undertake in common.

Article 3

Institutions of the Community

1. The institutions of the Community (established and regulated by Parts III and IV of this Treaty) shall be—

the East African Authority
the East African Legislative Assembly
the East African Ministers
the Common Market Council
the Common Market Tribunal
the Communications Council
the Finance Council
the Economic Consultative and Planning Council
the Research and Social Council,

and such other corporations, bodies, departments, and services as are established or provided for by this Treaty.

2. The institutions of the Community shall perform the functions and act within the limits of the powers conferred upon them by this Treaty or by any law.

3. The institutions of the Community shall be assisted in the exercise of their functions by a central secretariat of officers in the service of the Community.

4. Persons employed in the service of the Community, the Corporations or the Bank, and directors and alternate directors of the Bank—

(*a*) shall be immune from civil process with respect to acts performed by them in their official capacity; and

(*b*) shall be accorded such immunities from immigration restrictions or alien registration, and where they are not citizens of a Partner State, such facilities in relation to exchange regulations, as the Authority may determine.

5. Experts or consultants rendering services to the Community, the Corporations or the Bank shall be accorded such immunities and privileges in the Partner States as the Authority may determine.

Article 4

General undertaking as to implementation

The Partner States shall make every effort to plan and direct their policies with a view to creating conditions favourable for the development of the Common Market and the achievement of the aims of the Community and shall co-ordinate, through the institutions of the Community, their economic policies to the extent necessary to achieve such aims and shall abstain from any measure likely to jeopardize the achievement thereof.

PART II. THE EAST AFRICAN COMMON MARKET

CHAPTER II. EXTERNAL TRADE

Article 5

Common customs tariff

1. The Partner States, recognizing that a common external customs tariff is a basic requirement of the Common Market and subject to paragraphs 2 and 3 of this Article, agree to establish and maintain a common customs tariff in respect of all goods imported into the Partner States from foreign countries.

2. A Partner State may, with the agreement of the Ministers of the Partner States responsible for public finance, depart from the common external customs tariff in respect of the importation of a particular item into that State.

3. The Partner States agree to undertake early consultations in the Common Market Council with a view to the abolition generally of existing differences in the external customs tariff.

Article 6

Remission of customs duty

1. The Partner States agree not to exempt, remit or otherwise relieve from payment of customs duty any goods originating in a foreign country and imported by the Government of a Partner State if—

(a) such goods are imported for the purpose of resale or for any purpose other than consumption or use by that Government; and

(b) in the case of goods provided by way of aid, by any government or organization, either *gratis* or on terms less stringent than those appropriate to ordinary commercial transactions, such goods are intended for the purpose of resale or consumption in, or are transferred to, any country other than the Partner State which is the recipient of such goods.

2. The Partner States agree that the Community and the Corporations shall be enabled to import free of customs duty any goods required for the purpose of their operations except such goods as are intended for sale, or are sold, to the public.

Article 7

External trade arrangements

No Partner State shall enter into arrangements with any foreign country whereunder tariff concessions are available to that Partner State which are not available to the other Partner States.

Article 8

Deviation of trade resulting from barter agreements

1. If as a result of any barter agreement involving a particular kind of manufactured goods, entered into between a Partner State or any body or person therein, and a foreign country, or any body or person therein, there is, in respect of that kind of manufactured goods, a significant deviation of trade away from goods coming from and manufactured in another Partner State to goods imported in pursuance of that agreement, then the Partner State into which such goods are so imported shall take effective measures to counteract such deviation.

2. In paragraph 1 of this Article 'barter agreement' means any agreement or arrangement by which manufactured goods are imported into a Partner State, being goods for which settlement may be effected, in whole or in part, by the direct exchange of goods.

3. In order to determine whether a deviation of trade in a particular kind of manufactured goods has occurred for the purposes of this Article, regard shall be had to all relevant trade statistics and other records concerning that kind of manufactured goods of the East African Customs and Excise Department for the six months immediately preceding a complaint that a deviation has occurred and to the average of the two comparable periods of six months in the twenty-four months which preceded the first importation of goods under the barter agreement.

CHAPTER III. INTRA-EAST AFRICAN TRADE

Article 9

External goods—general principles

1. The Partner States agree that where customs duty has been charged and collected on any goods imported into a Partner State (hereinafter in this paragraph referred to as 'the importing State') from a foreign country then such goods shall not be liable to further customs duty on transfer to any other Partner State (hereinafter referred to as 'the receiving State'):

Provided that where the rate of customs duty applicable to such goods in the receiving State exceeds that charged and collected in the importing State any excess of duty so arising may be charged and collected.

2. Each of the Partner States shall grant full and unrestricted freedom of transit through its territory for goods proceeding to or from a foreign country indirectly through that territory to or from another Partner State; and such transit shall not be subject to any discrimination, quantitative restrictions, duties or other charges levied on transit.

3. Notwithstanding paragraph 2 of this Article—
   (*a*) goods in transit shall be subject to the customs laws; and
   (*b*) goods in transit shall be liable to the charges usually made for carriage and for any services which may be rendered, provided such charges are not discriminatory.

4. The Partner States agree that each Partner State shall be entitled to prohibit or restrict the import from a foreign country into it of goods of any particular description or derived from any particular source.

5. Where goods are imported from a foreign country into one Partner State, it shall be open to each of the other Partner States to restrict the transfer to it of such goods whether by a system of licensing and controlling importers or by other means:

Provided that, in the application of any restriction referred to in this paragraph, regard shall be had to the practicability of such restriction where goods have been repacked, blended, or otherwise processed.

6. The provisions of paragraphs 4 and 5 of this Article shall not apply to any goods which, under the provisions of Article 11 of this Treaty, fall to be accepted as goods originating in a Partner State.

Article 10

Customs duty collected to be paid to consuming State

1. Where any goods, which are imported into a Partner State from a foreign country and in respect of which customs duty has been charged

and collected in that State (in this paragraph referred to as 'the collecting State') are transferred to one of the other Partner States (in this paragraph referred to as 'the consuming State'), the following provisions shall apply—

(a) if the duty collected in the collecting State was a specific duty or if the goods are transferred to the consuming State in their original packages, the collecting State shall pay the full amount of the duty collected to the consuming State;

(b) if the duty collected in the collecting State was an *ad valorem* duty and the goods are transferred to the consuming State other than in their original packages, the collecting State shall pay to the consuming State an amount equal to 70 per cent of the duty which would have been payable if the value of the goods for duty had been taken to be the ordinary retail price; and for this purpose 'ordinary retail price' means the price at which the goods could be expected to sell at the time and place of their transfer to the consuming State:

Provided that the Authority may by order from time to time alter the amount to be paid by the collecting State to the consuming State under this sub-paragraph and the method of calculation thereof;

(c) if the duty collected was an *ad valorem* duty and the goods are transferred other than in their original packages and an alteration of the relevant tariff has been made in the collecting State within a material time, then, for the purpose of calculating the sum to be paid under sub-paragraph (b) of this paragraph, duty shall be deemed to have been collected in accordance with the tariff actually in force six weeks before the transfer of the goods.

2. Where any goods, which are imported from a foreign country into a Partner State (in this paragraph referred to as 'the importing State') are chargeable to customs duty in that State, but the duty has been remitted either in whole or in part, and are subsequently transferred to one of the other Partner States (in this paragraph referred to as 'the consuming State') the importing State shall, notwithstanding the said remission, pay to the consuming State the amount which would have been paid to the consuming State in accordance with paragraph 1 of this Article had the duty been collected but to the extent only that such duty would have been chargeable and collected if the goods had been imported directly into the consuming State.

Article 11

No internal tariff on East African goods

1. Except as is provided in paragraph 2 of this Article no Partner State shall impose a duty in the nature of a customs duty or import duty in

respect of goods which are transferred to that Partner State from one of the other Partner States and originate in the Partner States.

2. Paragraph 1 of this Article is subject to the rights and powers of Partner States to impose transfer taxes in accordance with and subject to the conditions contained in this Treaty.

3. For the purpose of this Treaty, goods shall be accepted as originating in the Partner States where—

(a) they have been wholly produced in the Partner States; or

(b) they have been produced in the Partner States and the value of materials imported from a foreign country or of undetermined origin which have been used at any stage of the production of the goods does not exceed 70 per cent of the ex-factory value of the goods.

4. Rules for the administration and application of this Article are contained in Annex I to this Treaty.

5. The Common Market Council shall from time to time examine whether the rules contained in Annex I to this Treaty can be amended to make them simpler and more liberal and to ensure their smooth and equitable operation, and the Authority may by order from time to time amend or add to Annex I.

Article 12
No quantitative restrictions on East African goods

1. Except as is provided in this Article, each of the Partner States undertakes that, at a time not later than the coming into force of this Treaty, it will remove all the then existing quota, quantitative or the like restrictions or prohibitions which apply to the transfer to that State of goods originating in the other Partner States (including agricultural products) and, except as may be provided for or permitted by this Treaty, will thereafter refrain from imposing any further restrictions or prohibitions:

Provided that this paragraph shall not preclude a Partner State introducing or continuing or executing restrictions or prohibitions affecting—

(a) the application of security laws and regulations;

(b) the control of arms, ammunition and other war equipment and military items;

(c) the protection of human, animal or plant health or life, or the protection of public morality;

(d) transfers of gold, silver and precious and semi-precious stones;

(e) the control of nuclear materials, radio-active products or any other material used in the development or exploitation of nuclear energy; or (*f*) the protection of its revenue where another Partner State has, in accordance with paragraph 2 of Article 17 of this Treaty, departed from a common excise tariff.

2. It is agreed that each of the Partner States shall have the right to impose restrictions and prohibitions against the transfer of goods from the other Partner States which originate in the other Partner States, in so far as may be necessary from time to time to give effect to the contractual and other obligations entered into by each of the States and listed in Annex II to this Treaty.

3. It is agreed that each of the Partner States shall have the right to impose quantitative restrictions or prohibitions in respect of certain agricultural products in the circumstances provided for by Article 13 of this Treaty.

4. If a Partner State encounters balance of payment difficulties, taking into account its overall position, that Partner State may, for the purpose only of overcoming such difficulties, impose quantitative restrictions on the goods of the other Partner States, subject to the following conditions being satisfied, namely that—

(*a*) the proposed quantitative restrictions do not contravene its obligations under the General Agreement on Tariffs and Trade or its obligations under the rules of the International Monetary Fund; and

(*b*) restrictions have been imposed on the import of goods from foreign countries and are inadequate to solve the difficulties; and

(*c*) the restrictions imposed under this paragraph shall in no case operate against the goods of Partner States more unfavourably than the restrictions imposed on the goods of foreign countries; and

(*d*) consultation concerning the proposed quantitative restrictions has first taken place within the Common Market Council and thereafter, while such restrictions remain in force, the Common Market Council shall keep the operation thereof under review.

Article 13

Exception for certain agricultural products

1. Notwithstanding the obligation of the Partner States in respect of agricultural products referred to in paragraph 1 of Article 12 of this Treaty, it is declared that each of the Partner States shall, to the extent set out in Annex III to this Treaty, have the right to impose quantitative restrictions against the transfer of the agricultural products of the other Partner States which are basic staple foods or major export crops, subject to special marketing arrangements and listed in that Annex.

2. The Authority may from time to time amend or add to Annex III to this Treaty.

Article 14

Long term aim as to agriculture

Notwithstanding Articles 12 and 13 of this Treaty, it is declared that, in the long term, it is the aim and intention of the Partner States that the provisions of this Treaty relating to the establishment and maintenance of the Common Market should extend to agriculture and trade in agricultural products and that the development of the Common Market in respect of agricultural products should be accompanied by co-operation and consultation in the field of agricultural policy among the Partner States so that in particular, within the framework of the Community, trade arrangements between the national agencies or marketing boards of the Partner States may be entered into directly within a single system of prices and a network within the Partner States as a whole of marketing services and facilities.

Article 15

Customs duty on goods used in manufacture

1. Where goods which are imported into a Partner State from a foreign country and in respect of which customs duty is charged and collected in that State (in this Article referred to as 'the collecting State') are wholly or in part used in the collecting State in the manufacture of other goods (in this Article referred to as 'the manufactured goods'), and the manufactured goods are subsequently transferred to another Partner State (in this Article referred to as 'the consuming State'), the collecting State shall pay to the consuming State the full amount of the duty collected in the collecting State in respect of the goods imported into the collecting State and used in the manufacture of the manufactured goods subsequently transferred to the consuming State.

2. Where goods which are imported into a Partner State (in this paragraph referred to as 'the importing State') from a foreign country are chargeable to customs duty in that State but the duty has been remitted either in whole or in part and the goods are wholly or in part used in the importing State in the manufacture of other goods (in this paragraph referred to as 'the manufactured goods'), and the manufactured goods are subsequently transferred to another Partner State (in this paragraph referred to as 'the consuming State'), the importing State shall, notwithstanding the said remission, pay to the consuming State the amount of the duty chargeable in respect of goods imported into the importing State and

used in the manufacture of the manufactured goods subsequently transferred to the consuming State to the extent that such duty would have been chargeable and collected if the goods had been imported into the consuming State.

3. Notwithstanding paragraphs 1 and 2 of this Article, if the value of the imported goods which are used in the manufacture of any manufactured goods transferred as a separate consignment is less than one hundred shillings in the currency of the State of manufacture, then in that case only no payment of duty shall be made to the consuming State under this Article.

Article 16

Discriminatory practices

1. The Partner States recognize that the following practices are incompatible with this Treaty to the extent that they frustrate the benefits expected from the removal or absence of duties and quantitative restrictions on trade between the Partner States—

(a) one channel marketing;
(b) discriminatory rates of taxes, duties or other charges levied in a Partner State on any goods originating in another Partner State;
(c) dumping; and
(d) discriminatory purchasing.

2. In paragraph 1 of this Article—

(a) 'one channel marketing' means any arrangement for the marketing of goods, whether regulated by law or otherwise, which, by limiting the channels by which such goods may be marketed, has effect to exclude competition in the marketing of such goods;
(b) 'discriminatory rates of taxes, duties or other charges' means rates of taxes, duties or other charges imposed upon goods by a Partner State which place such goods in an unfavourable position with regard to sale by comparison with similar goods originating in that Partner State or imported from any other country;
(c) 'dumping' means the transfer of goods originating in a Partner State to another Partner State for sale—

(i) at a price less than the comparable price charged for similar goods in the Partner State where such goods originate (due allowance being made for the differences in the conditions of sale or in taxation or for any other factors affecting the comparability of prices); and
(ii) under circumstances likely to prejudice the production of similar goods in that Partner State; and

(*d*) 'discriminatory purchasing' means any arrangement or practice whereby a Partner State or any body or person therein gives preference to the purchase of goods originating from a foreign country when suitable goods originating within the Partner States are available on comparable terms including price.

CHAPTER IV. EXCISABLE GOODS

Article 17

Common excise tariff

1. Subject to paragraphs 2 and 3 of this Article, the Partner States agree to establish and maintain a common excise tariff in respect of excisable goods manufactured, processed or produced in the Partner States.

2. For revenue purposes, a Partner State may, in special circumstances and after consultation between the Ministers of the Partner States responsible for public finance, depart from the common excise tariff in respect of the manufacture, processing or production of particular excisable goods in that State:

Provided that a Partner State before acting under this paragraph shall have due regard to the administrative practicability of enforcing the departure contemplated and to whether the proposed departure would be likely to affect detrimentally the proper functioning of the Common Market.

3. The Partner States acknowledge their intention to remove presently existing differences in the excise tariff which the Common Market Council may determine to be undesirable in the interests of the proper functioning of the Common Market.

Article 18

Excise duty to be paid to consuming State

1. Where goods which are liable to excise duty in one of the Partner States (in this Article referred to as 'the collecting State') are transferred to another Partner State (in this Article referred to as 'the consuming State') the East African Customs and Excise Department shall collect excise duty either at the rate in force in respect of the collecting State or, where the rate in force in respect of the consuming State is higher than that in force in respect of the collecting State, at that rate.

2. Where the rate of excise duty in force in respect of the consuming State is lower than that in force in respect of the collecting State, the owner or other transferor of goods referred to in paragraph 1 of this

Article shall receive from the East African Customs and Excise Department, on proof of transfer to the consuming State, a refund of the difference between those rates of duty.

3. The East African Customs and Excise Department shall, in respect of goods liable to excise duty transferred from the collecting State to the consuming State, pay to the consuming State the amount of the excise duty collected at the rate in force in that State.

CHAPTER V. MEASURES TO PROMOTE BALANCED INDUSTRIAL DEVELOPMENT

Article 19

Fiscal incentives

The Partner States declare that they shall use their best endeavours to agree upon a common scheme of fiscal incentives towards industrial development which shall apply within the Partner States.

Article 20

Transfer tax

1. As a measure to promote new industrial development in those Partner States which are less developed industrially transfer taxes may, with the aim of promoting industrial balance between the Partner States, be imposed, notwithstanding paragraph 1 of Article 11 of this Treaty, in accordance with and subject to the conditions and limitations imposed by this Treaty.

2. In this Article, 'manufactured goods' means the goods defined, or otherwise listed, in Annex IV to this Treaty. The Authority may by order from time to time amend or add to Annex IV.

3. Subject to this Article, a Partner State which is in deficit in its total trade in manufactured goods with the other two Partner States may impose transfer taxes upon manufactured goods which are transferred to that State and originate from either of the other Partner States.

4. Subject to this Article, a Partner State may impose transfer taxes upon the manufactured goods of a Partner State being goods of a value not exceeding the amount of the deficit in trade in manufactured goods between the State which is imposing the transfer tax and the State of origin of the goods upon which the tax is to be imposed.

5. For the purposes of paragraphs 3 and 4 of this Article the deficit in trade in manufactured goods between Partner States shall at any time be

taken to be that indicated in the most recently published annual trade statistics produced by the East African Customs and Excise Department and where, in any particular case, the manufactured goods of a Partner State upon which a transfer tax may under this Article be imposed are not readily identifiable within the trade statistics referred to in this paragraph, the Common Market Council may determine the extent to which any goods comprised in such statistics contribute to the amount of any deficit in any trade.

6. A Partner State may impose a transfer tax upon manufactured goods only if at the time the tax is imposed goods of a similar description are being manufactured in that State or are reasonably expected to be manufactured in that State within three months of the imposition of the tax, and for the purposes of this paragraph goods shall be deemed to be of a similar description to other goods if, in addition to similar function, constituent parts or content, they are of such a nature as will enable them actively to compete in the same market as those other goods:

Provided that this paragraph shall not preclude the imposition, but not the bringing into operation, of a suspended transfer tax at any time:

Provided further that, if a transfer tax is imposed in the reasonable expectation that the manufacture of particular goods will commence within three months of the imposition of the tax and such manufacture does not commence within that period—

(a) the Partner State imposing the transfer tax shall, within twenty-one days, revoke it unless, before the expiration of that period, that Partner State has obtained the directive of the Common Market Council that, conditional upon the commencement of manufacture within a further period of three months, the revocation of such tax may be deferred for such further period;

(b) notwithstanding that a transfer tax has been revoked, for the reason that the Common Market Council has not within three months of the imposition of such tax given the directive referred to in subparagraph (a) of this proviso, it shall be competent to that Council, where application in that behalf has been made by a Partner State within three months of the imposition of such tax, to direct that, conditional upon the commencement of manufacture within a further period of three months, such tax may be reimposed.

7. A Partner State may impose a transfer tax upon a particular kind of manufactured goods only if at the time the tax is imposed, or within three months thereafter if the tax is imposed in the reasonable expectation that the manufacture of such goods will commence within three months, the

industry within the tax imposing State has the capacity to produce in the ensuing year—

  (a) a quantity of goods equivalent to not less than 15 per cent of the domestic consumption within that Partner State of goods of that particular kind in the period of twelve months immediately preceding the imposition of the tax; or

  (b) goods of that particular kind having an ex-factory value of not less than 2,000,000 shillings.

8. The rate of transfer tax shall be determined by the Partner State which imposes it, but the rate for a particular item shall not exceed—

  (a) where the duty is chargeable *ad valorem* or *ad valorem* as an alternative to the specific duty, 50 per cent of the rate of duty prescribed by the customs tariff of the tax imposing State in respect of the import of the same kind of item; or

  (b) where the duty is a specific duty with no alternative *ad valorem*, 50 per cent of the *ad valorem* equivalent of the specific duty;

but if the same kind of item is not chargeable with any duty on import no transfer tax may be imposed.

9. For the purposes of paragraph 8 of this Article, the *ad valorem* equivalent of the specific duty on a particular item shall be the percentage which is equivalent to that proportion which the aggregate of the duties collected on all items of that kind imported into the tax imposing State in a period of one year bears to the total value of those items, calculated from the data used in compiling the most recently published annual trade statistics produced by the East African Customs and Excise Department:

Provided that, if in the course of the period covered by such annual trade statistics the relevant rate of specific duty was altered, the *ad valorem* equivalent of the specific duty shall be calculated with reference only to imports entered after the alteration of the rate of duty:

Provided further that, in the calculation of the *ad valorem* equivalent of the specific duty, no account shall be taken of manufactured goods which have been either exempted from the payment of customs duty or in respect of which the customs duty has been remitted:

Provided further that, in relation to goods subject to specific duty with no alternative *ad valorem*, where there has been no importation of such goods into the tax imposing State and consequently no *ad valorem* equivalent can be determined, the rate of transfer tax shall not exceed 50 per cent of the specific duty thereon.

10. Where, in accordance with this Article, a Partner State has imposed a transfer tax upon manufactured goods and subsequently the rate of

customs duty chargeable in that State of goods of the same kind is reduced, so that by virtue of paragraph 8 of this Article the tax falls to be reduced, that State shall, within twenty-one days of such reduction, reduce the tax accordingly:

Provided that, where the relevant item in the customs tariff is expressed only as a specific duty, the obligation to reduce the tax shall be performed as soon as the *ad valorem* equivalent of the specific duty as defined in paragraph 9 of this Article can be recalculated, on the basis of statistics produced by the East African Customs and Excise Department, in respect of imports into the tax imposing State for a period of three months following the reduction in the customs tariff.

11. Transfer tax shall be assessed on the value of the manufactured goods upon which it is imposed, which shall be taken to be the value set out in Annex V to this Treaty:

Provided that, in the case of manufactured goods transferred under a contract of sale and entered for the payment of transfer tax, tax shall be deemed to have been paid on that value if, before the goods are released after transfer, tax is tendered and accepted on a declared value based on the contract price and for the purposes of this proviso—

(a) the declared value of any goods shall be their value as declared by or on behalf of the buyer in the country to which the goods are being transferred in making entry of the goods for transfer tax;

(b) that value shall be deemed to be based on the contract price if, but only if, it represents that price properly adjusted to take account of circumstances differentiating the contract from such contract of sale as is contemplated by Annex V to this Treaty; and

(c) the rate of exchange to be used for determining the equivalent in the currency of the country to which the goods are transferred of any foreign currency shall be the current selling rate for sight drafts in the country to which the goods are transferred as last notified before the time when the goods are entered for transfer:

Provided further that, where under Article 15 of this Treaty the Partner State in which the goods are manufactured is liable to pay to the Partner State which has imposed the transfer tax the full amount of customs duty collected in respect of goods imported and used in the manufacture of the manufactured goods, the amount of such duty paid over shall be deducted from the value provided for by this Article:

Provided further that, where under Article 18 of this Treaty the Partner State in which the goods are manufactured is liable to pay to the Partner State which has imposed the transfer tax the full amount of excise duty collected in respect of goods manufactured or processed or used in the manufacture of the manufactured goods, the amount of such duty paid shall be deducted from the value provided for by this Article.

12. The Authority may from time to time make rules for the administration and operation of paragraph 11 of this Article and of Annex V to this Treaty and may from time to time amend or add to such rules.

13. Subject to this Treaty, the assessment, collection, administration and management generally of all transfer taxes imposed under this Treaty shall be performed by the East African Customs and Excise Department, but the costs and expenses thereof, including any costs and expenses incurred in establishing the system of such assessment and collection, shall be borne by the Partner States which impose such transfer taxes in such manner as the Finance Council may from time to time determine.

14. Every transfer tax shall expire, unless sooner revoked, eight years after the date of its first imposition; and for the purposes of this paragraph no regard shall be had, in the case of a suspended transfer tax, to the date when, if at all, such tax is brought into operation.

15. Every transfer tax imposed under this Treaty shall be revoked fifteen years after the coming into force of this Treaty unless such tax has sooner expired.

16. Notwithstanding paragraphs 14 and 15 of this Article, the Partner States agree that, for the purpose of evaluating the effectiveness of the transfer tax system as an instrument for attaining the aims of the Community, and in particular its effectiveness as a measure to promote a more balanced industrial development, they will undertake joint consultations to review and reappraise the system five years after the first imposition of a transfer tax under this Treaty.

17. If, as a result of a Partner State imposing a transfer tax upon a particular kind of manufactured goods, there is, in respect of manufactured goods of that kind coming into the Partner State which has imposed the transfer tax, a significant deviation of trade away from goods coming from and manufactured in the Partner State whose goods are subject to the transfer tax, to goods imported from a foreign country, then the Partner State which has imposed the transfer tax shall take measures to counteract such deviation and the other Partner States shall, where appropriate, take steps, in co-operation with that Partner State, to make such measures effective.

18. In order to determine whether a deviation of trade in a particular kind of manufactured goods has occurred for the purpose of paragraph 17 of this Article, regard shall be had to the information concerning that kind

of manufactured goods in the trade statistics of the East African Customs and Excise Department (or otherwise recorded by that Department) for the six months immediately preceding a complaint that a deviation has occurred and to the average of the two comparable periods of six months in the twenty-four months which preceded the imposition of the transfer tax.

19. If a transfer tax is imposed by a Partner State upon a particular kind of manufactured goods originating in one of the other Partner States, and subsequently not less than 30 per cent of the total ex-factory value of sales, in any period of twelve months, of manufactured goods of that kind originating in the tax imposing State is sold for transfer to the other Partner States, the transfer tax shall be revoked.

20. If a transfer tax is imposed by a Partner State upon a particular kind of manufactured goods originating in the other Partner States, or one of them, and subsequently not less than 30 per cent of the total ex-factory value of sales, in any period of twelve months, of manufactured goods of that kind originating in the tax imposing State is sold for transfer to the other Partner States or to a foreign country, a Partner State may, if it considers that in the circumstances the tax ought not to continue in force, having regard to all relevant matters and to this Treaty, raise the matter within the Common Market Council and the Council may direct that the Partner State which imposed the tax shall revoke it.

21. If a Partner State which is entitled to impose transfer taxes transfers to the other Partner States in any year beginning on the 1st January manufactured goods originating in that Partner State and amounting in total value to not less than 80 per cent of the total value (measured on a fair and comparable basis in accordance with the annual trade statistics produced by the East African Customs and Excise Department) of manufactured goods transferred into that Partner State from the other Partner States during that year (and originating in those Partner States), that Partner State shall not thereafter be entitled to impose any new transfer tax or bring any suspended transfer tax into operation; but this paragraph shall not affect any subsisting transfer tax.

22. If a transfer tax is imposed by a Partner State upon a particular kind of manufactured goods, the manufacture of which is regulated under the East African industrial licensing laws in operation in the Partner States (or any laws which may be enacted in replacement of those laws in pursuance of Article 23 of this Treaty), the Partner State whose goods are subject to the transfer tax may, if it considers that there are such exceptional circumstances that the tax ought not to continue in force, having

regard to all relevant matters and to this Treaty, raise the matter within the Common Market Council and if the Council after due consideration finds that such circumstances exist the Partner State which imposed the tax shall revoke it.

23. Each Partner State shall take effective action to prevent manufactured goods originating in a Partner State being transferred to another Partner State at a price lower than their true value if such transfer is likely to prejudice the production of similar goods by that other Partner State or retard or prevent the establishment of an industry to produce such goods in that State.

24. For the purpose of paragraph 23 of this Article—

(a) manufactured goods shall be considered to be transferred at a price lower than their true value if, due allowance having been made in each case for differences in conditions of sale, taxation or for any other factors affecting the comparability of prices, their price on transfer is less than—

(i) the comparable price, in ordinary trading conditions, of similar goods destined for domestic consumption in the State in which they were produced; or

(ii) the comparable price of similar goods on their export to a foreign country in ordinary trading conditions; or

(iii) the cost of production of the goods in the Partner State where they are produced, together with a reasonable addition in respect of distribution and sales costs and profit; and

(b) 'effective action' shall include the making available of facilities for enquiry relating to any allegation, by a Partner State, of transfer of goods to that Partner State at a price lower than the true value of such goods and where, on reference to the Common Market Council, the fact of such transfer at such lower value has been established, the taking of such measures as, in relation to any industry, shall be calculated to prevent its recurrence.

25. No Partner State shall directly or indirectly subsidize the transfer of any manufactured goods from that Partner State, or establish, maintain or support any system whereby such goods are sold for transfer to another Partner State at a price lower than the comparable price charged for similar goods on the domestic market, due allowance being made for differences in the conditions of sale or in taxation and for any other factors affecting the comparability of prices.

26. For the purpose of paragraph 25 of this Article, tax incentives or refunds of a general and non-discriminatory nature granted by a Partner

State with a view to encouraging production within that State of goods shall not constitute a transfer subsidy, provided they do not frustrate the purpose of the transfer tax system and are not inconsistent with this Treaty.

27. The Partner States agree that no transfer tax may be imposed upon manufactured goods which are required by the Community or by any of the Corporations for the purpose of their operations, otherwise than upon such goods as are intended for sale, or are sold, to the public.

Article 21

Establishment of the East African Development Bank

1. There is hereby established a Development Bank, to be known as the East African Development Bank.

2. The East African Development Bank is in this Treaty referred to as 'the Bank'.

Article 22

Charter of the Bank

The Charter of the Bank shall be that set out in Annex VI to this Treaty.

CHAPTER VI. INDUSTRIAL LICENSING

Article 23

Present system to continue

1. Subject to this Article, the Partner States agree to continue the industrial licensing system formulated in the three East African Industrial Licensing laws now in operation in the Partner States, whereby the manufacture of certain articles scheduled under the said laws is regulated and the East African Industrial Council is empowered to grant industrial licences in respect of the manufacture of such articles.

2. It is agreed that the industrial licensing system shall continue until the expiration of twenty years from the commencement of the said East African Industrial Licensing laws.

3. It is agreed that no additions shall be made to the schedules of articles, the manufacture of which is subject to industrial licensing under the said East African Industrial Licensing laws.

4. Subject to paragraph 5 of this Article, the Partner States agree to support the early replacement of the said East African Industrial Licensing laws by one law to be introduced into the East African Legislative Assembly for enactment as an Act of the Community.

5. It is agreed that the law proposed in paragraph 4 of this Article shall generally be in similar terms to the said East African Industrial Licensing laws, except that an appeal shall lie to the Industrial Licensing Appeal Tribunal on a matter of law only.

CHAPTER VII. CURRENCY AND BANKING

Article 24

No exchange commission

The Partner States undertake to make arrangements through their central banks, subject only to exchange control laws and regulations which do not conflict with this Treaty, whereby—

(*a*) their respective currency notes shall be exchanged without undue delay within the territories of the Partner States at official par value without exchange commission:

Provided that the Finance Council may at its discretion authorize the central banks to make such charge, upon the exchange of currency, as will be sufficient only to meet the cost of transfer of such currency to the Partner State of its origin; and

(*b*) remittances may be effected without undue delay between the Partner States at official par value of the respective currencies, that is to say without exchange commission.

Article 25

Payments and capital transfers

1. Each Partner State undertakes to permit, in the currency of the Partner State in which the creditor or beneficiary resides, all *bona fide* payments on current account falling within the definition of current account payments set out in Annex VII to this Treaty, and undertakes to ensure that all necessary permissions and authorities are given without undue delay.

2. Each Partner State undertakes to permit payments and transfers on capital account except to the extent that a Partner State may consider that control of certain categories of such payments and transfers is necessary for furthering its economic development and an increase in trade consistent with the aims of the Community:

Provided that no such control shall be imposed by a Partner State in such a manner as to prejudice the ability of the Community, the Bank or the Corporations to perform the functions conferred upon any of them by this Treaty or under any law.

3. The Authority may from time to time by order amend or add to Annex VII to this Treaty.

Article 26
Inter-State settlements

The central banks of the Partner States shall open accounts with each other over which settlements shall be effected between them in a currency acceptable to the creditor.

Article 27
Economic and monetary policy

1. Each of the Partner States agrees to pursue an economic policy aimed at ensuring the equilibrium of its overall balance of payments and confidence in its currency.

2. The Partner States will endeavour to harmonize their monetary policies to the extent required for the proper functioning of the Common Market and the fulfilment of the aims of the Community, and for this purpose agree that the Governors of the three central banks shall meet at least four times in every year to consult, and to co-ordinate and review their monetary and balance of payments policies.

Article 28
Reciprocal credits

1. If a Partner State is in difficulties as regards its balance of payments and has already exercised its drawing rights under the first credit tranche beyond the gold tranche with the International Monetary Fund, such State may, from time to time, request assistance in the way of credits for balance of payments support from any other Partner State with which it had a payments deficit in the last period of twelve months for which information is available and, subject to this Article, such a request shall be granted. Credits granted under this Article shall be in the currency of the Partner State granting the credits.

2. A Partner State shall not be obliged by this Article to allow credits at any one time to be outstanding in excess of an amount equivalent to the value of one-sixth of the goods transferred from the Partner State granting the credits to the recipient Partner State in the last period of twelve months for which information is available.

3. Except by agreement, a Partner State shall not be obliged by this Article to grant credits which in any year beginning on the 1st January exceed in total one-twelfth of the value of the goods transferred from the

Partner State granting the credits to the recipient Partner State in the preceding year.

4. Credits granted in pursuance of this Article shall be for a period not exceeding three years and interest shall be paid half-yearly on the amounts outstanding at the rate of 4 per cent per annum for the first year, 5 per cent per annum for the second year and 6 per cent per annum for the third year.

CHAPTER VIII. CO-OPERATION IN OTHER RESPECTS

Article 29

Co-operation in particular fields

The Partner States declare their intention to consult with one another through the appropriate institutions of the Community for the purpose of co-ordinating their respective policies in such fields of governmental activity as they may, from time to time, consider necessary or desirable for the efficient and harmonious functioning and development of the Common Market, and in particular, but without prejudice to the generality of the foregoing declaration, the Partner States agree—

(a) that the Tax Board established by Article 88 of this Treaty shall, if requested by any Partner State, render assistance in the study of and correlation between taxes managed and collected by the Community and taxes managed and collected directly by authorities in that Partner State, and shall render such further assistance in matters appertaining to fiscal planning as may be desired by any Partner State;

(b) that the Counsel to the Community shall advise the Partner States on, and endeavour to promote, the harmonization of the commercial laws in operation in the Partner States;

(c) that it is their intention to co-operate in the co-ordination of their surface transport policies and to consult thereon within the Communications Council as may from time to time be desirable; and

(d) in order to assist their respective national planning, to engage in consultations within the Economic Consultative and Planning Council and between the planning authorities of each of the Partner States and those of the Community.

PART III. PRINCIPAL COMMON MARKET MACHINERY

CHAPTER IX. THE COMMON MARKET COUNCIL

Article 30

Responsibilities of the Common Market Council

It shall be the responsibility of the Common Market Council established by Article 53 of this Treaty—

(a) to exercise such powers and perform such duties as are conferred or imposed upon it by this Treaty;

(b) to ensure the functioning and development of the Common Market in accordance with this Treaty and to keep its operation under review;

(c) to settle problems arising from the implementation of this Treaty concerning the Common Market;

(d) to receive and consider references making, refuting or concerning allegations as to the breach of any obligation under this Treaty in relation to the Common Market or as to any action or omission affecting the Common Market alleged to be in contravention of this Treaty and determine every such reference as follows—

(i) by issuing a binding directive to a Partner State or States; or

(ii) by making recommendations to a Partner State or States; or

(iii) by recording that the reference shall be deemed to be abandoned, settled or otherwise disposed of; or

(iv) by recording an inability to agree in relation to the reference;

(e) to consider what further action should be taken by Partner States and the Community in order to promote the attainment of the aims of the Community and to facilitate the establishment of closer economic and commercial links with other States, associations of States or international organizations;

(f) to request advisory opinions from the Common Market Tribunal in accordance with this Treaty.

Article 31

Common Market functions of the central secretariat

1. The central secretariat shall keep the functioning of the Common Market under continuous examination and may act in relation to any particular matter which appears to merit examination either on its own initiative or upon the request of a Partner State made through the Common

Market Council and the central secretariat shall, where appropriate, report the results of its examination to the Common Market Council.

2. The central secretariat shall undertake such work and studies and perform such services relating to the Common Market as may be assigned to it by the Common Market Council, and shall also make such proposals thereto as it considers may assist in the efficient and harmonious functioning and development of the Common Market.

3. For the performance of the functions imposed upon it by this Article, the central secretariat may collect information and verify matters of fact relating to the functioning of the Common Market and for that purpose may request a Partner State to provide information relating thereto.

4. The Partner States agree to co-operate with and assist the central secretariat in the performance of the functions imposed upon it by this Article and agree in particular to provide any information which may be requested under paragraph 3 of this Article.

CHAPTER X. THE COMMON MARKET TRIBUNAL

Article 32
Establishment of the Common Market Tribunal

1. There is hereby established a judicial body, to be known as the Common Market Tribunal, which shall ensure the observance of law and of the terms of this Treaty in the interpretation and application of so much of this Treaty as appertains to the Common Market.

2. The Common Market Tribunal is in this Treaty referred to as 'the Tribunal'.

Article 33
Composition of the Tribunal

1. Subject to this Article, the Tribunal shall be composed of a Chairman and four other members, all of whom shall be appointed by the Authority.

2. The Chairman of the Tribunal shall be chosen from among persons of impartiality and independence who fulfil the conditions required for the holding of the highest judicial office in their respective countries of domicile or who are jurists of a recognized competence.

3. Of the members of the Tribunal other than the Chairman, each of the Partner States shall choose one, and the fourth shall be chosen by the Chairman and the other three members acting in common agreement.

4. The members chosen under paragraph 3 of this Article shall be chosen from among persons of impartiality and independence who are qualified for appointment by reason of their knowledge or experience in industry, commerce or public affairs.

Article 34
Term of office and temporary membership of the Tribunal

1. The Chairman and the other members of the Tribunal shall hold office for such period, being not less than three years, as may be determined in their respective instruments of appointment, and in fixing such periods of office regard shall be had to the desirability of securing a measure of continuity in the membership of the Tribunal.

2. All members of the Tribunal shall be eligible for re-appointment.

3. If a member of the Tribunal is temporarily absent or otherwise unable to carry out his functions, the Authority shall, if such absence or inability to act appears to the Authority to be likely to be of such duration as to cause a significant delay in the work of the Tribunal, appoint a temporary member chosen in the same manner as was the absent or disabled member in accordance with Article 33 of this Treaty, to act in place of the said member.

4. If a member of the Tribunal, other than the Chairman, is directly or indirectly interested in a case before the Tribunal, he shall immediately report the nature of his interest to the Chairman, who, if he considers that the member's interest is such that it would be undesirable for him to take part in that case, shall make a report to the Authority; and the Authority shall appoint a temporary member, chosen in the same manner as was the interested member, to act for that case only in place of the interested member.

5. If the Chairman is directly or indirectly interested in a case before the Tribunal he shall, if he considers that the nature of his interest is such that it would be undesirable for him to take part in that case, make a report to the Authority; and the Authority shall appoint a temporary Chairman, chosen in the same manner as was the substantive Chairman, to act as Chairman for that case only in place of the substantive Chairman.

6. A temporary Chairman or temporary member appointed under this Article shall have, during the period he is acting, all the functions of the Chairman or member, as the case may be.

Article 35

Competence of the Tribunal

The Tribunal shall be competent to accept and adjudicate upon all matters which pursuant to this Treaty may be referred to it, and shall also possess the jurisdiction specifically conferred on it by this Chapter.

Article 36

References to the Tribunal by a Partner State

1. Where a Partner State has made a reference to the Common Market Council in pursuance of paragraph (*d*) of Article 30 of this Treaty, and the reference has not been determined by the Common Market Council in accordance with that paragraph within one month of the reference being made, that Partner State may refer the matter in dispute to the Tribunal.

2. Where a reference has been made to the Common Market Council in pursuance of paragraph (*d*) of Article 30 of this Treaty and the reference has been determined by the Council by recording an inability to agree in relation to the reference, a Partner State which is aggrieved by such determination may within two months thereof refer the matter in dispute to the Tribunal.

3. Where a reference has been made to the Common Market Council in pursuance of paragraph (*d*) of Article 30 of this Treaty, and a binding directive has been issued by the Common Market Council to a Partner State, and in the opinion of one of the other Partner States that directive is not complied with by the Partner State to which it is directed within the period fixed therein, that other Partner State may refer the question of such non-compliance to the Tribunal.

Article 37

Decisions of the Tribunal

1. The Tribunal shall consider and determine every reference made to it by a Partner State pursuant to this Treaty in accordance with the Statute of the Common Market Tribunal and its rules of procedure, and shall deliver in public session a reasoned decision which, subject to the provisions of the said Statute as to rectification and review, shall be final and conclusive and not open to appeal:

Provided that, if the Tribunal considers that in the special circumstances of the case it is undesirable that its decision be delivered in public, the Tribunal may make an order to that effect and deliver its decision before the parties privately.

2. The Tribunal shall deliver one decision only in respect of every reference to it, which shall be the decision of the Tribunal reached in private by majority verdict. In the event of the members of the Tribunal being equally divided, the Chairman shall have a casting vote.

3. If a member of the Tribunal does not agree with the majority verdict reached in respect of any reference, he shall not be permitted to deliver a dissenting opinion nor record his dissent in public.

Article 38
Advisory opinions of the Tribunal

The Common Market Council may request the Tribunal to give an advisory opinion regarding questions of law arising from the provisions of this Treaty affecting the Common Market, and the Partner States shall in the case of every such request have the right to be represented and take part in the proceedings.

Article 39
Interim orders and directions of the Tribunal

The Tribunal may, in any case referred to it, make any interim order or issue any directions which it considers necessary or desirable.

Article 40
Intervention

A Partner State which is not a party to a case before the Tribunal may intervene in that case, but its submissions shall be limited to supporting or opposing the arguments of a party to the case.

Article 41
Acceptance of the Tribunal's decisions

1. The Partner States undertake not to submit a dispute concerning the interpretation or application of this Treaty, so far as it relates to or affects the Common Market, to any method of settlement other than those provided for in this Treaty.

2. Where a dispute has been referred to the Common Market Council or to the Tribunal, the Partner States shall refrain from any action which might endanger the solution of the dispute or might aggravate the dispute.

3. A Partner State shall take, without delay, the measures required to implement a decision of the Tribunal.

Article 42

Statute and rules of the Tribunal

1. The Statute of the Tribunal shall be that set out in Annex VIII to this Treaty.

2. The Tribunal shall, after consultation with the Common Market Council, make its rules of procedure and may in like manner from time to time amend or add to any such rules.

PART IV. THE FUNCTIONS OF THE EAST AFRICAN COMMUNITY AND ITS INSTITUTIONS

CHAPTER XI. FUNCTIONS AND PROCEDURE

Article 43

Functions of the Community

1. The Community shall, on behalf of the Partner States, through its appropriate institutions, perform the functions given to it, and discharge the responsibilities imposed upon it, by this Treaty in relation to the establishment, functioning and development of the Common Market.

2. (*a*) The Community shall, on behalf of the Partner States, administer the services specified in Part A of Annex IX to this Treaty, and for that purpose shall, subject to this Treaty, take over from the Common Services Organization such of those services as are in existence at the date of the coming into force of this Treaty.

(*b*) The Authority may by order from time to time amend or add to Part A of Annex IX to this Treaty.

3. The Corporations shall, on behalf of the Partner States and in accordance with this Treaty and the laws of the Community, administer the services specified in Part B of Annex IX to this Treaty, and for that purpose shall take over from the Common Services Organization the corresponding services administered by the Common Services Organization at the date of the coming into force of this Treaty.

4. The Community shall provide machinery to facilitate the co-ordination of the activities of the Partner States on any matter of common interest.

5. Subject to this Treaty, the Community shall so regulate the distribution of its non-physical investments as to ensure an equitable contribution to the foreign exchange resources of each of the Partner States.

6. The Community shall so arrange its purchases within the Partner States as to ensure an equitable distribution of the benefits thereof to each of the Partner States.

7. Subject to this Treaty, the Community may enact measures with respect to the matters set out in Annex X to this Treaty.

8. The Community shall, in accordance with this Treaty, provide a Court of Appeal, a Common Market Tribunal and an East African Industrial Court.

Article 44

Provision of services on an agency basis

1. The Community and the Corporations may, with the approval of the Authority, enter into arrangements with any Government or international organization for providing services, and may provide and administer such services accordingly.

2. The Community may enter into arrangements with any of the Corporations for providing services, and may provide and administer such services accordingly.

3. Arrangements made under this Article shall normally provide for the Community or the Corporation concerned to be reimbursed for any expenditure incurred.

Article 45

Procedure within the Community

1. The procedural provisions set out in Annex XI to this Treaty shall be followed within the Community.

2. If there is a doubt as to the procedure to be followed in any particular case, or if no procedure is prescribed by or under this Treaty, the procedure to be followed may be determined by the Authority.

CHAPTER XII. THE EAST AFRICAN AUTHORITY

Article 46

Establishment of the East African Authority

There is hereby established an Authority to be known as the East African Authority, which shall, subject to this Treaty, be the principal executive authority of the Community.

Article 47

Composition of the Authority

1. The Authority shall consist of the President of the United Republic of Tanzania, the President of the Sovereign State of Uganda, and the President of the Republic of Kenya.

2. If a member of the Authority is unable to attend a meeting of the Authority and it is not convenient to postpone the meeting, he shall, after consultation with the other members of the Authority, appoint a person holding office as a Minister of his Government to represent him at such meeting only, and a person so appointed shall for the purpose of that meeting have all the powers, duties and responsibilities of the member of the Authority for whom he is acting.

Article 48

Functions of the Authority

1. The Authority shall be responsible for, and have the general direction and control of, the performance of the executive functions of the Community.

2. The Authority shall be assisted in the performance of its functions under this Article by the Councils and the East African Ministers.

3. The Authority may give directions to the Councils and to the East African Ministers as to the performance of any functions conferred upon them, and such directions shall be complied with.

Chapter XIII. East African Ministers

Article 49

Appointment of East African Ministers

1. There shall be three East African Ministers.

2. The Partner States shall each nominate one person, qualified under paragraph 3 of this Article, for appointment as an East African Minister, and the Authority shall appoint the persons so nominated to be East African Ministers.

3. A person shall be qualified to be appointed an East African Minister if he is qualified to vote under the national electoral laws of the Partner State nominating him:

Provided that if at the time of his appointment as an East African Minister a person holds office as a Minister, a Deputy, Junior or Assistant

Minister or a Parliamentary Secretary in the Government of a Partner State, he shall immediately resign from that office and may not thereafter hold such an office while he remains an East African Minister.

4. If an East African Minister is temporarily absent from the territories of the Partner States, or for some other reason is temporarily unable to perform his duties, the Partner State which nominated him for appointment may, and at the request of the other East African Ministers shall, nominate some other person, qualified to vote under its national electoral laws, for temporary appointment as an East African Minister; and the Authority shall appoint the person so nominated to be an Acting East African Minister in the place of the Minister who is absent or unable to act.

5. An Acting East African Minister shall hold office until the person in whose place he is acting returns to the territories of the Partner States or is able to resume his duties, as the case may be, and delivers notification thereof in writing to the Secretary-General for transmission to the Authority.

6. An Acting East African Minister shall while he is holding office have all the functions, responsibilities, powers, duties and privileges of the substantive East African Minister.

Article 50

Tenure of office of East African Ministers

An East African Minister shall not be appointed for a fixed term but shall vacate his office upon the happening of any of the following events—

(a) if he transmits his resignation in writing to the Authority and the Authority accepts his resignation;

(b) if he ceases to be qualified for appointment as an East African Minister;

(c) if the Authority terminates his appointment, which it shall do upon the request in writing of the Partner State which nominated him.

Article 51

Functions of East African Ministers

1. It shall be the responsibility of the East African Ministers to assist the Authority in the exercise of its executive functions to the extent required by and subject to the directions of the Authority, and to advise the Authority generally in respect of the affairs of the Community.

2. In addition to the responsibilities conferred on them by paragraph 1 of this Article, the East African Ministers shall perform the functions

conferred on them by this Treaty in respect of the Councils, the Assembly and other matters.

3. The Authority may allocate particular responsibilities to each of the East African Ministers.

4. The Authority may, in respect of any responsibilities which it confers upon the East African Ministers, specify which matters shall be performed by them acting in common agreement and which may be performed by a single East African Minister.

5. It shall be the responsibility of the East African Ministers, with the assistance of representatives of the East African Airways Corporation and such other persons as may be appropriate, to negotiate bi-lateral air services agreements on behalf of the Partner States and to conduct such negotiations in accordance with the criteria laid down by the Communications Ministerial Committee of the Common Services Organization and any amendment of such criteria which may be made by the Communications Council.

6. Each of the Partner States undertakes that it will grant to the East African Minister nominated by it a status within its territory commensurate with that of a Minister of its Government, and shall permit that East African Minister to attend and speak at meetings of its Cabinet.

Chapter XIV. Deputy East African Ministers

Article 52

Deputy East African Ministers

1. The Authority may, if at any time it considers it desirable, appoint three Deputy East African Ministers.

2. If the Authority decides to appoint three Deputy East African Ministers, the Partner States shall each nominate one person, qualified under paragraph 3 of this Article, for appointment as a Deputy East African Minister; and the Authority shall appoint the persons so nominated to be Deputy East African Ministers.

3. A person shall be qualified to be appointed a Deputy East African Minister if he is qualified to vote under the national electoral laws of the Partner State nominating him:

Provided that if, at the time of his appointment as a Deputy East African Minister, a person holds office as a Minister, a Deputy, Junior or Assistant Minister or a Parliamentary Secretary in the Government of a Partner

State, he shall immediately resign from that office and may not thereafter hold such an office while he remains a Deputy East African Minister.

4. A Deputy East African Minister shall not be appointed for a fixed term but shall vacate his office upon the happening of any of the following events—

(a) if he transmits his resignation in writing to the Authority and the Authority accepts his resignation;

(b) if he ceases to be qualified for appointment as a Deputy East African Minister;

(c) if the Authority terminates his appointment, which it shall do upon the request in writing of the Partner State which nominated him.

5. Where Deputy East African Ministers have been appointed and thereafter the number of Deputy East African Ministers falls below three, a person or persons shall be nominated and appointed in the manner provided by this Article to fill the vacancy or vacancies.

6. Subject to any directions given or instructions issued by the Authority, it shall be the responsibility of the Deputy East African Ministers to assist the East African Ministers in the performance of their functions and to perform such duties as may be imposed on them by the Authority or by this Treaty.

CHAPTER XV. THE COUNCILS

Article 53

Establishment of the Councils

There shall be established as institutions of the Community the following Councils—

(a) the Common Market Council;
(b) the Communications Council;
(c) the Economic Consultative and Planning Council;
(d) the Finance Council; and
(e) the Research and Social Council.

Article 54

Composition of the Councils

1. The composition of the Councils shall be as follows—

(a) the Common Market Council shall consist of the three East African Ministers, together with nine other members, of whom three shall be designated by each Partner State from among the persons holding office as Minister of its Government;

(b) the Communications Council shall consist of the three East African Ministers, together with three other members, being the persons holding office as Ministers responsible for matters relating to communications in the respective Governments of the Partner States;

(c) the Economic Consultative and Planning Council shall consist of the three East African Ministers, together with nine other members, of whom three shall be designated by each Partner State from among the persons holding office as Minister of its Government;

(d) the Finance Council shall consist of the three East African Ministers together with three other members, being the persons holding office as the Ministers responsible for matters relating to public finance in the respective Governments of the Partner States; and

(e) the Research and Social Council shall consist of the three East African Ministers, together with nine other members, of whom three shall be designated by each Partner State from among the persons holding office as Minister of its Government.

2. If an East African Minister is unable to attend a meeting of a Council, he may, if at the time there are persons holding office as Deputy East African Ministers, appoint one of them, by notice in writing delivered to the Secretary-General, to act as a member of that Council for that meeting and a person so appointed shall, in respect of the meeting for which he is appointed to act, have all the rights and duties of a member of the Council.

3. If a Minister of the Government of a Partner State is unable to attend a meeting of a Council of which he is a member, that Partner State may, by notice in writing delivered to the Secretary-General, appoint some other person who is a Minister, a Deputy, Junior or Assistant Minister or a Parliamentary Secretary of its Government to act as a member of that Council for that meeting, and a person so appointed shall, in respect of the meeting for which he is appointed to act, have all the rights and duties of a member of the Council.

4. If under paragraph 1 of this Article a Partner State designates one of its Ministers to be a member of a Council or terminates such a designation, it shall give notice thereof in writing to the Secretary-General.

Article 55

Functions of the Councils

The Common Market Council. 1. The function of the Common Market Council shall be the discharge of the responsibilities imposed upon it by Article 30 of this Treaty.

The Communications Council. 2. Subject to any directions given by the Authority, and subject to this Treaty and to any law of the Community, the Communications Council shall perform the duties and have the powers which are set out in Annex XIII to this Treaty, and shall provide a forum for consultation generally on communications matters.

The Economic Consultative and Planning Council. 3. The functions of the Economic Consultative and Planning Council shall be—

(a) to assist the national planning of the Partner States by consultative means; and

(b) to advise the Authority upon the long-term planning of the common services.

The Finance Council. 4. Subject to this Treaty, the functions of the Finance Council shall be to consult in common on the major financial affairs of the Community, and to consider and approve major financial decisions relating to the services administered by the Community, including their estimates of expenditure and related loan and investment programmes. In this paragraph 'the Community' shall not include the Bank.

The Research and Social Council. 5. The functions of the Research and Social Council shall be to assist, by consultative means, in the coordination of the policies of each of the Partner States and the Community regarding research and social matters.

CHAPTER XVI. THE EAST AFRICAN LEGISLATIVE ASSEMBLY

Article 56

Establishment and composition of the East African Legislative Assembly

1. There is hereby established for the Community a legislative body, to be known as the East African Legislative Assembly, which shall exercise the powers conferred upon it by this Treaty.

2. The members of the Assembly shall be—

(a) the three East African Ministers;

(b) the three Deputy East African Ministers (if any);

(c) twenty-seven appointed members; and

(d) the Chairman of the Assembly, the Secretary-General and the Counsel to the Community.

3. The Chairman of the Assembly shall preside over and take part in its proceedings in accordance with the rules of procedure of the Assembly made by the Authority in accordance with paragraph 17 of Annex XI to this Treaty.

4. The Assembly shall have a Public Accounts Committee, which shall be constituted in the manner provided in the rules of procedure of the Assembly and shall perform the functions provided in respect thereof in the said rules of procedure; and the Assembly may have such other committees as may be provided for or permitted under the said rules of procedure.

Article 57
Appointment of members of the Assembly

1. Of the twenty-seven appointed members of the Assembly each Partner State shall appoint nine in accordance with such procedure as each Partner State decides.

2. A person shall be qualified to be appointed a member by a Partner State if he is a citizen of that Partner State and is qualified to be elected a member of its legislature under its electoral laws, and is not an officer in the service of the Community or a servant of a Corporation or the Bank.

3. If an appointed member of the Assembly is temporarily absent from the territories of the Partner States, or for some other reason is temporarily unable to perform his duties, the Partner State which appointed him may appoint some other person, qualified under paragraph 2 of this Article, to be a temporary appointed member in his place; and a temporary appointed member shall, unless his period of office is terminated by the Partner State which appointed him, hold office until the person in whose place he is acting returns to the territories of the Partner States or is able to resume his duties, as the case may be, and so notifies the Chairman of the Assembly in writing.

4. A temporary appointed member of the Assembly shall, while holding office, have all the responsibilities, powers and privileges of the substantive appointed member.

Article 58
Tenure of office of appointed members

1. Subject to this Article, an appointed member of the Assembly shall hold office until the legislature of the Partner State which appointed him first meets after it is next dissolved.

2. An appointed member of the Assembly shall vacate his seat in the Assembly upon the happening of any of the following events—

(a) upon the delivery of his resignation in writing to the Chairman of the Assembly;

(b) upon his ceasing to be qualified for appointment as an appointed member;

(c) upon his appointment as a Minister, a Deputy, Junior or Assistant Minister or a Parliamentary Secretary in the Government of a Partner State;

(d) upon his appointment as an East African Minister or as a Deputy East African Minister;

(e) upon his having been absent from the Assembly for such period and in such circumstances as are prescribed by the rules of procedure of the Assembly.

Article 59

Acts of the Community

1. The enactment of measures of the Community shall be effected by means of Bills passed by the Assembly and assented to on behalf of the Community by the Heads of State of the Partner States and every measure that has been duly passed and assented to shall be styled an Act.

2. When a Bill has been duly passed by the Assembly the Chairman of the Assembly shall submit the Bill to the Heads of State of the Partner States.

3. Every Bill that is submitted to the Heads of State under paragraph 2 of this Article shall contain the following words of enactment—

'Enacted by the President of the United Republic of Tanzania, the President of the Sovereign State of Uganda and the President of the Republic of Kenya on behalf of the East African Community, with the advice and consent of the East African Legislative Assembly'.

Article 60

Assent to Bills

1. The President of the United Republic of Tanzania, the President of the Sovereign State of Uganda and the President of the Republic of Kenya may assent or withhold assent to a Bill.

2. A Bill that has not received the assent provided for in paragraph 1 of this Article within nine months of the date upon which it was passed by the Assembly shall lapse.

CHAPTER XVII. STAFF OF THE COMMUNITY

Article 61

Offices in the Community

1. There shall be the following offices in the service of the Community—

   (*a*) a Secretary-General, who shall be the principal executive officer of the Community;

   (*b*) a Counsel to the Community; and

   (*c*) an Auditor-General.

2. There shall be such other offices in the service of the Community as, subject to any Act of the Community, the Authority may determine.

3. In this Treaty, 'offices in the service of the Community' does not include an office in the service of a Corporation or of the Bank.

Article 62

Establishment of the East African Community Service Commission

1. There is hereby established a service commission to be known as the East African Community Service Commission for all offices in the service of the Community.

2. The Service Commission shall consist of such number of members as the Authority shall from time to time determine.

3. The Authority shall appoint the members of the Service Commission by instrument in writing, which shall specify the period of office of the member concerned.

4. A person shall not be qualified to be appointed a member of the Service Commission if he holds office as a Minister, a Deputy, Junior or Assistant Minister or a Parliamentary Secretary in the Government of a Partner State, or is a member of the Legislative Assembly or a member of the legislature of a Partner State.

5. A member of the Service Commission shall vacate his office—

   (*a*) upon the expiry of the period of office specified in his instrument of appointment;

   (*b*) if he delivers his resignation in writing to the Secretary-General for transmission to the Authority; or

   (*c*) if he ceases to be qualified for appointment as a member.

6. A member of the Service Commission may be removed from office by the Authority for inability to perform the functions of his office, whether

arising from infirmity of mind or body or for any other sufficient cause, or for misbehaviour, but shall not otherwise be removed from office.

Article 63

Appointment and disciplinary control of the Secretary-General and certain other officers

1. The Secretary-General of the Community shall be appointed by the Authority.

2. The Counsel to the Community and the holders of such other offices in the service of the Community as the Authority may, by notice in the Gazette, determine shall be appointed by the Authority after consultation with the Service Commission and with the Secretary-General.

3. If the Secretary-General or any person appointed under paragraph 2 of this Article is absent from the territories of the Partner States, or is unable through illness or for any other reason to perform the functions of his office, the Authority may appoint a person to act in the place of the Secretary-General or of such person, as the case may be, during the period of the absence or inability to act and the person so appointed shall have, while he is so acting, the same powers and responsibilities as the substantive holder of the office.

4. For the purposes of the exercise of the power of disciplinary control and dismissal, the persons appointed under paragraph 2 of this Article shall be subject to the jurisdiction of the Service Commission.

Article 64

Functions of the Service Commission

1. Subject to this Treaty and to any Act of the Community, the Service Commission shall, on behalf of the Community, make appointments to offices in the service of the Community, and shall exercise the powers of disciplinary control and dismissal over persons holding or acting in such offices.

2. For the purposes of paragraph 1 of this Article, references to appointments shall be construed as including references to appointments on promotion and on transfer, and appointments of persons in an acting capacity.

3. The Service Commission may, by order published in the Gazette, and with the approval of the Authority, delegate, subject to such conditions as it may think fit, any of its functions under this Article to any of its members or to any officer of the Community either generally or in respect of any particular class of cases.

4. This Article shall not apply to the Judges of the Court of Appeal for East Africa or to the members of the Common Market Tribunal.

CHAPTER XVIII. FINANCES OF THE COMMUNITY

Article 65

The General Fund and special funds

1. There shall be a General Fund of the Community, and such special funds as may from time to time be established by an Act of the Community.

2. Subject to this Treaty, all moneys received by the Community from whatever source shall be paid into the General Fund, except—

   (a) the divisible income tax, the remaining divisible income tax and the divisible customs and excise duties;

   (b) sums which fall to be paid into the Distributable Pool Fund under Article 67 of this Treaty; and

   (c) sums which are required by an Act of the Community to be paid into one of the special funds referred to in paragraph 1 of this Article.

Article 66

Expenditure from the General Fund

1. All expenditure of the Community, other than expenditure which is required by an Act of the Community to be met from one of the special funds referred to in Article 65 of this Treaty, shall be met from the General Fund.

2. There may be met from the General Fund—

   (a) the estimated net annual recurrent expenditure of the University of East Africa;

   (b) one-half of the estimated net annual recurrent expenditure of Makerere University College, the University College, Dar es Salaam, and University College, Nairobi; and

   (c) expenditure towards the cost of any service provided by the Community under Article 44 of this Treaty, or of any activity which the Authority declares to be in furtherance of the aims of the Community:

Provided that the expenditure under sub-paragraphs (a) and (b) of this paragraph shall cease on the 30th June 1970 or upon the cessation of the arrangements under which the University Colleges mentioned in sub-paragraph (*b*) of this paragraph are constituent colleges of the University of East Africa, whichever is the sooner.

3. No money shall be paid out of the General Fund unless—

    (*a*) the payment has been authorized by an Appropriation Act of the Community; or

    (*b*) the money is required to meet expenditure charged on the General Fund under this Treaty or by an Act of the Community:

Provided that, if an Appropriation Act for a particular financial year has not come into operation by the first day of that financial year, the Authority may from time to time authorize the payment of money out of the General Fund to meet any expenditure which may properly be met thereout, but so that—

    (i) the amount paid out in any particular month for any particular head of expenditure shall not exceed one-twelfth of the total appropriation for the previous financial year for that head;

    (ii) the authorization shall not extend beyond the 30th day of September in the same financial year or such earlier date as that on which the Appropriation Act may come into operation; and

    (iii) any money paid out under this proviso shall be brought into account when payments are being made under the Appropriation Act.

4. No money shall be paid out of the General Fund except in the manner prescribed by an Act of the Community.

5. The Authority shall cause detailed estimates of the receipts into and the payments out of the General Fund to be prepared for each financial year and shall cause them to be laid before a meeting of the Assembly in the financial year preceding that to which they relate.

6. A Bill for an Appropriation Act providing for the sums necessary to meet the estimated expenditure (other than expenditure charged on the General Fund under this Treaty or by an Act of the Community) to be paid out of the General Fund shall be introduced into the Assembly as soon as practicable after the estimates have been laid before a meeting of the Assembly under paragraph 5 of this Article.

7. If in any financial year it is found—

    (*a*) that the amount appropriated by the Appropriation Act is insufficient to meet any particular head of expenditure or that a need has arisen for expenditure from the General Fund for which no amount has been appropriated by that Act; or

    (*b*) that any expenditure has been incurred for any purpose in excess of the amount appropriated to that purpose by the Appropriation

Act, or for a purpose to which no amount has been appropriated by that Act,

the Authority shall cause a supplementary estimate of expenditure in respect thereof to be prepared and laid before the Assembly, and a Bill for a Supplementary Appropriation Act, providing for the sums necessary to meet the estimated expenditure (other than expenditure charged on the General Fund under this Treaty or by an Act of the Community) to be paid out of the General Fund, shall be introduced into the Assembly as soon as practicable after the supplementary estimate has been so laid before the Assembly.

8. Notwithstanding paragraph 3 of this Article, if at any time it appears to the East African Ministers to be necessary for money to be paid out of the General Fund to meet unforeseen expenditure which either—

(a) is of a special character, and may properly be provided for in an Appropriation Act but has not been so provided for; or

(b) will result in an excess on a vote contained in an Appropriation Act,

and which in either case cannot without serious injury to the public interest be postponed until a Supplementary Appropriation Act can be enacted, the East African Ministers may, in anticipation of such enactment, authorize payment from the General Fund of the sums required to meet such expenditure:

Provided that—

(i) the total sum so authorized shall not at any time exceed 500,000 Tanzania shillings; and

(ii) a Bill for a Supplementary Appropriation Act in respect of the payments shall be introduced into the Assembly as soon as practicable thereafter.

Article 67

The Distributable Pool Fund

1. There shall be a Distributable Pool Fund of the Community.

2. There shall be paid into the Distributable Pool Fund—

(a) a sum equal to 20 per cent of the income tax collected by the East African Income Tax Department on gains or profits of companies engaged in manufacturing or finance business (less 20 per cent of the proportion of the cost of collection referred to in paragraph 1 (b) of Article 68 of this Treaty):

Provided that, where the tax is collected on or after the effective date and before the final date, the percentages shall be 10 per cent; and

(b) a sum equal to 3 per cent of the amount of customs duty and excise duty collected by the East African Customs and Excise Department (less a rateable proportion of the cost of collection referred to in paragraph 3 of Article 68 of this Treaty):

Provided that, where the customs duty or excise duty is collected on or after the effective date and before the final date, the percentage shall be one and one half per cent.

3. Notwithstanding paragraph 2 of this Article, no payment shall be made into the Distributable Pool Fund in respect of income tax collected on or after the final date or in respect of customs duty or excise duty collected on or after the final date.

4. The Distributable Pool Fund shall be distributed among the Partner States in equal shares.

Article 68

Distribution of the principal revenue

1. From the amount of income tax collected by the East African Income Tax Department, there shall be deducted—

(a) the cost of collection, which shall be paid into the General Fund; and

(b) so much of the amount as represents income tax on gains or profits of companies engaged in manufacturing or finance business (less a rateable proportion of the cost of collection), which shall be dealt with in accordance with paragraph 4 of this Article,

and the balance (in this Treaty referred to as 'the divisible income tax') shall be divided among the Partner States in accordance with paragraph 7 of this Article.

2. In this Article and in Article 67 of this Treaty, the 'gains or profits of companies engaged in manufacturing or finance business' means the income defined in the provisions of Annex XII to this Treaty.

3. From the amount of customs duty and excise duty collected by the East African Customs and Excise Department, there shall be deducted the cost of collection, which shall be paid into the General Fund, and the balance shall be dealt with in accordance with paragraph 4 of this Article.

4. From the amounts which, under paragraph 1 (b) and paragraph 3 of this Article, are to be dealt with in accordance with this paragraph, there shall be deducted—

(a) the sums which, under Article 67 of this Treaty, fall to be paid into the Distributable Pool Fund; and

(b) such sums as are required to make up (with the moneys in the General Fund) the amount of expenditure to be met from the General Fund; and

(i) for the period from the coming into force of this Treaty until the final date as defined in Article 70 of this Treaty, such sums shall be charged against the moneys referred to in paragraph 1 (b) and paragraph 3 of this Article in the ratio which 20 per cent of the moneys referred to in paragraph 1 (b) bears to 3 per cent of the moneys referred to in paragraph 3 respectively; and

(ii) after the said final date, the proportions in which those sums shall be charged against the moneys referred to in paragraph 1 (b) and paragraph 3 of this Article respectively shall correspond to the relative sizes of those two amounts of money,

and the residue of the money referred to in paragraph 1 (b) of this Article (in this Treaty referred to as 'the remaining divisible income tax') and the residue of the money referred to in paragraph 3 of this Article (in this Treaty referred to as 'the divisible customs and excise duties') shall each be divided among the Partner States in accordance respectively with paragraphs 7 and 8 of this Article.

5. The money divided between the Partner States under paragraph 4 of this Article shall be paid direct by the East African Income Tax Department or the East African Customs and Excise Department, as the case may be, to the Partner States.

6. Revenue from transfer taxes payable to a Partner State under Article 20 of this Treaty, less the costs and expenses to be borne by that Partner State under paragraph 13 of that Article, shall be paid direct by the East African Customs and Excise Department to that Partner State, and the said costs and expenses shall be paid into the General Fund.

7. There shall be paid by the East African Income Tax Department to each of the Partner States that portion of the remaining divisible income tax as, according to law, may be ascertained as relating to income accruing in, or derived from, that Partner State.

8. There shall be paid by the East African Customs and Excise Department to each of the Partner States that portion of the divisible customs and excise duties which arises from customs and excise duties collected in respect of goods imported into, or manufactured in, that Partner State and consumed in that Partner State, together with such portion of the divisible customs and excise duties as falls to be paid to that State in accordance with Articles 10, 15, and 18 of this Treaty.

Article 69

Remuneration of the holders of certain offices

1. There shall be paid to the holders of the offices of—

(*a*) Judge of the Court of Appeal for East Africa;
(*b*) Chairman or other member of the Tribunal;
(*c*) Chairman of the Assembly;
(*d*) Chairman or other member of the Service Commission; and
(*e*) Auditor-General,

such salaries as may be prescribed by an Act of the Community.

2. The salaries payable to the holders of the offices specified in paragraph 1 of this Article shall be paid from and are hereby charged on the General Fund.

3. A holder of any of the offices specified in paragraph 1 of this Article shall not have his salary or any of his other terms and conditions of service altered to his disadvantage after his appointment.

Article 70

Interpretation of this Chapter

In this Chapter of this Treaty—

'cost of collection' means the expenditure of the East African Income Tax Department or the East African Customs and Excise Department, as the case may be, less appropriations in aid and less the costs and expenses referred to in paragraph 6 of Article 68 of this Treaty;

'divisible customs and excise duties' has the meaning given to it in paragraph 4 of Article 68 of this Treaty;

'divisible income tax' has the meaning given to it in paragraph 1 of Article 68 of this Treaty;

'effective date' means the first day of the month following the date on which a transfer tax is first imposed under this Treaty;

'final date' means the first day of the month following the first anniversary of the date on which the Republic of Kenya has paid in full the second instalment to the paid-in capital stock of the Bank pursuant to Article 5 of the Charter of the Bank;

'financial year' means the period from the 1st day of July to the succeeding 30th day of June;

'remaining divisible income tax' has the meaning given to it in paragraph 4 of Article 68 of this Treaty.

CHAPTER XIX. THE CORPORATIONS WITHIN THE COMMUNITY

Article 71

Establishment of the Corporations

1. There shall be within the Community, as institutions of the Community, the Corporations specified in paragraph 2 of this Article and the Corporations shall, subject to this Treaty, be constituted in such manner as shall be provided by law.

2. The Corporations shall be—

> The East African Railways Corporation;
> The East African Harbours Corporation;
> The East African Posts and Telecommunications Corporation; and
> The East African Airways Corporation.

Article 72

Principles of operation

1. It shall be the duty of each of the Corporations to conduct its business according to commercial principles and to perform its functions in such a manner as to secure that, taking one year with another, its revenue is not less than sufficient to meet its outgoings which are properly chargeable to revenue account, including proper allocations to the general reserve and provision in respect of depreciation of capital assets, pension liabilities, and interest and other provision for the repayment of loans and further to ensure that, taking one year with another, its net operating income is not less than sufficient to secure an annual return on the value of the net fixed assets in operation by the Corporation of such a percentage as the Authority may from time to time direct:

Provided that the Authority may at any time, if it thinks fit, relieve the East African Airways Corporation from any obligation to secure an annual return on the value of net fixed assets in operation by the Corporation.

2. For the purpose of paragraph 1 of this Article—

(*a*) 'net operating income' shall be determined by subtracting from gross operating revenues all operating and administrative expenses, including taxes (if any) and adequate provision for maintenance and depreciation; and

(*b*) 'value of the net fixed assets in operation' shall be the value of such assets less accumulated depreciation as shown in the statement of accounts of the Corporation:

Provided that, if the amounts shown in such statements of accounts do not reflect a true measure of value of the assets concerned because of currency revaluations, changes in prices or similar factors, the value of the fixed assets shall be adjusted adequately to reflect such currency revaluations, changes in prices or similar factors.

3. It shall be the duty of each Corporation, in performing its obligations under paragraph 1 of this Article, to have regard to its revenues in the territories of the Partner States as a whole and not to its revenues in any particular Partner State or area within the territories of the Partner States.

4. Subject to this Treaty, the Corporations shall so regulate the distribution of their non-physical investments as to ensure an equitable contribution to the foreign exchange resources of each of the Partner States, taking into account *inter alia* the scale of their operations in each Partner State.

5. The Corporations shall so arrange their purchases within the Partner States as to ensure an equitable distribution of the benefits thereof to each of the Partner States, taking into account *inter alia* the scale of their operations in each Partner State.

6. The Corporations shall be exempted from income tax and from stamp duty.

Article 73

Control of the Corporations

1. There shall be a Board of Directors for each of the Corporations which shall be, subject to this Treaty, responsible for its policy, control and management through the Director-General.

2. The Authority, the Communications Council and the Board of Directors and the Director-General of each Corporation shall, in respect of that Corporation, and in addition to any other powers and duties conferred or imposed on them by this Treaty or by any Act of the Community, have the powers and perform the duties specified in Annex XIII to this Treaty.

Article 74

Composition of Boards of Directors of the Corporations

1. Subject to this Article, the Boards of Directors of the Corporations, other than the East African Airways Corporation, shall each be composed of a Chairman, who shall be appointed by the Authority, the Director-General, who shall be a director *ex officio*, and six other members who shall be appointed in the manner provided by paragraph 2 of this Article.

2. Of the six members of the Boards of Directors to be appointed under paragraph 1 of this Article, three shall be appointed one each by the Partner States, and three shall be appointed by the Authority which shall have regard to the desirability of appointing persons with experience in commerce, industry, finance or administration or with technical experience or qualifications.

3. The Board of Directors of the East African Airways Corporation shall be composed of a Chairman, who shall be appointed by the Authority, the Director-General, who shall be a director *ex officio*, and eight other members of whom two each shall be appointed by the Authority and the Partner States, and the appointing authorities shall have regard to the desirability of appointing persons with experience in commerce, industry, finance or administration or with technical experience or qualifications.

4. A member of the legislature of a Partner State or a member of the Assembly shall not, while he remains such a member, be appointed to a Board of Directors.

Article 75

Resident Directors

1. The three directors appointed by the Partner States to the Board of Directors of the East African Railways Corporation shall be styled Resident Directors.

2. The Board of Directors of the East African Posts and Telecommunications Corporation may resolve (and may if it so desires rescind such a resolution) that the three directors appointed to the Board of Directors of that Corporation by the Partner States shall be styled Resident Directors and in that event paragraph 3 of this Article shall apply.

3. Each Resident Director shall have the duty of being the main link between the Partner State which appointed him and the Corporation of which he is a director, and for that purpose he shall reside and have his office in the capital of that Partner State and shall also be a member of the General Purposes Committee of the Board of Directors; but a Resident Director shall have no executive functions in relation to the Corporation other than his function as one of the directors of the Corporation.

Article 76

Directors-General of the Corporations.

1. There shall be a principal executive officer, who shall be styled the Director-General, for each of the Corporations and, subject to this Treaty,

a Director-General shall be responsible for the execution of the policy of the Board of Directors.

2. The Authority shall be responsible for the appointment, disciplinary control and termination of appointment of the Director-General of each of the Corporations:

Provided that, except in the case of the appointment of the first Director-General of a Corporation, the Authority shall exercise its powers under this paragraph after consultation with the Board of Directors.

Article 77

Appointment and disciplinary control of staff of the Corporations

1. The Corporations shall employ such staff as may be necessary for the efficient conduct of their operations.

2. The Board of Directors of each Corporation shall be responsible for the appointment, disciplinary control and dismissal of all staff of that Corporation other than the Director-General.

3. A Board of Directors may, subject to such conditions as it shall think fit, delegate any of its functions under paragraph 2 of this Article to the Director-General or to any other member of the staff of the Corporation or to any committee or board established by the Board of Directors.

4. The Board of Directors of each of the Corporations shall introduce and maintain procedures whereby staff aggrieved by the exercise of powers delegated under paragraph 3 of this Article may appeal to a higher authority.

5. For the purpose of Article 76 of this Treaty, and this Article, references to appointments shall be construed so as to include references to appointments on promotion and on transfer or secondment and appointments of persons in an acting capacity.

Article 78

Annual accounts of the Corporations

1. A Board of Directors shall ensure that proper accounts and proper records are kept in relation to the revenue and expenditure of the Corporation, and shall ensure that within six months of the end of each financial year of the Corporation, or such longer period as the Communications Council may allow in any particular case, a statement of accounts of the Corporation is prepared, in accordance with the best commercial

standards and any directions which may be issued by the Authority, and transmitted to the Auditor-General.

2. Upon the return of the statement of accounts, certified by the Auditor-General, and the receipt of his report thereon, the Board of Directors shall immediately transmit that statement of accounts and report of the Auditor-General to the Communications Council which shall cause the same to be presented to the Assembly without delay and, in any event, before the expiry of nine months from the end of the financial year to which they relate or such longer period as the Communications Council may allow in any particular case.

Article 79
Annual reports of the Corporations

A Board of Directors shall, within nine months after the end of each financial year, prepare a report upon the operations of the Corporation during that year and shall transmit such report to the Communications Council which shall cause the same to be presented to the Assembly with the statement of accounts and report of the Auditor-General referred to in Article 78 of this Treaty.

CHAPTER XX. THE COURT OF APPEAL FOR EAST AFRICA

Article 80
The Court of Appeal for East Africa

There shall be a Court of Appeal for East Africa which shall be constituted in such manner as may be provided by Act of the Community, and the Court of Appeal for Eastern Africa established by the East African Common Services Organization Agreements 1961 to 1966 shall continue in being under the name of the Court of Appeal for East Africa and shall be deemed to have been established by this Treaty, notwithstanding the abrogation of those Agreements by this Treaty.

Article 81
Jurisdiction of the Court of Appeal

The Court of Appeal for East Africa shall have jurisdiction to hear and determine such appeals from the courts of each Partner State as may be provided for by any law in force in that Partner State and shall have such powers in connection with appeals as may be so provided.

CHAPTER XXI. PENSIONS AND TRADE DISPUTES

Article 82

Pension rights

1. This Article applies to any benefit payable under any law providing for the grant of pensions, compensations, gratuities or like allowances to persons who are, or have been, officers or servants of the Community, the Corporations, the Common Services Organization or of the East Africa High Commission in respect of their services as such officers or servants, or to the widows, children or personal representatives of such persons in respect of such services.

2. The law applicable to any benefits to which this Article applies shall, in relation to any person who has been granted or is eligible for such benefits, be that in force on the relevant date or any later law that is no less favourable to the person.

3. In this Article, 'the relevant date' means—

(a) in relation to any benefits granted before the coming into force of this Treaty, the date upon which those benefits were granted;

(b) in relation to any benefits granted after the date upon which this Treaty comes into force, to or in respect of any person who was an officer or servant of the Common Services Organization before that date or any benefits for which any such person may be eligible, the date immediately preceding the date on which this Treaty comes into force; and

(c) in relation to any benefits granted to or in respect of any person who first becomes an officer or servant of the Community or of a Corporation after the date upon which this Treaty comes into force, the date upon which he first becomes such an officer or servant.

4. Where a person is entitled to exercise an option as to which of two or more laws might apply in his case, the law specified by him in exercising the option shall, for the purpose of this Article, be deemed to be more favourable to him than any other law.

5. Any benefits to which this Article applies shall—

(a) in the case of benefits that are payable in respect of the service of any person who at the time he ceased to be an officer or servant of the East Africa High Commission or the Common Services Organization was in the service of the East African Posts and Telecommunications Administration, be a charge upon the funds of the East African Posts and Telecommunications Corporation;

(b) in the case of benefits that are payable in respect of the service of any person who at the time he ceased to be an officer or servant of the East Africa High Commission or the Common Services Organization was in the service of the East African Railways and Harbours Administration, be a charge upon the funds of either the East African Railways Corporation or the East African Harbours Corporation as the Authority may, in respect of such person, by notice in the Gazette determine;

(c) in the case of benefits that are payable in respect of the service of any person who, immediately preceding his retirement, was an officer or servant of the East African Posts and Telecommunications Corporation, the East African Railways Corporation or the East African Harbours Corporation, be a charge upon the funds of that Corporation;

(d) in the case of any other benefits, be a charge upon the General Fund of the Community or such special fund as may be established for that purpose by an Act of the Community.

6. Where under any law any person or authority has a discretion—

(a) to decide whether or not any benefits to which this Article applies shall be granted; or

(b) to withhold, reduce in amount or suspend any amounts which have been granted,

those benefits shall be granted and may not be withheld, reduced in amount or suspended unless the appropriate body concurs in the refusal to grant the benefits or, as the case may be, the decision to withhold them, reduce them in amount or suspend them.

7. Where the amount of any benefit to which this Article applies that may be granted to any person is not fixed by law, the amount of the benefits to be granted to him shall be the greatest amount for which he is eligible unless the appropriate body concurs in his being granted benefits of a smaller amount.

8. For the purpose of this Article 'the appropriate body' means—

(a) in the case of benefits that have been granted or may be granted in respect of the services of any person who, at the time that he ceased to be an officer or servant of the Community, was subject to the jurisdiction of the Service Commission established by this Treaty, that Commission; and

(b) in the case of an officer or servant of any of the Corporations, the body appointed by that Corporation for the purpose of paragraphs 6 and 7 of this Article.

9. Reference in this Article to officers or servants of the Community shall include reference to the Judges, officers and servants of the Court of Appeal for East Africa.

Article 83
Investment of money accruing for the payment of pensions

Upon the coming into force of this Treaty, and until such time as the Authority may determine, the net accruals to money held by the Community or the Corporations for the payment of pensions shall be invested in such stock of the former East Africa High Commission as the Authority may specify; and thereafter such net accruals shall be invested in such stock of the Partner States as the Authority may specify, having regard to the relative proportions of the financial provisions made each year by the Community or the Corporations in respect of pensions for the citizens of each Partner State employed in their service.

Article 84
Settlement of trade disputes

The law relating to the settlement of trade disputes in force in any Partner State shall apply to employment or service under the Community and the Corporations, and to persons in such employment or service, within that State; so however that any such law shall provide that—

(a) any power therein conferred upon any tribunal, court or other authority to make binding awards or orders in respect of the salaries or other conditions of service of persons in employment or service under the Community or the Corporations, and any power incidental thereto, shall be conferred upon, and be exercised by, the East African Industrial Court provided for in Article 85 of this Treaty; and

(b) any award or order made by the East African Industrial Court which accords with paragraph 2 of Article 85 of this Treaty shall be binding.

Article 85
The East African Industrial Court

1. There shall be established a tribunal to be styled the East African Industrial Court, in this Article referred to as 'the Industrial Court', which shall be constituted by—

(a) the Chairman, or other member nominated by the Chairman, of the Permanent Labour Tribunal established under the Permanent Labour Tribunal Act 1967 of Tanzania;

(b) the president, or the deputy president if so nominated by the president, of the Industrial Court established under the Trade Disputes (Arbitration and Settlement) Act 1964 of Uganda; and

(c) the President, or other member nominated by the President, of the Industrial Court established under the Trade Disputes Act 1965 of Kenya.

2. The Industrial Court shall exercise the powers referred to in Article 84 of this Treaty in accordance with the principles laid down from time to time by the Authority.

3. The persons referred to in paragraph 1 of this Article shall, in the order set out therein, preside over the sittings of the Industrial Court.

4. The Industrial Court shall regulate its own procedure.

5. The Authority may determine the fees, emoluments or allowances to be paid to members of the Industrial Court.

Chapter XXII. Decentralization, The Location of Headquarters and The East African Tax Board

Article 86

Decentralization and related measures

The Partner States agree that the measures in Annex XIV to this Treaty, which relate to decentralization of the operations of the Corporations and of certain of the services administered by the Community, shall be put into effect by the authorities concerned in accordance with the said Annex.

Article 87

Location of headquarters

1. It is agreed that—
    (a) the headquarters of the Community, including the Tribunal and the central secretariat, shall be at Arusha in Tanzania;
    (b) the headquarters of the Bank shall be at Kampala in Uganda;
    (c) the headquarters of the East African Railways Corporation shall be at Nairobi in Kenya;
    (d) the headquarters of the East African Harbours Corporation shall be at Dar es Salaam in Tanzania;
    (e) the headquarters of the East African Posts and Telecommunications Corporation shall be at Kampala in Uganda; and
    (f) the headquarters of the East African Airways Corporation shall be at Nairobi in Kenya.

2. The authorities concerned shall implement paragraph 1 of this Article as soon as possible.

Article 88

The East African Tax Board

1. There is hereby established an advisory body, to be known as the East African Tax Board.

2. The Tax Board shall consist of—
   (a) three members appointed one each by the Minister responsible for public finance in each of the Partner States;
   (b) the Commissioner-General of the East African Income Tax Department;
   (c) the Commissioner-General of the East African Customs and Excise Department;
   (d) the three Commissioners of Income Tax in the Partner States;
   (e) the three Commissioners of Customs and Excise in the Partner States; and
   (f) a senior officer of the central secretariat of the Community designated by the Secretary-General.

3. The members appointed under sub-paragraph (a) of paragraph 2 of this Article shall hold the office of Chairman of the Tax Board in rotation.

4. The functions of the Tax Board shall be—
   (a) to render assistance as provided for in paragraph (a) of Article 29 of this Treaty;
   (b) to keep under review the administration of the East African Income Tax Department and the East African Customs and Excise Department including the allocation and distribution of revenue collected by those Departments;
   (c) to ensure the best possible co-operation between the East African Income Tax Department and the East African Customs and Excise Department;
   (d) to study the correlation between the taxes managed and collected by the Community and taxes managed and collected directly by authorities in the Partner States, to make proposals to improve this correlation and to report annually thereon to the Finance Council;
   (e) if requested by any Partner State, to render assistance in relation to taxation planning; and
   (f) to make an annual report to the Finance Council concerning the operation of the East African Income Tax Department and of the East African Customs and Excise Department, and the organization and the personnel situation in those Departments.

CHAPTER XXIII. AUDIT

Article 89

Audit of accounts

1. The public accounts of the Community and of all officers and authorities of the Community shall be audited and reported on by the Auditor-General and for that purpose the Auditor-General and any person authorized by him in that behalf shall have access to all books, records, returns and other documents relating to those accounts.

2. It shall be the duty of the Auditor-General to verify that the revenue collected by the East African Income Tax Department and the East African Customs and Excise Department has been allocated and distributed in accordance with this Treaty and to include a certificate to that effect in his report.

3. The Auditor-General shall submit his reports under paragraph 1 of this Article to the East African Ministers who shall cause the same to be laid before the Assembly.

4. The accounts of the Corporations and of all officers and authorities of the Corporations shall be audited by the Auditor-General, and for that purpose the Auditor-General and any person authorized by him in that behalf shall have access to all books, records, returns and other documents relating to those accounts and upon receipt of a statement of accounts transmitted to him under paragraph 1 of Article 78 of this Treaty the Auditor-General shall examine it, certify it and report on it and shall return the statement with his certificate and report to the Board of Directors of the Corporation concerned in sufficient time to enable compliance with paragraph 2 of Article 78 of this Treaty.

5. In the performance of his functions under this Article, the Auditor-General shall not be subject to the direction or control of any person or authority.

PART V. TRANSITIONAL AND GENERAL

CHAPTER XXIV. TRANSITIONAL

Article 90

Transitional provisions

The transitional provisions contained in Annex XV to this Treaty shall apply.

CHAPTER XXV. GENERAL

Article 91

Commencement of the Treaty

This Treaty shall come into force on the first day of December 1967.

Article 92

Duration of the Treaty

1. Parts II and III of this Treaty, together with so much of the other Parts of the Treaty as appertains to the Common Market or the Common Market Council, shall remain in force for 15 years after coming into force and shall be reviewed by the Partner States before the expiry of that period.

2. Subject to paragraph 1 of this Article, this Treaty shall have indefinite duration.

Article 93

Association of other countries with the Community

The Partner States may together negotiate with any foreign country with a view to the association of that country with the Community or its participation in any of the activities of the Community or the Corporations.

Article 94

Modification of the Treaty

1. This Treaty may be modified at any time by agreement of all the Partner States.

2. Notwithstanding paragraph 1 of this Article, Annex VI to this Treaty shall only be amended in accordance with Article 52 of that Annex.

Article 95

Implementation measures of the Partner States

1. Each of the Partner States undertakes to take all steps within its power to secure the enactment and the continuation of such legislation as is necessary to give effect to this Treaty, and in particular—

   (*a*) to confer upon the Community the legal capacity and personality required for the performance of its functions; and

   (*b*) to confer upon Acts of the Community the force of law within its territory.

2. A Partner State shall not, by or under any law of that Partner State, confer any power nor impose any duty upon an officer or authority of the Community, or of a Corporation as such, except with the prior consent of the Authority.

Article 96

Effect of Annexes, rules and orders

1. The Annexes to this Treaty shall form an integral part of this Treaty.

2. Rules and orders made by the Authority pursuant to this Treaty shall be binding on the institutions of the Community and the Partner States.

Article 97

Abrogation of existing agreements

1. Subject to this Treaty, the East African Common Services Organization Agreements 1961 to 1966 are hereby abrogated.

2. Subject to this Treaty, all the existing agreements between the Partner States or any of them concerning the imposition of customs and excise duties and the allocation and distribution of customs and excise revenue collected by the East African Customs and Excise Department are hereby abrogated.

3. Subject to this Treaty, all the existing agreements between the Partner States or any of them concerning the allocation and distribution of revenue collected by the East African Income Tax Department are hereby abrogated.

4. Subject to this Treaty, the Agreement dated the 22nd November 1961 made between the Governments of the Trust Territory of Tanganyika, the Protectorate of Uganda and the Colony and Protectorate of Kenya in pursuance of section 42A of the East Africa (High Commission) Order in Council 1947 with respect to payments into and out of the Distributable Pool Fund of the East Africa High Commission is hereby abrogated.

Article 98

Interpretation

1. In this Treaty, except where the context otherwise requires—

'Act of the Community' means an Act of the Community enacted in accordance with this Treaty or an Act of the Common Services Organization or an Act of the East Africa High Commission;

'appointed member' means an appointed member of the Assembly appointed under Article 57 of this Treaty;

'Assembly' means the East African Legislative Assembly established by Article 56 of this Treaty;

'Auditor-General' means the Auditor-General of the Community provided for by Article 61 of this Treaty;

'Authority' means the East African Authority established by Article 46 of this Treaty;

'Bank' means the East African Development Bank established by Article 21 of this Treaty;

'Board of Directors', except in Annex VI to this Treaty, means the Board of Directors of a Corporation;

'central banks' means the Bank of Tanzania, the Bank of Uganda and the Central Bank of Kenya;

'Chairman of the Assembly' means the Chairman of the East African Legislative Assembly provided for by paragraph 2 of Article 56 of this Treaty;

'Chairman of the Tribunal' means the Chairman of the Common Market Tribunal provided for by Article 33 of this Treaty;

'common customs tariff' and 'common excise tariff' imply an identical rate of tariff imposed in the same manner;

'Common Market' means the East African Common Market established by Article 1 of this Treaty;

'common services' means the services specified in Annex IX to this Treaty;

'Common Services Organization' means the East African Common Services Organization established by the East African Common Services Organization Agreements 1961 to 1966;

'Community' means the East African Community established by Article 1 of this Treaty;

'Corporation' means a corporation specified in paragraph 2 of Article 71 of this Treaty;

'Council' means a council established by Article 53 of this Treaty;

'Counsel to the Community' means the Counsel to the Community provided for by Article 61 of this Treaty;

'current account payments' means the payments so defined in Annex VII to this Treaty;

'customs duty' includes suspended duty;

'customs laws' means the East African Customs Management Act 1952;

'Deputy East African Ministers' means the Deputy East African Ministers appointed under Article 52 of this Treaty;

'Director-General', except in Annex VI to this Treaty, means the Director-General of a Corporation provided for by Article 76 of this Treaty;

'East African Ministers' means the East African Ministers appointed under Article 49 of this Treaty;

'foreign country' means any country other than a Partner State;

'Gazette' means the Official Gazette of the Community;

'General Fund' means the General Fund provided for by Article 65 of this Treaty;

'goods in transit' means goods being conveyed between a Partner State and a foreign country and passing through another Partner State or States, and 'transit' shall be construed accordingly;

'Heads of State' means the President of the United Republic of Tanzania, the President of the Sovereign State of Uganda and the President of the Republic of Kenya;

'import' with its grammatical variations and cognate expressions means to bring or cause to be brought into the territories of the Partner States from a foreign country;

'Industrial Licensing laws' means the East African Industrial Licensing Ordinance (Tanzania Cap. 324), the East African Industrial Licensing Act (Uganda Cap. 102) and the East African Industrial Licensing Act (Kenya Cap. 496);

'Industrial Licensing Tribunal' means the Tribunal established by the law referred to in paragraph 4 of Article 23 of this Treaty;

'manufactured goods' means the goods defined or otherwise listed in Annex IV to this Treaty;

'Minister' in relation to a Partner State includes the Vice-President of that Partner State;

'Partner States' means the United Republic of Tanzania, the Sovereign State of Uganda and the Republic of Kenya;

'Resident Director' means a director of a Corporation who is styled a Resident Director under Article 75 of this Treaty;

'salaries and other conditions of service' includes wages, overtime pay, salary and wage structures, leave, passages, transport for leave purposes, pensions and other retirement benefits, redundancy and severance payments, hours of duty, grading of posts, medical arrangements, housing, arrangements for transport and travelling on duty, and allowances;

'Secretary-General' means the Secretary-General of the Community provided for by Article 61 of this Treaty;

'Service Commission' means the East African Community Service Commission established by Article 62 of this Treaty;

'suspended transfer tax' means a transfer tax the operation of which is suspended at the time of its introduction;

'Tax Board' means the East African Tax Board established by Article 88 of this Treaty;

'transfer tax' includes suspended transfer tax;

'Tribunal' means the Common Market Tribunal established by Article 32 of this Treaty;

'University of East Africa' means the University of East Africa constituted by the University of East Africa Act 1962.

2. In this Treaty, a reference to a law shall be construed as a reference to that law as from time to time amended, added to or replaced.

2. *Annexes, including the Charter of the East African Development Bank and the Statute of the Common Market Tribunal*

(*Article* 11)

ANNEX I

RULES FOR THE ADMINISTRATION AND APPLICATION OF ARTICLE 11

Interpretation

1. (1) In these Rules—

'materials' includes products, parts and components used in the production of goods;

'produced' and 'a process of production' include the application of any operation or process with the exception of any operation or process which consist only of one or more of the following—

(*a*) packing, wherever the packing materials may have been produced;
(*b*) splitting up into lots;
(*c*) sorting or grading;
(*d*) marking;
(*e*) putting up into sets.

(2) Energy, fuel, plant, machinery and tools used in the production of goods within the Partner States and materials used in the maintenance of such plant, machinery and tools shall be regarded as wholly produced within the Partner States when determining the origin of such goods.

(3) In determining the place of production of marine products and goods in relation to a Partner State, a vessel of a Partner State shall be regarded as part of the territory of that State and in determining the place from which such goods originated, marine products taken from the sea, or goods produced therefrom at sea, shall be regarded as having their origin in the territory of a Partner State if they were taken by, or produced

in, a vessel of that State and have been brought directly to the territories of the Partner States.

(4) For the purposes of paragraph (3) of this rule, a vessel which is registered or licensed under any law in force within the Partner States shall be regarded as a vessel of the State in which it is so registered or licensed.

Goods wholly produced in the Partner States

2. For the purposes of paragraph 3 of Article 11 of this Treaty, the following are among the products which shall be regarded as wholly produced in the Partner States—

(*a*) mineral products extracted from the ground within the Partner States;

(*b*) vegetable products harvested within the Partner States;

(*c*) live animals born and raised within the Partner States;

(*d*) products obtained within the Partner States from live animals;

(*e*) products obtained by hunting or fishing conducted within the Partner States;

(*f*) marine products taken from the sea by a vessel of a Partner State;

(*g*) used articles fit only for the recovery of materials provided that they have been collected from users within the Partner States;

(*h*) scrap and waste resulting from manufacturing operations within the Partner States;

(*i*) goods produced within the Partner States exclusively from one or both of the following—

(i) products within sub-paragraphs (*a*) to (*h*);

(ii) materials containing no element imported from outside the Partner States or of undetermined origin.

Application of percentage criterion

3. For the purposes of sub-paragraph (*b*) of paragraph 3 of Article 11 of this Treaty, the following rules shall apply—

(*a*) any materials which meet the condition specified in sub-paragraph (*a*) of paragraph 3 of that Article shall be regarded as containing no element imported from outside the Partner States;

(*b*) the value of any materials which can be identified as having been imported from a foreign country shall be their c.i.f. value accepted by the East African Customs and Excise Department on clearance for home consumption less the amount of any transport costs incurred in transit through the territory of other Partner States;

(c) if the value of any materials imported from a foreign country cannot be determined in accordance with paragraph (b) of this rule, their value shall be the earliest ascertainable price paid for them in the territory of the Partner State where they were used in a process of production;

(d) if the origin of any materials cannot be determined, such materials shall be deemed to have been imported from a foreign country and their value shall be the earliest ascertainable price paid for them in the territory of the Partner State where they were used in a process of production;

(e) the ex-factory value of the goods shall be the price paid or payable for them to the exporter in the territory of the Partner State where the goods were produced, that price being adjusted where necessary to a f.o.b. or free at frontier basis in that territory;

(f) the value under paragraphs (b), (c) or (d) of this rule or the ex-factory value under paragraph (e) of this rule may be adjusted to correspond with the amount which would have been obtained on a sale in the open market between buyer and seller independent of each other; this amount shall also be taken to be the ex-factory value when the goods are not the subject of a sale.

Unit of Qualification

4. (a) Each article in a consignment shall be considered separately.

(b) For the purposes of paragraph (a) of this rule—

(i) tools, parts and accessories which are transferred with an article, the price of which is included in that of the article or for which no separate charge is made, shall be considered as forming a whole with the article so long as they constitute the standard equipment customarily included on the sale of articles of that kind;

(ii) in cases not within sub-paragraph (i) of this paragraph, goods shall be treated as a single article if they are so treated for the purpose of assessing customs duty on like articles.

(c) An unassembled or disassembled article which is imported in more than one consignment because it is not feasible for transport or production reasons to transfer it in a single consignment may, at the option of the transferee, be treated as one article.

Segregation of Materials

5. (a) For those products or industries where it would be impracticable to segregate physically materials of similar character but different origin used in the production of goods, such segregation may be replaced by an

appropriate accounting system which ensures that no more goods are deemed to originate in the Partner States than would have been the case if it had been possible physically to segregate the materials.

(b) Any such accounting system shall conform to such conditions as may be agreed upon by the Common Market Council in order to ensure that adequate control measures will be applied.

Treatment of mixtures

6. (a) In the case of mixtures, not being groups, sets or assemblies of separable articles dealt with under rule 4, a Partner State may refuse to accept as originating in the Partner States any product resulting from the mixing together of goods which would qualify as originating in the Partner States with goods which would not so qualify, if the characteristics of the product as a whole are not essentially different from the characteristics of the goods which have been mixed.

(b) In the case of particular products where it is recognized by the Common Market Council to be desirable to permit mixing of the kind described in paragraph (a) of this rule, such products shall be accepted as originating in the Partner States in respect of such part thereof as may be shown to correspond to the quantity of goods originating in the Partner States used in the mixing subject to such conditions as may be agreed by the Common Market Council.

Certificates of origin

7. The transferor of any goods from one Partner State to another Partner State shall, if required by law or by the appropriate authority, provide a certificate of the origin of such goods, determined in accordance with the provisions of paragraph 3 of Article 11 of this Treaty and of these rules, signed or otherwise authenticated by the manufacturer of such goods.

(*Article* 12)

ANNEX II

CONTRACTUAL AND OTHER OBLIGATIONS

Tanzania

Contracting Parties: The Government of Tanganyika
Anic S.P.A. of 12 Viale Dell'Arte, Rome, Italy
Hydrocarbons Holding Co. A.G. of Zurich, Switzerland
Tanganyikan & Italian Petroleum Refining Co. (Tiper) Ltd., of Dar es Salaam

Subject   (*a*) Petroleum products of the types made, or to be made, pursuant to the contract, by the Tanganyikan & Italian Petroleum Refining Company and those obtainable by blending two or more of these petroleum products;

                             (*b*) products which correspond commercially to the products aforesaid

Duration   Thirty years from the 19th June 1963

Uganda

Obligations: Those comprised in the Enguli (Manufacture and Licensing) Act (Cap. 96—Laws of Uganda) and the Jaggery and Enguli Base Tax Act, 1966

Subject   Jaggery and Enguli

Duration   Commencing respectively on 20th January 1965 and 1st July 1966—of indefinite duration

Kenya

1. Contracting Parties: The Government of Kenya and the Consolidated Petroleum Co. Ltd.

Subject   Crude oil and petroleum products

Duration   Indefinite duration from September 1959

2. Contracting Parties: The Government of Kenya, Ross Group (International) Ltd., F.A.A. Ellenberger, Lamu Fisheries Ltd., Sideswell and Co. (Mombasa) Ltd., and Kenya Inshore Fisheries

Subject   Crustacea

Duration   Five years from 1st January 1967

3. Contracting Parties: The Government of Kenya and Albatross Superfosfaatfabrikien, N.V., Covenant Industries Ltd., Imperial Chemical Industries Ltd.

Subject   Nitrogenous fertilizers

Duration   Indefinite duration

4. Contracting Parties: The Government of Kenya and, *inter alia*, Chemelil Sugar Company Ltd.

Subject   Sugar and sugar products

Duration   Indefinite duration from 6th August 1966

(*Article* 13)

ANNEX III

Agricultural Products

1. Period of operation—no limitation.

> Maize, including maize flour
> Wheat
> Rice, both paddy and husked
> Coffee, raw
> Pyrethrum flowers
> Cotton lint, cotton seed, and unginned cotton
> Sisal fibre, sisal tow, and sisal flume tow
> Beans, peas, lentils and other leguminous vegetables, split or dried
> Meat (including poultry) fresh, chilled or frozen
> Milk and cream, fresh
> Eggs
> Pineapples, fresh
> Passion fruit, fresh
> Groundnuts
> Millets
> Simsim (sesame seed)

2. Period of operation—three years from the coming into force of this Treaty.

> Onions

3. Period of operation—until 1st December 1968.

> Bixa
> Castor seed
> Copra
> Capsicum, dried
> Sunflower seed
> Cassava
> Cashew nuts
> Sorghum
> Wattle bark

(*Article* 20)

ANNEX IV

Manufactured Goods

Manufactured goods shall be all those goods referred to in those Sections, Divisions or Items of the Official Import and Export List, as specified in the Schedule to Legal Notice No. 68 of 1963 of the Common Services Organization, which are set out below, subject to the modifications expressly stated in the description of goods given below:—

Section, Division or Item	*Description of Goods*
012 (part)	Bacon, ham and other smoked meat, whether or not in airtight containers (excluding dried meat and salted meat)
013 (part)	Sausages and other prepared or preserved meat (exluding meat extracts and meat juices)
022 1 (part)	Milk or cream (in liquid or semi-solid form) evaporated or condensed, including buttermilk and whey but excluding skimmed milk
022 2	Milk and cream dry (in solid form such as blocks or powder,) including buttermilk, skimmed milk and whey
023	Butter, including clarified butter
024	Cheese and curd
032 (part)	Fish and fish preparations (including crustacea and molluscs) in airtight containers
046 (part)	Meal and flour of wheat (excluding meal and flour of meslin)
047 (part)	Meal and flour of other cereals (excluding meal and flour of maize)
048	Cereal preparations and preparations of flour and starch of fruits and vegetables
053	Fruit preserved and fruit preparations (excluding dried and artificially dehydrated fruit)
055	Vegetables, roots and tubers, preserved or prepared, not elsewhere specified, whether or not in airtight containers
06 (part)	Sugar, sugar preparations and honey (exluding item 061 6 0, natural honey)
071 1 8	Coffee, roasted, including ground, and coffee substitutes containing coffee
073	Chocolate and other food preparations containing cocoa or chocolate, not elsewhere specified
074 1 0	Tea (other than unprocessed leaf)
075 (part)	Spices, ground only
081	Feeding stuff for animals (excluding unmilled cereals)
091	Margarine and shortening
099	Food preparations, not elsewhere specified

11	Beverages
122	Tobacco manufactures
243 (part)	Wood, shaped or simply worked (excluding item 243 1 0, railway sleepers (ties))
251	Pulp and waste paper
266	Synthetic and regenerated (artificial) fibres (including waste of such fibres)
33	Petroleum and petroleum products
34	Gas, natural and manufactured
42	Fixed vegetable oils and fats
5 (part)	Chemicals (excluding item 532 4 1, wattle bark extract)
6 (part)	Manufactured goods classified chiefly by material, excluding the following items:—

        681 1 0 Silver, unworked or partly worked

        682 1 0 Copper and alloys, whether or not refined, unwrought

        683 1 0 Nickel and nickel alloys, unwrought

        684 1 0 Aluminium and aluminium alloys, unwrought

        685 1 0 Lead and lead alloys, unwrought

        686 1 0 Zinc and zinc alloys, unwrought

        687 1 0 Tin and tin alloys, unwrought

        688 0 0 Uranium and thorium and their alloys

        689 0 0 Miscellaneous non-ferrous base metals employed in metallurgy

7	Machinery and transport equipment
8	Miscellaneous manufactured articles

(Article 20)

ANNEX V

VALUE OF GOODS LIABLE TO TRANSFER TAX

1. (1) The value of any goods liable to transfer tax shall be taken to be the normal price, that is to say the price which they would fetch when they are entered for the payment of transfer tax (or, if they are not so entered, at the time of transfer) on a sale in the open market between a buyer in the country to which the goods are transferred and a seller in the country from which the goods are transferred independent of each other.

(2) The normal price of any goods liable to transfer tax shall be determined on the following assumptions—

(a) that the goods are treated as having been delivered to the buyer at the point of entry into the country to which the goods are being transferred; and (*b*) that the seller will bear freight, insurance, commission and all other costs, charges and expenses incidental to the sale and the delivery of the goods at that point of entry; but

(*c*) that the buyer will bear any tax chargeable in the country to which the goods are being transferred.

2. A sale in the open market between buyer and seller independent of each other presupposes—

(*a*) that the price is the sole consideration; and

(*b*) that the price paid is not influenced by any commercial, financial or other relationship, whether by contract or otherwise, between the seller or any person associated in business with him and the buyer or any person associated in business with him (other than the relationship created by the sale of the goods in question); and

(*c*) that no part of the proceeds of the subsequent resale, use or disposal of the goods will accrue directly or indirectly to the seller or any person associated with him.

3. Where the goods to be valued—

(*a*) are manufactured in accordance with any patented invention or are goods to which any registered design has been applied; or

(*b*) are transferred under a foreign trade mark or are transferred for sale (whether or not after further manufacture) under a foreign trade mark,

the normal price shall be determined on the assumption that the price covers the right to use the patent, design or trade mark in respect of the goods.

4. For the purposes of paragraph 3 of this Annex, the expression 'trade mark' includes a trade name and a get up, and a foreign trade mark is a trade mark used for the purpose of indicating that goods in relation to which it is used are those of—

(*a*) a person by whom the goods to be valued have been grown, produced, manufactured, selected, offered for sale or otherwise dealt with outside the country to which the goods are transferred; or

(*b*) a person associated in business with any such person as is referred to in sub-paragraph (*a*) of this paragraph; or

(*c*) a person to whom any such person as is mentioned in sub-paragraph (*a*) or (*b*) of this paragraph has assigned the goodwill of the business in connection with which the trade mark is used.

5. Two persons shall be deemed to be associated in business with one another if, whether directly or indirectly, either one of them has any

interest in the business or property of the other, or both have a common interest in any business or property, or some third person has an interest in the business or property of both of them.

(*Article* 22)

ANNEX VI

THE CHARTER OF THE EAST AFRICAN DEVELOPMENT BANK

WHEREAS the Governments of the United Republic of Tanzania, the Sovereign State of Uganda and the Republic of Kenya, who are referred to in the Treaty and this Charter as 'the Partner States', have in Article 21 of the Treaty agreed to establish a Development Bank to be known as the East African Development Bank:

AND WHEREAS the said Governments have agreed in Article 22 of the Treaty that the Charter of the East African Development Bank shall be set out in an Annex to the Treaty:

NOW THEREFORE it is agreed that the East African Development Bank (hereinafter referred to as 'the Bank') be established and operate in accordance with the following provisions:

CHAPTER I. OBJECTIVES AND MEMBERSHIP

Article 1

Objectives of the Bank

1. The objectives of the Bank shall be—
   (*a*) to provide financial and technical assistance to promote the industrial development of the Partner States;
   (*b*) to give priority, in accordance with the operating principles contained in this Charter, to industrial development in the relatively less industrially developed Partner States, thereby endeavouring to reduce the substantial industrial imbalances between them;
   (*c*) to further the aims of the East African Community by financing, wherever possible, projects designed to make the economies of the Partner States increasingly complementary in the industrial field;
   (*d*) to supplement the activities of the national development agencies of the Partner States by joint financing operations and by the use of such agencies as channels for financing specific projects;
   (*e*) to co-operate, within the terms of this Charter, with other institutions and organizations, public or private, national or international,

which are interested in the industrial development of the Partner States; and

(*f*) to undertake such other activities and provide such other services as may advance the objectives of the Bank.

2. In paragraph 1 of this Article, 'industry' with its grammatical variations and cognate expressions means manufacturing, assembling, and processing industries including processing associated with the agricultural, forestry and fishing industries but does not include the building, transport and tourist industries.

Article 2

Membership in the Bank

1. The original members of the Bank shall be the Partner States and such bodies corporate, enterprises or institutions who with the approval of the Governments of the Partner States become members on or before the date specified in Article 55 of this Charter.

2. Upon an affirmative decision of the Board of Directors by a majority of the voting power, any body corporate, enterprise or institution, which has not become a member under paragraph 1 of this Article, may, with the approval of the Authority, be admitted to membership of the Bank under such terms and conditions as the Bank may determine.

CHAPTER II. CAPITAL

Article 3

Authorized capital

1. The authorized capital stock of the Bank shall be 400,000,000 units of account and the value of the unit of account shall be 0·124414 grams of fine gold.

2. The authorized capital stock of the Bank shall be divided into 4,000 shares having a par value of 100,000 units of account each which shall be available for subscription only by members in accordance with Article 4 of this Chapter.

3. The original authorized capital stock of the Bank shall be divided equally into paid-in shares and callable shares.

4. The authorized capital stock of the Bank may, after consultation with the Board of Directors, be increased by the Authority.

Article 4

Subscription of shares

1. Each member of the Bank shall subscribe to shares of the capital stock of the Bank.

2. Each subscription to the original authorized capital stock of the Bank shall be for paid-in shares and callable shares in equal parts.

3. The initial subscription of each of the Partner States to the original authorized capital stock of the Bank shall be 800 shares and the initial subscriptions of other original members to the original authorized capital stock of the Bank shall be as determined by the Governments of the Partner States.

4. The initial subscriptions of members, other than original members, to the original authorized capital stock of the Bank shall be determined by the Bank but no subscription shall be authorized which would have the effect of reducing the percentage of capital stock held by the Partner States below 51 per cent of the total subscribed capital stock.

5. If the authorized capital stock of the Bank is increased, the following provisions shall apply—

   (*a*) subject to this Article, subscriptions to any increase of the authorized capital stock shall be subject to such terms and conditions as the Bank shall determine;

   (*b*) the Partner States shall subscribe to equal parts only of the increased capital stock; and

   (*c*) each member, other than a Partner State, shall be given a reasonable opportunity to subscribe to a proportion of the increase of stock equivalent to the proportion which its stock theretofore subscribed bears to the total subscribed capital stock immediately prior to such increase:

   Provided that no such member shall be obligated to subscribe to any part of an increase of capital stock; and

   Provided further that subscriptions shall be restricted proportionately to the extent necessary to ensure that the percentage of capital stock held by the Partner States remains not less than 51 per cent of the total subscribed capital stock.

6. Shares of stock initially subscribed for by the original members shall be issued at par. Other shares shall be issued at par unless the Bank, by a vote representing a majority of the total voting power of members, decides in special circumstances to issue them on other terms.

7. Shares of stock shall not be pledged or encumbered in any manner whatsoever and they shall not be transferable except to the Bank:

Provided that if any shares of stock which are transferred to the Bank are subsequently subscribed for by or otherwise transferred to the Partner States, they shall take up such shares in equal parts only.

8. The liability of the members on shares shall be limited to the unpaid portion of the issue price of the shares.

9. No member shall be liable, by reason of its membership in the Bank, for obligations of the Bank.

Article 5

Payment of subscriptions

1. Payment of the amount initially subscribed by the original members to the paid-in capital stock of the Bank shall be made in four instalments the first of which shall be 10 per cent of such amount and the remaining instalments shall each be 30 per cent of such amount. The first instalment payable by each Partner State shall be paid within 30 days after the coming into force of the Treaty to which this Charter is annexed and in the case of original members other than the Partner States, the first instalment shall be paid within 30 days of their becoming a member. The second instalment shall be paid six calendar months after the date on which the Treaty comes into force. The remaining two instalments shall each be paid successively six calendar months from the date on which the preceding instalment becomes due under this paragraph.

2. Notwithstanding the provisions of paragraph 1 of this Article, in respect of any instalment, other than the first instalment, of the initial subscriptions to the original paid-in capital stock, the Bank shall, if the funds are not immediately required, either defer the due date for payment of such instalment or require that part only of such instalment be payable on the due date and at the same time prescribe a due date for the remainder of such instalment.

3. Of each instalment for the payment of subscriptions by each of the Partner States to the original paid-in capital stock—

(*a*) 50 per cent shall be paid in convertible currency;

(*b*) 50 per cent shall be paid in the currency of the Partner State concerned.

4. Each payment of a Partner State in its own currency under subparagraph (*b*) of paragraph 3 of this Article shall be in such amount as the Bank, after such consultation with the International Monetary Fund as the Bank may consider necessary, determines to be equivalent to the full

value in terms of the unit of account as expressed in paragraph 1 of Article 3 of this Charter of the portion of the subscription being paid.

5. The initial payment of a Partner State under sub-paragraph (*b*) of paragraph 3 of this Article shall be in such amount as the member considers appropriate but shall be subject to such adjustment, to be effected within 90 days of the date on which such payment was made, as the Bank shall determine to be necessary to constitute the full value of such payment in terms of the unit of account as expressed in paragraph 1 of Article 3 of this Charter.

6. Each instalment for the payment of subscriptions by members other than Partner States to the original paid-in capital stock shall be paid in convertible currency.

7. Payment of the amount subscribed to the callable capital stock of the Bank shall be subject to call only as and when required by the Bank to meet its obligations incurred under paragraphs (*b*) and (*d*) of Article 10 of this Charter on borrowings of funds for inclusion in its ordinary capital resources or on guarantees chargeable to such resources.

8. In the event of a call being made in terms of paragraph 7 of this Article, payment may be made at the option of the member in convertible currency or in the currency required to discharge the obligations of the Bank for the purposes for which the call is made. Calls on unpaid subscriptions shall be uniform in percentage on all callable shares.

9. The Bank shall determine the place for any payment of subscriptions, provided that, until the first meeting of its Board of Directors, the payment of the first instalment referred to in paragraph 1 of this Article shall be made to the Bank of Uganda as Trustee for the Bank.

Chapter III. Ordinary Capital Resources and Special Funds

Article 6

Ordinary capital resources

In the context of this Charter, the term 'ordinary capital resources' of the Bank shall include—

(*a*) the authorized capital stock of the Bank including both paid-in and callable shares subscribed pursuant to Article 4 of this Charter;

(*b*) funds raised by borrowings of the Bank by virtue of powers conferred by Article 19 of this Charter to which the commitment to calls provided for in paragraph 7 of Article 5 of this Charter is applicable;

(c) funds received in repayment of loans or guarantees made with the resources specified in paragraphs (a) and (b) of this Article;

(d) income derived from loans made from the above-mentioned funds or from guarantees to which the commitment to calls provided for in paragraph 7 of Article 5 of this Charter is applicable; and

(e) any other funds or income received by the Bank which do not form part of its Special Funds referred to in Article 7 of this Charter.

Article 7

Special Funds

1. The Bank may accept for administration, from such sources as it considers appropriate, Special Funds which are designed to promote the objectives of the Bank.

2. Special Funds accepted by the Bank under paragraph 1 of this Article shall be used in such manner and on such terms and conditions as are not inconsistent with the objectives of the Bank and the agreement under which such funds are accepted by the Bank for administration.

3. The Board of Directors shall make such regulations as may be necessary for the administration and use of each Special Fund. Such regulations shall be consistent with the provisions of this Charter, other than those provisions which expressly relate only to the ordinary operations of the Bank.

4. The term 'Special Funds' as used in this Charter shall refer to the resources of any Special Fund and shall include—

(a) funds accepted by the Bank in any Special Fund;

(b) funds repaid in respect of loans or guarantees financed from any Special Fund which, under the regulations of the Bank covering that Special Fund, are received by such Special Fund; and

(c) income derived from operations of the Bank in which any of the above-mentioned resources or funds are used or committed if, under the regulations of the Bank covering the Special Fund concerned, that income accrues to such Special Fund.

CHAPTER IV. OPERATIONS OF THE BANK

Article 8

Use of resources

The resources and facilities of the Bank shall be used exclusively to implement the objectives of the Bank as set forth in Article 1 of this Charter.

Article 9

Ordinary and special operations

1. The operations of the Bank shall consist of ordinary operations and special operations. Ordinary operations shall be those financed from the ordinary capital resources of the Bank and special operations shall be those financed from the Special Funds referred to in Article 7 of this Charter.

2. The ordinary capital resources and the Special Funds of the Bank shall at all times and in all respects be held, used, committed, invested or otherwise disposed of entirely separately from each other.

3. The ordinary capital resources of the Bank shall not be charged with, or used to discharge, losses or liabilities arising out of special operations for which Special Funds were originally used or committed.

4. Expenses relating directly to ordinary operations shall be charged to ordinary capital resources of the Bank and those relating to special operations shall be charged to the Special Funds. Any other expenses shall be charged as the Bank shall determine.

Article 10

Methods of operation

Subject to the conditions set forth in this Charter, the Bank may provide finances or facilitate financing in any of the following ways to any agency, entity or enterprise operating in the territories of the Partner States—

    (*a*) by making or participating in direct loans with its unimpaired paid-in capital and, except in the case of its Special Reserve as defined in Article 17 of this Charter, with its reserves and undistributed surplus or with the unimpaired Special Funds;

    (*b*) by making or participating in direct loans with funds raised by the Bank in capital markets or borrowed or otherwise acquired by the Bank for inclusion in its ordinary capital resources;

    (*c*) by investment of funds referred to in paragraphs (*a*) and (*b*) of this Article in the equity capital of an institution or enterprise; or

    (*d*) by guaranteeing, in whole or in part, loans made by others for industrial development.

Article 11

Limitations on operations

1. The total amount outstanding of loans, equity investments and guarantees made by the Bank in its ordinary operations shall not at any time exceed one and a half times the total amount of its unimpaired subscribed

capital, reserves and surplus included in its ordinary capital resources, excluding the Special Reserve and any other reserves not available for ordinary operations.

2. The total amount outstanding in respect of the special operations of the Bank relating to any Special Fund shall not at any time exceed the total amount of the unimpaired special resources appertaining to that Special Fund.

3. In the case of loans made with funds borrowed by the Bank to which the commitment to calls provided for in paragraph 7 of Article 5 of this Charter is applicable, the total amount of principal outstanding and payable to the Bank in a specific currency shall not at any time exceed the total amount of the principal of outstanding borrowings by the Bank that are payable in the same currency.

4. In the case of funds invested in equity capital out of the ordinary capital resources of the Bank, the total amount invested shall not exceed 10 per cent of the aggregate amount of the unimpaired paid-in capital stock of the Bank actually paid up at any given time together with the reserves and surplus included in its ordinary capital resources, excluding the Special Reserve.

5. The amount of any equity investment in any entity or enterprise shall not exceed such percentage of the equity capital of that entity or enterprise as the Board of Directors shall in each specific case determine to be appropriate. The Bank shall not seek to obtain by such investment a controlling interest in the entity or enterprise concerned, except where necessary to safeguard the investment of the Bank.

6. In the case of guarantees given by the Bank in the course of its ordinary operations, the total amount guaranteed shall not exceed 10 per cent of the aggregate amount of the unimpaired paid-in capital stock of the Bank actually paid up at any given time together with the reserves and surplus included in its ordinary capital resources excluding the Special Reserve.

Article 12

Provision of currencies for direct loans

In making direct loans or participating in them, the Bank may provide finance in the following ways—

    (*a*) by furnishing the borrower with currencies other than the currency of the Partner State in whose territory the project is located, which are needed by the borrower to meet the foreign exchange costs of the project; or (*b*) by providing, when local currency required for the purposes of the loan cannot be raised by the borrower on reasonable terms, local currency but not exceeding a reasonable portion of the total local expenditure to be incurred by the borrower.

Article 13
Operating principles

The operations of the Bank shall be conducted in accordance with the following principles—

(*a*) the Bank shall be guided by sound banking principles in its operations and shall finance only economically sound and technically feasible projects, and shall not make loans or undertake any responsibility for the discharge or re-financing of earlier commitments by borrowers;

(*b*) in selecting projects, the Bank shall always be guided by the need to pursue the objectives set forth in Article 1 of this Charter;

(*c*) subject to this Article, the Bank shall ensure that, taken over consecutive periods of five years, the first of which shall begin upon the commencement of the operations of the Bank, it shall so conduct its operations that it shall have loaned, guaranteed or otherwise invested, as nearly as is possible, in the United Republic of Tanzania $38\frac{3}{4}$ per cent of the total sum which it has loaned, guaranteed or otherwise invested of its ordinary capital resources and the Special Funds, in the Sovereign State of Uganda $38\frac{3}{4}$ per cent thereof and in the Republic of Kenya $22\frac{1}{2}$ per cent thereof:

Provided that, after a period of ten years from the commencement of operations of the Bank, the Partner States shall review the percentages specified in this paragraph and thereafter the Authority, after consultation with the Board of Directors, may by order published in the Gazette of the Community alter the percentages specified in this paragraph;

(*d*) the operations of the Bank shall provide principally for the financing directly of specific projects within the Partner States but may include loans to or guarantees of loans made to the national development agencies of the Partner States so long as such loans or guarantees are in respect of and used for specific projects which are agreed to by the Bank;

(*e*) the Bank shall seek to maintain a reasonable diversification in its investments;

(*f*) the Bank shall seek to revolve its funds by selling its investments in equity capital to other investors wherever it can appropriately do so on satisfactory terms;

(g) the Bank shall not finance any undertaking in the territory of a Partner State if that Partner State objects to such financing;

(h) before a loan is granted or guaranteed or an investment made, the applicant shall have submitted an adequate proposal to the Bank, and the Director-General of the Bank shall have presented to the Board of Directors a written report regarding the proposal, together with his recommendations;

(i) in considering an application for a loan or guarantee, the Bank shall pay due regard to the ability of the borrower to obtain finance or facilities elsewhere on terms and conditions that the Bank considers reasonable for the recipient, taking into account all pertinent factors;

(j) in making or guaranteeing a loan, the Bank shall pay due regard to the prospects that the borrower and its guarantor, if any, will be able to meet their obligations under the loan contract;

(k) in making or guaranteeing a loan, the rate of interest, other charges and the schedule for repayment of principal shall be such as are, in the opinion of the Bank, appropriate for the loan concerned;

(l) in guaranteeing a loan made by other investors, the Bank shall charge a suitable fee or commission for its risk;

(m) in the case of a direct loan made by the Bank, the borrower shall be permitted by the Bank to draw the loan funds only to meet payments in connection with the project as they fall due;

(n) the Bank shall take all necessary measures to ensure that the proceeds of any loan made, guaranteed or participated in by the Bank are used only for the purpose for which the loan was granted and with due attention to considerations of economy and efficiency; and

(o) the Bank shall ensure that every loan contract entered into by it shall enable the Bank to exercise all necessary powers of entry, inspection and supervision of operations in connection with the project and shall further enable the Bank to require the borrower to provide information and to allow inspection of its books and records during such time as any part of the loan remains outstanding.

Article 14

Prohibition of political activity

1. The Bank shall not accept loans, Special Funds or assistance that may in any way prejudice, limit, deflect or otherwise alter its objectives or functions.

2. The Bank, its Director-General and officers and staff shall not interfere in the political affairs of any Partner State, nor shall they be influenced in their decisions by the political character of a Partner State. Only economic

considerations shall be relevant to their decisions and such considerations shall be weighed impartially to achieve and carry out the objectives and functions of the Bank.

Article 15

Terms and conditions for direct loans and guarantees

1. In the case of direct loans made or participated in or loans guaranteed by the Bank, the contract shall establish, in conformity with the operating principles set out above and subject to the other provisions of this Charter, the terms and conditions for the loan or the guarantee concerned, including payment of principal, interest, commitment fee and other charges, maturities and dates of payment in respect of the loan, or the fees and other charges in respect of the guarantee, respectively.

2. The contract shall provide that all payments to the Bank under the contract shall be made in the currency loaned, unless, in the case of a loan made or guaranteed as part of special operations, the regulations of the Bank provide otherwise.

3. Guarantees by the Bank shall also provide that the Bank may terminate its liability with respect to interest if, upon default by the borrower or any other guarantor, the Bank offers to purchase, at par and interest accrued to a date designated in the offer, the bonds or other obligations guaranteed.

4. Whenever it considers it appropriate, the Bank may require as a condition of granting or participating in a loan that the Partner State in whose territory a project is to be carried out, or a public agency or instrumentality of that Partner State acceptable to the Bank, guarantee the repayment of the principal and the payment of interest and other charges on the loan in accordance with the terms thereof.

5. The loan or guarantee contract shall specifically state the currency in which all payments to the Bank thereunder shall be made.

Article 16

Commission and fees

1. In addition to interest, the Bank shall charge a commission on direct loans made or participated in as part of its ordinary operations at a rate to be determined by the Board of Directors and computed on the amount outstanding on each loan or participation.

2. In guaranteeing a loan as part of its ordinary operations, the Bank shall charge a guarantee fee at a rate determined by the Board of Directors payable periodically on the amount of the loan outstanding.

3. Other charges, including commitment fee, of the Bank in its ordinary operations and any commission, fees or other charges in relation to its special operations shall be determined by the Board of Directors.

Article 17

Special Reserve

The amount of commissions and guarantee fees received by the Bank under the provisions of Article 16 of this Charter shall be set aside as a Special Reserve which shall be kept for meeting liabilities of the Bank in accordance with Article 18 of this Charter. The Special Reserve shall be held in such liquid form as the Board of Directors may decide but the Board of Directors shall ensure that any part of the Special Reserve which it may decide to invest in the territories of the Partner States shall be invested, as nearly as possible, in equal proportions in each Partner State.

Article 18

Defaults on loans and methods of meeting liabilities of the Bank

1. In cases of default on loans made, participated in or guaranteed by the Bank in its ordinary operations, the Bank shall take such action as it considers appropriate to conserve its investment including modification of the terms of the loan, other than any term as to the currency of repayment.

2. Payments in discharge of the Bank's liabilities on borrowings or guarantees chargeable to the ordinary capital resources shall be charged firstly against the Special Reserve and then, to the extent necessary and at the discretion of the Bank, against other reserves, surplus and capital available to the Bank.

3. Whenever necessary to meet contractual payments of interest, other charges or amortization on borrowings of the Bank in its ordinary operations, or to meet its liabilities with respect to similar payments in relation to loans guaranteed by it, chargeable to its ordinary capital resources, the Bank may call an appropriate amount of the uncalled subscribed callable capital in accordance with paragraphs 7 and 8 of Article 5 of this Charter.

Chapter V. Miscellaneous Powers and Duties of the Bank

Article 19

Miscellaneous powers

In addition to the powers specified elsewhere in this Charter, the Bank shall be empowered—

(*a*) to borrow funds in the territories of the Partner States, or elsewhere, and in this connection to furnish such collateral or other security therefor as the Bank shall determine:

Provided that—

(i) before selling its obligations or otherwise borrowing in the territory of a country, the Bank shall obtain the approval of the Government of that country to the sale; and

(ii) before deciding to sell its obligations or otherwise borrowing in a particular country, the Bank shall consider the amount of previous borrowing, if any, in that country with a view to diversifying its borrowing to the maximum extent possible;

(b) to buy and sell securities which the Bank has issued or guaranteed or in which it has invested;

(c) to guarantee securities in which it has invested in order to facilitate their sale;

(d) to invest funds not immediately needed in its operations in such obligations as it may determine and invest funds held by the Bank for pensions or similar purposes in marketable securities, but the Bank shall ensure that any funds which it may decide to invest in the territories of the Partner States shall be invested, as nearly as possible, in equal proportions in each Partner State;

(e) to provide technical advice and assistance which may serve its purposes and come within its functions and where appropriate, for example in the case of special feasibility studies, the Bank shall charge for such services; and

(f) to study and promote the investment opportunities within the Partner States.

Article 20

Allocation of net income

1. The Board of Directors shall determine annually what part of the net income of the Bank, including the net income accruing to the Special Funds, shall be allocated, after making provision for reserves, to surplus and what part, if any, shall be distributed to the members.

2. Any distributions to members made pursuant to paragraph 1 of this Article shall be in proportion to the number of shares held by each member and payments shall be made in such manner and in such currency as the Board of Directors shall determine.

Article 21

Power to make regulations

The Board of Directors may make such regulations, including financial regulations, being consistent with the provisions of this Charter as it considers necessary or appropriate to further the objectives and functions of the Bank.

Article 22

Notice to be placed on securities

Every security issued or guaranteed by the Bank shall bear on its face a conspicuous statement to the effect that it is not an obligation of any Government, unless it is in fact the obligation of a particular Government, in which case it shall so state.

CHAPTER VI. CURRENCIES

Article 23

Determination of convertibility

Whenever it shall become necessary under this Charter to determine whether any currency is convertible, such determination shall be made by the Bank after consultation with the International Monetary Fund.

Article 24

Use of currencies

1. The Partner States may not maintain or impose any restriction on the holding or use by the Bank or by any recipient from the Bank for payments in any country of the following—

   (a) currencies received by the Bank in payment of subscriptions to its capital stock;

   (b) currencies purchased with the currencies referred to in sub-paragraph (a) of this paragraph;

   (c) currencies obtained by the Bank by borrowing for inclusion in its ordinary capital resources;

   (d) currencies received by the Bank in payment of principal, interest, dividends or other charges in respect of loans or investments made out of any of the funds referred to in sub-paragraphs (a), (b) and (c) of this paragraph or in payment of fees in respect of guarantees made by the Bank; and

   (e) currencies received from the Bank in distribution of the net income of the Bank in accordance with Article 20 of this Charter.

2. The Partner States may not maintain or impose any restriction on the holding or use by the Bank or by any recipient from the Bank, for payments in any country, of currency received by the Bank which does not

come within the provisions of paragraph 1 of this Article unless such currency forms part of the Special Funds of the Bank and its use is subject to special regulations.

3. The Partner States may not maintain or impose any restriction on the holding or use by the Bank, for making amortisation payments or for re-purchasing in whole or in part the Bank's own obligations, of currencies received by the Bank in repayment of direct loans made out of its ordinary capital resources.

4. Each Partner State shall ensure, in respect of projects within its terri-tories, that the currencies necessary to enable payments to be made to the Bank in accordance with the provisions of the contracts referred to in Article 15 of this Charter shall be made available in exchange for currency of the Partner State concerned.

Article 25
Maintenance of value of currency holdings

1. Whenever the par value in the International Monetary Fund of the currency of a Partner State is reduced or the foreign exchange value of the currency of a Partner State has, in the opinion of the Bank, depreciated to a significant extent within the territory of that Partner State, such Partner State shall pay to the Bank within a reasonable time an additional amount of its own currency sufficient to maintain the value, as of the time of sub-scription, of the amount of the currency of such Partner State paid in to the Bank by that Partner State under sub-paragraph (b) of paragraph 3 of Article 5 of this Charter, and currency furnished under the provisions of this paragraph, provided, however, that the foregoing shall apply only so long as and to the extent that such currency shall not have been initially disbursed or exchanged for another currency.

2. Whenever the par value in the International Monetary Fund of the currency of a Partner State is increased, or the foreign exchange value of the currency of a Partner State has, in the opinion of the Bank, appreciated to a significant extent within the territory of that Partner State, the Bank shall return to such Partner State within a reasonable time an amount of the currency of that Partner State equal to the increase in the value of the amount of such currency to which the provisions of paragraph 1 of this Article are applicable.

Chapter VII. Organization and Management of the Bank

Article 26

Structure

The Bank shall have a Board of Directors, a Director-General and such other officers and staff as it may consider necessary.

Article 27

Board of Directors

1. All the powers of the Bank shall, subject to this Charter, be vested in the Board of Directors.

2. The Board of Directors shall consist of not more than five nor fewer than three members of whom—

   (*a*) three shall be appointed by the Partner States, each of which shall appoint one; and

   (*b*) up to two shall be elected by the members other than the Partner States in accordance with such procedure as the said members shall from time to time decide:

   Provided that no single member shall be represented by more than one director.

3. All directors shall be persons possessing high competence and wide experience in economic, financial and banking affairs.

4. Directors shall hold office for a term of three years and shall be eligible for re-appointment or re-election:

   Provided that—

   (*a*) of the first directors of the Bank two, who shall be chosen by the directors by lot, shall hold office for two years;

   (*b*) a director shall remain in office until his successor has been appointed or elected;

   (*c*) a director appointed or elected in place of one whose office has become vacant before the end of his term shall hold office only for the remainder of that term;

   (*d*) a director appointed by a Partner State may be required at any time by that Partner State to vacate his office.

5. There shall be appointed or elected, as the case may be, an alternate director in respect of each substantive director and an alternate director shall be appointed or elected in the same manner and for the same term of office as the director to whom he is an alternate; and an alternate director shall remain in office until his successor has been appointed or elected.

6. An alternate director may participate in meetings but may vote only when he is acting in place of and in the absence of the director to whom he is an alternate.

7. While the office of a director is vacant the alternate of the former director shall exercise the powers of that director.

Article 28

Procedure of the Board of Directors

1. The Board of Directors shall normally meet at the principal office of the Bank and shall meet at least once every three months or more frequently if the business of the Bank so requires.

2. Meetings of the Board of Directors shall be convened by the Director-General of the Bank.

3. Four directors, including the three directors appointed by the Partner States, or, if there is no member other than the Partner States, three directors, shall constitute a quorum for any meeting of the Board of Directors:

Provided that if within two hours of the time appointed for the holding of a meeting of the Board of Directors a quorum is not present, the meeting shall automatically stand adjourned to the next day, at the same time and place, or if that day is a public holiday, to the next succeeding day which is not a public holiday at the same time and place, and if at such adjourned meeting a quorum is not present within two hours from the time appointed for the meeting, the directors present shall constitute a quorum and may transact the business for which the meeting was called.

4. The Board of Directors may, by regulation, establish a procedure whereby a decision in writing signed by all the Directors of the Bank shall be as valid and effectual as if it had been made at a meeting of the Board of Directors.

Article 29

Voting

1. The voting power of each member of the Bank shall be equal to the number of shares of the capital stock of the Bank held by that member.

2. In voting in the Board of Directors—

    (*a*) an appointed director shall be entitled to cast the number of votes of the Partner State which appointed him;

    (*b*) each elected director shall be entitled to cast the number of votes of the members of the Bank whom he represents, which votes need not be cast as a unit; and

(c) except as otherwise expressly provided in this Charter, all matters before the Board of Directors shall be decided by a majority of the total voting power of the members of the Bank.

Article 30

Director-General of the Bank

1. There shall be a Director-General of the Bank who shall be appointed by the Authority after consultation with the Board of Directors, and who, while he remains Director-General, may not hold office as a Director or an alternate to a Director.

2. Subject to paragraph 3 of this Article, the Director-General shall hold office for a term of five years and may be re-appointed.

3. The Director-General shall vacate his office if the Authority after consultation with the Board of Directors so decides.

4. If the office of Director-General becomes vacant for any reason, a successor shall be appointed for a new term of five years.

5. The Director-General shall preside at meetings of the Board of Directors but shall have no vote.

6. The Director-General shall be the legal representative of the Bank.

7. The Director-General shall be chief of the staff of the Bank and shall conduct under the direction of the Board of Directors the current business of the Bank. He shall be responsible for the organization, appointment and dismissal of the officers and staff in accordance with regulations adopted by the Board of Directors.

8. In appointing officers and staff the Director-General shall, subject to the paramount importance of securing the highest standards of efficiency and technical competence, pay due regard to the recruitment of citizens of the Partner States.

Article 31

Loyalties of Director-General and officers and staff

The Director-General and officers and staff of the Bank, in the discharge of their offices, owe their duty entirely to the Bank and to no other authority. Each member of the Bank shall respect the international character of this duty and shall refrain from all attempts to influence the Director-General or any of the officers and staff in the discharge of their duties.

Article 32
Offices of the Bank

The principal office of the Bank shall be located at Kampala in Uganda and the Bank may establish offices or agencies elsewhere.

Article 33
Channel of communications, depositories

1. Each member of the Bank shall designate an appropriate official, entity or person with whom the Bank may communicate in connection with any matter arising under this Charter.

2. Each Partner State shall designate its central bank, or such other agency as may be agreed upon with the Bank, as a depository with which the Bank may keep its holdings of currency and other assets.

Article 34
Working language

The working language of the Bank shall be English.

Article 35
Accounts and reports

1. The Board of Directors shall ensure that proper accounts and proper records are kept in relation to the operations of the Bank and such accounts shall be audited in respect of each financial year by auditors of high repute selected by the Board of Directors.

2. The Bank shall prepare and transmit to the Authority and to the members of the Bank, and shall also publish, an annual report containing an audited statement of its accounts.

3. The Bank shall prepare and transmit to its members quarterly a summary statement of its financial position and a profit and loss statement showing the results of its operations.

4. All financial statements of the Bank shall show ordinary operations and the operations of each Special Fund separately.

5. The Bank may also publish such other reports as it considers desirable in carrying out its objectives and functions and such reports shall be transmitted to members of the Bank.

CHAPTER VIII. WITHDRAWAL AND SUSPENSION OF MEMBERS

Article 36

Withdrawal of members

1. A Partner State may not withdraw from the Bank.

2. Any member, other than a Partner State, may withdraw from the Bank at any time by delivering a notice in writing to the Bank at its principal office.

3. Withdrawal by a member under paragraph 2 of this Article shall become effective, and its membership shall cease, on the date specified in its notice but in no event less than six months after the date that notice has been received by the Bank. However, at any time before the withdrawal becomes finally effective, the member may notify the Bank in writing of the cancellation of its notice of intention to withdraw.

4. A withdrawing member shall remain liable for all direct and contingent obligations to the Bank to which it was subject at the date of delivery of the withdrawal notice. If the withdrawal becomes finally effective, the member shall not incur any liability for obligations resulting from operations of the Bank effected after the date on which the withdrawal notice was received by the Bank.

Article 37

Suspension of membership

1. If a member of the Bank, other than a Partner State, fails to fulfil any of its obligations to the Bank, the Board of Directors may suspend such member by a majority vote of the total number of Directors representing not less than 75 per cent of the total voting power of the members including the affirmative votes of each of the Partner States.

2. The member so suspended shall automatically cease to be a member of the Bank six months from the date of its suspension unless the Board of Directors decides, within that period and by the same majority necessary for suspension, to restore the member to good standing.

3. While under suspension, a member shall not be entitled to exercise any rights under this Charter but shall remain subject to all its obligations.

Article 38

Settlement of accounts

1. After the date on which a member ceases to be a member, it shall remain liable for its direct obligations to the Bank and for its contingent

liabilities to the Bank so long as any part of the loans or guarantees contracted before it ceased to be a member is outstanding; but it shall not incur liabilities with respect to loans and guarantees entered into thereafter by the Bank nor share either in the income or the expenses of the Bank.

2. At the time a member ceases to be a member, the Bank shall arrange for the repurchase of its shares by the Bank as a part of the settlement of accounts with such member in accordance with the provisions of paragraphs 3 and 4 of this Article. For this purpose, the repurchase price of the shares shall be the value shown by the books of the Bank on the date the member ceases to be a member.

3. The payment for shares repurchased by the Bank under this Article shall be governed by the following conditions—

(a) any amount due to the member concerned for its shares shall be withheld so long as that member remains liable, as a borrower or guarantor, to the Bank and such amount may, at the option of the Bank, be applied on any such liability as it matures. No amount shall be withheld on account of the contingent liability of the member for future calls on its subscription for shares in accordance with paragraph 7 of Article 5 of this Charter. In any event, no amount due to a member for its shares shall be paid until six months after the date on which the member ceases to be a member;

(b) payments for shares may be made from time to time, upon their surrender by the member concerned, to the extent by which the amount due as the repurchase price in accordance with paragraph 2 of this Article exceeds the aggregate amount of liabilities on loans and guarantees referred to in sub-paragraph (a) of this paragraph, until the former member has received the full repurchase price;

(c) payments shall be made in such available currencies as the Bank determines, taking into account its financial position; and

(d) if losses are sustained by the Bank on any guarantees or loans which were outstanding on the date when a member ceased to be a member and the amount of such losses exceeds the amount of the reserve provided against losses on that date, the member concerned shall repay, upon demand, the amount by which the repurchase price of its shares would have been reduced if the losses had been taken into account when the repurchase price was determined. In addition, the former member shall remain liable on any call for unpaid subscriptions in accordance with paragraph 7 of Article 5 of this Charter, to the same extent that it would have been required to respond if the impairment of capital had occurred and the call had been made at the time the repurchase price of its shares was determined.

4. If the Bank terminates its operations pursuant to Article 39 of this Charter within six months of the date upon which any member ceases to be a member, all rights of the member concerned shall be determined in accordance with the provisions of Articles 39 to 41 of this Charter. Such member shall be considered as still a member for the purposes of such Articles but shall have no voting rights.

CHAPTER IX. TERMINATION OF OPERATIONS

Article 39

Termination of operations

1. The Bank may terminate its operations by resolution of the Board of Directors approved by a vote representing not less than 85 per cent of the total voting power of the members and with the approval also of the Authority.

2. After such termination, the Bank shall forthwith cease all activities, except those incidental to the orderly realization, conservation and preservation of its assets and the settlement of its obligations.

Article 40

Liability of members and payment of claims

1. In the event of termination of the operations of the Bank, the liability of all members for uncalled subscriptions to the capital stock of the Bank shall continue until all claims of creditors, including all contingent claims, shall have been discharged.

2. All creditors holding direct claims shall first be paid out of the assets of the Bank and then out of payments to the Bank on unpaid or callable subscriptions. Before making any payments to creditors holding direct claims, the Board of Directors shall make such arrangements as are necessary, in its judgement, to ensure a *pro rata* distribution among holders of direct and contingent claims.

Article 41

Distribution of assets

1. No distribution of assets shall be made to members on account of their subscriptions to the capital stock of the Bank until all liabilities to creditors shall have been discharged or provided for and any such distribution shall

be approved by the Board of Directors by a vote representing not less than 85 per cent of the total voting power of the members.

2. Any distribution of the assets of the Bank to the members shall be in proportion to the capital stock held by each member and shall be effected at such times and under such conditions as the Bank shall consider fair and equitable. The shares of assets distributed need not be uniform as to type of asset. No member shall be entitled to receive its share in such a distribution of assets until it has settled all of its obligations to the Bank.

3. Any member receiving assets distributed pursuant to this Article shall enjoy the same rights with respect to such assets as the Bank enjoyed prior to their distribution.

CHAPTER X. STATUS, IMMUNITIES AND PRIVILEGES

Article 42

Purpose of Chapter

To enable the Bank effectively to fulfil its objectives and carry out the functions with which it is entrusted, the status, immunities, exemptions and privileges set forth in this Chapter shall be accorded to the Bank in the territories of each of the Partner States.

Article 43

Legal status

The Bank shall possess full juridical personality and, in particular, full capacity—

    (*a*) to contract;
    (*b*) to acquire, and dispose of, immovable and movable property; and
    (*c*) to institute legal proceedings.

Article 44

Judicial proceedings

1. Actions may be brought against the Bank in the territories of the Partner States only in a court of competent jurisdiction in a Partner State in which the Bank has an office, has appointed an agent for the purpose of accepting service or notice of process, or has issued or guaranteed securities.

2. No action shall be brought against the Bank by members or persons acting for or deriving claims from members. However, members shall have recourse to such special procedures for the settlement of controversies between the Bank and its members as may be prescribed in this Charter, in the regulations of the Bank or in contracts entered into with the Bank.

Article 45

Immunity of assets

1. Property and other assets of the Bank, wheresoever located and by whomsoever held, shall be immune from requisition, confiscation, expropriation or any other form of taking or foreclosure by executive or legislative action and premises used for the business of the Bank shall be immune from search.

2. The Bank shall prevent its premises from becoming refuges for fugitives from justice, or for persons subject to extradition, or persons avoiding service of legal process or a judicial proceeding.

Article 46

Immunity of archives

The archives of the Bank and all documents belonging to it, or held by it, shall be inviolable wherever located.

Article 47

Freedom of assets from restriction

To the extent necessary to carry out the objectives and functions of the Bank and subject to the provisions of this Charter, all property and other assets of the Bank shall be free from restrictions, regulations, controls, and moratoria of any nature.

Article 48

Personal immunities and privileges

Directors, alternates, officers and employees of the Bank and experts and consultants rendering services to the Bank shall have the immunities and privileges provided for under Article 3 of the Treaty to which this Charter is annexed.

Article 49

Exemption from taxation

1. The Bank shall be enabled to import free of customs duty any goods required for the purpose of its operations except such goods as are intended for sale, or are sold, to the public.

2. No transfer tax may be imposed upon manufactured goods which are required by the Bank for the purpose of its operations, otherwise than upon such goods as are intended for sale, or are sold, to the public.

3. The Bank shall be exempted from income tax and stamp duty.

Article 50

Implementation

Each Partner State shall promptly take such action as is necessary to make effective within that Partner State the provisions set forth in this Chapter and shall inform the Bank of the action which it has taken on the matter.

Article 51

Waiver of immunities

1. The Bank at its discretion may waive any of the privileges, immunities and exemptions conferred under this Chapter in any case or instance, in such manner and upon such conditions as it may determine to be appropriate in the best interests of the Bank.

2. The Bank shall take every measure to ensure that the privileges, immunities, exemptions and facilities conferred by this Charter are not abused and for this purpose shall establish such regulations as it may consider necessary and expedient.

CHAPTER XI. AMENDMENT, INTERPRETATION AND ARBITRATION

Article 52

Amendment of the Charter

1. This Charter may be amended only by a resolution of the Board of Directors approved by a vote representing not less than 85 per cent of the total voting power of the members and thereafter approved by the Authority.

2. An amendment to this Charter shall be published as a Legal Notice in the Gazette of the Community and shall enter into force three calendar months after the date of such publication unless the resolution referred to in paragraph 1 of this Article otherwise provides.

3. Notwithstanding the provisions of paragraph 1 of this Article, the unanimous agreement of the Board of Directors shall be required for the approval of any amendment of the Charter modifying—

(*a*) the right of a member, other than a Partner State, to withdraw from the Bank as provided in Article 36 of this Charter;

(*b*) the right to subscribe to capital stock of the Bank as provided in paragraph 5 of Article 4 of this Charter; and

(*c*) the limitation on liability as provided in paragraphs 8 and 9 of Article 4 of this Charter.

Article 53

Interpretation or application

Any question of interpretation or application of the provisions of this Charter arising between any member and the Bank or between two or more members of the Bank shall be submitted to the Board of Directors for decision.

Article 54

Arbitration

1. If a disagreement shall arise between the Bank and a member or between the Bank and a former member of the Bank including a disagreement in respect of a decision of the Board of Directors under Article 53 of this Charter, such disagreement shall be submitted to arbitration by a tribunal of three arbitrators. One of the arbitrators shall be appointed by the Bank, another by the member or former member concerned and the third, unless the parties otherwise agree, by the Executive Secretary of the Economic Commission for Africa or such other authority as may have been prescribed by regulations made by the Board of Directors.

2. A majority vote of the arbitrators shall be sufficient to reach a decision which shall be final and binding on the parties and a decision of the arbitrators may include an order as to payment of costs and expenses.

3. The third arbitrator shall be empowered to settle all questions of procedure in any case where the parties are in disagreement with respect thereto.

CHAPTER XII. FINAL PROVISIONS

Article 55

Signature and deposit

1. Upon the signature of the Treaty to which this Charter is annexed on behalf of all three Partner States, a copy of this Charter shall be deposited with the Secretary-General of the Common Services Organization where it shall remain open until the first day of December 1967 for signature by the bodies corporate, enterprises or institutions approved under paragraph 1 of Article 2 of this Charter.

2. Immediately after the first day of December 1967 the Secretary-General of the Community shall send certified copies of this Charter to all the Partner States and others who by signing this Charter become members of the Bank.

Article 56

Entry into force

This Charter shall enter into force at the same time as does the Treaty to which it is annexed.

Article 57

Commencement of operations

1. As soon as this Charter enters into force, the Directors shall be appointed or elected in accordance with the provisions of Article 27 of this Charter and the Secretary-General of the Community shall call the first meeting of the Board of Directors.

2. At its first meeting the Board of Directors shall determine the date on which the Bank shall commence its operations.

3. The Bank shall notify its members of the date of the commencement of its operations.

Article 58

Definitions

In this Charter, unless the context otherwise requires—

'Authority' means the East African Authority established by Article 46 of the Treaty to which this Charter is annexed;

'Board of Directors' means the Board of Directors of the Bank;

'Community' means the East African Community established by Article 1 of the Treaty to which this Charter is annexed;

'Director-General' means the Director-General of the Bank;

'Treaty' means the Treaty For East African Co-operation to which this Charter is annexed.

(Article 25)

ANNEX VII

CURRENT ACCOUNT PAYMENTS

1. Payments for goods of all kinds, including any payment of insurance in respect of such goods or any element in the price thereof in respect of such insurance, and payments for water and electricity, imported or to be imported into the Partner State from which payment is to be made.

2. Payments in respect of goods traded under transit or merchanting arrangements.

3. Payments in respect of the carriage of goods or passengers by any means of transport, including payments for the chartering of such transport.

4. Payments in respect of services incidental to the carriage of goods or passengers by any means of transport, including warehousing and storage and transit facilities.

5. Payments in respect of the operation of transport services, including bunkering and provisioning, maintenance, assembly and repair of equipment and installations, fuel and oil, garaging, and expenses of staff.

6. Payments in respect of postal and telecommunications services.

7. Payments in respect of business services, including payments for agency and representation services, advertising, banking commission and charges, insurance and reinsurance, commission and brokerage services, and assistance relating to the production and distribution of goods and services at all stages.

8. Payments for professional services, including legal, medical, dental, architectural, accounting and auditing and engineering services.

9. Payments in respect of travel, subsistence and accommodation.

10. Payments in respect of fees and remuneration for other services, including education and personal services.

11. Payments in respect of construction carried out in the Partner State from which payment is to be made.

12. Payments in respect of processing, finishing, servicing and maintenance work.

13. Payments of interest and other investment income on shares, loans, mortgages, overdrafts and debentures, of profits from business, and contractual amortization.

14. Payments by or to subsidiary concerns, branches or sub-branches in respect of overhead costs shared with a parent concern or branch.

15. Payments in respect of rentals.

16. Payments in respect of any tax, rate, fine, fee or charge levied or imposed under any law by any public authority, including charges for customs clearance, demurrage, licences and permits, court fees and fines, and fees for registration of companies, partnerships, business names, trade marks and patents.

17. Payments in respect of business expenses, including wages, salaries, allowances, directors' fees, gratuities and severance payments.

18. Payments of pensions, including any commuted portion thereof, and of superannuation and Provident Fund benefits.

19. Remittances from current income to, by or on behalf of persons (other than bodies corporate) in a Partner State who are not citizens of that Partner State.

20. Payments to, by or on behalf of persons visiting or residing in another Partner State whose personal income is not sufficient to cover their current expenses or the current expenses of their family.

21. Payments in respect of claims for damage, legal obligations for damages or for maintenance.

22. Payments in respect of subscriptions to and entrance and membership fees of any association.

23. Payments by persons having emigrated from the Partner State from which the payment is to be made to another Partner State, of amounts not less than those permitted for emigrants to any foreign country.

24. Payments in respect of royalties and of use of patent rights, designs, trade marks and inventions.

25. Donations out of current income towards charities.

26. Payments in respect of inheritances, subject to regulation of the timing of transfers of such payments.

27. Payments in respect of prizes, including premium bond, lottery and sports prizes.

(Article 42)

ANNEX VIII

STATUTE OF THE COMMON MARKET TRIBUNAL

Article 1
Preliminary

The Tribunal shall be constituted and shall perform its duties in accordance with this Treaty and this Statute.

Article 2
Oath and declaration

1. Before entering upon their duties, the members of the Tribunal shall in public session individually undertake, by oath or affirmation, to perform

their duties impartially and conscientiously and to preserve the secrecy of the Tribunal's deliberations.

2. When entering upon their duties, the members of the Tribunal shall make a declaration to the effect that they will, both during and after the termination of their office, respect the obligations resulting therefrom and in particular the duty of exercising honesty and discretion as regards the acceptance, after their term of office, of certain positions or benefits, and will abide by the direction of the Tribunal in cases of doubt.

Article 3

Holding of other offices

Except with the consent of the Authority, a member of the Tribunal shall neither hold any political office or any office in the service of a Partner State, the Community or a Corporation, nor engage in any trade, vocation or profession.

Article 4

Resignation

1. The Chairman of the Tribunal may at any time resign his office by letter delivered to the Secretary-General for transmission to the Authority, but his resignation shall not take effect until his successor enters upon his duties.

2. A member of the Tribunal other than the Chairman may at any time resign his office by letter delivered to the Chairman of the Tribunal for transmission to the Authority, but his resignation shall not take effect until his successor enters upon his duties.

Article 5

Replacement of member

A member of the Tribunal appointed to replace a member whose term of office has not expired shall be appointed in the same manner as was that member and for the remainder of that member's term of office.

Article 6

Registrar and staff

1. There shall be a Registrar of the Tribunal who shall hold office in the service of the Community and whose functions shall, subject to this Statute and to the rules of procedure of the Tribunal, be determined by the Tribunal.

2. Before entering upon his duties, the Registrar of the Tribunal shall undertake, by oath or affirmation sworn or made before the Tribunal in public session, to perform his duties impartially and conscientiously and to preserve the secrecy of the Tribunal's deliberations.

3. The Tribunal shall have such officials and staff, who shall hold office in the service of the Community, as may be necessary to enable it to perform its functions.

Article 7

Seat of the Tribunal

The seat of the Tribunal shall be at Arusha in Tanzania, but the Tribunal may in any particular case sit and exercise its functions elsewhere within the Partner States if it considers it desirable.

Article 8

Sessions of the Tribunal

1. The Tribunal shall remain permanently in session, except for judicial vacations, and the dates and length of such vacations shall be determined by the Chairman with due regard for its obligations.

2. Subject to this Statute and to the rules of procedure, the Tribunal shall sit in plenary session only with all its members present:

Provided that, in any case where the Tribunal has commenced the hearing of a case before it and not more than one member of the Tribunal is unable to continue such hearing and is temporarily absent therefrom, it shall be competent to the Tribunal, notwithstanding the temporary absence of such member and with the agreement of the parties to the case before it, to continue and determine the hearing of such case.

Article 9

Functions of the Chairman

Notwithstanding paragraph 2 of Article 8 of this Statute, the rules of procedure may impose functions upon the Chairman of the Tribunal sitting alone in relation to administrative, procedural and other preliminary matters not being matters falling to be dealt with by the Tribunal by interim order under Article 39 of this Treaty.

Article 10

Duty to attend

Members of the Tribunal shall be bound, unless they are prevented from attending by illness or other serious reasons duly explained to the Chairman, to hold themselves permanently at the disposal of the Tribunal.

Article 11

References

1. Matters in dispute shall be referred to the Tribunal by a reference addressed to the Registrar specifying the subject matter of the dispute and the parties to it.

2. The Registrar shall immediately send a copy of the reference to all concerned.

Article 12

Representation before the Tribunal

Every party to a case before the Tribunal shall be represented by a person appointed by that party for the case; a representative need not be an advocate but he may be assisted by an advocate entitled to appear before a superior court of any of the Partner States.

Article 13

Proceedings

1. The proceedings of the Tribunal shall consist of a written part and an oral part.

2. The written part of the proceedings shall include the reference, the application, the response to the application, the reply, the rejoinder and the submissions, together with all papers and documents in support.

3. The written part of the proceedings shall be presented to the Registrar, in the order and within the time fixed by the rules of procedure or by the Tribunal in any particular case, and a copy of every paper or document presented by one party shall be communicated to the other party.

4. The oral part of the proceedings shall consist of the hearing by the Tribunal of witnesses, experts, representatives and advocates.

Article 14

Hearings

The hearing before the Tribunal shall be under the control of the Chairman and shall be in public, unless the Tribunal decides otherwise or a party requests that the public be not admitted.

Article 15

Production of documents

1. The Tribunal may at any time request the parties to produce all documents and supply all information or explanations which the Tribunal considers desirable. Formal note shall be taken of any refusal.

2. The Tribunal may also request a Partner State, which is not a party to the case, or an institution of the Community to supply all information which the Tribunal considers necessary for the proceedings.

Article 16
Inquiries and expert opinions

The Tribunal may, in relation to any proceedings and at any time, charge any person, body or institution with the task of carrying out an inquiry or giving an expert opinion.

Article 17
Witnesses

1. During the hearing relevant questions may be put to the witnesses and experts under the conditions laid down by the rules of procedure.

2. During the hearing the Tribunal may examine the experts and witnesses and ask questions of the representatives and advocates.

3. The Tribunal shall have, with respect to defaulting witnesses, the powers granted to the superior court in the Partner State where it is at the relevant time sitting, and may impose sanctions accordingly.

4. Minutes shall be kept of each hearing and shall be signed by the Chairman and the Registrar.

Article 18
List of cases

The list of cases shall be fixed by the Chairman.

Article 19
Costs

Unless otherwise decided by the Tribunal, each party shall bear its own costs.

Article 20
Advisory opinions

1. A request for an advisory opinion under Article 38 of the Treaty shall be made by means of a written request containing an exact statement of the question upon which an opinion is required and shall be accompanied by all documents likely to be of assistance.

2. Upon receipt of a request under paragraph 1 of this Article, the Registrar shall forthwith give notice thereof to the Partner States and

notify them that the Tribunal will be prepared to accept, within a time to be fixed by the Chairman, written submissions, or to hear, at a hearing held for the purpose, oral submissions relating to the question.

3. The Tribunal shall, unless for special reasons it makes an order to the contrary, deliver an advisory opinion in public session.

4. In the exercise of its advisory function the Tribunal shall be guided by the provisions of this Statute relating to references to the extent which it considers them applicable.

Article 21

Interpretation of decisions

In the case of difficulty as to the meaning or scope of a decision or an advisory opinion, the Tribunal shall interpret it upon the request of any party or any institution of the Community establishing an interest therein.

Article 22

Revision

1. An application for revision of a decision may be made to the Tribunal only if it is based upon the discovery of some fact of such nature as to be a decisive factor, which fact was, when the decision was delivered, unknown to the Tribunal and to the party claiming revision.

2. On an application for revision, the procedure shall commence, where the application is admissible, with a decision of the Tribunal explicitly finding that the new fact alleged does exist and is of such a character as to lay the case open to revision, and declaring the application admissible on that ground.

3. Before declaring an application for revision of a decision to be admissible, the Tribunal may require prior compliance with the terms of the decision.

4. No application for revision of a decision may be made after the expiry of five years from the date of the decision.

Article 23

Amendment of the Statute

The Authority may, after consultation with the Tribunal, by order from time to time amend or add to this Statute, and the Tribunal may propose amendments or additions to this Statute.

(Article 43)

ANNEX IX

SERVICES TO BE ADMINISTERED BY THE COMMUNITY OR BY THE CORPORATIONS

Part A. Services to be Administered by the Community

1. The secretariat of the Community, including services relating to the Common Market and the Chambers of the Counsel to the Community.
2. The East African Directorate of Civil Aviation.
3. The East African Meteorological Department.
4. The East African Customs and Excise Department.
5. The East African Income Tax Department.
6. The East African Industrial Council.
7. The East African Literature Bureau.
8. The Auditor-General's Department.
9. The East African Community Service Commission.
10. The East African Legislative Assembly.
11. The East African Agriculture and Forestry Research Organization.
12. The East African Freshwater Fisheries Research Organization.
13. The East African Marine Fisheries Research Organization.
14. The East African Trypanosomiasis Research Organization.
15. The East African Veterinary Research Organization.
16. The East African Leprosy Research Centre.
17. The East African Institute of Malaria and Vector-Borne Diseases.
18. The East African Institute for Medical Research.
19. The East African Virus Research Organization.
20. The East African Industrial Research Organization.
21. The East African Tropical Pesticides Research Institute.
22. The East African Tuberculosis Investigation Centre.
23. Services arising from the operations of the East African Currency Board.
24. Services for the administration of grants or loans made by the government of any country, any organization or any authority, for the purposes of projects or services agreed between the Authority and the Partner States.

25. Services, including statistical services, for the purposes of co-ordinating the economic activities of the Partner States.

26. Services for the purposes of any body or authority established in pursuance of paragraph 4 of Article 43 of this Treaty.

27. Services for the purposes of the East African Industrial Court established by Article 85 of this Treaty.

Part B. Services to be Administered by the Corporations

1. The East African Railways Corporation—services and facilities relating to rail, road and inland waterways transport and inland waterways ports.

2. The East African Harbours Corporation—harbour services and facilities (other than inland waterways ports).

3. The East African Posts and Telecommunications Corporation—posts, telecommunications and other associated services.

4. The East African Airways Corporation—services and facilities relating to East African and international air transport.

(Article 43)

ANNEX X

MATTERS WITH RESPECT TO WHICH ACTS OF THE COMMUNITY MAY BE ENACTED

1. Finances of the Community.

2. Appropriations from the General Fund.

3. Audit of the accounts of the Community and the accounts of the Corporations.

4. Civil aviation.

5. Customs, excise and transfer tax—administrative and general provisions (but not including tariff, rates of tax and allowances).

6. Income tax—administrative and general provisions (but not including rates of tax and allowances).

7. Powers, privileges and immunities of the East African Legislative Assembly and the Chairman and members thereof.

8. Research within the Partner States.

9. Control of pesticides.

10. The University of East Africa; Makerere University College; the University College, Dar es Salaam; and University College, Nairobi.

11. The East African Staff College.

12. The East African Examinations Council.

13. Meteorology.

14. The East African Land Survey Certificate.

15. Pensions, gratuities and other retirement benefits payable out of the funds of the Community or the Corporations.

16. Staff of the Community, the East African Community Service Commission, and staff of the Corporations.

17. Posts and telegraphs, telephones, radio communications and other associated matters.

18. Services and facilities relating to rail, road and inland waterways transport and inland waterways ports.

19. Harbour services and facilities (other than inland waterways ports).

20. Borrowing for the purposes of the Community and the Corporations.

21. The Common Market Tribunal.

22. The Court of Appeal for East Africa (but not including the jurisdiction or powers of the Court).

23. Legal proceedings by or against the Community and the Corporations, or any officers or authorities thereof.

24. Statistics.

25. Industrial licensing in East Africa.

26. The establishment of advisory or consultative bodies in respect of any service or Corporation or in respect of any matter of common interest to the Partner States.

27. Any matter, not mentioned elsewhere in this Annex, which is incidental to the execution, performance or enforcement of any function conferred by this Treaty or by an Act of the Community upon any institution or authority, or officer in the service, of the Community, or upon any authority or servant of a Corporation.

(*Article* 45)

ANNEX XI

PROCEDURAL PROVISIONS

Procedure of Authority

1. (*a*) Subject to this Treaty, the Authority shall determine its own procedure, including that for convening its meetings, for the conduct of business thereat and at other times, and for the rotation of the office of Chairman among the members of the Authority.

(*b*) The East African Ministers shall attend meetings of the Authority (and speak at such meetings to the extent required or permitted by the Authority) unless, on any particular occasion, the Authority otherwise directs but the absence of an East African Minister or Ministers from a meeting of the Authority shall in no way invalidate its proceedings.

Delegation of the Authority's functions

2. (*a*) Subject to this Treaty, the Authority may delegate the exercise of any executive function, subject to any conditions which it may think fit to impose, to a member of the Authority, to the East African Ministers jointly or any one of them, to a Council, or to an officer in the service of the Community.

(*b*) An Act of the Community may make provision for the delegation of any powers, including legislative powers, conferred on the Authority by this Treaty or by any Act of the Community, to the East African Ministers jointly, or to any one of them, to an officer in the service of the Community or to a Director-General.

Decisions of the Authority

3. (*a*) Any member of the Authority may record his objection to a proposal submitted for the decision of the Authority and, if any such objection is recorded, the Authority shall not proceed with the proposal unless the objection is withdrawn.

(*b*) Subject to the provisions of any Act of the Community, the acts and decisions of the Authority may be signified under the hand of the Secretary-General or of any officer in the service of the Community authorized in that behalf by the Authority.

Procedure of the East African Ministers

4. (*a*) Subject to any directions which may be given by the Authority, the East African Ministers shall determine their procedure, including that for convening their meetings, for the conduct of business thereat and at

other times, and for the rotation of the office of Chairman among the East African Ministers, and such procedure may provide that a decision in writing signed by all the East African Ministers shall be as valid and effectual as if it had been made at a meeting of the East African Ministers.

(*b*) Subject to any Act of the Community, the acts and decisions of the East African Ministers may be signified by any East African Minister or by any officer in the service of the Community authorized by the East African Ministers in that behalf.

Meetings of the Councils

5. Subject to any directions which may be given by the Authority, the Councils shall determine the frequency of their meetings but the Chairman of any Council shall, at the request of any of the Partner States, summon that Council to meet within ten days.

Chairmanship of the Councils

6. (*a*) Subject to any directions which may be given by the Authority, within each Council the East African Ministers shall hold the office of Chairman in rotation for periods of four months in such order as may be determined by the Authority.

(*b*) If the person holding the office of Chairman of a Council is absent from a meeting of that Council, there shall preside at that meeting such member of the Council as the members present may elect for that purpose, unless the Authority otherwise directs.

Procedure of Councils

7. (*a*) Subject to any directions which may be given by the Authority, a Council shall determine its own procedure, including that for convening its meetings and the conduct of business thereat and at other times.

(*b*) The procedure determined by a Council under sub-paragraph (*a*) of this paragraph may include arrangements under which the exercise of any function of the Council is delegated, subject to such conditions as the Council may think fit to impose, to the East African Ministers jointly, or to any one of them, or to any officer in the service of the Community or to an authority or a servant of a Corporation.

(*c*) When the Communications Council is conducting business relating to any of the Corporations, the Chairman of the Board of Directors and the Director-General of that Corporation shall be entitled to attend and speak.

Decisions of Councils

8. (*a*) Any member of a Council may record his objection to a proposal submitted for the decision of that Council and, except where Article 36 of

this Treaty applies, unless such objection is withdrawn the proposal shall be referred to the Authority for its decision.

(*b*) If the Communications Council makes a decision which is contrary to a proposal submitted by the Board of Directors of a Corporation for the approval of that Council, that Board of Directors may refer the question at issue through the East African Ministers to the Authority for its decision.

(*c*) No further action shall be taken in relation to a proposal before a Council or a decision of a Council, as the case may be, in respect of which a reference has been made to the Authority whilst that reference is under consideration by the Authority, unless the reference is withdrawn and the Authority is notified accordingly.

(*d*) Subject to any Act of the Community, the acts and decisions of a Council may be signified by any member of the Council or by any officer in the service of the Community authorized by the Council in that behalf.

Questions as to membership of the Assembly

9. (*a*) Any questions that may arise whether any person is an appointed member of the Assembly or whether any seat in the Assembly is vacant shall be determined by the Partner State responsible for the appointment in question.

(*b*) The Partner States shall notify the Chairman of the Assembly of every determination made under sub-paragraph (*a*) of this paragraph, and for the information of the Chairman shall forward to him a copy of the instrument of appointment of every appointed member of the Assembly.

Chairman of the Assembly

10. (*a*) The Chairman of the Assembly shall be appointed by the Authority, by instrument in writing.

(*b*) A person shall not be qualified to hold the office of Chairman of the Assembly if he is an appointed member of the Assembly, a member of the legislature of a Partner State, a member of a Board of Directors, an officer in the service of the Community, a servant of a Corporation, an officer in the service of the Government of a Partner State, or a director, alternate director or a servant of the Bank.

(*c*) The Chairman of the Assembly shall vacate his office—

  (i) upon the expiry of the period of office specified in his instrument of appointment;

  (ii) if he delivers his resignation in writing to the Secretary-General for transmission to the Authority; or

  (iii) if he ceases to be qualified for appointment as Chairman.

(*d*) The Chairman of the Assembly may be removed from office by the Authority for inability to perform the functions of his office, whether arising from infirmity of mind or body or from any other cause, or for misbehaviour, but shall not otherwise be removed from office.

Invitation of persons to assist the Assembly

11. (*a*) The Chairman of the Assembly, at the request of the East African Ministers, shall invite any person to attend the Assembly, notwithstanding that he is not a member of the Assembly, if in the opinion of the East African Ministers the business before the Assembly renders his presence desirable.

(*b*) A person so invited shall be entitled to take part in the proceedings of the Assembly relating to the matters in respect of which he was invited as if he were a member of the Assembly, but he shall not have a right to vote in the Assembly.

Meetings of the Assembly

12. (*a*) The meetings of the Assembly shall be held at such times and places as the Authority may appoint.

(*b*) The Assembly shall meet at least once in every year and a period of twelve months shall not elapse between the commencement of the last meeting in any year and the first meeting in the following year.

Presiding in the Assembly

13. There shall preside at any sitting of the Assembly—

(*a*) the Chairman;
(*b*) in the absence of the Chairman, such member of the Assembly as the Authority may appoint; or
(*c*) in the absence of the Chairman or a person so appointed, such member as the Assembly may elect for the sitting.

Quorum and vacancies in the Assembly

14. (*a*) If, during any sitting of the Assembly, the attention of the person presiding is drawn to the fact that there are fewer than ten members present and if, after such interval as may be prescribed by the rules of procedure of the Assembly, the person presiding ascertains that there are present at the sitting fewer than ten members, he shall adjourn the Assembly.

(*b*) In reckoning the number of members who are present for the purposes of sub-paragraph (*a*) of this paragraph, the person presiding shall not be taken into account.

(*c*) The Assembly may transact business notwithstanding that there is a vacancy among its members, and the attendance or participation of any person not entitled to attend or participate in the proceedings of the Assembly shall not invalidate those proceedings.

Voting in the Assembly

15. (a) Subject to sub-paragraph (e) of this paragraph, all questions proposed for decision in the Assembly shall be determined by a majority of the votes of the members present and voting.

(b) The Chairman of the Assembly, the Secretary-General and the Counsel to the Community shall not be entitled to vote in the Assembly.

(c) When in the absence of a Chairman a member is presiding in the Assembly, the member presiding shall retain his right to vote.

(d) If the votes of the members are equally divided upon any motion before the Assembly, the motion shall be lost.

(e) A Bill for the amendment or repeal of the Court of Appeal for Eastern Africa Act 1962 shall not be passed in the Assembly unless it has received, on the second reading thereof, the votes of not less than two-thirds of all the members of the Assembly.

Bills and Motions in the Assembly

16. (a) Subject to the rules of procedure of the Assembly, any member may propose any motion or introduce any Bill in the Assembly:

Provided that a motion which does not relate to the functions of the Community shall not be proposed in the Assembly, and a Bill which does not relate to a matter with respect to which Acts of the Community may be enacted shall not be introduced into the Assembly.

(b) Except with the consent of the Authority, signified by an East African Minister, the Assembly shall not—

(i) proceed on any Bill, including an amendment to any Bill, that, in the opinion of the person presiding, makes provision for any of the following purposes—

(1) for the imposition of any charge upon any fund of the Community or any fund of a Corporation;

(2) for the payment, issue or withdrawal from any fund of the Community of any moneys not charged thereon or the increase in the amount of any such payment, issue or withdrawal; or

(3) for the remission of any debt due to the Community or a Corporation;

(ii) proceed upon any motion, including any amendment to a motion, the effect of which, in the opinion of the person presiding, would be to make provision for any of the said purposes.

Rules of Procedure of the Assembly

17. The Authority may make, amend, add to or revoke rules governing the procedure of the Assembly (including the Standing Orders thereof).

Publication of Acts of the Community

18. The Authority shall cause every Act of the Community to be published in the Gazette.

Publication and commencement of rules and orders of the Authority

19. The Authority shall cause all rules and every order made by it under this Treaty to be published in the Gazette; and such rules or order shall come into force on the date of publication unless otherwise provided therein.

(Article 68)

ANNEX XII

INCOME OF COMPANIES ENGAGED IN MANUFACTURING OR FINANCE BUSINESS

1. The expression 'income of companies engaged in manufacturing or finance business' means income of companies engaged within the Partner States in the business of manufacturing and income of companies engaged within the Partner States in the business of finance, being in either case income which is chargeable at the corporation rate under the laws in force in the Partner States.

2. For the purpose of the definition in paragraph 1 of this Annex, a company is engaged in the business of manufacturing if it is a company whose major activity, in terms of gross revenue, falls within one of the classifications in List A hereunder.

3. For the purposes of paragraph 2 of this Annex, where the end-product of an earlier activity is used as the raw material of a later activity and the major part of the company's revenue is from the sale of the final production, the company shall be classified according to the activity at the final stage.

4. For the purpose of the definition in paragraph 1 of this Annex, a company is engaged in the business of finance if it is a company whose major activity in terms of gross revenue falls within any one of the classifications in List B hereunder.

LIST A

Classifications	Examples of Activity
(i) Food manufacturing industries (except beverages)	Includes slaughtering, dressing, packing and canning, manufacture of prepared feeds for animals and fowls, the manufacture of ice other than dry ice.
(ii) Beverage industries	Production of distilled spirits, wines, malt liquors, soft drinks and carbonated beverages.
(iii) Tobacco manufacture	
(iv) Manufacture of textiles	Preparation of fibre, manufacture and finishing of fabrics (including carpets, linoleum, artificial leather, ropes and twine, and waterproofing of fabrics). Also includes the manufacture of garments in knitting mills (e.g. hosiery).
(v) Manufacture of footwear, other wearing apparel and made up textile goods	All types of footwear except vulcanized (which is included in (xi) manufacture of rubber products); all wearing apparel by cutting and sewing fabrics, leather, fur and other material, all made up textile goods.
(vi) Manufacture of wood and cork (except furniture)	Sawmills, manufacture of boxes, baskets, ladders and coffins.
(vii) Manufacture of furniture	Includes furniture for households, offices and restaurants.
(viii) Manufacture of pulp, paper and paperboard	
(ix) Printing, publishing and allied industries	Includes bookbinding, engraving and etching.
(x) Manufacture of leather and leather and fur products, except footwear and other wearing apparel	Tanning of hides, preparation of furs, manufacture of fur and skin, rugs, handbags, saddlery.
(xi) Manufacture of rubber products	Natural and synthetic rubber; tubes, tyres, vulcanized footwear.
(xii) Manufacture of chemical and chemical products	Basic chemicals, dyes, vegetable and animal oils and fats, paints, soap, ink, matches, insecticides (except lard and other edible fats from livestock).
(xiii) Manufacture of products of petroleum and coal	Petroleum refineries and other manufacturers of products from petroleum and coal.
(xiv) Manufacture of non-metallic mineral products (except petroleum and coal)	Pottery, cement, bricks, glass, china etc.
(xv) Basic metal industries	All processes from smelting to the semi-finished stage in rolling mills and foundries.
(xvi) Manufacture of metal products except machinery and transport equipment	Cutlery, hand tools, hardware, bolts and nuts; enamelling, galvanizing, blacksmithing and welding.
(xvii) Manufacture of machinery except electrical machinery	Tractors, refrigerators, airconditioning units, sewing machines, typewriters.

Classifications	*Examples of Activity*
(xviii) Manufacture of electrical machinery, apparatus, appliances and supplies	All machinery and apparatus for the generation, storage and transmission of electricity; vacuum cleaners, etc., insulated wire and cable, radios, electric lamps etc.
(xix) Manufacture of transport equipment	Does not include tyres and tubes (xi), agricultural and road building tractors (xvii), aeronautical instruments (xx).
(xx) Miscellaneous manufacturing industries	Scientific instruments, photographic and optical goods, watches and clocks, jewellery, musical instruments, lamp shades, tobacco pipes and cigarette holders, advertising displays, moulded or extruded plastic products.

LIST B

(i) Banks and other financial institutions	Banks, credit companies, investment companies.
(ii) Insurance	Insurance carriers of all kinds, life, fire, accident etc., insurance agents and brokers.

(Articles 55 *and* 73)

ANNEX XIII

CONTROL OF THE CORPORATIONS

Part A. The East African Posts and Telecommunications Corporation

The Director-General

1. It shall be the duty of the Director-General—

   (*a*) to conduct and manage, subject to the direction of the Board of Directors, the business and operations of the Corporation;

   (*b*) to keep the Board fully informed of the affairs of the Corporation, and to consult it where appropriate and give effect to its directions;

   (*c*) to submit to the Board annual estimates of revenue and expenditure; and

   (*d*) to submit annually a draft statement of accounts and a draft report for the consideration of the Board.

2. Subject to this Treaty and to the direction of the Board of Directors, the Director-General may—

   (*a*) establish and operate postal and telecommunications services and services, including agency services for the Partner States, which may conveniently be performed in association therewith;

   (*b*) regulate and control radio communications;

   (*c*) approve recurrent expenditure within limits which shall be determined by the Board;

(*d*) approve any individual capital work of which the estimated cost does not exceed 100,000 Uganda shillings or such other sum as the Authority may, by order, determine;

(*e*) approve any alteration in salaries or other conditions of service not involving expenditure in excess of the limits determined by the Board;

(*f*) approve any alteration in the establishment other than an alteration involving a major reorganization or a substantial reduction in the number of employees;

(*g*) if required by a Partner State, manage its Post Office Savings Bank;

(*h*) allocate functions and delegate powers to officers of the Corporation; and

(*i*) perform the duties and exercise the powers imposed on or vested in him by any Act of the Community.

The Board of Directors

3. Subject to this Treaty and to any directions of a general nature which may be given to the Board of Directors by the Communications Council, it shall be the duty of the Board of Directors—

(*a*) to provide postal and telecommunications services and services, including agency services for the Partner States, which may conveniently be performed in association therewith;

(*b*) to regulate and control radio communications;

(*c*) to determine policy regarding all the operations of the Corporation and to ensure the application of that policy;

(*d*) to keep the Communications Council informed of the affairs of the Corporation, and to consult it where appropriate and give effect to its directions;

(*e*) to approve annual estimates of revenue and expenditure;

(*f*) if required by a Partner State, to manage its Post Office Savings Bank;

(*g*) to establish a General Purposes Committee from among its members; and

(*h*) to publish the tariffs charged by the Corporation and the rules made by the Board of Directors.

4. Subject to this Treaty and to any directions of a general nature which may be given to the Board of Directors by the Communications Council, the Board of Directors may—

(*a*) approve any alteration in the tariff of a service which would not affect the gross revenue of the service concerned to an extent greater than two per cent;

(b) approve any alteration in salaries or other conditions of service of employees other than an alteration which would require a tariff increase of more than two per cent in the service concerned;

(c) approve any individual capital work of which the estimated cost does not exceed 2,000,000 Uganda shillings or such other sum as the Authority may, by order, determine;

(d) delegate functions to its General Purposes Committee;

(e) consider legislative proposals and recommend their enactment;

(f) refuse to provide a new service in a Partner State at a rate or charge which is insufficient to meet the costs involved in the provision of such service, unless the Partner State undertakes to make good the amount of the loss incurred by the provision of such service;

(g) approve any alteration in the organization or establishment which is beyond the competence of the Director-General; and

(h) give directions to the Director-General.

The Communications Council

5. It shall be the responsibility of the Communications Council—

(a) to receive and consider the information concerning the Corporation provided by the Board of Directors, and upon being consulted by the Board to assist it with advice or directions;

(b) to give to the Board of Directors directions of a general nature on matters of policy;

(c) to give effect to the directions of the Authority;

(d) to consider and approve the development plan and associated loan programme of the Corporation; and

(e) to consider and approve in principle legislative proposals submitted by the Board of Directors.

6. Subject to this Treaty and to any directions which may be given to the Communications Council by the Authority, the Communications Council may—

(a) give directions of a general nature to the Board of Directors;

(b) approve any alteration in the tariff of a service which is beyond the competence of the Board of Directors;

(c) approve any alteration in salaries or other conditions of service of employees of the Corporation which is beyond the competence of the Board of Directors; and

(d) approve any individual capital work of which the estimated cost exceeds 2,000,000 Uganda shillings or such other sum as the Authority may, by order, determine.

The Authority

7. Subject to this Treaty and to any Act of the Community, the Authority shall be responsible for the general direction and control of the Corporation.

8. The Authority may—

   (*a*) give directions of a general nature to the Communications Council; and

   (*b*) determine matters referred to it by the Communications Council.

Interpretation

9. In this Part, except where the context otherwise requires, 'service' means postal service, telephone service or telegraph service.

Part B. The East African Railways Corporation

The Director-General

1. It shall be the duty of the Director-General—

   (*a*) to conduct and manage, subject to the direction of the Board of Directors, the business and operations of the Corporation;

   (*b*) to keep the Board fully informed of the affairs of the Corporation, and to consult it where appropriate and give effect to its directions;

   (*c*) to submit to the Board annual estimates of revenue and expenditure; and

   (*d*) to submit annually a draft statement of accounts and a draft report for the consideration of the Board.

2. Subject to this Treaty and to the direction of the Board of Directors, the Director-General may—

   (*a*) establish and operate services and facilities relating to rail, road and inland waterways transport and inland waterways ports;

   (*b*) approve recurrent expenditure within limits which shall be determined by the Board;

   (*c*) approve any individual capital work of which the estimated cost does not exceed 400,000 Kenya shillings or such other sum as the Authority may, by order, determine;

   (*d*) approve any alteration in salaries or other conditions of service not involving expenditure in excess of the limits imposed by the Board;

   (*e*) approve any alteration in the establishment other than an alteration involving a major re-organization or a substantial reduction in the number of employees;

(*f*) allocate functions and delegate powers to officers of the Corporation; and

(*g*) perform the duties and exercise the powers imposed on or vested in him by any Act of the Community.

The Board of Directors

3. Subject to this Treaty and to any directions of a general nature which may be given to the Board of Directors by the Communications Council, it shall be the duty of the Board of Directors—

(*a*) to determine policy regarding all the operations of the Corporation and to ensure the application of that policy;

(*b*) to keep the Communications Council informed of the affairs of the Corporation, and to consult it where appropriate and give effect to its directions;

(*c*) to approve annual estimates of revenue and expenditure;

(*d*) to establish a General Purposes Committee from among its members; and

(*e*) to publish the tariff of rates, fares and other charges made by the Corporation and the rules made by the Board of Directors.

4. Subject to this Treaty and to any directions of a general nature which may be given to the Board of Directors by the Communications Council, the Board of Directors may—

(*a*) approve any minor alteration in the tariff of rates, fares and other charges;

(*b*) approve any minor alteration in salaries or other conditions of service of employees;

(*c*) approve any individual capital work, not included within a programme of works approved by the Communications Council, of which the estimated cost does not exceed 5,000,000 Kenya shillings or such other sum as the Authority may, by order, determine;

(*d*) delegate functions to its General Purposes Committee;

(*e*) consider legislative proposals and recommend their enactment;

(*f*) refuse to provide new transport services or inland waterways facilities in a Partner State at a rate or charge which is insufficient to meet the costs involved in the provision of such services or facilities, unless the Partner State undertakes to make good the amount of the loss incurred by the provision of such services or facilities;

(*g*) approve any alteration in the organization or establishment which is beyond the competence of the Director-General; and

(*h*) give directions to the Director-General.

The Communications Council

5. It shall be the responsibility of the Communications Council—

   (a) to receive and consider the information concerning the Corporation provided by the Board of Directors, and upon being consulted by the Board to assist it with advice or directions;

   (b) to give to the Board of Directors directions of a general nature on matters of policy;

   (c) to give effect to the directions of the Authority;

   (d) to consider and approve the development plan and associated loan programme of the Corporation; and

   (e) to consider and approve in principle legislative proposals submitted by the Board of Directors.

6. Subject to this Treaty and to any directions which may be given to the Communications Council by the Authority, the Communications Council may—

   (a) give directions of a general nature to the Board of Directors;

   (b) approve any major alteration in the tariff of rates, fares and other charges;

   (c) approve any major alteration in salaries or other conditions of service of employees of the Corporation;

   (d) approve any individual capital work of which the estimated cost exceeds 5,000,000 Kenya shillings or such other sum as the Authority may, by order, determine; and

   (e) give directions to the Board of Directors concerning any matter of policy involving agreement with, or the interests of, a foreign country.

The Authority

7. Subject to this Treaty and to any Act of the Community, the Authority shall be responsible for the general direction and control of the Corporation.

8. The Authority may—

   (a) give directions of a general nature to the Communications Council; and

   (b) determine matters referred to it by the Communications Council.

General

9. If there is a difference of opinion between the Communications Council and the Board of Directors concerning what constitutes a minor or a major alteration in the tariff of rates, fares and other charges, or a minor or major

G

alteration in salaries or other conditions of service of the employees of the Corporation, the difference shall be referred to the Authority to be resolved.

Part C. The East African Harbours Corporation

The Director-General

1. It shall be the duty of the Director-General—
   - (*a*) to conduct and manage, subject to the direction of the Board of Directors, the business and operations of the Corporation;
   - (*b*) to keep the Board fully informed of the affairs of the Corporation, and to consult it where appropriate and give effect to its directions;
   - (*c*) to submit to the Board annual estimates of revenue and expenditure; and
   - (*d*) to submit annually a draft statement of accounts and a draft report for the consideration of the Board.

2. Subject to this Treaty and to the direction of the Board of Directors, the Director-General may—
   - (*a*) establish and operate harbour services and facilities (other than inland waterways ports);
   - (*b*) approve recurrent expenditure within limits which shall be determined by the Board;
   - (*c*) approve any individual capital work of which the estimated cost does not exceed 400,000 Tanzania shillings or such other sum as the Authority may, by order, determine;
   - (*d*) approve any alteration in salaries or other conditions of service not involving expenditure in excess of the limits imposed by the Board;
   - (*e*) approve any alteration in the establishment other than an alteration involving a major re-organization or a substantial reduction in the number of employees;
   - (*f*) allocate functions and delegate powers to officers of the Corporation; and
   - (*g*) perform the duties and exercise the powers imposed on or vested in him by any Act of the Community.

The Board of Directors

3. Subject to this Treaty and to any directions of a general nature which may be given to the Board of Directors by the Communications Council, it shall be the duty of the Board of Directors—
   - (*a*) to determine policy regarding all the operations of the Corporation and to ensure the application of that policy;

(*b*) to keep the Communications Council informed of the affairs of the Corporation, and to consult it where appropriate and give effect to its directions;

(*c*) to approve annual estimates of revenue and expenditure;

(*d*) to establish a General Purposes Committee from among its members; and

(*e*) to publish the tariff of rates and other charges made by the Corporation and the rules made by the Board of Directors.

4. Subject to this Treaty and to any directions of a general nature which may be given to the Board of Directors by the Communications Council, the Board of Directors may—

(*a*) approve any minor alteration in the tariff of rates and other charges;

(*b*) approve any minor alteration in salaries or other conditions of service of employees;

(*c*) approve any individual capital work, not included within a programme of works approved by the Communications Council, of which the estimated cost does not exceed 5,000,000 Tanzania shillings or such other sum as the Authority may, by order, determine;

(*d*) delegate functions to its General Purposes Committee;

(*e*) consider legislative proposals and recommend their enactment;

(*f*) refuse to provide new harbour services or facilities in a Partner State at a rate or charge which is insufficient to meet the costs involved in the provision of such services or facilities, unless the Partner State undertakes to make good the amount of the loss incurred by the provision of such services or facilities;

(*g*) approve any alteration in the organization or establishment which is beyond the competence of the Director-General; and

(*h*) give directions to the Director-General.

The Communications Council

5. It shall be the responsibility of the Communications Council—

(*a*) to receive and consider the information concerning the Corporation provided by the Board of Directors, and upon being consulted by the Board to assist it with advice or directions;

(*b*) to give to the Board of Directors directions of a general nature on matters of policy;

(*c*) to give effect to the directions of the Authority;

(*d*) to consider and approve the development plan and associated loan programme of the Corporation; and

(*e*) to consider and approve in principle legislative proposals submitted by the Board of Directors.

6. Subject to this Treaty and to any directions which may be given to the Communications Council by the Authority, the Communications Council may—

(a) give directions of a general nature to the Board of Directors;

(b) approve any major alteration in the tariff of rates and other charges;

(c) approve any major alteration in salaries or other conditions of service of employees of the Corporation;

(d) approve any individual capital work of which the estimated cost exceeds 5,000,000 Tanzania shillings or such other sum as the Authority may, by order, determine; and

(e) give directions to the Board of Directors concerning any matter of policy involving agreement with or the interests of a foreign country.

The Authority

7. Subject to this Treaty and to any Act of the Community, the Authority shall be responsible for the general direction and control of the Corporation.

8. The Authority may—

(a) give directions of a general nature to the Communications Council; and

(b) determine matters referred to it by the Communications Council.

General

9. If there is a difference of opinion between the Communications Council and the Board of Directors concerning what constitutes a minor or a major alteration in the tariff of rates and other charges, or a minor or major alteration in salaries or other conditions of service of the employees of the Corporation, the difference shall be referred to the Authority to be resolved.

Part D. The East African Airways Corporation

The Director-General

1. It shall be the duty of the Director-General—

(a) to conduct and manage, subject to the direction of the Board of Directors, the business and operations of the Corporation;

(b) to keep the Board fully informed of the affairs of the Corporation, and to consult it where appropriate and give effect to its directions;

(c) to submit to the Board annually a programme of services and financial estimates for the ensuing year; and (*d*) to submit to the Board, in respect of every five-year period in the operations of the Corporation, a draft development plan including estimates of expected traffic growth, proposals for the development of air routes and for the use and operation of aircraft, and estimates of probable revenue and expenditure.

2. Subject to this Treaty and to the direction of the Board of Directors, the Director-General may—

(*a*) establish and operate air transport services, and facilities relating thereto, within the Partner States and elsewhere;

(*b*) approve recurrent expenditure within limits which shall be determined by the Board;

(*c*) approve any individual capital work of which the estimated cost does not exceed 200,000 Kenya shillings or such other sum as the Authority may, by order, determine;

(*d*) approve any alteration in salaries or other conditions of service not involving expenditure in excess of the limits imposed by the Board;

(*e*) approve any alteration in the establishment other than an alteration involving a major re-organization or a substantial reduction in the number of employees;

(*f*) allocate functions and delegate powers to officers of the Corporation; and

(*g*) perform the duties and exercise the powers imposed on or vested in him by any Act of the Community.

The Board of Directors

3. Subject to this Treaty and to any directions of a general nature which may be given to the Board of Directors by the Communications Council, it shall be the duty of the Board of Directors—

(*a*) to provide air transport services, and facilities relating thereto, within the Partner States and elsewhere;

(*b*) to determine policy governing the operation of the Corporation;

(*c*) to keep the Communications Council informed of the affairs of the Corporation, and to consult it where appropriate and give effect to its directions;

(*d*) to approve the annual programme of services and the financial estimates submitted by the Director-General;

(*e*) to prepare in respect of every five-year period in the operations of the Corporation a development plan, including estimates of expected traffic growth, proposals for the development of air routes and for the use and operation of aircraft, and estimates of probable revenue and expenditure for submission to the Communications Council;

(*f*) to submit to the Communications Council for approval any proposals affecting tariff policies in respect of international air services, which the Corporation wishes to put forward to the International Air Transport Association;

(*g*) to submit to the Communications Council for approval any proposals for an alteration in the tariff of rates, fares and other charges in respect of air transport services provided within the Partner States; and

(*h*) to give effect to any directions given to it by the Authority.

4. Subject to this Treaty and to any directions of a general nature which may be given to the Board of Directors by the Communications Council, the Board of Directors may—

(*a*) approve any minor alteration in the tariff of rates, fares and other charges in respect of any service or facility, other than an air transport service provided within the Partner States;

(*b*) approve any minor alteration in salaries or other conditions of service of employees;

(*c*) approve any individual capital work, not included within a development programme approved by the Communications Council or by the Authority, of which the estimated cost does not exceed 5,000,000 Kenya shillings or such other sum as the Authority may, by order, determine;

(*d*) consider legislative proposals and recommend their enactment;

(*e*) provide services or facilities requested by a Partner State so however that where the amount of the fares or other charges able to be recovered by the Corporation in respect of such services or facilities is less than the cost thereof, the Corporation shall not be obliged to provide such services or facilities unless that Partner State undertakes to make good the amount of such loss;

(*f*) approve any alteration in the organization or establishment of the Corporation which is beyond the competence of the Director-General; and

(*g*) give policy directions to the Director-General.

The Communications Council

5. It shall be the responsibility of the Communications Council—

(*a*) to receive and consider the information concerning the Corporation provided by the Board of Directors, and upon being consulted by the Board to assist it with advice or directions;

(*b*) to give to the Board of Directors directions of a general nature on matters of policy;

(c) to keep the Authority informed about the affairs of the Corporation, and to consult it where appropriate and give effect to its directions;

(d) to consider and approve in principle legislative proposals submitted by the Board of Directors.

6. Subject to this Treaty and to any directions which may be given to the Communications Council by the Authority, the Communications Council may—

(a) give directions of a general nature to the Board of Directors;

(b) approve any alteration in the tariff of rates, fares and other charges in respect of air transport services provided within the Partner States;

(c) approve any tariff proposals, in respect of international air services, which the Corporation wishes to put forward to the International Air Transport Association;

(d) approve the annual programme of services and the financial estimates of the Corporation;

(e) approve, in respect of every five-year period in the operations of the Corporation, the development plan submitted to it by the Board of Directors;

(f) approve any major alteration in salaries or other conditions of service of employees of the Corporation;

(g) approve any individual capital work of which the estimated cost exceeds 5,000,000 Kenya shillings or such other sum as the Authority may, by order, determine; and

(h) give directions to the Board of Directors concerning any matter of policy involving agreement with, or the interests of, a foreign country.

The Authority

7. Subject to this Treaty and to any Act of the Community, the Authority shall be responsible for the general direction and control of the Corporation.

8. The Authority may—

(a) give directions of a general nature to the Communications Council;

(b) give directions to the Board of Directors as to the exercise and performance of the functions of the Corporation in relation to any matter which appears to the Authority to affect the public interest; and

(c) determine matters referred to it by the Communications Council or by the Board of Directors.

General

9. If there is a difference of opinion between the Communications Council and the Board of Directors concerning what constitutes a minor or a major alteration in the tariff of rates, fares and other charges or a minor or major alteration in salaries or other conditions of service of the employees of the Corporation, the difference shall be referred to the Authority to be resolved.

Interpretation

10. In this Part, unless the context otherwise requires—

'air transport services and facilities relating thereto' includes, without prejudice to the generality of the expression, air transport services and services for the provision of hotel and catering facilities, for the carriage of passengers to and from airports and aerodromes, and for the collection, delivery and storage of baggage and freight;

'air transport services' means services for the transport of passengers or freight by air;

'international air services' means air transport services provided to or from any place outside the Partner States.

(*Article* 86)

ANNEX XIV

DECENTRALIZATION AND RELATED MEASURES

Part A. Services Administered by the Community

The East African Customs and Excise Department

1. (*a*) There shall be appointed for each Partner State a Commissioner of Customs and Excise who shall be an officer in the service of the Community.

(*b*) There shall be a Commissioner-General of the East African Customs and Excise Department who shall, subject to this Treaty and to any law, have the general control of the Department.

(*c*) Subject to the general control of the Commissioner-General, a Commissioner of Customs and Excise shall control the operations of the Department, including revenue collection, within the Partner State for which he is Commissioner, and shall have the duty to supply the Minister responsible for finance of that Partner State with such information, including statistical information, as may be required from time to time by that Minister.

(*d*) Notwithstanding sub-paragraph (*c*) of this paragraph, the Commissioner-General shall retain control over functions which are necessary to ensure effective co-ordination in the three Partner States.

The East African Income Tax Department

2. (*a*) There shall be appointed for each Partner State a Commissioner of Income Tax who shall be an officer in the service of the Community.

(*b*) There shall be a Commissioner-General of the East African Income Tax Department who shall, subject to this Treaty and to any law, have the general control of the Department.

(*c*) Subject to the general control of the Commissioner-General, a Commissioner of Income Tax shall control the operations of the Department, including revenue collection, within the Partner State for which he is Commissioner, and shall have the duty to supply the Minister responsible for finance of that Partner State with such information, including statistical information, as may be required from time to time by that Minister.

(*d*) Notwithstanding sub-paragraph (*c*) of this paragraph, the Commissioner-General shall retain control over functions which are necessary to ensure effective co-ordination in the three Partner States.

Directorate of Civil Aviation

3. (*a*) There shall be appointed for each Partner State a Director of Civil Aviation who shall be an officer in the service of the Community.

(*b*) There shall be a Director-General of Civil Aviation who shall, subject to this Treaty and to any law, have the general control of the Directorate.

(*c*) The Director of Civil Aviation for a Partner State shall be responsible to the Director-General but shall have as much control of the operations of the Directorate as is practical within the territory of the Partner State for which he is Director.

(*d*) The area of control of each Director shall be determined by the Director-General and need not correspond exactly with the territorial boundaries of the Partner States.

(*e*) In accordance with a programme to be agreed by the East African Ministers, Sub-Flight Information Centres shall be established at Dar es Salaam and Entebbe to handle air movements, in Tanzania and Uganda respectively, below flight level 145 as from time to time determined in accordance with the rules for international air navigation of the International Civil Aviation Organization.

(*f*) The programme referred to in sub-paragraph (*e*) of this paragraph shall give priority to the establishment of the Sub-Flight Information Centre at Dar es Salaam.

East African Meteorological Department

4. (*a*) The operations of the Department shall in each Partner State be placed under the control of a senior officer in the service of the Community.

(*b*) Each of the senior officers responsible for the operations of the Department in a Partner State shall have comparable status and responsibilities and their functions and the services which they control shall be gradually developed in accordance with the availability of staff and finance.

Part B. The Corporations

The East African Railways Corporation

1. (*a*) Strong and functionally comparable regional railway headquarters, including revenue and accounting services, shall be established in Dar es Salaam, Kampala and Nairobi.

(*b*) The Board of Directors and the Communications Council shall, when considering the capital development programme of the Corporation, give a high priority to sanctioning expenditure to enable—

(i) Mwanza to become the operating headquarters of the inland marine services (but the workshops and dockyard shall remain at Kisumu);

(ii) diesel locomotive facilities and carriage and wagon depots to be established in Uganda.

(*c*) The Board of Directors and the Communications Council shall, within sensible operating and financial parameters and for an initial period to be agreed, give preference to Tanzania and to Uganda in establishing new services and facilities.

(*d*) The Board of Directors and the Communications Council shall give consideration to the initiation of a preliminary economic and engineering survey of a possible new line of communication between Musoma, Arusha and Tanga.

The East African Harbours Corporation

2. The Board of Directors and the Communications Council shall, when considering the capital development programme of the Corporation, give special consideration to the development of harbours in Tanzania.

The East African Posts and Telecommunications Corporation

3. (*a*) Strong and functionally comparable regional headquarters, including revenue and accounting services, shall be established in Dar es Salaam, Kampala and Nairobi.

(*b*) The implementation of sub-paragraph (*a*) of this paragraph shall involve a measure of devolution of functions from the headquarters of the

Corporation to the regional headquarters in each Partner State and there shall be a corresponding adjustment of establishments.

The East African Airways Corporation

4. The Board of Directors and the Communications Council shall ensure that future development should, so far as possible, be sited in Uganda and Tanzania, the first priority being given to development in Uganda, and in particular that—

(i) a workshop be established in Uganda for the overhaul of all Pratt and Whitney piston engines; and

(ii) the maintenance and overhaul base for Friendship, Dakota and other piston-engined aircraft be transferred to Entebbe.

(Article 90)

ANNEX XV

TRANSITIONAL PROVISIONS

1. The amounts collected by the East African Income Tax Department and the East African Customs and Excise Department which immediately before the coming into force of this Treaty fall to be paid to the Distributable Pool Fund of the Common Services Organization but have not been so paid, shall, upon the coming into force of this Treaty, be paid to the Distributable Pool Fund of the Community.

2. Until rules governing the procedure of the Assembly are made under paragraph 17 of Annex XI to this Treaty, the Standing Orders of the Central Legislative Assembly, established by Article 16 of the Constitution of the Common Services Organization, shall apply for regulating the procedure of the Assembly with such modifications as the Authority may prescribe by order published in the Gazette of the Community.

3. The Service Commission established by Article 62 of this Treaty shall assume its functions under this Treaty on such date as may be appointed by the Authority by notice published in the Gazette of the Community and until that date those functions shall be performed by the Secretary-General.

4. Upon the coming into force of this Treaty, the Secretary-General and the Legal Secretary of the Common Services Organization shall assume the offices of Secretary-General of the Community and Counsel to the Community respectively and shall be deemed to have been appointed thereto under Article 63 of this Treaty.

5. Until provision is made by Act of the Community for the salary of an office to which Article 69 of this Treaty applies there shall be paid to the holder of that office such salary as shall be determined by the Authority.

6. Until the Assembly first meets after the coming into force of this Treaty, the Authority may, in anticipation of the enactment of an Appropriation Act in accordance with Article 66 of this Treaty and notwithstanding the provisions of that Article, authorize money to be paid from the General Fund for any purpose for which the Assembly might lawfully appropriate money in accordance with this Treaty in any case where the payment of such money is not already provided for in any law.

7. References—

(a) in sub-paragraph (a) of paragraph 5 of Article 82 of this Treaty, to a charge upon the funds of the East African Posts and Telecommunications Corporation shall, in respect of any period commencing on the day of the coming into force of this Treaty and ending on the day of the establishment of that Corporation, be construed as references to a charge upon the Posts and Telecommunications Fund; and

(b) in sub-paragraph (b) of paragraph 5 of Article 82 of this Treaty, to a charge upon the funds of the East African Railways Corporation or of the East African Harbours Corporation shall, in respect of any period commencing on the day of the coming into force of this Treaty and ending on the day of the establishment of those Corporations, be construed as references to a charge upon the Railways and Harbours Fund.

DONE AT KAMPALA, UGANDA, on the sixth day of June, in the year one thousand nine hundred and sixty-seven.

IN FAITH WHEREOF the undersigned have placed their signatures at the end of this Treaty and the Annexes thereto.

For the Government of the United Republic of Tanzania	For the Government of the Sovereign State of Uganda	For the Government of the Republic of Kenya
JULIUS K. NYERERE President	A. MILTON OBOTE President	JOMO KENYATTA President

PART TWO

ECONOMIC DEVELOPMENT AND INVESTMENT

I. REGIONAL CO-OPERATION AND INTEGRATION

REFER to Part One, sections III, IV, and V, and see generally United Nations, *Economic Co-operation and Integration in Africa, Three Case Studies*, 1969, U.N. Document, ST/ECA/109.

II. U.N. ECONOMIC COMMISSION FOR AFRICA: REPORT ON INVESTMENT LAWS AND REGULATIONS IN AFRICA

WHAT follows is Part I of a report of a study by the U.N. Economic Commission for Africa. The report was adopted on 27 February 1962 and appears in U.N. Document E/CN. 14/INR/28 (30 October 1963). The material reproduced raises major issues of development in relation to government planning of investment and is, of course, a survey of the legal structures affecting development plans. Further materials on economic development: Gunnar Myrdal, *Economic Theory and Under-developed Regions*, London, 1957 (University Paperbacks edition, 1963); *Towards a New Trade Policy for Development: Report by the Secretary-General of the United Nations Conference on Trade and Development*, 1964; Myint, *The Economics of the Developing Countries*, London, 3rd edn., 1967 (Hutchinson University Library); Eshag and Richards, 'An Analysis of the Divergent Paths of Economic Development in Ghana and the Ivory Coast since 1960', *Bulletin of the Oxford University Institute of Economics and Statistics*, vol. 29, no. 4, 1967; Special Issue, 'Development Aid', *Journal of World Trade Law*, vol. 4, no. 2, March–April 1970, especially Ewing at pp. 362–76; United Nations Economic Commission for Africa, *A Venture in Self-reliance, Ten Years of E.C.A.* (E/CN. 14/424), Addis Ababa, 1968; Green, *Journal of Modern African Studies*, vol. 5, 1967, p. 243; Seers and Joy (edd.), *Development in a Divided World*, Pelican Books, 1971.

TEXT

LEGAL FRAMEWORK FOR ECONOMIC DEVELOPMENT[1]

1. The year 1960 has been perhaps the most crucial date in the contemporary history of Africa. More than half the total number of new nations gained their political independence in that year. The next twelve months saw the formulation of economic policies and the drafting of development plans.

2. Almost simultaneously in early 1962, some seventeen countries had promulgated investment laws and modified the existing ones. Economic planning gives concrete expression to aspirations that lead to independence and investment legislation creates the framework that facilitates the realization of the development plans. It is not surprising, therefore, that the first set of laws to undergo rapid change happened to be those that affect investment.

3. In a developing economy, the function of investments is to push those factors which would lead to economic progress. Scarce capital, both domestic and foreign, must be channelled to provide for an infrastructure. The function of a comprehensive law is to announce and define the policy of the government with respect to areas of investments. The mechanism through which investments are administered and channelled brings in the consideration of strictly legal elements.

4. The purpose of investment laws is to enumerate and classify 'pioneering' or 'approved' industries. They describe the executive authority responsible for examining and supervising investments. They usually incorporate conditions of entry of foreign capital and the rules of remittance. Regulations also include tax provisions affecting investments which are applicable to beneficiary industries. Other features of these laws relate to employment of nationals, rules of compensation and the procedure of settlement of disputes. Investment laws thus serve not only to facilitate and often induce foreign and domestic investments but also create a recognizable structure of legal relationships involved. They provide the framework for government policy both for a potential investor and an administrator. The proper execution of these laws can lead to augmenting and ultimately influencing the level of economic development. To achieve a higher ratio of investment to product requires the adoption of an over-all investment target based on an expected relationship between the growth of investment and the growth of output.

[1] The text is reproduced with permission from *International Legal Materials*, vol. 3 (1964), p. 179.

5. In recent years, industrial development laws have become a universal instrument for promoting industrialization in developing countries. They provide an orderly framework by which societies today are organizing themselves to reach economic goals. Laws embody changes which the government hopes to make in carrying out their programmes of development. The responsibility of the government in creating conditions conducive to economic development is now generally accepted.

6. This decade in Africa is a period of trial and error in economic and legal planning. As new Development Plans are formulated and new experience is accumulated, investment codes and statutes will have to be modified to be in harmony with economic objectives. This study attempts to analyse some of these laws in a period of rapid economic transition.

A. Inter-dependence of Legal and Economic Processes

7. History does not offer any answer to the question whether codification of certain concepts into laws accelerates their general acceptance in society. Legal sanction, therefore, cannot be said to assist or help social sanction. What is clear, however, is that the major problem of the present era is economic development. It encompasses almost all sectors of society. A jurist as a member of this society in transition cannot afford to be a mere observer. He must also make some positive contribution towards the common action of eliminating poverty.

8. In the past century of rapid economic expansion in the industrial centres, law and economics proceeded in an entangled fashion; laws were codified as economic needs for them came to be recognized. During the process of industrialization, economic advance, in general, took place at a faster pace than the enactment of statutes. For often it meant going through cumbersome legal procedure. The fundamental transformations in society induced legal institutions to keep pace with it. But this was a hazardous process in an era where planning was not considered necessary. Now, it is considered to be a major instrument to achieve higher levels of economic and social well-being. Under this new situation, legal structure cannot be left to the wasteful process of accidental development. The jurist now has the possibility of evolving a structure of development laws which is suited to carry out the economic and social transition. The main advantage is that in the pre-industrial countries, political, economic and legal revolutions can be carried out almost simultaneously.

9. At present in the developing countries, planners rarely include legal framework in their concept of a nation's economic problems. It may be that the present generation of lawyers, have received their education in

universities, where the curricula are not yet adapted to the inter-dependence of economic needs and legal framework.[1] This attitude, of course, stems from historical reasons.

B. Legal Setting in Africa

10. Practically every State in Africa has had connections with some part of Europe. The intricacies of a dual and, in some cases, a plural legal system stems from the superimposition of varieties of European law. This is perhaps the most confusing legacy in Africa.[2]

11. The former British West African territories had legal systems derived from England.[3] Different local statutory variations were often maintained by courts and encouraged by legal training. The ex-French territories, on the other hand, developed under direct administration. In this process, the continental commercial laws were modified but slightly. The conflicts of European code systems as represented by France, Germany and Spain have left an imprint in Cameroun, Niger, Ivory Coast and Guinea.

12. If a chart were to be drawn of the conflicting legal systems of Africa today, the resulting picture would be a mosaic of laws zigzagging across the continent.[4] The main argument in the development era against dualism or even pluralism is that it leads to internal conflicts and uncertainties. One of the main objects of law is to offer certainty and flexibility in dealings. All systems of law at various times in history have been subjected to changes in social, economic and political conditions. Flexibility to meet the changing economic requirement is an essential attribute of modern law.

13. The main question, however, is whether the existing legal systems in Africa are suitable for development purposes. There may be a lot of differences in the political forms of government that exist in Africa today. But one common factor emerges in each case and that relates to the policy of independent countries to foster economic development. It is evident

[1] 'The teaching of law' it is beginning to be realized 'is totally incomplete if it is not accompanied by a background of economic, social and political sciences.' See 'Statement of the President of Ghana to the Faculty of Law', *Journal of African Law*, no. 6, 1962, and H. W. Chitepo, in *The African Conference on the Rule of Law* (Lagos, 3–7 January 1961), International Commission of Jurists, Geneva, 1961.

[2] A. N. Allott, *Judicial and Legal Systems in Africa*, 1962.

[3] The impact of English law upon Africa can be summarized in two ways: firstly, it had a modifying influence on certain aspects of local customary law and, secondly, it filled the gaps in the traditional law of usage brought about by new commercial and economic values. The latter bringing in its orbit mercantile law and commercial law.

[4] See recommendation of the Conference of International Jurists held in Venice in October 1963. The Conference called on all African countries to undertake research in their own traditions and customs to harmonize their legislations.

that economic progress can be retarded by a piecemeal system of law and may be accelerated by a coherent legal system.[1] This transformation could facilitate commercial transactions and thereby establish certainty of economic activities in general and investments in particular.

C. Some Aspects of Development Laws in Africa

14. The main provisions of the investment codes and related laws are incorporated in Part II of this study. These provisions vary from country to country, reflecting some of the differences in the past legal framework and the extent to which an attempt was made to modify it to meet new needs. It has not been possible to see clearly how the provisions have changed over time in the same country. The main reason is that most countries in Africa have so far had no time to assess the significance of the initial legal changes. But the need for putting together in an integrated law the main provisions concerning investments arose after each country had prepared its development plan. The investment code is thus becoming a legal counterpart of the development plan.

15. Out of the thirty countries under study in Africa, only ten do not have an integrated law or code on investments. Almost all the ex-French colonies have a codified law on investments except Togo.

16. The four States of ex-French Equatorial Africa: Gabon, Central African Republic, Chad and Congo (Brazzaville) have, except for small differences, similar investment codes.[2] The position is reversed as far as the ex-English colonies are concerned. Almost all of them do not have an integrated law on investments except Ghana. Sierra Leone has a Development Ordinance which was passed in 1960. Nigeria has several income tax and custom duties relief ordinances. In Tanganyika a bill affecting foreign investments is awaiting the approval of parliament.

17. Among the other countries of Africa, Ethiopia has recently passed an investment decree. Both the United Arab Republic and Liberia have various decrees and statutes which contain relevant provisions on investments.

18. It is not easy to fit so many diverse provisions of codes and laws into composite headings for analysis. In order to simplify the presentation, the

---

[1] It has been suggested that there is another positive factor in Africa. Since most of the local laws are unwritten, the existing flexibility may be utilized for new economic needs. See *The Future of Law in Africa*, Record of Proceedings of the London Conference, 28 December 1959–8 January 1960.

[2] They belong to the Equatorial Customs Union (Union douanière équatoriale) to which Cameroun is associated.

main topics of the material in Part II are discussed here under the following headings:

(a) Economic policy statements.
(b) 'Approved' enterprises.
(c) Patterns of administrative control.
(d) Foreign investments.
(e) Economic inducements.
(f) Arbitration.

(a) Economic policy statements

19. Most African countries are still in the process of formulating precisely their economic objectives. Even when these have been decided, it is not easy to locate them. In some cases, they have been embodied in the constitution or in the development plan or in the investment codes. But there are cases in which they are scattered in an important pronouncement by the President or the Prime Minister, in ministerial speeches, in parliamentary declarations and in various enactments. Thus, there is no single source through which one can discover the full expression of the national economic policy. Having said this, it is also important to add that government policy can only be related to a particular period of time. The pronouncements selected here, therefore, have value only in relation to a certain period when the Plan was formulated and investment code enacted.

20. The general impression on reading the pronouncements on national economic policy is that they have one dominant theme: to increase economic well-being mostly through a rapid industrialization. The means to attain this goal have often been spelled out in some detail. They relate to a better utilization of natural resources, to improving the infrastructure and social investments and to the development of one or other particular sector of the economy. These pronouncements are general and need not be interpreted as a comprehensive declaration of a national economic policy.

21. The Algerian Investment Code states that enterprises which encourage and aim at providing an infrastructure for the economy are 'of national significance'. The Ethiopian Development Plan spells out three basic aims: better utilization of resources, introduction of modern technology and increasing investments. Ivory Coast considers participation of government in developing unexploited resources as the main aim, while the United Arab Republic has underlined the desire to increase production in all sectors.

22. Some countries of the region have defined their aims in more detail. The Government of Sudan intends to concentrate its future programme

in developing public utilities and hydro-electric power, while Nigeria considers the development of transport, communication and higher education as its objective. The Tunisian statement gives priority to developing production of iron ore and chemicals. A number of countries, particularly those with comprehensive development plans have expressed their general aim in quantitative terms: such and such an increase in this or that sector over a given period.

23. Although the economic significance of these policy statements is general in character, they often give indication of areas of development which are pre-occupying the attention of the government at a given time. But there is one area in the statements which may be of considerable interest to the potential investor. This relates to the main channels of investment and economic growth which will be through public owner-ship, mixed ownership, co-operative enterprise or private enterprise.

24. Of course, no government in Africa has reserved any of these sectors exclusively. But there are important differences among countries concern-ing the emphasis they place on one or the other or a particular combination of them. Statements on public or private sector are normally found in development plans, but they are sometimes also expressed in investment codes.[1]

25. So far as the main social sectors, education, health and, to a varying extent, housing are concerned, all African Governments consider them as the proper field of public activity. Similar is the position in nearly all countries regarding public utilities, such as rail transport, communication, electric power, water supplies, etc. The same policy applies to construction of large projects such as irrigation dams, canals and ports.

26. The economic policies of the African Governments may be sub-divided in three groups depending upon the emphasis on a particular form of industrial organization.

27. At one extreme are the countries relying on the public sector as the main driving force for industrial development, and at the other, are those who expect to rely exclusively on private domestic as well as foreign enterprise. Between these two are a large number of countries where the attitude is more or less pragmatic: rely on private enterprise if possible, if it is not forthcoming, undertake the project in the public sector.

---

[1] There is an exception in the case of the Central African Republic where an article in the Constitution states *inter alia* that of property from the public to the private sector must be regulated by the authority of the law. Article 17, *Constitution de la République*, January 1963.

28. To the first group belong the United Arab Republic, Ghana, Algeria and Guinea. In these countries the construction of some form of socialist society has been accepted as a guiding principle of national policy. Emphasis on public enterprise stems from this, although private initiative offers a large and, in most cases, an expanded field of operation.

29. In Algeria, the State participates in all important activities, while in the United Arab Republic the right of establishing basic industries rests with the Government. Mining prospecting and research associated with it as well as ore utilization is reserved by the Government. The main reason given by the Government is that this kind of economic activity requires large investments which private enterprise cannot afford. Some of these important industries reserved by the Government of UAR are oil prospection, coal mining, etc. It has included in this category, fertilizers, caustic soda, paper, automobiles, tractors and other forms of transport. As far as iron and steel industries are concerned, co-ownership is practised in cases where private capital hesitates to invest owing to the likelihood of losses during the first years of operation.

30. Ghana and Guinea have classified their economic structure in their Development Plans into three or four sectors. They are: the state-owned sector, the private sector and joint state–private sector (also called the mixed sector). To these, Ghana has added a 'co-operative sector', the significance of which is that the Government initiates an industry until it can stand on its own feet when private enterprise takes it over. Sierra Leone's policy is to encourage the establishment of various industries, and in some cases to participate financially in the 'equity' which will eventually be handed over to nationals.

31. In some countries, like in Nigeria, Liberia, Libya, Morocco and Sudan, private enterprise is allocated the main role in promoting industrialization following the liberal tradition.

32. The Government of Liberia has stated that despite the fact that it pursues an 'open door investment policy' 'it has found it convenient to carry out investment in power production and will operate the plant when necessary'. Water supplies in Liberia are already being operated by the Government.

33. The policy of Libya aims, in the first instance, at making available 'an open range' where private capital can establish factories with 'technical and financial assistance' from the Government. After considering the national need, the Government embarks on an industrial project on the basis that 'private sector is abstaining from it for some economic, social, or other reasons'.

34. Morocco has stated in its investment code that private capital is welcome in economic sectors which have been given priority in the Development Plan. One of the proposals of the Plan is that the State will intervene to establish basic steel and chemical industries. Sudan has divided its economic structure by earmarking specific industries for public and private sectors. It has announced that private capital is welcome in investments on raw materials and light industries.

35. A sessional paper from Nigeria indicates that a 'mixed economy' is envisaged for the region, but private enterprise is 'responsible for the preponderant part of economic activity'. However, there are a few industries where Government has a monopoly. These are connected with generation and distribution of electricity, water supply and telecommunications.

36. There are other countries, however, who have declared themselves to be mixed economies in the sense of having both public and private sector overlap in several areas. The emphasis on either public or private sector in a given country, however, cannot be pushed too far. With the acceptance of some form of planning, it is obvious in all countries that the government has begun to play a role in guiding, directing, controlling and often directly undertaking various industrial projects.[1]

37. As discussed below, the State specified in some countries the industries and areas in which it will participate right from the beginning while in others the initiative is left with private enterprise even though later the government may decide to participate.

(b) 'Approved' enterprises[2]

38. As indicated earlier, the government not only points out the main area of operation in the public, private and mixed sectors, but often enumerates industries or undertakings which are accorded 'priority' in the process of industrialization. This is usually described in the investment codes and development plans. The beneficiary industries, because of the priority attached to them, are entitled to certain economic benefits. A scale of priority indicates the future pattern of industrial development of the given country and the range of choices available to the potential investor.

---

[1] See A. H. Hanson, *Public Enterprise and Economic Development*, London, 1960, p. 203. The author takes several examples from under-developed areas and concludes that 'the pattern of public enterprise cannot be drawn arbitrarily or solely in the light of ideological considerations'.

[2] The expressions 'priority' and 'approved' have been used inter-changeably in several laws. Strictly speaking 'priority' is an arbitrary selection of industries while 'approved' connotes that this 'priority' has been processed by some form of administrative procedure.

39. It is interesting to note that almost all the ex-French colonies who have integrated investment codes have enumerated 'approved' industries in great detail. Primarily, these countries have defined their basic economic objectives in terms of agriculture, mining, transformation of local raw materials or manufacturing industries. The majority of African countries have given priority to mining in their investment laws.

40. Some countries do not give a list of priorities in either their development plan or investment code. It may be found in a government publication as in the case of Nigeria. A long list of 'pioneering' industries includes mining, smelting and refining, canned foodstuffs, rubber soled shoes, tyres, hotel keeping, etc.

41. Algeria, Cameroun, Dahomey, Ghana, Central African Republic have incorporated a general condition in their laws according to which all prospective industries in adhering to the Plan, must channel investments in sectors defined by the plan. Liberia, Libya and Ethiopia have given priority to consumer goods industries, textiles and foodstuffs. Stock-farming and real estate industries are given priority in Chad, Guinea, Ivory Coast, Niger and Upper Volta. Those countries who intend to set up chemical industries are Ethiopia, Guinea, Morocco, United Arab Republic, Niger and Upper Volta. The building industry is specifically mentioned in the laws of Niger, Ethiopia and Liberia. Upper Volta, Chad and Guinea consider metallurgy as a 'priority' industry while the United Arab Republic and Morocco have included armaments in this category.

42. In certain cases the criteria of priority is also stated in the code. For example, the Investment Code of Madagascar lays down the conditions of approval of industries. According to its provisions, new enterprises must adhere to these rules. They are 'the contribution of the rectification of imports and the expansion of imports or the improvement of the balance of payments'. The Tunisian law specifies that any industry which intends to be 'approved' must satisfy the requirement of minimum capital per worker, least competition, import substitution. In Senegal, an approved enterprise must satisfy the following conditions: an investment of a minimum of one hundred million CFA realizable in three months or the direct creation of employment for at least one hundred persons per year.

43. The Investment Law of Ghana states that 'approval for capital investments under the Act may be granted' for the purposes of contributing to the attainment of four specific conditions. These concern the development of the productive capacity, its utilization and expansion, saving on imports and creating a high level of employment.

44. The meaning of the word 'priority' must not be misunderstood. In most cases it reflects the natural resource endowment and the stage of economic development in a given country. But 'approved' industries signify that a certain administrative procedure is involved which takes the form of a certificate or decree. The nature and function of this administrative machinery which grants 'approval' needs to be briefly examined.

(c) Patterns of administrative control

45. Although the organization of public enterprise in the industrially developed countries has often been a subject of controversy, they have evolved administrative systems which are more or less adapted to the needs of a complex and diversified economy. In the developing countries, on the other hand, the existing administrative machinery is not suited to the new tasks. Therefore, newly independent countries have established agencies which are specifically vested with authority to guide investments in channels which correspond to national requirements.

46. In most of the new nations of Africa, a new pattern of government control is emerging. It is now only in a minority that the authority to examine, guide and supervise investments still rests with the ministries of finance, industry and commerce. Such is the case in Ivory Coast, Liberia, Nigeria and Tanganyika. In the old pattern, one can discern a great deal of inter-ministerial rivalry between the ministries of finance and commerce to retain control over investments.

47. The new 'development' machinery, the 'investment commission', has been created by about half of the independent countries of Africa. Among them are Algeria, Cameroun, Ethiopia, Ghana, Madagascar, the United Arab Republic and Somalia. Constitutionally these commissions are quasi-government agencies whose relations with the government via the ministries is very close. Most of the investment commissions are created by the investment codes and, therefore, are statutory bodies established for special purposes.

48. In some cases this 'development' institution is established under a different title. In Guinea, for instance, it goes under the name of 'Commission of Economic Control' which is a member of 'Bureau politique national du PRG'. One of its functions is to initiate new enterprises. In Madagascar, there is a Technical Committee on private investment which is not created by the Code, but is an independent body. In addition it has an inter-ministerial Planning and Development Committee which assumes most of the functions of an investment commission in other countries.

49. This institution in Somalia is known as 'Committee on Foreign Investments'. It consists of ministers and directors of several governmental departments. Six experts who are technically competent to deal with questions of economic development are also appointed on this Committee. Tunisia has established an 'Economic and Social Council' in 1961, which is vested with the general authority to deal with all economic and social matters. The Council acts as an advisory body to the Government in the field of planning and its implementation.

50. In Somalia, Libya, Tanganyika, the Investment Commission is created specifically for foreign investments. In general, the function of these investment commissions is to encourage investments and supervise the areas in which they should be channelled. In Cameroun, the Investment Commission is the sole authority which reviews applications to be treated under priority schedules. It may reject or approve an application according to the criteria specified in the Code. In Ghana, the Capital Investment Board[1] initiates and organizes activities for the 'encouragement of investment of foreign capital'. The Board grants approval for capital investments, maintains liaison between investors, government departments and agencies. It is the responsibility of the Board to grant any exemptions and reduction facility or licence to assist an enterprise.

51. In Liberia, an institution called National Production Council, established in 1956, whose function is to co-ordinate policies, plans and programmes, is designed to strengthen the economy. The Commission established in Libya under the Foreign Capital Investment Law collects economic data on the possibilities of investing foreign capital in 'fields important to the economic development of the country'. In Morocco, the Investment Commission was specifically created to 'determine the industrial sector within the plan'.

52. In some countries, however, e.g. Ivory Coast, Nigeria, Senegal, the United Arab Republic and Tanganyika, the authority and control to examine, supervise and channel new investments still rests with the Ministry of Commerce, or Industry or Finance, and the traditional nucleus of economic control. In some of the new countries, the administrative structure is still based on the model of metropolitan powers. Interestingly enough, the developed countries are also finding the need to establish investment commissions and development corporations.[2] The reason is that it is no longer possible for a department in a ministry to handle the multifarious activities of an expanding economy.

[1] Created by the Capital Investment Act 1963.
[2] See United Nations, *Some Problems in the Organization and Administration of Public Enterprises in the Industrial Field.*

53. The composition of the investment commission follows a fairly uniform pattern. Usually, the Minister of Economy or Commerce is its President. The other members are a mixture of ministerial officials and representative members. In some cases, like in Dahomey, Cameroun, Chad and Congo (Brazzaville) two representatives from parliament are also included. In Gabon the number of members of parliament is four. In addition, Gabon has included two representatives of the trade associations and federations 'in whose field of activity the enterprise concerned is engaged'.

54. In most of the countries which have instituted investment commissions, members are not only drawn from the ministries but also from other fields. Directors of banks, commissioners of customs and taxation and presidents of chambers of commerce are also included.

55. The United Arab Republic has a 'Special Committee' which deals with and controls all aspects of national economic development. In the Upper Volta the power and authority to control investments rest with the Council of Ministers. In Ethiopia, the Investment Committee created by a government decree consists of the Minister of Commerce and Industry, the Governor of the National Bank and the General Secretary of the Planning Board.

56. Apart from the Investment Commission whose function is supervisory, few countries of Africa have created institutions which offer monetary assistance to 'approved' industries. About ten new institutions in the form of Credit Development Bank or 'Caisse' have been created in Africa in the last two or three years.

57. Industrial development and finance[1] cannot be easily separated. Therefore, some countries have created institutions which combine both of these functions. Liberia has created a Bank for Industrial Development and Investment. It is a statutory body the purpose of which is not only 'to develop Liberian economy by providing incentives for flow of private investment capital' but also to finance investments in loan and equity.[2]

58. In Somalia, an institution called Credito Somalo, government owned, operates a medium and long-term lending section to finance private industrial activities of all types. In the United Arab Republic, recently, the National Bank was split up in two separate bodies: the Central Bank and

[1] See *Mobilization of Domestic Capital*; Report of Second Working Party, where legal distinction is made between a finance corporation and development corporation. For other examples in Latin America and Asia see United Nations Economic Survey of Latin America, 1953, and ECAFE L/122, 12 March 1957.

[2] According to the rule it must not exceed an amount equivalent to 10 per cent of the Liberian Bank's total resources.

the National Bank. The former has the power to co-ordinate general credit
and banking policy, and the latter acts as a commercial bank to finance
industrial activities.

59. The Uganda Development Corporation established in 1952 is mainly
concerned with investigating and making recommendations on, new
projects that are submitted to it. A technical department is also available
to potential investors for assistance in technical matters. A project is
approved after exhaustive enquiries into all aspects of costing, marketing
and technical problems of production have been made.

60. There is a wide variety of procedures to determine specific benefits
granted to potential investors. In Africa, the typical procedure entails
application to the Investment Commission or any other authority designated by the law. This application is very often accompanied by supporting
documents of the legal and economic nature of investments. In some
cases the financial source must also be specified.

61. The Commission then investigates the nature and quality of investment particularly with regard to general requirements set out in the
investment laws. After examining several aspects of investment, the Commission may reject or approve an enterprise. The precise form of the
instrument varies in each country and is in the form of a decree or decision
of the Cabinet or a simple exemption certificate. As a rule this is granted
to domestic and foreign investors. The potential investor on his part also
undertakes certain obligations with regard to amount, period and form of
investments. Any failure to adhere to the conditions is subject to 'withdrawal of approval'. This usually means that an enterprise is deprived of
any economic benefits. In certain cases they are obliged to pay back the
benefits already derived.

(d) Foreign investments

62. The role of external assistance in terms of direct private investment
in Africa is essentially to release domestic resources. Provided a development programme is being carried out that implies a higher rate of investment, external financing will induce growth and capital formation. In this
sense all developing countries are in need of foreign capital.

63. One single dominant fear of the foreign investor is nationalization.
Others are low returns and inability to remit capital and profits. This is
what is usually termed as 'investment climate'. However, there exist real
fears of domination and exploitation on the part of capital importing
countries. This 'climate' of fear has somehow seeped into the new investment codes and laws of Africa.

64. The need of capital, and fear of exploitation faces a newly independent country with a dilemma. The investment laws under discussion have made several attempts in the direction of minimizing obstacles and encouraging foreign private investments through special incentives and guarantees. It is an interesting fact that the majority of the countries of Africa have addressed their laws to both domestic and foreign investments. Only a few countries have specifically enacted laws to attract exclusively foreign capital. Among these are Sudan, Libya, Togo and Somalia.

65. The rules concerning foreign investments encompass a very wide range. To a foreign investor, regulations concerning administrative procedures, tax incentives, rules relating to employment of nationals are all important. In general, investment laws contain guarantees of fair compensation, remittance of profits, non-discrimination and fiscal stability. Here we shall briefly deal with nationalization, repatriation of capital and profits, employment of nationals and non-discrimination.

(i) *Nationalization*[1]

66. The main factor responsible for the resistance of private capital in developing countries has been the fear of nationalization. One of the most important uses of nationalization has been to stimulate economic development in poor countries. Where a private enterprise has proved unable or unwilling to provide goods or services essential to industrial progress, government have stepped in to supply them.

67. Most countries in Africa have indicated their policy regarding nationalization in the investment laws or policy statements or constitutions. Those countries which provide a nationalization clause have also given a legal guarantee of fair compensation.[2] The majority of the countries who have integrated Codes have included a clause on nationalization.

68. The Investment Code of Dahomey provides a basic guarantee of equitable compensation in case of expropriation. The Foreign Investment Law of Somalia provides that 'property of the enterprises registered in Somalia is free from expropriation measures except in case of public interest'. This law further provides that the property of enterprises is not

---

[1] Nationalization is an economic expression used here in the sense of 'ownership and control by the State'. Most Investment Codes use the term 'expropriation' which legally means 'the compulsory acquisition of private property by the State'. There is an abundant literature on the subject. For a good summary see Friedmann, W., 'Some Impacts of Social Organization on International Law', *American Journal of International Law*, 1956.

[2] Most laws use the words 'just', 'appropriate', 'equitable', and 'fair' interchangeably.

subject to any administrative measures of seizure or requisition except in case of war and then 'only as long as it lasts in accordance with the relevant international convention in force'.

69. The Approved Enterprises (Concessions) Act 1956 of Sudan stipulates that 'if at any time any property belonging to an approved foreign enterprise is compulsorily acquired by the Sudan Government in furtherance of nationalization, ... the said compensation shall be remitted out of Sudan'.[1]

70. Constitutional guarantees to protect private enterprises have been provided in the constitutions of Ethiopia, Libya and the Central African Republic.[2]

71. According to the constitution of Libya, 'the property of any foreign investor cannot be expropriated except for "public good" in the circumstances defined and specified in the Expropriation Law'. The Ethiopian constitution provides that 'no one may be deprived of his property except upon a finding by ministerial order issued pursuant to the requirements of a special expropriation law . . . and except upon payment of just compensation determined, in the absence of agreement, by judicial procedures established by law'.

72. Liberia and Nigeria have made policy statements regarding nationalization. According to a government statement in Liberia, 'no expropriation of existing industries is envisaged'. The Government of Nigeria has indicated that there are 'no plans for nationalizing industry beyond the extent to which public utilities are already nationalized . . . Should this occur then fair compensation assessed by independent arbitration will be paid'.

73. 'Our Government', said the President of Ghana, 'has no plans whatever to take over industries in the private sector . . . Where Government has taken over private industry, it has done so either because—as in the case of the acquisition of the gold mines—the owners had indicated their intention of closing down, or—as in other cases—because the owners themselves had made proposition to the Government. The Government has in no case attempted to expropriate enterprise . . . Where it becomes necessary to take over private business at the request of private enterprise itself, the Government will . . . ensure that adequate compensation is paid to the owner'.[3]

74. The policy statement from Guinea declares that 'those who are ready to invest in the Republic of Guinea and who accept to participate in the economic development of our country, must be able to count on flawless

---

[1] There are virtually no restrictions in Sudan on the formation of foreign firms.
[2] Article 17, op. cit.   [3] *West Africa*, 6 October 1962, p. 1095.

social stability and benefits from guarantees protecting their capitals from all arbitrary acts and ensuring fair interests'.[1]

75. Laws of some countries state that certain industries will be nationalized for 'public interest'. But this does not exclude the payment of compensation.[2]

76. The mode of compensation is not normally provided in the Code. However, there are certain exceptions. In the investment code of the Central African Republic it is stipulated that the question of compensation is to be determined by the ordinary law. In Nigeria, the amount and adequacy of compensation is left to arbitration. A government statement from Tanganyika on nationalization gives a guarantee that in the event of nationalization, compensation will be paid in foreign currency.

77. It must be borne in mind that the intention of a government to nationalize is not always declared in a legal instrument. The basic difference between a policy statement and a legal provision on nationalization is that the latter is a formal declaration which is legally binding.

78. Briefly it must be added that the right of the State to nationalize in 'public interest' has been exercised by almost all States.[3] In some developed countries such as Italy, Norway, the United States, the right to seize private property for 'public use', subject to just compensation, is incorporated in the constitution, while in Iran, India and Mexico, the question of just compensation is under the jurisdiction of national courts.

79. The position in international law of the rights of the foreign investor who has entered an agreement with the government and whose property is seized is by no means clear. The only general statement one can make is that, in the event of nationalization in developing countries, equal treatment must be accorded to foreigners and nationals where a general confiscation of property occurs.

(ii) *Repatriation of capital and profits*

80. The main reason why the developing countries discourage foreign investment and encourage official loans is because investors want profits which had eventually to be transferred in hard currencies. Despite policy statements to this effect, it is interesting to note that investment laws reflect quite a different position.

---

[1] *Rapport de présentation du Code des investissements.*

[2] Senegal has specified that 'building' industries may be nationalized without guarantee.

[3] The two most famous cases in the contemporary world were the Anglo-Iranian Company and the Suez Canal Company, both of which were taken to the International Court of Justice. For conflicting opinions of judges, see *I.C.J. Reports*, 1953 and 1957.

[*Editor's note*. The Suez issue was not taken to the International Court. For the Anglo-Iranian case see *I.C.J. Reports*, 1952, p. 93.]

81. The provisions relating to repatriation of capital and profits in the investment laws of Africa reflect two main tendencies: a group of countries have placed no restrictions in remittance of profits and capital except the procedural requirement of permission for exchange.[1] Some countries of this group have free transferability of currency to the Franc Zone. The other group of countries have provided in their laws certain conditions before capital and profits can be transferred.

82. The Investment Code of Dahomey 'allows the free transfer of all earnings'. The Ethiopian Investment Decree states that capital, profits, interests as well as foreign loans can be remitted. The Codes of Ivory Coast and Madagascar stipulate that there are no restrictions of any kind on remitting to the Franc Zone.

83. The policy statement from Liberia indicates that 'there are no legal restrictions on repatriation of capital and profits including shareholder's dividends'. Tanganyika allows the remittance of profits, principal and interest irrespective of the monetary zone, but Nigeria gives this privilege of transfer only to sterling countries. However, prior permission for non-resident capital investment and 'approved status' must be obtained from the Federal Ministry of Finance.

84. Countries which have legally provided for free transferability include Gabon, Mauritania, Chad and Morocco.

85. In some countries, Algeria, Libya, Niger, Somalia and Tunisia, certain conditions have to be satisfied before any financial transfer can be made. These conditions generally relate to authorization or the proportion of percentage which is allowed by law.

86. Both Guinea and Ghana as a rule place no restrictions on remittances. But there are some exceptions to the rule. In Guinea beneficiary enterprises are entitled to transfer annually all of the interest and at least 20 per cent of their share of the annual net operating profits. A portion of 30 per cent of wages payable to foreign personnel are also transferable. The Investment Act of Ghana provides that there shall be no restriction on the remittance of capital, profits, payments in respect of principal interest and other financial charges, and remittances to the families of foreign personnel. But all these facilities are subject to *temporary restrictions* to safeguard the external payment position.

87. The Algerian Code allows transfer of both capital and profits up to 50 per cent *per annum*. All other remittances are subject to exchange control regulations. In Somalia profits, income, revenue accruing from

[1] See Annex III.

fixed assets on loan investments and the dividend and interest received on shares and bonds acquired can be freely transferred if the amount does not exceed 15 per cent of the capital invested. The big proviso is that these must accrue from 'investments which fall within the plans for economic development'.

88. Tunisia has classified the question of remittance in two classes: productive and non-productive enterprises. The former have to adhere to certain rules in obtaining permission, while the latter can only remit up to 8 per cent. In Libya, it is the Minister of Finance who has the authority and power to decide this question on the merits of the case, while in Senegal the right to transfer capital and its revenue by an enterprise depends upon its 'participation in the economic development of a country'.

(iii) *Employment of nationals*

89. That the need of skilled labour is a prerequisite of economic progress needs no emphasis. From the point of view of developing countries, not only capital but the import of trained personnel is equally important. If a foreign technician, during his stay, trains local manpower in a particular job, he has made a most valuable contribution. African Governments have, therefore, paid official attention to introducing legal provisions for the training of national staff by foreign enterprises.

90. Half the investment laws under study have provisions relating to employment of nationals. These provisions fall mainly into two categories: the first relates to those countries where it is obligatory for foreign firms to employ nationals,[1] and the second to those that restrict the participation of foreign personnel, thereby reserving places for nationals.[2]

91. In the laws of the Central African Republic, Ghana, Nigeria, Madagascar and the Sudan, it is obligatory for an approved foreign enterprise to employ nationals.

92. The Code of the Central African Republic states that 'the proposed investment must train nationals in specialized jobs', while the Sudan policy states that foreign industrialists must undertake to provide 'reasonable facilities for training'.

---

[1] 'Employment' is used in investment laws in the wider sense of training local labour in administrative, technical and managerial skills, sometimes defined in quantitative terms.
[2] This sometimes includes trade activities. In Senegal the law makes it obligatory that the direction of trade activities be in the hands of the nationals, although foreign nationals are allowed to participate in trade associations.

93. According to the Madagascar Code 'approved status' enterprises are required to 'create new jobs'. Both Ghana and Nigeria emphasize that nationals should be trained in technical and managerial skills. Nigeria has qualified this general statement by adding that this training should be accelerated, while Ghana has included administrative skills as a part of the legal obligations.

94. The Somalian Law on Foreign Investments provides that 'unskilled foreign personnel is not to exceed 5 per cent of the Somali personnel employed'. Furthermore, a foreign enterprise must, if requested, submit to the Committee on Investments a report on the results achieved in this field. The Libyan law makes all exemptions from taxes and duties conditional to the employment of a minimum of 90 per cent nationals of the total staff. The remaining 10 per cent must also be examined and approved by the Department of Industrial Organization. The United Arab Republic makes it obligatory to employ nationals for a minimum of 90 per cent of the workmen. This law further provides that the proportion of other employees, must be at least 75 per cent and their salaries must not be less than 65 per cent of the total salaries.

(iv) *Non-discrimination clause*

95. Certain codes have specific clauses on the rights of the foreign investor who is put on par with domestic investors. In Algeria, all foreign firms, by law are treated on a non-discriminatory basis with regard to legal rights and allocation of government contracts. The only general condition is that 'they contribute to the economic development of the country'.

96. The Code of Congo (Brazzaville) provides that foreign personnel can be represented on equal footing with nationals on 'Assemblées consulaires'. They are also accorded the same protection with respect to trade marks, patents, commercial labels and trade laws and other trade regulations under the ordinary law of the land. The Investment Code of Dahomey, without indicating the areas of equality, provides that there will be generally no discrimination in law between foreigners and nationals.

97. The Investment Law of Gabon has stated that there will be no discrimination on representation between foreign and domestic companies on 'Assemblées consulaires' (Commercial Councils). The labour and social law will not discriminate between domestic and foreign employees vis-à-vis trade union activities. No discrimination is applied as far as the liabilities to pay duties and taxes are concerned. A general provision of the Code protects new enterprises, foreign or domestic, against economic situations which might be prejudicial to them.

98. There are no restrictions upon the formation of new companies in Liberia by foreign firms, except that foreign nationals are not permitted to own real estate. A foreigner may lease real estate from a Liberian, but the lease may not exceed 21 years in the first place and two optional 21-year extensions.[1]

(e) Economic inducements

99. The African Governments have introduced a vast range of economic inducements to encourage 'new' and 'established' enterprises. These incentives are usually applicable to both domestic and foreign investments. There are a few exceptions in the case of those countries who have enacted investment laws specifically for foreign investments. These include Libya, Somalia and Tanganyika.

100. The underlying economic reason for inducements is that they guide investments into 'priority' or 'approved' industries. Economic inducements are thus a selective instrument in the hands of the State to guide and control the flow of capital in certain predetermined areas.

101. Economic inducements range from complete tax exemptions to a certain degree of concessions in the payment of taxes on income, profits, imports and exports for a fixed period of time. There are also provisions for generous depreciation allowances, including reductions in turnover tax, standard tax, business tax.[2]

102. The investment codes also include provisions guaranteeing unaltered continuation of many of these benefits for a contracted period.[3] All these provisions are too numerous and varied to be described here in detail.[4] Attention is therefore drawn to some of the most important features which are introduced with a view to inducing increased economic activity in developing sectors.

103. Foremost among economic inducements are tax benefits including the exoneration from payment of import duties on indispensation imports and of export duties on manufactured goods. Protection for the output of

---

[1] These restrictions, however, do not apply to concessions.

[2] It must be noted that the general concept of taxation is different in common law and civil law countries. Two types of taxes mentioned in Part II of this study are different in connotation from the Anglo-Saxon concepts. They are (a) Droit fiscal d'entrée or the Entry Tax, levied for revenue purposes on nearly all goods from foreign countries; (b) Taxe forfaitaire or the Standard Tax which is a type of transaction tax based on custom duties and fiscal entry tax.

[3] See Establishment Conventions.

[4] See Reports on national tax systems in World Tax Series, Harvard Law School, especially Brazil, Mexico, and India, 1957 and 1960. Also see E.C.O.S.O.C. resolution, 1951, on the need of system information on taxation.

beneficiary is also provided in some countries. In general, all tax benefits are granted after an enterprise has acquired a certificate of exemption or approval from a recognized government agency.

104. In the majority of countries influenced by the French legal system, the investment codes have established more than two regimes. The first general classification is between ordinary law and beneficiary enterprises.

105. These regimes in several cases are further sub-divided according to the importance of industries or of markets. Regime A in the countries of ex-Equatorial Africa applies to markets within the country;[1] regime B applies to countries within the Customs Union; and regime C is concerned with all markets.[2]

(i) *Exemption from taxes on income and profits*

106. The most prevalent tax exemption applies to income and profits for a minimum period of five years, a period which is widely regarded as reasonable for installing an industry and for beginning operations.

107. Although five year exemption is a usual practice in most of the countries of Africa, there are some exceptions.

108. In Ghana, this period is extended from five to ten years 'beginning from the date of production from the payment of Income Tax'.[3] Mauritania awards complete or partial tax exemption for a maximum of ten years to industries which are deemed particularly 'useful' for economic and social development.

109. In Senegal, the period of exemption on industrial and commercial profits is extended to eight years (outside the Cap-Vert area). The main condition for this exemption is that a new enterprise does not 'exercise harmful competitive pressure on the States which are signatory to a customs convention'.[4] The maximum period of tax exemption on profits granted to new industries is from five to sixteen and a half years in Liberia.

---

[1] Cameroun has four regimes: A, B, C, and D. All of these apply to enterprises according to the degree of their importance to economic development and the related type of economic benefits awarded.

[2] Discussed under *Establishment Conventions*.

[3] After this period of exemption the Investment Act of Ghana further provides that 'capital allowance' shall also be granted in respect of building, plant, machinery, structures, roads, furnitures, fixtures for the purpose of an approved project.

[4] Senegal is a member of the West African Customs Union which *inter alia* co-ordinates the tariff rates and customs regulations of member countries. Other members of the Union are Dahomey, Mali, Ivory Coast, Mauritania, Niger, and Upper Volta. The regulations for exemptions and tax relief can become effective only upon decision rendered by the Customs Union Committee.

110. Sudan tax legislation relates exemption on profits to a fixed percentage and not to a fixed period. According to the Business Profit Tax Ordinance, profits up to five per cent are exempt, but those in excess are taxed at half rates.

111. In Togo and Ethiopia, the period of tax exemption is related to the amount of investment. In Togo, if the amount of investment is from 20 to 500 million CFA the period of exemption is 15 years; from 500 to 1,500 million it is 20 years and above 1,500 million this duration goes up to 25 years. An investment of Eth. $200,000 is entitled to a normal period of five years exemption in Ethiopia, but if the amount is doubled, the tax exemption is reduced to three years.

112. In countries which have adopted the French system of separate fiscal regimes, both Chad and Congo (Brazzaville) exempt new enterprises on commercial and industrial profits for a period ranging from 10 to 15 years. In Gabon, permanent and temporary exemptions from tax are granted under the General Tax Code. Tax reduction of 50 per cent is also given for 'new' industrial, mining, agricultural or lumbering enterprises on profits from the second year of their establishment (may continue for the next three years). Niger grants under its Investment Code exemption from taxes on industrial and commercial income during ten years of the establishment of an industry.

113. Very few codes contain special provisions on reinvestments. Somalia's Law on Foreign Investments makes a special provision for reinvestment. Reinvested profits as capital are exempted from income tax up to five per cent. In Togo, failure to reinvest up to 10 per cent, increases liability to pay taxes up to 50 per cent.

(ii) Customs exonerations

114. As a general policy, the governments have undertaken to establish nil or low rates of duty for indispensable imports of machinery, equipment, raw materials, containers and packaging materials required for national industries.

115. In Algeria approved industries can get total or partial refund for taxes on the imported machinery and equipment. Congo (Brazzaville) has special customs legislation according to which import duties are reduced on equipment and machinery. This legislation also exempts from import duties certain raw materials which enter into the composition of finished or processed goods.

116. In Morocco, exemption from customs duty is granted if the enterprise has contributed to 'new exploitation of resources or expansion of an

existing industrial activity'. The imported material is entitled to customs benefits if it is a part of an investment programme.

117. In Tunisia and the United Arab Republic, customs exonerations apply only to certain products which are considered important for industrial development. There is a system entitled 'Admission temporaire' which permits the entry of certain industrial equipment and raw materials for a limited period in Tunisia. The United Arab Republic, under its new tariff structure,[1] allows machinery, equipment and raw materials for development, absolute exemption or a very reduced tariff of some two per cent.

118. Togo has retained its tax structure from Trusteeship status. Its customs legislation exempts mainly industrial goods from duties ranging from five to ten per cent.[2] In Libya, the criteria for customs exoneration is that essential materials and spare parts used in the industry 'are not to be found locally'. If this requirement is satisfied, 'new' enterprises are entitled to five years' exemption from all import duties.

119. Guinea has not specified any fixed rate in its Code, but has inserted a general principle that the reduction in tariff will depend on the nature of the enterprise. In Ivory Coast, all 'development material is exempted from custom duties up to ten years'.

120. The four equatorial states: Central African Republic, Chad, Congo (Brazzaville) and Gabon[3] grant reduced rates of import duty, under regime B, automatically on entry.

(iii) Export duties

121. Very few investment laws have special provisions relating to export duties. The Investment Act of Ghana grants exemption from taxes on export up to one hundred per cent on goods manufactured by approved projects. In Niger, reduction up to fifty per cent is given for export duties and connected taxes. In countries of the Equatorial Customs Union 'new' and 'established' enterprises are guaranteed preferential export duties. In addition, the markets of the Government and the armed forces are also reserved for them on a priority basis.

(iv) Long-term fiscal regimes

122. Most of the investment codes of ex-French colonies, as indicated above, have created special fiscal regimes of ordinary law and beneficiary

[1] Established in January 1962. For details see Part II.

[2] In addition, a few selected goods are exempted from import duties up to 40 per cent.

[3] Cameroun is an associate member of the 'Union douanière'.

enterprises. Mali, Guinea and Upper Volta are exceptions to this rule.[1] These three countries have enacted Investment Codes specially for priority enterprises.

123. The majority of the countries mentioned above including Cameroun, Dahomey, Gabon, Niger, Chad, Congo (Brazzaville) have established long-term fiscal regimes. In most of these cases the beneficiary enterprises are entitled to enter an establishment convention with the government. The main characteristic of the long-term fiscal regime is its importance to large industrial and mineral projects. In the main, the long-term regime grants stability of taxes to new enterprises for a stipulated period. This means that no new taxes can be levied during this period. Regime C is usually reserved for enterprises of 'economic importance' in the countries mentioned above. The period of stability varies from country to country, but the average ranged from 20 to 25 years. In Niger the minimum period of stability is ten years, while in Central African Republic it goes up to fifty.

(v) *Establishment conventions*

124. Companies involving large investments, which are entitled to long-term fiscal arrangements can sign a special contract with the governments according to the conditions provided in the investment laws. With slight variations, the same rules apply in Algeria, Cameroun, Dahomey, Gabon, Guinea, Ivory Coast, Madagascar and Niger. Already, certain large companies[2] are operating under this system.

125. Some of the conditions of entering into an agreement defining the obligations of the State and the enterprise are specified below.

126. Certain guarantees on the period of stability are given by the State. These assume unaltered continuation of certain legal, economic and financial conditions, particularly as regards to transfer of funds and non-discrimination with respect to legislation. The stability of the marketing of products, entry and freedom of movement of workers and employment, freedom in selecting suppliers, preference in obtaining supplies of raw materials and allocation of foreign exchange are often among the terms of contract. There is usually a clause precluding the State from any responsibility for losses, expenses and failure to make profits due to development of new techniques or any other development beyond its control.

---

[1] It may be noted that Upper Volta is a member of the West African Customs Union and Conseil de l'entente. It also has a special agreement regarding free trade zone with Ghana. Upper Volta is also an associate member of the European Community.

[2] For example, M.I.F.E.R.M.A. in Mauritania, F.R.I.A. in Guinea, Uranium de Franceville in Gabon.

127. A typical example may be taken from the Central African Republic.[1] The draft of this Convention is prepared by the mutual consent of the two parties and the Minister interested in the project. It is then submitted to the opinion of the Investment Commission. Finally the Council of Ministers issued a decree.

128. In English law, the procedure is slightly different. An example can be taken from the agreement of Volta Aluminium Company Ltd. The master agreement sets out the respective rights and obligations of the Company for a period ending thirty years following the commencement of the smelter operations. A special act entitled Volta River Development was passed to enable the Government to offer guarantees outside the ordinary law of contracts. As a result of the stabilized tax regime accorded to VALCO, a number of exemptive orders became necessary and these included a resolution by Parliament under the Customs Law, Minerals Duty Ordinance, Purchase Tax Act, Compulsory Saving Act, and Income Tax Ordinance.[2]

129. The legal character of these agreements is not very clear. Because of the fact that they often involve the State, they are not, strictly speaking, contracts of private law. The question whether violation of any clause gives rise to legal responsibility on the part of the State is not settled by law. The main reason is that when case law on this subject evolved, legal, political and economic conditions were very different. At the turn of the century, the questions of national control over national resources or nationalization of foreign property were rare.

(f) Arbitration

130. Arbitration signifies a process for the settlement of disputes based on the consent of the parties.[3] Not all the investment laws have provided for arbitration. Out of a total of twenty-six investment laws in Africa, twelve have specific provisions concerning arbitration. In Ivory Coast, Liberia, Libya, Sudan, Togo, Tunisia and the United Arab Republic, there are no special provisions on arbitration. In case of dispute, either

---

[1] There are several other examples in 'les codes d'investissement' by J. Loyrette in *Penant*, April–May 1963.

[2] E. A. K. Akuoko, *Impact of Legislation, Taxation Subsidies and Tariffs on the Volta River Project Negotiations*. Paper presented to United Nations Conference in the Application of Science and Technology for the Benefit of the Less Developed Areas, E/CONF. 3910/8, 26 September 1962.

[3] Arbitration is to be contrasted with conciliation or mediation in which the role of the third party is to persuade the parties in a dispute to accept a settlement rather than impose upon them a binding decision.

the parties resort to ordinary law or depend upon any remedies provided in the terms of contract.

131. Most of the codes, especially from ex-French colonies, contain procedures for the appointment of arbitrators. The general practice is that one arbitrator is appointed by each of the parties to the dispute. The third, according to the majority of Codes, is appointed by the consent of the two parties.

132. In the event that this consent is not forthcoming, as it happens quite often, the code or law indicates the procedure of choosing the third arbitrator. It is in the choice of the third member of the team of arbitrators that the laws of several countries show differences.

133. According to the Investment Code of Chad, the third arbitrator is appointed by the International Court of Justice. In Dahomey, this right is given to a highly qualified authority designated by the agreement or selected from the judiciary of the country of the investor. Niger recommends that the third arbitrator should be the Vice-President of the National Court, while Somalia designates the President of its Court of Justice. According to Upper Volta, the third arbitrator ought to be 'highly qualified', and must be named in the contract of investment.

134. The Code of Mauritania states that the settlement of disputes resulting from implementation of a commercial agreement may become subject to an international tribunal 'the terms of which will be set forth in the agreement'. But failure to meet the obligation stipulated under government licence can be submitted upon initial judgement by a Mauritanian tribunal to arbitration, which bars further proceedings.

135. In only two cases the law gives the parties the right to determine their own procedure in the contract. The Investment Code of Guinea stipulates that disputes arising over the validity, interpretation or application of the clauses of conventions of establishment of approved enterprises 'shall in each particular case be the subject of arbitration proceedings, the details of which shall be determined by agreement between the parties'. The Investment Code of the Central African Republic, while giving the right of settling the procedure to the parties, adds that the procedure must contain, *inter alia*, the method of appointment of the two arbitrators designated. The third arbitrator, in default of consent of the parties, is to be 'a highly qualified' person who should also be named in the convention.

136. In all the cases mentioned above, except in Chad, the parties to the dispute choose the panel of arbitrators. In Chad, the third arbitrator is

chosen by outside judicial agency such as the International Court of Justice. The new Investment Act in Ghana has introduced a new element. Rather than appoint national arbitrators or call in a judicial agency to appoint them, it stipulates that 'in case of dispute on the amount of compensation' in the event of nationalization, the matter shall be referred to an arbitrator appointed by the parties, and failing such appointment, to arbitration through the agency of the International Bank for Reconstruction and Development. In almost all cases the majority decision is binding.[1]

137. The existence of an arbitration clause signifies that the commercial agreement between the government and the enterprise is respected and will produce impartial results in case of controversies. Furthermore, the effect of an arbitration clause is that it leads to the development of settled practice. There may emerge gradually certain customs and principles which lend certainty to transactions. In the case of a foreign investor, an arbitration clause will entitle him to seek the intervention of his Government on the ground of denial of justice.

D. Direction of Legal Change

138. At any given moment in the process of defining economic policy or formulating a development plan, existing legislation has to be taken into account. The existing legislation may represent, as it does in several cases in Africa, survival of outmoded ideas on law and economics: some constitutional provisions protecting private property, some tax laws giving exclusive rights to produce, import or transport anything, some legislation affecting foreign exchange usually reflecting past political content. Whatever the merit of these rules and laws, at the time, they can hardly be expected to form an adequate legal basis for economic development in the years to come.

139. To implement a clearly defined development policy, it is necessary to spell out the detailed legislative needs in correspondence with the economic objectives. Present investment laws in Africa suffer from the same general weaknesses as the current development plans. The general requirement for both is a coherent strategy of development. The actual formulation of an investment programme envisages equally an outline of a clear legal strategy.

140. Although some of the ex-French territories have attempted in their codes to define and clarify their policy, there is still considerable room for

---

[1] In some cases there is a right to appeal to the National Court.

a better co-ordination between the development plan and investment law. These two are usually formulated by different ministries. It would not be untrue to state that the left hand often does not know what the right hand is doing. The countries under English influence suffer from nearly complete lack of cohesion on the legal level. Except in the case of Ghana, there is no country where it is easy to discover what the Investment Laws are. Even working through an assortment of regulations dealing with imports, customs, foreign exchange, taxation, etc., may not suffice to form a clear image. It may be suggested that in this age of the written word, investment laws need to be expressed in one easily accessible and understandable legal instrument. There is an urgent need, therefore, for African countries, acting at a continental or at a sub-regional level, to get together to co-ordinate their legal practices, procedures and provisions concerning the issue discussed below.

(a) One of the most important areas of investment law concerns approved or priority industries. The need for defining concrete areas of investment is extremely important so that in the mind of a potential investor there is no room for vagueness or misunderstanding. Once the areas of investments are clear-cut, the exact mechanism through which they would be channelled acquires considerable significance.

(b) The already existing investment commissions, development corporations, and other government agencies could be strengthened, administratively and structurally, to achieve the desired result. These agencies can then help adequately, in the formulation and implementation of the development plans. Their composition is important from the point of view of policy-making. If it is assumed that development involves the entire society, then it necessarily follows that decision-making should involve technical experts from all related fields. Some of the codes under study have already a nucleus for this type of development agencies.

(c) There exist abundant literature and controversy on the question of creating adequate climate for foreign investments. Yet neither in capital-exporting nor in capital-importing countries, is there clarity on the precise needs of the investor and the recipient. Investment laws can perhaps incorporate special and separate provisions defining the rights and obligations of a foreign investor. Local participation, treatment of foreign exchange, transfer of profits, tax benefits and, in general, the security of investments could all be defined point by point. Here again the countries influenced by English legal system need considerable consolidation of their legal provisions. It is customary in English law to leave questions of nationalization to conventions rather than written legal provisions. This tendency is still reflected in the investment laws of many countries in Africa. Concerning the question of repatriation of capital and profits, there appears to be no concrete policy on the part of the African Governments. There is often a tendency to use this as an economic inducement without having full regard of its future impact on the balance of payments situation of the capital-importing countries. Strict provisions regarding reinvestment of accrued earnings are, as a result, extremely rare in Africa. A positive tendency is visible in the African laws concerning a clause on employment of national labour. Several criteria have been used, regarding the amount of remuneration, type of jobs or number of employees. But there is great scope for incorporating in the laws a bolder programme of insisting on the training of nationals.

(d) The most complex and perhaps the most important subject relates to various types of economic incentives offered to the investors. It appears that tax laws, except for exemptions on import duties on certain products, so far have little relation to needs of future economic development. They have been generally drafted to obtain positive revenues without giving serious considerations to their economic effects. 'Tax holiday' and other concessions often tend to create a spirit of deliberate competitiveness on the part of capital-importing countries in Africa. There is thus a need to harmonize tax policies with a view to channel investments in selected areas and obtain revenues for defined public purposes. Fiscal policy in a developing country can be a much more effective tool in the hands of the State than it has been so far in Africa.[1]

(e) There are today as many tax laws as countries in Africa.[2] Perhaps there is a basis for the suggestion that fiscal incentives for industrial development could be unified so as to avoid harmful effects of a haphazard system of customs duties and taxation.[3]

141. The procedure of settling disputes needs to be regulated in a manner which creates confidence in the mind of the investor and yet does not infringe the long-term national interest. There are already countries who

---

[1] United Nations, *Financing of Economic Development* (Third Report), E/3665, 28 June 1962.
[2] With the exception of a few States who belong to the West African Customs Union and Equatorial Customs Union.
[3] E.C.L.A., Studies on Central America (CCE/GIF/1/D.T.I and E/CN. 12/CCE/110).

have provided an arbitration clause. There is always a difficulty in choosing the third arbitrator, thus creating the need in case of failure, to turn to some judicial agency. An African court of arbitration, along the lines of the Permanent Court of Arbitration created by the Hague Convention of 1899, could be established to give impartial awards.[1] It should also be possible for African countries to get together to draft an all-African convention on commercial arbitration, as has already been done in Europe.[2]

[1] Later followed by various treaties on compulsory arbitrations, e.g. The General Treaty of Inter-American Arbitration 1929.

[2] E.C.E., *Final Act and European Convention on International Commercial Arbitration*, 21 April 1961, Geneva.

III. AFRICAN DEVELOPMENT BANK

THE text below appears in *United Nations Treaty Series*, vol. 510, p. 46. The agreement entered into force on 10 September 1964, upon the deposit of instruments of ratification by the governments of twenty signatory states, whose initial subscriptions (Annex A, below) together constitute not less than 65 per cent of the authorized capital stock of the bank. The following states have ratified the agreement: Algeria, Burundi, Cameroon, Congo (Brazzaville), Congo (Kinshasa), Dahomey, Ethiopia, Ghana, Guinea, Ivory Coast, Kenya, Liberia, Malawi, Mali, Mauritania, Morocco, Niger, Nigeria, Rwanda, Senegal, Sierra Leone, Somalia, Sudan, Tanganyika, Togo, Tunisia, Uganda, United Arab Republic, Upper Volta and Zambia.

AGREEMENT ESTABLISHING THE AFRICAN DEVELOPMENT BANK. DONE AT KHARTOUM, ON 4 AUGUST 1963

The Governments on whose behalf this Agreement is signed,

Determined to strengthen African solidarity by means of economic co-operation between African States,

Considering the necessity of accelerating the development of the extensive human and natural resources of Africa in order to stimulate economic development and social progress in that region,

Realizing the importance of co-ordinating national plans of economic and social development for the promotion of the harmonious growth of African economies as a whole and the expansion of African foreign trade and, in particular, inter-African trade,

Recognizing that the establishment of a financial institution common to all African countries would serve these ends,

Have agreed to establish hereby the African Development Bank (hereinafter called the 'Bank') which shall be governed by the following provisions:

CHAPTER I. PURPOSE, FUNCTIONS, MEMBERSHIP AND STRUCTURE

Article 1

Purpose

The purpose of the Bank shall be to contribute to the economic development and social progress of its members—individually and jointly.

Article 2

Functions

(1) To implement its purpose, the Bank shall have the following functions:

(*a*) To use the resources at its disposal for the financing of investment projects and programmes relating to the economic and social development of its members, giving special priority to:

(i) Projects or programmes which by their nature or scope concern several members; and

(ii) Projects or programmes designed to make the economies of its members increasingly complementary and to bring about an orderly expansion of their foreign trade;

(*b*) To undertake, or participate in, the selection, study and preparation of projects, enterprises and activities contributing to such development;

(*c*) To mobilize and increase in Africa, and outside Africa, resources for the financing of such investment projects and programmes;

(*d*) Generally, to promote investment in Africa of public and private capital in projects or programmes designed to contribute to the economic development or social progress of its members;

(*e*) To provide such technical assistance as may be needed in Africa for the study, preparation, financing and execution of development projects or programmes; and

(*f*) To undertake such other activities and provide such other services as may advance its purpose.

(2) In carrying out its functions, the Bank shall seek to co-operate with national, regional and sub-regional development institutions in Africa. To the same end, it should co-operate with other international organizations pursuing a similar purpose and with other institutions concerned with the development of Africa.

(3) The Bank shall be guided in all its decisions by the provisions of Articles 1 and 2 of this Agreement.

Article 3

Membership and geographical area

(1) Any African country which has the status of an independent State may become a member of the Bank. It shall acquire membership in accordance with paragraph (1) or paragraph (2) of Article 64 of this Agreement.

(2) The geographical area to which the membership and development activities of the Bank may extend (referred to in this Agreement as

'Africa' or 'African', as the case may be) shall comprise the continent of Africa and African islands.

Article 4

Structure

The Bank shall have a Board of Governors, a Board of Directors, a President, at least one Vice-President and such other officers and staff to perform such duties as the Bank may determine.

CHAPTER II. CAPITAL

Article 5

Authorized capital

(1) (*a*) The authorized capital stock of the Bank shall be 250,000,000 units of account. It shall be divided into 25,000 shares of a par value of 10,000 units of account each share, which shall be available for subscription by members.

(*b*) The value of the unit of account shall be 0·88867088 gramme of fine gold.

(2) The authorized capital stock shall be divided into paid-up shares and callable shares. The equivalent of 125,000,000 units of account shall be paid up, and the equivalent of 125,000,000 units of account shall be callable for the purpose defined in paragraph (4) (*a*) of Article 7 of this Agreement.

(3) The authorized capital stock may be increased as and when the Board of Governors deems it advisable. Unless that stock is increased solely to provide for the initial subscription of a member, the decision of the Board shall be adopted by a two-thirds majority of the total number of Governors, representing not less than three-quarters of the total voting power of the members.

Article 6

Subscription of shares

(1) Each member shall initially subscribe shares of the capital stock of the Bank. The initial subscription of each member shall consist of an equal number of paid-up and callable shares. The initial number of shares to be subscribed by a State which acquires membership in accordance with paragraph (1) of Article 64 of this Agreement shall be that set forth in its respect in Annex A to this Agreement, which shall form an integral part thereof. The initial number of shares to be subscribed by other members shall be determined by the Board of Governors.

(2) In the event of an increase of the capital stock for a purpose other than solely to provide for an initial subscription of a member, each member shall have the right to subscribe, on such uniform terms and conditions as the Board of Governors shall determine, a proportion of the increase of stock equivalent to the proportion which its stock theretofore subscribed bears to the total capital stock of the Bank. No member, however, shall be obligated to subscribe to any part of such increased stock.

(3) A member may request the Bank to increase its subscription on such terms and conditions as the Board of Governors may determine.

(4) Shares of stock initially subscribed by States which acquire membership in accordance with paragraph (1) of Article 64 of this Agreement shall be issued at par. Other shares shall be issued at par unless the Board of Governors by a majority of the total voting power of the members decides in special circumstances to issue them on other terms.

(5) Liability on shares shall be limited to the unpaid portion of their issue price.

(6) Shares shall not be pledged nor encumbered in any manner. They shall be transferable only to the Bank.

Article 7
Payment of subscription

(1) (a) Payment of the amount initially subscribed to the paid-up capital stock of the Bank by a member which acquires membership in accordance with paragraph (1) of Article 64 shall be made in six instalments, the first of which shall be five per cent, the second thirty-five per cent, and the remaining four instalments each fifteen per cent of that amount.

(b) The first instalment shall be paid by the Government concerned on or before the date of deposit, on its behalf, of the instrument of ratification or acceptance of this Agreement in accordance with paragraph (1) of Article 64. The second instalment shall become due on the last day of a period of six months from the entry into force of this Agreement or on the day of the said deposit, whichever is the later day. The third instalment shall become due on the last day of a period of eighteen months from the entry into force of this Agreement. The remaining three instalments shall become due successively each on the last day of a period of one year immediately following the day on which the preceding instalment becomes due.

(2) Payments of the amounts initially subscribed by the members of the Bank to the paid-up capital stock shall be made in gold or convertible

currency. The Board of Governors shall determine the mode of payment of other amounts subscribed by the members to the paid-up capital stock.

(3) The Board of Governors shall determine the dates for the payment of amounts subscribed by the members of the Bank to the paid-up capital stock to which the provisions of paragraph (1) of this Article do not apply.

(4) (*a*) Payment of the amounts subscribed to the callable capital stock of the Bank shall be subject to call only as and when required by the Bank to meet its obligations incurred, pursuant to paragraph (1) (*b*) and (*d*) of Article 14, on borrowing of funds for inclusion in its ordinary capital resources or guarantees chargeable to such resources.

(*b*) In the event of such calls, payment may be made at the option of the member concerned in gold, convertible currency or in the currency required to discharge the obligation of the Bank for the purpose of which the call is made.

(*c*) Calls on unpaid subscriptions shall be uniform in percentage on all callable shares.

(5) The Bank shall determine the place for any payment under this Article provided that, until the first meeting of its Board of Governors provided in Article 66 of this Agreement, the payment of the first instalment referred to in paragraph (1) of this Article shall be made to the Trustee referred to in Article 66.

Article 8

Special Funds

(1) The Bank may establish, or be entrusted with the administration of, Special Funds which are designed to serve its purpose and come within its functions. It may receive, hold, use, commit or otherwise dispose of resources appertaining to such Special Funds.

(2) The resources of such Special Funds shall be kept separate and apart from the ordinary capital resources of the Bank in accordance with the provisions of Article 11 of this Agreement.

(3) The Bank shall adopt such special rules and regulations as may be required for the administration and use of each Special Fund, provided always that:

(*a*) Such special rules and regulations shall be subject to paragraph (4) of Article 7, Articles 9 to 11, and those provisions of this Agreement which expressly apply to the ordinary capital resources or ordinary operations of the Bank;

(b) Such special rules and regulations must be consistent with provisions of this Agreement which expressly apply to special resources or special operations of the Bank; and that

(c) Where such special rules and regulations do not apply, the Special Funds shall be governed by the provisions of this Agreement.

Article 9

Ordinary capital resources

For the purposes of this Agreement, the expression 'ordinary capital resources' of the Bank shall include:

(a) Authorized capital stock of the Bank subscribed pursuant to the provisions of Article 6 of this Agreement;

(b) Funds raised by borrowing of the Bank, by virtue of powers conferred in paragraph (a) of Article 23 of this Agreement, to which the commitment to calls provided for in paragraph (4) of Article 7 of this Agreement applies;

(c) Funds received in repayment of loans made with the resources referred to in paragraphs (a) and (b) of this article; and

(d) Income derived from loans made from the aforementioned funds; income from guarantees to which the commitment to calls provided for in paragraph (4) of Article 7 of this Agreement applies; as well as

(e) Any other funds or income received by the Bank which do not form part of its special resources.

Article 10

Special resources

(1) For the purposes of this Agreement, the expression 'special resources' shall refer to the resources of Special Funds and shall include:

(a) Resources initially contributed to any Special Fund;

(b) Funds borrowed for the purposes of any Special Fund, including the Special Fund provided for in paragraph (6) of Article 24 of this Agreement;

(c) Funds repaid in respect of loans or guarantees financed from the resources of any Special Fund which, under the rules and regulations governing that Special Fund, are received by that Special Fund;

(d) Income derived from operations of the Bank by which any of the aforementioned resources or funds are used or committed if, under the rules and regulations governing the Special Fund concerned, that income accrues to the said Special Fund; and

(e) Any other resources at the disposal of any Special Fund.

(2) For the purposes of this Agreement, the expression 'special resources appertaining to a Special Fund' shall include the resources, funds and income which are referred to in the preceding paragraph and are—as the case may be—contributed to, borrowed or received by, accruing to, or at the disposal of the Special Fund concerned in conformity with the rules and regulations governing that Special Fund.

Article 11

Separation of resources

(1) The ordinary capital resources of the Bank shall at all times and in all respects be held, used, committed, invested or otherwise disposed of, entirely separate from special resources. Each Special Fund, its resources and accounts shall be kept entirely separate from other Special Funds, their resources and accounts.

(2) The ordinary capital resources of the Bank shall under no circumstances be charged with, or used to discharge, losses or liabilities arising out of operations or other activities of any Special Fund. Special resources appertaining to any Special Fund shall under no circumstances be charged with, or used to discharge, losses or liabilities arising out of operations or other activities of the Bank financed from its ordinary capital resources or from special resources appertaining to any other Special Fund.

(3) In the operations and other activities of any Special Fund, the liability of the Bank shall be limited to the special resources appertaining to that Special Fund which are at the disposal of the Bank.

CHAPTER III. OPERATIONS

Article 12

Use of resources

The resources and facilities of the Bank shall be used exclusively to implement the purpose and functions set forth in Articles 1 and 2 of this Agreement.

Article 13

Ordinary and special operations

(1) The operations of the Bank shall consist of ordinary operations and of special operations.

(2) The ordinary operations shall be those financed from the ordinary capital resources of the Bank.

(3) The special operations shall be those financed from the special resources.

(4) The financial statements of the Bank shall show the ordinary operations and the special operations of the Bank separately. The Bank shall adopt such other rules and regulations as may be required to ensure the effective separation of the two types of its operations.

(5) Expenses appertaining directly to ordinary operations shall be charged to the ordinary capital resources of the Bank; expenses appertaining directly to special operations shall be charged to the appropriate special resources. Other expenses shall be charged as the Bank shall determine.

Article 14

Recipients and methods of operations

(1) In its operations, the Bank may provide or facilitate financing for any member, political sub-division or any agency thereof or for any institution or undertaking in the territory of any member as well as for international or regional agencies or institutions concerned with the development of Africa. Subject to the provisions of this chapter, the Bank may carry out its operations in any of the following ways:

(a) By making or participating in direct loans out of:

(i) Funds corresponding to its unimpaired subscribed paid-up capital and, except as provided in Article 20 of this Agreement, to its reserves and undistributed surplus; or out of

(ii) Funds corresponding to special resources; or

(b) By making or participating in direct loans out of funds borrowed or otherwise acquired by the Bank for inclusion in its ordinary capital resources or in special resources; or

(c) By investment of funds referred to in sub-paragraph (a) or (b) of this paragraph in the equity capital of an undertaking or institution; or

(d) By guaranteeing, in whole or in part, loans made by others.

(2) The provisions of this Agreement applying to direct loans which the Bank may make pursuant to sub-paragraph (a) or (b) of the preceding paragraph shall also apply to its participation in any direct loan undertaken pursuant to any of those sub-paragraphs. Equally, the provisions of this Agreement applying to guarantees of loans undertaken by the Bank pursuant to sub-paragraph (d) of the preceding paragraph shall apply where the Bank guarantees part of such a loan only.

Article 15

Limitations on operations

(1) The total amount outstanding in respect of the ordinary operations of the Bank shall not at any time exceed the total amount of its unimpaired

subscribed capital, reserves and surplus included in its ordinary capital resources excepting, however, the special reserve provided for in Article 20 of this Agreement.

(2) The total amount outstanding in respect of the special operations of the Bank relating to any Special Fund shall not at any time exceed the total amount of the unimpaired special resources appertaining to that Special Fund.

(3) In the case of loans made out of funds borrowed by the Bank to which the commitment to calls provided for in paragraph (4) (*a*) of Article 7 of this Agreement applies, the total amount of principal outstanding and payable to the Bank in a specific currency shall not at any time exceed the total amount of principal outstanding in respect of funds borrowed by the Bank that are payable in the same currency.

(4) (*a*) In the case of investments made by virtue of paragraph (1) (*c*) of Article 14 of this Agreement out of the ordinary capital resources of the Bank, the total amount outstanding shall not at any time exceed ten per cent of the aggregate amount of the paid-up capital stock of the Bank together with the reserves and surplus included in its ordinary capital resources excepting, however, the special reserve provided for in Article 20 of this Agreement.

(*b*) At the time it is made, the amount of any specific investment referred to in the preceding sub-paragraph shall not exceed a percentage of equity capital of the institution or undertaking concerned, which the Board of Governors shall have fixed for any investment to be made by virtue of paragraph (1) (*c*) of Article 14 of this Agreement. In no event shall the Bank seek to obtain by such an investment a controlling interest in the institution or undertaking concerned.

Article 16

Provision of currencies for direct loans

In making direct loans, the Bank shall furnish the borrower with currencies other than the currency of the member in whose territory the project concerned is to be carried out (the latter currency hereinafter to be called 'local currency'), which are required to meet foreign exchange expenditure on that project; provided always that the Bank may, in making direct loans, provide financing to meet local expenditure on the project concerned:

(*a*) Where it can do so by supplying local currency without selling any of its holdings in gold or convertible currencies; or (*b*) Where in the opinion of the Bank local expenditure on that project is likely to cause undue loss or strain on the balance of payments of the country where that project is to be carried out and the amount of such financing by the Bank does not exceed a reasonable portion of the total local expenditure incurred on that project.

Article 17

Operational principles

(1) The operations of the Bank shall be conducted in accordance with the following principles:

(*a*) (i) The operations of the Bank shall, except in special circumstances provide for the financing of specific projects, or groups of projects, particularly those forming part of a national or regional development programme urgently required for the economic or social development of its members. They may, however, include global loans to, or guarantees of loans made to, African national development banks or other suitable institutions, in order that the latter may finance projects of a specified type serving the purpose of the Bank within the respective fields of activities of such banks or institutions;

(ii) In selecting suitable projects, the Bank shall always be guided by the provisions of paragraph (1) (*a*) of Article 2 of this Agreement and by the potential contribution of the project concerned to the purpose of the Bank rather than by the type of the project. It shall, however, pay special attention to the selection of suitable multi-national projects;

(*b*) The Bank shall not provide for the financing of a project in the territory of a member if that member objects thereto;

(*c*) The Bank shall not provide for the financing of a project to the extent that in its opinion the recipient may obtain the finance or facilities elsewhere on terms that the Bank considers are reasonable for the recipient;

(*d*) Subject to the provisions of Articles 16 and 24 of this Agreement, the Bank shall not impose conditions enjoining that the proceeds of any financing undertaken pursuant to its ordinary operations shall be spent in the territory of any particular country nor that such proceeds shall not be spent in the territory of any particular country;

(*e*) In making or guaranteeing a loan, the Bank shall pay due regard to the prospects that the borrower and the guarantor, if any, will be in a position to meet their obligations under the loan;

(*f*) In making or guaranteeing a loan, the Bank shall be satisfied that the rate of interest and other charges are reasonable and such rate, charges and the schedule for the repayment of principal are appropriate for the project concerned;

(*g*) In the case of a direct loan made by the bank, the borrower shall be permitted by the Bank to draw its funds only to meet expenditure in connection with the project as it is actually incurred;

(*h*) The Bank shall make arrangements to ensure that the proceeds of any loan made or guaranteed by it are used only for the purposes for which the loan was granted, with due attention to considerations of economy and efficiency;

(*i*) The Bank shall seek to maintain a reasonable diversification in its investments in equity capital;

(*j*) The Bank shall apply sound banking principles to its operations and, in particular, to its investments in equity capital. It shall not assume responsibility for managing any institution or undertaking in which it has an investment; and

(*k*) In guaranteeing a loan made by other investors, the Bank shall receive suitable compensation for its risk.

(2) The Bank shall adopt such rules and regulations as are required for the consideration of projects submitted to it.

Article 18

Terms and conditions for direct loans and guarantees

(1) In the case of direct loans made by the Bank, the contract:

(*a*) Shall establish, in conformity with the operational principles set forth in paragraph (1) of Article 17 of this Agreement and subject to the other provisions of this chapter, all the terms and conditions for the loan concerned, including those relating to amortization, interest and other charges, and to maturities and dates of payment; and, in particular,

(*b*) Shall provide that—subject to paragraph (3) (*c*) of this Article— payments to the Bank of amortization, interest, commission and other charges shall be made in the currency loaned, unless—in the case of a direct loan made as part of special operations—the rules and regulations provide otherwise.

(2) In the case of loans guaranteed by the Bank, the contract of guarantee:

(*a*) Shall establish in conformity with the operational principles set forth in paragraph (1) of Article 17 of this Agreement and subject to the other provisions of this chapter, all the terms and conditions of the guarantee concerned including those relating to the fees, commission, and other charges of the Bank; and, in particular,

(*b*) Shall provide that—subject to paragraph (3) (*c*) of this Article—all payments to the Bank under the guarantee contract shall be made in the currency loaned, unless—in the case of a loan guaranteed as part of special operations—the rules and regulations provide otherwise; and

(c) Shall also provide that the Bank may terminate its liability with respect to interest if, upon default by the borrower and the guarantor, if any, the Bank offers to purchase, at par and interest accrued to a date designated in the offer, the bonds or other obligations guaranteed.

(3) In the case of direct loans made or loans guaranteed by the Bank, the Bank:

(a) In determining the terms and conditions for the operation, shall take due account of the terms and conditions on which the corresponding funds were obtained by the Bank;

(b) Where the recipient is not a member, may, when it deems it advisable, require that the member in whose territory the project concerned is to be carried out, or a public agency or institution of that member acceptable to the Bank, guarantee the repayment of the principal and the payment of interest and other charges on the loan;

(c) Shall expressly state the currency in which all payments to the Bank under the contract concerned shall be made. At the option of the borrower, however, such payments may always be made in gold or convertible currency or, subject to the agreement of the Bank, in any other currency; and

(d) May attach such other terms or conditions, as it deems appropriate, taking into account both the interest of the member directly concerned in the project and the interests of the members as a whole.

Article 19
Commission and fees

(1) The Bank shall charge a commission on direct loans made and guarantees given as part of its ordinary operations. This commission, payable periodically, shall be computed on the amount outstanding on each loan or guarantee and shall be at the rate of not less than one per cent per annum, unless the Bank, after the first ten years of its operations, decides to change this minimum rate by a majority of two-thirds of its members representing not less than three-quarters of the total voting power of the members.

(2) In guaranteeing a loan as part of its ordinary operations, the Bank shall charge a guarantee fee, at a rate determined by the Board of Directors, payable periodically on the amount of the loan outstanding.

(3) Other charges of the Bank in its ordinary operations and the commission, fees and other charges in its special operations shall be determined by the Board of Directors.

Article 20
Special reserve

The amount of commissions received by the Bank pursuant to Article 19 of this Agreement shall be set aside as a special reserve which shall be kept for meeting liabilities of the Bank in accordance with its Article 21. The special reserve shall be held in such liquid form, permitted under this Agreement, as the Board of Directors may decide.

Article 21
Methods of meeting liabilities of the Bank (ordinary operations)

(1) Whenever necessary to meet contractual payments of interest, other charges or amortization on the borrowing of the Bank, or to meet its liabilities with respect to similar payments in respect of loans guaranteed by it and chargeable to its ordinary capital resources, the Bank may call an appropriate amount of the unpaid subscribed callable capital in accordance with paragraph (4) of Article 7 of this Agreement.

(2) In cases of default in respect of a loan made out of borrowed funds or guaranteed by the Bank as part of its ordinary operations, the Bank may, if it believes that the default may be of long duration, call an additional amount of such callable capital not to exceed in any one year one per cent of the total subscriptions of the members, for the following purposes:

(*a*) To redeem before maturity, or otherwise discharge, its liability on all or part of the outstanding principal of any loan guaranteed by it in respect of which the debtor is in default; and

(*b*) To repurchase, or otherwise discharge, its liability on all or part of its own outstanding borrowing.

Article 22
Methods of meeting liabilities on borrowings for Special Funds

Payments in satisfaction of any liability in respect of borrowings of funds for inclusion in the special resources appertaining to a Special Fund shall be charged:

(i) First, against any reserve established for this purpose for or within the Special Fund concerned; and

(ii) Then, against any other assets available in the special resources appertaining to that Special Fund.

CHAPTER IV. BORROWING AND OTHER ADDITIONAL POWERS

Article 23

General powers

In addition to the powers provided elsewhere in this Agreement, the Bank shall have power to:

(*a*) Borrow funds in member countries or elsewhere, and in that connection to furnish such collateral or other security as it shall determine provided always that:

    (i) Before making a sale of its obligations in the market of a member, the Bank shall have obtained its approval;

    (ii) Where the obligations of the Bank are to be denominated in the currency of a member, the Bank shall have obtained its approval; and

    (iii) Where the funds to be borrowed are to be included in its ordinary capital resources, the Bank shall have obtained, where appropriate, the approval of the members referred to in sub-paragraphs (i) and (ii) of this paragraph that the proceeds may be exchanged for any other currency without any restrictions;

(*b*) Buy and sell securities the Bank has issued or guaranteed or in which it has invested provided always that it shall have obtained the approval of any member in whose territory the securities are to be bought or sold;

(*c*) Guarantee or underwrite securities in which it has invested in order to facilitate their sale;

(*d*) Invest funds not needed in its operations in such obligations as it may determine and invest funds held by the Bank for pensions or similar purposes in marketable securities;

(*e*) Undertake activities incidental to its operations such as, among others, the promotion of consortia for financing which serves the purpose of the Bank and comes within its functions;

(*f*) (i) Provide all technical advice and assistance which serve its purpose and come within its functions; and

(ii) Where expenditure incurred by such a service is not reimbursed, charge the net income of the Bank therewith and, in the first five years of its operations use up to one per cent of its paid-up capital on such expenditure; provided always that the total expenditure of the Bank on such services in each year of that period does not exceed one-fifth of that percentage; and

(*g*) Exercise such other powers as shall be necessary or desirable in furtherance of its purpose and functions, consistent with the provisions of this Agreement.

Article 24

Special borrowing powers

(1) The Bank may request any member to loan amounts of its currency to the Bank in order to finance expenditure in respect of goods or services produced in the territory of that member for the purpose of a project to be carried out in the territory of another member.

(2) Unless the member concerned invokes economic and financial difficulties which, in its opinion, are likely to be provoked or aggravated by the granting of such a loan to the Bank, that member shall comply with the request of the Bank. The loan shall be made for a period to be agreed with the Bank, which shall be in relation to the duration of the project which the proceeds of that loan are designed to finance.

(3) Unless the member agrees otherwise, the aggregate amount outstanding in respect of its loans made to the Bank pursuant to this Article shall not, at any time, exceed the equivalent of the amount of its subscription to the capital stock of the Bank.

(4) Loans to the Bank made pursuant to this Article shall bear interest, payable by the Bank to the lending member, at a rate which shall correspond to the average rate of interest paid by the Bank on its borrowings for Special Funds during a period of one year preceding the conclusion of the loan agreement. This rate shall in no event exceed a maximum rate which the Board of Governors shall determine from time to time.

(5) The Bank shall repay the loan, and pay the interest due in respect thereof, in the currency of the lending member or in a currency acceptable to the latter.

(6) All resources obtained by the Bank by virtue of the provisions of this Article shall constitute a Special Fund.

Article 25

Warning to be placed on securities

Every security issued or guaranteed by the Bank shall bear on its face a conspicuous statement to the effect that it is not an obligation of any government unless it is in fact the obligation of a particular government in which case it shall so state.

Article 26

Valuation of currencies and determination of convertibility

Whenever it shall become necessary under this Agreement:

(i) To value any currency in terms of another currency, in terms of gold or of the unit of account defined in paragraph (1) (*b*) of Article 5 of this Agreement, or

(ii) To determine whether any currency is convertible,

such valuation or determination, as the case may be, shall be reasonably made by the Bank after consultation with the International Monetary Fund.

Article 27

Use of currencies

(1) Members may not maintain or impose any restrictions on the holding or use by the Bank or by any recipient from the Bank, for payments anywhere, of the following:

(*a*) Gold or convertible currencies received by the Bank in payment of subscriptions to the capital stock of the Bank from its members;

(*b*) Currencies of members purchased with the gold or convertible currencies referred to in the preceding sub-paragraph;

(*c*) Currencies obtained by the Bank by borrowing, pursuant to paragraph (*a*) of Article 23 of this Agreement, for inclusion in its ordinary capital resources;

(*d*) Gold or currencies received by the Bank in payment on account of principal, interest, dividends or other charges in respect of loans or investments made out of any of the funds referred to in sub-paragraphs (*a*) to (*c*) or in payment of commissions or fees in respect of guarantees issued by the Bank; and

(*e*) Currencies, other than its own, received by a member from the Bank in distribution of the net income of the Bank in accordance with Article 42 of this Agreement.

(2) Members may not maintain or impose any restrictions on the holding or use by the Bank or by any recipient from the Bank, for payments anywhere, of currency of a member received by the Bank which does not come within the provisions of the preceding paragraph, unless:

(*a*) That member declares that it desires the use of such currency to be restricted to payments for goods or services produced in its territory; or

(*b*) Such currency forms part of the special resources of the Bank and its use is subject to special rules and regulations.

(3) Members may not maintain or impose any restrictions on the holding or use by the Bank, for making amortization or anticipatory payments or for repurchasing—in whole or in part—its obligations, of currencies received by the Bank in repayment of direct loans made out of its ordinary capital resources.

(4) The Bank shall not use gold or currencies which it holds for the purchase of other currencies of its members except:

(*a*) In order to meet its existing obligations; or

(*b*) Pursuant to a decision of the Board of Directors adopted by a two-thirds majority of the total voting power of the members.

Article 28

Maintenance of value of the currency holdings of the Bank

(1) Whenever the par value of the currency of a member is reduced in terms of the unit of account defined in paragraph (1) (*b*) of Article 5 of this Agreement, or its foreign exchange value has, in the opinion of the Bank, depreciated to a significant extent, that member shall pay to the Bank within a reasonable time an amount of its currency required to maintain the value of all such currency held by the Bank, excepting currency derived by the Bank from its borrowing.

(2) Whenever the par value of the currency of a member is increased in terms of the said unit of account, or its foreign exchange value has, in the opinion of the Bank, appreciated[1] to a significant extent, the Bank shall pay to that member within a reasonable time an amount of that currency required to adjust the value of all such currency held by the Bank, excepting currency derived by the Bank from its borrowing.

(3) The Bank may waive the provisions of this Article where a uniform proportionate change in the par value of the currencies of all its members takes place.

CHAPTER V. ORGANIZATION AND MANAGEMENT

Article 29

Board of Governors: Powers

(1) All the powers of the Bank shall be vested in the Board of Governors. In particular, the Board shall issue general directives concerning the credit policy of the Bank.

(2) The Board of Governors may delegate to the Board of Directors all its powers except the power to:

(*a*) Decrease the authorized capital stock of the Bank;

(*b*) Establish or accept the administration of Special Funds;

(*c*) Authorize the conclusion of general arrangements for co-operation with the authorities of African countries which have not yet attained independent status or of general agreements for co-operation with African Governments which have not yet acquired membership of the Bank, as

---

[1] As corrected: *United Nations Treaty Series*, vol. 569, p. 353.

well as of such agreements with other Governments and with other international organizations;

(*d*) Determine the remuneration of directors and their alternates;

(*e*) Select outside auditors to certify the General Balance Sheet and the Statement of Profit and Loss of the Bank and to select such other experts as may be necessary to examine and report on the general management of the Bank;

(*f*) Approve, after reviewing the report of the auditors, the General Balance Sheet and Statement of Profit and Loss of the Bank; and

(*g*) Exercise such other powers as are expressly provided for that Board in this Agreement.

(3) The Board of Governors shall retain full powers to exercise authority over any matter delegated to the Board of Directors pursuant to paragraph (2) of this Article.

Article 30

Board of Governors: Composition

(1) Each member shall be represented on the Board of Governors and shall appoint one governor and one alternate governor. They shall be persons of the highest competence and wide experience in economic and financial matters and shall be nationals of the member States. Each governor and alternate shall serve for five years, subject to termination of appointment at any time, or to reappointment, at the pleasure of the appointing member. No alternate may vote except in the absence of his principal. At its annual meeting, the Board shall designate one of the governors as Chairman who shall hold office until the election of the Chairman at the next annual meeting of the Board.

(2) Governors and alternates shall serve as such without remuneration from the Bank, but the Bank may pay them reasonable expenses incurred in attending meetings.

Article 31

Board of Governors: Procedure

(1) The Board of Governors shall hold an annual meeting and such other meetings as may be provided for by the Board or called by the Board of Directors. Meetings of the Board of Governors shall be called, by the Board of Directors, whenever requested by five members of the Bank, or by members having one-quarter of the total voting power of the members.

(2) A quorum for any meeting of the Board of Governors shall be a majority of the total number of governors or their alternates, representing not less than two-thirds of the total voting power of the members.

(3) The Board of Governors may by regulation establish a procedure whereby the Board of Directors may, when it deems such action advisable, obtain a vote of the governors on a specific question without calling a meeting of the Board.

(4) The Board of Governors, and the Board of Directors to the extent authorized, may establish such subsidiary bodies and adopt such rules and regulations as may be necessary or appropriate to conduct the business of the Bank.

Article 32

Board of Directors: Powers

Without prejudice to the powers of the Board of Governors as provided in Article 29 of this Agreement, the Board of Directors shall be responsible for the conduct of the general operations of the Bank and for this purpose shall, in addition to the powers provided for it expressly in this Agreement, exercise all the powers delegated to it by the Board of Governors, and in particular:

(*a*) Elect the President and, on his recommendation, one or more Vice-Presidents of the Bank and determine their terms of service;

(*b*) Prepare the work of the Board of Governors;

(*c*) In conformity with the general directives of the Board of Governors, take decisions concerning particular direct loans, guarantees, investments in equity capital and borrowing of funds by the Bank;

(*d*) Determine the rates of interest for direct loans and of commissions for guarantees;

(*e*) Submit the accounts for each financial year and an annual report for approval to the Board of Governors at each annual meeting; and

(*f*) Determine the general structure of the services of the Bank.

Article 33

Board of Directors: Composition

(1) The Board of Directors shall be composed of nine members who shall not be governors or alternate governors. They shall be elected by the Board of Governors in accordance with Annex B to this Agreement, which shall form an integral part thereof. In electing the Board of Directors, the Board of Governors shall have due regard to the high competence in economic and financial matters required for the office.

(2) Each director shall appoint an alternate who shall act for him when he is not present. Directors and their alternates shall be nationals of member States; but no alternate may be of the same nationality as his

director. An alternate may participate in meetings of the Board but may vote only when he is acting in place of his director.

(3) Directors shall be elected for a term of three years and may be re-elected. They shall continue in office until their successors are elected. If the office of a director becomes vacant more than 180 days before the end of his term, a successor shall be elected in accordance with Annex B to this Agreement, for the remainder of the term by the Board of Governors at its next session. While the office remains vacant the alternate of the former director shall exercise the powers of the latter except that of appointing an alternate.

Article 34

Board of Directors: Procedure

(1) The Board of Directors shall function in continuous session at the principal office of the Bank and shall meet as often as the business of the Bank may require.

(2) A quorum for any meeting of the Board of Directors shall be a majority of the total number of directors representing not less than two-thirds of the total voting power of the members.

(3) The Board of Governors shall adopt regulations under which, if there is no director of its nationality, a member may be represented at a meeting of the Board of Directors when a request made by, or a matter particularly affecting, that member is under consideration.

Article 35

Voting

(1) Each member shall have 625 votes and, in addition, one vote for each share of the capital stock of the Bank held by that member.

(2) In voting in the Board of Governors, each governor shall be entitled to cast the votes of the member he represents. Except as otherwise expressly provided in this Agreement, all matters before the Board of Governors shall be decided by a majority of the voting power represented at the meeting.

(3) In voting in the Board of Directors, each director shall be entitled to cast the number of votes that counted towards his election, which votes shall be cast as a unit. Except as otherwise provided in this Agreement, all matters before the Board of Directors shall be decided by a majority of the voting power represented at the meeting.

Article 36
The President: Appointment

The Board of Directors, by a majority of the total voting power of the members, shall elect the President of the Bank. He shall be a person of the highest competence in matters pertaining to the activities, management and administration of the Bank and shall be a national of a member State. While holding office, neither he nor any Vice-President shall be a governor or a director or alternate for either. The term of office of the President shall be five years. It may be renewed. He shall, however, cease to hold office if the Board of Directors so decides by a two-thirds majority of the voting power of the members.

Article 37
The Office of the President

(1) The President shall be Chairman of the Board of Directors but shall have no vote except a deciding vote in case of an equal division. He may participate in meetings of the Board of Governors but shall not vote.

(2) The President shall be chief of the staff of the Bank and shall conduct, under the direction of the Board of Directors, the current business of the Bank. He shall be responsible for the organization of the officers and staff of the Bank whom he shall appoint and release in accordance with regulations adopted by the Bank. He shall fix the terms of their employment in accordance with rules of sound management and financial policy.

(3) The President shall be the legal representative of the Bank.

(4) The Bank shall adopt regulations which shall determine who shall legally represent the Bank and perform the other duties of the President in the event that he is absent or that his office should become vacant.

(5) In appointing the officers and staff, the President shall make it his foremost consideration to secure the highest standards of efficiency, technical competence and integrity. He shall pay full regard to the recruitment of personnel among nationals of African countries, especially as far as senior posts of an executive nature are concerned. He shall recruit them on as wide a geographical basis as possible.

Article 38
Prohibition of political activity; the international character of the Bank

(1) The Bank shall not accept loans or assistance that could in any way prejudice, limit, deflect or otherwise alter its purpose or functions.

(2) The Bank, its President, Vice-Presidents, officers and staff shall not interfere in the political affairs of any member; nor shall they be influenced in their decisions by the political character of the member concerned. Only economic considerations shall be relevant to their decisions. Such considerations shall be weighed impartially in order to achieve and carry out the functions of the Bank.

(3) The President, Vice-Presidents, officers and staff of the Bank, in discharge of their offices, owe their duty entirely to the Bank and to no other authority. Each member of the Bank shall respect the international character of this duty and shall refrain from all attempts to influence any of them in the discharge of their duties.

Article 39

Office of the Bank

(1) The principal office of the Bank shall be located in the territory of a member State. The choice of the location of the principal office of the Bank shall be made by the Board of Governors at its first meeting, taking into account the availability of facilities for the proper functioning of the Bank.

(2) Notwithstanding the provisions of Article 35 of this Agreement, the choice of the location of the principal office of the Bank shall be made by the Board of Governors in accordance with the conditions that applied to the adoption of this Agreement.

(3) The Bank may establish branch offices or agencies elsewhere.

Article 40

Channel of communications; depositories

(1) Each member shall designate an appropriate authority with which the Bank may communicate in connection with any matter arising under this Agreement.

(2) Each member shall designate its central bank or such other institution as may be agreed by the Bank, as a depository with which the Bank may keep its holdings of currency of that member as well as other assets of the Bank.

(3) The Bank may hold its assets, including gold and convertible currencies, with such depositories as the Board of Directors shall determine.

Article 41

Publication of the Agreement, working languages, provision of information and reports

(1) The Bank shall endeavour to make available the text of this Agreement and all its important documents in the principal languages used in Africa. The working languages of the Bank shall be, if possible, African languages, English and French.

(2) Members shall furnish the Bank with all information it may request of them in order to facilitate the performance of its functions.

(3) The Bank shall publish and transmit to its members an annual report containing an audited statement of the accounts. It shall also transmit quarterly to the members a summary statement of its financial position and a profit and loss statement showing the results of its operations. The Annual Report and the Quarterly Statements shall be drawn up in accordance with the provisions of paragraph (4) of Article 13 of this Agreement.

(4) The Bank may also publish such other reports as it deems desirable to carry out its purpose and functions. They shall be transmitted to the members of the Bank.

Article 42

Allocation of net income

(1) The Board of Governors shall determine annually what part of the net income of the Bank, including the net income accruing to its Special Funds, shall be allocated—after making provision for reserves—to surplus and what part, if any, shall be distributed.

(2) The distribution referred to in the preceding paragraph shall be made in proportion to the number of shares held by each member.

(3) Payments shall be made in such manner and in such currency as the Board of Governors shall determine.

CHAPTER VI. WITHDRAWAL AND SUSPENSION OF MEMBERS; TEMPORARY SUSPENSION AND TERMINATION OF OPERATIONS OF THE BANK

Article 43

Withdrawal

(1) Any member may withdraw from the Bank at any time by transmitting a notice in writing to the Bank at its principal office.

(2) Withdrawal by a member shall become effective on the date specified in its notice but in no event less than six months after the date that notice has been received by the Bank.

Article 44

Suspension

(1) If it appears to the Board of Directors that a member fails to fulfil any of its obligations to the Bank, that member shall be suspended by that Board unless the Board of Governors at a subsequent meeting, called by the Board of Directors for that purpose, decides otherwise by a decision taken by a majority of the governors exercising a majority of the total voting power of the members.

(2) A member so suspended shall automatically cease to be a member of the Bank one year from the date of suspension unless a decision is taken by the Board of Governors by the same majority to restore the member to good standing.

(3) While under suspension, a member shall not be entitled to exercise any rights under this Agreement, except the right of withdrawal, but shall remain subject to all obligations.

Article 45

Settlement of accounts

(1) After the date on which a State ceases to be a member (hereinafter in this Article called the 'termination date'), the member shall remain liable for its direct obligations to the Bank and for its contingent liabilities to the Bank so long as any part of the loans or guarantees contracted before the termination date is outstanding; but it shall cease to incur liabilities with respect to loans and guarantees entered into thereafter by the Bank and to share either in the income or the expenses of the Bank.

(2) At the time a State ceases to be a member, the Bank shall arrange for the repurchase of its shares as a part of the settlement of accounts with that State in accordance with the provisions of paragraphs (3) and (4) of this Article. For this purpose, the repurchase price of the shares shall be the value shown by the books of the Bank on the termination date.

(3) The payment for shares repurchased by the Bank under this Article shall be governed by the following conditions:

(*a*) Any amount due to the State concerned for its shares shall be withheld so long as that State, its central Bank or any of its agencies remains liable, as borrower or guarantor, to the Bank and such amount may, at the option of the Bank, be applied on any such liability as it matures. No amount shall be withheld on account of the liability of the State resulting from its subscription for shares in accordance with paragraph (4) of Article 7 of this Agreement. In any event, no amount due to a member for its shares shall be paid until six months after the termination date.

(*b*) Payments for shares may be made from time to time, upon their surrender by the Government of the State concerned, to the extent by which the amount due as the repurchase price in accordance with paragraph (2) of this Article exceeds the aggregate amount of liabilities on loans and guarantees referred to in sub-paragraph (*a*) of this paragraph until the former member has received the full repurchase price.

(*c*) Payments shall be made in the currency of the State receiving payment or, if such currency is not available, in gold or convertible currency.

(*d*) If losses are sustained by the Bank on any guarantees or loans which were outstanding on the termination date and the amount of such losses exceeds the amount of the reserve provided against losses on that date, the State concerned shall repay, upon demand, the amount by which the repurchase price of its shares would have been reduced, if the losses had been taken into account when the repurchase price was determined. In addition, the former member shall remain liable on any call for unpaid subscriptions in accordance with paragraph (4) of Article 7 of this Agreement, to the extent that it would have been required to respond if the impairment of capital had occurred and the call had been made at the time the repurchase price of its shares was determined.

(4) If the Bank terminates its operations pursuant to Article 47 of this Agreement within six months of the termination date, all rights of the State concerned shall be determined in accordance with the provisions of its Articles 47 to 49.

Article 46

Temporary suspension of operations

In an emergency, the Board of Directors may suspend temporarily operations in respect of new loans and guarantees pending an opportunity for further consideration and action by the Board of Governors.

Article 47

Termination of operations

(1) The Bank may terminate its operations in respect of new loans and guarantees by a decision of the Board of Governors exercising a majority of the total voting power of the members.

(2) After such termination, the Bank shall forthwith cease all activities except those incident to the orderly realization, conservation and preservation of its assets and settlement of its obligations.

Article 48

Liability of members and payment of claims

(1) In the event of termination of the operations of the Bank, the liability of all members for uncalled subscriptions to the capital stock of the Bank and in respect of the depreciation of their currencies shall continue until all claims of creditors, including all contingent claims, shall have been discharged.

(2) All creditors holding direct claims shall be paid out of the assets of the Bank and then out of payments to the Bank on calls on unpaid subscriptions. Before making any payments to creditors holding direct claims, the Board of Directors shall make such arrangements as are necessary, in its judgement, to ensure a *pro rata* distribution among holders of direct and contingent claims.

Article 49

Distribution of assets

(1) In the event of termination of operations of the Bank, no distribution shall be made to members on account of their subscriptions to the capital stock of the Bank until:

  (i) All liabilities to creditors have been discharged or provided for; and
  (ii) The Board of Governors has taken a decision to make a distribution. This decision shall be taken by the Board exercising a majority of the total voting power of the members.

(2) After a decision to make a distribution has been taken in accordance with the preceding paragraph, the Board of Directors may by a two-thirds majority vote make successive distributions of the assets of the Bank to members until all assets have been distributed. This distribution shall be subject to the prior settlement of all outstanding claims of the Bank against each member.

(3) Before any distribution of assets is made, the Board of Directors shall fix the proportionate share of each member according to the ratio of its shareholding to the total outstanding shares of the Bank.

(4) The Board of Directors shall value the assets to be distributed at the

date of distribution and then proceed to distribute in the following manner:

(*a*) There shall be paid to each member in its own obligations or those of its official agencies or legal entities within its territories, to the extent that they are available for distribution, an amount equivalent in value to its proportionate share of the total amount to be distributed.

(*b*) Any balance due to a member after payment has been made in accordance with the preceding sub-paragraph shall be paid in its currency, to the extent that it is held by the Bank, up to an amount equivalent in value to such balance.

(*c*) Any balance due to a member after payment has been made in accordance with sub-paragraphs (*a*) and (*b*) of this paragraph shall be paid in gold or currency acceptable to that member, to the extent that they are held by the Bank, up to an amount equivalent in value to such balance.

(*d*) Any remaining assets held by the Bank after payments have been made to members in accordance with sub-paragraphs (*a*) to (*c*) of this paragraph shall be distributed *pro rata* among the members.

(5) Any member receiving assets distributed by the Bank in accordance with the preceding paragraph shall enjoy the same rights with respect to such assets as the Bank enjoyed before their distribution.

CHAPTER VII. STATUS, IMMUNITIES, EXEMPTIONS AND PRIVILEGES

Article 50

Status

To enable it to fulfil its purpose and the functions with which it is entrusted, the Bank shall possess full international personality. To those ends, it may enter into agreements with members, non-member States and other international organizations. To the same ends, the status, immunities, exemptions and privileges set forth in this chapter shall be accorded to the Bank in the territory of each member.

Article 51

Status in member countries

In the territory of each member the Bank shall possess full juridical personality and, in particular, full capacity:

(*a*) To contract;
(*b*) To acquire and dispose of immovable and movable property; and
(*c*) To institute legal proceedings.

Article 52

Judicial proceedings

(1) The Bank shall enjoy immunity from every form of legal process except in cases arising out of the exercise of its borrowing powers when it may be sued only in a court of competent jurisdiction in the territory of a member in which the Bank has its principal office, or in the territory of a member or non-member State where it has appointed an agent for the purpose of accepting service or notice of process or has issued or guaranteed securities. No actions shall, however, be brought by members or persons acting for or deriving claims from members.

(2) The property and assets of the Bank shall, wherever located and by whomsoever held, be immune from all forms of seizure, attachment or execution before the delivery of final judgement against the Bank.

Article 53

Immunity of assets and archives

(1) Property and assets of the Bank, wherever located and by whomsoever held, shall be immune from search, requisition, confiscation, expropriation or any other form of taking or foreclosure by executive or legislative action.

(2) The archives of the Bank and, in general, all documents belonging to it, or held by it, shall be inviolable, wherever located.

Article 54

Freedom of assets from restriction

To the extent necessary to carry out the purpose and functions of the Bank and subject to the provisions of this Agreement, all property and other assets of the Bank shall be exempt from restrictions, regulations, controls and moratoria of any nature.

Article 55

Privilege for communications

Official communications of the Bank shall be accorded by each member the same treatment that it accords to the official communications of other members.

Article 56

Personal immunities and privileges

(1) All governors, directors, alternates, officers and employees of the Bank:

  (i) Shall be immune from legal process with respect to acts performed by them in their official capacity;

  (ii) Where they are not local nationals, shall be accorded the same immunities from immigration restrictions, alien registration requirements and national service obligations, and the same facilities as regards exchange regulations as are accorded by members to the representatives, officials and employees of comparable rank of other members; and

  (iii) Shall be granted the same treatment in respect of travelling facilities as is accorded by members to representatives, officials and employees of comparable rank of other members.

(2) Experts and consultants performing missions for the Bank shall be accorded such immunities and privileges as are, in the opinion of the Bank, necessary for the independent exercise of their functions during the period of their mission, including the time spent on journeys in connection therewith.

Article 57

Exemption from taxation

(1) The Bank, its property, other assets, income and its operations and transactions shall be exempt from all taxation and from all customs duties. The Bank shall also be exempt from any obligation relating to the payment, withholding or collection of any tax or duty.

(2) No tax shall be levied on or in respect of salaries and emoluments paid by the Bank to directors, alternates, officers and other professional staff of the Bank.

(3) No tax of any kind shall be levied on any obligation or security issued by the Bank, including any dividend or interest thereon, by whomsoever held:

  (i) Which discriminates against such obligation or security solely because it is issued by the Bank; or

  (ii) If the sole jurisdictional basis for such taxation is the place or currency in which it is issued, made payable or paid, or the location of any office or place of business maintained by the Bank.

(4) No tax of any kind shall be levied on any obligation or security guaranteed by the Bank, including any dividend or interest thereon, by whomsoever held:

    (i) Which discriminates against such obligation or security solely because it is guaranteed by the Bank; or

    (ii) If the sole jurisdictional basis for such taxation is the location of any office or place of business maintained by the Bank.

Article 58

Notification of implementation

Each member shall promptly inform the Bank of the specific action which it has taken to make effective in its territory the provisions of this chapter.

Article 59

Application of immunities, exemptions and privileges

The immunities, exemptions and privileges provided in this chapter are granted in the interests of the Bank. The Board of Directors may waive, to such extent and upon such conditions as it may determine, the immunities and exemptions provided in Articles 52, 54, 56, and 57 of this Agreement in cases where its action would in its opinion further the interests of the Bank. The President shall have the right and the duty to waive the immunity of any official in cases where, in his opinion, the immunity would impede the course of justice and can be waived without prejudice to the interests of the Bank.

CHAPTER VIII. AMENDMENTS, INTERPRETATION, ARBITRATION

Article 60

Amendments

(1) Any proposal to introduce modifications to this Agreement, whether emanating from a member, a governor or the Board of Directors, shall be communicated to the Chairman of the Board of Governors, who shall bring the proposal before that Board. If the proposed amendment is approved by the Board, the Bank shall, by circular letter or telegram, ask the members whether they accept the proposed amendment. When two-thirds of the members, having three-quarters of the total voting power of the members, have accepted the proposed amendment, the Bank shall certify the fact by formal communication addressed to the members.

(2) Notwithstanding paragraph (1) of this Article, acceptance by all the members is required for any amendment modifying:

   (i) The right secured by paragraph (2) of Article 6 of this Agreement;

  (ii) The limitation on liability provided in paragraph (5) of that Article; and

 (iii) The right to withdraw from the Bank provided in Article 43 of this Agreement.

(3) Amendments shall enter into force for all members three months after the date of the formal communication provided for in paragraph (1) of this Article unless the Board of Governors specifies a different period.

(4) Notwithstanding the provisions of paragraph (1) of this Article, three years at the latest after the entry into force of this Agreement and in the light of the experience of the Bank, the rule according to which each member should have one vote shall be examined by the Board of Governors or at a meeting of Heads of State of the member countries in accordance with the conditions that applied to the adoption of this Agreement.

Article 61

Interpretation

(1) The English and French texts of this Agreement shall be regarded as equally authentic.

(2) Any question of interpretation of the provisions of this Agreement arising between any member and the Bank or between any members of the Bank shall be submitted to the Board of Directors for decision. If there is no director of its nationality on that Board, a member particularly affected by the question under consideration shall be entitled to direct representation in such cases. Such right of representation shall be regulated by the Board of Governors.

(3) In any case where the Board of Directors has given a decision under paragraph (2) of this Article, any member may require that the question be referred to the Board of Governors, whose decision shall be sought—under a procedure to be established in accordance with paragraph (3) of Article 31 of this Agreement—within three months. That decision shall be final.

Article 62

Arbitration

In the case of a dispute between the Bank and the Government of a State which has ceased to be a member, or between the Bank and any member upon the termination of the operations of the Bank, such dispute shall be submitted to arbitration by a tribunal of three arbitrators. One of the arbitrators shall be appointed by the Bank, another by the Government of the State concerned, and the third arbitrator, unless the parties otherwise agree, shall be appointed by such other authority as may have been prescribed by regulations adopted by the Board of Governors. The third arbitrator shall have full power to settle all questions of procedure in any case where the parties are in disagreement with respect thereto.

CHAPTER IX. FINAL PROVISIONS

Article 63

Signature and deposit

(1) This Agreement, deposited with the Secretary-General of the United Nations (hereinafter called the 'Depositary'), shall remain open until 31 December 1963 for signature by the Governments of States whose names are set forth in Annex A to this Agreement.

(2) The Depositary shall communicate certified copies of this Agreement to all the Signatories.

Article 64

Ratification, acceptance, accession and acquisition of membership

(1) (*a*) This Agreement shall be subject to ratification or acceptance by the Signatories. Instruments of ratification or acceptance shall be deposited by the Signatory Governments with the Depositary before 1 July 1965. The Depositary shall notify each deposit and the date thereof to the other Signatories.

(*b*) A State whose instrument of ratification or acceptance is deposited before the date on which this Agreement enters into force shall become a member of the Bank on that date. Any other Signatory which complies with the provisions of the preceding paragraph shall become a member on the date on which its instrument of ratification or acceptance is deposited.

(2) States which do not acquire membership of the Bank in accordance with the provisions of paragraph (1) of this Article may become members —after the Agreement has entered into force—by accession thereto on such terms as the Board of Governors shall determine. The Government of any such State shall deposit, on or before a date appointed by that Board, an instrument of accession with the Depositary who shall notify such deposit and the date thereof to the Bank and to the Parties to this

Agreement. Upon the deposit, the State shall become member of the Bank on the appointed date.

Article 65

Entry into force

This Agreement shall enter into force upon the deposit of instruments of ratification or acceptance by twelve signatory Governments whose initial subscriptions, as set forth in Annex A to this Agreement, in aggregate comprise not less than sixty-five per cent of the authorized capital stock of the Bank;[1] provided always that 1 January 1964 shall be the earliest date on which this Agreement may enter into force in accordance with the provisions of this Article.

Article 66

Commencement of operations

(1) As soon as this Agreement enters into force, each member shall appoint a governor, and the Trustee appointed for this purpose and for the purpose indicated in paragraph (5) of Article 7 of this Agreement shall call the first meeting of the Board of Governors.

(2) At its first meeting, the Board of Governors:

(*a*) Shall elect nine directors of the Bank in accordance with paragraph (1) of Article 33 of this Agreement; and

(*b*) Make arrangements for the determination of the date on which the Bank shall commence its operations.

(3) The Bank shall notify its members of the date of the commencement of its operations.

DONE IN KHARTOUM, this fourth day of August nineteen hundred and sixty-three, in a single copy in the English and French languages.

---

[1] According to the Memorandum on the interpretation of Article 65 of the Agreement, the words 'authorized capital stock of the Bank' shall be understood to refer to such authorized capital stock of the Bank as is equivalent to 211·2 million units of account and as corresponds to the aggregate initial number of shares to be subscribed by the States that may acquire its membership in accordance with paragraph (1) of Article 64 of the Agreement. See *United Nations Treaty Series*, vol. 510, p. 124, for the text.

ANNEX A

INITIAL SUBSCRIPTIONS TO THE AUTHORIZED CAPITAL STOCK OF THE BANK

Member	Paid-up shares	Callable shares	Total subscription (in million of units of account)
1. Algeria	1,225	1,225	24·50
2. Burundi	60	60	1·20
3. Cameroon	200	200	4·00
4. Central African Republic	50	50	1·00
5. Chad	80	80	1·60
6. Congo (Brazzaville)	75	75	1·50
7. Congo (Leopoldville)	650	650	13·00
8. Dahomey	70	70	1·40
9. Ethiopia	515	515	10·30
10. Gabon	65	65	1·30
11. Ghana	640	640	12·80
12. Guinea	125	125	2·50
13. Ivory Coast	300	300	6·00
14. Kenya	300	300	6·00
15. Liberia	130	130	2·60
16. Libya	95	95	1·90
17. Madagascar	260	260	5·20
18. Mali	115	115	2·30
19. Mauritania	55	55	1·10
20. Morocco	755	755	15·10
21. Niger	80	80	1·60
22. Nigeria	1,205	1,205	24·10
23. Rwanda	60	60	1·20
24. Senegal	275	275	5·50
25. Sierra Leone	105	105	2·10
26. Somalia	110	110	2·20
27. Sudan	505	505	10·10
28. Tanganyika	265	265	5·30
29. Togo	50	50	1·00
30. Tunisia	345	345	6·90
31. Uganda	230	230	4·60
32. U.A.R. (Egypt)	1,500	1,500	30·00
33. Upper Volta	65	65	1·30

ANNEX B

ELECTION OF DIRECTORS

(1) At the election of directors each governor shall cast all votes of the member he represents for a single person.

(2) The nine persons receiving the highest number of votes shall be directors, except that no person who receives less than ten per cent of the total voting power of the members shall be considered as elected.

(3) If nine persons are not elected at the first ballot, a second ballot shall be held in which the person who received the lowest number of votes in the preceding ballot shall be ineligible and in which votes shall be cast only by:

(a) Governors who voted in the preceding ballot for a person who is not elected; and

(b) Governors whose votes for a person who is elected are deemed, in accordance with paragraph 4 of this Annex, to have raised the votes for that person above twelve per cent of the total voting power of the members.

(4) (a) In determining whether the votes cast by a governor shall be deemed to have raised the total number of votes for any person above twelve per cent, the said twelve per cent shall be deemed to include, first, the votes of the governor casting the highest number of votes for that person, and then, in diminishing order, the votes of each governor casting the next highest number until twelve per cent is attained.

(b) Any governor part of whose votes must be counted in order to raise the votes cast for any person above ten per cent shall be considered as casting all his votes for that person even if the total number of votes cast for that person thereby exceeds twelve per cent.

(5) If, after the second ballot, nine persons are not elected, further ballots shall be held in conformity with the principles laid down on this Annex, provided that after eight persons are elected, the ninth may be elected—notwithstanding the provisions of paragraph 2 of this Annex—by a simple majority of the remaining votes. All such remaining votes shall be deemed to have counted towards the election of the ninth director.

IV. DAHOMEY: INVESTMENT CODE, 1961

THE background to the Investment Code is provided by the Report of the U.N. Economic Commission for Africa; an excerpt of which appears above, p. 196. The Code was issued on 31 December 1961. The English text set out here is not official: it is reproduced with permission from *International Legal Materials*, vol. 7 (1968), p. 334.

TEXT

LAW NUMBER 61–53
ESTABLISHING AN INVESTMENT CODE[1]

THE NATIONAL ASSEMBLY has deliberated and adopted:

THE PRESIDENT OF THE REPUBLIC promulgates the law the tenor of which follows:

Article 1. The arrangements relative to investments in the Republic of Dahomey include common law status and privileged statuses.

The three privileged statuses offer enterprises progressive advantages according to the interest and importance which they have for national development:

Statuses A and B apply to small and medium enterprises.

Status C: This is directed to large enterprises which are important to the economic development of the Nation and which require a long installation period prior to beginning normal operation and the establishment of which is only possible through exceptional, preferential measures.

BOOK I

COMMON LAW STATUS

Article 2. The Republic of Dahomey, desiring to see private investment contribute to national development, in respect to law and order, guarantees to enterprises established or about to be established:

—fair indemnification in case of expropriation;
—non-discrimination between foreign nationals and nationals before the law;

[1] [Edited in co-operation with the Dahomey Embassy, Washington, D.C., by Frank E. Samuel, Jr., member of the District of Columbia Bar, from an English translation of the French text issued by the Government of the Republic of Dahomey.]

—within the framework of the exchange control, liberty to transfer properly accounted profits and capital realized in case of the transfer or cessation of the enterprise;

—preservation, up to December 31st, 1975, of those provisions in the General Tax Code relative to exonerations for the investment of profits.

BOOK II

PRIVILEGED STATUSES

TITLE I. GENERAL PROVISIONS

CHAPTER I. GRANTING OF PRIVILEGED STATUSES

Article 3. Any new enterprise of an industrial, agricultural or mining character, by reason of the interest or the importance which it affords for the economic development of Dahomey, after advice given by the Investment Commission provided for in Article 12 hereafter, may be considered as possessing priority and thus benefit from one of the privileged statuses provided for in Title II. In exceptional cases, the Council of Ministers may decide to extend the provisions of the present law to a commercial enterprise.

Article 4. The same advantages may be granted to enterprises of an industrial, agricultural or mining character already established in Dahomey, when they expand or reconvert, as a function of the new programme which they introduce.

Article 5. The following points will be taken into account in examining requests:

—participation in the implementation of the economic and social development plan;

—contribution to redressing the balance of trade or to an improvement in the balance of payments;

—creation of employment, particularly when recourse is to be had to qualified labour and national executives;

—volume of investments.

Article 6. No approval shall be granted to enterprises which are not able to afford formal guarantees in financial and technical matters.

Article 7. The request for approval is addressed to the Minister of Economy. This must specify the privileged status for which the request is made and must contain all relevant justification (see instructions attached in Annex 1).[1]

Article 8. After advice from the Investment Commission, the project of approval is presented to the Council of Ministers.

Statuses A and B are granted by decree of the Council of Ministers. Status C is granted by law.

Article 9. For each enterprise, the text of approval:

—fixes the status granted and its duration;

—enumerates the activities for which approval is granted;

—specifies the obligations incumbent upon it, particularly with regard to its equipment programme;

—provides for the possible application of the benefits of Articles 15, 20 and 21; and fixes special conditions for the application of status A, Article 26, and for status B, Article 27;

—defines, in the case of status C the manner of arbitration procedure relative to the validity, interpretation and application of the clauses of the contract;

—determines the amount of deposit provided for in Article 14 hereafter.

Those operations effected by the approved Company, which do not expressly pertain to activities enumerated in the decision of approval, shall remain subject to fiscal provisions and other provisions of common law.

Article 10. Approval is granted for periods varying with the status which are not renewable. On the expiration date, the enterprise loses its privileged character and becomes subject to the provisions of common law.

Article 11. The approval granted to an enterprise is not transferable.

Article 12. The Investment Commission consists of the representatives from the following ministerial departments:

—President:

   Ministry in charge of Development and Planning;

—Members:

   Ministry of Commerce, Economy and Tourism;

   Ministry of Finance and Budget;

   Ministry of Labour and Civil Service;

   Ministry of Agriculture and Co-operation;

   Two Members of the National Assembly designated by it;

   A representative from the Chamber of Commerce and Industry;

   A representative from the Chamber of Agriculture;

   The Director of the Central Bank;

[1] Annex omitted.

The Director of the Exchange Control Office;
The Director of the Dahomey Development Bank.

The Committee may call on the advice of any person qualified by his competence as a consultant.

Article 13. Benefiting enterprises generally undertake to act in a spirit of co-operation with public authorities and to respect the interests of the State and the population.

Article 14. The benefit from the grant of privileged status is conditional on the opening, by the enterprise, of a deposit account with the National Treasury of Dahomey. The average quarterly amount of the credit balance of this account shall be fixed by the text of approval.

CHAPTER II. MISCELLANEOUS MEASURES

Article 15. The State shall make efforts to conclude bilateral agreements concerning double taxation with the countries from which foreign investors originate.

Article 16. The Ministry of Labour and Civil Service shall facilitate for approved enterprises the study of conditions of employment and recruitment for local labour which the enterprise undertakes to use on a priority basis. Certain exceptions to labour legislation may be granted in the approval contract or the establishment agreement.

Article 17. The entry of foreign labour is subject to prior authorization which is only granted in the case where the man-power requirements of the enterprise are not satisfied quantitatively or qualitatively by nationals.

Article 18. Concerning high technical executives and specialized foremen, the enterprise shall state its requirements in its request for approval. Adequate authorization is granted in the decree of approval.

Article 19. According to the terms to be agreed in each particular case, the technical and professional educational establishment shall co-operate with enterprises in the selection, guidance and supplementary training of labour.

Article 20. Within the framework of exchange control, there may be reserved to approved enterprises priorities for granting currency.

Article 21. There may be instituted in their favour:

—restrictions on imports which compete with their products;
—preferential rates for exit duties and taxes or for indirect taxes.

Administrative and military contracts shall be granted to them by preference for equal quality and equal price.

Article 22. No legislative or regulatory decision, taking effect at a date later than that of approval, may have the effect of restricting, with regard to the benefiting enterprise, the arrangements made in its favour.

Article 23. An approved enterprise may request to benefit from any more favourable arrangement which may intervene in fiscal and customs legislation.

CHAPTER III. WITHDRAWAL OF APPROVAL

Article 24. In the case of grave breach by an enterprise of the arrangements resulting from the decree of approval, the benefit of the status may be withdrawn under the following conditions:

I. On the report of the Minister of Economy, the President of the Republic issues a warning to the enterprise for it to take the necessary measures to end the situation created by its breach. In default of sufficient effect within sixty days from receipt of the warning, the President of the Republic orders an investigation into the above-mentioned grave breach. In the course of this investigation the enterprise in question is invited to present its explanations.

II. After the substantiated opinion of the Investment Commission, and if necessary, a decree of withdrawal of approval issued by the Council of Ministers, the enterprise has sixty days from notification of this decree to exercise its right of recourse before the administrative court.

TITLE II. VARIOUS PRIVILEGED STATUSES

CHAPTER I. STATUS 'A'

Article 25. Status 'A' is granted for a period which may not exceed five years.

Article 26. Approval to status 'A' includes the following:

1. Exoneration from duties and taxes levied at import:

   (*a*) on equipment and material, machines and tooling directly necessary to the production and transformation of products,

   (*b*) on raw materials and products entering entirely or partially into the composition of worked or processed products,

   (*c*) on raw materials or products which, although these do not constitute tooling and do not enter into worked or processed products, are destroyed or lose their specific properties in the course of direct manufacturing operations,

   (*d*) on raw materials and products for conditioning and on packaging, which cannot be re-used, of worked or processed products.

2. Reduction of exit duties applicable to prepared, manufactured or industrial products exported by the enterprise. Rates are laid down in the establishment contract.

3. Exemption from consumption tax; however, if the product is already manufactured, transformed and sold in Dahomey by another approved enterprise, the exoneration shall only be applicable for the period remaining before the first enterprise becomes liable for the said tax.

CHAPTER II. STATUS 'B'

Article 27. Approval to status 'B' is granted for a period which may not exceed eight years and includes, apart from the advantages of status 'A', the following terms:

(a) exoneration from the tax on industrial and commercial profits for the first five periods of operation, the first period being that during the course of which the first sale or delivery took place either locally in Dahomey or for export.

Normally accounted for depreciation during these first five periods can be fiscally offset against the three following periods on express authority of the Minister of Finance.

(b) exoneration for the same period and under the same conditions from the trading licence and the mining or forest royalty.

CHAPTER III. STATUS 'C'

Article 28. Status 'C' is directed to very important enterprises requiring a long installation period prior to beginning normal operation, the establishment of which is of capital importance to the economic development of the Nation and thus requiring exceptional measures. These enterprises enter into 'Establishment Agreements' with the Government of the Republic of Dahomey the period of which may not exceed 25 years.

Article 29. Status 'C' includes various guarantees on the part of the Government:

(a) guarantee of stability with regard to the marketing of products;

(b) guarantees of access to the circulation of labour, of liberty of employment, as well as the free choice of suppliers and goods and services in respect of the principles laid down above in Article 5, paragraph 2, and Article 17;

(c) guarantees concerning the renewal of forest and mine exploitation licences;

(d) if necessary, conditions for the use of hydraulic, electrical or other resources necessary for operation as well as those means of evacuation of products to an embarkation point and the use of installations existing or created by or for the enterprise at this point of embarkation.

Article 30. Status 'C' makes it possible to benefit, by right, from the advantages authorized within the frameworks of statuses A and B and for the same periods.

Article 31. These enterprises shall benefit, apart from those advantages enumerated in Article 29, from stabilization of their fiscal status for 25 years extended, if necessary, by normal delays for installation which, apart from projects taking exceptionally long to establish, cannot exceed, on principle, five years.

Article 32. During the period of stabilized fiscal status, stability of direct taxation, as exists at the time of establishment of the agreement, is granted both as regards rules for basis and rates as well as manner of recovery.

The benefit of this arrangement may be extended to other contributions, taxes and fiscal dues for varying periods.

These last conditions shall be discussed during the preparation of each text of approval.

Article 33. Stabilization of fiscal status may also concern the taxes due to Dahomey by the founding companies or shareholders of the said enterprises.

Article 34. The establishment agreement granting the benefit of stabilized fiscal status must be approved by a law which fixes the starting date of the said status.

Article 35. During the period of application of stabilized fiscal status, any legislative or regulatory provision which would have the effect of countermanding the provisions of Article 32 or the text of approval resulting therefrom, shall not be applicable to enterprises benefiting from status 'C'.

Article 36. The establishment agreement may not include, on the part of the State, an undertaking the effect of which would relieve the enterprise from loss, expenses, or loss of profit due to technical development or the economic situation or factors proper to the enterprise.

Article 37. Special fiscal statuses granted prior to the promulgation of the present law, to enterprises already exercising their activities in Dahomey by virtue of the Law of July 13th, 1960 relative to the Investment Code, remain expressly in force.

All enterprises subject to these special statuses may at any time solicit the benefits of the provisions of the present law. Requests shall be granted after endorsement by the Investment Commission.

CHAPTER IV. ARBITRATION PROCEDURE

Article 38. The settlement of disputes relating to the validity, interpretation or application of the clauses of the contract or agreement provided in chapters 2 and 3 of Title II and possible determination of the indemnity due for disregard of undertakings entered into shall be the object of arbitration procedure the terms of which shall be fixed in each contract or agreement and which must include the following provisions:

—designation of an arbitrator by each of the parties,

—designation of a third arbitrator by agreement between both parties or, in default, by a highly qualified authority, which shall be designated in the agreement and which could be the highest judicial authority in the investor's country,

—definitive and executory character of the decision rendered by a majority of the arbitrators establishing their own procedure and judging with equity. This decision must be accompanied by the executive ordinance.

Article 39. The present law abrogates all prior and contradictory provisions and, in particular, Law No. 60–18 of July 13th, 1960.

Article 40. Decrees by the Council of Ministers shall fix, insofar as required, the manner of application of the present law, which shall be enacted as a law of the State.

V. ECONOMIC AND CUSTOMS UNION OF CENTRAL AFRICA: COMMON CONVENTION ON INVESTMENTS, 1965

THE heads of state of the Economic and Customs Union of Central Africa (on which see p. 46 above) adopted the Common Convention on 14 December 1965, and the Convention entered into force on 1 January 1966. The text was published in the *Official Gazette of the Federal Republic of Cameroon*, 1 April 1966, p. 609, and is reproduced with permission from *International Legal Materials*, vol. 7 (1968), p. 221.

COMMON CONVENTION

*on investments in the States of the Customs and Economic Union
of Central Africa*

Federal Republic of Cameroon,
Central African Republic,
Republic of Congo-Brazzaville,
Republic of Gabon,
Republic of Chad.

PART I

GENERAL GUARANTEES

1. The acquired rights of any kind shall be guaranteed to undertakings lawfully established in the countries forming the Customs and Economic Union of Central Africa hereafter referred to as the 'Union'.

2. Within the framework of their exchange regulations, the member States of the Union shall guarantee the free transfer of:

(*a*) Capital;
(*b*) Profits lawfully acquired;
(*c*) Funds arising from the transfer or winding-up of business activities.

3. Undertakings whose capital derives from other countries, shall be able to acquire rights of any kind deemed necessary for the exercise of their activities: real property and industrial rights, concessions, official authorizations and permits, participations in government contracts under the same conditions as undertakings in the member countries of the Union.

4. In the exercise of their professional activities foreign employers and workers shall rank as nationals of the member States of the Union.

They shall benefit from Labour and Social Welfare legislation under the same conditions as the nationals of the States of the Union. They may participate in trade union activities and be members of organizations for defending their professional interests within the framework of existing laws.

In addition, foreign undertakings and their management shall be represented under the same conditions as the undertakings or nationals of the member countries of the Union in the commercial assemblies and in organizations representing professional and economic interests within the framework of the laws of each State.

5. Foreign employers and workers may not in their private capacity be subject to duties, taxes or contributions of any kind other than or higher than those levied on the nationals of countries of the Union.

Foreign undertakings shall enjoy the same rights and protection regarding trade-marks and patents, trade labels and names and any other industrial properties as undertakings possessing the nationality of the member countries of the Union.

The conditions of access to judicial or administrative courts applicable to foreign undertakings and workers shall be the same as those guaranteed to nationals of the States of the Union by their respective laws.

PART II

PREFERENTIAL SCHEDULES

CHAPTER I. COMMON PROVISIONS

SECTION I

6. Subject to the conditions laid down in the following articles, any undertaking wishing to launch a new activity or to expand to an important extent an activity already existing in a country of the Union, excluding commercial activities, may benefit from a special decision admitting it to a preferential schedule. The undertaking must undertake to utilize in priority local raw materials and in general local products.

7. Undertakings which may benefit from preferential schedule must belong to one of the following categories:

(1) Industrial-plantation undertakings engaged in the processing or conditioning of products;

(2) Stock-farming undertakings equipped with installations for protecting the health of livestock;

(3) Industrial undertakings that prepare or process animal or vegetable products;

(4) Lumbering industries;

(5) Fishing undertakings equipped with installations for the conservation or the processing of products;

(6) Industries for the manufacture or assembly of finished articles or goods;

(7) Undertakings engaged in the mining activities of extracting, improving or processing mineral substances and allied operations;

(8) Petroleum prospecting undertakings;

(9) Power-production undertakings;

(10) Undertakings engaged in the development of touristic regions.

8. The following criteria shall in particular be taken into consideration during the examination of projects:

(1) The importance of the investments;

(2) Participation in the implementation of the economic and social plans;

(3) Creation of employment and vocational training;

(4) Participation of nationals of the countries of the Union in the formation of capital;

(5) The use of technically guaranteed equipment;

(6) Priority use of local raw materials and, in general, local products;

(7) Registered office established in a country of the Union.

SECTION 2. *Approval procedure*

9. This convention comprises two categories of investment schedules:

(1) The first category concerns undertakings established in a State of the Union, the market of which does not include the other member States of the Union.

Schedules I and II set forth in Part III of this convention which concern the above undertakings shall be granted in accordance with the procedure peculiar to each State.

(2) The second category concerns companies the market of which includes or is likely to include the territories of two or more States. It comprises schedules III and IV which shall be granted according to a procedure common to all the member States.

In addition establishment conventions may be concluded with undertakings according to the procedure determined either by national laws or by this convention.

10. The application for approval shall be addressed to the appropriate Ministry of the State concerned and presented in the forms laid down in Article 1 of Act No. 12/65-UDEAC-34 regulating the single tax rules (standard form Annex 1).

The Minister shall as the case may be transmit the application file to an investments board for its advice.

11. For each undertaking, the decision of approval:

—shall specify the preferential schedule to which the approved undertaking is admitted and shall fix its term,

—shall list the activities for which the approval is granted,

—shall specify the obligations incumbent on the undertaking, particularly its equipment programme,

—shall stipulate the special rules for international arbitration.

Any operations effected by the approved undertaking which do not fall within the scope of those listed by the decision of approval shall remain subject to the fiscal and other provisions of ordinary law.

Chapter II. Economic Advantages

Section 1. *Installations and supplies*

12. The assistance of public credit institutions may be granted to undertakings admitted to preferential schedules upon the intervention of the appropriate authorities of each State.

13. Within the framework of exchange regulations, approved undertakings may be given priority in the granting of foreign currency in order to buy equipment goods and raw materials, products and containers necessary for their operations.

Section 2. *Sale of products*

14. Protective customs measures with regard to imports of similar competitive goods may, if necessary, be instituted in favour of undertakings admitted to a preferential schedule.

Government and Army contracts shall, as far as possible, be reserved for them in priority.

PART III

SPECIAL PROVISIONS TO WHICH NATIONAL INVESTMENT CODES MUST CONFORM IN THE CASE OF UNDERTAKINGS BELONGING TO ONLY ONE STATE OF THE UNION

CHAPTER I. GENERAL

15. Having regard to the decision regarding the harmonization of development plans and in respect for the general principles laid down by this text, admission to any one of the preferential schedules provided for priority undertakings of all kinds classified in categories *a*, *b* and *c* of Article 51 of the Treaty instituting the Union, shall be granted according to the procedure peculiar to the State, where the undertaking is established.

In the case of undertakings defined in category *c* of Article 51 of the Treaty instituting the Union, applications for approval shall be transmitted beforehand to the Secretary-General of the Union, in conformity with the provisions of Article 53 of the Treaty.

The grant of an internal preferential schedule may only be effected at the end of the consultation procedure laid down by Article 55 of the Treaty.

The Management Committee of the Union shall be informed of each approval in respect of these categories of undertakings by the Government of the State where they are established or will be established.

16. Preferential tariff provisions may be granted by the Government of the State concerned to industries already established which wish to expand their production capacity. Such provision comprises the application of a reduced overall rate of 5% of the duties and taxes collected on imports of plant (excluding building materials, furniture and spare parts) provided that they conform with an equipment programme approved by the Government and that their value exceeds 10 million francs.

The conditions and procedure for according this tariff shall be governed by national legislation.

17. The undertakings classified in categories *a*, *b* and *c* of Article 51 of the Treaty instituting the Union may be admitted to one of the schedules defined below.

Chapter II. Schedule I

18. Schedule I shall entail for the companies admitted to it:

(1) The application of an overall reduced rate of 5% of the duties and taxes collected on imports or a nil rate on equipment and building materials, machinery and tools directly necessary for the production and the processing of products.

(2) Total exemption from import duties and taxes as well as from single taxes and indirect taxes levied inland:

(a) On raw materials and products which enter either in whole or in part into the composition of finished or processed goods.

(b) On raw materials or products which while not constituting equipment and not entering into the composition of finished or processed goods are used up or lose their specific quality in the course of direct manufacturing operations.

(c) On raw materials and products intended for the handling and non-reusable packing of finished or processed products.

Equipment and building materials, machinery, plants, raw materials or products benefiting from a reduction or exemption in respect of import duties and taxes shall be fixed in a list drawn up in accordance with the procedure proper to each State.

This list shall be published officially.

(d) As the case may be on electric power.

(3) The benefit of reduced or nil rates of export duties in the case of prepared or manufactured goods.

(4) Goods manufactured by an undertaking admitted to schedule I shall be exempted from the inland tax on turnover and any other similar tax; they shall be subject to an internal consumption tax, the rate of which shall be subject to revision and the dates for the application of which shall be fixed by the decision of approval.

This tax shall be defined and applied according to Act No. 12/65-UDEAC-34 of the 14th December 1965. The duration of the benefits provided for under paragraphs 1, 2 and 3 of this Article shall be fixed by the decision of approval. It may not exceed ten years.

19. Taking into consideration the economic social importance of the undertaking and the special conditions of its installation, schedule I may further compromise the following benefits:

(a) Exemption from the tax on industrial and commercial profit during the first five years of operation, the first year being that in which the first sale or delivery was made either within the national market or for export.

Depreciation normally accounted for during the first five years may for tax purposes be charged against the three following years according to a procedure determined by the appropriate authorities of the State where the undertaking is established.

(*b*) Exemption during the same period and under the same conditions from the business licence and land, mining or lumbering taxes.

20. The decision of approval may provide that for the duration of schedule I as defined above, no import duty or tax, no new tax or duty or additional part thereof of a fiscal nature may be collected in addition to the duties and taxes in force on the date of grant of the approval.

No law or regulation coming into force on a date subsequent to the date of admission of an undertaking to the provisions of schedule I may result in the restriction of the aforedefined provisions regarding the undertaking.

In addition, undertakings licensed under schedule I may request the benefit of any more favourable provisions which may be provided for by customs and fiscal laws of the States in accordance with Article 43 of the Treaty setting up the Union and of Article 6 of this convention.

CHAPTER II. SCHEDULE II

21. The provisions of schedule II may be granted to undertakings of cardinal importance to national economic development, involving exceptionally high investments.

It comprises the stabilization of the fiscal provisions, whether special or under common law, which are applicable to them according to the conditions set down below.

22. Tax stabilization may likewise apply to the taxes due by the parent or stockholding companies of the undertakings defined in Article 21 above.

23. The tax provisions thus defined shall remain in force for a term not exceeding twenty-five years to which may be added, if need be, the normal periods required for installation.

24. During the period it is in force, the tax stabilization provisions shall guarantee the beneficiary undertaking against any increase in the direct or indirect taxation which is applicable to it on the date of approval with regard to the basis of assessment, rate and the method of collection.

In addition all or part of the fiscal or customs provisions concerning schedule I may be extended to schedule II with the exception of the land consumption tax, the rate of which remains subject to revision.

The schedule of stabilized taxes and duties, as well as the rates applicable during the term of validity of schedule I shall be defined in the decision of approval.

~ Insofar as customs duties and taxes are concerned, the provisions of tax stabilization may only apply to the fiscal import duty and the turnover tax on imports. Imported equipment and building materials benefiting from the stabilization of these two duties shall form the subject of a limitation list appended to the decision of approval.

In case of modifications being introduced into the fiscal provisions fixed by ordinary law in pursuance of the provisions of Article 43 of the Treaty instituting the Union and Article 6 of this convention, the undertaking benefiting from tax stabilization may apply for the benefit of such modifications.

Such undertaking may further apply to revert to the tax provisions of ordinary law.

25. No legislation or regulation which would nullify these provisions shall apply, during the same period, to undertakings benefiting from the provisions of tax stabilization.

Chapter IV. Establishment Conventions

26. Any undertaking approved under one of the schedules I or II or considered as being especially important to the social and economic development plans of the member States of the Union, may benefit from an establishment convention granting it certain guarantees and imposing certain obligations on it in accordance with the following conditions:

The parent or stockholding companies of the aforementioned undertakings may likewise be parties to the convention.

Nothing in the establishment convention may constitute any undertaking, on the part of the States of the Union, to compensate the undertaking for losses, debts or deficiencies due to technical developments, economic circumstances or factors attributable to the undertaking itself.

27. The establishment convention shall define its term of validity and as the case may be:

(a) The general conditions of operation, the minimum equipment and production programmes, the commitments of the undertaking regarding vocational training or social works provided for in the aforesaid programme as well as any obligation accepted by the two parties;

(b) Various guarantees by the Government other than fiscal or customs guarantees such as:

—guarantees as to financial, legal and economic stability and stable conditions for financial transfers and the marketing of goods;

—guarantees as to entry and movement of labour, freedom of employment, and the free choice of suppliers and services;

—guarantees as to the renewal of lumbering and mining permits if necessary;

(c) Facilities for the use of hydraulic, electric, and other resources necessary for the exploitation, as well as the facilities for conveying products to the place of shipment and the use of installations, whether already existing or to be built by or for the undertaking at the place of shipment;

(d) The procedure for extending the term of the convention and the circumstances which will entail a cancellation or the forfeiture of all rights and the penalties designed to ensure that both parties fulfil their obligations.

28. The provisions regarding import taxes and duties laid down in schedule I may likewise be included either in whole or in part in the establishment convention for the term of validity of the latter.

If the establishment convention comprises provisions regarding internal taxation as set forth in schedule I they shall be restricted to the term of validity of the aforesaid schedule.

CHAPTER V

29. Any grant of benefits similar to those laid down by the foregoing schedule but granted according to rules other than those defined below or any grant of higher benefits shall be subject to the preliminary agreement of the Council of Heads of State of the Union, after consultation with the Management Committee.

PART IV

SPECIAL PROVISIONS APPLICABLE TO UNDERTAKINGS AND ESTABLISHMENTS OF INTEREST TO TWO OR MORE STATES OF THE UNION

CHAPTER I. SCOPE

30. This part applies to the undertakings classified in categories d and e of Article 51 of the Treaty instituting the Union and defined in Article 7 of this convention.

31. Such undertakings may apply for admission to either of the two following schedules.

Chapter II. Schedule III

32. Admission to schedule III shall confer right to the following benefits:

(*a*) Application during the period of installation of an overall reduced rate of 5% of the duties and taxes collected on imports of equipment goods. Total exemption may in exceptional cases be granted by the Management Committee;

(*b*) Benefit of the single tax system in force in the Union.

33. The following fiscal benefits may in addition be granted:

(1) Exemption from the tax on industrial and commercial profits during the first five years of operation, the first year being that during which the first sale or delivery was made.

Depreciation normally accounted for during the first five years may for tax purposes be charged against the following three years.

(2) Rates on structures: temporary exemption (for a maximum period of ten years) on new buildings, rebuilding or additions to buildings.

(3) Rates on land plots. Temporary exemption (for a maximum period of ten years) on land newly used for stockrearing or on reclaimed and sown land.

(4) Exemption for five years from the business patent licence.

(5) Exemption for five years from land, mining or lumbering taxes.

Chapter III. Schedule IV

34. Schedule IV shall further comprise the customs and fiscal benefits set forth in schedule III and in particular the application of the single tax and the benefit of an establishment convention.

35. The establishment convention shall define:

(1) its term of validity and procedure for its extension,

(2) where necessary, various commitments by the undertakings, in particular:

—the general conditions of operation;

—minimum programmes of equipment and production;

—vocational training or social works provided for by the aforesaid programme as well as any other obligations accepted by the undertaking with regard to the state of its establishment and the other States of the Union,

(3) various guarantees by the State of its establishment and the member States of the Union, in particular:

—guarantees as to stability in the judicial, economic and financial fields as well as in the matter of financial transfers and the marketing of products;

—guarantees as to entry and movement of labour, freedom of employment and the free choice of suppliers and services;

—guarantees as to the renewal of lumbering and mining permits;

—guarantees as to facilities in the use of hydraulic, electric and other resources necessary for operations and facilities for the evacuation of products to the place of shipment and the use of installations existing or those to be created by or for the undertaking at this place of shipment.

36. In addition, undertakings of cardinal importance to the economic and social development of the States of the Union and involving exceptionally high investments may be granted stabilization of the special or ordinary fiscal provisions applicable to them.

37. The applications drawn up as provided by Article 11 shall be submitted to the appropriate authorities of the State of establishment.

After the appropriate examination, enquiry and fuller investigation, the appropriate authorities of the State of establishment shall transmit to the Secretary-General of the Union these applications and, as the case may be, the data concerning the project of the establishment convention accompanied by the presentation report as provided under Article 13 of the Treaty.

38. The Secretary-General of the Union shall where necessary undertake in liaison with the appropriate authorities of the State of establishment of fuller investigation of the application with a view to its transmission to the States, in conformity with the provisions of Article 55 of the Treaty.

39. Where the Management Committee receives an application as provided under Article 55 of the Treaty it shall decide as the case may be on the rate or rates of the single tax to be applied to the project and shall determine the benefits and guarantees to be granted to the undertaking.

Where necessary, it shall give its decision on the data of the establishment convention, the final draft of which it shall approve.

40. The draft of the convention thus approved shall be transmitted to the Government of the State of establishment for signature. The convention shall be made enforceable within the territory of the Union by a decision of the Management Committee.

PART V

SETTLEMENT OF DISPUTES

CHAPTER I. PROCEDURE OF WITHDRAWAL

41. In the case of serious deficiencies on the part of an undertaking with regard to the provisions of the decision of approval:

(1) The benefit of the advantages provided under either of schedules I or II may be withdrawn in accordance with the procedures established by the legislation of each nation.

(2) The benefit of the advantages laid down by either of schedules III or IV may be withdrawn by the Management Committee at the justifiable request of the State of establishment.

The Management Committee may seek the advice of a board of experts composed as follows:

—an expert designated by the Government of the State of establishment,
—an expert designated by the undertaking,
—an expert designated by the Government of the State of establishment,
—an expert designated by agreement between the aforesaid Government and the undertaking.

CHAPTER II. PROCEDURE FOR APPEAL

42. Undertakings which form the subject of a decision to withdraw approval may seek appeal.

In the case of an undertaking benefiting from the advantages provided under schedules I or II, the appeal shall be referred to an administrative court of the State of establishment within a maximum period of sixty days, with effect from the date of notification of the decision of withdrawal.

In the case of an undertaking benefiting from the advantages provided under schedules III or IV, the appeal shall be referred to the Council of Heads of State of the Union within a maximum period of ninety days with effect from the notification of the decision of withdrawal.

CHAPTER III. ARBITRATION

43. Disputes arising out of the application of the clauses of an establishment convention and the calculation of any penalty due for nonfulfilment of the obligations assumed may be settled by arbitration the procedure for which shall be established by each convention.

Such procedure of arbitration shall always comprise the following provisions:

(*a*) The nomination of an arbitrator by each party;

(*b*) In the case of disagreement between the arbitrators, the nomination of a third arbitrator by agreement between the two parties or, in default thereof, by a highly qualified authority who shall be named in the convention;

(*c*) The final and binding nature of the award rendered by a majority of the arbitrators who shall determine their own procedure and decide cases in equity;

(*d*) Notwithstanding the foregoing provisions, in the case of undertakings, the initial capital of which was subscribed in the major part from abroad, the decision of approval may provide for a procedure of international arbitration in replacement of the above procedure.

44. Any disputes arising out of the application of the decisions of approval to the various schedules may if necessary be settled by the arbitration procedure laid down by Article 43 above if the latter exists in the national legislation.

PART VI

TRANSITIONAL PROVISIONS

45. Any preferential schemes and establishment conventions granted prior to the promulgation of this convention to undertakings operating in the States of the Union shall specifically remain in force.

Provided always that such schemes and conventions may, on the initiative either of the Government or the undertakings concerned, form the subject of negotiations with a view to their adaptation to the provisions of this convention.

The procedure to be followed shall be that defined by Articles 37 to 44 above.

YAOUNDÉ, the 14th December 1965.

VI. CERTAIN TANZANIAN NATIONALIZATION LAWS, 1967

THE two pieces of legislation set out below are taken from the *Acts Supplement, Gazette of the United Republic of Tanzania*, no. 8, vol. 48, 17 February 1967. They are nos. 1 and 2 of 1967 and the assent of the President was given on 15 February 1967.

1. *An Act to establish the National Bank of Commerce and to vest in that Bank the Assets and Liabilities of Banks hitherto carrying on Banking Business in the United Republic*

[6th February, 1967]

ENACTED by the Parliament of the United Republic of Tanzania.

PART I

PRELIMINARY

Short title, commencement and application

1. (1) This Act may be cited as the National Bank of Commerce (Establishment and Vesting of Assets and Liabilities) Act, 1967.

(2) This Act shall be deemed to have come into operation on the sixth day of February, 1967.

(3) This Act shall extend to Zanzibar as well as to Tanganyika.

Interpretation

2. (1) In this Act, unless the context otherwise requires—'assets' means real and personal property of every kind including:

(*a*) rights under contracts and agreements;

(*b*) books, books of account and records;

(*c*) choses in action; and

(*d*) all other rights, interests and claims in or to real or personal property, whether liquidated or unliquidated, certain or contingent, accrued or accruing;

but does not include any right to a refund of taxation under any law in force in the United Republic or elsewhere;

'bank' means a body corporate the name of which is set out in the
  Schedule;

'Board' means the Board of Directors established under section 5;

'effective date' means the time at which the banks closed for business on
  the 6th February, 1967;

'liabilities' includes obligations under contracts or agreements but does
  not include—

  (a) any liability of a bank to a director or member of that bank in his
      capacity as such a director or member;

  (b) any liability in respect of taxation under any law in force in the
      United Republic or elsewhere;

'Minister' means the Minister for the time being responsible for finance;

'National Bank of Commerce' means the body corporate established by
  section 3;

'Tanzanian assets' means assets, situated or deemed by law to be situated,
  in the United Republic;

'Tanzanian liabilities' means liabilities situated, or deemed by law to be
  situated, in the United Republic.

(2) For the purposes of this Act, a chose in action, wherever situate,
relating to the banking business of a bank in the United Republic shall be
deemed to be situate in the United Republic.

PART II

THE NATIONAL BANK OF COMMERCE

Establishment of the National Bank of Commerce

3. There is hereby established a corporation to be known as 'the National
Bank of Commerce' which shall—

  (a) have perpetual succession and a common seal;

  (b) in its corporate name be capable of suing and being sued;

  (c) subject to this Act, be capable of purchasing and otherwise ac-
      quiring, and of alienating, any movable or immovable property.

Objects of the National Bank of Commerce

4. (1) As from the effective date it shall be the duty of the National Bank
of Commerce (in this Act referred to as 'the National Bank')—

  (a) to provide in accordance with the conditions appropriate in the
      normal and proper conduct of banking business, adequate and
      proper banking services and facilities throughout the United
      Republic;

(*b*) to conduct its business without discrimination except on such grounds as are appropriate in the normal and proper conduct of banking business;

(*c*) not to divulge any information relating to, or to the affairs of, a customer of the National Bank, except in circumstances in which it is, in accordance with any written law or the practices and usages customary among bankers, necessary or proper for the National Bank to divulge that information.

(2) Without prejudice to the generality of paragraph (*a*) of subsection (1), the National Bank may, within the United Republic and elsewhere—

(*a*) carry on the business of banking in all its branches and departments, including borrowing, raising or taking up money; lending or dealing in bills of exchange, promissory notes, coupons, drafts, bills of lading, warrants, debentures, certificates, scrip and other instruments and securities, whether transferable or negotiable, or not; granting and issuing letters of credit and circular notes; buying, selling and dealing in bullion and species; acquiring, holding and issuing on commission, underwriting and dealing with stocks, funds, shares, debentures, debenture stock, bonds, obligations, securities and investments of all kinds, the negotiating of loans and advances; receiving money and valuables on deposit, or for safe custody, or otherwise; collecting and transmitting money and securities; managing property, and transacting all kinds of agency business commonly transacted by bankers;

(*b*) undertake and execute any trusts the undertaking whereof may seem desirable, and also to undertake the office of executor, administrator, receiver, treasurer, registrar or auditor, and to keep for any company, Government authority, or body, any register relating to any stocks, funds, shares or securities, or to undertake any duties in relation to the registration of transfers and the issue of certificates;

(*c*) take or concur in taking all such steps and proceedings as may seem best calculated to uphold and support the credit of the National Bank, and to obtain and justify public confidence, and to avert or minimize financial disturbances which might affect the National Bank.

Management of the National Bank

5. (1) There shall be a Board of Directors for the National Bank, which shall, subject to this Act, be responsible for the policy, control and management of the National Bank.

(2) The Board of Directors shall consist of:

(*a*) a chairman who shall be appointed by the President;

(*b*) the General Manager of the National Bank;

(*c*) such other members being not less than five nor more than nine as the Minister may appoint.

(3) The Chairman and the other members of the Board shall be appointed from amongst persons who have had experience of, and shown capacity in industrial, commercial or financial matters, administration or the organization of workers.

(4) The General Manager of the National Bank shall be appointed by the Board acting with the approval of the Minister:

Provided that the first General Manager shall be appointed by the Minister.

(5) The Board may, with the approval of the Minister, appoint a Deputy General Manager.

(6) The Minister may make regulations with respect to—

(*a*) the appointment of, and the tenure and vacation of office by, the members of the Board;

(*b*) the quorum, proceedings and meetings of the Board and determinations of the Board;

(*c*) the execution of instruments and the mode of entering into contracts by or on behalf of the National Bank, and the proof of documents purporting to be executed, issued or signed by the National Bank, or a Director, officer, or servant of the National Bank.

(7) Subject to the provisions of any regulations made under subsection (6), the Board shall have power to regulate their own procedure.

Powers of Minister in relation to the Board

6. (1) The Minister may, after consultation with the Governor of the Bank of Tanzania, give to the Board directions of a general character as to the exercise and performance by the Board of their functions in relation to matters appearing to the Minister to affect the national interest and the Board shall give effect to any such directions.

(2) The Board shall afford to the Minister facilities for obtaining information with respect to the property and activities of the National Bank and shall furnish him with returns, accounts and other information with respect thereto and afford to him facilities for the verification of information furnished, in such manner and at such times as the Minister may require.

Accounts and audit

7. (1) The Board shall ensure that proper accounts and other records in relation thereto are kept by the National Bank and shall prepare in respect of each financial year of the Bank a statement of accounts in such form as the Minister may direct, being a form which shall conform with the best commercial standards.

(2) The accounts of the National Bank shall be audited by auditors of high repute who shall be appointed by the Minister.

(3) As soon as the accounts of the National Bank have been audited, the Board shall send a copy of the statement of accounts to the Minister together with a copy of any report made by the auditors.

(4) The Minister shall lay a copy of every such statement of account and auditors' report before the National Assembly.

PART III

NATIONALIZATION OF BANKS IN TANZANIA

Nationalization of banking business in Tanzania

8. (1) The National Bank shall take over the banking business of the banks in the United Republic and shall be deemed to have taken over such business as from the effective date.

(2) All the assets of the banks, which are Tanzanian assets, subsisting upon the effective date, shall by virtue of this section and without further assurance be vested in the National Bank and shall be deemed to have so vested upon the effective date.

(3) All the liabilities of the banks, which are Tanzanian liabilities, subsisting at the effective date, shall by virtue of this section and without further assurance be vested in the National Bank and shall be deemed to have so vested upon the effective date and the banks shall be discharged from their obligations in respect of those liabilities.

(4) The Minister may by Regulations make such provisions supplementary to or consequential on the provisions of this section as appear to him to be necessary or expedient.

(5) Notwithstanding the other provisions of this section, the Minister may by Order exclude from the operation of the preceding subsections any asset, in whole or in part, of any bank and where an order under this subsection is made, any property and rights which would otherwise have been vested in the National Bank shall be deemed never to have been so vested.

Operation of contracts etc.

9. (1) The instruments to which this section applies are instruments (including contracts, guarantees, agreements, bonds, authorities, mortgages, charges, bills of exchange, promissory notes, bank drafts, bank cheques, letters of credit and securities)—

(*a*) to which a bank is a party;

(*b*) under which any money is or may become payable or any other property is to be, or may become liable to be transferred, conveyed or assigned to that bank; or

(*c*) under which any money is, or may become, payable as any other property is to be, or may become liable to be transferred, conveyed or assigned, by that bank,

which are subsisting at the effective date and which relate to the business which has been taken over by virtue of this Act, but not including any contract or agreement between a bank and a director of or a person employed by the bank other than as a local employee (as defined in Part IV) in his capacity as such a director or person.

(2) An instrument to which this section applies shall, by virtue of this section, continue in full force and effect and the National Bank shall by this section—

(*a*) be substituted for the bank as a party thereto;

(*b*) be entitled to receive, and enforce payment of, any money payable thereunder;

(*c*) be entitled to obtain a transfer, conveyance or assignment of, and enforce possession of any property which is to be transferred, conveyed or assigned thereunder;

(*d*) be liable to make payment of any money payable thereunder; or

(*e*) be liable to transfer, convey or assign any property which is to be transferred, conveyed or assigned thereunder,

as the case requires.

Compensation to be paid

10. (1) The United Republic shall pay full and fair compensation in respect of the net value of the assets taken over under section 8 after taking into account the liabilities also taken over under that section.

(2) When the amount of compensation payable to any person entitled thereto by virtue of subsection (1) has been determined, the Minister shall issue to that person a certificate setting out such amount and that amount shall constitute a charge on and be paid out of the Consolidated Fund:

Provided that the said amount of compensation shall be payable in such manner and in such instalments as the Minister, after consultation with the person entitled, shall determine.

PART IV

EXISTING STAFF OF THE BANKS

Interpretation of Part IV

11. (1) In this Part, unless the context otherwise requires—

'employee of the banks' includes every officer or servant of a bank employed in connection with the banking business of that bank in the United Republic on the effective date and who is resident in, or is ordinarily resident in, the United Republic on that date;

'local employee' means an employee of a bank who is a citizen of the United Republic or whose terms and conditions of service require the person concerned to serve within East Africa only;

'other employee' means an employee of a bank who is not a citizen of the United Republic and whose terms and conditions of service require the person concerned to serve the bank within East Africa or elsewhere.

(2) Notwithstanding the definitions contained in subsection (1), a person who is an employee of a bank in consequence of an agreement or arrangement with a foreign government for technical aid or is seconded or otherwise made available temporarily by a bank not listed in the Schedule shall be deemed to be an 'other employee' and not a 'local employee'.

Local employees

12. (1) Each person employed by a bank as a local employee immediately preceding the effective date shall be employed, and as from the effective date shall be deemed to have been employed, by the National Bank.

(2) After a person becomes employed by the National Bank by virtue of subsection (1), the terms and conditions of service applicable thereafter to him shall be not less favourable than those which were applicable to him immediately before his transfer to the service of the National Bank and such a person shall be deemed to have been appointed to the service of the National Bank in such employment as the Board shall determine (being employment in a like office to that in which he was serving immediately prior to the effective date); and for the purposes of determining any right to gratuity or other superannuation benefit, his service with the

National Bank shall be regarded as continuous with his service immediately preceding the effective date.

(3) After a person becomes employed by the National Bank by virtue of subsection (1), his employment immediately prior to the effective date and his employment by the National Bank shall be deemed to be continuous employment by one employer within the meaning of section 8A of the Severance Allowance Act, 1962, and that Act shall apply to the parties in the same manner as it applies to the cases set out in subsection (1) of the said section 8A.

Existing staff other than local staff

13. If a bank notifies the National Bank that it is willing to second other employees to the service of the National Bank, the National Bank may enter into arrangements with such bank and with the staff concerned whereby such employees are seconded to the service of the National Bank upon terms and conditions to be agreed but not in any case less favourable than those which were applicable to the employees concerned immediately before the effective date.

PART V

OFFENCES

Prohibition of banking business of banks

14. (1) Notwithstanding anything contained in any other written law, or in any licence or other instrument, a bank listed in the Schedule to this Act shall not carry on banking business in the United Republic on or after the effective date.

(2) Any bank which contravenes the provisions of subsection (1) shall commit an offence and on conviction shall be liable to a fine not exceeding two hundred thousand shillings (Shs. 200,000).

Staff to assist in respect of transfer of business

15. (1) A bank, and every director of and person employed by such bank in relation to its banking business in the United Republic immediately preceding the effective date, shall do or join in doing all acts or things which it is necessary or convenient to do for or in relation to the operation of any of the provisions of this Act, and, in particular, for or in relation to—

(a) the taking over by the National Bank under this Act of the assets and business of that bank;

(*b*) the assumption by the National Bank under this Act of the liabilities of that bank.

(2) Any bank or person who contravenes the provisions of subsection (1) shall be guilty of an offence and on conviction shall be liable to a fine not exceeding ten thousand shillings in respect of each day that the contravention continues.

PART VI

GENERAL

Banking Ordinance (Cap. 430) not to apply

16. The Banking Ordinance shall not apply in any respect to the National Bank.

Regulations

17. The Minister may make Regulations prescribing all matters which are by this Act required or permitted to be prescribed, or for carrying out or giving effect to the purposes and provisions of this Act and in particular for prescribing penalties not exceeding twenty thousand shillings for offences against the Regulations.

SCHEDULE

National and Grindlays Bank Limited.
The Standard Bank Limited.
Barclays Bank D.C.O.
Algemene Bank Nederland N.V.
The Bank of India Limited.
The Bank of Baroda Limited.
Commercial Bank of Africa Limited.
National Bank of Pakistan.
Tanzania Bank of Commerce Limited.

Passed in the National Assembly on the fourteenth day of February, 1967.

P. Msekwa,
Clerk of the National Assembly

2. *An Act to establish the State Trading Corporation and to vest in that Corporation the Assets and Liabilities and Shareholdings of certain Firms and Companies carrying on business in Tanganyika*

[11th February, 1967]

ENACTED by the Parliament of the United Republic of Tanzania.

PART I

PRELIMINARY

Short title and commencement

1. (1) This Act may be cited as the State Trading Corporation (Establishment and Vesting of Interests) Act, 1967.

(2) This Act shall be deemed to have come into operation on the eleventh day of February, 1967.

Interpretation

2. In this Act, unless the context otherwise requires—

'assets' means real and personal property of every kind including:

(*a*) rights under contracts and agreements;

(*b*) books, books of account and records;

(*c*) stock-in-trade;

(*d*) choses in action; and

(*e*) all other rights, interests and claims in or to real or personal property, whether liquidated or unliquidated, certain or contingent, accrued or accruing,

but does not include any right to a refund of taxation under any law in force in the United Republic or elsewhere;

'Board' means the Board of Directors established under section 5;

'the Corporation' means the body corporate established by section 3;

'effective date' means midday of the eleventh day of February, 1967;

'firm' means any person or body of persons, whether corporate or incorporate, carrying on business in Tanganyika;

'liabilities' includes obligations under contracts or agreements but does not include any liability in respect of taxation under any law in force in the United Republic or elsewhere;

'Minister' means the Minister for the time being responsible for commerce;

'scheduled firm' means a firm specified in the Schedule to this Act;

'Tanganyika assets' means assets, situated or deemed by law to be situated in Tanganyika;

'Tanganyika liabilities' means liabilities situated or deemed by law to be situated in Tanganyika.

(2) For the purpose of this Act, a chose in action, wherever situate, relating to the business of a scheduled firm shall be deemed to be situated in Tanganyika.

PART II

THE STATE TRADING CORPORATION

Establishment of the Corporation

3. There is hereby established a corporation to be known as 'the State Trading Corporation' which shall—

(*a*) have perpetual succession and a common seal;

(*b*) in its corporate name be capable of suing and being sued;

(*c*) subject to this Act, be capable of purchasing and otherwise acquiring, and of alienating, any movable or immovable property.

Functions of the Corporation

4. (1) As from the effective date it shall be the function of the Corporation—

(*a*) to conduct the business of importers, exporters, wholesale dealers and retailers of such merchandise as the Board may, from time to time, decide;

(*b*) to conduct its business in an efficient manner and in accordance with the best mercantile traditions;

(*c*) to conduct its business without discrimination except on such grounds as are appropriate in the normal and proper conduct of mercantile business.

(2) Without prejudice to the generality of paragraph (*a*) of subsection (1) the Corporation may—

(*a*) acquire by agreement and hold interests in any mercantile firm;

(b) establish branches within the United Republic or elsewhere;

(c) manage the affairs of any firm the interests of which are vested in or acquired by the Corporation under the provisions of this Act;

(d) do anything or enter into any transaction which in its opinion is calculated to facilitate the proper and efficient carrying on of its activities and the proper exercise of its functions under the provisions of this Act;

(e) do all such acts and things as may be necessary to uphold and support the credit of the Corporation and to obtain and justify public confidence, and to avert or minimize any loss to the Corporation.

(3) Nothing in this section shall be construed as imposing on the Corporation, either directly or indirectly, any form of duty or liability enforceable by proceedings before any court.

Management of the Corporation

5. (1) There shall be a Board of Directors for the Corporation, which shall, subject to this Act, be responsible for the policy, control and management of the Corporation.

(2) The Board of Directors shall consist of:

(a) a chairman who shall be appointed by the President;

(b) a General Manager who shall be appointed by the Minister, except in the case of the first appointment, after consultation with the Board of Directors;

(c) such other members being not less than five nor more than nine as the Minister may appoint.

(3) The Chairman and the other members of the Board shall be appointed from amongst persons who have had experience of, and shown capacity in, industrial, commercial or financial matters, administration or the organization of workers.

(4) The Board shall elect one of their members to act as deputy chairman.

(5) The Minister may make regulations with respect to—

(a) the appointment of, and the tenure and vacation of office by, the members of the Board;

(b) the quorum, proceedings and meetings of the Board and determinations of the Board;

(c) the execution of instruments and the mode of entering into contracts by or on behalf of the Corporation, and the proof of documents purporting to be executed, issued or signed by the Corporation, or a Director, officer, or servant of the Corporation.

(6) Subject to the provisions of any regulations made under subsection (5), the Board shall have power to regulate their own procedure.

Powers of Minister in relation to the Board

6. (1) The Minister may give to the Board directions of a general character as to the exercise and performance by the Board of their functions in relation to matters appearing to the Minister to affect the national interest and the Board shall give effect to any such directions.

(2) The Board shall afford to the Minister facilities for obtaining information with respect to the property and activities of the Corporation and shall furnish him with returns, accounts and other information with respect thereto and afford to him facilities for the verification of information furnished, in such manner and at such times as the Minister may require.

Accounts and audit

7. (1) The Board shall ensure that proper accounts and other records in relation thereto are kept by the Corporation and shall prepare in respect of each financial year of the Corporation a statement of accounts in such form as the Minister may direct, being a form which shall conform with the best commercial standards.

(2) The accounts of the Corporation shall be audited by auditors of high repute who shall be appointed by the Minister.

(3) As soon as the accounts of the Corporation have been audited, the Board shall send a copy of the statement of accounts to the Minister together with a copy of any report made by the auditors.

(4) The Minister shall lay a copy of every such statement of accounts and auditors' report before the National Assembly.

PART III

VESTING OF INTERESTS OF CERTAIN SCHEDULED FIRMS

Interpretation

8. In this Part, unless the context otherwise requires—

'employee of a scheduled firm' includes every officer or servant of a scheduled firm employed in connection with the business of that firm in Tanganyika on the effective date and who is resident in or ordinarily resident in Tanganyika on that date;

'expatriate employee' means an employee of a scheduled firm who is not a citizen of the United Republic of Tanzania and whose terms and conditions of service require him to serve the scheduled firm within Tanganyika or elsewhere;

'local employee' means an employee of a scheduled firm who is a citizen of the United Republic of Tanzania or whose terms and conditions of service require the person concerned to serve within Tanganyika only;

'scheduled firm' means any firm specified in Part I of the Schedule to this Act.

(a) Nationalization

Nationalization of scheduled firms

9. (1) As from the effective date, the Corporation shall take over the respective businesses in Tanganyika of the scheduled firms.

(2) All the assets of the scheduled firms which are Tanganyika assets, subsisting upon the effective date, shall, by virtue of this section and without further assurance, be vested in the Corporation and shall be deemed to have so vested upon the effective date.

(3) All the liabilities of the scheduled firms, which are Tanganyika liabilities, subsisting at the effective date, shall, by virtue of this section and without further assurance, be vested in the Corporation and shall be deemed to have so vested upon the effective date and the scheduled firms shall be discharged from their obligations in respect of those liabilities.

(4) For the avoidance of doubts it is hereby declared that—

(a) all the assets of the scheduled firms which relate to mercantile transactions and become Tanganyika assets after the effective date shall be vested in the Corporation upon the date upon which they so become Tanganyika assets;

(b) all the liabilities of the scheduled firms which relate to mercantile transactions and become Tanganyika liabilities after the effective date shall become liabilities of the Corporation upon the date upon which they so become Tanganyika liabilities and the scheduled firms shall be discharged from their obligations in respect of those liabilities.

(5) The Minister may by Regulations make such provisions supplementary to or consequential on the provisions of this section as appear to him to be necessary or expedient.

(6) Notwithstanding the other provisions of this section, the Minister may by order exclude from the operation of the preceding subsections any asset, in whole or in part, of any scheduled firm and where an order under this subsection is made, any property and rights which would otherwise have been vested in the Corporation shall be deemed never to have been so vested.

Operation of contract, etc.

10. (1) The instruments to which this section applies are instruments (including contracts, guarantees, agreements, bonds, authorities, mortgages, charges, bills of exchange, promissory notes, bank drafts, bank cheques, letters of credit and securities)—

(a) to which a scheduled firm the business of which in Tanganyika has been nationalized under this Act is a party;

(b) under which any money is or may become payable or any other property is to be, or may become liable to be transferred, conveyed or assigned to that scheduled firm; or

(c) under which any money is, or may become, payable or any other property is to be, or may become liable to be, transferred, conveyed or assigned, by that scheduled firm,

which are subsisting at the effective date or come into existence after that date and which relate to that business, but not including any contract or agreement between a scheduled firm and a partner, director or member of the scheduled firm or a person employed by the scheduled firm, other than a local employee, in his capacity as such partner, director, member or person.

(2) An instrument to which this section applies shall, by virtue of this section, continue in full force and effect and the Corporation shall by this Act—

(a) be substituted for the scheduled firm as a party thereto;

(b) be entitled to receive, and enforce payment of, any money payable thereunder;

(c) be entitled to obtain a transfer, conveyance or assignment of, and enforce possession of any property which is to be transferred, conveyed or assigned thereunder;

(d) be liable to make payment of any money payable thereunder; or

(e) be liable to transfer, convey or assign any property which is to be transferred, conveyed or assigned thereunder,

as the case may be.

Power of the Corporation

11. For the avoidance of doubts and without prejudice to the generality of the foregoing provisions of this Part it is hereby declared that the Corporation shall have all such powers necessary to take possession and recover any property, to ascertain, perfect and enforce any right, and to discharge any liability or obligation, vested in the Corporation by section 9, and to deal therewith, as would have been enjoyed by the scheduled firm concerned had the same remained vested in the scheduled firm.

(b) Compensation

Compensation to be paid

12. (1) The United Republic shall pay full and fair compensation in respect of the net value of the assets taken over under section 9 after taking into account the liabilities also taken over under that section.

(2) When the amount of compensation payable to any person entitled thereto by virtue of subsection (1) has been determined the Minister for Finance shall issue a certificate setting out such amount and that amount shall constitute a charge on and be paid out of the Consolidated Fund:

Provided that the said amount of compensation shall be payable in such manner and in such instalments as the Minister for Finance, after consultation with the person entitled, shall determine.

(3) Nothing in this Act shall be construed so as to affect in any way the rights of the holder of a certificate issued under the Foreign Investments (Protection) Act, 1963.

(c) Employees of scheduled firms

Local employees

13. (1) Each person employed by a scheduled firm as a local employee immediately preceding the effective date shall, as from the effective date be, and be deemed to have been employed by the Corporation.

(2) After a person becomes employed by the Corporation by virtue of subsection (1), the terms and conditions of service applicable thereafter to him shall be not less favourable than those which were applicable to him immediately before his transfer to the service of the Corporation and such a person shall be deemed to have been appointed to the service of the Corporation in such employment as the Board shall determine; and for the purposes of determining any right to gratuity or other superannuation benefit, his service with the Corporation shall be regarded as continuous with his service immediately preceding the effective date.

(3) After a person becomes employed by the Corporation by virtue of subsection (1), his employment immediately prior to the effective date and his employment by the Corporation shall be deemed to be continuous employment by one employer within the meaning of section 8A of the Severance Allowance Act, 1962 and that Act shall apply to the parties in the same manner as it applies to the cases set out in subsection (1) of the said section 8A.

Existing expatriate employees

14. If a scheduled firm notifies the Corporation that it is willing to second expatriate employees to the service of the Corporation, the Corporation may enter into arrangements with such firm and with the expatriate staff concerned whereby such employees are seconded to the service of the Corporation upon terms and conditions to be agreed but not in any case less favourable than those which were applicable to the employees concerned immediately before the effective date.

(d) General

Staff to assist in respect of transfer of business

15. (1) Every scheduled firm and every partner, director and member thereof, and every person employed by such firm in relation to its business in Tanganyika immediately preceding the effective date, shall do or join in doing all acts or things which it is necessary or convenient to do for or in relation to the operation of any of the provisions of this Act, and, in particular, for or in relation to—

    (a) the taking over by the Corporation under this Act of the assets and business of that scheduled firm;

    (b) the assumption by the Corporation under this Act of the liabilities of that scheduled firm.

(2) Any scheduled firm or person who contravenes the provisions of subsection (1) shall be guilty of an offence and on conviction shall be liable to a fine not exceeding ten thousand shillings in respect of each day that the contravention continues.

PART IV

VESTING OF SHARES OF CERTAIN SCHEDULED FIRMS

Interpretation

16. In this Part, unless the context otherwise requires, 'scheduled firms' means the firms specified in Part II of the Schedule to this Act.

Vesting of shares

17. As from the effective date all the shares in each of the scheduled firms shall by virtue of this section and without further assurance vest, free of any trust, mortgage, charge, lien, interest or other incumbrance whatso-

ever, in the Corporation and shall be deemed to have so vested as from the effective date and the Corporation shall be the sole shareholder of the firm.

Directors to retire from office

18. (1) As from the effective date the directors of every scheduled firm shall cease to hold office.

(2) A director who ceases to hold office by virtue of subsection (1) shall not, notwithstanding any provision to the contrary in any law or in any Articles of Association, charter, agreement, contract or other instrument whatsoever, be entitled to any damages or compensation in respect of the loss of office.

Board to be the Board of Directors

19. As from the effective date and notwithstanding any provision to the contrary in any law or in any Articles of association, charter, agreement, contract or other instrument whatsoever—

(a) the Board shall be the Board of Directors of each of the scheduled firms;

(b) the Board may, with the approval of the Minister, appoint a manager of a scheduled firm;

(c) the proceedings of the Board when meeting as the Board of Directors of a scheduled firm shall be regulated by the provisions of section 5 and regulations made under subsection (5) thereof;

(d) the seal of the scheduled firm shall be affixed in such manner as the Minister may direct or, failing any such direction, as the Board may decide.

Minister may make regulations modifying provisions of the Companies Ordinance or Articles of Association, Cap. 212

20. (1) The Minister may make regulations modifying in their application to a scheduled firm any of the provisions of the Companies Ordinance or of any subsidiary legislation made thereunder or of the Articles of Association or other charter or instrument of the scheduled firm.

(2) Nothing in subsection (1) shall be construed as limiting the power of the Corporation as the sole member of a scheduled firm to amend the Articles of the Association of the scheduled firm where such power exists under such Articles.

Effect of reduction in the membership of a scheduled firm

21. Every provision in any law or in any Articles of Association or any other charter or instrument of a scheduled firm, providing for any consequence to follow, or requiring any act or thing to be done, or entitling

any person to do any act or thing or to take any action whatsoever, as a result of a reduction in the number of the members of the firm below a certain number, shall be of no effect in relation to the scheduled firms.

Compensation

22. (1) The United Republic shall pay full and fair compensation in respect of the shares vested in the Corporation under section 17.

(2) When the amount of compensation payable to any person entitled thereto by virtue of subsection (1) has been determined the Minister for Finance shall issue a certificate setting out such amount and that amount shall constitute a charge on and be paid out of the Consolidated Fund:

Provided that the said amount of compensation shall be payable in such manner and in such instalments as the Minister for Finance, after consultation with the person entitled, shall determine.

(3) Nothing in this Act shall be construed so as to affect in any way the rights of the holder of a certificate issued under the Foreign Investments (Protection) Act, 1963.

Construction of instruments affecting shares

23. (1) Any disposition—
   (a) which was effected by a testamentary instrument executed before the effective date; and
   (b) which would have operated as a bequest of all or any of the shares vested in the Corporation under the provisions of this Part,

shall have effect as a bequest of the right of the testator to be paid compensation in respect of the acquisition of the shares in relation to which that disposition would have operated.

(2) Any power of attorney or other instrument—
   (a) which was executed before the effective date upon which any shares became vested in the Corporation under the provisions of this Part; and
   (b) which operates in relation to all or any of those shares,

shall have the like operation in relation to the right to payment of compensation in respect of the acquisition of the shares to which that power of attorney or other instrument relates.

Retiring directors to assist in the take over

24. (1) Every person who immediately before the effective date was a director, member or employee of a scheduled firm shall do all such lawful things and acts as he may be called upon in writing to do by the Board

in order to assist the Board in the taking over of the shares and in assuming an effective control of the scheduled firm.

(2) Any person who contravenes the provisions of subsection (1) shall be guilty of an offence and shall be liable on conviction to a fine not exceeding ten thousand shillings in respect of each day that the contravention continues.

PART V

MISCELLANEOUS

Trades Licensing Ordinance not to apply

25. The Trades Licensing Ordinance shall not apply in any respect to the Corporation.

Regulations

26. The Minister may make regulations prescribing all matters which are by this Act required or permitted to be prescribed, or for carrying out or giving effect to this Act and in particular for prescribing penalties not exceeding twenty thousand shillings for offences against the regulations.

SCHEDULE

PART I

Name of Firm	Country of Incorporation
Smith Mackenzie & Company Limited	Kenya.
Dalgety and Company Limited.	England.
Dalgety (East Africa) Limited	England.
A. Baumann and Company Limited	Kenya.
Twentsche Overseas Trading Co. (E.A.) Limited	Kenya.
African Mercantile Company (Overseas) Limited	England.
Wigglesworth & Co. Limited	England.
Co-operative Supply Association of Tanganyika Limited	Co-operative Society registered in Tanganyika under Cap. 211.
East African Cotton Exporters Limited	Uganda.

PART II

Name of Firm	Country of Incorporation
Smith Mackenzie & Company (Tanganyika) Limited	Tanganyika.
Dalgety (Tanzania) Limited	Tanganyika.
International Trading and Credit Company of Tanganyika Limited	Tanganyika.
A. Baumann and Company (Tanganyika) Limited	Tanganyika.
Twentsche Overseas Trading Company (Tanzania) Limited	Tanganyika.
TOM Laboratories Limited	Tanganyika.
Wigglesworth & Co. (Africa) Limited	Tanganyika.
Wigglesworth & Co. Tanzania Limited	Tanganyika.

Passed in the National Assembly on the fourteenth day of February, 1967.

P. MSEKWA,
Clerk of the National Assembly

VII. RESOLUTIONS OF THE U.N. GENERAL ASSEMBLY ON PERMANENT SOVEREIGNTY OVER NATURAL RESOURCES

THE law concerning expropriation of foreign assets on State territory has always been the subject of controversy, and Resolution 1803 (XVII) of the General Assembly of the United Nations provides an important index, albeit not always very precise, of the present position. In 1955 the Third Committee of the General Assembly adopted a draft article, as a part of the Human Rights Covenants, on the right of self-determination. The second paragraph of the draft article provided: 'The peoples may, for their own ends, freely dispose of their natural wealth and resources without prejudice to any obligations arising out of international economic co-operation, based upon the principle of mutual benefit, and international law. In no case may a people be deprived of its own means of subsistence.' General Assembly Resolution 626 (VII) of 21 December 1952 supported a concept of economic self-determination. This resolution was cited in *Anglo-Iranian Oil Co. Ltd.* v. *S.U.P.O.R.*, 22 International Law Reports (1955), p. 23 at p. 40, and *Anglo-Iranian Oil Co. Ltd.* v. *Idemitsu Kosan Kabushiki Kaisha*, ibid., vol. 20 (1953), p. 305 at p. 313. See also resolutions 1314 (XIII), 12 December 1958, and 1515 (XV), 15 December 1960. After a hiatus in development, the Commission on Permanent Sovereignty over Natural Resources was established in 1958 and work in that body and in the Economic and Social Council resulted in the adoption of Resolution 1803 (XVII). In 1964 a Report by the Secretary-General on the subject was considered by the Economic and Social Council which submitted the Report, together with its comments, to the General Assembly. See generally Hyde, 50 *American Journal of International Law* (1956), pp. 854–67; U.N. Secretariat Study, *The Status of Permanent Sovereignty over Natural Wealth and Resources*, 1962; Gess, 13 *International and Comparative Law Quarterly* (1964), pp. 398–449; Brownlie, *Principles of Public International Law*, pp. 431–44; Fischer, *Annuaire français de droit international*, 1962, pp. 516–28.

Resolution 1803 (XVII) was adopted on 14 December 1962: 87 votes in favour; 2 against; 12 abstentions.

Resolution 2158 (XXI) was adopted on 25 November 1966: 104 votes in favour; none against; 6 abstentions.

1. *Resolution 1803 (XVII)*

The General Assembly,

Recalling its resolutions 523 (VI) of 12 January 1952 and 626 (VII) of 21 December 1952,

Bearing in mind its resolution 1314 (XIII) of 12 December 1958, by which it established the Commission on Permanent Sovereignty over Natural Resources and instructed it to conduct a full survey of the status of permanent sovereignty over natural wealth and resources as a basic constituent of the right to self-determination, with recommendations, where necessary, for its strengthening, and decided further that, in the conduct of the full survey of the status of the permanent sovereignty over peoples and nations over their natural wealth and resources, due regard should be paid to the rights and duties of States under international law and to the importance of encouraging international co-operation in the economic development of developing countries,

Bearing in mind its resolution 1515 (XV) of 15 December 1960, in which it recommended that the sovereign right of every State to dispose of its wealth and its natural resources should be respected,

Considering that any measure in this respect must be based on the recognition of the inalienable right of all States freely to dispose of their natural wealth and resources in accordance with their national interests, and on respect for the economic independence of States,

Considering that nothing in paragraph 4 below in any way prejudices the position of any Member State on any aspect of the question of the rights and obligations of successor States and Governments in respect of property acquired before the accession to complete sovereignty of countries formerly under colonial rules,

Noting that the subject of succession of States and Governments is being examined as a matter of priority by the International Law Commission,

Considering that it is desirable to promote international co-operation for the economic development of developing countries, and that economic and financial agreements between the developed and the developing countries must be based on the principles of equality and of the right of peoples and nations to self-determination,

Considering that the provision of economic and technical assistance, loans and increased foreign investment must not be subject to conditions which conflict with the interests of the recipient State,

Considering the benefits to be derived from exchanges of technical and scientific information likely to promote the development and use of such resources and wealth, and the important part which the United Nations and other international organizations are called upon to play in that connection,

Attaching particular importance to the question of promoting the economic development of developing countries and securing their economic independence,

Noting that the creation and strengthening of the inalienable sovereignty of States over their natural wealth and resources reinforces their economic independence,

Desiring that there should be further consideration by the United Nations of the subject of permanent sovereignty over natural resources in the spirit of international co-operation in the field of economic development, particularly that of the developing countries.

I

Declares that:

1. The right of peoples and nations to permanent sovereignty over their natural wealth and resources must be exercised in the interest of their national development and of the well-being of the people of the State concerned;

2. The exploration, development and disposition of such resources, as well as the import of the foreign capital required for these purposes, should be in conformity with the rules and conditions which the peoples and nations freely consider to be necessary or desirable with regard to the authorization, restriction or prohibition of such activities;

3. In cases where authorization is granted, the capital imported and the earnings on that capital shall be governed by the terms thereof, by the national legislation in force, and by international law. The profits derived must be shared in the proportions freely agreed upon, in each case, between the investors and the recipient State, due care being taken to ensure that there is no impairment, for any reason, of that State's sovereignty over its natural wealth and resources;

4. Nationalization, expropriation or requisitioning shall be based on grounds or reasons of public utility, security or the national interest which are recognized as overriding purely individual or private interests, both domestic and foreign. In such cases the owner shall be paid appropriate compensation, in accordance with the rules in force in the State taking such measures in the exercise of its sovereignty and in accordance with international law. In any case where the question of compensation gives rise to a controversy, the national jurisdiction of the State taking such measures shall be exhausted. However, upon agreement by sovereign States and other parties concerned, settlement of the dispute should be made through arbitration or international adjudication;

5. The free and beneficial exercise of the sovereignty of peoples and nations over their natural resources must be furthered by the mutual respect of States based on their sovereign equality;

6. International co-operation for the economic development of developing countries, whether in the form of public or private capital investments, exchange of goods and services, technical assistance, or exchange of scientific information, shall be such as to further their independent national development and shall be based upon respect for their sovereignty over their natural wealth and resources;

7. Violation of the rights of peoples and nations to sovereignty over their natural wealth and resources is contrary to the spirit and principles of the Charter of the United Nations and hinders the development of international co-operation and the maintenance of peace;

8. Foreign investment agreements freely entered into by, or between, sovereign States shall be observed in good faith; States and international organizations shall strictly and conscientiously respect the sovereignty of peoples and nations over their natural wealth and resources in accordance with the Charter and the principles set forth in the present resolution.

II

Welcomes the decision of the International Law Commission to speed up its work on the codification of the topic of responsibility of States for the consideration of the General Assembly.

III

Requests the Secretary-General to continue the study of the various aspects of permanent sovereignty over natural resources, taking into account the desire of Member States to ensure the protection of their sovereign rights while encouraging international co-operation in the field of economic development, and to report to the Economic and Social Council and to the General Assembly, if possible at its eighteenth session.

2. *Resolution 2158 (XXI)*

The General Assembly,

Recalling its resolutions 523 (VI) of 12 January 1952, 626 (VII) of 21 December 1952 and 1515 (XV) of 15 December 1960,

Recalling further its resolution 1803 (XVII) of 14 December 1962 on permanent sovereignty over natural resources,

Recognizing that the natural resources of the developing countries constitute a basis of their economic development in general and of their industrial progress in particular,

Bearing in mind that natural resources are limited and in many cases exhaustible and that their proper exploitation determines the conditions of the economic development of the developing countries both at present and in the future,

Considering that, in order to safeguard the exercise of permanent sovereignty over natural resources, it is essential that their exploitation and marketing should be aimed at securing the highest possible rate of growth of the developing countries,

Considering further that this aim can better be achieved if the developing countries are in a position to undertake themselves the exploitation and marketing of their natural resources so that they may exercise their freedom of choice in the various fields related to the utilization of natural resources under the most favourable conditions,

Taking into account the fact that foreign capital, whether public or private, forthcoming at the request of the developing countries, can play an important role inasmuch as it supplements the efforts undertaken by them in the exploitation and development of their natural resources, provided that there is government supervision over the activity of foreign capital to ensure that it is used in the interests of national development.

I

1. *Reaffirms* the inalienable right of all countries to exercise permanent sovereignty over their natural resources in the interest of their national development, in conformity with the spirit and principles of the Charter of the United Nations and as recognized in General Assembly resolution 1803 (XVII);

2. *Declares*, therefore, that the United Nations should undertake a maximum concerted effort to channel its activities so as to enable all countries to exercise that right fully;

3. *States* that such an effort should help in achieving the maximum possible development of the natural resources of the developing countries and in strengthening their ability to undertake this development themselves, so that they might effectively exercise their choice in deciding the manner in which the exploitation and marketing of their natural resources should be carried out;

4. *Confirms* that the exploitation of natural resources in each country shall always be conducted in accordance with its national laws and regulations;

5. *Recognizes* the right of all countries, and in particular of the developing countries, to secure and increase their share in the administration of enterprises which are fully or partly operated by foreign capital and to have a greater share in the advantages and profits derived therefrom on an equitable basis, with due regard to the development needs and objectives of the peoples concerned and to mutually acceptable contractual practices, and calls upon the countries from which such capital originates to refrain from any action which would hinder the exercise of that right;

6. *Considers* that, when natural resources of the developing countries are exploited by foreign investors, the latter should undertake proper and accelerated training of national personnel at all levels and in all fields connected with such exploitation;

7. *Calls upon* the developed countries to make available to the developing countries, at their request, assistance, including capital goods and know-how, for the exploitation and marketing of their natural resources in order to accelerate their economic development, and to refrain from placing on the world market non-commercial reserves of primary commodities which may have an adverse effect on the foreign exchange earnings of the developing countries;

8. *Recognizes* that national and international organizations set up by the developing countries for the development and marketing of their natural resources play a significant role in ensuring the exercise of the permanent sovereignty of those countries in this field, and on that account should be encouraged;

9. *Recommends* to the Economic Commissions for Asia and the Far East, the Economic Commission for Latin America, the Economic Commission for Africa and the United Nations Economic and Social Office in Beirut that, in the execution of their functions, they keep under review the question of permanent sovereignty over natural resources in the countries of the regions concerned, as well as the problem of the economic utilization of these resources in the national interests of their peoples.

II

Requests the Secretary-General:

(*a*) To co-ordinate the activities of the Secretariat in the field of natural resources with those of other United Nations organs and programmes, including the United Nations Conference on Trade and Development, the United Nations Development Programme, the regional economic commissions, the United Nations Economic and Social Office in Beirut, the specialized agencies and the International Atomic Energy Agency, and in particular with those of the United Nations Industrial Development Organization;

(*b*) To take the necessary steps to facilitate, through the work of the Centre for Development Planning, Projections and Policies, the United Nations Conference on Trade and Development, the United Nations Industrial Development Organization and the Advisory Committee on the Application of Science and Technology to Development, the inclusion of the exploitation of the natural resources of the developing countries in programmes for their accelerated economic growth;

(*c*) To submit to the General Assembly at its twenty-third session a progress report on the implementation of the present resolution.

VIII. NOTE ON ASSOCIATION AGREEMENTS WITH THE EUROPEAN ECONOMIC COMMUNITY

A GOOD number of African states have a trade pattern deriving from continued economic links with the former colonial powers. In addition, African states have in some cases increased trade with E.E.C. states in cases where the former colonial power is not an E.E.C. member. Several Association Agreements between African states and the E.E.C. have been concluded, the first and best known being the Yaoundé Convention which expired on 31 May 1969. For the text of the Yaoundé Convention: *International Legal Materials*, vol. 3 (1963), p. 971; Campbell, *Common Market Law*, vol. 2, p. 271.

See also the Lagos Convention, signed on 16 July 1966; *International Legal Materials*, vol. 5 (1966), p. 828; *Journal of Common Market Studies*, vol. 5, p. 200; the East African Association Agreement, signed on 26 July 1968; *International Legal Materials*, vol. 8 (1969), p. 741; and the E.E.C., African and Malagasy States Convention of Association, signed on 29 July 1969; *International Legal Materials*, vol. 8 (1969), p. 741.

See further Okigbo, *Africa and the Common Market*, 1967; Ingrid Doimi di Delupis, *The East African Community and Common Market*, 1970, pp. 129 et seq.; Institut d'Études européennes, Université Libre de Bruxelles, *L'Association à la Communauté économique européenne: Aspects Juridiques*, Bruxelles, 1970, and especially pp. 113–317; Elias, *Journal of World Trade Law*, vol. 2 (1968), p. 189; Tromm, *Common Market Law Review*, vol. 5, p. 50.

IX. INTERNATIONAL COFFEE AGREEMENT, 1968

THE text of the Agreement has been published in the United Kingdom *Treaty Series*, no. 103 (1969), Cmnd. 4211. The Agreement came into force provisionally on 1 October 1968 and definitively on 30 December 1968. It supersedes the agreement adopted in 1962: United Kingdom *Treaty Series*, no. 31 (1965), Cmnd. 2640. At least 20 African States are parties.

Since many underdeveloped countries derive much of their income from export of primary products, agreements intended to regulate and stabilize trade and prices have an obvious importance. Generally on commodity agreements see *Law and Contemporary Problems*, vol. 28 (1963), no. 2 (Duke University School of Law).

On the background to the 1968 Coffee Agreement see John Woodland, *The Times*, 31 May 1967; Bilder, *Law and Contemporary Problems*, vol. 28, p. 328; Chayes, Ehrlich, and Lowenfeld, *International Legal Process*, vol. 1 (1968), p. 576. On the possibility of a Cocoa Agreement see Ursula Wassermann, *Journal of World Trade Law*, vol. 2 (1968), p. 521. In November 1970 the Board of the African and Malagasy Coffee Organization proposed that negotiations should start with the International Coffee Organization with the aim of preparing the guidelines for a third International Coffee Agreement.

TEXT

INTERNATIONAL COFFEE AGREEMENT, 1968

PREAMBLE

The Governments Parties to this Agreement,

Recognizing the exceptional importance of coffee to the economies of many countries which are largely dependent upon this commodity for their export earnings and thus for the continuation of their development programmes in the social and economic fields;

Considering that close international co-operation on coffee marketing will stimulate the economic diversification and development of coffee-producing countries and thus contribute to a strengthening of the political and economic bonds between producers and consumers;

Finding reason to expect a tendency toward persistent disequilibrium between production and consumption, accumulation of burdensome stocks, and pronounced fluctuations in prices, which can be harmful both to producers and to consumers;

Believing that, in the absence of international measures, this situation cannot be corrected by normal market forces; and

Noting the renegotiation by the International Coffee Council of the International Coffee Agreement, 1962,

Have agreed as follows:

CHAPTER I. OBJECTIVES

Article 1

Objectives

The objectives of the Agreement are:

(1) to achieve a reasonable balance between supply and demand on a basis which will assure adequate supplies of coffee to consumers and markets for coffee to producers at equitable prices and which will bring about long-term equilibrium between production and consumption;

(2) to alleviate the serious hardship caused by burdensome surpluses and excessive fluctuations in the prices of coffee which are harmful both to producers and to consumers;

(3) to contribute to the development of productive resources and to the promotion and maintenance of employment and income in the Member countries, thereby helping to bring about fair wages, higher living standards, and better working conditions;

(4) to assist in increasing the purchasing power of coffee-exporting countries by keeping prices at equitable levels and by increasing consumption;

(5) to encourage the consumption of coffee by every possible means; and

(6) in general, in recognition of the relationship of the trade in coffee to the economic stability of markets for industrial products, to further international co-operation in connection with world coffee problems.

CHAPTER II. DEFINITIONS

Article 2

Definitions

For the purposes of the Agreement:

(1) 'Coffee' means the beans and berries of the coffee tree, whether parchment, green or roasted, and includes ground, decaffeinated, liquid and soluble coffee. These terms shall have the following meaning:

    (*a*) 'green coffee' means all coffee in the naked bean form before roasting;

(*b*) 'coffee berries' means the complete fruit of the coffee tree; to find the equivalent of coffee berries to green coffee, multiply the net weight of the dried coffee berries by 0·50;

(*c*) 'parchment coffee' means the green coffee bean contained in the parchment skin; to find the equivalent of parchment coffee to green coffee, multiply the net weight of the parchment coffee by 0·80;

(*d*) 'roasted coffee' means green coffee roasted to any degree and includes ground coffee; to find the equivalent of roasted coffee to green coffee, multiply the net weight of roasted coffee by 1·19;

(*e*) 'decaffeinated coffee' means green, roasted or soluble coffee from which caffein has been extracted; to find the equivalent of decaffeinated coffee to green coffee, multiply the net weight of the decaffeinated coffee in green, roasted or soluble form by 1·00, 1·19 or 3·00 respectively;

(*f*) 'liquid coffee' means the water-soluble solids derived from roasted coffee and put into liquid form; to find the equivalent of liquid to green coffee, multiply the net weight of the dried coffee solids contained in the liquid coffee by 3·00;

(*g*) 'soluble coffee' means the dried water-soluble solids derived from roasted coffee; to find the equivalent of soluble coffee to green coffee, multiply the net weight of the soluble coffee by 3·00.

(2) 'Bag' means 60 kilogrammes or 132·276 pounds of green coffee; 'ton' means a metric ton of 1,000 kilogrammes or 2,204·6 pounds; and 'pound' means 453·597 grammes.

(3) 'Coffee year' means the period of one year, from 1 October through 30 September.

(4) 'Export of Coffee' means, except as otherwise provided in Article 39, any shipment of coffee which leaves the territory of the country where the coffee was grown.

(5) 'Organization', 'Council' and 'Board' mean, respectively, the International Coffee Organization, the International Coffee Council, and the Executive Board referred to in Article 7 of the Agreement.

(6) 'Member' means a Contracting Party; a dependent territory or territories in respect of which separate Membership has been declared under Article 4; or two or more Contracting Parties or dependent territories or both, which participate in the Organization as a Member group under Articles 5 or 6.

(7) 'Exporting Member' or 'exporting country' means a Member or country, respectively, which is a net exporter of coffee; that is, whose exports exceed its imports.

(8) 'Importing Member' or 'importing country' means a Member or country, respectively, which is a net importer of coffee; that is, whose imports exceed its exports.

(9) 'Producing Member' or 'producing country' means a Member or country, respectively, which grows coffee in commercially significant quantities.

(10) 'Distributed simple majority vote' means a majority of the votes cast by exporting Members present and voting, and a majority of the votes cast by importing Members present and voting, counted separately.

(11) 'Distributed two-thirds majority vote' means a two-thirds majority of the votes cast by exporting Members present and voting and a two-thirds majority of the votes cast by importing Members present and voting, counted separately.

(12) 'Entry into force' means, except as otherwise provided, the date on which the Agreement enters into force, whether provisionally or definitively.

(13) 'Exportable production' means the total production of coffee of an exporting country in a given coffee year less the amount destined for domestic consumption in the same year.

(14) 'Availability for export' means the exportable production of an exporting country in a given coffee year plus accumulated stocks from previous years.

(15) 'Export entitlement' means the total quantity of coffee which a Member is authorized to export under the various provisions of the Agreement, but excluding exports which under the provisions of Article 40 are not charged to quotas.

(16) 'Authorized exports' means actual exports covered by the export entitlement.

(17) 'Permitted exports' means the sum of authorized exports and exports which under the provisions of Article 40 are not charged to quotas.

CHAPTER III. MEMBERSHIP

Article 3

Membership in the Organization

(1) Each Contracting Party, together with those of its dependent territories to which the Agreement is extended under paragraph (1) of Article

65, shall constitute a single Member of the Organization, except as otherwise provided under Articles 4, 5 and 6.

(2) A Member may change its category of Membership previously declared on approval, ratification, acceptance or accession to the Agreement, on such conditions as the Council may agree.

(3) On application by two or more importing Members for a change in the form of their participation in the Agreement and/or their representation in the Organization, and notwithstanding other provisions of the Agreement, the Council may, after consultation with the Members concerned, determine the conditions which shall be applicable to such changed participation and/or representation.

Article 4
Separate membership in respect of dependent territories

Any Contracting Party which is a net importer of coffee may, at any time, by appropriate notification in accordance with paragraph (2) of Article 65, declare that it is participating in the Organization separately with respect to any of its dependent territories which are net exporters of coffee and which it designates. In such case, the metropolitan territory and its non-designated dependent territories will have a single Membership, and its designated dependent territories, either individually or collectively as the notification indicates, will have separate Membership.

Article 5
Group membership upon joining the Organization

(1) Two or more Contracting Parties which are net exporters of coffee may, by appropriate notification to the Secretary-General of the United Nations at the time of deposit of their respective instruments of approval, ratification, acceptance or accession and to the Council, declare that they are joining the Organization as a Member group. A dependent territory to which the Agreement has been extended under paragraph (1) of Article 65 may constitute part of such a Member group if the Government of the State responsible for its international relations has given appropriate notification thereof under paragraph (2) of Article 65. Such Contracting Parties and dependent territories must satisfy the following conditions:

(a) they shall declare their willingness to accept responsibility for group obligations in an individual as well as a group capacity;

(b) they shall subsequently provide sufficient evidence to the Council that the group has the organization necessary to implement a common coffee policy, and that they have the means of complying, together with the other parties to the group, with their obligations under the Agreement; and

(c) they shall subsequently provide evidence to the Council either:

(i) that they have been recognized as a group in a previous international coffee agreement; or

(ii) that they have:

(a) a common or co-ordinated commercial and economic policy in relation to coffee; and

(b) a co-ordinated monetary and financial policy, as well as the organs necessary for implementing such a policy, so that the Council is satisfied that the Member group can comply with the spirit of group membership and the group obligations involved.

(2) The Member group shall constitute a single Member of the Organization, except that each party to the group shall be treated as if it were a single Member as regards all matters arising under the following provisions:

(a) Chapters XII, XIII and XVI;

(b) Articles 10, 11 and 19 of Chapter IV; and

(c) Article 68 of Chapter XX.

(3) The Contracting Parties and dependent territories joining as a Member group shall specify the Government or organization which will represent them in the Council as regards all matters arising under the Agreement other than those specified in paragraph (2) of this Article.

(4) The Member group's voting rights shall be as follows:

(a) the Member group shall have the same number of basic votes as a single Member country joining the Organization in an individual capacity. These basic votes shall be attributed to and exercised by the Government or organization representing the group;

(b) in the event of a vote on any matters arising under provisions specified in paragraph (2) of this Article, the parties to the Member group may exercise separately the votes attributed to them by the provisions of paragraph (3) of Article 12 as if each were an individual Member of the Organization, except for the basic votes, which shall remain attributable only to the Government or organization representing the group.

(5) Any Contracting Party or dependent territory which is a party to a Member group may, by notification to the Council, withdraw from that Group and become a separate Member. Such withdrawal shall take effect upon receipt of the notification by the Council. In case of such withdrawal

from a group, or in case a party to a group ceases, by withdrawal from the Organization or otherwise, to be such a party, the remaining parties to the group may apply to the Council to maintain the group, and the group shall continue to exist unless the Council disapproves the application. If the Member group is dissolved, each former party to the group will become a separate Member. A Member which has ceased to be a party to a group may not, as long as the Agreement remains in force, again become a party to a group.

Article 6

Subsequent group membership

Two or more exporting Members may, at any time after the Agreement has entered into force with respect to them, apply to the Council to form a Member group. The Council shall approve the application if it finds that the Members have made a declaration, and have provided evidence, satisfying the requirements of paragraph (1) of Article 5. Upon such approval the Member group shall be subject to the provisions of paragraphs (2), (3), (4) and (5) of that Article.

Chapter IV. Organization and Administration

Article 7

Seat and structure of the International Coffee Organization

(1) The International Coffee Organization established under the 1962 Agreement shall continue in being to administer the provisions and supervise the operation of the Agreement.

(2) The seat of the Organization shall be in London unless the Council by a distributed two-thirds majority vote decides otherwise.

(3) The Organization shall function through the International Coffee Council, its Executive Board, its Executive Director and its staff.

Article 8

Composition of the International Coffee Council

(1) The highest authority of the Organization shall be the International Coffee Council, which shall consist of all the Members of the Organization.

(2) Each Member shall be represented on the Council by a representative and one or more alternates. A Member may also designate one or more advisers to accompany its representative or alternates.

Article 9

Powers and functions of the Council

(1) All powers specifically conferred by the Agreement shall be vested in the Council, which shall have the powers and perform the functions necessary to carry out the provisions of the Agreement.

(2) The Council shall, by a distributed two-thirds majority vote, establish such rules and regulations, including its own rules of procedure and the financial and staff regulations of the Organization, as are necessary to carry out the provisions of the Agreement and are consistent therewith. The Council may, in its rules of procedure, provide a procedure whereby it may, without meeting, decide specific questions.

(3) The Council shall also keep such records as are required to perform its functions under the Agreement and such other records as it considers desirable. The Council shall publish an annual report.

Article 10

Election of the Chairman and Vice-Chairmen of the Council

(1) The Council shall elect, for each coffee year, a Chairman and a first, a second and a third Vice-Chairman.

(2) As a general rule, the Chairman and the first Vice-Chairman shall both be elected either from among the representatives of exporting Members, or from among the representatives of importing Members, and the second and the third Vice-Chairmen shall be elected from representatives of the other category of Members. These offices shall alternate each coffee year between the two categories of Members.

(3) Neither the Chairman nor any Vice-Chairman acting as Chairman shall have the right to vote. His alternate will in such case exercise the Member's voting rights.

Article 11

Sessions of the Council

As a general rule, the Council shall hold regular sessions twice a year. It may hold special sessions if it so decides. Special sessions shall also be held when either the Executive Board, or any five Members, or a Member or Members having at least 200 votes so request. Notice of sessions shall be given at least thirty days in advance, except in cases of emergency. Sessions shall be held at the seat of the Organization, unless the Council decides otherwise.

Article 12

Votes

(1) The exporting Members shall together hold 1,000 votes and the importing Members shall together hold 1,000 votes, distributed within each category of Members—that is, exporting and importing Members, respectively—as provided in the following paragraphs of this Article.

(2) Each Member shall have five basic votes, provided that the total number of basic votes within each category of Members does not exceed 150. Should there be more than thirty exporting Members or more than thirty importing Members, the number of basic votes for each Member within that category of Members shall be adjusted so as to keep the number of basic votes for each category of Members within the maximum of 150.

(3) The remaining votes of exporting Members shall be divided among those Members in proportion to their respective basic export quotas, except that in the event of a vote on any matter arising under the provisions specified in paragraph (2) of Article 5, the remaining votes of a Member group shall be divided among the parties to that group in proportion to their respective participation in the basic export quota of the Member group. Any exporting Member to which a basic quota has not been allotted shall receive no share of these remaining votes.

(4) The remaining votes of importing Members shall be divided among those Members in proportion to the average volume of their respective coffee imports in the preceding three-year period.

(5) The distribution of votes shall be determined by the Council at the beginning of each coffee year and shall remain in effect during that year, except as provided in paragraph (6) of this Article.

(6) The Council shall provide for the redistribution of votes in accordance with this Article whenever there is a change in the Membership of the Organization, or if the voting rights of a Member are suspended or regained under the provisions of Articles 25, 38, 45, 48, 54 or 59.

(7) No Member shall hold more than 400 votes.

(8) There shall be no fractional votes.

Article 13

Voting procedure of the Council

(1) Each representative shall be entitled to cast the number of votes held by the Member represented by him, and cannot divide its votes. He may,

however, cast differently any votes which he exercises pursuant to paragraph (2) of this Article.

(2) Any exporting Member may authorize any other exporting Member, and any importing Member may authorize any other importing Member, to represent its interests and to exercise its right to vote at any meeting or meetings of the Council. The limitation provided for in paragraph (7) of Article 12 shall not apply in this case.

Article 14
Decisions of the Council

(1) All decisions of the Council shall be taken, and all recommendations shall be made, by a distributed simple majority vote unless otherwise provided in the Agreement.

(2) The following procedure shall apply with respect to any action by the Council which under the Agreement requires a distributed two-thirds majority vote:

(a) if a distributed two-thirds majority vote is not obtained because of the negative vote of three or less exporting or three or less importing Members, the proposal shall, if the Council so decides by a majority of the Members present and by a distributed simple majority vote, be put to a vote again within 48 hours;

(b) if a distributed two-thirds majority vote is again not obtained because of the negative vote of two or less importing or two or less exporting Members, the proposal shall, if the Council so decides by a majority of the Members present and by a distributed simple majority vote, be put to a vote again within 24 hours;

(c) if a distributed two-thirds majority vote is not obtained in the third vote because of the negative vote of one exporting Member or one importing Member, the proposal shall be considered adopted;

(d) if the Council fails to put a proposal to a further vote, it shall be considered rejected.

(3) The Members undertake to accept as binding all decisions of the Council under the provisions of the Agreement.

Article 15
Composition of the Board

(1) The Executive Board shall consist of eight exporting Members and eight importing Members, elected for each coffee year in accordance with Article 16. Members may be re-elected.

(2) Each member of the Board shall appoint one representative and one or more alternates.

(3) The Chairman of the Board shall be appointed by the Council for each coffee year and may be re-appointed. He shall not have the right to vote. If a representative is appointed Chairman, his alternate will have the right to vote in his place.

(4) The Board shall normally meet at the seat of the Organization, but may meet elsewhere.

Article 16
Election of the Board

(1) The exporting and the importing Members on the Board shall be elected in the Council by the exporting and the importing Members of the Organization respectively. The election within each category shall be held in accordance with the following paragraphs of this Article.

(2) Each Member shall cast all the votes to which it is entitled under Article 12 for a single candidate. A Member may cast for another candidate any votes which it exercises pursuant to paragraph (2) of Article 13.

(3) The eight candidates receiving the largest number of votes shall be elected; however, no candidate shall be elected on the first ballot unless it receives at least 75 votes.

(4) If under the provisions of paragraph (3) of this Article less than eight candidates are elected on the first ballot, further ballots shall be held in which only Members which did not vote for any of the candidates elected shall have the right to vote. In each further ballot, the minimum number of votes required for election shall be successfully diminished by five until eight candidates are elected.

(5) Any Member who did not vote for any of the Members elected shall assign its votes to one of them, subject to paragraphs (6) and (7) of this Article.

(6) A Member shall be deemed to have received the number of votes originally cast for it when it was elected and, in addition, the number of votes assigned to it, provided that the total number of votes shall not exceed 499 for any Member elected.

(7) If the votes deemed received by an elected Member would otherwise exceed 499, Members which voted for or assigned their votes to such elected Member shall arrange among themselves for one or more of them to withdraw their votes from that Member and assign or reassign them to

another elected Member so that the votes received by each elected Member shall not exceed the limit of 499.

Article 17

Competence of the Board

(1) The Board shall be responsible to and work under the general direction of the Council.

(2) The Council by a distributed simple majority vote may delegate to the Board the exercise of any or all of its powers, other than the following:

    (a) approval of the administrative budget and assessment of contributions under Article 24;

    (b) determination of quotas under the Agreement with the exception of adjustments made under the provisions of Article 35 paragraph (3) and of Article 37;

    (c) suspension of the voting rights of a Member under Article 45 or 59;

    (d) establishment or revision of individual country and world production goals under Article 48;

    (e) establishment of a policy relative to stocks under Article 49;

    (f) waiver of the obligations of a Member under Article 57;

    (g) decision of disputes under Article 59;

    (h) establishment of conditions for accession under Article 63;

    (i) a decision to require the withdrawal of a Member under Article 67;

    (j) extension or termination of the Agreement under Article 69; and

    (k) recommendation of amendments to Members under Article 70.

(3) The Council by a distributed simple majority vote may at any time revoke any delegation of powers to the Board.

Article 18

Voting procedure of the Board

(1) Each member of the Board shall be entitled to cast the number of votes received by it under the provisions of paragraphs (6) and (7) of Article 16. Voting by proxy shall not be allowed. A member may not split its votes.

(2) Any action taken by the Board shall require the same majority as such action would require if taken by the Council.

Article 19

Quorum for the Council and the Board

(1) The quorum for any meeting of the Council shall be the presence of a majority of the Members representing a distributed two-thirds majority

of the total votes. If there is no quorum on the day appointed for the opening of any Council session, or if in the course of any Council session there is no quorum at three successive meetings, the Council shall be convened seven days later; at that time and throughout the remainder of that session the quorum shall be the presence of a majority of the Members representing a distributed simple majority of the votes. Representation in accordance with paragraph (2) of Article 13 shall be considered as presence.

(2) The quorum for any meeting of the Board shall be the presence of a majority of the members representing a distributed two-thirds majority of the total votes.

Article 20

The Executive Director and the staff

(1) The Council shall appoint the Executive Director on the recommendation of the Board. The terms of appointment of the Executive Director shall be established by the Council and shall be comparable to those applying to corresponding officials of similar inter-governmental organizations.

(2) The Executive Director shall be the chief administrative officer of the Organization and shall be responsible for the performance of any duties devolving upon him in the administration of the Agreement.

(3) The Executive Director shall appoint the staff in accordance with regulations established by the Council.

(4) Neither the Executive Director nor any member of the staff shall have any financial interest in the coffee industry, coffee trade, or coffee transportation.

(5) In the performance of their duties, the Executive Director and the staff shall not seek or receive instructions from any Member or from any other authority external to the Organization. They shall refrain from any action which might reflect on their position as international officials responsible only to the Organization. Each Member undertakes to respect the exclusively international character of the responsibilities of the Executive Director and the staff and not to seek to influence them in the discharge of their responsibilities.

Article 21

Co-operation with other organizations

The Council may make whatever arrangements are desirable for consultation and co-operation with the United Nations and its specialized agencies and with other appropriate inter-governmental organizations.

The Council may invite these organizations and any organizations concerned with coffee to send observers to its meetings.

CHAPTER V. PRIVILEGES AND IMMUNITIES

Article 22

Privileges and immunities

(1) The Organization shall have legal personality. It shall in particular have the capacity to contract, acquire and dispose of movable and immovable property and to institute legal proceedings.

(2) The Government of the country in which the headquarters of the Organization is situated (hereinafter referred to as 'the host Government') shall conclude with the Organization as soon as possible an agreement to be approved by the Council relating to the status, privileges and immunities of the Organization, of its Executive Director and its staff and of representatives of Members while in the territory of the host Government for the purpose of exercising their functions.

(3) The agreement envisaged in paragraph (2) of this Article shall be independent of the present Agreement and shall prescribe the conditions for its termination.

(4) Unless any other taxation arrangements are implemented under the agreement envisaged in paragraph (2) of this Article the host Government:

    (*a*) shall grant exemption from taxation on the remuneration paid by the Organization to its employees, except that such exemption need not apply to nationals of that country; and

    (*b*) shall grant exemption from taxation on the assets, income and other property of the Organization.

(5) Following the approval of the agreement envisaged in paragraph (2) of this Article, the Organization may conclude with one or more other Members agreements to be approved by the Council relating to such privileges and immunities as may be necessary for the proper functioning of the International Coffee Agreement.

CHAPTER VI. FINANCE

Article 23

Finance

(1) The expenses of delegations to the Council, representatives on the Board, and representatives on any of the committees of the Council or the Board shall be met by their respective Governments.

(2) The other expenses necessary for the administration of the Agreement shall be met by annual contributions from the Members assessed in accordance with Article 24. However, the Council may levy fees for specific services.

(3) The financial year of the Organization shall be the same as the coffee year.

Article 24
Determination of the budget and assessment of contributions

(1) During the second half of each financial year the Council shall approve the administrative budget of the Organization for the following financial year and shall assess the contribution of each Member to that budget.

(2) The contribution of each Member to the budget for each financial year shall be in the proportion which the number of its votes at the time the budget for that financial year is approved bears to the total votes of all the Members. However, if there is any change in the distribution of votes among Members in accordance with the provisions of paragraph (5) of Article 12 at the beginning of the financial year for which contributions are assessed, such contributions shall be correspondingly adjusted for that year. In determining contributions, the votes of each Member shall be calculated without regard to the suspension of any Member's voting rights or any redistribution of votes resulting therefrom.

(3) The initial contribution of any Member joining the Organization after the entry into force of the Agreement shall be assessed by the Council on the basis of the number of votes to be held by it and the period remaining in the current financial year, but the assessments made upon other Members for the current financial year shall not be altered.

Article 25
Payment of contributions

(1) Contributions to the administrative budget for each financial year shall be payable in freely convertible currency, and shall become due on the first day of that financial year.

(2) If any Member fails to pay its full contribution to the administrative budget within six months of the date on which the contribution is due, both its voting rights in the Council and its right to have its votes cast in the Board shall be suspended until such contribution has been paid. However, unless the Council by a distributed two-thirds majority vote so decides, such Member shall not be deprived of any if its other rights nor relieved of any of its obligations under the Agreement.

(3) Any Member whose voting rights have been suspended, either under paragraph (2) of this Article or under Articles 38, 45, 48, 54 or 59 shall nevertheless remain responsible for the payment of its contribution.

Article 26

Audit and publication of accounts

As soon as possible after the close of each financial year an independently audited statement of the Organization's receipts and expenditures during that financial year shall be presented to the Council for approval and publication.

CHAPTER VII. REGULATION OF EXPORTS

Article 27

General undertakings by Members

(1) The Members undertake to conduct their trade policy so that the objectives set forth in Article 1, and in particular paragraph (4) of that Article, may be achieved. They agree on the desirability of operating the Agreement in a manner such that the real income derived from the export of coffee could be progressively increased so as to make it consonant with their needs for foreign exchange to support their programmes for social and economic progress.

(2) To attain these purposes through the fixing of quotas as provided for in this Chapter and in other ways carrying out the provisions of the Agreement, the Members agree on the necessity of assuring that the general level of coffee prices does not decline below the general level of such prices in 1962.

(3) The Members further agree on the desirability of assuring to consumers prices which are equitable and which will not hamper a desirable increase in consumption.

Article 28

Basic export quotas

Beginning on 1 October 1968 the exporting countries shall have the basic export quotas specified in Annex A.

Article 29

Basic export quota of a Member group

Where two or more countries listed in Annex A form a Member group in accordance with Article 5, the basic export quotas specified for those countries in Annex A shall be added together and the combined total treated as a single basic quota for the purposes of this Chapter.

Article 30

Fixing of annual export quotas

(1) At least 30 days before the beginning of each coffee year the Council by a two-thirds majority vote shall adopt an estimate of total world imports and exports for the following coffee year and an estimate of probable exports from non-member countries.

(2) In the light of these estimates the Council shall forthwith fix annual export quotas for all exporting Members. Such annual export quotas shall be the same percentage of the basic export quotas specified in Annex A, save for those exporting Members whose annual quotas are subject to the provisions of paragraph (2) of Article 31.

Article 31

Additional provisions concerning basic and annual export quotas

(1) A basic quota shall not be allotted to an exporting Member whose average annual authorized exports of coffee for the preceding three-year period were less than 100,000 bags and its annual export quota shall be calculated in accordance with paragraph (2) of this Article. When the annual export quota of any such Member reaches 100,000 bags the Council shall establish a basic quota for the exporting Member concerned.

(2) Without prejudice to the provisions of footnote (2) of Annex A to the Agreement each exporting Member to which a basic quota has not been allotted shall have in the coffee year 1968–69 the quota indicated in footnote (1) of Annex A to the Agreement. In each of the subsequent years the quota, subject to the provisions of paragraph (3) of this Article, shall be increased by 10 per cent of that initial quota until the maximum of 100,000 bags mentioned in paragraph (1) of this Article is reached.

(3) Not later than 31 July of each year, each Member concerned shall notify the Executive Director, for the information of the Council, of the amount of coffee likely to be available for export under quota during the next coffee year. The quota for the next coffee year shall be the amount thus indicated by the exporting Member provided that such amount is within the permissible limit defined in paragraph (2) of this Article.

(4) Exporting Members to which basic quotas have not been allotted shall be subject to the provisions of Article 27, 29, 32, 34, 35, 38 and 40.

(5) Any Trust Territory, administered under a trusteeship agreement with the United Nations, whose annual exports to countries other than the Administering Authority do not exceed 100,000 bags shall not be subject

to the quota provisions of the Agreement so long as its exports do not exceed that quantity.

Article 32

Fixing of quarterly export quotas

(1) Immediately following the fixing of the annual export quotas the Council shall fix quarterly export quotas for each exporting Member for the purpose of keeping supply in reasonable balance with estimated demand throughout the coffee year.

(2) These quotas shall be, as nearly as possible, 25 per cent of the annual export quota of each Member during the coffee year. No Member shall be allowed to export more than 30 per cent in the first quarter, 60 per cent in the first two quarters, and 80 per cent in the first three quarters of the coffee year. If exports by any Member in one quarter are less than its quota for that quarter, the outstanding balance shall be added to its quota for the following quarter of that coffee year.

Article 33

Adjustment of annual export quotas

If market conditions so require, the Council may review the quota situation and may vary the percentage of basic export quotas fixed under paragraph (2) of Article 30. In so doing, the Council shall have regard to any likely shortfalls by Members.

Article 34

Notification of shortfalls

(1) Exporting Members undertake to notify the Council as early in the coffee year as possible but not later than the end of the eighth month thereof, as well as at such later dates as the Council may require, whether they have sufficient coffee available to export the full amount of their quota for that year.

(2) The Council shall take into account these notifications in determining whether or not to adjust the level of export quotas in accordance with Article 33.

Article 35

Adjustment of quarterly export quotas

(1) The Council shall in the circumstances set out in this Article vary the quarterly export quotas fixed for each Member under paragraph (1) of Article 32.

(2) If the Council varies the annual export quotas as provided in Article 33, then that change shall be reflected in the quotas for the current quarter, current and remaining quarters, or the remaining quarters of the coffee year.

(3) Apart from the adjustment provided for in the preceding paragraph, the Council may, if it finds the market situation so requires, make adjustments among the current and remaining quarterly export quotas for the same coffee year, without, however, altering the annual export quotas.

(4) If on account of exceptional circumstances an exporting Member considers that the limitations provided in paragraph (2) of Article 32 would be likely to cause serious harm to its economy, the Council may, at the request of that Member, take appropriate action under Article 57. The Member concerned must furnish evidence of harm and provide adequate guarantees concerning the maintenance of price stability. The Council shall not, however, in any event, authorize a Member to export more than 35 per cent of its annual export quota in the first quarter, 65 per cent in the first two quarters, and 85 per cent in the first three quarters of the coffee year.

(5) All Members recognize that marked price rises or falls occurring within brief periods may unduly distort underlying trends in price, cause grave concern to both producers and consumers, and jeopardize the attainment of the objectives of the Agreement. Accordingly, if such movements in general price levels occur within brief periods, Members may request a meeting of the Council which, by a distributed simple majority vote, may revise the total level of the quarterly export quotas in effect.

(6) If the Council finds that a sharp and unusual increase or decrease in the general level of prices is due to artificial manipulation of the coffee market through agreements among importers or exporters or both, it shall then by a simple majority vote decide on what corrective measures should be applied to readjust the total level of the quarterly export quotas in effect.

Article 36

Procedure for adjusting export quotas

(1) Except as provided for in Articles 31 and 37 annual export quotas shall be fixed and adjusted by altering the basic export quota of each Member by the same percentage.

(2) General changes in all quarterly export quotas, made pursuant to paragraphs (2), (3), (5) and (6) of Article 35, shall be applied *pro rata* to individual quarterly export quotas in accordance with appropriate rules

established by the Council. Such rules shall take account of the different percentages of annual export quotas which the different Members have exported or are entitled to export in each quarter of the coffee year.

(3) All decisions by the Council on the fixing and adjustment of annual and quarterly export quotas under Articles 30, 32, 33 and 35 shall be taken, unless otherwise provided, by a distributed two-thirds majority vote.

Article 37
Additional provisions for adjusting export quotas

(1) In addition to fixing annual export quotas in accordance with estimated total world imports and exports as required by Article 30, the Council shall seek to ensure that:

(a) supplies of the types of coffee that consumers require are available to them;

(b) the prices for the different types of coffee are equitable; and

(c) sharp price fluctuations within brief periods do not occur.

(2) To achieve these objectives the Council may, notwithstanding the provisions of Article 36, adopt a system for the adjustment of annual and quarterly quotas in relation to the movement of the prices of the principal types of coffee. The Council shall annually set a limit not exceeding five per cent by which annual quotas may be reduced under any system so established. For the purposes of such a system the Council may establish price differentials and price brackets for the various types of coffee. In so doing the Council shall take into consideration, among other things, price trends.

(3) Decisions of the Council under the provisions of paragraph (2) of this Article shall be taken by a distributed two-thirds majority vote.

Article 38
Compliance with export quotas

(1) Exporting Members subject to quotas shall adopt the measures required to ensure full compliance with all provisions of the Agreement relating to quotas. In addition to any measures it may itself take, the Council by a distributed two-thirds majority vote may require such Members to adopt additional measures for the effective implementation of the quota system provided for in the Agreement.

(2) Exporting Members shall not exceed the annual and quarterly export quotas allocated to them.

(3) If an exporting Member exceeds its quota for any quarter, the Council shall deduct from one or more of its subsequent quotas a quantity equal to 110 per cent of that excess.

(4) If an exporting Member for the second time while the Agreement remains in force exceeds its quarterly quota, the Council shall deduct from one or more of its subsequent quotas a total amount equal to twice that excess.

(5) If an exporting Member for a third or subsequent time while the Agreement remains in force exceeds its quarterly quota, the Council shall make the same deduction as provided in paragraph (4) of this Article and the voting rights of the Member shall be suspended until such time as the Council decides whether to take action in accordance with Article 67 to require the withdrawal of such a Member from the Organization.

(6) In accordance with rules established by the Council the deductions in quotas provided for in paragraphs (3), (4) and (5) of this Article and the additional action required by paragraph (5) shall be effected by the Council as soon as the necessary information is received.

Article 39
Shipments of coffee from dependent territories

(1) Subject to paragraph (2) of this Article, the shipment of coffee from any of the dependent territories of a Member to its metropolitan territory or to another of its dependent territories for domestic consumption therein or in any other of its dependent territories shall not be considered as the export of coffee, and shall not be subject to any export quota limitations, provided that the Member concerned enters into arrangements satisfactory to the Council with respect to the control of re-exports and such other matters as the Council may determine to be related to the operation of the Agreement and which arise out of the special relationship between the metropolitan territory of the Member and its dependent territories.

(2) The trade in coffee between a Member and any of its dependent territories which, in accordance with Article 4 or 5, is a separate Member of the Organization or a party to a Member group, shall however be treated, for the purposes of the Agreement, as the export of coffee.

Article 40
Exports not charged to quotas

(1) To facilitate the increase of coffee consumption in certain areas of the world having a low *per capita* consumption and considerable potential for expansion, exports to countries listed in Annex B shall not, subject to the

provisions of sub-paragraph 2 (*f*) of this Article, be charged to quotas. The Council shall review Annex B annually to determine whether any country or countries should be deleted or added, and may, if it so decides, take action accordingly.

(2) The provisions of the following sub-paragraphs shall be applicable to exports to the countries listed in Annex B:

(*a*) The Council shall prepare annually an estimate of imports for internal consumption by the countries listed in Annex B after reviewing the results obtained in the previous year with regard to the increase of coffee consumption in those countries and taking into account the probable effect of promotion campaigns and trade arrangements. The Council may revise this estimate in the course of the year. Exporting Members shall not in the aggregate export to the countries listed in Annex B more than the quantity set by the Council and for that purpose the Organization shall keep Members informed of current exports to such countries. Exporting Members shall inform the Organization not later than thirty days after the end of each month of all exports made to each of the countries listed in Annex B during that month.

(*b*) Members shall supply such statistics and other information as the Organization may require to assist it in controlling the flow of coffee to countries listed in Annex B and to ensure that it is consumed in such countries.

(*c*) Exporting Members shall endeavour to renegotiate existing trade agreements as soon as possible in order to include in them provisions designed to prevent re-exports of coffee from the countries listed in Annex B to traditional markets. Exporting Members shall also include such provisions in all new trade agreements and in all new sales contracts not covered by trade agreements, whether such contracts are negotiated with private traders or with government organizations.

(*d*) To maintain control at all times of exports to countries listed in Annex B, exporting Members shall clearly mark all coffee bags destined to those countries with the words 'New Market' and shall require adequate guarantees to prevent re-exportation or diversion to countries not listed in Annex B. The Council may establish appropriate rules for this purpose. All Members other than those listed in Annex B, shall prohibit, without exception, the entry of all shipments of coffee consigned directly from, or diverted from, any country listed in Annex B, or which bear evidence on the bags or the export documents of having been originally destined to a country listed in Annex B, or which are accompanied by a Certificate showing a destination in a country listed in Annex B or marked 'New Market'.

(e) The Council shall annually prepare a comprehensive report on the results obtained in the development of coffee markets in the countries listed in Annex B.

(f) If coffee exported by a Member to a country listed in Annex B is re-exported, or diverted to any country not listed in Annex B, the Council shall charge the corresponding amount to the quota of that exporting Member and in addition may, in accordance with rules established by the Council, apply the provisions of paragraph (4) of Article 38. Should there again be a re-exportation from the same country listed in Annex B, the Council shall investigate the case and, if it deems necessary, may at any time delete that country from Annex B.

(3) Exports of coffee beans as raw material for industrial processing for any purposes other than human consumption as a beverage or foodstuff shall not be charged to quotas, provided that the Council is satisfied from information supplied by the exporting Member that the coffee beans are in fact used for such other purposes.

(4) The Council may, upon application by an exporting Member, decide that coffee exports made by that Member for humanitarian or other non-commercial purposes shall not be charged to its quota.

Article 41

Regional and inter-regional price arrangements

(1) Regional and inter-regional price arrangements among exporting Members shall be consistent with the general objectives of the Agreement and shall be registered with the Council. Such arrangements shall take into account the interests of both producers and consumers and the objectives of the Agreement. Any Member of the Organization which considers that any of these arrangements are likely to lead to results not in accordance with the objectives of the Agreement may request that the Council discuss them with the Members concerned at its next session.

(2) In consultation with Members and with any regional organization to which they belong, the Council may recommend a scale of price differentials for various grades and qualities of coffee which Members should strive to achieve through their pricing policies.

(3) Should sharp price fluctuations occur within brief periods in respect of those grades and qualities of coffee for which a scale of price differentials

has been adopted as the result of recommendations made under paragraph (2) of this Article, the Council may recommend appropriate measures to correct the situation.

Article 42

Survey of market trends

The Council shall keep under constant survey the trends of the coffee market with a view to recommending price policies, taking into consideration the results achieved through the quota mechanism of the Agreement.

CHAPTER VIII. CERTIFICATES OF ORIGIN AND RE-EXPORT

Article 43

Certificates of origin and re-export

(1) Every export of coffee from any Member in whose territory that coffee has been grown shall be accompanied by a valid Certificate of Origin in accordance with rules established by the Council and issued by a qualified agency chosen by that Member and approved by the Organization. Each Member shall determine the number of copies of the Certificate it will require and each original Certificate and all copies thereof shall bear a serial number. Unless the Council decides otherwise the original of the Certificate shall accompany the documents of export and a copy shall be furnished immediately to the Organization by that Member, except that original Certificates issued to cover exports of coffee to non-member countries shall be despatched directly to the Organization by that Member.

(2) Every re-export of coffee from a Member shall be accompanied by a valid Certificate of Re-export, in accordance with the rules established by the Council, issued by a qualified agency chosen by that Member and approved by the Organization, certifying that the coffee in question was imported in accordance with the provisions of the Agreement. Each Member shall determine the number of copies of the Certificate it will require and each original Certificate and all copies thereof shall bear a serial number. Unless the Council decides otherwise, the original of the Certificate of Re-export shall accompany the documents of re-export and a copy shall be furnished immediately to the Organization by the re-exporting Member, except that original Certificates of Re-export issued to cover re-exports of coffee to a non-member country shall be despatched directly to the Organization.

(3) Each Member shall notify the Organization of the government or non-government agency which is to administer and perform the functions speci-

fied in paragraphs (1) and (2) of this Article. The Organization shall specifically approve any such non-government agency upon submission of satisfactory evidence by the Member country of the agency's ability and willingness to fulfil the Member's responsibilities in accordance with the rules and regulations established under the provisions of this Agreement. The Council may at any time, for cause, declare a particular non-government agency to be no longer acceptable to it. The Council shall, either directly or through an internationally recognized world-wide organization, take all necessary steps so that at any time it will be able to satisfy itself that Certificates of Origin and Certificates of Re-export are being issued and used correctly and to ascertain the quantities of coffee which have been exported by each Member.

(4) A non-government agency approved as a certifying agency under the provisions of paragraph (3) of this Article shall keep records of the Certificates issued and the basis for their issue, for a period of not less than two years. In order to obtain approval as a certifying agency under the provisions of paragraph (3) of this Article a non-government agency must previously agree to make the above records available for examination by the Organization.

(5) Members shall prohibit the entry of any shipment of coffee from any other Member, whether imported direct or via a non-member, which is not accompanied by a valid Certificate of Origin or of Re-export issued in accordance with the rules established by the Council.

(6) Small quantities of coffee in such forms as the Council may determine, or coffee for direct consumption on ships, aircraft and other international carriers, shall be exempt from the provisions of paragraphs (1) and (2) of this Article.

CHAPTER IX. PROCESSED COFFEE

Article 44

Measures relating to processed coffee

(1) No Member shall apply governmental measures affecting its exports and re-exports of coffee to another Member which, when taken as a whole in relation to that other Member, amount to discriminatory treatment in favour of processed coffee as compared with green coffee. In the application of this provision, Members may have due regard to:

(a) the special situation of markets listed in Annex B of the Agreement;
(b) differential treatment in an importing Member as far as imports or re-exports of the various forms of coffee are concerned.

(2) (*a*) If a Member considers that the provisions of paragraph (1) of this Article are not being complied with, it may notify the Executive Director in writing of its complaint with a detailed report of the reasons for its opinion together with a description of the measures it considers should be taken. The Executive Director shall forthwith inform the Member against which the complaint has been made and seek its views. He shall encourage the Members to reach a mutually satisfactory solution and as soon as possible make a full report to the Council including the measures the complaining Member considers should be taken and the views of the other party.

(*b*) If a solution has not been found within 30 days after receipt of the notification by the Executive Director, he shall not later than 40 days after the receipt of the notification establish an arbitration panel. The panel shall consist of:

   (i) one person designated by the complaining Member;
   (ii) one person designated by the Member against which the complaint has been made; and
   (iii) a chairman mutually agreed upon by the Members involved or, failing such agreement, by the two persons designated under (i) and (ii).

(*c*) If the panel is not fully constituted within 45 days after the receipt of the notification by the Executive Director, the remaining arbitrators shall be appointed within 10 further days by the Chairman of the Council after consultation with the Members involved.

(*d*) None of the arbitrators shall be officials of any Government involved in the case or have any interest in its outcome.

(*e*) The Members concerned shall facilitate the work of the panel and make available all relevant information.

(*f*) The arbitration panel shall, on the basis of all the information at its disposal, determine, within three weeks after its establishment whether, and if so to what extent, there exists discriminatory treatment.

(*g*) Decisions of the panel on all questions, whether of substance or procedure, shall if necessary be by majority vote.

(*h*) The Executive Director shall forthwith notify the Members concerned and inform the Council of the panel's conclusions.

(*i*) The costs of the arbitration panel shall be charged to the administrative budget of the Organization.

(3) (*a*) If discriminatory treatment is found to exist the Member concerned will be given a period of 30 days after it has been notified of

the conclusions of the arbitration panel, to correct the situation in accordance with the panel's conclusions. The Member shall inform the Council of the measures it intends to take.

(b) If after this period, the complaining Member considers that the situation has not been corrected it may, after informing the Council, take counter measures which shall not go beyond what is necessary to counteract the discriminatory treatment determined by the arbitration panel and shall last no longer than the discriminatory treatment exists.

(c) The Members concerned shall keep the Council informed of the measures being taken by them.

(4) In applying the counter measures Members undertake to have due regard to the need of developing countries to practise policies designed to broaden the base of their economies through, *inter alia*, industrialization and the export of manufactured products and to do what is necessary to ensure that the provisions of this Article are applied equitably to all Members in a like situation.

(5) None of the provisions of this Article shall be deemed to prevent a Member from raising in the Council an issue under this Article or having recourse to Article 58 or 59, provided that any such action shall not interrupt any procedure that has been started under this Article without the consent of the Members concerned, nor prevent such procedure from being initiated unless a procedure under Article 59 in regard to the same issue has been completed.

(6) Any time limit in this Article may be varied by agreement of the Members concerned.

CHAPTER X. REGULATION OF IMPORTS

Article 45

Regulation of imports

(1) To prevent non-member exporting countries from increasing their exports at the expense of Members, each Member shall limit its annual imports of coffee produced in non-member exporting countries to a quantity not in excess of its average annual imports of coffee from those countries during the calendar years 1960, 1961 and 1962.

(2) The Council by a distributed two-thirds majority may suspend or vary these quantitative limitations if it finds such action necessary to further the purposes of the Agreement.

(3) The Council shall prepare annual reports of the quantity of permissible imports of coffee of non-member origin and quarterly reports of imports by each importing Member under the provisions of paragraph (1) of this Article.

(4) The obligations of the preceding paragraphs of this Article shall not derogate from any conflicting bilateral or multilateral obligations which importing Members entered into with non-member countries before 1 August 1962 provided that any importing Member which has such conflicting obligations shall carry them out in such a way as to minimize the conflict with the obligations of the preceding paragraphs, take steps as soon as possible to bring its obligations into harmony with those paragraphs, and inform the Council of the details of the conflicting obligations and of the steps taken to minimize or eliminate the conflict.

(5) If an importing Member fails to comply with the provisions of this Article the Council by a distributed two-thirds majority may suspend both its voting rights in the Council and its right to have its votes cast in the Board.

CHAPTER XI. INCREASE OF CONSUMPTION

Article 46

Promotion

(1) The Council shall sponsor the promotion of coffee consumption. To achieve this purpose it may maintain a separate committee with the objective of promoting consumption in importing countries by all appropriate means without regard to origin, type or brand of coffee and of striving to achieve and maintain the highest quality and purity of the beverage.

(2) The following provisions shall apply to such committee:

  (*a*) The cost of the promotion programme shall be met by contributions from exporting Members.

  (*b*) Importing Members may also contribute financially to the promotion programme.

  (*c*) Membership in the committee shall be limited to Members contributing to the promotion programme.

  (*d*) The size and cost of the promotion programme shall be reviewed by the Council.

  (*e*) The bye-laws of the committee shall be approved by the Council.

  (*f*) The committee shall obtain the approval of a Member before conducting a campaign in that Member's country.

  (*g*) The committee shall control all resources of promotion and approve all accounts related thereto.

(3) The ordinary administrative expenses relating to the permanent staff of the Organization employed directly on promotion activities, other than the costs of their travel for promotion purposes, shall be charged to the administrative budget of the Organization.

Article 47

Removals of obstacles to consumption

(1) The Members recognize the utmost importance of achieving the greatest possible increase of coffee consumption as rapidly as possible, in particular through the progressive removal of any obstacles which may hinder such increase.

(2) The Members recognize that there are presently in effect measures which may to a greater or lesser extent hinder the increase in consumption of coffee, in particular:

(a) import arrangements applicable to coffee, including preferential and other tariffs, quotas, operations of Government import monopolies and official purchasing agencies, and other administrative rules and commercial practices;

(b) export arrangements as regards direct or indirect subsidies and other administrative rules and commercial practices; and

(c) internal trade conditions and domestic legal and administrative provisions which may affect consumption.

(3) Having regard to the objectives stated above and to the provisions of paragraph (4) of this Article, the Members shall endeavour to pursue tariff reductions on coffee or to take other action to remove obstacles to increased consumption.

(4) Taking into account their mutual interest and in the spirit of Annex A.II.1 of the Final Act of the First United Nations Conference on Trade and Development, the Members undertake to seek ways and means by which the obstacles to increased trade and consumption referred to in paragraph (2) of this Article could be progressively reduced and eventually wherever possible eliminated, or by which their effects could be substantially diminished.

(5) Members shall inform the Council of all measures adopted with a view to implementing the provisions of this Article.

(6) The Council may, in order to further the purposes of this Article, make any recommendations to Members, and shall examine the results achieved at the first session of the coffee year 1969-70.

CHAPTER XII. PRODUCTION POLICY AND CONTROLS

Article 48

Production policy and controls

(1) Each producing Member undertakes to adjust its production of coffee to a level not exceeding that needed for domestic consumption, permitted exports and stocks as referred to in Article 49.

(2) Prior to 31 December 1968 each exporting Member shall submit to the Executive Board its proposed production goal for coffee year 1972–73, based on the elements set forth in paragraph (1) of this Article. Unless rejected by the Executive Board by a distributed simple majority vote prior to the first session of the Council after 31 December 1968 such goal shall be considered as approved. The Executive Board shall inform the Council of the production goals which have been approved in this manner. If the production goal proposed by an exporting Member is rejected by the Executive Board, the Board shall recommend a production goal for that exporting Member. At its first session after 31 December 1968, which shall be not later than 31 March 1969, the Council by a distributed two-thirds majority vote and in the light of the Board's recommendations shall establish individual production goals for exporting Members whose own proposed goals have been rejected by the Board or who have not submitted proposed production goals.

(3) Until its production goal has been approved by the Organization or established by the Council, in accordance with paragraph (2) of this Article, no exporting Member shall enjoy any increase in its annual export entitlement above the level of its annual export entitlement in effect on 1 April 1969.

(4) The Council shall establish production goals for exporting Members acceding to the Agreement and may establish production goals for producing Members which are not exporting Members.

(5) The Council shall keep the production goals, established or approved under the terms of this Article, under constant review and shall revise them to the extent necessary to ensure that the aggregate of the individual goals is consistent with estimated world requirements.

(6) Members undertake to conform with the individual production goals established or approved under the terms of this Article and each producing Member shall apply whatever policies and procedures it deems necessary for this purpose. Individual production goals established or approved

under the terms of this Article are not binding minima nor do they confer any entitlement to specific levels of exports.

(7) Producing Members shall submit to the Organization, in such form and at such times as the Council shall determine, periodic reports on the measures taken to control production and to conform with their individual production goals established or approved under the terms of this Article. In the light of its appraisal of this and other relevant information the Council shall take such action, general or particular, as it deems necessary or appropriate.

(8) If the Council determines that any producing Member is not taking adequate steps to comply with the provisions of this Article such Member shall not enjoy any subsequent increase in its annual export entitlement and may have its voting rights suspended under the terms of paragraph (7) of Article 59 until the Council is satisfied that the Member is fulfilling its obligations in respect of this Article. If, however, after the elapse of such additional period as the Council shall determine it is established that the Member concerned has still not taken the steps necessary to implement a policy to conform with the objectives of this Article, the Council may require the withdrawal of such Member from the Organization under the terms of Article 67.

(9) The Organization shall, under such conditions as may be determined by the Council, extend to those Members so requesting it all possible assistance within its powers to further the purposes of this Article.

(10) Importing Members undertake to co-operate with exporting Members in their plans for adjusting the production of coffee in accordance with paragraph (1) above. In particular, Members shall refrain from offering directly financial or technical assistance or from supporting proposals for such assistance by any international body to which they belong, for the pursuit of production policies which are contrary to the objectives of this Article, whether the recipient country is a Member of the International Coffee Organization or not. The Organization shall maintain close contact with the international bodies concerned, with a view to securing their maximum co-operation in the implementation of this Article.

(11) Except as specified in paragraph (2) hereof, all decisions provided for in this Article shall be taken by a distributed two-thirds majority vote.

CHAPTER XIII. REGULATION OF STOCKS

Article 49

Policy relative to coffee stocks

(1) To complement the provisions of Article 48 the Council by a distributed two-thirds majority may establish a policy relating to coffee stocks in producing Member countries.

(2) The Council shall take measures to ascertain annually the volume of coffee stocks in the hands of individual exporting Members in accordance with procedures which it shall establish. Members concerned shall facilitate this annual survey.

(3) Producing Members shall ensure that adequate facilities exist in their respective countries for the proper storage of coffee stocks.

CHAPTER XIV. MISCELLANEOUS OBLIGATIONS OF MEMBERS

Article 50

Consultation and co-operation with the trade

(1) The Organization shall maintain close liaison with appropriate non-governmental organizations concerned with international commerce in coffee and with experts in coffee matters.

(2) Members shall conduct their activities within the framework of the Agreement in a manner consonant with established trade channels. In carrying out these activities they shall endeavour to take due account of the legitimate interests of the coffee trade.

Article 51

Barter

In order to avoid jeopardizing the general price structure, Members shall refrain from engaging in direct and individually linked barter transactions involving the sale of coffee in the traditional markets.

Article 52

Mixtures and substitutes

(1) Members shall not maintain any regulations requiring the mixing, processing or using of other products with coffee for commercial resale as coffee. Members shall endeavour to prohibit the sale and advertisement of

products under the name of coffee if such products contain less than the equivalent of 90 per cent green coffee as the basic raw material.

(2) The Executive Director shall submit to the Council an annual report on compliance with the provisions of this Article.

(3) The Council may recommend to any Member that it take the necessary steps to ensure observance of the provisions of this Article.

CHAPTER XV. SEASONAL FINANCING

Article 53

Seasonal financing

(1) The Council shall, upon the request of any Member who is also a party to any bilateral, multilateral, regional or inter-regional agreement in the field of seasonal financing, examine such agreement with a view to verifying its compatibility with the obligations of the Agreement.

(2) The Council may make recommendations to Members with a view to resolving any conflict of obligations which might arise.

(3) The Council may, on the basis of information obtained from the Members concerned, and if it deems appropriate and suitable, make general recommendations with a view to assisting Members which are in need of seasonal financing.

CHAPTER XVI. DIVERSIFICATION FUND

Article 54

Diversification Fund

(1) There is hereby established the Diversification Fund of the International Coffee Organization to further the objectives of limiting the production of coffee in order to bring supply into reasonable balance with world demand. The Fund shall be governed by Statutes to be approved by the Council not later than 31 December 1968.

(2) Participation in the Fund shall be compulsory for each Contracting Party that is not an importing Member and has an export entitlement of over 100,000 bags. Voluntary participation in the Fund by Contracting Parties to which this provision does not apply, and contributions from other sources, shall be under such conditions as may be agreed between the Fund and the parties concerned.

(3) An exporting Participant liable to compulsory participation shall contribute to the Fund in quarterly instalments an amount equivalent to

US$0·60 times the number of bags it actually exports in excess of 100,000 bags each coffee year to quota markets. Contributions shall be made for five consecutive years commencing with coffee year 1968–69. The Fund by a two-thirds majority vote may increase the rate of contribution to a level not exceeding US$1·00 per bag. The annual contribution of each exporting Participant shall be assessed initially on the basis of its export entitlement for the year of assessment as at 1 October. This initial assessment shall be revised on the basis of the actual quantity of coffee exported to quota markets by the Participant during the year of assessment and any necessary adjustment in contribution shall be effected during the ensuing coffee year. The first quarterly instalment of the annual contribution for coffee year 1968–69 becomes due on 1 January 1969 and shall be paid not later than 28 February 1969.

(4) The contribution of each exporting Participant shall be utilized for programmes or projects approved by the Fund carried out inside its territory, but in any case twenty per cent of the contribution shall be payable in freely convertible currency for use in any programmes or projects approved by the Fund. In addition a percentage of the contribution within limits to be established in the Statutes shall be payable in freely convertible currency for the administrative expenses of the Fund.

(5) The percentage of the contribution to be made in freely convertible currency in accordance with paragraph (4) may be increased by mutual agreement between the Fund and the exporting Participant concerned.

(6) At the commencement of the third year of operation of the Fund the Council shall review the results obtained in the first two years and may then revise the provisions of this Article with a view to improving them.

(7) The Statutes of the Fund shall provide for:
  (a) the suspension of contributions in relation to stipulated changes in the level of coffee prices;
  (b) the payment to the Fund in freely convertible currency of any part of the contribution which has not been utilized by the Participant concerned;
  (c) arrangements that would permit the delegation of appropriate functions and activities of the Fund to one or more international financial institutions.

(8) Unless the Council decides otherwise, an exporting Participant which fails to meet its obligations under this Article shall have its voting rights in the Council suspended and shall not enjoy any increase in its export entitlement. If the exporting Participant fails to meet the obligations for

a continuous period of one year, it shall cease to be a Party to the Agreement ninety days thereafter, unless the Council decides otherwise.

(9) Decisions of the Council under the provisions of this Article shall be taken by a distributed two-thirds majority vote.

Chapter XVII. Information and Studies

Article 55

Information

(1) The Organization shall act as a centre for the collection, exchange and publication of:

(a) statistical information on world production, prices, exports and imports, distribution and consumption of coffee; and

(b) in so far as is considered appropriate, technical information on the cultivation, processing and utilization of coffee.

(2) The Council may require Members to furnish such information as it considers necessary for its operations, including regular statistical reports on coffee production, exports and imports, distribution, consumption, stocks and taxation, but no information shall be published which might serve to identify the operations of persons or companies producing, processing or marketing coffee. The Member shall furnish information requested in as detailed and accurate a manner as is practicable.

(3) If a Member fails to supply, or finds difficulty in supplying, within a reasonable time, statistical and other information required by the Council for the proper functioning of the Organization, the Council may require the Member concerned to explain the reasons for non-compliance. If it is found that technical assistance is needed in the matter, the Council may take any necessary measures.

Article 56

Studies

(1) The Council may promote studies in the fields of the economics of coffee production and distribution, the impact of governmental measures in producing and consuming countries on the production and consumption of coffee, the opportunities for expansion of coffee consumption for traditional and possible new uses, and the effects of the operation of the Agreement on producers and consumers of coffee, including their terms of trade.

(2) The Organization may study the practicability of establishing minimum standards for exports of coffee from producing Members. Recommendations in this regard may be discussed by the Council.

CHAPTER XVIII. WAIVER

Article 57

Waiver

(1) The Council by a distributed two-thirds majority vote may relieve a Member of an obligation, on account of exceptional or emergency circumstances, *force majeure*, constitutional obligations, or international obligations under the United Nations Charter for territories administered under the trusteeship system.

(2) The Council, in granting a waiver to a Member, shall state explicitly the terms and conditions on which and the period for which the Member is relieved of such obligation.

(3) The Council shall not consider a request for a waiver of quota obligations on the basis of the existence in a Member country, in one or more years, of an exportable production in excess of its permitted exports, or which is the consequence of the Member having failed to comply with the provisions of Articles 48 and 49.

CHAPTER XIX. CONSULTATIONS, DISPUTES AND COMPLAINTS

Article 58

Consultations

Each Member shall accord sympathetic consideration to, and shall afford adequate opportunity for, consultation regarding such representations as may be made by another Member with respect to any matter relating to the Agreement. In the course of such consultation, on request by either party and with the consent of the other, the Executive Director shall establish an independent panel which shall use its good offices with a view to conciliating the parties. The costs of the panel shall not be chargeable to the Organization. If a party does not agree to the establishment of a panel by the Executive Director, or if the consultation does not lead to a solution, the matter may be referred to the Council in accordance with Article 59. If the consultation does lead to a solution, it shall be reported to the Executive Director who shall distribute the report to all Members.

Article 59

Disputes and complaints

(1) Any dispute concerning the interpretation or application of the Agreement which is not settled by negotiation shall, at the request of any Member party to the dispute, be referred to the Council for decision.

(2) In any case where a dispute has been referred to the Council under paragraph (1) of this Article, a majority of Members, or Members holding not less than one-third of the total votes, may require the Council, after discussion, to seek the opinion of the advisory panel referred to in paragraph (3) of this Article on the issues in dispute before giving its decision.

(3) (*a*) Unless the Council unanimously agrees otherwise, the panel shall consist of:

> (i) two persons, one having wide experience in matters of the kind in dispute and the other having legal standing and experience, nominated by the exporting Members;
>
> (ii) two such persons nominated by the importing Members; and
>
> (iii) a chairman selected unanimously by the four persons nominated under (i) and (ii) or, if they fail to agree, by the Chairman of the Council.

(*b*) Persons from countries whose Governments are Contracting Parties to this Agreement shall be eligible to serve on the advisory panel.

(*c*) Persons appointed to the advisory panel shall act in their personal capacities and without instructions from any Government.

(*d*) The expenses of the advisory panel shall be paid by the Organization.

(4) The opinion of the advisory panel and the reasons therefor shall be submitted to the Council which, after considering all the relevant information, shall decide the dispute.

(5) Any complaint that any Member has failed to fulfil its obligations under the Agreement shall, at the request of the Member making the complaint, be referred to the Council, which shall make a decision on the matter.

(6) No Member shall be found to have committed a breach of its obligations under the Agreement except by a distributed simple majority vote. Any finding that a Member is in breach of the Agreement shall specify the nature of the breach.

(7) If the Council finds that a Member has committed a breach of the Agreement, it may, without prejudice to other enforcement measures provided for in other Articles of the Agreement, by a distributed two-thirds majority vote, suspend that Member's voting rights in the Council and its right to have its votes cast in the Board until it fulfils its obligations, or the Council may take action requiring compulsory withdrawal under Article 67.

(8) A Member may seek the prior opinion of the Executive Board in a matter of dispute or complaint before the matter is discussed by the Council.

CHAPTER XX. FINAL PROVISIONS

Article 60

Signature

The Agreement shall be open for signature at the United Nations Headquarters until and including 31 March 1968 by any Government which is a Contracting Party to the International Coffee Agreement, 1962.

Article 61

Ratification

The Agreement shall be subject to approval, ratification or acceptance by the signatory Governments or by any other Contracting Party to the International Coffee Agreement, 1962, in accordance with their respective constitutional procedures. Except as provided in paragraph (2) of Article 62 instruments of approval, ratification or acceptance shall be deposited with the Secretary-General of the United Nations not later than 30 September 1968.

Article 62

Entry into force

(1) The Agreement shall enter into force definitively on 1 October 1968 among those Governments that have deposited instruments of approval, ratification or acceptance if, on that date, such Governments represent at least twenty exporting Members holding at least 80 per cent of the votes of the exporting Members and at least ten importing Members holding at least 80 per cent of the votes of the importing Members.[1] The votes for this purpose shall be as distributed in Annex C. Alternatively, it shall enter into force definitively at any time after it is provisionally in force and the aforesaid requirements of this paragraph are satisfied. The Agreement shall enter into force definitively for any Government that deposits an instrument of approval, ratification, acceptance or accession subsequent to the definitive entry into force of the Agreement for other Governments on the date of such deposit.

(2) The Agreement may enter into force provisionally on 1 October 1968.[2] For this purpose a notification by a signatory Government or by any other

---

[1] The Agreement entered into force definitively on 30 December 1968.
[2] The Agreement entered into force provisionally on 1 October 1968.

Contracting Party to the International Coffee Agreement, 1962, containing an undertaking to apply the Agreement provisionally and to seek approval, ratification or acceptance in accordance with its constitutional procedures, as rapidly as possible, that is received by the Secretary-General of the United Nations not later than 30 September 1968, shall be regarded as equal in effect to an instrument of approval, ratification or acceptance. A Government that undertakes to apply the Agreement provisionally will be permitted to deposit an instrument of approval, ratification or acceptance and shall be provisionally regarded as a party thereto until either it deposits its instruments of approval, ratification or acceptance or up to and including 31 December 1968, whichever is the earlier.

(3) If the Agreement has not entered into force definitively or provisionally by 1 October 1968, those Governments that have deposited instruments of approval, ratification or acceptance or notifications containing an undertaking to apply the Agreement provisionally and to seek approval, ratification or acceptance may immediately after that date consult together to consider what action the situation requires and may, by mutual consent, decide that it shall enter into force among themselves. Likewise, if the Agreement has entered into force provisionally but has not entered into force definitively by 31 December 1968, those Governments that have deposited instruments of approval, ratification, acceptance or accession may consult together to consider what action the situation requires and may, by mutual consent, decide that it shall continue in force provisionally or enter into force definitively among themselves.

Article 63

Accession

(1) The Government of any State Member of the United Nations or of any of its specialized agencies may accede to this Agreement upon conditions that shall be established by the Council. In establishing such conditions the Council shall, if such country is an exporting country and is not named in Annex A, establish quota provisions for it. If such exporting country is named in Annex A, the respective quota provisions specified therein shall be applied to that country unless the Council by a distributed two-thirds majority vote decides otherwise. Not later than 31 March 1969 or such other date as may be determined by the Council, any importing Member of the International Coffee Agreement, 1962, may accede to the Agreement on the same conditions under which it could have approved, ratified or accepted the Agreement and, if it applies the Agreement provisionally, it shall provisionally be regarded as a party thereto until either

it deposits its instrument of accession or up to and including the above date, whichever is the earlier.

(2) Each Government depositing an instrument of accession shall, at the time of such deposit, indicate whether it is joining the Organization as an exporting Member or an importing Member, as defined in paragraphs (7) and (8) of Article 2.

Article 64

Reservations

Reservations may not be made with respect to any of the provisions of the Agreement.

Article 65

Notifications in respect of dependent territories

(1) Any Government may, at the time of signature or deposit of an instrument of approval, ratification, acceptance or accession, or at any time thereafter, by notification to the Secretary-General of the United Nations, declare that the Agreement shall extend to any of the territories for whose international relations it is responsible and the Agreement shall extend to the territories named therein from the date of such notification.

(2) Any Contracting Party which desires to exercise its rights under Article 4 in respect of any of its dependent territories, or which desires to authorize one of its dependent territories to become part of a Member group formed under Article 5 or 6, may do so by making a notification to that effect to the Secretary-General of the United Nations, either at the time of the deposit of its instrument of approval, ratification, acceptance or accession, or at any later time.

(3) Any Contracting Party which has made a declaration under paragraph (1) of this Article may at any time thereafter, by notification to the Secretary-General of the United Nations, declare that the Agreement shall cease to extend to the territory named in the notification and the Agreement shall cease to extend to such territory from the date of such notification.

(4) The Government of a territory to which the Agreement has been extended under paragraph (1) of this Article and which has subsequently become independent may, within 90 days after the attainment of independence, declare by notification to the Secretary-General of the United Nations that it has assumed the rights and obligations of a Contracting Party to the Agreement. It shall, as from the date of such notification, become a party to the Agreement.

Article 66
Voluntary withdrawal

Any Contracting Party may withdraw from the Agreement at any time by giving a written notice of withdrawal to the Secretary-General of the United Nations. Withdrawal shall become effective 90 days after the notice is received.

Article 67
Compulsory withdrawal

If the Council determines that any Member has failed to carry out its obligations under the Agreement and that such failure significantly impairs the operations of the Agreement, it may by a distributed two-thirds majority vote require the withdrawal of such Member from the Organization. The Council shall immediately notify the Secretary-General of the United Nations of any such decision. Ninety days after the date of the Council's decision that Member shall cease to be a Member of the Organization and, if such Member is a Contracting Party, a party to the Agreement.

Article 68
Settlement of accounts with withdrawing Members

(1) The Council shall determine any settlement of accounts with a withdrawing Member. The Organization shall retain any amounts already paid by a withdrawing Member and such Member shall remain bound to pay any amounts due from it to the Organization at the time the withdrawal becomes effective: provided, however, that in the case of a Contracting Party which is unable to accept an amendment and consequently either withdraws or ceases to participate in the Agreement under the provisions of paragraph (2) of Article 70, the Council may determine any settlement of accounts which it finds equitable.

(2) A Member which has withdrawn or which has ceased to participate in the Agreement shall not be entitled to any share of the proceeds of liquidation or the other assets of the Organization upon termination of the Agreement under Article 69.

Article 69
Duration and termination

(1) The Agreement shall remain in force until 30 September 1973 unless extended under paragraph (2) of this Article, or terminated earlier under paragraph (3).

(2) The Council after 30 September 1972 may, by a vote of a majority of the Members having not less than a distributed two-thirds majority of the total votes, either renegotiate the Agreement or extend it, with or without modification, for such period as the Council shall determine. Any Contracting Party, or any dependent territory which is either a Member or a party to a Member group, on behalf of which notification of acceptance of such a renegotiated or extended Agreement has not been made by the date on which such renegotiated or extended Agreement becomes effective, shall as of that date cease to participate in the Agreement.

(3) The Council may at any time, by vote of a majority of the Members having not less than a distributed two-thirds majority of the total votes, decide to terminate the Agreement. Such termination shall take effect on such date as the Council shall decide.

(4) Notwithstanding termination of the Agreement, the Council shall remain in being for as long as necessary to carry out the liquidation of the Organization, settlement of its accounts and disposal of its assets, and shall have during that period such powers and functions as may be necessary for those purposes.

Article 70

Amendment

(1) The Council by a distributed two-thirds majority vote may recommend an amendment of the Agreement to the Contracting Parties. The amendment shall become effective 100 days after the Secretary-General of the United Nations has received notifications of acceptance from Contracting Parties representing at least 75 per cent of the exporting countries holding at least 85 per cent of the votes of the exporting Members, and from Contracting Parties representing at least 75 per cent of the importing countries holding at least 80 per cent of the votes of the importing Members. The Council may fix a time within which each Contracting Party shall notify the Secretary-General of the United Nations of its acceptance of the amendment and if the amendment has not become effective by such time, it shall be considered withdrawn. The Council shall provide the Secretary-General with the information necessary to determine whether the amendment has become effective.

(2) Any Contracting Party, or any dependent territory which is either a Member or a party to a Member group, on behalf of which notification of acceptance of an amendment has not been made by the date on which such amendment becomes effective, shall as of that date cease to participate in the Agreement.

Article 71

Notifications by the Secretary-General

The Secretary-General of the United Nations shall notify all Contracting Parties to the International Coffee Agreement, 1962, and all other Governments of States Members of the United Nations or of any of its specialized agencies, of each deposit of an instrument of approval, ratification, acceptance or accession and of the dates on which the Agreement comes provisionally and definitively into force. The Secretary-General of the United Nations shall also notify all Contracting Parties of each notification under Articles 5, 62 paragraph (2), 65, 66 or 67; of the date to which the Agreement is extended or on which it is terminated under Article 69; and of the date on which an amendment becomes effective under Article 70.

Article 72

Supplementary and transitional provisions

(1) The present Agreement shall be considered as a continuation of the International Coffee Agreement, 1962.

(2) In order to facilitate the uninterrupted continuation of the 1962 Agreement:

(*a*) All acts by or on behalf of the Organization or any of its organs under the 1962 Agreement, in effect on 30 September 1968 and whose terms do not provide for expiry on that date, shall remain in effect unless changed under the provisions of the present Agreement.

(*b*) All decisions required to be taken by the Council during coffee year 1967–68 for application in coffee year 1968–69 shall be taken during the last regular session of the Council in coffee year 1967–68 and applied on a provisional basis as if the present Agreement had already entered into force.

IN WITNESS WHEREOF the undersigned, having been duly authorized to this effect by their respective Governments, have signed this Agreement on the dates appearing opposite their signatures.

The texts of this Agreement in the English, French, Portuguese, Russian and Spanish languages shall all be equally authentic. The originals shall be deposited in the archives of the United Nations and the Secretary-General of the United Nations shall transmit certified copies thereof to each signatory and acceding Government.

ANNEX A

BASIC EXMPORT QUOTAS[1]

(thousands of 60–kilo bags)

Brazil	20,926
Burundi[2]	233
Cameroon	1,000
Central African Republic	200
Colombia	7,000
Congo (Democratic Republic)[2]	1,000
Costa Rica	1,100
Dominican Republic	520
Ecuador	750
El Salvador	1,900
Ethiopia	1,494
Guatemala	1,800
Guinea (basic export quota to be established by the Council)	
Haiti	490
Honduras	425
India	423
Indonesia	1,357
Ivory Coast	3,073
Kenya	860
Malagasy Republic	910
Mexico	1,760
Nicaragua	550
Peru	740
Portugal	2,776
Rwanda[2]	150
Tanzania	700
Togo	200
Uganda	2,379
Venezuela[2]	325
Grand Total	55,041

[1] According to the provisions of Article 31 (1), the following exporting countries do not have a basic export quota and shall receive in coffee year 1968–9 export quotas of: Bolivia 50,000 bags; Congo (Brazzaville) 25,000 bags; Cuba 50,000 bags; Dahomey 33,000 bags; Gabon 25,000 bags; Ghana 51,000 bags; Jamaica 25,000 bags; Liberia 60,000 bags; Nigeria 52,000 bags; Panama 25,000 bags; Paraguay 70,000 bags; Sierra Leone 82,000 bags; Trinidad and Tobago 69,000 bags.

[2] Burundi, Congo (Democratic Republic), Cuba, Rwanda, and Venezuela, after presentation to the Executive Board of acceptable evidence of an exportable production

ANNEX B

Non-Quota Countries of Destination referred to in Article 40, Chapter VII

The geographical areas which are non-quota countries for the purposes of this Agreement are:

Bahrain	Poland
Botswana	Qatar
Ceylon	Romania
China (Taiwan)	Saudi Arabia
China (mainland)	Somalia
Hungary	South Africa, Republic of
Iran	Southern Rhodesia
Iraq	South-West Africa
Japan	Sudan
Korea, Republic of	Swaziland
Kuwait	Thailand
Lesotho	Trucial Oman
Malawi	Union of Soviet Socialist Republics
Muscat and Oman	Zambia
North Korea	

Note. The abbreviated names above are intended to be of purely geographical significance and to convey no political implications whatsoever.

larger than 233,000; 1,000,000; 50,000; 150,000, and 325,000 bags respectively shall each be granted an annual export entitlement not exceeding the annual export entitlement it would receive with a basic quota of 350,000; 1,300,000; 200,000; 260,000, and 475,000 bags respectively. In no event, however, shall the increases allowed to these countries be taken into account for the purpose of calculating the distribution of votes.

ANNEX C

DISTRIBUTION OF VOTES

Country	Exporting	Importing
Argentina	—	16
Australia	—	9
Austria	—	11
Belgium[1]	—	28
Bolivia	4	—
Brazil	332	—
Burundi	8	—
Canada	—	32
Colombia	114	—
Congo (Democratic Republic of)	20	—
Costa Rica	21	—
Cuba	4	—
Cyprus	—	5
Czechoslovakia	—	9
Denmark	—	23
Dominican Republic	12	—
Ecuador	16	—
El Salvador	34	—
Ethiopia	27	—
Federal Republic of Germany	—	101
Finland	—	21
France	—	84
Ghana	4	—
Guatemala	32	—
Guinea	4	—
Haiti	12	—
Honduras	11	—
India	11	—
Indonesia	25	—
Israel	—	7
Italy	—	47
Jamaica	4	—
Japan	—	18
Kenya	17	—
Liberia	4	—
Mexico	32	—
Netherlands	—	35
New Zealand	—	6
Nicaragua	13	—
Nigeria	4	—
Norway	—	16

[1] Includes Luxembourg.

ANNEX C—*continued*

Country	Exporting	Importing
OAMCAF	(88)	—
OAMCAF	(4)[1]	—
Cameroon	15	—
Central African Republic	3	—
Congo (Brazzaville)	1	—
Dahomey	1	—
Gabon	1	—
Ivory Coast	47	—
Malagasy Republic	13	—
Togo	3	—
Panama	4	—
Peru	16	—
Portugal	48	—
Rwanda	6	—
Sierra Leone	4	—
Spain	—	21
Sweden	—	38
Switzerland	—	19
Tanzania	15	—
Trinidad and Tobago	4	—
Tunisia	—	6
Uganda	41	—
U.S.S.R.	—	16
United Kingdom	—	32
United States of America	—	400
Venezuela	9	—
TOTAL	996	1,000

[1] Basic votes not attributable to individual contracting parties under Article 5 (4) (*b*).

PART THREE

NON-PROLIFERATION OF NUCLEAR WEAPONS

THE Resolution of the U.N. General Assembly set out below was adopted on 3 December 1965: 105 votes in favour; none against; 2 abstentions (France and Portugal). The aims of the resolution accord closely with those of the non-aligned states and the resolution itself is a part of a general effort on the part of states to control the testing and spread of nuclear weapons. A treaty on the Non-Proliferation of Nuclear Weapons was adopted in U.N. General Assembly resolution 2373 (XXII) on 12 June 1968.

Generally, on the problems of non-proliferation see Younger, *International Affairs*, 1966, p. 14; Brownlie, the same volume, p. 600; Willrich, *Non-Proliferation Treaty: Framework for Nuclear Arms Control*, 1969; Fischer, *La Non-Prolifération des armes nucléaires*, 1969; Delcoigne and Rubinstein, *Non-Prolifération des armes nucléaires et systèmes de contrôle*, 1970; Burns, *International Organization*, vol. 23 (1969), p. 788.

U.N. RESOLUTION 2033 (XX)
GENERAL ASSEMBLY

Declaration on the denuclearization of Africa

The General Assembly,

Believing in the vital necessity of saving contemporary and future generations from the scourge of a nuclear war,

Recalling its resolution 1652 (XVI) of 24 November 1961, which called upon all Member States to refrain from testing, storing or transporting nuclear weapons in Africa and to consider and respect the continent as a denuclearized zone,

Recalling its resolution 2028 (XX) of 19 November 1965 on the non-proliferation of nuclear weapons,

Observing that proposals for the establishment of denuclearized zones in various other areas of the world have also met with general approval,

Convinced that the denuclearization of various areas of the world would help to achieve the desired goal of prohibiting the use of nuclear weapons,

Considering that the Assembly of Heads of State and Government of the Organization of African Unity, at its first regular session, held at Cairo from 17 to 21 July 1964, issued a solemn declaration on the denuclearization of Africa in which the Heads of State and Government announced their readiness to undertake in an international treaty to be concluded under the auspices of the United Nations not to manufacture or acquire control of nuclear weapons,

Noting that this declaration on the denuclearization of Africa was endorsed by the Heads of State or Government of Non-Aligned Countries in the Declaration issued on 10 October 1964, at the close of their Second Conference, held at Cairo,

Recognizing that the denuclearization of Africa would be a practical step towards the prevention of the further spread of nuclear weapons in the world and towards the achievement of general and complete disarmament and of the objectives of the United Nations,

1. *Reaffirms* its call upon all States to respect the continent of Africa as a nuclear-free zone;

2. *Endorses* the declaration on the denuclearization of Africa issued by the Heads of State and Government of African countries;

3. *Calls upon* all States to respect and abide by the aforementioned declaration;

4. *Calls upon* all States to refrain from the use, or the threat of use, of nuclear weapons on the African continent;

5. *Calls upon* all States to refrain from testing, manufacturing, using or deploying nuclear weapons on the continent of Africa, and from acquiring such weapons or taking any action which would compel African States to take similar action;

6. *Urges* those States possessing nuclear weapons and capability not to transfer nuclear weapons, scientific data or technological assistance to the national control of any State, either directly or indirectly, in any form which may be used to assist such States in the manufacture or use of nuclear weapons in Africa;

7. *Expresses the hope* that the African States will initiate studies, as they deem appropriate, with a view to implementing the denuclearization of Africa, and take the necessary measures through the Organization of African Unity to achieve this end;

8. *Urges* the African States to keep the United Nations informed of any further developments in this regard;

9. *Requests* the Secretary-General to extend to the Organization of African Unity such facilities and assistance as may be requested in order to achieve the aims of the present resolution.

PART FOUR

TERRITORIAL PROBLEMS

I. O.A.U. RESOLUTION ON BORDER DISPUTES, 1964

THE European expansion in Africa produced a territorial division which bore little or no relation to the character and distribution of the populations of the colonies and protectorates. Tribes, such as the Ewe in West Africa, and the Masai and Makonde in East Africa, had their lands intersected by arbitrary political boundaries based on historical accident and the bargains of external interests. One of the strands of Pan-Africanist thought has been political unity and the changing of arbitrary frontiers. However, after independence it soon became clear that the best policy was to confirm colonial boundaries in principle and thus give priority to the avoidance of disputes and threats to the peace in Africa. The O.A.U. resolution on respect for frontiers existing at independence is very similar to the policy adopted in Latin America in the wake of the Spanish Empire and its internal administrative divisions. The solution does not affect disputes about demarcation, frontiers which were in dispute in colonial times, or frontiers in dispute before the colonial intervention (e.g. relations between Morocco and Algeria). The policy on frontiers is a qualification of the principle of self-determination.

See further Saadia Touval, *International Organization*, vol. 21 (1967), p. 102; Patricia Berko Wild, ibid., vol. 20 (1966), p. 18; Widstrand (ed.), *African Boundary Problems*, Uppsala, 1969; Catherine Hoskyns, *The Ethiopia–Somali–Kenya Dispute 1966–1967.*

TEXT

BORDER DISPUTES AMONG AFRICAN STATES

The Assembly of Heads of State and Government at its First Ordinary Session, held in Cairo, U.A.R., from 17 to 21 July 1964;

Considering that the border problems constitute a grave and permanent factor of dissension;

Conscious of the existence of extra-African manœuvres aiming at dividing the African States;

Considering further that the borders of African States, on the day of their independence, constitute a tangible reality;

Recalling the establishment in the course of the Second Ordinary Session of the Council of the Committee of Eleven in charge of studying the means of strengthening African Unity;

Recognizing the imperious necessity of settling, by peaceful means and within a strictly African framework, all disputes between African States;

Recalling further that all Member States have pledged, under Article VI, to scrupulously respect all principles laid down in Article III of the Charter of the Organization of African Unity;

1. Solemnly reaffirms the strict respect by all Member States of the Organization for the principles laid down in Article III, paragraph 3 of the Charter of the Organization of African Unity;

2. Solemnly declares that all Member States pledge themselves to respect the frontiers existing on their achievement of national independence.

II. O.A.U. DECLARATION ON KENYA–SOMALI RELATIONS, 1967

THIS resolution was adopted at the Assembly of Heads of State and Government of the O.A.U. at Kinshasa, 11–14 September 1967. For the background see the note on p. 360 above.

TEXT

The Assembly of Heads of State and Government meeting in its Fourth Ordinary Session in Kinshasa, Congo, from 11 to 14 September 1967;

Desirous of consolidating the fraternal links that unite us;

Recalling resolution CM/Res. 17 (II) of 29 February 1964;

Recalling further the attempts that have been made by the Governments of Kenya and Somalia at Arusha in December, 1965, through the Good Offices of His Excellency President Julius K. Nyerere of the Republic of Tanzania;

Mindful of the new and welcome initiative taken by His Excellency President Kenneth D. Kaunda of the Republic of Zambia in Kinshasa during the Fourth Ordinary Session of the Assembly of Heads of State and Government;

Notes with pleasure the joint Declaration mutually and amicably reached between the Governments of Kenya and Somalia, as represented by Vice-President Daniel Arap Moi and Prime Minister Mohamed Ibrahim Egal, respectively, through the Good Offices of the President of Zambia, which reads as follows:

1. Both Governments have expressed their desire to respect each other's sovereignty and territorial integrity in the spirit of paragraph 3 of Article III of the OAU Charter;
2. The two Governments have further undertaken to resolve any outstanding differences between them in the spirit of paragraph 4 of Article III of the OAU Charter;
3. The two Governments have pledged to ensure maintenance of peace and security on both sides of the border by preventing destruction of human life and property;
4. Furthermore, the two Governments have agreed to refrain from conducting hostile propaganda through mass media such as radio and the press against each other;

5. The two Governments have accepted the kind invitation of President Kaunda to meet in Lusaka, during the later part of October, 1967, in order to improve, intensify and consolidate all forms of co-operation;

Resolves to express its sincere gratitude and congratulations to President Kenneth D. Kaunda of Zambia as well as the Governments of Kenya and Somalia for their positive efforts to overcome differences in a fraternal manner;

Requests the Governments of Kenya and Somalia, as parties to the Declaration, and the Government of the Republic of Zambia as host and convenor, to submit a progress report on the proposed meeting in Lusaka to the Secretary-General of the OAU.

III. O.A.U. RESOLUTION ON THE SITUATION IN NIGERIA, 1967

MANY African states are plural societies comparable to Austria–Hungary before 1919 in terms of diversity of populations, and with tribal divisions to complicate ethnic and cultural divisions. Thus, if the original goal of pan-African unity is postponed, perhaps indefinitely, the members of the O.A.U. at the very least are concerned to avoid balkanization. This over-all concern explains the hostile attitude of the vast majority of O.A.U. toward the attempt at secession by Biafra. It will be remembered that the crisis in the Congo involved an externally sponsored secession by certain elements in Katanga. See, in particular, Post, *International Affairs*, vol. 44 (1968), p. 26. On the Congo crisis see further below, Part Seven.

The resolution printed below was adopted at the Assembly of Heads of State and Government of the O.A.U. at Kinshasa, 11–14 September 1967.

TEXT

The Assembly of Heads of State and Government meeting in its Fourth Ordinary Session, at Kinshasa, Congo, from 11 to 14 September 1967,

Solemnly reaffirming their adherence to the principle of respect for the sovereignty and territorial integrity of Member States;

Reiterating their condemnation of secession in any Member States;

Concerned at the tragic and serious situation in Nigeria;

Recognizing that situation as an internal affair, the solution of which is primarily the responsibility of Nigerians themselves;

Reposing their trust and confidence in the Federal Government of Nigeria;

Desirous of exploring the possibilities of placing the services of the Assembly at the disposal of the Federal Government of Nigeria;

Resolves to send a consultative mission of 6 Heads of State (Cameroon, Congo (Kinshasa), Ethiopia, Ghana, Liberia and Niger) to the Head of the Federal Government of Nigeria to assure him of the Assembly's desire for the territorial integrity, unity and peace of Nigeria.

PART FIVE

SELF-DETERMINATION AND RACIAL DISCRIMINATION IN SOUTHERN AFRICA

I. RESOLUTIONS OF THE
U.N. GENERAL ASSEMBLY AND THE O.A.U.

THE political drive against colonialism in Africa has rested on the principle of self-determination. The independent states of Africa not ruled by racial minorities have continued the struggle against both colonialism in the Portuguese territories of Angola and Mozambique and the racially exclusive minority regimes in Rhodesia and South Africa. An associated issue is the administration of South-West Africa by South Africa. For materials on racial discrimination see Brownlie, *Basic Documents on Human Rights*, 1971. The O.A.U. has modified the principle of self-determination in its application to ethnic claims to changes in existing frontiers: see above, p. 360. Issues affecting Southern Africa under white rule have highlighted the difficulties of making Afro-Asian voting strength in the United Nations effective in the face of the reluctance of the United States and other powers to give whole-hearted support to practical measures, including economic sanctions, directed against Portugal, Rhodesia, and South Africa.

1. *Declaration on the Granting of Independence to Colonial Countries and Peoples: U.N. General Assembly Resolution 1514 (XV)*

THE Declaration set out below was adopted by the United Nations General Assembly in Resolution 1514 (XV) on 14 December 1960. Eighty-nine States voted for the resolution and none against: but there were nine abstentions, viz., Portugal, Spain, Union of South Africa, United Kingdom, United States, Australia, Belgium, Dominican Republic, and France. The Declaration relates the normative development in the field of human rights to the rights of national groups, and, in particular, the right of self-determination. The Declaration, in conjunction with the United Nations Charter, supports the view that self-determination is now a legal principle, and, although its precise ramifications are not yet determined, the principle has great significance as a root of particular legal developments. The resolution on permanent sovereignty over natural resources (*supra*,) p. 303 is an aspect of the principle. See also the Declaration on the Inadmissibility of Intervention in Resolution 2131 (XX) of 14 January 1966, 5 *International Legal Materials*, 1966, p. 374. Generally on self-determination see Nawaz, *Duke Law Journal* (1965), pp. 82–101; Scelle, *Spiropoulos Festschrift*, 1957, pp. 385–91; Tunkin, *Droit international public, problèmes théoriques*, 1965, pp. 42–51; Whiteman, *Digest*, vol. 5, pp. 38–87; Brownlie, *Principles of Public International Law*, 1967, pp. 482–6. Resolution 1514 (XV) is in the form of an authoritative interpretation of the Charter rather than a recommendation. For earlier resolutions see Resolutions 637 A (VII) of 16 December 1952 and 1314 (XIII) of 12 December 1958.

The General Assembly established as a subsidiary organ a Special Committee on the Situation with regard to the Implementation of the Declaration on the Granting of Independence by Resolution 1654 (XVI) of 27 November 1961. This consisted at first of seventeen and later of twenty-four states. In 1964 the Special Committee examined situations and made recommendations in respect to fifty-five territories. In 1963 the General Assembly decided to discontinue the Committee on information from non-self-governing territories and to transfer its functions to the Special Committee. As a result, apart from the Trusteeship Council, the Special Committee is the only body responsible for matters relating to dependent territories.

TEXT

The General Assembly,

Mindful of the determination proclaimed by the peoples of the world in the Charter of the United Nations to reaffirm faith in fundamental human rights, in the dignity and worth of the human person, in the equal rights of men and women and of nations large and small and to promote social progress and better standards of life in larger freedom,

Conscious of the need for the creation of conditions of stability and well-being and peaceful and friendly relations based on respect for the principles of equal rights and self-determination of all peoples, and of universal respect for, and observance of, human rights and fundamental freedom for all without distinction as to race, sex, language or religion,

Recognizing the passionate yearning for freedom in all dependent peoples and the decisive role of such peoples in the attainment of their independence,

Aware of the increasing conflicts resulting from the denial of or impediments in the way of the freedom of such peoples, which constitute a serious threat to world peace,

Considering the important role of the United Nations in assisting the movement for independence in Trust and Non-Self-Governing Territories,

Recognizing that the peoples of the world ardently desire the end of colonialism in all its manifestations,

Convinced that the continued existence of colonialism prevents the development of international economic co-operation, impedes the social, cultural and economic development of dependent peoples and militates against the United Nations ideal of universal peace,

Affirming that peoples may, for their own ends, freely dispose of their natural wealth and resources without prejudice to any obligations arising out of international economic co-operation, based upon the principle of mutual benefit, and international law,

Believing that the process of liberation is irresistible and that, in order to avoid serious crises, an end must be put to colonialism and all practices of segregation and discrimination associated therewith,

Welcoming the emergence in recent years of a large number of dependent territories into freedom and independence, and recognizing the increasingly powerful trends towards freedom in such territories which have not yet attained independence,

Convinced that all peoples have an inalienable right to complete freedom, the exercise of their sovereignty and the integrity of their national territory, *Solemnly proclaims* the necessity of bringing to a speedy and unconditional end colonialism in all its forms and manifestations;

And to this end

Declares that:

1. The subjection of peoples to alien subjugation, domination and exploitation constitutes a denial of fundamental human rights, is contrary to the Charter of the United Nations and is an impediment to the promotion of world peace and co-operation.

2. All peoples have the right to self-determination; by virtue of that right they freely determine their political status and freely pursue their economic, social and cultural development.

3. Inadequacy of political, economic, social or educational preparedness should never serve as a pretext for delaying independence.

4. All armed action or repressive measures of all kinds directed against dependent peoples shall cease in order to enable them to exercise peacefully and freely their right to complete independence, and the integrity of their national territory shall be respected.

5. Immediate steps shall be taken, in Trust and Non-Self-Governing Territories or all other territories which have not yet attained independence, to transfer all powers to the peoples of those territories, without

any conditions or reservations, in accordance with their freely expressed will and desire, without any distinction as to race, creed or colour, in order to enable them to enjoy complete independence and freedom.

6. Any attempt aimed at the partial or total disruption of the national unity and the territorial integrity of a country is incompatible with the purposes and principles of the Charter of the United Nations.

7. All States shall observe faithfully and strictly the provisions of the Charter of the United Nations, the Universal Declaration of Human Rights and the present Declaration on the basis of equality, non-interference in the internal affairs of all States, and respect for the sovereign rights of all peoples and their territorial integrity.

2. *U.N. General Assembly Resolution 1541 (XV)*

THIS resolution was adopted on 15 December 1960: 89 votes in favour; 2 against (Portugal and South Africa); and 21 abstentions. For a commentary see Gutteridge, *The United Nations in a Changing World*, 1969, pp. 58–60.

The General Assembly,

Considering the objectives set forth in Chapter XI of the Charter of the United Nations,

Bearing in mind the list of factors annexed to General Assembly resolution 742 (VIII) of 27 November 1953,

Having examined the report of the Special Committee of Six on the Transmission of Information under Article 73*e* of the Charter, appointed under General Assembly resolution 1467 (XIV) of 12 December 1959 to study the principles which should guide Members in determining whether or not an obligation exists to transmit the information called for in Article 73*e* of the Charter and to report on the results of its study to the Assembly at its fifteenth session,

1. *Expresses its appreciation* of the work of the Special Committee of Six on the Transmission of Information under Article 73*e* of the Charter;

2. *Approves* the principles set out in section V, part B, of the report of the Committee, as amended and as they appear in the annex to the present resolution;

3. *Decides* that these principles should be applied in the light of the facts and the circumstances of each case to determine whether or not an obligation exists to transmit information under Article 73*e* of the Charter.

ANNEX

Principles which should guide Members in determining whether or not an obligation exists to transmit the information called for in Article 73*e* of the Charter of the United Nations

Principle I

The authors of the Charter of the United Nations had in mind that Chapter XI should be applicable to territories which were then known to be of the colonial type. An obligation exists to transmit information under Article 73*e* of the Charter in respect of such territories whose peoples have not yet attained a full measure of self-government.

Principle II

Chapter XI of the Charter embodies the concept of Non-Self-Governing Territories in a dynamic state of evolution and progress towards a 'full measure of self-government'. As soon as a territory and its peoples attain a full measure of self-government, the obligation ceases. Until this comes about, the obligation to transmit information under Article 73*e* continues.

Principle III

The obligation to transmit information under Article 73*e* of the Charter constitutes an international obligation and should be carried out with due regard to the fulfilment of international law.

Principle IV

Prima facie there is an obligation to transmit information in respect of a territory which is geographically separate and is distinct ethnically and/or culturally from the country administering it.

Principle V

Once it has been established that such a *prima facie* case of geographical and ethnical or cultural distinctness of a territory exists, other elements may then be brought into consideration. These additional elements may be, *inter alia*, of an administrative, political, juridical, economic or historical nature. If they affect the relationship between the metropolitan State and the territory concerned in a manner which arbitrarily places the latter in a position or status of subordination, they support the presumption that there is an obligation to transmit information under Article 73*e* of the Charter.

Principle VI

A Non-Self-Governing Territory can be said to have reached a full measure of self-government by:

(*a*) Emergence as a sovereign independent state;

(*b*) Free association with an independent state; or

(*c*) Integration with an independent state.

Principle VII

(*a*) Free association should be the result of a free and voluntary choice by the peoples of the territory concerned expressed through informed and democratic processes. It should be one which respects the individuality and the cultural characteristics of the territory and its peoples, and retains for the peoples of the territory which is associated with an independent state the freedom to modify the status of that territory through the expression of their will by democratic means and through constitutional processes.

(*b*) The associated territory should have the right to determine its internal constitution without outside interference, in accordance with due constitutional processes and the freely expressed wishes of the people. This does not preclude consultations as appropriate or necessary under the terms of the free association agreed upon.

Principle VIII

Integration with an independent State should be on the basis of complete equality between the peoples of the erstwhile Non-Self-Governing Territory and those of the independent country with which it is integrated. The peoples of both territories should have equal status and rights of citizenship and equal guarantees of fundamental rights and freedoms without any distinction or discrimination; both should have equal rights and opportunities for representation and effective participation at all levels in the executive, legislative and judicial organs of government.

Principle IX

Integration should have come about in the following circumstances:

(*a*) The integrating territory should have attained an advanced stage of self-government with free political institutions, so that its people would have the capacity to make a responsible choice through informed and democratic processes;

(*b*) The integration should be the result of the freely expressed wishes of the territory's peoples acting with full knowledge of the change in their status, their wishes having been expressed through informed and demo-

cratic processes, impartially conducted and based on universal adult suffrage. The United Nations could, when it deems it necessary, supervise
these processes.

Principle X

The transmission of information in respect of Non-Self-Governing
Territories under Article 73*e* of the Charter is subject to such limitation
as security and constitutional considerations may require. This means
that the extent of the information may be limited in certain circumstances,
but the limitation in Article 73*e* cannot relieve a Member State of the
obligations of Chapter XI. The 'limitation' can relate only to the quantum
of information of economic, social and educational nature to be transmitted.

Principle XI

The only constitutional considerations to which Article 73*e* of the Charter refers are those arising from constitutional relations of the territory
with the Administering Member. They refer to a situation in which the
constitution of the territory gives it self-government in economic, social
and educational matters through freely elected institutions. Nevertheless,
the responsibility for transmitting information under Article 73*e* continues, unless these constitutional relations preclude the Government or
parliament of the Administering Member from receiving statistical and
other information of a technical nature relating to economic, social and
educational conditions in the territory.

Principle XII

Security considerations have not been invoked in the past. Only in very
exceptional circumstances can information on economic, social and educational conditions have any security aspect. In other circumstances,
therefore, there should be no necessity to limit the transmission of information on security grounds.

3. Resolutions of the First Assembly of the Heads of State and Government of the O.A.U., Cairo, 1964

REPORT OF THE COMMITTEE OF LIBERATION

Recalling Resolution No. CIAS/Plen./Rev/2(A) adopted by the Assembly
of Heads of State and Government in Addis Ababa on 25 May 1963 and
Resolution 15 (II) of the Second Session of the Council of Ministers held
in Lagos, Nigeria;

Having examined the report of the Committee for the Liberation Movement of Africa;

Noting with satisfaction the work so far accomplished by the Co-ordination Committee;

Noting that some progress has been made by some nationalist liberation movements with the assistance of the Co-ordination Committee to establish common action fronts with a view to strengthening the effectiveness of their actions;

Regretting the continued existence of multiple rival movements in the territories under foreign domination in spite of efforts of the Committee;

Considering that certain Member States have not yet paid their voluntary contribution for 1963 to the Special Fund;

Reaffirming the will of Member States to continue by all means the intensification of the struggle for the independence of the territories under foreign domination;

1. Maintains the Liberation Committee as presently composed;

2. Decides the budget of the Special Fund[1] to be £800,000 for the budget year 1964 which shall be collected from Member States in accordance with Article XXIII of the Charter of the Organization of African Unity;

3. Requests each Member State to pay its obligatory contribution in accordance with operative paragraph 2 above to the Special Liberation Fund in Dar-es-Salaam;

4. Requests the Administrative Secretary-General to exercise supervisory powers over the Committee Secretariat.

APARTHEID AND RACIAL DISCRIMINATION

Recalling the previous resolutions of the Council of Ministers on apartheid and racial discrimination and in particular the resolution adopted by the Summit Conference held in Addis Ababa in May 1963;

Reaffirming resolution CM/Res.13 (II);

Having examined the reports of the Administrative Provisional Secretary-General of the Organization of African Unity, the Resolutions of the International Conference on Economic Sanctions against South Africa which was held in London, in April 1964, the report of the Delegation of Foreign Ministers of Liberia, Tunisia, Madagascar and Sierra Leone appointed by the Conference of Heads of State and Government at Addis Ababa in May 1963, and the report of the African Group at the United Nations;

Noting with grave concern the consistent refusal of the South African Government to give consideration to appeals made by every sector of

---

[1] For the recent position regarding contributions see *The Guardian*, 5 May 1971. In the last contribution year, payments amounted to approximately £440,000.

world opinion and their non-compliance with the resolutions of the United Nations Security Council and the General Assembly;

Noting further that the attitude of certain states towards the Government of South Africa and their continued close relations with that Government only encourages it to persist in its policies of apartheid and its contempt for the United Nations;

Convinced of the desirability of stepping up as a matter of urgency the action of the African States in regard to the application of sanctions against the South African Government;

Expressing its deep concern for the trials conducted according to the arbitrary and inhuman laws of the Government of South Africa against the opponents of policies of apartheid and for the recent convictions and sentences passed on African nationalists, particularly Nelson Mandela and Walter Sisulu;

1. Calls for the release of Nelson Mandela, Walter Sisulu, Mangalisso Sobukue and all other Nationalists imprisoned or detained under the arbitrary laws of South Africa;

2. Extends the mandate of the four Foreign Ministers of Liberia, Madagascar, Sierra Leone and Tunisia to continue their action before the Security Council;

3. Appeals to all oil producing countries to cease, as a matter of urgency, their supply of oil and petroleum products to South Africa;

4. Calls on all African States to implement forthwith the decision taken in Addis Ababa in May 1963 to boycott South African goods and to cease the supply of mineral and other raw materials and the importation of South African goods;

5. Requests the co-operation of all countries and in particular that of the Major Trading Partners in the boycott of South Africa;

6. Establishes a body within the OAU General Secretariat, entrusted, among others, with the following functions:

(*a*) to plan co-ordination among the Member States and to ensure the strictest implementation of the resolutions of the Organization of African Unity;

(*b*) to harmonize co-operation with friendly States with a view to implementing an effective boycott of South Africa;

(*c*) to collect and disseminate information about States, foreign financial, economic and commercial institutions which trade with the Government of South Africa;

(*d*) to promote, in co-operation with other international bodies, the campaign for international economic sanctions against South Africa by all appropriate means, in particular countering the propaganda and pressures of the South African Government.

II. DOCUMENTS CONCERNING TERRITORIES UNDER PORTUGUESE ADMINISTRATION

THE resolutions set out below speak for themselves to a considerable extent. They are the two most important of the U.N. General Assembly's resolutions concerning Portuguese colonial territories.

Resolution 1542 (XV) was adopted on 15 December 1960: 68 votes in favour; 6 against (Belgium, Brazil, France, Portugal, Spain, South Africa); 17 abstentions (including the U.S. and the United Kingdom).

Resolution 2270 (XXII) was adopted on 17 November 1967: 82 votes in favour; 7 against (Australia, Netherlands, Portugal, South Africa, Spain, United Kingdom, United States); 21 abstentions.

For an excellent account of one of the liberation movements (F.R.E.L.I.M.O.), see Eduardo Mondlane, *The Struggle for Mozambique* (Penguin African Library), 1969. See also Amilcar Cabral, *Revolution in Guinea*, 1969.

1. *Resolution 1542 (XV)*

The General Assembly,

Recalling that, by resolution 742 (VIII) of 27 November 1953, the General Assembly approved a list of factors to be used as a guide in determining whether a Territory is or is no longer within the scope of Chapter XI of the Charter of the United Nations,

Recalling also that differences of views arose among Member States concerning the status of certain territories under the administrations of Portugal and Spain and described by these two states as 'overseas provinces' of the metropolitan state concerned, and that with a view to resolving those differences the General Assembly, by resolution 1467 (XIV) of 12 December 1959, appointed the Special Committee of Six on the Transmission of Information under Article 73*e* of the Charter to study the principles which should guide Members in determining whether or not an obligation exists to transmit the information called for in Article 73*e*,

Recognizing that the desire for independence is the rightful aspiration of peoples under colonial subjugation and that the denial of their right to self-determination constitutes a threat to the well-being of humanity and to international peace,

Recalling with satisfaction the statement of the representative of Spain at the 1048th meeting of the Fourth Committee that his Government agrees to transmit information to the Secretary-General in accordance with the provisions of Chapter XI of the Charter,

Mindful of its responsibilities under Article 14 of the Charter,

Being aware that the Government of Portugal has not transmitted information on the territories under its administration which are enumerated in operative paragraph 1 below and has not expressed any intention of doing so, and because such information as is otherwise available in regard to the conditions in these territories gives cause for concern,

1. *Considers* that, in the light of the provisions of Chapter XI of the Charter, General Assembly resolution 742 (VIII) and the principles approved by the Assembly in resolution 1541 (XV) of 15 December 1960, the territories under the administration of Portugal listed hereunder are Non-Self-Governing Territories within the meaning of Chapter XI of the Charter:

(*a*) The Cape Verde Archipelago;

(*b*) Guinea, called Portuguese Guinea;

(*c*) São Tomé and Príncipe, and their dependencies;

(*d*) São João Batista de Ajudá;

(*e*) Angola, including the enclave of Cabinda;

(*f*) Mozambique;

(*g*) Goa and dependencies, called the State of India;

(*h*) Macau and dependencies;

(*i*) Timor and dependencies;

2. *Declares* that an obligation exists on the part of the Government of Portugal to transmit information under Chapter XI of the Charter concerning these territories and that it should be discharged without further delay;

3. *Requests* the Government of Portugal to transmit to the Secretary-General information in accordance with the provisions of Chapter XI of the Charter on the conditions prevailing in the territories under its administration enumerated in paragraph 1 above;

4. *Requests* the Secretary-General to take the necessary steps in pursuance of the declaration of the Government of Spain that it is ready to act in accordance with the provisions of Chapter XI of the Charter;

5. *Invites* the Governments of Portugal and Spain to participate in the work of the Committee on Information from Non-Self-Governing Territories in accordance with the terms of paragraph 2 of General Assembly resolution 1332 (XIII) of 12 December 1958.

2. *Resolution 2270 (XXII)*

The General Assembly,

Having examined the question of Territories under Portuguese domination,

Having heard the statements of the petitioners,

Recalling its resolution 1514 (XV) of 14 December 1960 containing the Declaration on the Granting of Independence to Colonial Countries and Peoples,

Recalling also all the relevant resolutions concerning the Territories under Portuguese domination adopted by the General Assembly, the Security Council and the Special Committee on the Situation with regard to the Implementation of the Declaration on the Granting of Independence to Colonial Countries and Peoples,

Taking note of the report of the International Seminar on *Apartheid*, Racial Discrimination and Colonialism in Southern Africa, held at Kitwe, Zambia, from 25 July to 4 August 1967,

Deeply disturbed by the negative attitude of the Government of Portugal and its persistent refusal to implement the relevant United Nations resolutions,

Gravely concerned about the critical and explosive situation which is threatening international peace and security owing to the methods of oppression and the military operations which continue to be used against the African peoples of the Territories under Portuguese domination,

Noting once more with deep concern that the activities of the foreign economic and financial interests in those Territories are being pursued as intensively as ever and continue to impede the realization of the legitimate aspirations of the African peoples,

Noting further with profound concern that Portugal continues to receive aid and weapons from certain States, and in particular from its military allies, which it uses against the population of those territories,

Noting with satisfaction the progress towards national independence and freedom made by the liberation movements both through their struggle and through a reconstruction programme,

Taking note of the report of the Secretary-General relating to his consultations with the International Bank for Reconstruction and Development in pursuance of General Assembly resolutions 2184 (XXI) of 12 December 1966 and 2202 (XXI) of 16 December 1966,

1. *Reaffirms* the inalienable right of the peoples of the Territories under Portuguese domination to achieve freedom and independence, in accordance with General Assembly resolution 1514 (XV), and the legitimacy of their struggle to achieve this right;

2. *Approves* the chapter of the report of the Special Committee on the Situation with regard to the Implementation of the Declaration on the Granting of Independence to Colonial Countries and Peoples relating to the Territories under Portuguese domination and endorses the conclusions and recommendations contained therein;

3. *Strongly condemns* the persistent refusal of the Government of Portugal to implement the relevant resolutions adopted by the General Assembly, the Security Council and the Special Committee, as well as that Government's actions which are designed to perpetuate its oppressive foreign rule;

4. *Strongly condemns* the colonial war being waged by the Government of Portugal against the peaceful peoples of the Territories under its domination, which constitutes a crime against humanity and a grave threat to international peace and security;

5. *Condemns* the policy of the Government of Portugal, which violates the economic and political rights of the indigenous population by the settlement of foreign immigrants in the Territories and by the forcible exporting of African workers to South Africa, and calls upon that Government to stop immediately the systematic influx of foreign immigrants into these Territories and the forcible exporting of African workers to South Africa;

6. *Strongly condemns* the activities of the financial interests operating in the Territories under Portuguese domination, which exploit the human and material resources of the Territories and impede the progress of their peoples towards freedom and independence;

7. *Urges* the Government of Portugal to apply without delay to the peoples of the Territories under its domination the principle of self-determination in accordance with General Assembly resolution 1514 (XV) and other relevant resolutions of the General Assembly and the Security Council, and, in particular, to take the following action:

(*a*) To recognize solemnly the right of the peoples under its domination to self-determination and independence;

(*b*) To desist forthwith from all acts of repression and to withdraw all military and other forces which it is using for that purpose;

(*c*) To proclaim an unconditional political amnesty and create the conditions which will enable authority to be transferred to freely elected institutions representative of the populations, in accordance with General Assembly resolution 1514 (XV);

8. *Once again requests* all States, particularly the military allies of Portugal in the North Atlantic Treaty Organization, to take the following measures:

(*a*) To desist forthwith from giving the Government of Portugal any assistance, including the training of Portuguese military personnel within or outside the framework of the North Atlantic Treaty Organization, which encourages that Government to continue its repression of the African people in the Territories under its domination;

(*b*) To prevent any sale or supply of weapons and military equipment to the Government of Portugal;

(*c*) To stop the sale or shipment to the Government of Portugal of equipment and materials for the manufacture or maintenance of weapons and ammunition;

(*d*) To put an end to the activities referred to in paragraph 6 above;

9. *Condemns* the policies of Portugal for using the Territories under its domination for violations of the territorial integrity and sovereignty of independent African States, in particular the Democratic Republic of the Congo;

10. *Draws the urgent attention* of the Security Council to the continued deterioration of the situation in the Territories under Portuguese domination, as well as to the consequences of these violations by Portugal of the territorial integrity and sovereignty of the neighbouring independent African States that border its colonies;

11. *Recommends* the Security Council to consider urgently the adoption of the necessary measures to make mandatory the provisions of its resolutions concerning this question, particularly resolution 218 (1965) of 23 November 1965, and those of General Assembly resolutions 2107 (XX) of 21 December 1965 and 2184 (XXI) of 12 December 1966;

12. *Appeals again* to all States to grant the peoples of the Territories under Portuguese domination the moral and material assistance necessary for the restoration of their inalienable rights;

13. *Appeals once again* to all the specialized agencies, in particular to the International Bank for Reconstruction and Development and the International Monetary Fund, to refrain from granting Portugal any financial, economic or technical assistance as long as the Government of Portugal fails to implement General Assembly resolution 1514 (XV);

14. *Expresses its appreciation* to the United Nations High Commissioner for Refugees, the specialized agencies concerned and other international relief organizations for the help they have given so far, and requests them, in co-operation with the Organization of African Unity and through it with the national liberation movements, to increase their assistance to the refugees from the Territories under Portuguese domination and to those who have suffered and are still suffering as a result of military operations;

15. *Requests* the Secretary-General, in consultation with the Special Committee, to promote through the various United Nations bodies and agencies the widespread and continuous publicizing of the work of the United Nations concerning this question so that world opinion may be sufficiently and accurately informed of the situation in the Territories under Portuguese domination and of the continuing struggle waged by the

peoples of these Territories for their liberation and, for this purpose, to prepare periodically special publications to be widely distributed in various languages;

16. *Requests* the Secretary-General to enter into consultations with the specialized agencies referred to in paragraph 13 above with regard to its implementation and to report thereon to the Special Committee;

17. *Requests* the Special Committee to continue to keep the situation in the Territories under review and to examine the extent of compliance by States with the relevant resolutions of the United Nations.

III. DOCUMENTS CONCERNING SOUTHERN RHODESIA

THE situation in Southern Rhodesia has the following elements: the territory has been declared to be a non-self-governing territory by the United Nations; the situation since the Unilateral Declaration of Independence in 1965 has been regarded as a threat to international peace by the United Nations; mandatory economic sanctions have been imposed by decision of the Security Council; and the United Kingdom government regards Southern Rhodesia as under British sovereignty and, apart from the threat to peace, a matter of domestic jurisdiction.

See Barber, *Rhodesia: The Road to Rebellion*, London, 1967; Jane Symonds, *Southern Rhodesia, Background to Crisis*, Chatham House Memoranda, 1965; Young, *Rhodesia and Independence*, New York, 1967; Zacklin, *International Conciliation*, no. 575, 1969; Margery Perham, *International Affairs*, 1966, p. 1; Fawcett, *British Year Book of International Law* (1965–6), p. 103; *Madzimbamuto v. Lardner-Burke* (Rhodesian High Court, General Division, 1966; Rhodesian High Court, Appellate Division, 1968; Judicial Committee of the Privy Council, 1968), International Law Reports (ed. E. Lauterpacht), vol. 39, p. 61; Sithole, *African Nationalism*, 2nd edn. rev., 1968; Shamuyarira, *Crisis in Rhodesia*, 1965.

1. *United Kingdom Proposals, 1966*

These were set out in Cmnd. Paper 3159 presented to the United Kingdom Parliament on 5 December 1966. Appendix A (the Commonwealth Prime Ministers' Communiqué of September 1966 relating to Rhodesia) has been omitted. The British Government accepted the document set out in Appendix B on 4 December 1966 and the Smith regime rejected the document the next day. On 20 December 1966 the United Kingdom government withdrew its offer. See *Keesing's Contemporary Archives*, vol. 16 (1967–8), p. 21836. On the *Fearless* talks in October 1968 see *Keesing*, vol. 17 (1969–70), pp. 23121–7.

RHODESIA[1]

PROPOSALS FOR A SETTLEMENT—1966

The six principles

The approach of successive British Governments towards the problem of granting independence to Rhodesia has throughout been governed by

---

[1] [Reproduced with the permission of the Controller of Her Britannic Majesty's Stationery Office from Command Paper 3159. The paper was presented to Parliament by the Secretary of State for Commonwealth Affairs on 5 December 1966.]

certain basic requirements. These have been formulated as five principles, to which the present Government subsequently added a sixth. These are as follows:

(1) The principle and intention of unimpeded progress to majority rule, already enshrined in the 1961 Constitution, would have to be maintained and guaranteed.

(2) There would also have to be guarantees against retrogressive amendment of the Constitution.

(3) There would have to be immediate improvement in the political status of the African population.

(4) There would have to be progress towards ending racial discrimination.

(5) The British Government would need to be satisfied that any basis proposed for independence was acceptable to the people of Rhodesia as a whole.

(6) It would be necessary to ensure that, regardless of race, there was no oppression of majority by minority or of minority by majority.

Commonwealth Prime Ministers' Meeting

2. At the Commonwealth Prime Ministers' Meeting in London in September this year the British Government notified to the Conference their decisions as regards a settlement of the Rhodesian problem, and stated that they proposed to communicate their intentions through the Governor to all sections of opinion in Rhodesia, and to inform the illegal régime that, if they were not prepared to take the initial and indispensable steps whereby the rebellion was brought to an end and executive authority was vested in the Governor, certain related consequences would ensue. The section of the Commonwealth Prime Ministers' communiqué relating to Rhodesia is reproduced at Appendix A.

Discussions in Salisbury

3. The Commonwealth Secretary and the Attorney-General visited Salisbury from 19 to 28 September for the purposes explained in the communiqué. During the course of their visit they met, under the aegis of the Governor, a cross-section of representative opinion in the country including Mr. Smith and members of the régime. In these talks they made clear the British Government's requirements for a settlement of the Rhodesian problem and what the consequences of rejection of the British proposals would be.

4. Discussion of those proposals continued during a visit to Rhodesia in October by Sir Morrice James, Deputy Under-Secretary of State, Commonwealth Office; and in a further effort to resolve the problem the Commonwealth Secretary again visited Rhodesia between 25 and 27 November, 1966.

5. In the light of the Commonwealth Secretary's report on his return, the British Government decided that a further meeting with Mr. Smith should be arranged with the purpose of ascertaining whether or not a settlement of the Rhodesian problem could be reached, on the basis of the principles and within the programme of action to which they were committed by the communiqué of the Commonwealth Prime Ministers' Meeting.

Prime Minister's meeting with Mr. Smith

6. The meeting took place in H.M.S. *Tiger* off Gibraltar from 2 to 4 December, 1966. There were present the Prime Minister, the Secretary of State for Commonwealth Affairs and the Attorney-General; the Governor and the Chief Justice of Rhodesia; and Mr. Smith and Mr. Howman representing the illegal régime. The meeting resulted in a working document covering all the essential elements of the problem. A statement was signed by the Prime Minister and Mr. Smith, in the presence of the Governor, on 4 December, indicating that this document was without commitment on either side and that both sides would decide by 12 noon (Salisbury time) on Monday, 5 December, whether it was accepted in its entirety. The texts of the statement and of the document are reproduced at Appendix B.

7. In the view of the British Government the document forms the basis for an acceptable settlement. It sets out proposals for an independence constitution which satisfy the six principles. It provides for unimpeded progress to majority rule (*i.e.*, the first principle), while finding a means of introducing European reserved seats (to give effect to the sixth principle). It meets the second principle by establishing an effective blocking mechanism in a Senate and Lower House voting together, and by providing a right of appeal against the amendment of specially entrenched clauses of the constitution, in the first instance to a Constitutional Commission in Rhodesia and from that Commission, as of right, to the Judicial Committee of the Privy Council. It meets the third principle (*i.e.*, an immediate improvement of the political status of the Africans) by an extension of the 'B' Roll franchise to cover all Africans over 30 years of age; by increasing 'B' Roll seats in the Lower House from 15 to 17, and by a total of 14 African seats in the Senate of which eight would be elected and six would be Chiefs.

8. The fourth principle is met by a Royal Commission to study and make recommendations on the problems of racial discrimination and land apportionment.

9. Finally, satisfactory arrangements are suggested, within the requirements indicated in the Commonwealth Prime Ministers' communiqué, for a return to legality by means of the appointment by the Governor of a broad-based administration, and for the testing of the opinion of the people of Rhodesia as a whole as required by the fifth principle after constitutional Government has been restored.

10. The British Government accordingly instructed the Head of the British Residual Staff in Salisbury on the evening of 4 December to inform Mr. Smith, through the Governor, that they accepted the document in its entirety.

11. On the evening of 5 December, the Head of the British Residual Staff in Salisbury was informed by the régime that they were unwilling to accept the document in its entirety. As was made clear to Mr. Smith in H.M.S. *Tiger*, and as he recognised in signing the document at Appendix B, the illegal régime have thus rejected that document.

Conclusion

12. Throughout the constitutional discussions before the illegal declaration of independence on 11 November, 1965, and in the exploratory talks which have taken place since that event culminating in the meeting in H.M.S. *Tiger*, the British Government have sought a solution which would be fair to Europeans and Africans alike and which would win the acceptance of the people of Rhodesia as a whole. If such a solution could have been agreed they would have been prepared to commend it to the British people and Parliament as a just and honourable settlement which would be calculated to establish Rhodesia as an independent State with the general goodwill of the world community. By their refusal to accept in its entirety the document which the British Government have accepted the illegal régime have made it clear that they are not prepared to take the necessary steps to bring the rebellion to an end. The responsibility for the situation which now arises rests wholly upon them. The related consequences foreshadowed in the communiqué of the Commonwealth Prime Ministers' Meeting in London in September will now ensue.

APPENDIX B

The attached document was worked out by the British Prime Minister and Mr. Smith in H.M.S. *Tiger* off Gibraltar on 2nd/3rd December, 1966.

It is without commitment on either side and both sides will decide by 12 noon (Salisbury time) on Monday, 5th December, 1966, whether it is accepted in its entirety.

HAROLD WILSON
I. DOUGLAS SMITH

Signed in my presence

HUMPHREY GIBBS
(Governor)
On board H.M.S. Tiger
4th December, 1966

RHODESIA—INDEPENDENCE CONSTITUTION

I

The following are the principal changes which are to be made in the 1961 Constitution to meet the first, second, third and sixth principles:

1. *The Governor*

Governor-General to be appointed on the advice of the Rhodesian Government.

2. *The Legislature*

The composition to be:

Legislative Assembly

33 'A' Roll seats
17 'B' Roll seats   } Each block of seats to cover the
17 Reserved European seats } whole country

Senate

The composition to be:

12 European seats (elected by Europeans on the 'A' Roll. Six members to represent Mashonaland and six members to represent Matabeleland).

8 African (elected by Africans on the 'A' and 'B' Rolls voting together. Four members to represent Mashonaland and four members to represent Matabeleland).

6 Chiefs (elected by Chiefs' Council).

3. *Franchise*

The 'B' Roll franchise—to be extended to include all Africans over 30 who satisfy the citizenship and residence qualifications.

Reserved European seats—to be elected by the European electorate.

Cross voting to be retained and applied to all seats.

4. *Delimitation*

Alteration in the composition of both Houses and in number of seats to be effected by special entrenchment procedure. But the terms of reference of the Delimitation Commission are to incorporate the agreed formula as follows:

The overriding objective of the Commission is so to divide the constituencies that the proportion of those with a majority of African voters on the 'A' Roll at the time of delimitation is the same as the proportion of African voters then on the 'A' Roll for the country as a whole.

Subject to this, the Commission is to take into account the factors specified in Section 38.

5. *Terms of office of Senators*

20 Elected members—as for Legislative Assembly.

6 Chiefs—as for Legislative Assembly although a Chief will vacate his office as a Senator if he ceases to be a Chief.

Chiefs are only to be removed from office on the recommendation of an impartial judicial tribunal.

6. *Powers of Senate*

The powers of the Senate will be:

(*a*) Review of legislation.

(*b*) Special legislative powers in respect of Tribal Land, Law and Custom.

(*c*) Amendment of Constitution—see below.

Members of the Senate may be appointed as Ministers.

7. *Executive powers*

The Governor-General will act on Ministers' advice in all matters.

8. *Amendment of the Constitution*

Ordinary amendments of the Constitution will require, as now, a vote of two-thirds of the total membership of the Legislative Assembly.

The amendment of the Specially Entrenched provisions of the Constitution will require a vote of at least three-quarters of the total membership of both Houses voting together. In addition there will be a system of appeal against such an amendment. The amendment will not come into force until the time for appeal has expired or the appeal has been finally disposed of. The appeal will lie in the first instance to a Constitutional Commission in Rhodesia, consisting of the Chief Justice and other judges: with further appeal as of right to the Judicial Committee of the Privy Council. The permitted grounds of appeal will be that the amendment discriminates unjustly or has the effect of discriminating unjustly between the races or contravenes any of the provisions of the Declaration of Rights contained in the Constitution.

II

9. *Fourth principle*

As a minimum requirement to give effect to the fourth principle, a Royal Commission will be set up without delay to study and make recommendations on the problems of racial discrimination, in particular Land Apportionment in Rhodesia, and the possibility of extending the competence of the Constitutional Council to embrace pre-1961 legislation: and a Standing Commission will keep the problems of racial discrimination under regular review.

III

10. *Return to legality and the fifth principle*

An Order in Council will be made as soon as possible permitting the appointment by the Governor of a Prime Minister and other Ministers in Rhodesia.

11. The existing Legislature will be dissolved. The Governor will be invested with legislative powers, to be used on the advice of Ministers except in those cases where he is empowered to act in his own discretion. No later than four months from the date of dissolution of the Legislature, and on the assumption that the test of acceptability referred to in paragraph 17 below will have been completed in that interval, new elections will be held. If that test has shown that the new constitution is acceptable to the people of Rhodesia as a whole, a further election, on the basis of that constitution, will be held as soon as possible either immediately before or immediately after independence.

12. As soon as the Order in Council mentioned in paragraph 10 above is made, the Governor, in the full exercise of his constitutional powers, will invite Mr. Smith to head a broad-based interim Government which will

include, in addition to representatives of existing political parties, independent members and Africans.

13. This Government will be appointed by the Governor in his discretion.

14. The restored constitutional government will be based upon the 1961 Constitution, modified (by Order in Council which will be made as soon as possible) to provide that during the interim period before the first election is held Rhodesian Ministers will be appointed by and responsible to the Governor, who will normally act on their advice in all internal matters of administration but, as regards his ultimate responsibility for the maintenance of law and order and the protection of human rights, will be advised, in his capacity as Commander-in-Chief of the Defence Forces, by a Defence and Security Council, comprising the responsible Ministers, together with the heads of the Defence Forces, the Chief of Police, and a representative of the British Government.

15. During the interim period, and before any testing of opinion under the Fifth Principle is carried out, censorship will be removed; and normal political activities will be permitted, provided they are conducted peacefully and democratically and without intimidation from any quarter. In this connection an impartial judicial tribunal, appointed by the Rhodesian Government, but including one British representative nominated by the Lord Chancellor, will be set up to consider the detention and restriction of persons on security grounds. Such detention and restriction will not be authorized unless the tribunal are affirmatively satisfied that the persons concerned have committed, or incited the commission of, acts of violence or intimidation.

16. As soon as possible after the return to legality, the British Government will negotiate with the legal Government the details of the constitutional settlement for an independent Rhodesia in accordance with the arrangements already agreed informally and described in Part I of this document.

17. The agreed settlement will be submitted to the test of acceptability to the people of Rhodesia as a whole by a Royal Commission whose composition and terms of reference will be agreed by the British Government with the legal interim administration.

18. If the settlement is shown to be acceptable to the people of Rhodesia as a whole, the British Government will at the earliest possible date introduce the necessary legislation to grant independence to Rhodesia on this basis and will commend this legislation to Parliament.

19. The two Governments will also negotiate the terms of a Treaty guaranteeing the independence constitution. They will also enter into

discussions on the desirability of negotiating an appropriate Defence Agreement for the purpose of regulating future defence relations between the two Governments.

20. If however the settlement is shown to be unacceptable to the people of Rhodesia as a whole, the two Governments will immediately confer together to consider what steps should be taken to devise alternative proposals for an independence constitution.

21. On the restoration of legal government, the British Government will take all action in their power to bring about the immediate discontinuance of the economic and other sanctions at present in force.

2. U.N. General Assembly Resolutions

Resolution of 12 October 1965

The Resolution was adopted by 107 votes to 2 (Portugal and South Africa). France abstained and the United Kingdom did not participate in the vote.

2012 (XX). QUESTION OF SOUTHERN RHODESIA

The General Assembly,

Deeply concerned at the situation in Southern Rhodesia,

Noting with particular concern the repeated threats of the present authorities in Southern Rhodesia immediately to declare unilaterally the independence of Southern Rhodesia, in order to perpetuate minority rule in Southern Rhodesia,

Noting the attitude of the Government of the United Kingdom of Great Britain and Northern Ireland that a unilateral declaration of independence for Southern Rhodesia would be an act of rebellion and that any measure to give it effect would be an act of treason,

1. *Condemns* any attempt on the part of the Rhodesian authorities to seize independence by illegal means in order to perpetuate minority rule in Southern Rhodesia;

2. *Declares* that the perpetuation of such minority rule would be incompatible with the principle of equal rights and self-determination of peoples proclaimed in the Charter of the United Nations and in the Declaration on the Granting of Independence to Colonial Countries and Peoples contained in General Assembly resolution 1514 (XV) of 14 December 1960;

3. *Requests* the United Kingdom of Great Britain and Northern Ireland and all Member States not to accept a declaration of independence for

Southern Rhodesia by the present authorities, which would be in the sole interest of the minority, and not to recognize any authorities purporting to emerge therefrom;

4. *Calls upon* the United Kingdom to take all possible measures to prevent a unilateral declaration of independence and, in the event of such a declaration, to take all steps necessary to put an immediate end to the rebellion, with a view to transferring power to a representative government in keeping with the aspirations of the majority of the people;

5. *Decides* to keep the question of Southern Rhodesia under urgent and continued review during the twentieth session and to consider what further steps may be necessary.

Resolution of 5 November 1965

The Resolution was adopted by 82 votes to 9 (Australia, Belgium, Canada, Luxembourg, Netherlands, New Zealand, Portugal, South Africa, and the United States). There were 18 abstentions and the United Kingdom did not participate in the vote.

2022 (XX). QUESTION OF SOUTHERN RHODESIA

The General Assembly,

Having examined the chapters of the reports of the Special Committee on the Situation with regard to the Implementation of the Declaration on the Granting of Independence to Colonial Countries and Peoples relating to Southern Rhodesia,[1]

Recalling its resolutions 1514 (XV) of 14 December 1960, 1747 (XVI) of 28 June 1962, 1760 (XVII) of 31 October 1962, 1883 (XVIII) of 14 October 1963, 1889 (XVIII) of 6 November 1963, 1956 (XVIII) of 11 December 1963 and 2012 (XX) of 12 October 1965, the resolutions adopted by the Special Committee on 22 April 1965[2] and 28 May 1965,[3] and Security Council resolution 202 (1965) of 6 May 1965,

Considering that the administering Power has not implemented the above resolutions and that no constitutional progress has been made,

Noting that the increasing co-operation between the authorities of Southern Rhodesia, South Africa and Portugal is designed to perpetuate racist minority rule in southern Africa and constitutes a threat to freedom, peace and security in Africa,

Noting with grave concern the manifest intention of the present authorities in Southern Rhodesia to proclaim independence unilaterally, which

---

[1] A/5800/Add. 1 and A/5800/Add. 1 (Part II); and A/6000/Add. 1.
[2] A/6000/Add. 1, para. 292.   [3] Ibid., para. 513.

would continue the denial to the African majority of their fundamental rights to freedom and independence,

Deeply concerned about the explosive situation in Southern Rhodesia,

1. *Approves* the chapters of the reports of the Special Committee on the Situation with regard to the Implementation of the Declaration on the Granting of Independence to Colonial Countries and Peoples relating to Southern Rhodesia and endorses the conclusions and recommendations contained therein;

2. *Reaffirms* the right of the people of Southern Rhodesia to freedom and independence and recognizes the legitimacy of their struggle for the enjoyment of their rights as set forth in the Charter of the United Nations, the Universal Declaration of Human Rights and the Declaration on the Granting of Independence to Colonial Countries and Peoples contained in General Assembly resolution 1514 (XV);

3. *Solemnly warns* the present authorities in Southern Rhodesia and the United Kingdom of Great Britain and Northern Ireland, in its capacity as administering Power, that the United Nations will oppose any declaration of independence which is not based on universal adult suffrage;

4. *Condemns* the policies of racial discrimination and segregation practised in Southern Rhodesia, which constitute a crime against humanity;

5. *Condemns* any support or assistance rendered by any State to the minority régime in Southern Rhodesia;

6. *Calls upon* all States to refrain from rendering any assistance whatsoever to the minority régime in Southern Rhodesia;

7. *Requests* that the administering Power effect immediately:

(a) The release of all political prisoners, political detainees and restrictees;

(b) The repeal of all repressive and discriminatory legislation and, in particular, the Law and Order (Maintenance) Act and the Land Apportionment Act;

(c) The removal of all restrictions on African political activity and the establishment of full democratic freedom and equality of political rights;

8. *Requests once more* the Government of the United Kingdom to suspend the Constitution of 1961 and to call immediately a constitutional conference in which representatives of all political parties will take part, with a view to making new constitutional arrangements on the basis of universal adult suffrage and fixing the earliest possible date for independence;

9. *Appeals* to all States to use all their powers against a unilateral declaration of independence and, in any case, not to recognize any govern-

ment in Southern Rhodesia which is not representative of the majority of the people;

10. *Requests* all States to render moral and material help to the people of Zimbabwe in their struggle for freedom and independence;

11. *Calls upon* the Government of the United Kingdom to employ all necessary measures, including military force, to implement paragraphs 7 and 8 above;

12. *Draws the attention* of the Security Council to the threats made by the present authorities in Southern Rhodesia, including the threat of economic sabotage against the independent African States adjoining Southern Rhodesia;

13. *Further draws the attention* of the Security Council to the explosive situation in Southern Rhodesia which threatens international peace and security, and decides to transmit to the Council the records and resolutions of the twentieth session of the General Assembly on this question;

14. *Decides* to keep the question of Southern Rhodesia under urgent and continuing review.

Resolution of 12 November 1965

The Resolution was adopted by 107 votes to 2 (Portugal and South Africa). France abstained and the United Kingdom did not participate in the vote.

2024 (XX). QUESTION OF SOUTHERN RHODESIA

The General Assembly,

Considering the explosive situation created in Southern Rhodesia following the unilateral declaration of independence,

Noting the measures taken by the Government of the United Kingdom of Great Britain and Northern Ireland,

1. *Condemns* the unilateral declaration of independence made by the racialist minority in Southern Rhodesia;

2. *Invites* the United Kingdom of Great Britain and Northern Ireland to implement immediately the relevant resolutions adopted by the General Assembly and the Security Council in order to put an end to the rebellion by the unlawful authorities in Southern Rhodesia;

3. *Recommends* the Security Council to consider this situation as a matter of urgency.

Resolution of 17 November 1966

The Resolution was adopted by 89 votes to 2 (Portugal and South Africa), with 17 abstentions.

2151 (XXI). QUESTION OF SOUTHERN RHODESIA

The General Assembly,

Having considered the question of Southern Rhodesia,

Having examined the chapter of the report of the Special Committee on the Situation with regard to the Implementation of the Declaration on the Granting of Independence to Colonial Countries and Peoples relating to Southern Rhodesia,[1]

Having heard the statements of the administering Power,

Recalling its resolution 1514 (XV) of 14 December 1960 containing the Declaration on the Granting of Independence to Colonial Countries and Peoples,

Recalling its resolutions 2022 (XX) of 5 November 1965, 2105 (XX) of 20 December 1965 and 2138 (XXI) of 22 October 1966 and the various resolutions of the Security Council, in particular resolution 217 (1965) of 20 November 1965, which declared, *inter alia*, that the racist minority régime in Southern Rhodesia is illegal,

Recalling further that, since the illegal declaration of independence by the racist minority régime in Southern Rhodesia, the Government of the United Kingdom of Great Britain and Northern Ireland has declared, on several occasions, that that régime is illegal and that it would not negotiate with the régime on the future of Southern Rhodesia,

Reiterating its serious concern about the implications which the pourparlers between the administering Power and the representatives of the illegal racist minority régime have for the right of the African people of Zimbabwe to freedom and independence,

Noting with concern the increasingly harmful role played by those foreign monopolies and financial interests in Southern Rhodesia whose support for the illegal racist minority régime constitutes an impediment to the attainment of independence by the people of Zimbabwe,

Noting with deep regret that the administering Power has failed to take effective and concrete measures to bring down the illegal racist minority régime in Southern Rhodesia, and to grant independence to the people of Zimbabwe in accordance with General Assembly resolution 1514 (XV) and other relevant resolutions,

1. *Reaffirms* the inalienable right of the people of Zimbabwe to freedom

[1] A/6300/Add. 1 (Parts I and II).

and independence, and the legitimacy of their struggle for the exercise of that right;

2. *Deplores* the failure of the Government of the United Kingdom of Great Britain and Northern Ireland so far to put an end to the illegal racist minority régime in Southern Rhodesia;

3. *Condemns* any arrangement between the administering Power and the illegal racist minority régime in the Territory which would transfer power to the latter on any basis and which would fail to recognize the inalienable right of the people of Zimbabwe to self-determination and independence in accordance with General Assembly resolution 1514 (XV);

4. *Condemns* the Governments of Portugal and South Africa for their support of the illegal racist minority régime in Southern Rhodesia;

5. *Condemns* the activities of those foreign financial and other interests which, by supporting and assisting the illegal racist minority régime in Southern Rhodesia, are preventing the African people of Zimbabwe from attaining freedom and independence in accordance with General Assembly resolution 1514 (XV), and calls upon the Governments of the States concerned to take all necessary measures to bring to an end such activities;

6. *Draws the attention* of the Security Council once again to the grave situation prevailing in Southern Rhodesia, in order that it may decide to apply the necessary enforcement measures envisaged under Chapter VII of the Charter of the United Nations;

7. *Calls upon* the Government of the United Kingdom to take prompt and effective measures to prevent any supplies, including oil and petroleum products, from reaching Southern Rhodesia;

8. *Calls once again upon* the Government of the United Kingdom to take all necessary measures, including in particular the use of force, in the exercise of its powers as the administering Power, to put an end to the illegal racist minority régime in Southern Rhodesia and to ensure the immediate application of General Assembly resolution 1514 (XV) and other relevant resolutions;

9. *Calls upon* the administering Power to report on its actions in the implementation of the present resolution to the Special Committee on the Situation with regard to the Implementation of the Declaration on the Granting of Independence to Colonial Countries and Peoples;

10. *Calls upon* all States to render all moral and material support to the people of Zimbabwe in their legitimate struggle to overthrow the illegal racist régime and to achieve freedom and independence;

11. *Requests* the specialized agencies concerned and other international assistance organizations to aid and assist the refugees from Zimbabwe and those who are suffering from oppression by the illegal racist minority régime in Southern Rhodesia;

12. *Requests* the Special Committee to continue its study of the situation in Southern Rhodesia;

13. *Decides* to keep the question of Southern Rhodesia on its agenda.

3. Security Council Resolutions

Resolution of 12 November 1965
RESOLUTION 216 (1965)[1]

The Security Council

1. *Decides to condemn* the unilateral declaration of independence made by the racist minority in Southern Rhodesia;

2. *Decides to call upon* all States not to recognize this illegal racist minority régime in Southern Rhodesia and to refrain from rendering any assistance to this illegal régime.

Resolution of 20 November 1965
RESOLUTION 217 (1965)[1]

The Security Council,

Deeply concerned about the situation in Southern Rhodesia,

Considering that the illegal authorities in Southern Rhodesia have proclaimed independence and that the Government of the United Kingdom of Great Britain and Northern Ireland, as the administering Power, looks upon this as an act of rebellion,

Noting that the Government of the United Kingdom has taken certain measures to meet the situation and that to be effective these measures should correspond to the gravity of the situation,

1. *Determines* that the situation resulting from the proclamation of independence by the illegal authorities in Southern Rhodesia is extremely grave, that the Government of the United Kingdom of Great Britain and Northern Ireland should put an end to it and that its continuance in time constitutes a threat to international peace and security;

2. *Reaffirms* its resolution 216 (1965) of 12 November 1965 and General Assembly resolution 1514 (XV) of 14 December 1960;

3. *Condemns* the usurpation of power by a racist settler minority in Southern Rhodesia and regards the declaration of independence by it as having no legal validity;

---

[1] Adopted by 10 votes to 0 with 1 abstention (France).

4. *Calls upon* the Government of the United Kingdom to quell this rebellion of the racist minority;

5. *Further calls upon* the Government of the United Kingdom to take all other appropriate measures which would prove effective in eliminating the authority of the usurpers and in bringing the minority régime in Southern Rhodesia to an immediate end;

6. *Calls upon* all States not to recognize this illegal authority and not to entertain any diplomatic or other relations with this illegal authority;

7. *Calls upon* the Government of the United Kingdom, as the working of the Constitution of 1961 has broken down, to take immediate measures in order to allow the people of Southern Rhodesia to determine their own future consistent with the objectives of General Assembly resolution 1514 (XV);

8. *Calls upon* all States to refrain from any action which would assist and encourage the illegal régime and, in particular, to desist from providing it with arms, equipment and military material, and to do their utmost in order to break off economic relations with Southern Rhodesia, including an embargo on oil and petroleum products;

9. *Calls upon* the Government of the United Kingdom to enforce urgently and with vigour all the measures it has announced, as well as those mentioned in paragraph 8 above;

10. *Calls upon* the Organization of African Unity to do all in its power to assist in the implementation of the present resolution, in conformity with Chapter VIII of the Charter of the United Nations;

11. *Decides* to keep the question under review in order to examine what other measures it may deem necessary to take.

Resolution of 9 April 1966

RESOLUTION 221 (1966)[1]

The Security Council,

Recalling its resolutions Nos. 216 of 12 November 1965 and 217 of 20 November 1965 and in particular its call to all States to do their utmost to break off economic relations with Southern Rhodesia, including an embargo on oil and petroleum products,

Gravely concerned at reports that substantial supplies of oil may reach Rhodesia as the result of an oil tanker having arrived at Beira and the approach of a further tanker which may lead to the resumption of pumping through the CPMR pipeline with the acquiescence of the Portuguese authorities,

[1] This resolution was adopted by 10 votes to 0, with 5 abstentions (Bulgaria, France, Mali, U.S.S.R., Uruguay).

Considering that such supplies will afford great assistance and encouragement to the illegal regime in Southern Rhodesia, thereby enabling it to remain longer in being,

1. *Determines* that the resulting situation constitutes a threat to the peace;

2. *Calls upon* the Portuguese Government not to permit oil to be pumped through the pipeline from Beira to Rhodesia;

3. *Calls upon* the Portuguese Government not to receive at Beira oil destined for Rhodesia;

4. *Calls upon* all States to ensure the diversion of any of their vessels reasonably believed to be carrying oil destined for Rhodesia which may be en route for Beira;

5. *Calls upon* the Government of the United Kingdom to prevent by the use of force if necessary the arrival at Beira of vessels reasonably believed to be carrying oil destined for Rhodesia, and empowers the United Kingdom to arrest and detain the tanker known as the Joanna V upon her departure from Beira in the event her oil cargo is discharged there.

Resolution of 16 December 1966

RESOLUTION 232 (1966)[1]

The Security Council,

Reaffirming its resolutions 216 (1965) of 12 November 1965, 217 (1965) of 20 November 1965 and 221 (1966) of 9 April 1966, and in particular its appeal to all States to do their utmost in order to break off economic relations with Southern Rhodesia,

Deeply concerned that the Council's efforts so far and the measures taken by the administering Power have failed to bring the rebellion in Southern Rhodesia to an end,

Reaffirming that to the extent not superseded in this resolution, the measures provided for in resolution 217 (1965) of 20 November 1965, as well as those initiated by Member States in implementation of that resolution, shall continue in effect,

Acting in accordance with Articles 39 and 41 of the United Nations Charter,

1. *Determines* that the present situation in Southern Rhodesia constitutes a threat to international peace and security;

2. *Decides* that all States Members of the United Nations shall prevent:

(*a*) the import into their territories of asbestos, iron ore, chrome, pig-iron, sugar, tobacco, copper, meat and meat products and hides, skins and

[1] Adopted by 11 votes to 0, with 4 abstentions (Bulgaria, France, Mali, U.S.S.R.).

leather originating in Southern Rhodesia and exported therefrom after the date of this resolution;

(*b*) any activities by their nationals or in their territories which promote or are calculated to promote the export of these commodities from Southern Rhodesia and any dealings by their nationals or in their territories in any of these commodities originating in Southern Rhodesia and exported therefrom after the date of this resolution, including in particular any transfer of funds to Southern Rhodesia for the purposes of such activities or dealings;

(*c*) shipment in vessels or aircraft of their registration of any of these commodities originating in Southern Rhodesia and exported therefrom after the date of this resolution;

(*d*) any activities by their nationals or in their territories which promote or are calculated to promote the sale or shipment to Southern Rhodesia of arms, ammunition of all types, military aircraft, military vehicles, and equipment and materials for the manufacture and maintenance of arms and ammunition in Southern Rhodesia;

(*e*) any activities by their nationals or in their territories which promote or are calculated to promote the supply to Southern Rhodesia of all other aircraft and motor vehicles and of equipment and materials for the manufacture, assembly or maintenance of aircraft and motor vehicles in Southern Rhodesia: the shipment in vessels and aircraft of their registration of any such goods destined for Southern Rhodesia: and any activities by their nationals or in their territories which promote or are calculated to promote the manufacture or assembly of aircraft or motor vehicles in Southern Rhodesia;

(*f*) participation in their territories or territories under their administration or in land or air transport facilities or by their nationals or vessels of their registration in the supply of oil or oil products to Southern Rhodesia; notwithstanding any contracts entered into or licences granted before the date of this resolution;

3. *Reminds* Member States that the failure or refusal by any of them to implement the present resolution shall constitute a violation of Article 25 of the Charter;

4. *Reaffirms* the inalienable rights of the people of Southern Rhodesia to freedom and independence in accordance with the Declaration on the Granting of Independence to Colonial Countries and Peoples contained in General Assembly resolution 1514 (XV); and recognizes the legitimacy of their struggle to secure the enjoyment of their rights as set forth in the Charter of the United Nations;

5. *Calls upon* all States not to render financial or other economic aid to the illegal racist régime in Southern Rhodesia;

6. *Calls upon* all States Members of the United Nations to carry out this decision of the Security Council in accordance with Article 25 of the United Nations Charter;

7. *Urges*, having regard to the principles stated in Article 2 of the United Nations Charter, States not Members of the United Nations to act in accordance with the provisions or[1] paragraph 2 of the present resolution;

8. *Calls upon* States Members of the United Nations or of the specialized agencies to report to the Secretary-General the measures each has taken in accordance with the provisions of paragraph 2 of the present resolution;

9. *Requests* the Secretary-General to report to the Council on the progress of the implementation of the present resolution, the first report to be submitted not later than 1 March 1967;

10. *Decides* to keep this item on its agenda for further action as appropriate in the light of developments.

Resolution of 29 May 1968

This resolution was adopted unanimously. Resolution 217 (above) in effect recommended the application of economic sanctions (see the wording of its paragraph 8). Resolution 221 had the narrow if rather dramatic object of authorizing and requiring the use of force if necessary to enforce the oil embargo. In Resolution 232 of 16 December 1966 the Security Council decided to impose mandatory though selective economic sanctions under Articles 39 and 41 of the United Nations Charter (the first time these powers have been used). Resolution 253, set out below, establishes comprehensive mandatory economic sanctions.

See further Zacklin, *International Conciliation*, no. 575 (1969), pp. 36–63. The sanctions policy is undermined by the support given to the Rhodesian minority régime by Portugal and South Africa. For a further development within the Security Council in March 1970, see below, p. 460. See also General Assembly Resolution 2262 (XXII) of 3 November 1967.

RESOLUTION 253 (1968)

The Security Council,

Recalling and reaffirming its resolutions 216 (1965) of 12 November 1965, 217 (1965) of 20 November 1965, 221 (1966) of 9 April 1966, and 232 (1966) of 16 December 1966,

Taking note of resolution 2262 (XXII) adopted by the General Assembly on 3 November 1967,

---

[1] Corrected by United Nations Document S/RES/232/Corr. 1 (1966) (17 December 1966) to read 'of'.

Noting with great concern that the measures taken so far have failed to bring the rebellion in Southern Rhodesia to an end,

Reaffirming that, to the extent not superseded in this resolution, the measures provided for in resolutions 217 (1965) of 20 November 1965, and 232 (1966) of 16 December 1966, as well as those initiated by Member States in implementation of those resolutions, shall continue in effect,

Gravely concerned that the measures taken by the Security Council have not been complied with by all States and that some States, contrary to resolution 232 (1966) of the Security Council and to their obligations under Article 25 of the Charter, have failed to prevent trade with the illegal régime in Southern Rhodesia,

Condemning the recent inhuman executions carried out by the illegal régime in Southern Rhodesia which have flagrantly affronted the conscience of mankind and have been universally condemned,

Affirming the primary responsibility of the Government of the United Kingdom to enable the people of Southern Rhodesia to achieve self-determination and independence, and in particular their responsibility for dealing with the prevailing situation,

Recognizing the legitimacy of the struggle of the people of Southern Rhodesia to secure the enjoyment of their rights as set forth in the Charter of the United Nations and in conformity with the objectives of General Assembly resolution 1514 (XV),

Reaffirming its determination that the present situation in Southern Rhodesia constitutes a threat to international peace and security,

Acting under Chapter VII of the United Nations Charter,

1. *Condemns* all measures of political repression, including arrests, detentions, trials and executions which violate fundamental freedoms and rights of the people of Southern Rhodesia, and calls upon the Government of the United Kingdom to take all possible measures to put an end to such actions;

2. *Calls upon* the United Kingdom as the administering Power in the discharge of its responsibility to take urgently all effective measures to bring to an end the rebellion in Southern Rhodesia, and enable the people to secure the enjoyment of their rights as set forth in the Charter of the United Nations and in conformity with the objectives of General Assembly resolution 1514 (XV);

3. *Decides* that, in furtherance of the objective of ending the rebellion, all States Members of the United Nations shall prevent:

(*a*) The import into their territories of all commodities and products originating in Southern Rhodesia and exported therefrom after the date of this resolution (whether or not the commodities or products are for consumption or processing in their territories, whether or not they are imported in bond and whether or not any special legal status with respect to the import of goods is enjoyed by the port or other place where they are imported or stored);

(b) Any activities by their nationals or in their territories which would promote or are calculated to promote the export of any commodities or products from Southern Rhodesia; and any dealings by their nationals or in their territories in any commodities or products originating in Southern Rhodesia and exported therefrom after the date of this resolution, including in particular any transfer of funds to Southern Rhodesia for the purposes of such activities or dealings;

(c) The shipment in vessels or aircraft of their registration or under charter to their nationals, or the carriage (whether or not in bond) by land transport facilities across their territories of any commodities or products originating in Southern Rhodesia and exported therefrom after the date of this resolution;

(d) The sale or supply by their nationals or from their territories of any commodities or products (whether or not originating in their territories, but not including supplies intended strictly for medical purposes, educational equipment and material for use in schools and other educational institutions, publications, news material and, in special humanitarian circumstances, food-stuffs) to any person or body in Southern Rhodesia or to any other person or body for the purposes of any business carried on in or operated from Southern Rhodesia, and any activities by their nationals or in their territories which promote or are calculated to promote such sale or supply;

(e) The shipment in vessels or aircraft of their registration, or under charter to their nationals, or the carriage (whether or not in bond) by land transport facilities across their territories of any such commodities or products which are consigned to any person or body in Southern Rhodesia, or to any other person or body for the purposes of any business carried on in or operated from Southern Rhodesia;

4. *Decides* that all States Members of the United Nations shall not make available to the illegal régime in Southern Rhodesia or to any commercial, industrial or public utility undertaking, including tourist enterprises, in Southern Rhodesia any funds for investment or any other financial or economic resources and shall prevent their nationals and any persons within their territories from making available to the régime or to any such undertaking any such funds or resources and from remitting any other funds to persons or bodies within Southern Rhodesia except payments exclusively for pensions or for strictly medical, humanitarian or educational purposes or for the provision of news material and in special humanitarian circumstances, food-stuffs;

5. *Decides* that all States Members of the United Nations shall:

(*a*) Prevent the entry into their territories, save on exceptional humanitarian grounds, of any person travelling on a Southern Rhodesian passport, regardless of its date of issue, or on a purported passport issued by or on behalf of the illegal régime in Southern Rhodesia; and

(*b*) Take all possible measures to prevent the entry into their territories of persons whom they have reason to believe to be ordinarily resident in Southern Rhodesia and whom they have reason to believe to have furthered or encouraged, or to be likely to further or encourage, the unlawful actions of the illegal régime in Southern Rhodesia or any activities which are calculated to evade any measure decided upon in this resolution or resolution 232 (1966) of 16 December 1966;

6. *Decides* that all States Members of the United Nations shall prevent airline companies constituted in their territories and aircraft of their registration or under charter to their nationals from operating to or from Southern Rhodesia and from linking up with any airline company constituted or aircraft registered in Southern Rhodesia;

7. *Decides* that all States Members of the United Nations shall give effect to the decisions set out in operative paragraphs 3, 4, 5 and 6 of this resolution notwithstanding any contract entered into or licence granted before the date of this resolution;

8. *Calls upon* all States Members of the United Nations or of the specialized agencies to take all possible measures to prevent activities by their nationals and persons in their territories promoting, assisting or encouraging emigration to Southern Rhodesia, with a view to stopping such emigration;

9. *Requests* all States Members of the United Nations or of the specialized agencies to take all possible further action under Article 41 of the Charter to deal with the situation in Southern Rhodesia, not excluding any of the measures provided in that Article;

10. *Emphasizes* the need for the withdrawal of all consular and trade representation in Southern Rhodesia, in addition to the provisions of operative paragraph 6 of resolution 217 (1965);

11. *Calls upon* all States Members of the United Nations to carry out these decisions of the Security Council in accordance with Article 25 of the United Nations Charter and reminds them that failure or refusal by any one of them to do so would constitute a violation of that Article;

12. *Deplores* the attitude of States that have not complied with their obligations under Article 25 of the Charter, and censures in particular those States which have persisted in trading with the illegal régime in defiance of the resolutions of the Security Council, and which have given active assistance to the régime;

13. *Urges* all States Members of the United Nations to render moral and material assistance to the people of Southern Rhodesia in their struggle to achieve their freedom and independence;

14. *Urges*, having regard to the principles stated in Article 2 of the United Nations Charter, States not Members of the United Nations to act in accordance with the provisions of the present resolution;

15. *Requests* States Members of the United Nations, the United Nations Organization, the specialized agencies, and other international organizations in the United Nations system to extend assistance to Zambia as a matter of priority with a view to helping her solve such special economic problems as she may be confronted with arising from the carrying out of these decisions of the Security Council;

16. *Calls upon* all States Members of the United Nations, and in particular those with primary responsibility under the Charter for the maintenance of international peace and security, to assist effectively in the implementation of the measures called for by the present resolution;

17. *Considers* that the United Kingdom as the administering Power should ensure that no settlement is reached without taking into account the views of the people of Southern Rhodesia, and in particular the political parties favouring majority rule, and that it is acceptable to the people of Southern Rhodesia as a whole;

18. *Calls upon* all States Members of the United Nations or of the specialized agencies to report to the Secretary-General by 1 August 1968 on measures taken to implement the present resolution;

19. *Requests* the Secretary-General to report to the Security Council on the progress of the implementation of this resolution, the first report to be made not later than 1 September 1968;

20. *Decides* to establish, in accordance with rule 28 of the provisional rules of procedure of the Security Council, a committee of the Security Council to undertake the following tasks and to report to it with its observations:

(*a*) To examine such reports on the implementation of the present resolution as are submitted by the Secretary-General;

(*b*) To seek from any States Members of the United Nations or of the specialized agencies such further information regarding the trade of that State (including information regarding the commodities and products exempted from the prohibition contained in operative paragraph 3 (*d*) above) or regarding any activities by any nationals of that State or in its territories that may constitute an evasion of the measures decided upon in this resolution as it may consider necessary for the proper discharge of its duty to report to the Security Council;

21. *Requests* the United Kingdom, as the administering Power, to give maximum assistance to the committee, and to provide the committee with any information which it may receive in order that the measures envisaged in this resolution and resolution 232 (1966) may be rendered fully effective;

22. *Calls upon* all States Members of the United Nations, or of the specialized agencies, as well as the specialized agencies themselves, to supply such further information as may be sought by the Committee in pursuance of this resolution;

23. *Decides* to maintain this item on its agenda for further action as appropriate in the light of developments.

4. O.A.U. Resolution, 9 November 1966

The Assembly of Heads of State and Government meeting in its Third Ordinary Session in Addis Ababa, Ethiopia, from 5 to 9 November 1966,

HAVING REVIEWED events in Southern Rhodesia covering a period of nearly one year since the illegal seizure of independence by British racist, minority settlers in that country;

HAVING OBSERVED the hypocritical attitude and vacillation of the British Government towards the rebel regime in Southern Rhodesia;

CONVINCED that the programme of sanctions against the British colony of Southern Rhodesia as conceived and directed by the British Government will not and cannot bring down the illegal regime at Salisbury;

MORE CONVINCED than ever that the Southern Rhodesia independence crisis constitutes a threat to international peace and security;

(1) *Bitterly and unreservedly* condemns the current talks between the British Government and the rebel settler regime in Southern Rhodesia as a conspiracy aimed at recognizing the independence seized illegally by the rebel settlers;

(2) *Calls upon* all Member States of the OAU and all other States to continue to refuse recognition to the present government of Southern Rhodesia and to refuse recognition to any independent regime which the present talks between Britain and the Southern Rhodesian rebels may bring about unless such a government is based on majority rule;

(3) *Strongly condemns* Britain for her refusal to crush the Southern Rhodesian rebel regime and repeats its demands to the United Kingdom Government to bring about the immediate downfall of that regime by any means including the use of force;

(4) *Re-iterates* the terms of paragraph 4 of the Resolution of 5th March 1966, and accordingly recommends to the OAU, and to all friendly governments, to give material and financial aid to the Zimbabwe people who are actually fighting inside Zimbabwe;

(5) *Condemns* those States especially those of Portugal and South Africa which render support to the rebel regime in Southern Rhodesia;

(6) *Invites* Member countries in consultation with each other to take measures against those persons, companies and institutions in their own countries which, in pursuance of colonialist interests continue to have dealings with or business under, the illegal regime in Southern Rhodesia.

(7) *Calls upon* all Member countries and all countries which wish to see human dignity and freedom in Africa and throughout the world to support a programme of mandatory and comprehensive sanctions against Southern Rhodesia under Chapter VII of the Charter of the United Nations;

(8) *Repeats* its calls upon all Member countries to contribute to a Special Southern Rhodesia Liberation Fund to enable all Zimbabwe Nationalists to intensify the fighting against the rebels;

(9) *Calls upon* Member States to give practical implementation to paragraph 3 of the Resolution of March 5th, 1966 which states:

> 'Decides to establish a "Committee of Solidarity for Zambia" composed of five Members whose task shall be to seek appropriate measures of technical and economic assistance by Member States to Zambia.'

so as to enable Zambia not only to withstand the effects of U.D.I. but also to help all Zimbabwe Freedom Fighters more effectively;

(10) *Re-iterates* its call upon all Member States of the OAU and UNO, who have not taken any notice, to implement the United Nations Security Council Resolution of 20th November, 1965 and to intensify their efforts for the adoption of other more effective measures, including the release of all Zimbabwe leaders from the Nazi type concentration camps of Southern Rhodesia;

(11) *Expresses* its appreciation here to the Foreign Ministers of Algeria, Senegal and Zambia and all African delegations at the United Nations for their efforts to move the Security Council to consider the Southern Rhodesian situation under Chapter VII of the United Nations Charter; and requests the Ministers to continue with their efforts in the Security Council and submit reports to the Council of Ministers;

(12) *Pays tribute* to the sons of Zimbabwe who have died in battle with the racist settler regime's usurper forces.

IV. DOCUMENTS CONCERNING NAMIBIA
(SOUTH-WEST AFRICA)

THE Union of South Africa retained control of the Mandated Territory of South-West Africa in 1946 without an agreement to create a trusteeship within the Charter of the United Nations. The usurpation of a territory of which South Africa was not the sovereign, the introduction of *apartheid*, and the economic exploitation of the territory in the interests of white South Africa resulted in action by the United Nations to terminate the mandate in order to deprive South Africa of any legal basis for her administration. See generally Wellington, *South West Africa and its Human Issues*, 1967. The O.A.U. supports the African Nationalists who are developing a resistance movement within South-West Africa or Namibia, the name used lately by the nationalists (South-West African People's Organization) and organs of the United Nations.

The resolutions of the U.N. General Assembly and the Security Council set out below are the principal recent resolutions on the subject. More recent General Assembly resolutions are 2324 (XVIII) of 16 December 1967 (condemning the trial in Pretoria of 37 South-West Africans); 2325 (XVII) of the same date (condemning the refusal of South Africa to comply with Resolutions 2145 (XXI) and 2248 (S-V)). The Security Council dealt with these same matters in Resolutions 245 (1968), 264 (1969), and 276 (1970).

The General Assembly adopted the name 'Namibia' in Resolution 2372 (XXII) of 12 June 1968.

For further materials see the following publications of the International Court of Justice: *International Status of South West Africa*, I.C.J. Reports, 1950, p. 128; *South West Africa Cases* (Preliminary Objections), I.C.J. Reports, 1962, p. 319; *South West Africa Cases* (Second Phase), I.C.J. Reports, 1966, p. 6; and the Report of the United Nations Council for South-West Africa, U.N. Document A/6897, 10 November 1967.

1. *U.N. General Assembly Resolutions*

Resolution of 27 October 1966

The Resolution was adopted by 114 votes to 2 (Portugal and South Africa). France, Malawi, and the United Kingdom abstained. Botswana and Lesotho were absent.

2145 (XXI). QUESTION OF SOUTH WEST AFRICA

The General Assembly,

Reaffirming the inalienable right of the people of South West Africa to freedom and independence in accordance with the Charter of the United

Nations, General Assembly resolution 1514 (XV) of 14 December 1960 and earlier Assembly resolutions concerning the Mandated Territory of South West Africa,

Recalling the advisory opinion of the International Court of Justice of 11 July 1950,[1] which was accepted by the General Assembly in its resolution 449 A (V) of 13 December 1950, and the advisory opinions of 7 June 1955[2] and 1 June 1956[3] as well as the judgement of 21 December 1962,[4] which have established the fact that South Africa continues to have obligations under the Mandate which was entrusted to it on 17 December 1920 and that the United Nations as the successor to the League of Nations has supervisory powers in respect of South West Africa,

Gravely concerned at the situation in the Mandated Territory, which has seriously deteriorated following the judgement of the International Court of Justice of 18 July 1966,[5]

Having studied the reports of the various committees which had been established to exercise the supervisory functions of the United Nations over the administration of the Mandated Territory of South West Africa,

Convinced that the administration of the Mandated Territory by South Africa has been conducted in a manner contrary to the Mandate, the Charter of the United Nations and the Universal Declaration of Human Rights,

Reaffirming its resolution 2074 (XX) of 17 December 1965, in particular paragraph 4 thereof which condemned the policies of *apartheid* and racial discrimination practised by the Government of South Africa in South West Africa as constituting a crime against humanity,

Emphasizing that the problem of South West Africa is an issue falling within the terms of resolution 1514 (XV),

Considering that all the efforts of the United Nations to induce the Government of South Africa to fulfil its obligations in respect of the administration of the Mandated Territory and to ensure the well-being and security of the indigenous inhabitants have been of no avail,

Mindful of the obligations of the United Nations towards the people of South West Africa,

---

[1] *International status of South West Africa, Advisory Opinion*: I.C.J. Reports 1950, p. 128.

[2] *South West Africa—Voting procedure, Advisory Opinion of June 7th, 1955*: I.C.J. Reports 1955, p. 67.

[3] *Admissibility of hearings of petitioners by the Committee on South West Africa, Advisory Opinion of June 1st, 1956*: I.C.J. Reports 1956, p. 23.

[4] *South West Africa Cases (Ethiopia v. South Africa; Liberia v. South Africa), Preliminary Objections, Judgment of 21 December 1962*: I.C.J. Reports 1962, p. 319.

[5] *South West Africa, Second Phase, Judgment*: I.C.J. Reports 1966, p. 6.

Noting with deep concern the explosive situation which exists in the southern region of Africa,

Affirming its right to take appropriate action in the matter, including the right to revert to itself the administration of the Mandated Territory,

1. *Reaffirms* that the provisions of General Assembly resolution 1514 (XV) are fully applicable to the people of the Mandated Territory of South West Africa and that, therefore, the people of South West Africa have the inalienable right to self-determination, freedom and independence in accordance with the Charter of the United Nations;

2. *Reaffirms further* that South West Africa is a territory having international status and that it shall maintain this status until it achieves independence;

3. *Declares* that South Africa has failed to fulfil its obligations in respect of the administration of the Mandated Territory and to ensure the moral and material well-being and security of the indigenous inhabitants of South West Africa, and has, in fact, disavowed the Mandate;

4. *Decides* that the Mandate conferred upon His Britannic Majesty to be exercised on his behalf by the Government of the Union of South Africa is therefore terminated, that South Africa has no other right to administer the Territory and that henceforth South West Africa comes under the direct responsibility of the United Nations;

5. *Resolves* that in these circumstances the United Nations must discharge those responsibilities with respect to South West Africa;

6. *Establishes* an *Ad Hoc* Committee for South West Africa—composed of fourteen Member States to be designated by the President of the General Assembly—to recommend practical means by which South West Africa should be administered, so as to enable the people of the Territory to exercise the right of self-determination and to achieve independence, and to report to the General Assembly at a special session as soon as possible and in any event not later than April 1967;

7. *Calls upon* the Government of South Africa forthwith to refrain and desist from any action, constitutional, administrative, political or otherwise, which will in any manner whatsoever alter or tend to alter the present international status of South West Africa;

8. *Calls the attention* of the Security Council to the present resolution;

9. *Requests* all States to extend their whole-hearted co-operation and to render assistance in the implementation of the present resolution;

10. *Requests* the Secretary-General to provide all assistance necessary to implement the present resolution and to enable the *Ad Hoc* Committee for South West Africa to perform its duties.

Resolution of 19 May 1967

The Resolution was adopted by 85 votes to 2 (Portugal and South Africa) with 30 abstentions.

2248 (S-V). QUESTION OF SOUTH WEST AFRICA

The General Assembly,

Having considered the report of the *Ad Hoc* Committee for South West Africa,[1]

Reaffirming its resolution 1514 (XV) of 14 December 1960 containing the Declaration on the Granting of Independence to Colonial Countries and Peoples,

Reaffirming its resolution 2145 (XXI) of 27 October 1966, by which it terminated the Mandate conferred upon His Britannic Majesty to be exercised on his behalf by the Government of the Union of South Africa and decided that South Africa had no other right to administer the Territory of South West Africa,

Having assumed direct responsibility for the Territory of South West Africa in accordance with resolution 2145 (XXI),

Recognizing that it has thereupon become incumbent upon the United Nations to give effect to its obligations by taking practical steps to transfer power to the people of South West Africa,

I

Reaffirms the territorial integrity of South West Africa and the inalienable right of its people to freedom and independence, in accordance with the Charter of the United Nations, General Assembly resolution 1514 (XV) and all other resolutions concerning South West Africa;

II

1. *Decides* to establish a United Nations Council for South West Africa (hereinafter referred to as the Council) comprising eleven Member States to be elected during the present session and to entrust to it the following powers and functions, to be discharged in the Territory:

   (*a*) To administer South West Africa until independence, with the maximum possible participation of the people of the Territory;

   (*b*) To promulgate such laws, decrees and administrative regulations as are necessary for the administration of the Territory until a

[1] A/6640.

legislative assembly is established following elections conducted on the basis of universal adult suffrage;

(c) To take as an immediate task all the necessary measures, in consultation with the people of the Territory, for the establishment of a constituent assembly to draw up a constitution on the basis of which elections will be held for the establishment of a legislative assembly and a responsible government;

(d) To take all the necessary measures for the maintenance of law and order in the Territory;

(e) To transfer all powers to the people of the Territory upon the declaration of independence;

2. *Decides* that in the exercise of its powers and in the discharge of its functions the Council shall be responsible to the General Assembly;

3. *Decides* that the Council shall entrust such executive and administrative tasks as it deems necessary to a United Nations Commissioner for South West Africa (hereinafter referred to as the Commissioner), who shall be appointed during the present session by the General Assembly on the nomination of the Secretary-General;

4. *Decides* that in the performance of his tasks the Commissioner shall be responsible to the Council;

III

1. *Decides* that:

(a) The administration of South West Africa under the United Nations shall be financed from the revenues collected in the Territory;

(b) Expenses directly related to the operation of the Council and the Office of the Commissioner—the travel and subsistence expenses of members of the Council, the remuneration of the Commissioner and his staff and the cost of ancillary facilities—shall be met from the regular budget of the United Nations;

2. *Requests* the specialized agencies and the appropriate organs of the United Nations to render to South West Africa technical and financial assistance through a co-ordinated emergency programme to meet the exigencies of the situation;

IV

1. *Decides* that the Council shall be based in South West Africa;

2. *Requests* the Council to enter immediately into contact with the authorities of South Africa in order to lay down procedures, in accordance with General Assembly resolution 2145 (XXI) and the present resolution,

for the transfer of the administration of the Territory with the least possible upheaval;

3. *Further requests* the Council to proceed to South West Africa with a view to:

(*a*) Taking over the administration of the Territory;

(*b*) Ensuring the withdrawal of South African police and military forces;

(*c*) Ensuring the withdrawal of South African personnel and their replacement by personnel operating under the authority of the Council;

(*d*) Ensuring that in the utilization and recruitment of personnel preference be given to the indigenous people;

4. *Calls upon* the Government of South Africa to comply without delay with the terms of resolution 2145 (XXI) and the present resolution and to facilitate the transfer of the administration of the Territory of South West Africa to the Council;

5. *Requests* the Security Council to take all appropriate measures to enable the United Nations Council for South West Africa to discharge the functions and responsibilities entrusted to it by the General Assembly;

6. *Requests* all States to extend their whole-hearted co-operation and to render assistance to the Council in the implementation of its task;

V

Requests the Council to report to the General Assembly at intervals not exceeding three months on its administration of the Territory, and to submit a special report to the Assembly at its twenty-second session concerning the implementation of the present resolution;

VI

Decides that South West Africa shall become independent on a date to be fixed in accordance with the wishes of the people and that the Council shall do all in its power to enable independence to be attained by June 1968.

2. *Security Council Resolution, 29 July 1970*

Resolution 283 (1970) was adopted with 13 votes in favour, none against and 2 abstentions (France and the United Kingdom). In Resolution 284 (1970) of the same date the Security Council submitted the following question to the International Court of Justice with a request for an advisory opinion: 'What are the legal consequences for states of the continued presence of South Africa in

Namibia, notwithstanding Security Council resolution 276 (1970)?' The latter item is referred to in the resolution set out below.

RESOLUTION 283 (1970)

The Security Council,

Reaffirming once more the inalienable right of the people of Namibia to freedom and independence recognized in General Assembly resolution 1514 (XV) of 14 December 1960,

Reaffirming its resolution 264 (1969) and 276 (1970) by which the Security Council recognized the decision of the General Assembly to terminate the mandate of South West Africa and assume direct responsibility for the territory until its independence and in which the continued presence of the South African authority in Namibia as well as all acts taken by that Government on behalf of or concerning Namibia after the termination of the mandate were declared illegal and invalid,

Recalling its resolution 269 (1969),

Noting with great concern the continued flagrant refusal of the Government of South Africa to comply with the decisions of the Security Council demanding the immediate withdrawal of South Africa from the territory,

Deeply concerned that the enforcement of South African laws and juridical procedures in the territory have continued in violation of the international status of the territory,

Reaffirming its resolution 282 (1970) on the arms embargo against the Government of South Africa and the significance of that resolution with regard to the territory and people of Namibia,

Recalling the decisions taken by the Security Council on 30 January 1970 to establish, in accordance with rule 28 of the provisional rules of procedure, an *Ad Hoc* Sub-Committee of the Security Council to study, in consultation with the Secretary-General, ways and means by which the relevant resolutions of the Council, including resolution 276 (1970), could be effectively implemented in accordance with the appropriate provisions of the Charter in the light of the flagrant refusal of South Africa to withdraw from Namibia, and to submit its recommendations to the Council,

Having examined the report submitted by the *Ad Hoc* Sub-Committee (S/9863) and the recommendations contained in that report,

Bearing in mind the special responsibility of the United Nations with regard to the territory of Namibia and its people,

1. *Requests* all States to refrain from any relations—diplomatic, consular or otherwise—with South Africa implying recognition of the authority of the South African Government over the territory of Namibia;

2. *Calls upon* all States maintaining diplomatic or consular relations with South Africa to issue a formal declaration to the Government of

South Africa to the effect that they do not recognize any authority of South Africa with regard to Namibia and that they consider South Africa's continued presence in Namibia illegal;

3. *Calls upon* all States maintaining such relations to terminate existing diplomatic and consular representation as far as they extend to Namibia and to withdraw any diplomatic or consular mission or representative residing in the territory;

4. *Calls upon* all States to ensure that companies and other commercial and industrial enterprises owned by, or under direct control of the State, cease all dealings with respect to commercial or industrial enterprises or concessions in Namibia;

5. *Calls upon* all States to withhold from their nationals or companies of their nationality not under direct government control, government loans, credit guarantees and other forms of financial support that would be used to facilitate trade or commerce with Namibia;

6. *Calls upon* all States to ensure that companies and other commercia enterprises owned by the State or under direct control of the State cease all further investment activities including concessions in Namibia;

7. *Calls upon* all States to discourage their nationals or companies of their nationality not under direct governmental control from investing or obtaining concessions in Namibia, and to this end withhold protection of such investment against claims of a future lawful government of Namibia;

8. *Requests* all States to undertake without delay a detailed study and review of all bilateral treaties between themselves and South Africa in so far as these treaties contain provisions by which they apply to the territory of Namibia;

9. *Requests* the Secretary-General of the United Nations to undertake without delay a detailed study and review of all multilateral treaties to which South Africa is a party, and which either by direct reference or on the basis of relevant provisions of international law might be considered to apply to the territory of Namibia;

10. *Requests* the United Nations Council for Namibia to make available to the Security Council the results of its study and proposals with regard to the issuance of passports and visas for Namibians and to undertake a study and make proposals with regard to special passport and visa regulations to be adopted by States concerning travel of their citizens to Namibia;

11. *Calls upon* all States to discourage the promotion of tourism and emigration to Namibia;

12. *Requests* the General Assembly at its twenty-fifth session to set up a United Nations Fund for Namibia to provide assistance to Namibians who have suffered from persecution and to finance a comprehensive education

and training programme for Namibians with particular regard to their future administrative responsibilities of the territory;

13. *Requests* all States to report to the Secretary-General on measures they have taken in order to give effect to the provisions set forth in the present resolution;

14. *Decides* to re-establish, in accordance with rule 28 of the provisional rules of procedure, the *Ad Hoc* Sub-Committee on Namibia and request the *Ad Hoc* Sub-Committee to study further effective recommendations on ways and means by which the relevant resolutions of the Council can be effectively implemented in accordance with the appropriate provisions of the Charter, in the light of the flagrant refusal of South Africa to withdraw from Namibia;

15. *Requests* the *Ad Hoc* Sub-Committee to study the replies submitted by Governments to the Secretary-General in pursuance of operative paragraph 13 of the present resolution and to report to the Council as appropriate;

16. *Requests* the Secretary-General to give every assistance to the *Ad Hoc* Sub-Committee in the performance of its tasks;

17. *Decides* to remain actively seized of this matter.

3. *O.A.U. Resolution, 9 November 1966*

The Assembly of Heads of State and Government meeting in its Third Ordinary Session in Addis Ababa, Ethiopia, from 5 to 9 November 1966,

Recalling Article II (*d*) and Article III (6) of the Charter of the Organization of African Unity, and resolution CIAS/PLEN. 2/Rev. 2 of May 1963 on the question of South West Africa,

Reaffirming the inalienable right of the people of South West Africa to freedom and independence, in accordance with the Charter of the O.A.U., the United Nations Charter and the relevant resolutions of the O.A.U. and the United Nations, in particular, the United Nations General Assembly Resolution 1514 (XV) containing the Declaration on the granting of independence to colonial countries and peoples,

Taking note of the resolution of 27 October 1966 by the General Assembly of the United Nations:

(*a*) reaffirming that the people of South West Africa have the inalienable right to self-determination, freedom and independence in accordance with the Charter of the United Nations, and that South West Africa shall maintain its international status until it achieves independence;

(*b*) deciding that the mandate conferred upon His Britannic Majesty to be exercised on his behalf by the Government of the Union of South Africa is terminated, that South Africa has no other right to administer the territory, and that henceforth South West Africa comes under the direct responsibility of the United Nations;

(*c*) resolving that in these circumstances the United Nations must discharge those responsibilities with respect to South West Africa, and

(*d*) calling upon the South African Government forthwith to refrain and desist from any action, constitutional, administrative, political or otherwise, which may in any manner whatsoever alter or tend to alter the present international status of South West Africa,

Welcoming with satisfaction the fact that by this resolution the United Nations General Assembly has unequivocally terminated the mandate of the Government of South Africa over South West Africa and, therefore, the Government of South Africa has no right whatever to exercise authority in any form in South West Africa,

1. *Considers* that the continued domination of South West Africa by South Africa constitutes an illegal military occupation of an African sister country;

2. *Calls upon* all Member States to spare no effort in helping the people of South West Africa to rid themselves of foreign occupation in order to exercise their inalienable right to freedom and independence, and urges the Co-ordinating Committee for the Liberation of Africa to give priority to the termination of the occupation of South West Africa;

3. *Calls upon* the various organs of the United Nations to take all measures deemed necessary under its Charter to put into immediate effect the General Assembly's resolution of 27 October 1966 on South West Africa to terminate this oppressive illegal occupation of South West Africa;

4. *Pledges* wholehearted co-operation with the United Nations in discharging its responsibilities with respect to South West Africa and urges all its Member States, in the light of the aforementioned United Nations General Assembly resolution, to communicate to the Secretary-General of the United Nations the manner and the extent of material support they are ready to place before the United Nations for the effective implementation of the United Nations resolution;

5. *Urges* all States which have not yet done so to refrain from supplying arms, military equipment, petroleum or petroleum products to South Africa.

V. DOCUMENTS CONCERNING SOUTH AFRICA

1. *The Bantu Education Act, 1953*

RACIALIST laws and practices were enforced by various European regimes in Africa and were not introduced by South African Nationalists like Malan: see Macmillan, *Africa Emergent*, 1938 (rev. edn., 1949). What happened in South Africa after 1948 was the application of a more doctrinal and oppressive regime of separate development or *apartheid*. The institutions of *apartheid* affront ordinary conceptions of human dignity, create demoralization among Africans (the 'natives'), and support a highly developed system of economic exploitation of the non-whites by the white minority. There is a great deal of material on *apartheid* in the *South West Africa Cases* (Second Phase), 1966, *Pleadings*, published by the International Court of Justice. See also the *South West Africa Cases* (Second Phase), I.C.J. Reports, 1966, p. 6 at pp. 139–93 (Van Wyk), 232–5 (Wellington Koo), 284–316 (Tanaka), 464–70 (Padilla Nervo), 486–9 (Mbanefo); Hahlo and Kahn, *The Union of South Africa: The Development of its Laws and Constitution*, 1960, pp. 793–813; Davis, Melunsky, and Du Randt, *Urban Native Law*, Port Elizabeth, 1959; McEwan (ed.), *Twentieth-Century Africa*, 1968, pp. 252–99; U.N. Unit on *Apartheid*, *Repressive Legislation of the Republic of South Africa*, 1969, U.N. Document ST/PSCA/SER.A/7.

The Bantu Education Act is a typical and also fundamental measure of *apartheid* policy.

TEXT

ACT

To provide for the transfer of the administration and control of native education from the several provincial administrations to the Government of the Union, and for matters incidental thereto.

(*English text signed by the Governor-General.*)
(*Assented to 5th October, 1953.*)

BE IT ENACTED by the Queen's Most Excellent Majesty, the Senate and the House of Assembly of the Union of South Africa, as follows:

Definitions

1. In this Act, unless the context otherwise indicates—

    (i) 'Bantu' shall be synonymous with 'native'; (ii)

    (ii) 'Department' means the Department of Native Affairs; (iii)

    (iii) 'education' means education other than 'higher education' within the meaning of section *seventeen* of the Financial Relations Consolidation and Amendment Act, 1945 (Act No. 38 of 1945); (viii)

(iv) 'Minister' means the Minister of Native Affairs; (v)

(v) 'native' means any person who is or is generally accepted as a member of any aboriginal race or tribe of Africa; (vi)

(vi) 'native school' or 'Bantu school' means any school, class, college, or institution for the education of Bantu children or persons, or for the instruction and training of Bantu persons who desire to become teachers or to improve their qualifications as teachers; (vii)

(vii) 'officer' means an officer on the fixed establishment of the public service; (i)

(viii) 'prescribed' means prescribed by regulation; (xi)

(ix) 'regulation' means any regulation made under this Act; (ix)

(x) 'Secretary' means the Secretary for Native Affairs and includes any Under-Secretary of the Department; (x)

(xi) 'this Act' includes any regulation. (iv)

Transfer of control of native education from the provincial administrations to the Union Government

2. As from the date of commencement of this Act—

(a) the control of native education shall vest in the Government of the Union subject to the provisions of this Act;

(b) there shall cease to be vested in the executive committee of a province any powers, authorities and functions, and the provincial council of a province shall cease to be competent to make ordinances, in relation to native education:

Provided that, subject to the provisions of section *eleven*—

(i) a provincial administration shall continue to administer any pension, retirement or provident fund established or conducted by such administration in connection with native education;

(ii) a provincial council shall continue to be competent to make ordinances for the proper administration of any such fund.

Administration

3. (1) It shall be the function of the Department under the direction and control of the Minister, to perform all the work necessary for or incidental to the general administration of native education.

(2) The Minister may, subject to the laws governing the public service, from time to time appoint such officers and employees as he may deem necessary for the proper performance by the Department of its functions under this Act.

Transfer of officers employed by a province in connection with native education to the service of the Union Government

4. Every officer who, on or after the first day of July, 1953, was serving under a provincial administration mainly in connection with native education, and who on the date of promulgation of this Act is still serving under a provincial administration, shall, as from the date of commencement of this Act, be transferred to the Department, unless any such officer, at the request or with the approval of the Minister, acting in consultation with the Administrator of the province concerned, is transferred to another post in the public service or is in like manner excluded from the operation of this section.

Transfer of certain employees of a province to the service of the Union Government

5. (1) Every person, other than an officer or a teacher, who immediately prior to the date of commencement of this Act, was employed by a provincial administration mainly in connection with native education, shall, as from that date, become an employee of the Department, unless the Minister, acting in consultation with the Administrator of the province concerned, decides otherwise.

(2) The continuous employment by a provincial administration immediately prior to the commencement of this Act, of any person who becomes an employee of the Department in terms of sub-section (1), shall, except as hereinafter provided, be deemed to have been employment in the service of the Department.

(3) Notwithstanding any limitation in respect of age or educational qualifications prescribed by or under the Public Service Act, 1923 (Act No. 27 of 1923), any person who becomes an employee of the Department in terms of sub-section (1), who is a South African citizen and who has not attained the prescribed age of retirement, may, on the recommendation of the Public Service Commission, be appointed, on probation or otherwise, to a post in the public service.

(4) Any person appointed to the public service in terms of sub-section (3) shall be adjusted to the scale of salary applicable to the post to which he is appointed at such notch on that scale as may be recommended by the Public Service Commission: Provided that, except with his own consent or in accordance with the provisions of any law, the salary or the scale of salary at or in accordance with which any such person was remunerated immediately prior to the commencement of this Act, shall not be reduced.

(5) (a) Any person who becomes an employee of the Department in terms of sub-section (1) and who, immediately prior to the date

of commencement of this Act, was subject to a law relating to pensions administered by a provincial administration, shall retain his rights and obligations under any such pensions law and shall continue to contribute to the pension, retirement, or provident fund to which he contributed prior to such date; and there shall be contributed to the said fund, out of moneys appropriated by Parliament for the purpose, in respect of every such person, an amount equal to the amount which the provincial administration would have contributed to that fund in respect of every such person if he had remained in its service.

(b) The provisions of section *forty-seven* of the Pension Laws Amendment Act, 1943 (Act No. 33 of 1943), shall *mutatis mutandis* apply to any person referred to in paragraph (a) or any dependant of any such person who becomes entitled to a pension under this sub-section.

Financial assistance to Bantu community schools

6. (1) Subject to the provisions of this Act, the Minister may, on such special conditions as he may stipulate and in accordance with such general principles as he may determine in consultation with the Minister of Finance, out of moneys appropriated or set aside by Parliament for native education—

(a) subsidize any Bantu school established or maintained by any Bantu authority, or any native council, tribe or community (hereinafter called a Bantu community school); or

(b) assist in the establishment or maintenance of any such school.

(2) The Minister may, in his discretion, at any time suspend, reduce, or withdraw any subsidy or assistance granted to any such school under this section.

Establishment of Government Bantu schools

7. (1) The Minister may, out of moneys appropriated or set aside by Parliament for native education—

(a) establish and maintain Bantu schools which shall be known as Government Bantu schools;

(b) establish and maintain any hostel, teachers' quarters, school clinic, or any other accessory to a Government Bantu school.

(2) Every native school or accessory thereto which was established and maintained by a provincial administration and which is in existence on the date of commencement of this Act, shall, as from that date, be deemed to

have been established in terms of sub-section (1) as a Government Bantu School or as an accessory to a Government Bantu School.

(3) The Minister may at any time, whenever he considers it expedient to do so, close or disestablish any such Government Bantu school, hostel, teachers' quarters, school clinic or other accessory to a Government Bantu school.

Grants-in-aid to State-aided native schools

8. (1) Subject to the provisions of this Act, the Minister may, on such special conditions as he may stipulate and in accordance with such general principles as he may determine in consultation with the Minister of Finance, out of moneys appropriated or set aside by Parliament for native education, make grants-in-aid to any native school approved by him for the purposes of this section: Provided that before approving any such school the Minister may consider—

(*a*) in respect of any native school situate in a scheduled native area or a released area referred to in the Native Trust and Land Act, 1936 (Act No. 18 of 1936), after consultation with the Bantu authority, or the native council, tribe, or community concerned; or

(*b*) in respect of any native school situate outside a scheduled native area and a released area, with due regard to the interests of the Bantu people,

whether the establishment or existence of any such native school precludes, retards, or renders impracticable, or is likely to preclude, retard, or render impracticable, the establishment of a Bantu community school or a Government Bantu school for the area concerned.

(2) The Minister may, in his discretion, at any time suspend, reduce, or withdraw any grant made under this section or revoke his approval of any native school for the purposes of this section: Provided that before so exercising his discretion the Minister may cause an inquiry to be held at which the person or committee or other body in charge of the said school shall be entitled to be heard.

Registration of Bantu or native schools

9. (1) As from a date to be fixed by the Minister by notice in the *Gazette*, no person shall establish, conduct, or maintain any Bantu or native school, other than a Government Bantu school, unless it is registered as prescribed.

(2) The registration of any such school shall be refused or cancelled if the Minister, acting on the advice and recommendation of the Native Affairs Commission constituted under the Native Affairs Act, 1920 (Act No. 23 of 1920), given after due enquiry by the said Commission is of

opinion that its establishment or continued existence is not in the interests of the Bantu people or any section of such people or is likely to be detrimental to the physical, mental or moral welfare of the pupils or students attending or likely to attend such school.

(3) Any person who, after the date fixed under sub-section (1), admits any Bantu child or person to, or establishes, conducts or maintains, any Bantu or native school which is not registered in terms of this Act, shall be guilty of an offence and liable on conviction to a fine not exceeding fifty pounds, or, in default of payment, to imprisonment for a period not exceeding six months.

Appointment, conditions of service and retirement benefits of teachers in Government Bantu schools

10. (1) The teaching establishment at any Government Bantu school shall be determined by the Minister on a basis to be laid down from time to time in consultation with the Minister of Finance and on the recommendation of the Public Service Commission.

(2) (a) The power of appointment, promotion, transfer, or discharge of teachers in Government Bantu schools shall, subject to the provisions of this Act, vest in the Minister, who may delegate any or all of the said powers to the Secretary.

(b) In respect of any post designated by the Minister, he may delegate the power of appointment or discharge of any teacher to any officer of the Department.

(3) Every person who immediately prior to the date of commencement of this Act was employed by a provincial administration as a teacher on the establishment of a native school referred to in sub-section (2) of section *seven*, shall, as from that date, be transferred to the service of the Department.

(4) Unless and until the Minister prescribes otherwise, the conditions of service, including the emoluments and leave privileges, of any teacher referred to in sub-section (3), shall continue in force as if the said teacher had remained in the service of the provincial administration.

(5) Unless and until the Minister prescribes otherwise—

(a) the retirement or pension benefits of any teacher referred to in sub-section (3) shall continue in force as if such teacher had remained in the service of the provincial administration by which he was employed immediately prior to the coming into operation of this Act and the provisions of section *forty-seven* of the Pension Laws Amendment Act, 1943 (Act No. 33 of 1943), shall *mutatis mutandis* apply to any such teacher or any dependant of any such teacher who becomes entitled to a pension under this paragraph;

(b) every such teacher shall continue to contribute to the pension, retirement, or provident fund which is administered by the provincial administration concerned and to which he contributed prior to the commencement of this Act, as if he had not been transferred to the service of the Department, and there shall be contributed to the said fund, out of moneys appropriated by Parliament for the purpose, in respect of every such teacher, an amount which the provincial administration concerned would have contributed to that fund in respect of every such teacher: Provided that, in the case of the pension fund established under Act No. 43 of 1887 (Cape), there may each year be contributed out of moneys similarly appropriated, towards pension benefits payable to retired native teachers, an amount determined by the Minister in consultation with the Minister of Finance.

(6) Subject to the foregoing provisions of this section, the conditions of service, including the scales of salary, leave privileges, and retirement or pension benefits, of teachers in Government Bantu schools, shall be prescribed by the Minister in consultation with the Minister of Finance and on the recommendation of the Public Service Commission.

(7) Any disciplinary proceedings in respect of misconduct committed by any teacher referred to in sub-section (3) before the date of commencement of this Act, may be continued or instituted by the Department as if such misconduct had been committed after the said date.

Transfer of administration of Natal non-European Teachers' Provident Fund

11. The Minister may, after consultation with the Minister of Finance and the Administrator of the Province of Natal, by notice in the *Gazette*, direct that subject to such conditions as he may determine, the moneys of the Natal non-European Teachers' Provident Fund, constituted by Ordinance No. 10 of 1930 (Natal), shall in respect of native teachers vest in and be administered *mutatis mutandis* by the Commissioner of Pensions in accordance with the provisions of the said Ordinance or as prescribed and thereafter, as from the date of the said notice, all contributions payable to the said Fund in terms of the said Ordinance or this Act by or in respect of native teachers shall be paid to the Commissioner of Pensions, who shall be responsible for the payment out of the said moneys and contributions of all liabilities of the said Fund arising, or which have arisen, in terms of the said Ordinance or this Act, in respect of native teachers.

Management of Government Bantu schools

12. (1) The Minister may, with due regard to the principle of providing for active participation by the Bantu people in the control and management of Government Bantu schools, establish such regional, local, and domestic councils, boards, or other bodies as he may deem expedient, or may for this purpose entrust the control and management of any Government Bantu school to any Bantu authority or native council established by or under any other law.

(2) The constitution, duties, powers, privileges, and functions of any such council, board, or body, or the duties, powers, privileges, and functions of any Bantu authority or native council to whom the control and management of any Government Bantu school is entrusted, shall be as prescribed.

Certain assets and liabilities transferred to Union Government

13. As from the date of commencement of this Act—

(*a*) all the property, movable or immovable, which immediately prior to the said date was used or had been acquired by a provincial administration solely for the purposes of or in connection with native education, shall vest in the Government of the Union, subject to any conditions or obligations upon or under which such property was held immediately prior to the said date in so far as such conditions or obligations do not lapse by merger as a result of this vesting;

(*b*) all the liabilities lawfully incurred by a provincial administration for the purposes of or in connection with native education and existing immediately prior to the said date, including any liability to pay a bonus or allowance to any retired teacher or employee or any dependant of any such teacher or employee in supplementation of any pension payable to any such person, shall become the liabilities of the Government of the Union, subject to the provisions of this Act and to the conditions under which those liabilities were incurred:

Provided that, save as is provided in section *eleven*, the provisions of this section shall not be deemed to include any asset acquired or liability incurred in connection with any pension, retirement or provident fund administered by a provincial administration.

Power to expropriate land for native education purposes

14. The Minister may expropriate any land required for the purposes of a Government Bantu school or any accessory thereto, and the Expropriation of Lands and Arbitration Clauses Proclamation, 1902 (Proclamation No. 5 of 1902), of the Transvaal, shall *mutatis mutandis* apply to any such expropriation in any part of the Union.

Regulations

15. (1) The Minister may from time to time make regulations—

(*a*) prescribing, subject to the laws governing the public service, the powers and duties of the Secretary and any other officer or employee of the Department in connection with the administration of native education;

(*b*) prescribing the conditions of appointment and service, including the rights, duties and privileges, of teachers in Government Bantu schools;

(*c*) prescribing a code of discipline for teachers in Government Bantu schools, the punishments which may be imposed for, and the procedure to be followed in connection with, any contravention of or failure to comply with the provisions of such code, and the circumstances in which the services of any such teacher may be terminated;

(*d*) prescribing courses of training or instruction in Government Bantu schools and the fees, if any, payable in respect of such courses or any examination held by or under the supervision or control of the Department;

(*e*) prescribing the medium of instruction in Government Bantu schools;

(*f*) prescribing the conditions governing the establishment, control and maintenance of any hostel, school clinic, or other accessory to a Government Bantu school;

(*g*) relating to the admission of pupils or students to, the control, and treatment of pupils or students at, and the discharge of pupils or students from, any Government Bantu school;

(*h*) providing for the medical examination of teachers, pupils or students in Government Bantu schools, including the particulars to be contained in medical certificates;

(*i*) providing for the control of funds collected for any Government Bantu school;

(*j*) providing for religious instruction in Government Bantu schools;

(*k*) prescribing the circumstances in which the suspension or expulsion of any pupil or student from any Government Bantu school may take place or any other punishment may be administered or imposed;

(*l*) prescribing the conditions under which Bantu community schools may be subsidized or assisted under section *six*;

(*m*) providing for the approval of State-aided native schools, under section *eight*, and prescribing the conditions under which grants-in-aid may be made;

(*n*) providing for the registration of Bantu community schools or other native schools;

(*o*) providing for the award of bursaries to Bantu pupils or students and prescribing the conditions under which such bursaries may be awarded;

(*p*) providing for the establishment of an advisory board or advisory boards on Bantu education for the Union and prescribing the constitution, duties, powers, privileges and functions of such a board and the fees and allowances, if any, payable to any member of a board who is not in the full-time employment of the State;

(*q*) providing for the constitution, duties, powers, privileges and functions of regional, local and domestic councils, boards or other bodies or the duties, powers, privileges and functions of any Bantu authority or native council to whom the control and management of a Government Bantu school is entrusted and prescribing the fees and allowances, if any, payable to any members thereof who are not in the full-time employment of the State;

(*r*) providing, subject to the approval of the Minister of Finance, for the establishment and management of a pension or provident fund or scheme for teachers in Government Bantu schools to be administered by the Commissioner of Pensions and prescribing the contributions to be made to such fund or scheme out of moneys appropriated by Parliament and by teachers;

(*s*) providing generally for any other matter relating to the establishment, maintenance, management and control of Government Bantu schools or which the Minister may deem necessary or expedient to prescribe for achieving the purposes of this Act, the generality of the powers conferred by this paragraph not being limited by the provisions of the preceding paragraphs.

(2) Different regulations may be made in respect of different teachers, groups, classes or races of teachers, or different schools or areas.

(3) The regulations may provide penalties for any contravention thereof or failure to comply therewith not exceeding a fine of fifty pounds or, in default of payment, imprisonment for a period not exceeding six months.

(4) Until the Minister makes regulations, the laws in force in the respective provinces immediately prior to the date of commencement of this Act, other than the law repealed by section *seventeen*, shall, in so far as they relate to native education and are not inconsistent with the provisions of this Act, continue to apply *mutatis mutandis* in respect of native education: Provided that in any such law, any reference to the 'Governor'

or the 'Administrator' shall be construed as a reference to the Minister, and any reference to the 'Superintendent-General', 'Superintendent' or 'Director' as a reference to the Secretary, and any reference to the 'Department' as a reference to the Department, and any reference to the 'Controller' as a reference to the Principal Accountant of the Department.

(5) Whenever the Minister makes regulations with regard to any of the matters referred to in sub-section (1), that part of the laws referred to in sub-section (4) relating to any matter dealt with in the regulations, shall then cease to apply to native education.

Amendment of section 85 of the South Africa Act, 1909

16. Section *eighty-five* of the South Africa Act, 1909, is hereby amended by the insertion in paragraph (iii) after the words 'higher education' of the words 'and native education'.

Repeal of Act 29 of 1945

17. The Native Education Finance Act, 1945 (Act No. 29 of 1945), is hereby repealed.

Short title and date of commencement

18. This Act shall be called the Bantu Education Act, 1953, and shall come into operation on a date to be fixed by the Governor-General by proclamation in the *Gazette*.

2. *U.N. General Assembly and Security Council Resolutions*

The reaction of the United Nations to the racial policies of South Africa provides a general guide to the development of racial conflict as a major factor in international relations. It is no doubt often true that 'racial conflict' is a superficial reference behind which lies an issue of economic inequality or historical rivalry between groups. In any case in African affairs analysis of racial issues must take into account the special aggressiveness of *apartheid*, together with the historical background of European colonialism and racial assumptions and practices. In other words, sociological analysis should take into account the issue of justice, both as a current issue and as a matter of past affronts.

See generally Segal (ed.), *Sanctions Against South Africa*, Penguin Special, 1964; Mason, *Patterns of Dominance*, 1970 (this contains a useful reading list); Fanon, *The Wretched of the Earth*, 1965; Hill, *Bantustans: The Fragmentation of South Africa*, 1964; Luthuli, *Let My People Go: An Autobiography*, 1962; Preiswerk, *Year Book of World Affairs*, 1970, p. 54; Study of Apartheid and Racial Discrimination in Southern Africa, U.N. Document E/CN. 4/949/Add. 4, 23 January 1968; U.N. Unit on *Apartheid*, *Review of United Nations Consideration of Apartheid*, 1967, U.N. Document ST/PSCA/SER.A/2.

There have been numerous General Assembly resolutions on South African affairs, commencing with resolution 44 (I) adopted on 8 December 1946 concerning the treatment of Indians in South Africa. After 1952 resolutions began to appear referring to South African policies in a general way and characterizing these policies as in contravention of the U.N. Charter in particular, Article 56: see Resolutions 616 (B) (VII), 5 December 1952; 820 (IX), 14 December 1954; 917 (X), 6 December 1955; 1178 (XII), 26 November 1957; 1248 (XIII), 30 October 1958.

In 1960 the situation altered, partly as a result of incidents like the shootings at Sharpeville and partly as a result of increased African participation in international affairs as Black Africa became independent. For the first time the Security Council showed concern, on the basis that the situation 'if continued might endanger international peace and security': Res. S/4300, 1 April, 1960.

The General Assembly now began to urge the taking of measures against South Africa to bring about the abandonment of her policies. The resolutions concerned involved permitting and urging states to take economic and other measures but were not binding on states since they only had the force of recommendations: see Resolutions 1598 (XV), 13 April 1961; 1663 (XVI), 28 November 1961; and 1761 (XVII), 6 November 1962, set out below.

Eventually the Security Council adopted a resolution of 7 August 1963 calling upon all states to cease the sale and shipment of arms, ammunition of all types, and military vehicles to South Africa. (9 votes to 0; 2 abstentions—U.K. and France). Further resolutions on similar lines were adopted on 4 December 1963, 9 June 1964 (set out below), 18 June 1964 (set out below). There, essentially, the matter has rested and Resolution 2054 (XX), adopted by the General Assembly on 15 December 1965 (set out below) summarizes the position. The central point is the refusal of the major Western powers to introduce a mandatory sanctions policy against South Africa. This refusal, coupled with Western investment in Southern Africa, is the basis of the strength of South Africa, Portugal, and Rhodesia. The most recent development is the Security Council resolution of 23 July 1970 (set out below). See further below, p. 539.

Further General Assembly resolutions have been adopted as follows: Resolution 2202 (XXI) of 16 December 1966; and 2307 (XXII) of 13 December 1967.

U.N. GENERAL ASSEMBLY RESOLUTION 1761 (XVII)

The Resolution was adopted by 67 votes to 16 with 23 abstentions, on 6 November 1962.

The General Assembly,

Recalling its previous resolutions on the question of race conflict in South Africa resulting from the policies of *apartheid* of the Government of the Republic of South Africa,

Further recalling its resolutions 44 (I) of 8 December 1946, 395 (V) of 2 December 1950, 615 (VII) of 5 December 1952, 1179 (XII) of 26 November 1957, 1302 (XIII) of 10 December 1958, 1460 (XIV) of 10 December 1959, 1597 (XV) of 13 April 1961 and 1662 (XVI) of 28 November 1961, on the question of the treatment of peoples of Indian and Indo-Pakistan origin,

Noting the reports of the Governments of India and Pakistan on that subject,

Recalling that the Security Council in its resolution of 1 April 1960 recognized that the situation in South Africa was one that had led to international friction and, if continued, might endanger international peace and security,

Recalling further that the Security Council in its aforesaid resolution called upon the Government of South Africa to initiate measures aimed at bringing about racial harmony based on equality in order to ensure that the present situation does not continue or recur, and to abandon its policies of *apartheid* and racial discrimination,

Regretting that the actions of some Member States indirectly provide encouragement to the Government of South Africa to perpetuate its policy of racial segregation, which has been rejected by the majority of that country's population,

1. *Deplores* the failure of the Government of the Republic of South Africa to comply with the repeated requests and demands of the General Assembly and of the Security Council and its flouting of world public opinion by refusing to abandon its racial policies;

2. *Strongly deprecates* the continued and total disregard by the Government of South Africa of its obligations under the Charter of the United Nations and, furthermore, its determined aggravation of racial issues by enforcing measures of increasing ruthlessness involving violence and bloodshed;

3. *Reaffirms* that the continuance of those policies seriously endangers international peace and security;

4. *Requests* Member States to take the following measures, separately or collectively, in conformity with the Charter, to bring about the abandonment of those policies:

(*a*) Breaking off diplomatic relations with the Government of the Republic of South Africa or refraining from establishing such relations;

(*b*) Closing their ports to all vessels flying the South African flag;

(*c*) Enacting legislation prohibiting their ships from entering South African ports;

(*d*) Boycotting all South African goods and refraining from exporting goods, including all arms and ammunition, to South Africa;

(e) Refusing landing and passage facilities to all aircraft belonging to the Government of South Africa and companies registered under the laws of South Africa;

5. *Decides* to establish a Special Committee consisting of representatives of Member States nominated by the President of the General Assembly, with the following terms of reference:

(a) To keep the racial policies of the Government of South Africa under review when the Assembly is not in session;

(b) To report either to the Assembly or to the Security Council or to both, as may be appropriate, from time to time;

6. *Requests* all Member States:

(a) To do everything in their power to help the Special Committee to accomplish its task;

(b) To refrain from any act likely to delay or hinder the implementation of the present resolution;

7. *Invites* Member States to inform the General Assembly at its eighteenth session regarding actions taken, separately or collectively, in dissuading the Government of South Africa from pursuing its policies of *apartheid*;

8. *Requests* the Security Council to take appropriate measures, including sanctions, to secure South Africa's compliance with the resolutions of the General Assembly and of the Security Council on this subject and, if necessary, to consider action under Article 6 of the Charter.

SECURITY COUNCIL RESOLUTION 190 (1964)

This was adopted on 9 June 1964 by 7 votes to 0, with 4 abstentions (Brazil, France, United Kingdom, United States).

The Security Council,

Recalling General Assembly resolution 1881 (XVIII) of 11 October 1963, which condemns the Government of the Republic of South Africa for its failure to comply with the repeated resolutions of the General Assembly and of the Security Council and which requests it to abandon the arbitrary trial in progress and forthwith to grant unconditional release to all political prisoners and to all persons imprisoned, interned or subjected to other restrictions for having opposed the policy of *apartheid*,

Further recalling that the Security Council in its resolutions of 7 August 1963 (S/5386) and 4 December 1963 (S/5471) called upon the Government of South Africa to liberate all persons imprisoned, interned or subjected to other restrictions for having opposed the policy of *apartheid*,

Noting with great concern that the arbitrary Rivonia trial instituted against the leaders of the anti-*apartheid* movement has been resumed, and that the imminent verdict to be delivered under arbitrary laws prescribing long terms of imprisonment and the death sentence may have very serious consequences,

Noting with regret that the Government of South Africa has rejected the appeal of the Secretary-General of 27 March 1964,

1. *Urges* the South African Government:

(*a*) to renounce the execution of the persons sentenced to death for acts resulting from their opposition to the policy of *apartheid*;

(*b*) to end forthwith the trial in progress, instituted within the framework of the arbitrary laws of *apartheid*; and

(*c*) to grant an amnesty to all persons already imprisoned, interned or subjected to other restrictions for having opposed the policy of *apartheid*, and particularly to the defendants in the Rivonia trial;

2. *Invites* all States to exert all their influence in order to induce the South African Government to comply with the provisions of this resolution;

3. *Invites* the Secretary-General to follow closely the implementation of the resolution and to report thereon to the Security Council at the earliest possible date.

SECURITY COUNCIL RESOLUTION 191 (1964)

This was adopted on 18 June 1964 by 8 votes to 0, with 3 abstentions (Czechoslavakia, France, U.S.S.R.

The Security Council,

Having considered the question of race conflict in South Africa resulting from the policies of *apartheid* of the Government of the Republic of South Africa, brought to the attention of the Security Council by fifty-eight Member States in their letter of 27 April 1964,

Being gravely concerned with the situation in South Africa arising out of the policies of *apartheid* which are contrary to the principles and purposes of the Charter of the United Nations and inconsistent with the provisions of the Universal Declaration of Human Rights as well as South Africa's obligations under the Charter,

Taking note with appreciation of the reports of the Special Committee on the Policies of *Apartheid* of the Government of the Republic of South Africa and the report of the Group of Experts appointed by the Secretary-General pursuant to the Security Council resolution of 4 December 1963 (S/5471),

Recalling the resolutions of the Security Council of 7 August 1963 (S/5386), 4 December 1963 (S/5471) and 9 June 1964 (S/5761),

Convinced that the situation in South Africa is continuing seriously to disturb international peace and security,

Deploring the refusal of the Government of the Republic of South Africa to comply with pertinent Security Council resolutions,

Taking into account the recommendations and conclusions of the Group of Experts,

1. *Condemns* the *apartheid* policies of the Government of the Republic of South Africa and the legislation supporting these policies, such as the General Law Amendment Act, and in particular its ninety-day detention clause;

2. *Urgently reiterates* its appeal to the Government of the Republic of South Africa to liberate all persons imprisoned, interned or subjected to other restrictions for having opposed the policies of *apartheid*;

3. *Notes* the recommendations and the conclusions in the Report of the Group of Experts;

4. *Urgently appeals* to the Government of the Republic of South Africa to:

(*a*) renounce the execution of any persons sentenced to death for their opposition to the policy of *apartheid*;

(*b*) grant immediate amnesty to all persons detained or on trial, as well as clemency to all persons sentenced for their opposition to the Government's racial policies;

(*c*) abolish the practice of imprisonment without charges, without access to counsel or without the right of prompt trial;

5. *Endorses* and subscribes in particular to the main conclusion of the Group of Experts that 'all the people of South Africa should be brought into consultation and should thus be enabled to decide the future of their country at the national level';

6. *Requests* the Secretary-General to consider what assistance the United Nations may offer to facilitate such consultations among representatives of all elements of the population in South Africa;

7. *Invites* the Government of the Republic of South Africa to accept the main conclusion of the Group of Experts referred to in paragraph 5 above and to co-operate with the Secretary-General and to submit its views to him with respect to such consultations by 30 November 1964;

8. *Decides* to establish an Expert Committee, composed of representatives of each present member of the Security Council, to undertake a technical and practical study, and report to the Security Council as to the feasibility, effectiveness, and implications of measures which could, as appropriate, be taken by the Security Council under the United Nations Charter;

9. *Requests* the Secretary-General to provide to the Expert Committee the Secretariat's material on the subjects to be studied by the Committee, and to co-operate with the Committee as requested by it;

10. *Authorizes* the Expert Committee to request all United Nations Members to co-operate with it and to submit their views on such measures to the Committee no later than 30 November 1964, and the Committee to complete its report not later than three months thereafter;

11. *Invites* the Secretary-General in consultation with appropriate United Nations specialized agencies to establish an educational and training programme for the purpose of arranging for education and training abroad for South Africans;

12. *Reaffirms* its call upon all States to cease forthwith the sale and shipment to South Africa of arms, ammunition of all types, military vehicles, and equipment and materials for the manufacture and maintenance of arms and ammunition in South Africa;

13. *Requests* all Member States to take such steps as they deem appropriate to persuade the Government of the Republic of South Africa to comply with this resolution.

GENERAL ASSEMBLY RESOLUTION 2054 (XX)

This was adopted by 80 votes to 2 (Portugal and South Africa), with 16 abstentions, on 15 December 1965.

2054 (XX). *The policies of* apartheid *of the Government of the Republic of South Africa*

A

The General Assembly,

Recalling its resolutions on the policies of *apartheid* of the Government of the Republic of South Africa,

Having considered the reports of the Special Committee on the Policies of *apartheid* of the Government of the Republic of South Africa,[1]

Considering the recommendations and conclusions contained in the report[2] of the Group of Experts established under Security Council resolution 182 (1963) of 4 December 1963,

Recalling Security Council resolution 191 (1964) of 18 June 1964,[3]

---

[1] *Official Records of the General Assembly, Nineteenth Session, Annexes*, Annex no. 12, documents A/5692, A/5707, A/5825 and Add. 1; A/5932 and A/5957.

[2] See *Official Records of the Security Council, Nineteenth Year, Supplement for April, May and June 1964*, document S/5658, Annex.

[3] S/5773.

Gravely concerned at the aggravation of the explosive situation in the Republic of South Africa as a result of the continued implementation of the policies of *apartheid* by the Government of South Africa in violation of its obligations under the Charter of the United Nations and in defiance of the resolutions of the Security Council and the General Assembly,

Profoundly disturbed at the fact that the policies and actions of the Government of South Africa are thus aggravating the situation in neighbouring territories in southern Africa,

Noting the measures taken by Member States in pursuance of the resolutions of the General Assembly and the Security Council,

Having studied the notes, annexed to the Special Committee's report of 17 June 1965, on the build-up of military and police forces in the Republic of South Africa and on recent investments by foreign-owned corporations in that country,[1]

Considering that prompt and effective international action is imperative in order to avert the grave danger of a violent racial conflict in Africa, which would inevitably have grave repercussions throughout the world,

Recalling its resolution 1761 (XVII) of 6 November 1962 recommending the application of economic and diplomatic sanctions against South Africa,

1. *Urgently appeals* to the major trading partners of the Republic of South Africa to cease their increasing economic collaboration with the Government of South Africa, which encourages that Government to defy world opinion and to accelerate the implementation of the policies of *apartheid*;

2. *Expresses its appreciation* to the Special Committee on the Policies of apartheid of the Government of the Republic of South Africa and requests it to continue to perform its functions;

3. *Decides* to enlarge the Special Committee by the addition of six members, to be appointed by the President of the General Assembly on the basis of the following criteria:

(*a*) Primary responsibility with regard to world trade;

(*b*) Primary responsibility under the Charter for the maintenance of international peace and security;

(*c*) Equitable geographical distribution;

4. *Condemns* the Government of South Africa for its refusal to comply with the resolutions of the Security Council and the General Assembly and its continued implementation of the policies of *apartheid*;

5. *Firmly supports* all those who are opposing the policies of *apartheid* and particularly those who are combating such policies in South Africa;

[1] See A/5932, Annexes I and II.

6. *Draws the attention* of the Security Council to the fact that the situation in South Africa constitutes a threat to international peace and security, that action under Chapter VII of the Charter is essential in order to solve the problem of apartheid and that universally applied economic sanctions are the only means of achieving a peaceful solution;

7. *Deplores* the actions of those States which, through political, economic and military collaboration with the Government of South Africa, are encouraging it to persist in its racial policies;

8. *Again requests* all States to comply fully with all the resolutions of the Security Council on this question and to halt forthwith the sale and delivery to South Africa of arms, ammunition of all types, military vehicles, and equipment and materials intended for their manufacture and maintenance;

9. *Requests* the Secretary-General, in consultation with the Special Committee, to take appropriate measures for the widest possible dissemination of information on the policies of *apartheid* of the Government of South Africa and on United Nations efforts to deal with the situation, and requests all Member States, specialized agencies and non-governmental organizations to co-operate with the Secretary-General and the Special Committee in this regard;

10. *Invites* the specialized agencies:

(a) To take the necessary steps to deny technical and economic assistance to the Government of South Africa, without, however, interfering with humanitarian assistance to the victims of the policies of *apartheid*;

(b) To take active measures, within their fields of competence, to compel the Government of South Africa to abandon its racial policies;

(c) To co-operate with the Special Committee in the implementation of its terms of reference;

11. *Requests* the Secretary-General to provide the Special Committee with all the necessary means, including appropriate financial means, for the effective accomplishment of its task.

B

The General Assembly,

Recalling its resolution 1978 B (XVIII) of 16 December 1963,

Taking note of the reports of the Secretary-General in pursuance of that resolution,[1]

---

[1] *Official Records of the General Assembly, Nineteenth Session, Annexes*, Annex no. 12, documents A/5850; A/5850/Add. 1, A/6025 and Add. 1.

Considering the recommendation contained in paragraphs 161 to 164 of the report of 16 August 1965 submitted by the Special Committee on the Policies of *Apartheid* of the Government of the Republic of South Africa,[1]

Deeply concerned at the plight of numerous persons persecuted by the Government of South Africa for their opposition to the policies of *apartheid* and repression, and at the plight of their families,

Considering that humanitarian assistance to such persons and their families is in keeping with the purposes of the United Nations,

1. *Expresses its great appreciation* to the Governments which have made contributions in response to resolution 1978 B (XVIII) and the Special Committee's appeal of 26 October 1964;[2]

2. *Requests* the Secretary-General to establish a United Nations trust fund, made up of voluntary contributions from States, organizations and individuals, to be used for grants to voluntary organizations, Governments of host countries of refugees from South Africa and other appropriate bodies, towards:

(*a*) Legal assistance to persons charged under discriminatory and repressive legislation in South Africa;

(*b*) Relief for dependants of persons persecuted by the Government of South Africa for acts arising from opposition to the policies of *apartheid*;

(*c*) Education of prisoners, their children and other dependants;

(*d*) Relief for refugees from South Africa;

3. *Requests* the President of the General Assembly to nominate five Member States, each of which should appoint a person to serve on a committee of trustees which will decide on the uses of the trust fund;

4. *Authorizes and requests* the committee of trustees to take steps to promote contributions to the fund, and to promote co-operation and co-ordination in the activities of voluntary organizations concerned with relief and assistance to the victims of the policies of *apartheid* of the Government of South Africa;

5. *Requests* the Secretary-General to provide the necessary assistance to the committee of trustees in the discharge of its responsibilities;

6. *Appeals* to Governments, organizations and individuals to contribute generously to the trust fund.

[1] See A/5957.   [2] A/AC. 115/L. 98.

SECURITY COUNCIL RESOLUTION 282 (1970)

This was adopted on 23 July 1970 by 12 votes to 0, with 3 abstentions (France, United Kingdom, and United States). For the background see below, p. 539.

The Security Council,

Having considered the question of race conflict in South Africa resulting from the policies of *apartheid* of the Government of the Republic of South Africa as submitted by forty Member States,

Reiterating its condemnation of the evil and abhorrent policies of *apartheid* and the measures being taken by the Government of South Africa to enforce and extend those policies beyond its borders,

Recognizing the legitimacy of the struggle of the oppressed people of South Africa in pursuance of their human and political rights as set forth in the Charter of the United Nations and of the Universal Declaration of Human Rights,

Gravely concerned by the persistent refusal of the Government of South Africa to abandon its racist policies and to abide by the resolutions of the Security Council and of the General Assembly on this question and others relating to southern Africa,

Gravely concerned with the situation arising from violations of the arms embargo called for in its resolutions 181 (1963) of 7 August 1963, 182 (1963) of 4 December 1963 and 191 (1964) of 18 June 1964,

Convinced of the need to strengthen the arms embargo called for in the above resolutions,

Convinced further that the situation resulting from the continued application of the policies of *apartheid* and the constant build-up of the South African military and police forces made possible by the continued acquisition of arms, military vehicles and other equipment and of spare parts for military equipment from a number of Member States and by local manufacture of arms and ammunition under licences granted by some Member States constitutes a potential threat to international peace and security,

Recognizing that the extensive arms build-up of the military forces of South Africa poses a real threat to the security and sovereignty of independent African States opposed to the racial policies of the Government of South Africa, in particular the neighbouring States,

1. *Reiterates* its total opposition to the policies of *apartheid* of the Government of the Republic of South Africa;

2. *Reaffirms* its resolutions 181 (1963), 182 (1963) and 191 (1964);

3. *Condemns* the violations of the arms embargo called for in resolutions 181 (1963), 182 (1963) and 191 (1964);

4. *Calls upon* all States to strengthen the arms embargo

(*a*) by implementing fully the arms embargo against South Africa unconditionally and without reservations whatsoever;

(*b*) by withholding supply of all vehicles and equipment for use of the armed forces and paramilitary organizations of South Africa;

(*c*) by ceasing supply of spare parts for all vehicles and military equipment used by the armed forces and paramilitary organizations of South Africa;

(*d*) by revoking all licences and military patents granted to the South African Government or to South African companies for the manufacture of arms and ammunition, aircraft and naval craft or other military vehicles and by refraining from further granting such licences and patents;

(*e*) by prohibiting investment in or technical assistance for the manufacture of arms and ammunition, aircraft, naval craft, or other military vehicles;

(*f*) by ceasing provision of military training for members of the South African armed forces and all other forms of military co-operation with South Africa;

(*g*) by undertaking the appropriate action to give effect to the above measures;

5. *Requests* the Secretary-General to follow closely the implementation of the present resolution and report to the Security Council from time to time; and

6. *Calls upon* all States to observe strictly the arms embargo against South Africa and to assist effectively in the implementation of this resolution.

3. *African National Congress: The Freedom Charter*

The title of this document is *The Freedom Charter: Revolutionary Programme of the African National Congress of South Africa*. It is based upon the original Freedom Charter and appears in *Sechaba* (the official organ of the A.N.C.), Special Issue on the Consultative Conference of A.N.C., vol. 3, no. 7 (July 1969), p. 11. The A.N.C. is the most senior of the African liberation movements and its programme is typical of the tendency to link liberation and socialist objectives of economic justice. The close associates of A.N.C. in this respect are F.R.E.L.I.M.O. (Frente de Libertação de Mocambique), M.P.L.A. (Movimento Popular para Libertação da Angola), S.W.A.P.O. (South-West Africa People's Organization), Z.A.P.U. (Zimbabwe African People's Union), and P.A.I.G.C. (Partido Africano da Independencia da Guiné e Cabo Verde). This list by no means exhausts the tally of liberation movements. Thus in the case of Rhodesia the Zimbabwe African National Union is a rival of Z.A.P.U.

TEXT

For over two hundred and fifty years the African people fought wars of resistance against the European invaders in defence of their motherland— South Africa. Despite their heroism, courage and tenacity our people were defeated on the battlefield by the superior arms and organization of the Europeans.

Although the conflicts and problems of South Africa have largely centred on the relationships between the Africans and Europeans, they are not the only peoples who form the South African population. The Coloured and Indian people are, like the Africans, oppressed by the dominant European minority.

The South Africa of today is the product of the common labour of all its peoples. The cities, industries, mines and agriculture of the country are the result of the efforts of all its peoples. But the wealth is utilized by and for the interests of the white minority only.

The African National Congress was formed in 1912 to unite the Africans as a nation and to forge an instrument for their liberation. From the outset the African National Congress asserted the right of the African people as the indigenous owners of the country, entitled to determine its direction and destiny. Simultaneously our forefathers recognized that the other groups in the country—the Europeans, Indians and Coloureds were historically part and parcel of South Africa.

Democratic principles

The ANC rejected the claims of the European settlers to domination, and fought against all attempts to subjugate them in the land of their birth. But in the face of the gravest injustices the ANC never once abandoned the principle that all those who had their home in the country of the Africans, were welcome, provided only that they accepted full and consistent equality and freedom for all. In this the ANC was not merely bowing to history and reality but believed that it was correct in principle to make this position clear. Over and over again in the face of manifest inhumanity the ANC absolutely refused to be provoked into abandoning its democratic principles.

The ruling white minority rejected the concepts of the ANC and to that extent the movement and the people fought and will fight them.

Congress of the people

In the early fifties when the struggle for freedom was reaching new intensity the need was seen for a clear statement of the future South Africa as the ANC saw it. Thus was born the Congress of the People campaign.

In this campaign the African National Congress and its allies invited the whole of South Africa to record their demands which would be incorporated in a common document called the Freedom Charter. Literally millions of people participated in the campaign and sent in their demands of the kind of South Africa they wished to live in. These demands found final expression in the Freedom Charter. The Freedom Charter was adopted at the Congress of the People representative of all the people of South Africa which met at Kliptown, Johannesburg, on June 25 and 26, 1955. The three thousand delegates who gathered at Kliptown were workers, peasants, intellectuals, women, youth and students of all races and colours. The Congress was the climax of the campaign waged by the African National Congress, the South African Indian Congress, the Coloured People's Organization, the South African Congress of Trade Unions and the Congress of Democrats. Subsequently all these organizations adopted the Freedom Charter in their national conferences as their official programme. Thus the Freedom Charter became the common programme enshrining the hopes and aspirations of all the progressive people of South Africa.

'High Treason'

From the moment the idea of the Congress of the People and the Freedom Charter was mentioned the white government of South Africa termed it 'High Treason'. After the Congress of the People was held and the Charter adopted, fresh threats were uttered by the government. Eventually 156 leaders of the liberation movement were arrested on December 5, 1956 and charged with plotting to overthrow the state and to replace it by a new one along the lines laid down in the Charter. This long trial which lasted four-and-a-half years resulted in the acquittal of all the accused. By that time the Freedom Charter had become one of the most famous documents in the history of man's struggle for freedom.

The Charter was not the statement of this or that section of the population. It was a declaration of all the people of South Africa. It was a simple, honest, unpretentious document reflecting the desires and ideas of millions of common people. Therein lay the power of its revolutionary message. And always it should be borne in mind that both in its wording and intent the Charter projected the view not of present-day South Africa but that of the country as it should and will be after the victory of the revolution.

Today the African National Congress and its allies are engaged in an armed struggle for the overthrow of the racist regime. In its place the ANC will establish a democratic state along the lines indicated in the Freedom Charter. Although the Charter was adopted 14 years ago its words remain as fresh and relevant as ever. Some who have forgotten its actual terms or the kind of document it is, or, who detach this or that phrase from the document taken as a whole, imagine that the conditions of armed struggle somehow invalidate some provisions of the Charter. What we believe is that the Charter may require elaboration of its revolutionary message. But what is even more meaningful, it requires to be achieved and put into practice. This cannot be done until state power has been seized from the fascist South African government and transferred to the revolutionary forces led by the ANC.

The preamble of the Freedom Charter

The first lines of the Charter declare that South Africa belongs to all who live in it, Black and White, and that no government can justly claim authority unless it is based on the will of the people.

The expression 'South Africa belongs to all who live in it, Black and White' embodies the historical principle which has characterized the policy of the African National Congress towards the peoples who have settled in the country in the past centuries. The African people as the indigenous owners of the country have accepted that all the people who have made South Africa and helped build it up, are components of its multi-national population, are and will be in a democratic South Africa, one people inhabiting their common home. No government can justly claim authority unless it is based on the will, not just of the whites, but of all the people of the country. The Freedom Charter thus begins by an assertion of what is and has been a cardinal democratic principle that all can live in South Africa whatever their origin, in equality and democracy. That the South Africa of the future will not be a country divided unto itself and dominated by a particular racial group. It will be the country of all its inhabitants. It is the white people who in the past as now have rejected this principle leaving the people no alternative but to convince them by the truth of revolutionary struggle. The preamble ends by calling on the people, Black and White, as equals, countrymen and brothers to pledge to strive together sparing neither strength nor courage until the democratic changes set out in the Freedom Charter had been won.

The preamble couched in terms similar to many famous documents reflecting man's aspiration for freedom called for a new state resting on the will of the people—a repudiation of the existing state and a call for revolution. Hereunder we examine, briefly, each section of our Charter.

The people shall govern!

The Republican constitution of South Africa passed in 1961 is a monument to racialism and despotism. In terms of this constitution supreme legislative authority is vested in the White fascist State President, the House of Assembly and the Senate. Only a White person can be elected State President. The House of Assembly and the Senate consist exclusively of White representatives elected by an exclusively White electorate. Therefore the power to make laws in our country is a monopoly of the White minority.

The same applies to other organs of government such as the four provincial councils of Natal, Cape, Orange Free State and Transvaal which are headed by a White Administrator assisted by an all White executive Council. Organs of local government such as District Councils, Municipal Councils, boroughs are manned entirely by White people. Such organs of local government as there are for non-Whites consist of the Transkei Legislative Council and an executive; the Indian Council; the Coloured Council; urban Bantu authorities, Territorial Authorities and other such bodies. These are all undemocratic institutions with little or no power and serving merely as a sounding board for the White minority government.

The administration in South Africa is similarly manned at all significant levels by White persons.

A successful armed revolution will put an end to this state of affairs.

The Parliament of South Africa will be wholly transformed into an Assembly of the People. Every man and woman in our country shall have the right to vote for and stand as a candidate for all offices and bodies which make laws. The present administration will be smashed and broken up. In its place will be created an administration to which all people irrespective of race, colour or sex can take part. The bodies of minority rule shall be abolished and in their place will be established democratic organs of self-government in all the Provinces, districts and towns of the country.

All national groups shall have equal rights!

In South Africa not only does the system at present enforce discrimination against individuals by reason of their colour or race but in addition some national groups are privileged, as such, over others. At the moment the Afrikaner national group is lording it over the rest of the population with the English group playing second-fiddle to them. For all the non-White groups—the Africans, Indians and the Coloureds the situation is one of humiliation and oppression. As far as languages are concerned only Afrikaans and English have official status in the bodies of state such as Parliament or Provincial Councils; in the courts, schools and in the administration. The culture of the African, Indian and Coloured people is barely tolerated. In fact everything is done to smash and obliterate the genuine cultural heritage of our people. If there is reference to culture by the oppressors it is for the purpose of using it as an instrument to maintain our people in backwardness and ignorance.

Day in and day out White politicians and publicists are regaling the world with their theories of national, colour and racial discrimination and contempt for our people. Enshrined in the laws of South Africa are a host of insulting provisions directed at the dignity and humanity of the oppressed people.

A Democratic government of the people shall ensure that all national groups have equal rights, as such, to achieve their destiny in a united South Africa.

There shall be equal status in the bodies of state, in the courts and in the schools for the African, Indian, Coloured and Whites as far as their national rights are concerned. All people shall have equal right to use their own languages, and to develop their own folk culture and customs; all national groups shall be protected by laws against insults to their race or national pride; the preaching and practice of national, racial or colour discrimination and contempt shall be a punishable crime; and all laws and practices based on *apartheid* or racial discrimination shall be set aside.

The people shall share in the country's wealth!

Today most of the wealth of South Africa is flowing into the coffers of a few in the country and others in foreign lands. In addition the White minority as a group have over the years enjoyed a complete monopoly of economic rights, privileges and opportunities.

An ANC government shall restore the wealth of our country, the heritage of all South Africans to the people as a whole. The mineral wealth beneath the soil, the banks and monopoly industry shall be transferred to the ownership of the people as a whole.

At the moment there are vast monopolies whose existence affects the livelihood of large numbers of our people and whose ownership is in the hands of Europeans only. It is necessary for monopolies which vitally affect the social well-being of our people such as the mines, the sugar and wine industry to be transferred to public ownership so that they can be used to uplift the life of all the people. All other industry and trade which is not monopolistic shall be allowed with controls to assist the well-being of the people.

All restriction on the right of the people to trade, to manufacture and to enter all trades, crafts and professions shall be ended.

The land shall be shared among those who work it!

The indigenous people of South Africa after a series of resistance wars lasting hundreds of years were deprived of their land. Today in our country all the land is controlled and used as a monopoly by the White minority. It is often said that 87% of the land is 'owned' by the Whites and 13% by the Africans. In fact the land occupied by Africans and referred to as 'Reserves' is state land from which they can be removed at any time but which for the time being the fascist government allows them to live on. The Africans have always maintained their right to the country and the land as a traditional birthright of which they have been robbed. The ANC slogan 'Mayibuye i-Afrika' was and is precisely a demand for the return of the land of Africa to its indigenous inhabitants. At the same time the liberation movement recognizes that other oppressed people deprived of land live in South Africa. The White people who now monopolize the land have made South Africa their home and are historically part of the South African population and as such entitled to land. This made it perfectly correct to demand that the land be shared among those who work it. But who work the land? Who are the tillers?

The bulk of the land in our country is in the hands of land barons, absentee landlords, big companies and state capitalist enterprises. The land must be taken away from exclusively European control and from these groupings and divided among the small farmers, peasants and land-less of all races who do not exploit the labour of others. Farmers will be prevented from holding land in excess of a given area, fixed in accordance with the concrete situation in each locality. Lands held in communal ownership be increased so that they can afford a decent livelihood to the people and their ownership shall be guaranteed. Land obtained from land barons and the monopolies shall be distributed to the landless and land-poor peasants. State land shall be used for the benefit of all the people.

Restrictions of land ownership on a racial basis shall be ended and all land shall be open to ownership and use to all people, irrespective of race.

The State shall help farmers with implements, seeds, tractors and dams to save soil and assist the tillers. Freedom of movement shall be guaranteed to all who work on the land. Instruments of control such as the 'Trek Pass', private gaols on farms, forced labour shall be abolished. The policy of robbing people of their cattle in order to enforce them to seek work in order to pay taxes shall be stopped.

All shall be equal before the Law!

In terms of such laws as the notorious Suppression of Communism Act; the Native Administration Act; the Riotous Assemblies Act; the Terrorism and Sabotage Acts and many other laws our people suffer imprisonment, deportation and restriction without fair trials. These laws shall be abolished. No one shall suffer imprisonment, deportation or restriction without fair trial.

In our country petty government officials are invested with vast powers in their discretion to condemn people. These powers shall be ended.

The courts of South Africa are manned by White officials, magistrates, judges. As a result the courts serve as instruments of oppression. The democratic state shall create courts representative of all the people.

South Africa has the highest proportion of prisoners of any state in the world. This is because there are so many petty infringements to which a penalty of imprisonment is attached. In a new South Africa, imprisonment shall only be for serious crimes against the people, and shall aim at re-education, not vengeance.

It has been a standing policy of White governments in South Africa to prevent Africans and other non-Whites from holding responsible positions in the police force. The present police force and army are instruments of coercion to protect White supremacy. Their whole aim is punitive and terroristic against the majority of the population.

It is the major aim of the armed revolution to defeat and destroy the police force, army and other instruments of coercion of the present state.

In a Democratic South Africa the army and police force shall be open to people of all races. Already Umkhonto We Sizwe—the nucleus of our future people's army is an armed force working in the interests of people drawn from the land for their liberation. It consists of people drawn from all population groups in South Africa.

All shall enjoy equal human rights!

South Africa has numerous laws which limit or infringe the human rights of the people. One need only mention the notorious Suppression of Communism Act; Proclamation 400 which imposes a state of emergency in the Transkei; the Proclamation of 1953 which bans meetings of more than ten Africans in scheduled areas; the Native Laws Amendment Act which introduces racial discrimination in churches and places of worship; the Bantu Education Act which makes education without a government permit an offence—surely an offence unique in the world—to educate without a permit!

All the above Acts and regulations will be swept away by a peoples' government. The law shall guarantee to all, their right to speak, to organ-ize to meet together, to publish, to preach, to worship and to educate their children.

The Pass Laws of South Africa result in the arrest of an average of 1,100 persons a day. These laws control and prohibit movement of our people in the country. There are also laws which restrict movement from one province to another. As part of their checking of the people numerous police raids are organized during which homes are broken into at any time of the day or night. Many laws give the police powers to enter people's homes without warrant and for no apparent reason except to terrorize them.

All this shall be abolished. The privacy of the home from police raids shall be protected by law.

All shall be free to travel without restrictions from countryside to town, from province to province and from South Africa abroad.

Pass laws, permits and all other laws restricting these freedoms shall be abolished.

There shall be work and security!

As with everything else the rights of collective bargaining of workers in South Africa have been twisted and warped by racial ideas and practices. Africans do not have the right to form registered trade unions and are prohibited from going on strike. Other workers are forced to belong to racially divided unions. The government has the power to determine what jobs shall be reserved for what racial groups. People of different races are paid differential wage rates for the same work. Migratory labour is a chief feature of the South African economy and leads to massive social up-heaval and distress particularly among Africans. In the Democratic State the ANC is determined to achieve, all who work shall be free to form trade unions, to elect their officers and to make wage agreements with their employers.

The State shall recognize the right and duty of all to work and to draw full unemployment benefits. Men and women of all races shall receive equal pay for equal work. There shall be a forty-hour working week, a national minimum wage, paid annual leave, and sick leave for all workers and maternity leave on full pay for all working mothers. Miners, domestic workers, farm workers, and civil servants shall have the same rights as all others who work to form trade unions, and join political organizations.

The use of child labour, the housing of male workers in single men's compounds, the system whereby workers on wine farms are paid tots of wine as part payment on their wages, contract labour—all these pernicious practices shall be abolished by a victorious revolutionary government.

The doors of learning and culture shall be opened!

One of the biggest crimes of the system of White supremacy is the damage it has done to the development of the people of South Africa in the fields of learning and culture. On the one hand the minds of White people have been poisoned with all manner of unscientific and racialist twaddle in their separate schools, colleges and universities. There has been made available to them all the worst forms of so-called Western culture. The best creations of art, writing, the theatre and cinema which extol the unity of the human family and the need for liberty are only made available in dribs and drabs, whilst the general position is one of a cultural desert.

As far as the non-White people are concerned the picture is one of deprivation all along the line. One has to think hard to discover whether or not there is even one single theatre, drama school, ballet school, college of music to which non-Whites are admitted in South Africa. In Cape Town there is some ridiculously slight opening for Coloured people. Otherwise eighty per cent of the people of South Africa are by and large confined to patronizing the few cinemas whose fare is the most inferior type of American cinema art.

A vigilant censorship system exists to ensure that these racially separate cinemas do not show non-Whites anything that is considered to be bad for them by the authorities.

It is not only that non-Whites are virtually debarred from the cultural productions of mankind, but in addition everything has been done to prevent them developing their own national cultures. Publishing is strictly controlled. Apart from the most banal forms of music, the people are not encouraged or allowed to produce such music as enhances their spirit. Such music as contains protest against conditions of life are searched for and prohibited. The languages of the people are not permitted to be developed by them in their own way. Ignorant and officious White professors sit in education committees as arbiters of African languages and books without consultation with the people concerned. The grotesque spectacle is seen of the White government of South Africa posing as a 'protector' of so-called Bantu culture and traditions of which they know nothing. The arrogance of the fascists knows no bounds! They apparently love African culture more than the Africans themselves! The truth is that they wish to preserve these aspects of the African tradition which contain divisive tendencies likely to prevent the consolidation of the African people as a nation.

The forces represented in the present state after combating education of non-Whites for over one hundred years suddenly decided to take over all education as a state responsibility. The result was the introduction of a racially motivated ideological education; a lowering of standards; the emergence of tribal colleges; and the intensification of racial separation in university education. Science and technology are hardly taught to non-Whites. The training of doctors and other medical personnel is derisory.

The Democratic State shall discover, develop and encourage national talent for the enhancement of our cultural life; all cultural treasures of mankind shall be open to all, by free exchange of books, ideas and contact with other lands. The aim of education shall be to teach the youth to love their people and their culture, to honour human brother-hood, liberty and peace.

Education shall be free, compulsory, universal and equal for all children.

High education and technical training shall be opened to all by means of state allowances and scholarships awarded on the basis of merit.

Adult illiteracy shall be ended by a mass state education plan.

Teachers shall have the rights of other citizens to organize themselves and participate in political life. The colour bar in cultural life, in sport and education shall be abolished.

There shall be houses, security and comfort!

Migratory labour and its concomitant of separation of families, social problems and distress, is one of the tragedies of South Africa. Residential segregation is the order of the day throughout South Africa. Massive shortage and bad housing for non-Whites and huge homes and flats most of which are either empty or not fully used for the White minority. The infant mortality rate in our country is among the highest in the world, and the life expectancy of Africans among the lowest. Medical services are haphazard and costly.

The Democratic state established after the victory of the revolution shall ensure the right of the people to live where they choose, to be decently housed, and to bring up their families in comfort and security. The vast unused housing space in such areas as the flatlands of Hillbrow and Johannesburg shall be made available to the people. Rent and prices shall be lowered, and adequate amounts of food shall be made available to the people. A preventive health scheme shall be run by the state. Free medical care and hospitalization shall be provided for all, with medical care for mothers and young children. Slums, which have to some extent been demolished in the nine major centres of the country shall be eliminated in the middle of towns and rural areas where the majority of the people live.

New suburbs shall be built where proper facilities shall be provided of transport, lighting, playing fields, creches and social centres.

The aged, the orphans, the disabled and the sick shall be cared for by the State.

Every person shall have the right to leisure, rest and recreation.

Fenced locations, and racial ghettoes shall be abolished and laws which result in the break-up of families shall be repealed.

There shall be peace and friendship!

On the wake of the victorious revolution a Democratic People's Republic shall be proclaimed in South Africa. This shall be a fully independent state which respects the rights and sovereignty of nations.

South Africa shall strive to maintain world peace and the settlement of international disputes by negotiation—not war.

Peace and friendship amongst all people shall be secured by upholding the equal rights, opportunities and status of all.

The Democratic state shall maintain close neighbourly relations with the states of Lesotho, Botswana and Swaziland in place of the present veiled threats and economic pressure applied against our brothers and sisters in these states by White supremacy.

Democratic South Africa shall take its place as a member of the OAU and work to strengthen Pan-African unity in all fields. Our country will actively support national liberation movements of the peoples of the world against imperialism, colonialism and neo-colonialism.

Diplomatic relations will be established with all countries regardless of their social and political systems on the principles of mutual respect for each other's independence, sovereignty and territorial integrity.

The economic and cultural interests of those countries which sympathize with and support the struggle of South Africa for freedom shall be respected.

The revolutionary struggle is in its infancy. It will be a long hard road. To accomplish the glorious task of the revolution maximum unity among all national groups and revolutionary forces must be created and maintained. All South African patriots whatever their race must take their place in the revolution under the banner of the African National Congress. Forward to revolution and the victory of the people's programme of liberation!

VI. ASSISTANCE TO PORTUGAL AND SOUTH AFRICA BY THE INTERNATIONAL BANK AND INTERNATIONAL MONETARY FUND

THE documents set out below represent a special facet of the struggle by the so-called Third World to apply pressure to South Africa and Portugal. The provision of financial aid by the International Bank and International Monetary Fund to projects in Portuguese colonies and South Africa is regarded as incompatible with the status of these institutions as specialized agencies in a special relation with the United Nations. In practice both bodies are autonomous and their policies are in line with those of the United States and its associates. The issue is thus linked with the general problem of persuading Western states to bring their economic policies into accord with the principles they have accepted, especially with regard to South African policies.

The General Assembly is concerned with the over-all problem of foreign investment in Southern Africa: see Resolution 2288 (XXII) of 7 December 1967. See also Resolution 2311 (XXII) of 14 December 1967 on 'Implementation of the Declaration on the Granting of Independence to Colonial Countries and Peoples by the specialized agencies and the international institutions associated with the United Nations'.

On the attempt to suspend South Africa from membership of the United Nations Conference on Trade and Development in 1968 see *International Legal Materials*, vol. 8 (1969), p. 209.

1. *U.N. General Assembly Resolution 2426 (XXIII)*

This was adopted on 18 December 1968, by 82 votes to 7 (Brazil, Costa Rica, Honduras, Portugal, South Africa, United Kingdom, and the United States), with 25 abstentions.

2426 (XXIII). IMPLEMENTATION OF THE DECLARATION ON THE GRANTING OF INDEPENDENCE TO COLONIAL COUNTRIES AND PEOPLES BY THE SPECIALIZED AGENCIES AND THE INTERNATIONAL INSTITUTIONS ASSOCIATED WITH THE UNITED NATIONS

The General Assembly,

Having considered the item entitled 'Implementation of the Declaration on the Granting of Independence to Colonial Countries and Peoples by the specialized agencies and the international institutions associated with the United Nations',

Recalling the Declaration on the Granting of Independence to Colonial Countries and Peoples contained in General Assembly resolution 1514 (XV) of 14 December 1960,

Recalling its resolution 2311 (XXII) of 14 December 1967 and other relevant General Assembly resolutions,

Taking into account the relevant reports submitted by the Secretary-General,[1] the Economic and Social Council[2] and the Special Committee on the Situation with regard to the Implementation of the Declaration on the Granting of Independence to Colonial Countries and Peoples[3] concerning the implementation of the Declaration by the specialized agencies and international institutions associated with the United Nations,

Bearing in mind that the national liberation movements in several colonial Territories, and particularly in Africa, require the urgent assistance of the specialized agencies, particularly in the field of education, health and nutrition, in their struggle to attain freedom and independence,

Noting with regret that some of the specialized agencies and international institutions associated with the United Nations, and in particular the International Bank for Reconstruction and Development and the International Monetary Fund, have not so far implemented General Assembly resolution 2311 (XXII) and other relevant resolutions,

Considering that, by virtue of the Charter of the United Nations, in particular Chapters IX and X, the United Nations shall make recommendations for the co-ordination of the policies and activities of the specialized agencies,

1. *Reiterates* its appeal to the specialized agencies, the International Atomic Energy Agency and the international institutions associated with the United Nations to extend their full co-operation to the United Nations in the achievement of the objectives and provisions of General Assembly resolution 1514 (XV) and other relevant resolutions;

2. *Expresses its appreciation* to the Office of the United Nations High Commissioner for Refugees and to those specialized agencies and the international institutions which have co-operated with the United Nations in the implementation of the relevant General Assembly resolutions;

3. *Recommends* that the specialized agencies and international institutions concerned should assist the peoples struggling for their liberation from colonial rule and, in particular, should work out, within the scope of their respective activities and in co-operation with the Organization of African Unity and, through it, with the national liberation movements,

---

[1] A/7301.

[2] *Official Records of the General Assembly, Twenty-third Session, Supplement No. 3* (A/7203), chapter XVI, section C; A/7203/Add. 1 (Part IV).

[3] A/7200 (Part II) and Corr. 1.

concrete programmes for assisting the oppressed peoples of Southern Rhodesia, Namibia and the Territories under Portuguese domination;

4. *Appeals once again* to all the specialized agencies and international institutions, and in particular the International Bank for Reconstruction and Development and the International Monetary Fund, to take all necessary steps to withhold from the Governments of Portugal and South Africa financial, economic, technical and other assistance until they renounce their policies of racial discrimination and colonial domination;

5. *Recommends* that the International Bank for Reconstruction and Development should withdraw the loans and credits it has granted to the Governments of Portugal and South Africa, which are being used by those Governments to suppress the national liberation movement in the Portuguese colonies and in Namibia, and against the African population of South Africa;

6. *Requests* all States, through action in the specialized agencies and international institutions of which they are members, to facilitate the full and speedy implementation of the relevant General Assembly resolutions;

7. *Requests* the Economic and Social Council to consider, in consultation with the Special Committee on the Situation with regard to the Implementation of the Declaration on the Granting of Independence to Colonial Countries and Peoples, appropriate measures for the coordination of the policies and activities of the specialized agencies in implementing the relevant General Assembly resolutions;

8. *Invites* the Secretary-General:

(*a*) To continue to assist the specialized agencies and international institutions concerned in working out appropriate measures for implementing the relevant General Assembly resolutions and to report thereon to the Assembly at its twenty-fourth session;

(*b*) To obtain and transmit to the Special Committee for its consideration concrete suggestions from the specialized agencies and international institutions concerned regarding the best ways and means of achieving the full and speedy implementation of the relevant resolutions;

9. *Requests* the Special Committee to continue to examine the question and to report to the General Assembly at its twenty-fourth session.

2. *I.B.R.D. Responses*[1]

LETTERS FROM THE INTERNATIONAL BANK (I.B.R.D.)
TO THE U.N. SECRETARY-GENERAL

I

17 December 1968

Dear Mr. Secretary-General:

I would like very briefly to comment on operative paragraph 5 in the resolution contained in document A/7424 which was adopted by the Fourth Committee on 13 December. This new operative paragraph would ask the Bank to act in contravention of formal loan agreements which it has entered into and which are registered with the United Nations Secretariat. The Bank's General Counsel had advised me that under these agreements the Bank could not legally do what the amendment would ask it to do. I am further advised that if the Bank tried to act illegally in the manner suggested by the amendment, the borrowers in question could take legal action against the Bank before the international arbitral tribunals established by the loan agreements. I trust that the General Assembly would not wish to recommend to the Bank that it disregard the obligations it has undertaken in its loan agreements.

I would be grateful if you were to bring this letter to the attention of the General Assembly, before it considers the report of the Fourth Committee (A/7424) on this item.

Yours sincerely,
(*Signed*) FEDERICO CONSOLO
Special Representative for
United Nations Organizations

U Thant
Secretary-General
United Nations
New York

II

14 May 1969

In respect of operative paragraph 4, I would like to confirm that the Bank's position remains as set forth in the letter which my predecessor, Mr. Woods, wrote to you on 18 August 1967, a copy of which is attached for convenience.

Operative paragraph 5 recommends that the Bank 'should withdraw the loans and credits it has granted to the Governments of Portugal and South Africa, which are being used by those Governments to suppress

[1] See U.N. Documents A/7446, 17 December 1968; A/AC. 109/333, 3 July 1969.

the national liberation movement in the Portuguese colonies and in Namibia, and against the African population of South Africa'. The loans extended by the Bank to, or with the guarantee of, South Africa and Portugal, the most recent of which was made in 1966, were for specific projects of economic development and the Bank, in accordance with its normal practice, took appropriate steps to ensure that the proceeds of the loans would be used only for those projects.

The loans were made under formal loan or guarantee agreements which were entered into by the Bank with its members in accordance with its Articles of Agreement and these agreements are registered with the United Nations Secretariat. There are no contractual or other legal grounds which would permit the Bank now to withdraw these loans.

You have drawn our attention to paragraph 8 of the resolution. While appreciating your kind offer of assistance pursuant to paragraph 8 (a), we are unable under the circumstances to avail ourselves of it. We do not have, at this moment, any suggestions for the consideration of the Special Committee pursuant to paragraph 8 (b).

Finally, I want to confirm that, as Mr. Woods assured you in the attached letter, it is the desire and intention of the Bank, despite its inability to comply with the particular resolution which is the subject of your letter, to co-operate with the United Nations to the maximum extent possible, consistent with its own mandate.

The resolution has been brought to the attention of the Executive Directors of the Bank and they have approved this letter.

Enclosure

The Legal Counsel of the United Nations has, as you know, sent us a paper containing a closely reasoned legal argument why the World Bank should take certain actions under the General Assembly's requests for the withholding of economic assistance to Portugal and South Africa. The Bank's General Counsel has replied with legal arguments to show that, under the terms of its Agreement with the United Nations, the Bank is not obligated to comply with such requests and indeed, under the terms of its own Articles of Agreement, is not free to do so. The Legal Counsel of the United Nations has since written that he continues to adhere to his original views, to which the United Nations organs concerned will doubtless give great weight. However, the Executive Directors of the Bank who, as you know, are responsible for interpreting the Articles of Agreement, having carefully considered all the arguments advanced, have, although with some dissents, endorsed the position taken by the Bank's General Counsel. It seems to me unlikely that additional legal argumentation would change the situation.

In the circumstances, I should like at this point to leave legal argumentation aside and to assure you—and through you the various United Nations organs concerned—that the World Bank is keenly aware and proud of being part of the United Nations family. Its earnest desire is to co-operate with the United Nations by all legitimate means and to the extent consistent with its Articles of Agreement, to avoid any action that might run counter to the fulfilment of the great purposes of the United Nations. I give you this assurance in the hope that it may be helpful in dissipating any misunderstanding of the Bank's attitude.

PART SIX

RELATIONS WITH NON-AFRICAN
POWERS

THE material which follows is necessarily of modest proportions. It is merely intended to lead the reader toward certain issues and further materials. The O.A.U. has forty-one member states and the external relations of the continent of Africa are more complicated than might be expected if too much emphasis is placed on the concept of an African bloc. In this Part and indeed in this volume as a whole the special relations of the Arab states of North Africa with each other and with other Arab states are not considered. There is a useful study by Macdonald, *The League of Arab States*, 1965.

I. ECONOMIC TIES

A GOOD proportion of African states have a considerable connection with the banking and credit system dominated by the Western powers. Loans and credits are derived from the United States and other Western countries, and also from the International Bank and other institutions with the objective of furthering private capital investment. See further above, p. 195. Loans and credits are obtained from China and the U.S.S.R. on a lesser scale. It is to be noted that China, in particular, provides very favourable terms. Aid from Communist countries has two special features: it is not devoted to furthering development outside the public sector and it does not result in a foreign-owned investment or other asset.

The association agreements with the E.E.C. have been noted already: see above, p. 310.

A number of states formerly under British rule are members of the sterling area. In other words they have their monetary reserves centralized in the form of gold, sterling securities, or cash, in London: see further Fawcett, *The British Commonwealth in International Law*, 1963, p. 235.

Former French territories are members of the franc zone and, in some cases, the West African Monetary Union and the West African Economic Community. France thus maintains substantial economic and political influence in certain African states, a circumstance indicated by their voting behaviour in the United Nations and O.A.U.

II. MILITARY ASSISTANCE AGREEMENTS

FRANCE has military assistance agreements with a number of states. For the defence agreement between France, Central African Republic, Congo (Brazzaville), and Republic of Chad, 15 August 1960, see *Documents on International Affairs 1960*, R.I.I.A. (ed. Gott, Major, and Warner), p. 333. Gabon joined the arrangement on 20 June 1961. France has similar agreements with the Cameroon, Mauritania, Togo, Malagasy Republic, Ivory Coast, Dahomey, and Niger. On a number of occasions French forces have intervened in civil strife under the provisions of such agreements. French assistance has been given to government forces in Chad engaged in a civil war. The United Kingdom has an agreement on mutual defence and assistance with Mauritius (1968), and assists in the training and development of the armed forces in Kenya (U.K. *Treaty Series*, no. 33 (1968), Cmnd. 3582). In 1967 the United Kingdom and South Africa concluded an agreement concerning the Simonstown naval base and related matters: see further below, p. 539 (Appendix III).

III. NON-ALIGNMENT

In the 1950s a number of states which were not attached to either of the Cold War camps began a loose form of political association described as 'neutralism' or 'non-alignment'. Leading members of this group were India, Indonesia, Yugoslavia, and Egypt. The basic outlook of non-alignment appears in the Declaration of the Bandung Conference in 1955:

'1. Respect for fundamental human rights and for the purposes and principles of the Charter of the United Nations.

2. Respect for the sovereignty and territorial integrity of all nations.

3. Recognition of the equality of all races and of the equality of all nations large and small.

4. Abstention from intervention or interference in the internal affairs of another country.

5. Respect for the right of each nation to defend itself singly or collectively, in conformity with the Charter of the United Nations.

6. (a) Abstention from the use of arrangements of collective defence to serve the particular interests of any of the big Powers.

   (b) Abstention by any country from exerting pressures on other countries.

7. Refraining from acts or threats of aggression or the use of force against the territorial integrity or political independence of any country.

8. Settlement of all international disputes by peaceful means, such as negotiations, conciliations, arbitration or judicial settlement as well as other peaceful means of the parties' own choice, in conformity with the Charter of the United Nations.

9. Promotion of mutual interest and co-operation.

10. Respect for justice and international obligations.

   The Asian African Conference declares its conviction that friendly co-operation in accordance with these principles would effectively contribute to maintenance and promotion of international peace and security, while co-operation in the economic, social and cultural fields would help bring about the common prosperity and well-being of all.'

For material on 'non-alignment' see Legum, *Pan-Africanism*, 1965, pp. 59–63, 112–18; Lyon, *Neutralism*, 1963; Hovet, *Africa in the United Nations*, 1963; Jansen, *Afro-Asia and Non-alignment*, 1966; Margaret Legum, *Non-alignment*, 1966.

Non-alignment has in practice involved a principle of association based on the 'third world' or world of underdeveloped states: thus China was involved in some of the conferences. Certain common factors in foreign policy persisted: anti-colonialism; pressure for measures against South Africa and her associates; opposition to nuclear testing and proliferation of nuclear weapons; a desire for economic self-determination, in other words means of development without foreign ownership of natural resources; and emphasis on the five principles of peaceful coexistence and the principles of the Charter of the United Nations. At the most recent conference of non-aligned states, held at Lusaka, in September 1970, sixty-four countries took part, thirty-two being African states, members of the OAU. The two previous conferences were at Belgrade in 1961 and Cairo in 1964. See on the Belgrade Conference, *Documents on International Affairs 1960*, R.I.I.A., pp. 604 seq.; *Keesing's Contemporary Archives*, vol. 13 (1961–2), 18601A. On the Cairo Conference, 1964, see Keesing, vol. 14 (1963–4), 20431A. On the Lusaka Conference, 1970, see *International Legal Materials*, vol. 10 (1971), p. 215.

For a well-informed examination of the policies of a state which practises non-alignment see Catherine Hoskyns, *International Affairs*, R.I.I.A., 1968, p. 446: 'Africa's Foreign Relations: The Case of Tanzania'.

IV. THE BRITISH COMMONWEALTH

ABOUT two-thirds of the states present at the 1970 Conference of non-aligned States were members of the British Commonwealth. The political significance of membership is not, perhaps, very great. Specific economic relations, arising from membership of the sterling area, are of more significance. The non-renewal of South African membership in 1961 indicated that there was a condition of membership concerning equality of races apart from the more formal conditions, namely, recognition of the Queen either as Head of State or Head of the Commonwealth, and readiness to consult on matters of common concern. See further Fawcett, *The British Commonwealth in International Law*, 1963, especially chapter 3; Whiteman, *Digest of International Law*, i. 476–544; Wheare, *The Constitutional Structure of the Commonwealth*, 1960; De Smith, *The New Commonwealth and Its Constitutions*, 1964; Miller, *The Commonwealth in the World*, 3rd edn., 1965. For the text of the 'Declaration of Principles' adopted unanimously by the thirty-one States represented at the Commonwealth Conference held at Singapore in 1971, see *The Times*, 23 January 1971.

V. THE FRENCH COMMUNITY

IN 1960 the French Constitution was altered to allow independent states to remain members of the French Community. The Central African Republic, Chad, Congo (Brazzaville), Gabon, the Malagasy Republic, and Senegal remained in the Community at independence. However, the conclusion of various economic and other agreements between former French territories now independent outside the Community, and France, has meant that the practical difference between membership and non-membership is negligible. Important relations arise from association with the E.E.C. and membership of the franc zone. However, not all members of the franc zone are members of the French Community. The franc zone provides for free currency movements and a guaranteed franc exchange rate.

VI. UNITED STATES POLICY

THE documents reproduced below provide a recent and very full guide to American policy on Africa. Since March 1961 the United States has supported the principles of decolonization and racial equality. It is more than probable that this position depends in part on the need to prevent liberation movements turning exclusively to Socialist and Communist states for support. In any event the United States has been reluctant to support effective measures against the minority regimes in Southern Africa and has attracted criticism and bitterness as a consequence of the role of American capital in South Africa and Portuguese territories. Moreover, Portugal is regarded as gaining indirect military support through her membership of N.A.T.O. See further Mondlane, *The Struggle for Mozambique*, 1969, pp. 144–5, 197–214. Mondlane writes (at p. 209): 'Western diplomacy pays lip-service to multiracialism and democracy, while the governments quietly continue to act against both.' See further Emerson, *Africa and United States Policy*, 1967; Hance and others (edd.), *Southern Africa and the United States*, 1968.

1. *Security Council Debate on Rhodesia, March 1970:*
U.S. Statements

These statements are reproduced from the *U.S. Department of State Bulletin*, vol. 62, no. 1607, 13 April 1970, p. 501. The outcome of the debate was the use of United States and United Kingdom veto to reject a five-power draft resolution (see below) and the adoption of a compromise resolution on 18 March (see below). The situation in Rhodesia was considered by the Security Council in response to the implementation on 2 March of a new constitution by the Smith regime and repudiation of the British Crown as Head of State.

TEXTS OF U.S. STATEMENTS

Statement by Ambassador Yost, March 13
U.S./U.N. press release 31 dated March 13

I have listened with great care and interest to the statements made before this Council and in particular to the statements made by the Minister of State for Foreign Affairs of Zambia and previous speakers. I also listened with great interest to the interventions made by my distinguished colleague Lord Caradon, who stressed the importance and need for urgency in acting in unison in not recognizing the so-called Republic of Rhodesia.

To say that we are meeting at a sad or shocking or deplorable time in the history of the Rhodesian question is but to state a truism. For indeed these adjectives apply to the entire period since the unilateral declaration of independence in November of 1965. And yet the situation with which we are confronted now does have a special significance, for we are told that a constitution which was approved by 1 per cent of the Rhodesian population is now in effect and that a 'republic' which was approved by a similarly small percentage of the electorate has been established.

I commented in some detail at our meeting last June on the specifics of that constitution—on the provisions which assure that political power will forever remain in white hands and on the ironically entitled Declaration of Rights. I would only like to remind the members of the Council of what I said at that time:

Since these proposals—despite all the trappings of law in which they are dressed—are intrinsically unjust and since they emanate from an unlawful regime, they will be without legal effect regardless of the results of the voting on June 20.

My Government's view, Mr. President, has not changed since that time. Illegal acts perpetrated by an illegal regime can in no way be considered to lend any air of legitimacy to that regime. Attaching the word 'republic' to the illegal minority regime in Salisbury will deceive no one.

My Government has assured the United Kingdom that we continue to regard it as the legal sovereign in Rhodesia. Consistent with this position and following the Smith regime's severance of the last formal ties with the United Kingdom, the Secretary of State on March 9 announced that the United States consulate general in Salisbury would be closed as of March 17 and that the staff would depart. We believe that this was an important step at a crucial time, a step which again made clear the posture of the United States toward the Smith regime's pretentions to legitimacy. This step may, we hope, help to discourage any prospect that the newly instituted republic might begin to gain acceptance by the nations of the world. We have not recognized, and we have no intention of recognizing, the illegal regime in Salisbury. I repeat these assurances to the members of this Council.

Mr. President, the United States has supported every resolution passed by the Security Council concerning Rhodesia since the unilateral declaration of independence by the Smith regime in 1965. We have implemented strictly the mandatory economic sanctions imposed by Resolutions 232 and 253. We believe that our implementation of the sanctions has been second to none.

We and six other members of the Council regretfully found ourselves unable to support the last resolution placed before the Council concerning Rhodesia last June. I pointed out at that time that the Council had 'exerted an effective influence on the Rhodesian situation only when it worked on the basis of unanimity' and that the only ones who would find any solace in the division within the Council would be Mr. Smith and his friends.

Mr. President, I hope and trust that this will not be the situation we face during this Council session. The United States supports the view expressed by the distinguished delegate of the United Kingdom that we should urgently act in not recognizing the 'Republic' of Rhodesia, and we support the draft resolution which was introduced by the United Kingdom at our meeting March 6.[1] I hope that all other members of the Council will do so as well and that we will not become bogged down in attempts to call for measures which will divide the Council and will not assist the people of Rhodesia.

Let us, rather, pass this resolution speedily and unanimously so that Mr. Smith and his followers will be fully aware that the mind of the international community has not been changed by the 'purported assumption of a republic status', that we still refuse to recognize his regime, and that we remain firm in our belief that majority rule will eventually come to Southern Rhodesia.

Mr. President, my Government shares the desire felt around this table for the need to achieve an equitable solution to the situation. This is indeed a most difficult and complex problem. We are convinced that all of us here in this Council must meet our responsibilities concerning Rhodesia with perseverance but also with prudence.

The Security Council has steadfastly condemned the actions of the present Salisbury regime and taken the unprecedented step of imposing mandatory economic sanctions. These sanctions must be firmly maintained and strictly enforced. We must persevere in our opposition to racism and repression. In charting our course for the future, Mr. President, we will want to take particular care that we continue to act with unanimity. My delegation is aware that the failure of South Africa and Portugal to adhere to the sanctions program provided for in Resolution 253 is a major source of concern. It is regrettable that these two countries continue to flout the sanctions. Minister Nkama [Minister of State for Foreign Affairs, Moto Nkama, of Zambia], when speaking the other day, made a direct reference to this unfortunate situation, and I note that this particular question is included in the draft resolution tabled by the Afro-Asian members of this Council.[1] My delegation has had the occasion

[1] See below.

to state that the application of sanctions to countries neighbouring Southern Rhodesia would be only following a dubious course which would introduce new and grave complications in an already complicated situation.

There is no doubt that, in view of the continued refusal of the Smith regime to heed the calls of the international community to alter its course we all would prefer to take more effective and decisive measures. The question, however, arises whether these more extreme measures which have been suggested would be sufficiently supported by the international community, especially those most directly concerned, to make them in fact effective or whether in seeking such action against economically powerful states under existing circumstances they would merely demonstrate the limitations of the U.N. and further entrench the Smith regime and its supporters in southern Africa. We must therefore seek to avoid embarking on unrealistic courses of action which, because they would overextend the capacity of the U.N. for effective action, would reflect adversely on this body and give aid and comfort to Ian Smith and his collaborators.

Mr. President, my delegation also doubts the wisdom and the effectiveness of imposing a communications ban as envisaged in the draft resolution. We in the United States have consistently attached the greatest importance to the maintenance of communications with other states, even those with whom our relations were greatly strained and in some cases even when hostilities were in progress between us. The United States has a long history and tradition of freedom of movement and of speech and would view most seriously the prospect of leaving United States citizens anywhere in the world without the means to travel or communicate. Furthermore, we do not believe that the cutting off of communications, the stemming of a free flow of information, would contribute to a solution of the difficult problem with which we are faced. Rather, it might tend to further harden the attitude of the white minority.

In our view, such measures tear the very fabric of international relations and would tend to foreclose the free exchange of information and ideas upon which progress in this unfortunate situation in part depends.

I should like to close my remarks, Mr. President, by quoting from President Nixon's recent report to the Congress on U.S. foreign policy for the 1970's:

Clearly there is no question of the United States condoning, or acquiescing in, the racial policies of the white-ruled regimes. For moral as well as historical reasons, the United States stands firmly for the principles of racial equality and self-determination.

Statement by Ambassador Buffum, March 13

U.S./U.N. press release 32 dated March 13

Mr. President, I shall be very brief indeed. Naturally we will wish to give very careful consideration to the remarks we have just heard from the distinguished Minister of State for Foreign Affairs of Zambia. I should like to say, however, by way of introducing this very brief comment, that the one thing that pleases me most about his intervention was that I think all of his remarks reflect—and, indeed, this is an accurate reflection that we do share, both of us—a very common objective in dealing with the problem of Southern Rhodesia. If I may say so, it emerges equally clearly that where we differ is with regard to the means of achieving that objective, and I think it is very frequently on such differences of tactics and methods that friends can honestly disagree. But I do appreciate the spirit in which he made his remarks, and we shall study them in exactly the same spirit.

There is only one specific that I should like to comment on at this point and would reserve a right, if I may, to intervene at a later stage with regard to the other questions which he has raised, some of which we will need to investigate. But he did, in his comment with regard to the purchase of chrome, imply that the United States is in fact still purchasing chrome in Southern Rhodesia. I can assure him and the members of the Council categorically that this is not the case; in fact, just the contrary is true. As a result of our prohibition on the importation of chrome from Southern Rhodesia, it has been necessary for us to secure alternative sources in other countries, often at considerable extra expense and difficulty and in many instances in a less satisfactory manner and quality, I think. But nevertheless we do abide scrupulously by the sanctions imposed by this Council. We do so willingly and wholeheartedly.

Just to make quite clear this is fully understood in all of its ramifications, I should like to add that chrome arriving in the United States from any source in southern Africa is carefully tested, and we have through a consistent and stringent checking system of this kind determined that there has been no disguised Rhodesian chrome entering this country. I would just like to submit that information as a partial reply to the remarks of the Minister this afternoon.

Statement by Ambassador Yost, March 17

U.S./U.N. press release 35 dated March 17

Mr. President, under these rather extraordinary circumstances I should like to make another suggestion, and since I wish to be sure that we have time to consider it seriously, with all the seriousness that I think these circumstances warrant, I am going to ask for consecutive interpretation, and I announce that in advance.

I very deeply regret the decision of the Council. It is a procedural one, of course, but I must say I find it out of keeping with the normal spirit in which we conduct our operations.

I have had a great deal of experience on this Council, and I remember any number of occasions in which members, for reasons that seemed good to them because they were confronting difficult decisions on important matters, have requested postponements. The distinguished Representative of the Soviet Union, for example, has frequently done so, in my recollection. Almost invariably this request is granted in the spirit of courtesy and mutual accommodation which governs the business of this Council.

There are many differences of substance between us, and we try to resolve those as best we can over time. In order to help us do so, we try to conduct our procedures in such a way as to give rise to as little difference and as little dissatisfaction and resentment as possible.

Therefore, I must say that I do find this a legitimate request designed to give several members of the Council an opportunity to reflect on a new situation. This was not simply the text of a resolution with which, of course, as the distinguished Representative of Sierra Leone points out, we have been fully familiar for a long time. But a new situation was created by private consultations after the meeting had begun, I believe, as far as we are aware, in which we were not involved. This has presented a new set of circumstances of great gravity and moment on which we certainly would have wished to have further instructions from our Government.

Voting on a resolution of this magnitude, importance, and scope is not a matter to be undertaken lightly. We had previously considered, and I had explained in my comment on the resolution, some of the difficulties that confronted us.

As we are all quite aware, the exact composition and balance of the resolution makes a difference to some delegations; some can vote for one paragraph and not for others; and in other cases the situation is different. Therefore, a fundamental change may occur in the course of paragraph-by-paragraph voting.

We entirely agree with the statement of the distinguished representative of the United Kingdom, made earlier in this meeting, in which he explained that it would be impossible for his Government to undertake to apply force under the special circumstances which exist in Southern Rhodesia. We think that his explanation was a convincing one. We think that it would not be in the interest of the United Nations or the people of Southern Rhodesia—and I speak, of course, of the people as a whole—if any such action were undertaken, the repercussions and consequences of which none of us can fully foresee.

As I mentioned in my remarks the other day, the United States also finds it extremely difficult to join in a decision of this Council which would sever postal, telegraphic, and wireless communications with Southern Rhodesia. The United States has not taken such extreme measures as rupture of communications even at the worst periods of our relations with a number of countries. In fact, we have maintained postal service even with North Korea and North Viet-Nam. It does not seem to us that the cutting off of the channels of communication and information is an appropriate way to deal with the problem or is likely to assist in its resolution.

We did, of course, close our consulate general in Salisbury as a consequence of the recent action of the illegal regime there, and we did so with the feeling that this was a necessary, appropriate, and proper action. Nevertheless, we did so with some hesitation, because there are American citizens in Rhodesia who need access to consular and related services, who need to be in communication with their relatives in this country, and with whom our Government might need to be in communication. The prospect of simply cutting them off totally from communications is one that we would find very, very difficult, if not impossible, to support.

There are all sorts of ramifications of these two paragraphs, as well as the paragraphs relating to the application of sanctions against the Republic of South Africa and Portugal, which Lord Caradon also referred to, it seemed to us, with eminent good sense.

It is hard to imagine that any such measures could be effective without the comprehensive sort of blockade which we indeed find it difficult to imagine the world community is prepared at this stage of its evolution to support and carry out effectively.

Therefore, as I say, this resolution, which we treat with the utmost seriousness, which we do not wish to deal with in any way lightly or precipitantly, gives us most serious problems and requires the most careful reflection.

Finally, Mr. President, since the majority of the Council, to our deep regret, has been unwilling to grant the request of a 24-hour delay, we would at least appeal once again, as a matter of courtesy, that there be a suspension of the meeting for half an hour, in order at least to give us that much time to reflect on the new situation which has been created.[1]

[1] The U.S. proposal for suspension was rejected by a vote of 7 against, 6 (U.S.) in favour, with 2 abstentions.

[In a further intervention, Ambassador Yost said:]

Mr. President, I shall not delay the meeting long.

I appreciate the wise and friendly remarks of the distinguished Representative of Sierra Leone.

I would like to comment just a moment on the remarks of the distinguished Minister of State of Zambia.

We all are in a great hurry to proceed when it happens to suit our convenience; but on the other hand, we all are ready to delay our proceedings for several days if that suits our convenience.

I would just like to remind him that I think the first meeting of the Council in this series on this question was first asked for on March 2 or 3. It was delayed first to the end of that week, in order to meet the convenience of our African members. Then after a brief meeting on that Friday, it was delayed again until the following Tuesday, in the expectation that three African Foreign Ministers would then have time to arrive. We were happy to endeavor to meet their convenience. During that period of a week or 10 days there seemed to be no terrible hurry, as far as we could gather. Suddenly, there now seems to be such a terrific haste to act that even a request for a further half-hour's delay is not granted. I regret this, but I am quite prepared to proceed to the vote.

Statement by Ambassador Yost, in Explanation of Vote, March 17

U.S./U.N. press release 36 dated March 17

Mr. President, only the most serious of considerations would cause us to take the step of casting our negative vote on a resolution of such importance.

The United States has stanchly supported the economic sanctions which had been imposed on Rhodesia. We were prepared to look with favor on the suggestions put forward earlier in the debate by the distinguished Ambassador of Finland for taking further action in common. We shall still continue, of course, to explore all possibilities in this sense.

However, we are not able to support the resolution which, by implication, calls upon the United Kingdom to use force. We have repeatedly stated the view that force is not the answer to this problem. For this reason we oppose a resolution condemning the United Kingdom for failure to use it.

We closed our consulate in Southern Rhodesia, thus leaving our citizens in that country with no direct protection. We did so in the belief that it remained possible for our citizens at least to be in contact with their own country and with consulates elsewhere in Africa. We cannot now agree not only to cut off all their communications with the rest of the world but even to cut off all means by which they might leave Southern Rhodesia. Paragraph 6, in our view, would amount to barring American citizens in Rhodesia from contact with the outside world, and this we cannot support. Besides the grave effect this action would have on United States citizens, many of whom are there for the sole purpose of alleviating suffering among the black majority of the population, we do not think that such an action is in the interests of the oppressed majority in Rhodesia, nor indeed that it would have any decisive effect on the illegal minority regime.

It is with very great reluctance, therefore, that we take this step. We have felt, and continue to feel, that a little greater effort to find common ground might have obviated this necessity. Let us not now abandon the search for common ground but resolve to try all the harder to grapple together with the problem of Rhodesia, which so deeply concerns us all and which, sooner or later, must and will be resolved in the interest of the oppressed majority.

Statement by Ambassador Yost, March 18
U.S./U.N. press release 38 dated March 18

I should again like to pay tribute to the distinguished Representative of Finland for his efforts to make this Council once more a center for harmonizing the actions of nations. We are grateful to him for his skill and wisdom, which, after the unfortunate divisions of yesterday, have restored the prospect of unanimous action. It is, in the view of my delegation, on such unanimous action and not on outwitting each other that progress on this difficult and important problem depends.

Mr. President, I believe that we are all agreed on fundamentals. We all believe in democracy and brotherhood, in the words of the distinguished Minister of State of Zambia. My own nation is founded on the proposition that all men, everywhere, are born with equal rights. It flows from this that the United States is opposed to any form of racial discrimination anywhere and to any regime which uses racial discrimination as its basis. The United States has not condoned, is not condoning, and will not condone any attempts by a minority and racist regime, either in Southern Rhodesia or elsewhere in southern Africa, to impose its will on the majority or to thwart the aspirations of that majority to exercise their civil, political, and human rights without any restriction whatsoever.

It is for these reasons that the United States has steadfastly condemned and opposed the illegal declaration of independence proclaimed by the Smith regime. It is for these reasons that the United States has chosen not to recognize the so-called Republic of Rhodesia and has closed its consulate. It is for these same reasons that the United States has steadfastly supported the imposition of mandatory economic sanctions against the Smith regime, has cooperated fully with the United Nations in their application, and will continue to do so.

President Nixon, in his report to Congress on foreign policy last month, reiterated United States policy toward southern Africa in a way which is pertinent to our present discussions here. He said:

Clearly there is no question of the United States condoning, or acquiescing in, the racial policies of the white-ruled regimes. For moral as well as historical reasons, the United States stands firmly for the principles of racial equality and self-determination.

. . . . .

These problems must be solved. But there remains a real issue in how best to achieve their resolution. Though we abhor the racial policies of the white regimes, we cannot agree that progressive change in Southern Africa is furthered by force. The history of the area shows all too starkly that violence and the counter-violence it inevitably provokes will only make more difficult the task of those on both sides working for progress on the racial question.

The United States warmly welcomes, therefore, the recent Lusaka Manifesto, a declaration by African leaders calling for a peaceful settlement of the tensions in Southern Africa. That statesmanlike document combines a commitment to human dignity with a perceptive understanding of the depth and complexity of the racial problem in the area—a combination which we hope will guide the policies of Africa and her friends as they seek practical policies to deal with this anguishing question.

Mr. President, I have already expressed my regret over the unfortunate division of the Council yesterday. To a considerable extent this division no doubt arises from honest differences of perspective. It is natural and proper that the African members of our organization should feel deep frustration at the inability of our organization, thus far, to bring about the compliance of a regime, representing only 200,000 whites, and not even all of them, among $4\frac{1}{2}$ million blacks, with the legitimate demands and decisions of this Council. It is equally natural that they should seek further means to make our decisions prevail.

However, as we are all aware, the United Nations does not have unlimited powers. The charter does not convey such powers upon it, nor have members been able to agree among themselves to give it in fact all the authority which the charter conveys in principle. As long as this situation obtains, we who believe in and cherish this organization, who place great hope in its future growth and reinforcement, must take great care not to place impossible burdens upon it, not to demand of it more than it can deliver. To do so will only emphasize its shortcomings, bring it into contempt, and lessen that public confidence and support on which its future growth and reinforcement depend.

In the present instance it seems to us both improper and futile to call upon the United Kingdom to overthrow the Smith regime by force— improper because starting a war anywhere is hardly what the United Nations should recommend and starting a war in southern Africa would be particularly risky business; futile because we all know perfectly well that the United Kingdom is not going to engage in any such hazardous enterprise. As to cutting off communications, we have also expressed our view. Even if it were possible, we should not want to cut off all the inhabitants of Rhodesia, blacks as well as whites, foreigners as well as nationals, from the free flow of information from the outside. There might be nothing which would be more agreeable to the minority regime than to have our help in bringing down an iron curtain around its people. Certainly such an act would be totally ineffective in inducing the regime to change its oppressive policies.

Unpalatable as it may be to all of us, I think we have no alternative but to recognize the fact that the process of making the rule of law and the rights of the majority prevail in Rhodesia will not be a quick one. We must persist firmly and patiently in the course we are pursuing, in the strict and comprehensive application of the sanctions we have all agreed upon. In the long run, if they are persisted in, they are bound to have their effect.

My delegation has examined with great care the resolution[1] tabled by the Representative of Finland. While we have reservations about some provisions, we support the resolution as a whole, believing it would make a substantial contribution to achieving the ends we all seek and would help to restore harmony and unanimity among us. Concerning operative paragraph 3, I should note that under our constitutional system our courts must be free to take judicial notice. We have serious doubts about the wisdom of seeking to impose a complete ban on all surface transportation, as envisaged in paragraph 9 (b), having in mind the practical problems of implementation, the serious practical problems created for United States citizens in Rhodesia, and the economic consequences which would fall particularly on the neighbouring state of Zambia, and would not very probably be without unforeseen consequences on others. We would have wished to have a separate vote on this paragraph and, if there had been such a separate vote, we would have abstained. However, as long as it is clear that the humanitarian and medical exceptions provided for in Resolution 253 are maintained, as the sponsor of the resolution has pointed out they would be, we will not oppose the resolution on account of this provision.

[1] See below.

Having in mind the broader considerations I mentioned a moment ago, particularly the capital importance of harmony among us for the effect that harmony must have on the minority regime, my delegation is prepared to support the resolution tabled by Finland.

2. *Texts of Resolutions in the Security Council*

U.K. DRAFT RESOLUTION, S/9676/Rev. 1

This was rejected: 5 votes in favour (including the U.S.); none against; 10 abstentions.

The Security Council,

Recalling and reaffirming its resolutions 216 (1965) of 12 November 1965, 217 (1965) of 20 November 1965, 221 (1966) of 9 April 1966, 232 (1966) of 16 December 1966 and 253 (1968) of 29 May 1968,

1. *Condemns* the illegal acts of the racist minority régime in Southern Rhodesia, including the purported assumption of a republican status;

2. *Decides*, in accordance with Article 41 of the United Nations Charter, that all Member States of the United Nations shall refrain from recognizing this illegal régime or from rendering any assistance to it, and urges States not Members of the United Nations, having regard to the principles stated in Article 2 of the United Nations Charter, to act accordingly.

FIVE-POWER DRAFT RESOLUTION, S/9696/Corr. 1 and 2

On 17 March in two separate votes paragraphs 8 and 9 were rejected by 7 votes to 0, with 8 abstentions (including the U.S.). The modified resolution was rejected as follows: 9 votes in favour; 2 against (vetoes by U.S. and U.K.); 4 abstentions.

The Security Council,

Recalling and reaffirming its resolutions 216 (1965) of 12 November 1965, 217 (1965) of 20 November 1965, 221 (1966) of 9 April 1966, 232 (1966) of 16 December 1966 and 253 (1968) of 29 May 1968,

Reaffirming in particular its resolution 232 (1966), in which it determined that the situation in Southern Rhodesia constitutes a threat to international peace and security,

Deeply concerned that the situation in Southern Rhodesia has deteriorated further as a result of the proclamation of a so-called republic and that the measures so far taken have proved inadequate to resolve the situation in Southern Rhodesia,

Gravely concerned further that the decisions taken by the Security Council have not been fully complied with by all States,

Noting that the Governments of the Republic of South Africa and Portugal, in particular, in contravention of their obligation under Article 25 of the Charter of the United Nations, have not only continued to trade with the illegal racist minority régime of Southern Rhodesia, contrary to the terms of Security Council resolutions 232 (1966) and 253 (1968), but have in fact given active assistance to that régime, enabling it to counter the effects of measures decided upon by the Security Council,

Noting in particular the continued presence of South African forces in the territory of Zimbabwe,[1]

Affirming the primary responsibility of the Government of the United Kingdom to enable the people of Zimbabwe to exercise their right of self-determination and independence,

Reaffirming the inalienable right of the people of Zimbabwe to freedom and independence and the legitimacy of their struggle for the enjoyment of that right,

Acting under Chapter VII of the Charter of the United Nations,

1. *Condemns* the proclamation of a so-called republic in Zimbabwe by the racist minority régime in Salisbury and declares null and void any form of government which is not based on the principle of majority rule;

2. *Decides* that all States Members of the United Nations shall refrain from recognizing this illegal régime and urges States not Members of the Organization, having regard to the principles set out in Article 2 of the Charter of the United Nations, to act accordingly;

3. *Calls upon* all States to take measures as appropriate, at the national level, to ensure that any act performed by officials and institutions of the illegal régime in Southern Rhodesia or by persons and organizations purporting to act for it or in its behalf shall not be accorded any official recognition, including judicial notice, by the competent organs of their State;

4. *Emphasizes* the responsibility of the Government of the United Kingdom, as the administering Power, with regard to the situation prevailing in Southern Rhodesia;

5. *Condemns* the persistent refusal of the Government of the United Kingdom, as the administering Power, to use force to bring an end to the rebellion in Southern Rhodesia and enable the people of Zimbabwe to exercise their right to self-determination and independence in accordance with General Assembly resolution 1514 (XV);

6. *Decides* that all States shall immediately sever all diplomatic, consular, economic, military and other relations with the illegal racist minority

[1] The African name for Southern Rhodesia.

régime in Southern Rhodesia, including railway, maritime, air transport, postal, telegraphic and wireless communications and other means of communication;

7. *Requests* the Government of the United Kingdom, as the administering Power, to rescind or withdraw any existing agreements on the basis of which foreign consular, trade and other representations may at present be maintained in or with Southern Rhodesia;

8. *Condemns* the assistance given by the Governments of Portugal and South Africa and by other imperialist Powers to the illegal racist minority régime in defiance of resolutions of the Security Council and demands the immediate withdrawal of the troops of the South African aggressors from the territory of Zimbabwe;

9. *Decides* that Member States and members of the specialized agencies shall apply against the Republic of South Africa and Portugal the measures set out in resolution 253 (1968) and in the present resolution;

10. *Calls upon* all Member States and members of the specialized agencies to carry out the decisions of the Security Council in accordance with their obligations under the Charter of the United Nations;

11. *Calls upon* all States Members of the United Nations, and, in particular, those with primary responsibility under the Charter for the maintenance of international peace and security, to assist effectively in the implementation of the measures called for by the present resolution;

12. *Urges all* States to render moral and material assistance to the national liberation movements of Zimbabwe in order to enable them to regain their freedom and independence;

13. *Requests* all States to report to the Secretary-General on the measures taken to implement the present resolution;

14. *Requests* the Secretary-General to report to the Security Council on the progress made in implementing the present resolution.

DRAFT RESOLUTION OF FINLAND, S/RES/277 (1970)/Corr. 1
(S/9709/Rev. 1)

This compromise resolution was adopted on 18 March 1970 by 14 votes to 0, with 1 abstention (Spain).

The Security Council,

Reaffirming its resolutions 216 (1965) of 12 November 1965, 217 (1965) of 20 November 1965, 221 (1966) of 9 April 1966, 232 (1966) of 16 December 1966 and 253 (1968) of 29 May 1968,

Reaffirming that, to the extent not superseded in this resolution, the measures provided for in resolutions 217 (1965) of 20 November 1965, 232 (1966) of 16 December 1966 and 253 (1968) of 29 May 1968, as well as those initiated by Member States in implementation of those resolutions, shall continue in effect,

Taking into account the reports of the Committee established in pursuance of Security Council resolution 253 (1968) (S/8954 and S/9252),

Noting with grave concern:

(*a*) That the measures so far taken have failed to bring the rebellion in Southern Rhodesia to an end,

(*b*) That some States, contrary to resolutions 232 (1966) and 253 (1968) of the Security Council and to their obligations under Article 25 of the Charter, have failed to prevent trade with the illegal régime of Southern Rhodesia,

(*c*) That the Governments of the Republic of South Africa and Portugal have continued to give assistance to the illegal régime of Southern Rhodesia, thus diminishing the effects of the measures decided upon by the Security Council,

(*d*) That the situation in Southern Rhodesia continues to deteriorate as a result of the introduction by the illegal régime of new measures, including the purported assumption of republican status, aimed at repressing the African people in violation of General Assembly resolution 1514 (XV),

Recognizing the legitimacy of the struggle of the people of Southern Rhodesia to secure the enjoyment of their rights as set forth in the Charter of the United Nations and in conformity with the objectives of General Assembly resolution 1514 (XV),

Reaffirming that the present situation in Southern Rhodesia constitutes a threat to international peace and security,

Acting under Chapter VII of the United Nations Charter,

1. *Condemns* the illegal proclamation of republican status of the Territory by the illegal régime in Southern Rhodesia;

2. *Decides* that Member States shall refrain from recognizing this illegal régime or from rendering any assistance to it;

3. *Calls upon* Member States to take appropriate measures, at the national level, to ensure that any act performed by officials and institutions of the illegal régime in Southern Rhodesia shall not be accorded any recognition, official or otherwise, including judicial notice, by the competent organs of their State;

4. *Reaffirms* the primary responsibility of the Government of the United Kingdom for enabling the people of Zimbabwe to exercise their right to self-determination and independence, in accordance with the Charter of the United Nations and in conformity with General Assembly resolution 1514 (XV), and urges that Government to discharge fully its responsibility;

5. *Condemns* all measures of political repression, including arrests, detentions, trials and executions, which violate fundamental freedoms and rights of the people of Southern Rhodesia;

6. *Condemns* the policies of the Governments of South Africa and Portugal, which continue to have political, economic, military, and other relations with the illegal régime in Southern Rhodesia in violation of the relevant United Nations resolutions;

7. *Demands* the immediate withdrawal of South African police and armed personnel from the Territory of Southern Rhodesia;

8. *Calls upon* Member States to take more stringent measures in order to prevent any circumvention by their nationals, organizations, companies and other institutions of their nationality, of the decisions taken by the Security Council in resolutions 232 (1966) and 253 (1968), all provisions of which shall fully remain in force;

9. *Decides*, in accordance with Article 41 of the Charter and in furthering the objective of ending the rebellion, that Member States shall:

(*a*) Immediately sever all diplomatic, consular, trade, military and other relations that they may have with the illegal régime in Rhodesia, and terminate any representation that they may maintain in the Territory;

(*b*) Immediately interrupt any existing means of transportation to and from Southern Rhodesia;

10. *Requests* the Government of the United Kingdom as the administering Power, to rescind or withdraw any existing agreements on the basis of which foreign consular, trade and other representation may at present be maintained in or with Southern Rhodesia;

11. *Requests* Member States to take all possible further action under Article 41 of the Charter to deal with the situation in Southern Rhodesia, not excluding any of the measures provided in that Article;

12. *Calls upon* Member States to take appropriate action to suspend any membership or associate membership that the illegal régime of Southern Rhodesia has in specialized agencies of the United Nations;

13. *Urges* Member States of any international or regional organizations to suspend the membership of the illegal régime of Southern Rhodesia from their respective organizations and to refuse any request for membership from that régime;

14. *Urges* Member States to increase moral and material assistance to the people of Southern Rhodesia in their legitimate struggle to achieve freedom and independence;

15. *Requests* specialized agencies and other international organizations concerned, in consultation with the Organization of African Unity, to

give aid and assistance to refugees from Southern Rhodesia and those who are suffering from oppression by the illegal régime of Southern Rhodesia;

16. *Requests* Member States, the United Nations, the specialized agencies and other international organizations in the United Nations system to make an urgent effort to increase their assistance to Zambia as a matter of priority with a view to helping her solve such special economic problems as she may be confronted with arising from the carrying out of the decisions of the Security Council in this question;

17. *Calls upon* Member States, and in particular those with primary responsibility under the Charter for the maintenance of international peace and security, to assist effectively in the implementation of the measures called for by the present resolution;

18. *Urges*, having regard to the principle stated in Article 2 of the United Nations Charter, States not Members of the United Nations, to act in accordance with the provisions of the present resolution;

19. *Calls upon* Member States to report to the Secretary-General by 1 June 1970 on the measures taken to implement the present resolution;

20. *Requests* the Secretary-General to report to the Security Council on the progress of the implementation of this resolution, the first report not to be made later than 1 July 1970;

21. *Decides* that the Committee of the Security Council established by resolution 253 (1968), in accordance with rule 28 of the provisional rules of procedure of the Security Council, shall be entrusted with the responsibility of:

(*a*) Examining such reports on the implementation of the present resolution as will be submitted by the Secretary-General;

(*b*) To seek from Member States such further information regarding the effective implementation of the provisions laid down in the present resolution as it may consider necessary for the proper discharge of its duty to report to the Security Council;

(*c*) To study ways and means by which Member States could carry out more effectively the decisions of the Security Council regarding sanctions against the illegal régime of Southern Rhodesia and to make recommendations to the Security Council;

22. *Requests* the United Kingdom, as the administering Power, to continue to give maximum assistance to the Committee and to provide the Committee with any information which it may receive in order that the measures envisaged in this resolution as well as resolutions 232 (1966), and 253 (1968) may be rendered fully effective;

23. *Calls upon* Member States as well as the specialized agencies to supply such information as may be sought by the Committee in pursuance of this resolution;

24. *Decides* to maintain this item on its agenda for further action as appropriate in the light of developments.

3. *Policy Statement on Africa, 28 March 1970*

The following items are reproduced from the *U.S. Department of State Bulletin*, vol. 72, no. 1608, 20 April 1970, p. 513. See also the *Bulletin*, no. 1615, 8 June 1970, p. 716.

THE UNITED STATES AND AFRICA IN THE SEVENTIES

Following is an exchange of letters between Secretary Rogers and President Nixon on March 26, together with a policy statement on Africa which was submitted to the President with Secretary Rogers' letter.

Press release 105 dated March 27 for release March 28

Secretary Rogers' Letter

March 26, 1970

DEAR MR. PRESIDENT: We have prepared and are submitting for your approval the attached statement on our policies in Africa. This is the first full statement of this kind by the United States Government in recent years. It represents, as you know, the results of numerous discussions with African leaders, a reflection of your own observations and interests regarding the continent, and conclusions arising from my own recent tour of Africa.[1] It reflects with greater detail the principles of our African policy set forth in the Report on Foreign Policy in the 1970's.[2]

The report emphasizes elements of our relationship to Africa both economic and political which will be of special importance in the coming months.

We believe the actions and objectives set forth in this paper represent a positive program within current budgetary and legislative guidelines. We have not suggested precise levels for the economic programs in view of the current studies of the worldwide foreign assistance policy. We feel it important, however, that our programs be certainly not less than the

[1] For statements and remarks by Secretary Rogers during his trip to Africa, 7–23 February, see *Bulletin* of 23 March, 1970, p. 365.

[2] The complete text of President Nixon's foreign policy report to the Congress on 18 February appears in the *Bulletin* of 9 March 1970; the section entitled 'Africa' begins on p. 305.

present level. We intend, within that level, to demonstrate herein how our current capabilities can respond more fully to Africa's stated needs.

In the ensuing weeks we shall be discussing aspects of the program with members of the Congress. We shall be developing other aspects in direct consultation with African governments, governments of other countries participating in African development and significant regional and international institutions.

As time goes on, we shall be building on this foundation, expanding where we can to increase the total effectiveness of our relationship with this significant continent. I believe you will find in our approach the basis for the positive expression of U.S. interest in Africa which you have so strongly encouraged.

Respectfully yours,
WILLIAM P. ROGERS

THE PRESIDENT
The White House

Enclosure:
African Policy Statement

President Nixon's Letter

THE WHITE HOUSE
WASHINGTON, March 26, 1970

DEAR MR. SECRETARY: Your thoughtfully prepared policy statement on Africa is wholeheartedly approved.

You know of my keen personal interest in relations with the African countries. We have both felt the spirit and dynamism of this continent and its people. I believe we now have a special opportunity to maintain and to expand our present relationships and am pleased that you and your staff have made so complete and positive an examination of the paths that are available to us.

You may count on my full support in the fulfillment of this program. It establishes a good foundation upon which we can respond to African needs and build that relationship of cooperation and understanding which we desire.

Sincerely,

RICHARD NIXON

The Honorable WILLIAM P. ROGERS
The Secretary of State
Washington, D.C. 20520

Text of Statement

U.S. AND AFRICA IN THE 70'S

A. *Africa and the U.S.*

Africa, for many reasons, deserves the active attention and support of the United States. It is in our national interest to cooperate with African countries in their endeavors to improve conditions of life and to help in their efforts to build an equitable political and economic order in which all can effectively share.

The energy and talent of the peoples of Africa represent a significant force in world development and world trade. It is a continent of impressive opportunities for future growth and development—one destined to play an increasingly important role in the world. Africans have taken much of their political inspiration from the United States. Their thousands of students in the United States today—and the many Americans studying and teaching in Africa—continue the tradition of this exchange. More than a few Africans who studied in America became leaders of independence of their countries.

Many of our ties to Africa have been longstanding. The Sultan of Morocco recognized our own independence at an early date and exchanged diplomatic correspondence with George Washington. The oldest American treaty which has been continuously in force was signed with Morocco in 1787. We signed a similar treaty with Tunisia in 1797. Close U.S. ties to Liberia date from 1816 and with Ethiopia from 1903. And Americans have long identified themselves with the pursuit of independence and freedom in Africa, as elsewhere.

Africa is growing closer to the United States. Communications with Africa are rapidly developing, and communication links with other continents through Intelsat are now in operation and more African earth stations are being constructed. Two major American airlines serve the continent. Overflight rights are important to our commerce and to our scientific efforts. We have important communications facilities in both West and East Africa. Our space and scientific programs rely on the cooperation of the peoples and governments of Africa.

The resources of Africa are products which we purchase substantially in international trade: rubber, petroleum, bauxite, timber, coffee, cocoa, minerals and precious stones, to name a few. They are important to the Africans as a primary source of their wealth.

America's links with the peoples of Africa have been extensive. Missionaries have established schools and hospitals throughout the continent and have lived and worked in Africa many years before official relations were established. We have demonstrated humanitarian concern for the people of the continent in our provision of help and relief in countless ways.

And, finally, we are linked by the cultural fact that one out of every ten Americans has his origins in Africa.

B. *What We Seek*

We seek a relationship of constructive cooperation with the nations of Africa—a cooperative and equal relationship with all who wish it. We are prepared to have diplomatic relations under conditions of mutual respect with all the nations of the continent. We want no military allies, no spheres of influence, no big power competition in Africa. Our policy is a policy related to African countries and not a policy based upon our relations with non-African countries.

As early as 1957, when he returned from a mission to Africa on behalf of President Eisenhower, the then Vice President Nixon recommended that the U.S. assign a higher priority to our relations with an Africa, which he recognized to be of growing importance to the United States. Specifically he said:[1]

> The United States must come to know these leaders better, to understand their hopes and aspirations, and to support them in their plans and programs for strengthening their own nations and contributing to world peace and stability. To this end, we must encourage the greatest possible interchange of persons and ideas with the leaders and peoples of these countries. We must assure the strongest possible diplomatic and consular representation to those countries and stand ready to consult these countries on all matters affecting their interests and ours.

Personal relationships between members of the Administration and African leaders have been widely expanded. President Nixon met leaders from 10 African countries during the past year. I met a number of African leaders during 1969 and in the fall met and discussed common issues with 26 African Foreign Ministers at the United Nations General Assembly. The meetings included and contributed to closer understanding even with states with which we have no current diplomatic relations; in the case of Mauritania the discussion with the Foreign Minister in New York was the first step toward a resumption of relations which has now taken place. In February I became the first Secretary of State to tour Africa. I visited 10 African countries. I also spoke with leaders of the Organization of African Unity, the UN Economic Commission for Africa

[1] For a report to President Eisenhower from Vice President Nixon, see *Bulletin* of 22 April 1957, p. 635.

and other regional bodies. I met in Kinshasa with the American chiefs of mission and principal officers from the African countries in which we are represented.

It is through open and honest exchanges such as these that we can better understand the needs and aspirations of the peoples and governments of Africa and they can learn of the objectives and problems we Americans face at this time and place in history.

Some of my countrymen used to long for the luxury of isolation behind the protection of two great oceans. But the time for that has passed. The continental size of the United States, its vast productive power, its technological capabilities, its interdependence with other parts of this planet impel us into active participation in world affairs.

But in this participation we do not seek any kind of domination. We seek with all nations the closest relationship which is mutually acceptable and beneficial, but seek it with full respect for diversity among nations.

C. *What Africans Seek*

An effective relationship with Africa depends on an understanding of Africa and its needs. We have sought in our discussions and visits with African leaders and African peoples to determine how they define these needs.

They have spoken to us first of their strong desire to satisfy the aspirations of their people for a better life. They want to do this through economic cooperation. They want economic assistance now to make themselves less dependent later on foreign resources. They look to trade as a more equitable relationship than aid. They want investment in which they are partners.

After decades of being governed from afar, they want respect for human dignity. They want to abolish discrimination. They want equality throughout the continent.

They want self-determination throughout the continent. They want respect for the independence of the new nations and for their sovereignty. They welcome cooperation with other nations but they do not want intervention.

They want to build political and social institutions based on their own cultural patterns. They want to adapt ideas from abroad to their own psychology and spirit.

They want respect for the boundaries of Africa and security for each nation within these boundaries. They want recognition that, within its infinite diversity, Africa has a cohesion and a unity of its own, such as represented by the Organization of African Unity.

D. *The U.S. Response*

The United States desires to be responsive to Africa, even though there are limitations on our capacities and our resources.

We desire economic relations on a basis of mutual benefit and respect. Recognizing the need for capital and technical assistance, the United States directly and in cooperation with others will continue to help. The U.S. will pursue more active programs of trade and private investment, with full recognition of African sovereignty.

We will continue to support wider cooperation on a regional and continental basis among African countries.

The United States will continue to stand for racial equality and self-determination looking for peaceful and evolutionary solutions to advance these goals. We will help to provide economic alternatives for the small independent states in southern Africa.

We will avoid supplying arms in southern Africa, and we will persist in our support for self-determination.

We will respect the institutions which the Africans themselves create. While we in this country have a preference for democratic procedures, we recognize that the forces for change and nation-building which operate in Africa may create governmental patterns not necessarily consistent with such procedures.

We are impressed with the growing force of youth in Africa. In country after country, governments are headed by young leaders—each with constituencies made up overwhelmingly of people even younger than themselves. Leaders and led, they are to an impressive degree post-World War II men, all shaped by the forces of this era of rapid, unprecedented change.

The opportunities for progress, and the prospects for difficulties, are immense: More educated, more aware, more confident, more competent than any African generation before, the youth of that continent cannot help but exert a restless pressure for change, for greater opportunity to improve their lives.

Their percentage of the population is enormous and growing. Today, 45 per cent of Africa's population is 15 years old or younger. But it is not through strength of numbers alone that these youths will change the face of the continent. All of us are conscious of the vastly changing nature of our times, but for Africa perhaps even more than for the rest of the world, one era ended and another began while this generation was growing up. The city attracts the villager; school and university challenge ancient customs and ritual; the transistor radio brings the farthest points of the world instantly to the smallest village. Better trained in modern techniques and modern concepts than previous generations, today's young African will be the key to progress.

United States policies and programs in Africa will be affected by the force of youth and its potential for the future of the continent. As we review and try to strengthen our educational exchange, our technical training and assistance programs, and our Peace Corps support, we shall give special attention to programs to cooperate with these youths in preparation for their present and future responsibilities.

E. *Economic Assistance Policy*

An American economic assistance program in Africa is in United States national interests. We wish to see African countries develop and take their rightful place in cooperative international efforts to resolve worldwide problems. The drive and determination to develop must come from the African countries themselves. But at this point in their development, when per capita annual incomes average about $135, most of these countries need substantial external assistance to achieve rates of progress responsive to the minimum aspirations of their more than 300 million people for a better life. Our principal concern, therefore, is how most effectively to make capital assistance and technical knowledge from the developed nations available to these developing nations.

Ever since the wave of independence swept through Africa in the late '50's and early '60's, Western European nations and multidonor organizations have provided 60 to 70 per cent of economic assistance to Africa. Because of their strong traditional and historic links to Africa, we hope the European nations will continue to provide the bulk of foreign assistance to Africa. But the United States also has deep and special ties to Africa. We should do our fair share in support of the independence and growth of African nations.

F. *U.S. Assistance*

The total U.S. share has, in fact, averaged about $350 million a year for the past several years. This is about 20 per cent of all external assistance to Africa. We intend to maintain a substantial contribution, hopefully with a larger share in economic development programs.

Our bilateral assistance program has included resources from A.I.D., PL-480, the Export-Import Bank and the Peace Corps. In the form of loans, grants and personnel, it has reached some thirty-five African countries. It has assisted national development programs, as well as regional projects. We have worked through regional organizations, and jointly with other donors. The United States will continue to provide assistance to those nations which have been given emphasis in the past.

At the same time, mindful of needs throughout the continent, we have decided to make our approach to African assistance more flexible than it has recently been:

—We will to the extent permitted by legislation also provide limited assistance in other African countries to projects which contribute significantly to increased production and revenues.

—We will continue to emphasize aid to regional programs and projects, giving special attention to innovative ways to make our efforts effective.

—We wish to do more to strengthen African economic institutions including the UN Economic Commission for Africa, the African Development Bank, the OAU's Scientific, Technical, and Research Commission and sub-regional organizations.

—We will utilize food aid to advance economic development objectives and to help tide nations over emergency food shortages.

—We will more and more orient the program of the Peace Corps to meet the technical, educational and social development needs of African nations.

—We will concentrate our economic assistance in the coming years in the fields of agriculture, education, health including demographic and family planning, transportation and communications.

—We are actively studying the requirement that U.S. loans to Africa be used almost exclusively for the purchase of American goods and services.

We intend to provide more assistance to Africa through international institutions and multidonor arrangements. We contribute 40 per cent of the budget of the UN Development Program; 40 per cent of its program is now being directed to Africa. We also contribute 40 per cent of the budget of the International Development Association; in the past year its loans to Africa have risen substantially to 20 per cent of all its loans, and the prospect is that this proportion will continue to rise.

We are seeking a substantial increase in the absolute amount of United States contributions to these institutions. The United States is now engaged in discussions with other members of IDA, under the leadership of the World Bank, which we hope will lead to larger contributions by all donor members of IDA. We have proposed to Congress an increased contribution to UNDP.

In addition to our participation in international organizations, we are working more closely with other donors in World Bank and IMF [International Monetary Fund] sponsored consultative groups for several African countries, and in projects involving several donors. With limited total aid resources, we believe these mechanisms greatly increase the effectiveness of foreign aid.

We also look forward to joining with other non-African donors in support of the African Development Bank. This young institution, which has the financial backing of thirty-one African governments, has prospects for promoting significant pan-African cooperation in economic progress. It has already raised $67 million from its members in fully convertible currencies. It needs, however, a source of funds that could be loaned to its members on concessional terms. We are participating in discussions with other non-African donors which we hope will lead to the creation of special funds for this purpose. In the meantime, we are assisting the Bank directly in its efforts to develop and carry out urgently needed projects in its member countries.

An important portion of our assistance to Africa supports regional projects and regional institutions. In Addis Ababa, in the United Nations Economic Commission for Africa, one sees one of the most successful forms of international economic cooperation. Any serious appraisal of the development prospects in Africa makes clear the need for much greater regional cooperation. Many African nations are small; their national boundaries frequently split natural economic regions. Most national markets are too small to support industry using modern technology. Africans have already demonstrated their recognition of the need for regional cooperation by establishing regional educational, technical and research institutes, economic communities, common markets, common financial arrangements and even common currencies. We hope to remain in the forefront of cooperative efforts to foster regional cooperation in Africa.

Our Food for Peace programs have been a major means of economic assistance in many African countries, through credit sales, food-for-work, donations and emergency relief efforts. In the past few years, 40 per cent of our aid to Africa has taken these forms. We will maintain this assistance wherever food aid can make an important contribution to economic development or help meet serious emergencies.

The Peace Corps conducts programs in twenty-three African countries. This, too, will be continued as long as African governments find the Peace Corps' efforts useful to them. The Peace Corps is seeking to intensify its recruitment of experienced and highly qualified personnel in order to emphasize technically oriented positions needed in development efforts. The Peace Corps is also moving ahead to make qualified volunteers available to international organizations working in the development field.

In our programs for youth, we shall intensify our efforts to establish personal relationships between African and American young political leaders, technicians, students and businessmen.

We shall expand inter-African scholarships and third-country training programs for youth within Africa, while maintaining traditional exchanges with the United States.

We shall encourage more of our own country's diverse public and private groups to learn about and from Africans.

G. *Joint Public–Private Technical Cooperation*

We shall encourage the greater utilization of American citizens from the private sector to meet development needs in Africa. The International Executive Service Corps, an American private organization which recruits American businessmen for short-term service in developing nations has pointed the way. This technique has already proven its usefulness in a number of countries as a means of offering American management experience to budding private industry and to government in African countries. We desire to see what can be done further to encourage this approach.

I have also called for a study of how the United States Government can establish a clearing house for requests from the more advanced developing nations for the provision of technical and professional services to meet scientific, technological and industrial requirements. Such a clearing house should be able to draw on both public and private personnel, and should have sufficient funds available where necessary to 'top-off' salaries offered by these developing nations to foreign experts, so that the total earnings of the American specialists would continue to match their current value in the United States.

In these and other fashions we should like to share some of the positive aspects of our science, technology and management experience, as well as some of the lessons we have been learning from our own development. I have in mind not only our achievements in communications, industry and science, but some of the grave by-products of these accomplishments, such as over-urbanization and pollution.

The U.S. Government recognizes the great potential of African labor to play a constructive role in the sound economic development of free and independent African nations. We have, therefore, consistently sought friendly understanding of the labor movements of African countries. We hope we can continue to make some significant contributions.

It is our policy to continue to support and encourage African governments in the development and execution of comprehensive labor manpower programs. And while recognizing African preferences for a distinctive African approach to trade union matters, we encourage close fraternal relations between the leaders and members of the African trade unions and Western national and international labor organizations.

H. *Private Investment*

There has been a steady growth in U.S. private investment in Africa since most of the African nations achieved their independence. By the end of 1968 the value of U.S. private investment in OAU member states was almost $2 billion. Between 1963 and 1968, U.S. private investment in Africa grew at an average annual rate of about 14 per cent.

We believe that private investment can and should play a growing role, above and beyond public assistance, in African development. Africans themselves desire to participate in such investment. In many countries, in the face of limited capital resources, it is the government rather than the private sector which has the financial wherewithal to join with foreign private investors. Thus, 'joint ventures' frequently involve a combination of foreign private and African governmental capital. We are prepared to encourage American investors to cooperate in such endeavours under adequate investment protection.

Our investment policy should be creative and flexible. It should be deeply concerned with the social environment in which it operates. When investing abroad, modern American businessmen offer training, profit-sharing and other opportunities. At the same time, as businessmen, they expect stability for the enterprises in which they join and a reasonable return on their investments. While the United States Government has guaranty programs available to many American investors, these are insurance and not the basis on which businessmen make investment. Thus, they pay great heed to African government programs to foster a favorable investment climate. Therefore, an investment code, assurances from the African government and reasonable entry, work and tax arrangements, can make the difference between an American's willingness or unwillingness to work out an investment.

Mineral and petroleum development account for nearly three-fourths of current U.S. private investment in Africa. The industry is exceptionally able to seek out new sources and new opportunities to meet growing demands.

The same is not the case, however, for investments in manufacturing, agro-business and commerce. Thus, we are already conducting certain programs to stimulate American private efforts in these fields.

—We have an increasingly successful, albeit modest, effort at getting American investors to look at integrated, large-unit agricultural schemes in Africa. In the past three years, American companies have made 27 preliminary studies, leading to ten in-depth studies and four investment commitments. Several more are currently being negotiated.

—We are also seeking to interest medium size American investors to look at opportunities to help contribute to African markets, i.e., flour milling, bus transportation; and for meeting specialized markets which Africa could fill, such as plywood, shrimp fishing and food processing.

Success in these and other programs depends on the already-mentioned favorable investment climate, on enterprises tailored to realistic market size, and ultimately on getting the prospective American investor to go to Africa to see for himself what the conditions are and what his opportunity costs are.

The new Overseas Private Investment Corporation is authorized to provide guaranties, some equity, local currency loans and sound investment project advice to form the basis for a more efficient, flexible and aggressive approach to the promotion of U.S. investment in developing nations. It will be an important element in stimulating further American private investment in Africa.

I. *Increased and Improved Trade Relations*

I was deeply impressed on my recent trip by the great dependence of so many African countries on exports of one or two agricultural or mineral commodities. Sudden changes in world market prices for these commodities can cause violent fluctuations in export earnings and can disrupt development programs. In recognition of this instability the United States over the years has participated in international efforts to stabilize prices and incomes of primary products. We were one of the initial signatories of the International Coffee Agreement. The President is now recommending to the Congress renewal of the legislative authority for our continued adherence to this agreement. By the same token, we are continuing to participate in the discussions within UNCTAD [United Nations Conference on Trade and Development] working toward an international agreement on cocoa.

But the problem of prices affects other commodities as well. We have joined international efforts, such as those recently conducted at African initiative in the World Bank and IMF, to see whether new and additional measures can be taken to stabilize prices and incomes.

Several months ago the President set forth proposals for generalized tariff preferences for all developing nations, so that they could more readily find markets for their manufactured and semi-manufactured products in the developed nations, including the United States. To this end, we are actively seeking agreement with other developed nations on some generalized preference scheme.

We are mindful of the special relationship which exists between some African and some European countries. Our purpose, however, is to give all developing nations much improved access for exports of their manufactures to the markets of all developed nations on an equal basis. We are also urging the elimination of discriminatory tariffs—sometimes called 'reverse preferences'—which put our goods at a competitive disadvantage in many African markets. We hope that European nations see no linkage between eliminating the preferences they currently receive in some twenty African nations and their levels of aid to those countries.

In the meantime, we have been most encouraged to learn of the important first step taken by the member nations of the Central African Customs and Economic Union (UDEAC), to reduce their general tariffs on most imported goods by 50 per cent. They thus move closer to a nondiscriminatory tariff position.

This measure offers the prospect of greater American trade with these countries.

J. *The Problem of Southern Africa*

One of the most critical political problems of continental concern relates to southern Africa. The problems of southern Africa are extremely stubborn. Passions are strong on both sides. We see no easy solutions.

Yet the modern world demands a community of nations based on respect for fundamental human rights. These are not only moral and legal principles; they are powerful and ultimately irresistible political and historical forces. We take our stand on the side of those forces of fundamental human rights in southern Africa as we do at home and elsewhere.

In Southern Rhodesia, we have closed our consulate. Our representatives in Salisbury were accredited to the Queen of England. When the Queen's authority was no longer recognized by the regime we withdrew our consulate. We have also determined not to recognize the white-minority regime in Salisbury and will continue to support UN economic sanctions.

To alleviate the difficulties of certain refugees in the United States, particularly of those from southern Africa, with respect to travel abroad, the United States expects in the near future to issue travel documentation as provided under the Protocol to the 1951 Geneva Convention on the Status of Refugees.

In the matter of Namibia (South West Africa), the United States has respected the international status of that territory since 1920. It has sought in the United Nations, before the International Court of Justice and in direct exchanges with South Africa, to defend that status. We have sought equally to defend the rights of the inhabitants, which that status was established to protect. We are now participating in UN deliberations on this matter. Any further actions which the U.S. may take, in the UN or elsewhere, will continue to be consistent with our historic support of the law.

Our relations with the Republic of South Africa have been a matter of particular attention. We do not believe cutting our ties with this rich, troubled land would advance the cause we pursue or help the majority of the people of that country. We continue to make known to them and the world our strong views on *apartheid*. We are maintaining our arms embargo. We oppose their continued administration of Namibia (South West Africa) and their implementation of *apartheid* and other repressive legislation there. We will continue to make clear that our limited governmental activities in South Africa do not represent any acceptance or condoning of its discriminatory system.

As for the Portuguese Territories, we shall continue to believe that their peoples should have the right of self-determination. We will encourage peaceful progress toward that goal. The declared Portuguese policy of racial toleration is an important factor in this equation. We think this holds genuine hope for the future. Believing that resort to force and violence is in no one's interest, we imposed an embargo in 1961 against the shipment of arms for use in the Portuguese territories. We have maintained this embargo and will continue to do so.

The smaller independent states south of the Zambesi also deserve attention. They are seeking to create multiracial societies free of the predominant influence of the minority-dominated states adjoining and surrounding them. They cannot exist without a realistic relationship with their neighbours. At the same time it is in the interest of all those who wish to see these states develop and prosper to provide alternative sources of assistance and means of access to these states. This the United States, in cooperation with other donors, will seek to do. At the same time, the United States will seek to be responsive to requests from these states for a higher level of U.S. diplomatic representation.

In all these ways, as well as in positions taken in the United Nations and through diplomatic channels, we shall work to bring about a change of direction in parts of Africa where racial oppression and residual colonialism still prevail.

At the same time, we cannot accept the fatalistic view that only violence can ultimately resolve these issues. Rather we believe that solution lies in the constructive interplay of political, economic and social forces which will inevitably lead to changes.

Conclusion

As the President said in his Report to the Congress on Foreign Policy: 'We want the Africans to build a better life for themselves and their children. We want to see an Africa free of poverty and disease, and free too of economic or political dependence on any outside power. And we want Africans to build this future as they think best, because in that way both our help and their efforts will be most relevant to their needs.'

VII. SOVIET POLICY

THE Soviet Union has supported the movement against colonialism in the United Nations but has entered into close relations with only a very small number of African states since independence. The fact is that since independence Western ties with a number of the new states have discouraged them from improving relations with China and the Soviet Union. In any case many African governments are conservative in political terms and fear socialist influences. The Soviet Union in the recent past has supported general O.A.U. policy on the Nigerian war and other issues. The Report on the international situation and Soviet foreign policy made to the Supreme Soviet by the Foreign Minister, Andrei Gromyko, on 10 July 1969, does not give great emphasis to African affairs. It does, however, refer directly to the principle of supporting the national liberation movement. For the text of the Report see *Soviet News* (Press Dept. of the London Embassy), 15 July 1969. The documents presented below are regarded as symptomatic of Soviet policies. See below, p. 520, on Soviet attitudes toward events in the Congo, 1960–2. See further Morison, *The U.S.S.R. and Africa*, 1964; Brzezinski (ed.), *Africa and the Communist World*, 1963; Thompson, *Ghana's Foreign Policy, 1957–1966*, 1969; Legvold, *Soviet Policy in West Africa*, 1970; Hamrell and Widstrand (edd.), *The Soviet Bloc, China and Africa*, 1964.

1. *Soviet Memorandum to U.N. General Assembly, 26 September 1961*

This concerns the implementation of the Declaration on the Granting of Independence to Colonial Countries and Peoples (for which see p. 365 above). The text is taken from *Soviet News*, 12 October 1961.

1. Having discussed, on the initiative of the Soviet government, the problem of the liquidation of the colonial system, the General Assembly of the United Nations adopted, on December 14, 1960, the historic Declaration on Granting Independence to Colonial Countries and Peoples in which it solemnly proclaimed the need to put an end, immediately and unconditionally, to colonialism in all its forms and manifestations.

Expressing the will of the peoples, the United Nations stated in the declaration that 'the subjugation of the peoples to foreign oppression and domination and their exploitation deny the fundamental human rights, contradict the United Nations Charter, and impede the development of co-operation and the establishment of peace throughout the world'.

All countries of the world, except for the colonial powers—the United States of America, Britain, France, Portugal, Belgium, the Union of South

Africa, Spain and Australia and the Dominican Republic, which joined them—unanimously supported the declaration and thereby voted for the complete liquidation of the ignominious colonial system, for the inauguration of an independent and free life for all the peoples of the colonies. That was a major victory for all progressive mankind and an outstanding success of the socialist countries and the independent states of Asia, Africa and Latin America in their joint struggle against colonialism and imperialism.

The United Nations Declaration on Granting Independence to Colonial Countries and Peoples was warmly approved by all peoples of the globe. The peoples of the colonies hailed the declaration as a harbinger of the nearing end of age-old slavery.

The adoption of the declaration was also met with great satisfaction by all peoples because the total elimination of colonialism would deliver mankind from the painful legacy of the past and do away with one of the most dangerous sources of wars. Not a single year passes without the colonialists unleashing armed conflicts in Asia, Africa or Latin America, in their attempt to keep the peoples of the colonies in subjugation by force. Each such conflict confronts the world with a serious international crisis, a real threat of world war.

The system of colonialism has always been condemned by all honest people. Now that the Declaration on Granting Independence to Colonial Countries and Peoples has been adopted, preserving the system, pressing on with the policy of terrorism and reprisals against the fighters for national self-determination and fomenting colonial wars cannot be regarded in any other way than as the gravest crime against all mankind, as a gross violation of international law, as an open challenge to the United Nations.

2. A fairly long period has passed since the declaration was adopted. There has been enough time and ample opportunity for taking genuine measures to liberate the peoples wherever they are still languishing in the fetters of colonialism, to fulfil the requirements of the declaration on the transfer of all power to the peoples of the colonies on their territories and on the elimination of the colonial administration, with the simultaneous cessation of all military operations and reprisals against the peoples of the colonies and also all attempts to violate their territorial integrity and national unity. There is no doubt that if the colonial powers had complied with the requirements of the declaration, the vestiges of the colonial system would have been eliminated by now and the United Nations members could have stated at the General Assembly session that this major decision of the United Nations had been successfully fulfilled.

Yet there is irrefutable factual evidence that the colonial powers are in fact ignoring the demands of the declaration, and their crimes against the peoples, fighting for their freedom and independence, far from being nipped in the bud are on the contrary becoming ever more extensive and dangerous.

The declaration demanded that all peoples of the colonies should be granted the right to self-determination, that is, the right to the establishment of independent national states, immediately and unconditionally. In fact, not even a tenth part of this main requirement of the declaration has been fulfilled.

It is known, of course, that the independence of the former British colony Sierra Leone was proclaimed on April 27, 1961, and that British trusteeship over the British Cameroons has ended; it has been declared that Tanganyika, a British trusteeship territory, would obtain independence by the end of 1961, and West Samoa, a trusteeship territory of New Zealand, from January 1962. But that is all!

Allowing for all the changes which have occurred on these territories or will occur before the end of this year, *88 territories with a population of 71,100,000 will still be under colonial rule by January 1, 1962.* If independence continues to be granted at such a pace, the fulfilment of the declaration may drag out for decades, and this is impermissible.

Human conscience cannot tolerate the fact that on the great African continent, the peoples of which are now playing an outstanding role in the life of human society, there are still 27 colonial and trusteeship territories where 50 million Africans live under the conditions of cruel colonial oppression.

It is there that the largest tracts of Britain's colonial possessions lie— Kenya, Uganda, the Federation of Rhodesia and Nyasaland and others, with a total population of 23 million. Over 11 million Africans are oppressed by Portugal and over 10 million by France.

The preservation in Asia of 16 colonial territories with a population of about 10 million is another fact that arouses indignation. Britain alone continues to keep there 12 colonies with a population of about seven million. Next come the colonialists of the Netherlands and Portugal who have enslaved millions on the territories they wrested from Indonesia and India.

About seven million are languishing under colonial rule on the American continent and nearby islands, and over three million live in conditions of enslavement in Oceania.

All these territories should, in accordance with the declaration, have been granted freedom and independence immediately. And yet they are still colonies.

3. The Declaration on Granting Independence to Colonial Countries and Peoples contained a clear and unequivocal demand to end armed actions and repressive measures of any kind against the peoples of colonies. How is this highly humanistic demand of the declaration being carried out? The colonialists have cynically replied to it with new colonial wars and intensified repressions against the colonial peoples.

Almost the day after the adoption of the declaration the government of Portugal launched a bloody colonial war against the people of Angola fighting for national independence. Day after day the heavily armed Portuguese army is killing heroic sons and daughters of Angola and turning the territory of that country into a scorched desert. As objective observers testify, the Portuguese colonialists are deliberately pursuing a policy designed to destroy the native population of that country.

According to witnesses, the Portuguese colonialists subject captured freedom-fighters to medieval tortures; they cut off their arms and legs, flay them with bludgeons set with nails and starve or kill even their kinsmen if the latter try to bury their bodies. In the first four months of the colonial war in Angola more than 50,000 Angolese were killed, and since then the war has been going on for another four months. Trying to prolong their domination in Angola and conceal the atrocities committed there from the world public, the Portuguese government refuses to comply with the decisions of the Security Council and the General Assembly providing, among other things, for the dispatch of a United Nations investigation commission to Angola.

Currently the Portuguese colonialists are out to spread the colonial war also to Mozambique and Portuguese Guinea. Portuguese terror is becoming more and more ferocious and ruthless in Goa, to which large numbers of troops and modern weapons are being shipped, creating a serious threat to security in that region of Asia.

France is continuing her criminal war against the people of Algeria. An army of the French colonialists, more than half a million strong, is committing more and more crimes on the soil of Algeria, soaked in blood and tears. Some 800,000 people killed, 200,000 thrown into prisons and concentration camps, more than a million forcibly herded into 'migration centres', 300,000 driven by repressions to Tunisia and Morocco—such is the far from complete list of victims of the French colonialists in Algeria, a list to which new additions are being made every day.

It appeared at one time that the Algerian question could be settled in a peaceful way, for the French government had expressed, in words, its readiness to end the war against the Algerian people on the basis of recognition of the principle of Algeria's self-determination and to come to agreement with the provisional government of the Algerian Republic regarding the order for carrying out self-determination. Hardly had the talks begun, however, when it became clear that the French colonialists wanted, not the termination of the war in Algeria, but the dismemberment of the country, that they wanted to tear away from it an inalienable part, the Sahara with its oil, to rob the Algerian people of the riches of their country.

And all that after the adoption of the declaration, in which any attempt partially or fully to undermine the national unity and territorial integrity of any colony while granting it independence was condemned as being incompatible with the aims and principles of the United Nations Charter! But what do the French government and the United States, West German and other western oil companies standing behind it care for the United Nations Charter, for the demands of the peoples, for right and justice, if Sahara oil promises them fabulous profits!

The government of Britain has declared repeatedly, and declares now, that it favours the granting of independence to colonies. But in effect Britain, as before, remains the world's biggest colonial power, with almost 35 million people languishing under the colonial yoke in her possessions.

In defiance of the demands of the United Nations declaration, British colonial authorities continue to destroy fighters for the freedom of Northern Rhodesia and carry on mass-scale repressions against the patriots of Kenya; British planes are bombing peaceful villages of East Aden. For the sixth year running Britain is waging a colonial war against the people of Oman, and there seems to be no end to this war.

On June 19, 1961, making a formal concession to the spirit of the times, the British government declared the abolition of its protectorate over Kuwait, but immediately followed this up with the dispatch of its troops there. One could hardly find a more convincing example of the hypocrisy of the colonialists in making a mockery of the Declaration on Granting Independence to Colonial Countries and Peoples.

The Congo, which, through the fault of the imperialist powers, has not been able to enjoy even a day of tranquil life in conditions of their hard-won independence, has been subjected to open intervention by a united front of the Belgian and other colonialists. Facts testify that Belgium has never abandoned her interventionist plans in the Congo and continues to weave a spider's web of conspiracy against the young Republic of the Congo, relying in her criminal activities against the Congolese people on puppets of the Tshombe type, in an attempt to retain, with their help, key positions in the Congo, especially in the province of Katanga, with its colossal mineral wealth.

Seeking to preserve at any cost their rule over the trusteeship territory of Ruanda-Urundi, situated in the centre of Africa, the Belgian colonialists are resorting to the poisoned weapon of national and tribal strife, provoking conflicts between local tribes so as to split the national liberation movement and thus prevent the implementation of the United Nations General Assembly's resolution on holding elections in Ruanda-Urundi and granting freedom and independence to the people of that territory. According to refugees from Ruanda-Urundi, the colonialists have started the physical destruction of people there with the use of modern weapons, flame-throwers included.

The government of the Netherlands is shipping increasing numbers of troops and armaments to West Irian.

4. In adopting the declaration, the United Nations demanded immediate measures for turning over all power to the peoples of colonial and trusteeship territories, without any conditions or reservations and irrespective of race, religion or colour of skin. The colonialists are ignoring this demand as well.

In French Somali, Spanish Sahara, British-oppressed Basutoland, Portuguese Guinea and the overwhelming majority of other colonies, not only have no measures been taken to transfer power to the native population, but this population also remains completely deprived of elementary political rights and freedoms, including the freedom of speech, press and assembly and the right to establish national political parties and elect its organs of power.

Wherever elections do take place—as, for instance, in Rhodesia—the colonialists bar almost the entire local population from taking part in them. The laws establishing racial discrimination in the colonies have not been abolished, and the local black and other coloured population, as before, does not enjoy equal political and civil rights with the white settlers.

Particularly monstrous outrages against the most elementary rights of the people are perpetrated in the Republic of South Africa, that domain of slave-owners, where white masters, as in ancient Rome, build all their prosperity on the exploitation of millions of black and other coloured slaves. Racial discrimination and apartheid are the cornerstones of the ruling circles' policy in the Republic of South Africa.

The racialist government of the Republic of South Africa is implanting a régime of terror and racial discrimination also in South-West Africa, which has been turned into a disfranchised colony. The tyranny of the Republic of South Africa over the people of that country has assumed such dangerous forms that the United Nations committee for South-West Africa declared, with full responsibility, in its memorandum of July 28, 1961, that the situation in South-West Africa continued to be a serious threat to universal peace and security and stated that by its criminal actions on that territory the Republic of South Africa had 'confronted the United Nations Organization with a fact of the use of force calling for action on the part of the Security Council'.

By grossly rejecting all United Nations appeals and decisions demanding an end to the policy of apartheid and racial discrimination in the Republic of South Africa and the granting of freedom to the people of South-West Africa, the government of the Republic of South Africa is alienating its country from the community of member-states of the United Nations Organization.

5. The colonialists' actions aimed at preventing the implementation of the Declaration on Granting Independence to Colonial Countries and Peoples are so provocative that the legitimate question arises: How do they dare go against the will of the peoples expressed in the United Nations declaration, where do they find confidence in their impunity?

Life itself provides an answer to this question: The Portuguese and French, British and Belgian, South African, Dutch and Spanish colonialists rely in everything on the support of the United States, that mainstay of modern colonialism.

The United States government exerts no little effort in trying to convince the world that it is a champion of freedom and independence of the peoples. Each day, however, brings fresh evidence of the fact that it is the United States that not only supports the British, French, Portuguese, Belgian, Dutch and other colonialists but also comes out itself as the chief gendarme and strangler of the colonial peoples.

No manœuvres or propaganda tricks can hide this fact. What, for example, is the use of the United States' formal support in the United Nations of the demand that Portugal should stop mass reprisals against the people of Angola, if the very same United States has granted Portugal armaments and military equipment to the sum of almost 300 million dollars and continues its military aid to her, if American-made bombs marked 'Property of the U.S. Air Force' are dropped on peaceful villages in Angola!

Who will believe the statements of United States official circles about the United States government being interested in the peaceful settlement of the Algerian problem, if the planes strafing Algerian peaceful residents bear the trade-mark 'Made in the United States'! The representatives of the French government had every grounds for declaring that they were satisfied with the position of their United States ally with regard to the events in Algeria: after all, French pilots bombed Bizerta from American B-26 planes, and when the Bizerta problem was discussed at the special session of the United Nations General Assembly the United States delegation actually supported the French aggressors.

The other colonial powers also get extensive support from the United States. The United States has, for example, granted military assistance in a sum exceeding 1,000 million dollars to Britain, almost 4,500 million dollars to France, 1,200 million dollars to Belgium and almost 500 million dollars to Spain, and it is common knowledge that a considerable part of this aid, in the form of tanks, artillery guns, planes, aviation bombs, napalm, machine-guns and other military equipment, is used by the armies waging colonial wars.

It means that the United States is an accomplice in all the heinous atrocities perpetrated by other colonial powers in their colonies. Everywhere where the blood of people's fighters is spilt—in Algeria, Tunisia, Angola, Oman, Rhodesia, Aden and South-West Africa, everywhere where lawlessness and the racialists' arbitrary rule reign, this is the fault not only of the bellicose colonialists of France, Britain, Portugal and the South African Republic but also of their ally and patron, the United States of America.

The United States is also an accomplice of the government of the South African Republic, which is carrying out the barbarous policy of apartheid and racial discrimination; it was the United States that granted the government of the South African Republic three-quarters of all the loans it has received since the Second World War.

The entire system of the United States-led aggressive military blocs of N.A.T.O., Cento and S.E.A.T.O. is placed at the service of colonialism. It is precisely within the framework of these military blocs that the colonialists' mutual guarantee is shaped, that they work out joint plans for combating the national liberation movement in the colonies. It is rather significant, for example, that N.A.T.O. has an African committee among its other bodies. This committee is called upon to co-ordinate the measures of the colonial powers for suppressing the African people's movement for freedom and independence. As soon as any of the N.A.T.O. members face the danger of losing their colonies the United States and other allies in the bloc hurry to the rescue.

The military machine of the aggressive blocs is also completely at the colonialists' disposal. The troops used by France in Algeria and by Portugal in Angola for waging war against the peoples of those countries are a part of the so-called N.A.T.O. joint armed forces, and they could not have been transferred from Western Europe to the African continent without the consent and direct approval of the N.A.T.O. Supreme Command, headed by the Americans.

By defending and supporting the colonialists of Britain, France,

Portugal and other powers the United States is thereby defending the huge profits derived by the American monopolies from the exploitation of the natural resources and cheap manpower in the colonial possessions of these states. There, in the colonies of European states, a secret United States colonial empire, a sphere of domination of American monopoly capital, emerged a long time ago and has been expanding ever since. According to official United States data, the profits of United States companies in Africa piled up to 1,234 million dollars in 15 years after the Second World War. It is not for nothing that the Africans say that the United States government is ready to support not only the Portuguese colonialists and South African slave-owners but the devil himself, so as to allow United States monopolies to go on pumping hundreds of millions of dollars out of the colonial countries of Africa.

The United States supports its N.A.T.O. allies in their colonial gambles also because it itself has colonies, no matter how hard United States government representatives may try to deny it. What, if not a colony in the true sense of the word, is Puerto Rico, where two and a half million people live in the conditions of ruthless exploitation? And what about Okinawa, with its population of almost a million—a Japanese island seized by the United States and literally strewn all over with military bases? Or the hundreds of islands in the Pacific whose population has been driven from its native areas in connection with the creation of proving grounds for testing United States atomic and thermonuclear weapons? It is an indisputable fact that the United States has 12 colonial possessions with a population of 3,300,000 at present.

In common with the other colonial powers, the United States not only clings fast to its possessions but is not averse to laying its hands on other territories either. It has become known, for example, that the United States government has launched active back-stage activity in the United Nations with a view to joining to its territory, or the territory of its colony Guam, the Pacific islands transferred to United States trusteeship by decision of the United Nations after the Second World War.

The history of the United States for many decades and to the present day is a history of colonial wars and imperialist aggressions. Now, too, the so-called special task troops—designated first of all for suppressing the national liberation movement in the colonies and undermining from within the young Afro-Asian states which have wrested their independence from the colonialists—are being built up actively and drilled in special military centres. The special task troops are complemented by the United States 'peace corps', the task of which is to supply the colonies and independent Afro-Asian and Latin American states with preachers of humbleness and propagandists for the United States way of life, the very same way of life under which the United States Negroes are subjected to humiliating racial discrimination and diplomats of African countries, including representatives of these countries in the United Nations, become victims of base outrages only because their skin is black.

6. There is yet another country which, as time passes, is adhering ever more closely to the colonialists' common front against the peoples of the colonies. This is the Federal Republic of Germany, a state of revenge-seekers and militarists, which has granted 'assistance' to the French government in the sum of 2,000 million marks to finance the colonial war against the Algerian people; which is furnishing cadres of former S.S.-men for the foreign legions of Spain, France, Belgium and other colonial powers, a country which maintains the very closest relations with the South African Republic of racialists and slave-owners.

As a member of the N.A.T.O. military bloc, the Federal Republic of Germany takes an active part in the implementation of all joint measures of the colonial powers against the national liberation movement of the peoples of the colonies. And it does not merely help other colonialists, its ruling circles are again hatching plans for colonial conquests. None other than the Chancellor of the Federal Republic of Germany, Dr. Adenauer, announced as far back as in 1953 that the West German youth would have to 'recolonize' the countries of the East.

The nations have not forgotten that similar delirious plans were nurtured by the leaders of the Kaiser's and then Hitler's Germany. The peoples remember how much blood the practical implementation of these plans cost mankind. And now these plans are again being advanced by the West German revenge-seekers. Of course, it is not easy in our time to re-enslave independent countries, to turn them into colonies. Therefore, the ruling circles of the Federal Republic of Germany, waiting for a suitable moment for some colonial gamble, are meanwhile creating a secret colonial empire of West German banks and industrial and trade companies, following the example of the United States in Asia, Africa and Latin America.

7. In the course of the year which has passed since the United Nations General Assembly adopted the Declaration on Granting Independence to the Colonial Countries and Peoples, the role assigned by the United States and other colonial powers to their military bases on foreign territories, as bases of colonialism, has become still more obvious.

The most vivid symbol of colonialism nowadays is the French military base at Bizerta in Tunisia, directed against all the countries of Maghrib. The French aggression against Tunisia, launched with the aim of keeping

Bizerta, showed to the whole of Africa, and not only to Africa, what a tremendous danger colonialism represents to the cause of safeguarding universal peace and the security of nations. This aggression has also shown that the military bases on the territories of the young countries which have won their right to an independent national life in a hard struggle, are being utilized by the colonialists as springboards for the restoration of colonialism.

The French colonialists continue to occupy the area of Bizerta, although in the United Nations General Assembly's resolution of August 25, 1961, the overwhelming majority of countries declared once again that 'the presence of French armed forces on Tunisian territory, against the clearly expressed will of the Tunisian government and people, is a violation of the sovereignty of Tunisia, serves as a constant source of international tensions, and threatens international peace and security'.

For the same purposes the colonialists are also using their own military bases on foreign territories. A British special task brigade was dispatched from the British military base at Kahawa (Kenya) to Kuwait. British planes take off from the military base at Mukalla (Aden) to bomb the defenceless towns and villages of Oman. The American military base at Willis Field in Libya served as a transit station for the Belgian troops sent from Europe to Africa in July 1960 to carry out the aggression against the Republic of the Congo.

In their effort to maintain a foothold on the African continent, the colonialists are trying to extend the system of military bases wherever that is possible. Who does not know, for instance, that the French government has concluded with a number of African countries that have recently gained independence a 'defence' treaty granting France the right to station her troops on the territories of those countries and thus set up strongholds for fresh colonial wars? It is also known that Britain has forced analogous treaties on Cyprus, Nigeria and certain other young independent states.

8. Such is the state of affairs. From whichever aspect one approaches the question of fulfilment of the Declaration on Granting Independence to Colonial Countries and Peoples, there is only one conclusion: there is no crime at which the colonial powers will stop short in order to frustrate the fulfilment of the declaration, in order to maintain their domination over the colonies.

The colonialists are not giving up their booty, and they delude themselves that the peoples will not find ways of keeping them in check. But they are mistaken. The globe is not their patrimonial estate, and the 20th century is the century of the atom and manned space flights, not the age of the slave trade and piracy. Nowadays there are no peoples who are not ready for freedom, but there are peoples who are still forcibly deprived of freedom. And they must be given freedom. It is the duty of the United Nations Organization, the duty of the United Nations member-countries, to help them to achieve their aspirations. One must not wait passively for the rusty bars of the colonial prisons to crumble of themselves. These bars must be broken as soon as possible, and for ever—broken by the joint efforts of all freedom-loving countries.

In this noble and just cause great responsibility rests with the United Nations Organization, the Charter of which is based on the just principles of the equality of nations, the freedom of the peoples, and the sovereignty of countries. A year ago, in its declaration, the United Nations Organization expressed itself in favour of the unconditional and immediate granting of independence to the colonial countries and peoples.

The past year has shown the great vital power, the great strength of this declaration. But at the same time it is now clearer than ever that a statement by the United Nations in favour of the freedom and independence of the peoples of the colonies is not yet sufficient in itself—it is necessary to work out concrete measures ensuring the fulfilment of the declaration, to oblige the colonialists to carry out these measures, and to control their implementation.

Having in mind the adoption of appropriate decisions precisely of this nature by the General Assembly, the Soviet government has submitted for the consideration of the Assembly the question: 'The course of the implementation of the Declaration on Granting Independence to Colonial Countries and Peoples.' What are the measures which have to be taken?

In the first place, the Soviet government proposes that the General Assembly declare 1962 to be the year of the final liquidation of colonialism. To complete, towards the end of 1962, the liquidation of the colonial system on the global scale is a quite feasible task, if all the freedom-loving states and peoples unite to break the resistance of the colonialists.

But to specify the time limits is not enough. It is necessary to define precisely what has to be done in the course of this period in all the colonies and trusteeship and other non-self-governing territories without exception, in order to implement the demands of the Declaration on Granting Independence to Colonial Countries and Peoples.

According to this practical approach to the question of carrying out the declaration, it is self-evident that the first demand, already contained in the declaration itself, is to terminate immediately all colonial wars and all repressions against participants in the national liberation movement and to withdraw all foreign troops from the colonies and dismantle all foreign bases there.

To demand that these measures be taken is a direct duty of the United Nations Organization. As long as colonial wars go on, as long as the territories of colonies are occupied by the colonialist troops, as long as their military bases exist there, there can be no question of the liberation of the colonies and, more than that, none of the African, Asian or Latin American states that have won independence in recent years can consider themselves safe.

Last year's experience has testified convincingly, however, to the fact that it is not enough for the United Nations merely to demand that the colonialists stop wars against the colonial peoples. It must be made clear to the colonialists that if they do not comply with this demand they will be punished, that sanctions provided for by the United Nations Charter will be taken against them with all the strictness of international law.

The Soviet government considers that the General Assembly and the Security Council would be acting correctly if they decided already now to take sanctions against Portugal, which refuses to comply with the United Nations demand that the war against the people of Angola be ended.

Along with the demand for the immediate discontinuance of colonial wars and all other means of pressure upon the colonial peoples with the use of force, the United Nations Organization must, in the Soviet government's opinion, make it encumbent upon the colonial powers to undertake such steps in the colonies which would ensure, not later than the end of 1962, the actual transition of all colonies to the status of independent states.

It goes without saying that the establishment of national organs of power in the colonies must be uppermost among these steps, and the United Nations Organization must demand that this task be carried out unconditionally in all colonies and trusteeship and other non-self-governing territories in the course of the next few months.

The establishment of national organs of power in the colonies is a serious and responsible task. In this matter the colonialists cannot be relied upon, of course; compelled to agree to the establishment of national organs of power in the colonies, they are sure to try to plant their stooges and puppets there. National organs of power must be established by the colonial peoples themselves.

To enable them to do so, the United Nations must demand the immediate granting to the population of every colony of broad democratic rights and freedoms, including universal suffrage, freedom of speech, the press and assembly, and freedom to establish their national political parties, trade unions and other public organizations. It is equally necessary to secure the immediate abolition in all colonial territories of all laws and regulations allowing racial, religious and other kinds of discrimination.

On the question of the democratic rights of the native population, just as on the question of ending wars against the colonial peoples, the United Nations must show firmness if it is to achieve any results. If, for instance, the government of the Republic of South Africa persists in the policy of racial discrimination and *apartheid*, the General Assembly would be justified in declaring the expulsion of the Republic of South Africa from the United Nations and the Security Council would be justified in taking proper sanctions against it, as is envisaged in the United Nations Charter. Let it be a lesson to all colonialists and racialists!

The termination of colonial wars and repressions, the withdrawal of foreign troops from the colonies, the liquidation of foreign military bases and the granting of democratic rights and freedoms to the population of the colonies will provide conditions for holding there, in the course of 1962, truly democratic general elections to all democratic organs of power, in keeping with the only just principle: 'One man—one voice.'

It is to these democratically elected organs that the colonial administration will have to transfer, before the end of 1962, all power in the territories of the colonies becoming independent states. From the moment of the transfer of power and the liquidation of the colonial administration the countries that are still colonies today will embark upon the road of independence.

It is essential to ensure, however, that this should not be a fictitious independence, that the new independent states should not remain direct or indirect vassals of their former parent states. On this question as well the United Nations must say its clear and weighty word by demanding the unconditional abrogation of all agreements, including secret ones, with colonies and trusteeship territories designed to restrict the sovereignty of future independent states. All acts aimed at joining colonies and trusteeship territories in any form to the parent states must also be unconditionally abrogated.

All forms of seizing and keeping colonial territories, even under the pretext of joining them to the parent state, must be ruled out. The United Nations Organization could not and did not believe the false assertion of the Portuguese government to the effect that Angola was a part of Portugal. It must not allow, for instance, Pacific islands or Okinawa to be declared a part of United States territory and retained for ever as colonies under this pretext.

Such, in the Soviet government's opinion, are the minimum measures whose implementation must be demanded by the United Nations from all the colonial powers, so as to ensure the actual implementation of the historic Declaration on Granting Independence to Colonial Countries and Peoples.

The carrying out of all these measures must be undertaken by the United Nations under strict and constant control; otherwise the colonialists will find thousands of loopholes and pretexts to evade their implementation.

In view of this, the Soviet government considers it necessary that the United Nations should set up a commission for observation and control over the implementation of the declaration in all colonies and trusteeship and other non-self-governing territories. So as to cope successfully with these important tasks, this commission must include, on an equal footing, representatives of all three main groups of states: the socialist states, the countries aligned with the western military blocs, and the neutralist states.

Being firmly convinced that the complete and final liquidation of colonialism is one of the most important and pressing tasks of today, in the solution of which all the peoples are vitally interested, the Soviet government calls upon the governments of all the member-states of the United Nations to support the Soviet Union's proposals on measures to implement the Declaration on Granting Independence to Colonial Countries and Peoples.

2. Soviet–Senegalese Joint Communiqué, 14 June 1962

This is typical of statements on talks with African states. For another example see the Soviet–Guinean Joint Communiqué, 8 September 1960, text in Soviet News, 10 September 1960. A further Soviet–Guinean Joint Communiqué of 15 February 1961 appears in Documents on International Affairs 1961, R.I.I.A., p. 643.

Mamadou Dia, Prime Minister and Minister of National Defence of the Republic of Senegal, paid an official visit to the U.S.S.R. at the invitation of the Soviet government from June 5 to June 15, 1962. The Prime Minister was accompanied by Ousmane N'Gom, Vice-Chairman of the National Assembly of the Republic of Senegal, Ibrahim Sarn, Minister of Public Services and Labour, and other officials.

During their stay in the Soviet Union the Prime Minister and Minister of National Defence of the Republic of Senegal and the party accompanying him visited Moscow, Tashkent, Baku and Leningrad. Everywhere the representatives of Senegal were given a friendly and hearty welcome.

The guests from Senegal were provided with opportunities for becoming broadly acquainted with different aspects of the life of the Soviet people. They saw the U.S.S.R. Exhibition of Economic Achievements and a number of industrial and agricultural undertakings and cultural establishments.

Mamadou Dia and his party expressed great satisfaction with their tour of the Soviet Union.

Mamadou Dia, Prime Minister of the Republic of Senegal, had meetings and talks with N. S. Khrushchov, Chairman of the U.S.S.R. Council of Ministers, and paid a visit to L. I. Brezhnev, President of the Presidium of the U.S.S.R. Supreme Soviet.

During the talks between N. S. Khrushchov and Mamadou Dia—talks which took place in an atmosphere of sincerity and good will—views were exchanged on questions concerning Soviet–Senegalese relations and on a number of important problems of the present international situation.

The exchange of opinion brought out the identity of views of the two sides on a number of topical international problems.

The governments of the two countries stated their firm intention of continuing to take all measures in their power for the preservation and consolidation of world peace. Both sides emphasized, in particular, that general and complete disarmament under strict international control would be of decisive importance for safeguarding world peace and international security. The implementation of general and complete disarmament would not only rid mankind for ever of the threat of a new war, but would also help to allocate substantial additional resources for rendering aid to the countries which have recently embarked on the path of independent development.

The governments of the Soviet Union and the Republic of Senegal have a high appreciation of the importance of the United Nations General Assembly's Declaration on Granting Independence to Colonial Countries and Peoples and consider that effective steps have to be taken for the earliest possible implementation of this declaration so that colonialism may be completely and finally abolished both in Africa and in other parts of the world.

The governments of the Soviet Union and the Republic of Senegal have proclaimed their solidarity with the peoples of Angola, Mozambique and so-called Portuguese Guinea, who are fighting for national freedom and independence, and express their profound indignation at the methods of terror employed by the Portuguese colonialists. Portugal's actions in her colonies create a serious threat to world peace and security.

The two sides consider that the United Nations and the peace-loving states should take urgent and effective measures to put an end to the colonial war being waged by Portugal in Africa and to ensure independence for the peoples of Angola, Mozambique and so-called Portuguese Guinea, and other nations which are still under the yoke of the Portuguese colonialists.

Both sides have expressed satisfaction in connection with the real prospects which are emerging for a final settlement of the Algerian problem and the setting up of an independent Algerian state. They resolutely condemn the criminal activities of those who are trying to wreck the implementation of the Evian agreements with bloody acts of terrorism.

Both the Soviet and Senegalese sides angrily condemn the policy of racial discrimination in the South African Republic and in South-West Africa and call for an immediate end to the acts of repression against the African population of these countries who are striving for freedom and equality.

During the discussion on questions concerning Soviet–Senegalese relations, the two sides stated that they attached great importance to the development of reciprocal trade contacts, economic co-operation and cultural exchanges. In view of this, the Soviet Union and the Republic of Senegal concluded a trade agreement, an agreement on economic and technical co-operation and a convention on cultural co-operation.

Prompted by a desire to develop relations of friendship and co-operation between the Union of Soviet Socialist Republics and the Republic of Senegal, the governments of the two countries decided to establish diplomatic relations and exchange diplomatic missions at Embassy level. Both sides expressed confidence that in this way they would promote better understanding between the peoples of the two countries, as well as the development of international co-operation and the consolidation of world peace.

Both sides consider that the visit paid by Mamadou Dia, Prime Minister of the Republic of Senegal, to the U.S.S.R. will be of great importance in the development of friendly relations between the two countries.

N. KHRUSHCHOV
Chairman of the U.S.S.R.
Council of Ministers

MAMADOU DIA
Prime Minister of the
Republic of Senegal

Moscow, June 14, 1962.

VIII. CHINESE POLICY

THE Chinese People's Republic has been involved with the group of non-aligned states from the outset and participated in the Bandung Conference in 1955. Good relations have been established with some African states in spite of strong opposition to this from the Western powers. The Chinese support the liberation movements in Southern Africa by both words and deeds and provide technical assistance and credits on very favourable terms. Chinese policy rests on the goodwill generated by practical assistance. Western reaction to Chinese activity verges at times on the hysterical. In the period 1964–9 Tanzania was host to Chinese technical experts and consequently was regarded in some quarters as an instrument of the Chinese. However, during the same period technical experts from a large number of Western states were in the country and the army was trained and armed by Canada. The ministries do not have many foreign experts at policy level and the few that exist appear to be British or American. The International Bank were asked and refused to finance the Tan-Zam railway and instead the Chinese have agreed to provide finance and assist generally in its construction. The Friendship Textile Mill outside Dar es Salaam in Tanzania is typical of Chinese activity. The Chinese financed the project, installed machinery, trained local personnel to staff the mill, and then went away, leaving a publicly owned Tanzanian asset.

For discussion and further references see Yu, *Year Book of World Affairs*, 1970, p. 125. On treaties of economic assistance concluded by China with Guinea, Ghana, Mali, the United Arab Republic, Algeria, Congo (Brazzaville), and Tanzania, see also Lee, *China and International Agreements*, 1969, pp. 92–5.

China has concluded four Treaties of Friendship: with Guinea (set out below), Ghana (1961), Congo (Brazzaville) (1964), and Tanzania (1965). The text below is reproduced from *Peking Review*, 14 September 1960, p. 10. The Treaty of Friendship was accompanied by an Agreement on Economic and Technical Co-operation and an Agreement on Trade and Payments.

Treaty of Friendship, China & Guinea,
13 September 1960

The Chairman of the People's Republic of China and the President of the Republic of Guinea,

Desiring to consolidate and further develop the profound friendship between the People's Republic of China and the Republic of Guinea,

Convinced that the strengthening of friendly co-operation between the People's Republic of China and the Republic of Guinea conforms to the fundamental interests of the peoples of the two countries, conduces to strengthening the friendship and solidarity between the peoples of China and Guinea as well as among Asian and African peoples, and is in the interest of world peace,

Have decided for this purpose to conclude the present Treaty.

Article I

The Contracting Parties will maintain and develop peaceful and friendly relations between the People's Republic of China and the Republic of Guinea.

Article II

The Contracting Parties decide to take the Five Principles of mutual respect for sovereignty and territorial integrity, mutual non-aggression, non-interference in each other's internal affairs, equality and mutual benefit and peaceful co-existence as the principles guiding the relations between the two countries.

The Contracting Parties will settle all disputes between them by means of peaceful negotiation.

Article III

The Contracting Parties agree to develop the economic and cultural relations between the two countries in the spirit of equality, mutual benefit and friendly co-operation.

Article IV

The present Treaty is subject to ratification and the instruments of ratification shall be exchanged in Conakry as soon as possible.

The present Treaty will come into force immediately on the exchange of the instruments of ratification and will remain in force for a period of ten years.

Unless either of the Contracting Parties gives the other notice in writing to terminate it one year before the expiration of this period, it will remain in force indefinitely, subject to the right of either Party to terminate it by giving to the other notice of its intention to do so one year in advance.

Done in duplicate in Peking on the thirteenth day of September, nineteen sixty, in the Chinese and French languages, both texts being equally authentic.

PART SEVEN

THE SITUATION IN THE CONGO
1960–1964

It is hardly possible to explain the elements in the conflicts which arose in the Congo after independence in an introductory note. Apart from the many issues arising from the role of the United Nations force in the Congo (O.N.U.C.), the situation indicates the extent to which external forces can control affairs of African states through local intermediaries, who may use the standard rhetoric of nationalism and self-determination. The story of the earlier period is told very well by Catherine Hoskyns, *The Congo Since Independence, January 1960–December 1961*, 1965. On the O.A.U. involvement see Catherine Hoskyns, *The Organization of African Unity and the Congo Crisis, 1964–1965*, 1969. See also Bowett (ed.), *United Nations Forces*, 1964, chapter 6; Crawford Young, *Politics in the Congo*, 1965; *Documents on International Affairs 1960*, R.I.A.I., pp. 259–326; *Documents on International Affairs 1961*, R.I.A.I., pp. 734–71; Nkrumah, *Challenge of the Congo*, 1967; Young, *Politics in the Congo*, 1965.

I. SECURITY COUNCIL RESOLUTIONS ADOPTED IN JULY 1960

The first resolution, S/4387, was adopted on 14 July 1960 by 8 votes to 0, with 3 abstentions. The second, S/4405, was adopted unanimously on 22 July 1960.

(i)

The Security Council,
    Considering the report of the Secretary-General on a request for United Nations action in relation to the Republic of the Congo,
    Considering the request for military assistance addressed to the Secretary-General by the President and the Prime Minister of the Republic of the Congo (document S/4382),
    1. *Calls upon* the Government of Belgium to withdraw their troops from the territory of the Republic of the Congo;
    2. *Decides* to authorize the Secretary-General to take the necessary steps, in consultation with the Government of the Republic of the Congo, to provide the Government with such military assistance, as may be neces-

sary, until, through the efforts of the Congolese Government with the technical assistance of the United Nations, the national security forces may be able, in the opinion of the Government, to meet fully their tasks;

3. *Requests* the Secretary-General to report to the Security Council as appropriate.

(ii)

The Security Council,

Having considered the first report by the Secretary-General on the implementation of Security Council resolution S/4387 of 14 July 1960 (document S/4389),

Appreciating the work of the Secretary-General and the support so readily and so speedily given to him by all Member States invited by him to give assistance,

Noting that as stated by the Secretary-General the arrival of the troops of the United Nations Force in Leopoldville has already had a salutary effect,

Recognizing that an urgent need still exists to continue and to increase such efforts,

Considering that the complete restoration of law and order in the Republic of the Congo would effectively contribute to the maintenance of international peace and security,

Recognizing that the Security Council recommended the admission of the Republic of the Congo to membership in the United Nations as a unit,

1. *Calls upon* the Government of Belgium to implement speedily the Security Council resolution of 14 July 1960, on the withdrawal of their troops and authorizes the Secretary-General to take all necessary action to this effect;

2. *Requests* all States to refrain from any action which might tend to impede the restoration of law and order and the exercise by the Government of the Congo of its authority and also to refrain from any action which might undermine the territorial integrity and the political independence of the Republic of the Congo;

3. *Commends* the Secretary-General for the prompt action he has taken to carry out resolution S/4387 of the Security Council and his first report;

4. *Invites* the specialized agencies of the United Nations to render to the Secretary-General such assistance as he may require;

5. *Requests* the Secretary-General to report further to the Security Council as appropriate.

II. SECURITY COUNCIL RESOLUTIONS ADOPTED IN AUGUST AND SEPTEMBER 1960

THE first resolution, S/4426, was adopted on 9 August 1960, by 9 votes to 0, with 2 abstentions. The second, S/4526, was adopted on 17 September 1960.

(i)

The Security Council,

Recalling its resolution of 22 July 1960 (S/4405), *inter alia*, calling upon the Government of Belgium to implement speedily the Security Council resolution of 14 July (S/4387) on the withdrawal of their troops and authorizing the Secretary-General to take all necessary action to this effect,

Having noted the second report by the Secretary-General on the implementation of the aforesaid two resolutions and his statement before the Council,

Having considered the statements made by the representatives of Belgium and the Republic of the Congo to this Council at this meeting,

Noting with satisfaction the progress made by the United Nations in carrying out the Security Council resolutions in respect of the territory of the Republic of the Congo other than the Province of Katanga,

Noting however that the United Nations had been prevented from implementing the aforesaid resolutions in the Province of Katanga although it was ready, and in fact attempted, to do so,

Recognizing that the withdrawal of Belgian troops from the Province of Katanga will be a positive contribution to and essential for the proper implementation of the Security Council resolutions,

1. *Confirms* the authority given to the Secretary-General by the Security Council resolutions of 14 July and 22 July 1960 and requests him to continue to carry out the responsibility placed on him thereby;

2. *Calls upon* the Government of Belgium to withdraw immediately its troops from the Province of Katanga under speedy modalities determined by the Secretary-General and to assist in every possible way the implementation of the Council's resolutions;

3. *Declares* that the entry of the United Nations Force into the Province of Katanga is necessary for the full implementation of this resolution;

4. *Reaffirms* that the United Nations Force in the Congo will not be a party to or in any way intervene in or be used to influence the outcome of any internal conflict, constitutional or otherwise;

5. *Calls upon* all Member States, in accordance with Articles 25 and 49 of the Charter, to accept and carry out the decisions of the Security Council and to afford mutual assistance in carrying out measures decided upon by the Security Council;

6. *Requests* the Secretary-General to implement this resolution and to report further to the Security Council as appropriate.

(ii)

The Security Council,

Having considered the item on its agenda as contained in document S/Agenda 906,

Taking into account that the lack of unanimity of its permanent members at the 906th meeting of the Security Council has prevented it from exercising its primary responsibility for the maintenance of international peace and security,

Decides to call an emergency special session of the General Assembly as provided in General Assembly resolution 377 A (V) of 3 November 1950, in order to make appropriate recommendations.

III. RESOLUTION OF THE FOURTH EMERGENCY SPECIAL SESSION OF THE U.N. GENERAL ASSEMBLY, 1960

This resolution, 1474 (ES-IV) was adopted on 20 September 1960, by 70 votes to 0, with 11 abstentions (the Communist States, France, and South Africa).

The General Assembly,

Having considered the situation in the Republic of the Congo,

Taking note of the resolutions of 14 July, 22 July and 9 August 1960 of the Security Council,

Taking into account the unsatisfactory economic and political conditions that continue in the Republic of the Congo,

Considering that, with a view to preserving the unity, territorial integrity and political independence of the Congo, to protecting and advancing the welfare of its people, and to safeguarding international peace, it is essential for the United Nations to continue to assist the Central Government of the Congo,

1. *Fully supports* the resolutions of 14 and 22 July and 9 August 1960 of the Security Council;

2. *Requests* the Secretary-General to continue to take vigorous action in accordance with the terms of the aforesaid resolutions and to assist the Central Government of the Congo in the restoration and maintenance of law and order throughout the territory of the Republic of the Congo and to safeguard its unity, territorial integrity and political independence in the interests of international peace and security;

3. *Appeals* to all Congolese within the Republic of the Congo to seek a speedy solution by peaceful means of all their internal conflicts for the unity and integrity of the Congo, with the assistance, as appropriate, of Asian and African representatives appointed by the Advisory Committee on the Congo, in consultation with the Secretary-General, for the purpose of conciliation;

4. *Appeals* to all Member Governments for urgent voluntary contributions to a United Nations Fund for the Congo to be used under United Nations control and in consultation with the Central Government for the purpose of rendering the fullest possible assistance to achieve the objective mentioned in the preamble;

5. *Requests:*

(*a*) All States to refrain from any action which might tend to impede the restoration of law and order and the exercise by the Government of the Republic of the Congo of its authority and also to refrain from any action which might undermine the unity, territorial integrity and the political independence of the Republic of the Congo;

(*b*) All Member States in accordance with Articles 25 and 49 of the Charter of the United Nations, to accept and carry out the decisions of the Security Council and to afford mutual assistance in carrying out measures decided upon by the Security Council;

6. Without prejudice to the sovereign rights of the Republic of the Congo, *calls upon* all States to refrain from the direct and indirect provision of arms or other materials of war and military personnel and other assistance for military purposes in the Congo during the temporary period of military assistance through the United Nations, except upon the request of the United Nations through the Secretary-General for carrying out the purposes of this resolution and of the resolutions of 14 and 22 July and 9 August 1960 of the Security Council.

IV. SECURITY COUNCIL RESOLUTIONS ADOPTED ON 20–21 FEBRUARY 1961 AND 24 NOVEMBER 1961

THE first resolution, S/4741, was adopted by 9 votes to 0, with 2 abstentions. The second, S/5002, was adopted by 9 votes to 0, with 2 abstentions.

(i) A

The Security Council,

Having considered the situation in the Congo,

Having learnt with deep regret the announcement of the killing of the Congolese leaders, Mr. Patrice Lumumba, Mr. Maurice Mpolo and Mr. Joseph Okito,

Deeply concerned at the grave repercussions of these crimes and the danger of wide-spread civil war and bloodshed in the Congo and the threat to international peace and security,

Noting the Report of the Secretary-General's Special Representative (S/4691) dated 12 February 1961 bringing to light the development of a serious civil war situation and preparations therefor,

1. *Urges* that the United Nations take immediately all appropriate measures to prevent the occurrence of civil war in the Congo, including arrangements for cease-fires, the halting of all military operations, the prevention of clashes, and the use of force, if necessary, in the last resort;

2. *Urges* that measures be taken for the immediate withdrawal and evacuation from the Congo of all Belgian and other foreign military and para-military personnel and political advisers not under the United Nations Command, and mercenaries;

3. *Calls upon* all States to take immediate and energetic measures to prevent the departure of such personnel for the Congo from their territories, and for the denial of transit and other facilities to them;

4. *Decides* that an immediate and impartial investigation be held in order to ascertain the circumstances of the death of Mr. Lumumba and his colleagues and that the perpetrators of these crimes be punished;

5. *Reaffirms* the Security Council resolutions of 14 July, 22 July and 9 August 1960 and the General Assembly resolution 1474 (ES-IV) of 20 September 1960 and reminds all States of their obligation under these resolutions.

B

The Security Council,

Gravely concerned at the continued deterioration in the Congo, and the prevalence of conditions which seriously imperil peace and order, and the unity and territorial integrity of the Congo, and threaten international peace and security,

Noting with deep regret and concern the systematic violations of human rights and fundamental freedoms and the general absence of rule of law in the Congo,

Recognizing the imperative necessity of the restoration of parliamentary institutions in the Congo in accordance with the fundamental law of the country, so that the will of the people should be reflected through the freely elected Parliament,

Convinced that the solution of the problem of the Congo lies in the hands of the Congolese people themselves without any interference from outside and that there can be no solution without conciliation,

Convinced further that the imposition of any solution, including the formation of any government not based on genuine conciliation would, far from settling any issues, greatly enhance the dangers of conflict within the Congo and threat to international peace and security,

1. *Urges* the convening of the Parliament and the taking of necessary protective measures in that connection;

2. *Urges* that Congolese armed units and personnel should be re-organized and brought under discipline and control, and arrangements be made on impartial and equitable bases to that end and with a view to the elimination of any possibility of interference by such units and personnel in the political life of the Congo;

3. *Calls upon* all States to extend their full co-operation and assistance and take such measures as may be necessary on their part, for the implementation of this resolution.

(ii)

The Security Council,

Recalling its resolutions S/4387, S/4405, S/4426 and S/4741,

Recalling further General Assembly resolutions 1474 (ES-IV), 1592 (XV), 1599 (XV), 1600 (XV) and 1601 (XV),

Reaffirming the policies and purposes of the United Nations with respect to the Congo (Leopoldville) as set out in the aforesaid resolutions, namely:

(*a*) To maintain the territorial integrity and the political independence of the Republic of the Congo;

(*b*) To assist the Central Government of the Congo in the restoration and maintenance of law and order;

(*c*) To prevent the occurrence of civil war in the Congo;

(*d*) To secure the immediate withdrawal and evacuation from the Congo of all foreign military, para-military and advisory personnel not under the United Nations Command, and all mercenaries; and

(*e*) To render technical assistance,

Welcoming the restoration of the national Parliament of the Congo in accordance with the *Loi fondamentale* and the consequent formation of a Central Government on 2 August 1961,

Deploring all armed action in opposition to the authority of the Government of the Republic of the Congo, specifically secessionist activities and armed action now being carried on by the Provincial Administration of Katanga with the aid of external resources and foreign mercenaries, and *completely rejecting* the claim that Katanga is a 'sovereign independent nation',

Noting with deep regret the recent and past actions of violence against United Nations personnel,

Recognizing the Government of the Republic of the Congo as exclusively responsible for the conduct of the external affairs of the Congo,

Bearing in mind the imperative necessity of speedy and effective action to implement fully the policies and purposes of the United Nations in the Congo to end the unfortunate plight of the Congolese people, necessary both in the interests of world peace and international co-operation, and stability and progress of Africa as a whole,

1. *Strongly deprecates* the secessionist activities illegally carried out by the provincial administration of Katanga, with the aid of external resources and manned by foreign mercenaries;

2. *Further deprecates* the armed action against United Nations forces and personnel in the pursuit of such activities;

3. *Insists* that such activities shall cease forthwith, and *calls upon* all concerned to desist therefrom;

4. *Authorizes* the Secretary-General to take vigorous action, including the use of requisite measure of force, if necessary, for the immediate apprehension, detention pending legal action and/or deportation of all foreign military and para-military personnel and political advisers not under the United Nations Command, and mercenaries as laid down in paragraph A-2 of the Security Council resolution of 21 February 1961;

5. *Further requests* the Secretary-General to take all necessary measures to prevent the entry or return of such elements under whatever guise and also of arms, equipment or other material in support of such activities;

6. *Requests* all States to refrain from the supply of arms, equipment or other material which could be used for warlike purposes, and to take the necessary measures to prevent their nationals from doing the same, and

also to deny transportation and transit facilities for such supplies across their territories, except in accordance with the decisions, policies and purposes of the United Nations;

7. *Calls upon* all Member States to refrain from promoting, condoning, or giving support by acts of omission or commission, directly or indirectly, to activities against the United Nations often resulting in armed hostilities against the United Nations forces and personnel;

8. *Declares* that all secessionist activities against the Republic of the Congo are contrary to the *Loi fondamentale* and Security Council decisions and specifically *demands* that such activities which are now taking place in Katanga shall cease forthwith;

9. *Declares* full and firm support for the Central Government of the Congo, and the determination to assist that Government in accordance with the decisions of the United Nations to maintain law and order and national integrity, to provide technical assistance and to implement those decisions;

10. *Urges* all Member States to lend their support, according to their national procedures, to the Central Government of the Republic of the Congo, in conformity with the Charter and the decisions of the United Nations;

11. *Requests* all Member States to refrain from any action which may directly or indirectly impede the policies and purposes of the United Nations in the Congo and is contrary to its decisions and the general purpose of the Charter.

V. SOVIET STATEMENT, 9 SEPTEMBER 1960

THE text is taken from *Soviet News*, 13 September 1960.

The developments in the Republic of Congo indicate that the conspiracy of the colonialists against the independence and integrity of this African state, against its people and legitimate government, is assuming an increasingly dangerous nature.

Events, and in particular the events of recent days, prove incontrovertibly that the Belgian colonialists, their N.A.T.O. allies, in the first place the United States, and the command of the troops sent to the Congo in accordance with the resolution of the Security Council—a command which in point of fact has become a servant of the colonialists—are acting in collusion in an attempt to strangle the freedom of the Congolese people.

The flagrant interference in the internal affairs of the Congo Republic is in fact a direct mockery of the resolutions of the Security Council designed to protect the independence and integrity of the Congo.

Here are the facts: The imperialist powers, relying on traitors to the Congolese people such as Tshombe, Kalonji and others, are pursuing a policy of fomenting civil war in the Congo Republic.

The Congolese province of Katanga, seized by stooges of the colonialists, is before everyone's eyes being turned by Belgium, with the support of her N.A.T.O. allies, into a military camp of forces hostile to the legitimate government of the Congo Republic. The army of the Tshombe puppet government is being formed and equipped with the direct participation of the Belgian interventionists. The entire Belgian male population is being mobilized in Katanga on orders from the Belgian command, and detachments of 'volunteers' are being set up, with Belgian military personnel being included in them under the disguise of technical advisers. The anti-government Kalonji bands active in Kasai province are armed with Belgian weapons issued from N.A.T.O. stores.

Belgian planes of the Sabena Company, repainted in United Nations blue, are providing an airlift carrying arms for the Tshombe bands.

During his stay in the Congo, the United Nations Secretary-General even found it possible to negotiate with the traitor Tshombe without notifying the lawful Congo government. On Hammarskjöld's orders, as soon as the Kamina military base in Katanga was evacuated by the Belgians, it was occupied by troops under the United Nations command. Instead of being transferred to the government of the Congo Republic, this base was occupied under the artificial pretext of 'neutralizing' it.

In spite of the fact that United Nations troops were sent to the Congo at the request of the Congolese government, and although the resolutions of the Security Council have clearly stated that they may be used only with the knowledge and consent of the Congo government, this important provision is being systematically violated by the United Nations command in the Congo and by Secretary-General Hammarskjöld. The United Nations representatives in the Congo, far from helping, are in every way interfering with the efforts of the Congo government to restore order and normal conditions in the country.

The actions of the United Nations command have become especially wanton in the past few days. On the orders of this command, troops operating under the United Nations flag, in face of resolute protests from the Congo government, have occupied and blocked the aerodromes of Leopoldville, the capital of the Republic, and other Congolese towns. The United Nations command has even forbidden the landing of a plane carrying the commander of the national army of the Congo on the Leopoldville aerodrome. Moreover, it was announced that if the plane attempted to land, it would be fired upon.

There is in fact no limit to the overbearing colonialist attitude of representatives sent by Hammarskjöld to the Congo. In face of protests from the government, troops of the United Nations command occupied the central radio station of Leopoldville. Representatives of the legitimate government of the country are barred from access to this radio station.

Moreover, persons who style themselves representatives of the United Nations in the Congo have even refused to enter into negotiations with the Congolese government, which has demanded the immediate evacuation of the aerodromes and the radio station. And this is being done in conditions in which these representatives are on Congolese soil at the request of the government of that country.

N.A.T.O. countries, and in the first place the United States, jointly with the United Nations command, which is in charge of the troops who were sent to the Congo in accordance with the resolutions of the Security Council but who are actually used to sabotage those resolutions, are openly attempting to discredit the legitimate government of the Congo Republic headed by Prime Minister Lumumba.

They are following a policy of encouraging secessionist, anti-popular elements who, in order to curry favour with the colonialists, are ready to sacrifice the independence of the country and to sell its territory. They have also resorted to the insidious tactics of setting the troops placed by certain countries at the disposal of the United Nations command at loggerheads with Congolese government troops.

In fact there has been formed a coalition of colonialists which aims to suppress the young African state—the Congo Republic—by the hands of African soldiers from Tunisia, Morocco, Ethiopia and Ghana. The real purposes of the coalition of the interventionists are obvious from its arrogant actions. The whole of Africa, the entire world, now sees that an attempt is being made to replace one kind of colonialism in the Congo by another kind, in the form of the collective colonialism of N.A.T.O. countries, with the blue flag of the United Nations as a cover.

The United Nations Security Council, which has repeatedly discussed the situation in the Congo, has taken good, correct decisions aimed at ensuring the independence and integrity of the Republic of Congo, at helping the Congo government to restore normal life in that country, which has been disrupted by the colonialists. At the present time, however, attempts are being made to sabotage the implementation of these decisions, to deceive the peoples and use to the detriment of the Congo the troops placed by a number of states at the disposal of the United Nations command.

Undoubtedly most of the states which sent their contingents to the Congo in accordance with the Security Council resolution, did so with the best of intentions, striving to assist in the preservation of the freedom, independence and integrity of the Congolese state.

Now that it is becoming increasingly clear that the present United Nations command in the Congo is using the contingents of those troops for entirely different purposes and is aiding those who oppressed the Congo in the past and who are now encroaching on the independence of that country, the states which have sent their troops to the Congo are in duty bound to see that their soldiers who arrived on Congo soil to help that country, should really be used in accordance with the direct purpose for which they were destined and should help the government of the Republic of Congo to consolidate the independence of that country in full conformity with the Security Council resolutions. If the United Nations command refuses to comply with these resolutions, they must be carried out over the head of this command.

It is worth noting the unseemly role assumed with regard to the Congo by United Nations Secretary-General Hammarskjöld.

There is every reason to say that the events in the Congo and the participation of United Nations representatives in the carrying out of the resolutions of the Security Council concerning that country have been a serious test of the impartiality of the United Nations apparatus. And it must be said outright that the most highly-placed official of this apparatus —the United Nations Secretary-General—has failed to display a minimum of the impartiality which the present situation has demanded of him. In the general mechanism of the United Nations apparatus, its head has proved to be precisely that component which has been most openly working in favour of the colonialists, thus compromising the United Nations in the eyes of the peoples.

In view of the situation in the Congo, the Soviet government has instructed its representative in the Security Council to insist on the immediate convocation of the Council in order to take measures to terminate forthwith interference in the Congo's internal affairs in any form whatsoever.

For this purpose it is essential, in the first place, to evacuate the armed forces at the disposal of the United Nations command from all the aerodromes they are occupying at the present time.

National radio stations must again be placed at the complete and unrestricted disposal of the Congo government.

The command, which is using for purposes for which they were not intended the troops sent to the Congo in accordance with the resolution of the Security Council, must be dismissed.

The legitimate government of the Republic of Congo must be allowed to exercise its sovereign rights and authority over the entire territory of the Congo without any interference or hindrance from the United Nations representatives.

The Soviet government will press for all this at the meeting of the Security Council and it expects that its efforts will be supported by all states which cherish the cause of the national independence and security of the peoples and which do not want the name of the United Nations to be besmirched by disgraceful complicity with the colonialists.

If, however, the Security Council, for some reason, is unable to do its duty, the states which respect the earlier resolutions on assistance to the Congo, in this hour of trial for the Congolese people must render every support to the legitimate government of the Republic of Congo.

VI. THE STANLEYVILLE OPERATION: SECURITY COUNCIL RESOLUTION ADOPTED ON 30 DECEMBER 1964

IN 1963 the United Nations Secretary-General decided on a policy of military disengagement in the Congo and complete withdrawal of U.N. forces took place on 30 June 1964. The secession of Katanga had ended some time before this but the Congo was divided between the authority of Tshombe's government in the capital and the surviving Lumumbaist nationalists based upon Stanleyville. By a mysterious series of events Tshombe had acquired the backing of the Western powers and indirect military support for his operations against his nationalist opponents. The threat to the lives of foreign residents held as hostages by the insurgents was the reason advanced for intervention by Belgian parachute forces, carried by U.S. aircraft, at Stanleyville on 24 November 1964. This operation had the permission of Tshombe's government and was opportune for him. However, the majority of O.A.U. members were incensed by the outside interference in African affairs and the bypassing of O.A.U. decisions concerning the Congo situation. For an account of the Security Council debate see the *Year Book of the United Nations*, 1964, pp. 95–100. For further materials see below, p. 534 (Appendix 2).

Resolution Adopted on 30 December 1964

This resolution, S/6129, was adopted by 10 votes to 0, with 1 abstention (France).

The Security Council,
   Noting with concern the aggravation of the situation in the Democratic Republic of the Congo,
   Deploring the recent events in the Democratic Republic of the Congo,
   Convinced that the solution of the Congolese problem depends on national reconciliation and the restoration of public order,
   Recalling the pertinent resolutions of the General Assembly and the Security Council,
   Reaffirming the sovereignty and territorial integrity of the Democratic Republic of the Congo,
   Taking into consideration the resolution of the Organization of African Unity dated 10 September, in particular paragraph 1 relating to the mercenaries,
   Convinced that the Organization of African Unity should be able, in the context of Article 52 of the Charter, to help find a peaceful solution to all

the problems and disputes affecting peace and security in the continent of Africa,

Having in mind the efforts of the Organization of African Unity to help the Government of the Democratic Republic of the Congo and the other political factions in the Congo to find a peaceful solution to their dispute,

1. *Requests* all States to refrain or desist from intervening in the domestic affairs of the Congo;

2. *Appeals* for a cease-fire in the Congo in accordance with the Organization of African Unity's resolution dated 10 September 1964;

3. *Considers*, in accordance with the Organization of African Unity's resolution dated 10 September 1964, that the mercenaries should as a matter of urgency be withdrawn from the Congo;

4. *Encourages* the Organization of African Unity to pursue its efforts to help the Government of the Democratic Republic of the Congo to achieve national reconciliation in accordance with resolution CM/Resolution 5 (III) dated 10 September 1964 of the Organization of African Unity;

5. *Requests* all States to assist the Organization of African Unity in the attainment of these objectives;

6. *Requests* the Organization of African Unity, in accordance with Article 54 of the Charter, to keep the Security Council fully informed of any action it may take under this resolution;

7. *Requests* the Secretary-General of the United Nations to follow the situation in the Congo, and to report to the Security Council at the appropriate time.

APPENDIX 1

THE LUSAKA MANIFESTO, 1969

IN April 1969 fourteen East and Central African States issued a manifesto on the future of Southern Africa, the text of which appears below: see text in *The Times*, 22 May 1969, issued by the Zambian High Commissioner's Office in London. The objectives of the manifesto were adopted by the Assembly of Heads of State and Government of the O.A.U. at its sixth ordinary session, 6–10 September 1969. On 20 November 1969 the United Nations General Assembly adopted a resolution sponsored by forty-eight states which welcomed the manifesto and recommended it to the attention of all States and peoples: 113 votes in favour, 2 against (Portugal and South Africa), and 2 abstentions (Cuba and Malawi). Recent tentative proposals for 'a dialogue with South Africa' should be placed in relation to the manifesto.

TEXT

MANIFESTO ON SOUTHERN AFRICA

1. When the purpose and the basis of States' international policies are misunderstood, there is introduced into the world a new and unnecessary disharmony. Disagreements, conflicts of interest, or different assessments of human priorities, which already provoke an excess of tension in the world, and disastrously divide mankind at a time when united action is necessary to control modern technology and put it to the service of man. It is for this reason, that discovering widespread misapprehension of our attitudes and purposes in relation to Southern Africa, we the leaders of East and Central African States meeting at Lusaka, 16th April, 1969, have agreed to issue this Manifesto.

2. By this Manifesto we wish to make clear, beyond all shadow of doubt, our acceptance of the belief that all men are equal, and have equal rights to human dignity and respect, regardless of colour, race, religion, or sex. We believe that all men have the right and the duty to participate, as equal members of the society, in their own government. We do not accept that any individual or group has any right to govern any other group of sane adults, without their consent, and we affirm that only the people of a society, acting together as equals, can determine what is, for them, a good society and a good social, economic, or political organization.

3. On the basis of these beliefs we do not accept that any one group within a society has the right to rule any society without the continuing

consent of all the citizens. We recognize that at any one time there will be, within every society, failures in the implementation of these ideals. We recognize that for the sake of order in human affairs, there may be transitional arrangements while a transformation from group inequalities to individual equality is being effected. But we affirm that without an acceptance of these ideals—without a commitment to these principles of human equality and self-determination—there can be no basis for peace and justice in the world.

4. None of us would claim that within our own States we have achieved that perfect social, economic, and political organization which would ensure a reasonable standard of living for all our people and establish individual security against avoidable hardship or miscarriage of justice. On the contrary, we acknowledge that within our own States the struggle towards human brotherhood and unchallenged human dignity is only beginning. It is on the basis of our commitment to human equality and human dignity, not on the basis of achieved perfection, that we take our stand of hostility towards the colonialism and racial discrimination which is being practised in Southern Africa. It is on the basis of their commitment to these universal principles that we appeal to other members of the human race for support.

5. If the commitment to these principles existed among the States holding power in Southern Africa, any disagreements we might have about the rate of implementation, or about isolated acts of policy, would be matters affecting only our individual relationships with the States concerned. If these commitments existed, our States would not be justified in the expressed and active hostility towards the regimes of Southern Africa such as we have proclaimed and continue to propagate.

6. The truth is, however, that in Mozambique, Angola, Rhodesia, South-West Africa, and the Republic of South Africa, there is an open and continued denial of the principles of human equality and national self-determination. This is not a matter of failure in the implementation of accepted human principles. The effective Administrations in all these territories are not struggling towards these difficult goals. They are fighting the principles; they are deliberately organizing their societies so as to try to destroy the hold of these principles in the minds of men. It is for this reason that we believe the rest of the world must be interested. For the principle of human equality, and all that flows from it, is either universal or it does not exist. The dignity of all men is destroyed when the manhood of any human being is denied.

7. Our objectives in Southern Africa stem from our commitment to this principle of human equality. We are not hostile to the Administrations

of these States because they are manned and controlled by white people. We are hostile to them because they are systems of minority control which exist as a result of, and in the pursuance of, doctrines of human inequality. What we are working for is the right of self-determination for the people of those territories. We are working for a rule in those countries which is based on the will of all the people, and an acceptance of the equality of every citizen.

8. Our stand towards Southern Africa thus involves a rejection of racialism, not a reversal of the existing racial domination. We believe that all the peoples who have made their homes in the countries of Southern Africa are Africans, regardless of the colour of their skins: and we would oppose a racialist majority government which adopted a philosophy of deliberate and permanent discrimination between its citizens on grounds of racial origin. We are not talking racialism when we reject the colonialism and apartheid policies now operating in those areas; we are demanding an opportunity for all the people of these States, working together as equal individual citizens to work out for themselves the institutions and the system of government under which they will, by general consent, live together and work together to build a harmonious society.

9. As an aftermath of the present policies, it is likely that different groups within these societies will be self-conscious and fearful. The initial political and economic organizations may well take account of these fears, and this group self-consciousness. But how this is to be done must be a matter exclusively for the peoples of the country concerned, working together. No other nation will have a right to interfere in such affairs. All that the rest of the world has a right to demand is just what we are now asserting— that the arrangements within any State which wishes to be accepted into the community of nations must be based on an acceptance of the principles of human dignity and equality.

10. To talk of the liberation of Africa is thus to say two things: First, that the peoples in the territories still under colonial rule shall be free to determine for themselves their own institutions of self-government. Secondly, that the individuals in Southern Africa shall be freed from an environment poisoned by the propaganda of racialism, and given an opportunity to be men—not white men, brown men, yellow men, or black men.

11. Thus the liberation of Africa for which we are struggling does not mean a reverse racialism. Nor is it an aspect of African Imperialism. As far as we are concerned the present boundaries of the States of Southern Africa are the boundaries of what will be free and independent African States. There is no question of our seeking or accepting any

alterations to our own boundaries at the expense of these future free African nations.

12. On the objective of liberation as thus defined, we can neither surrender nor compromise. We have always preferred and we still prefer, to achieve it without physical violence. We would prefer to negotiate rather than destroy, to talk rather than kill. We do not advocate violence; we advocate an end to the violence against human dignity which is now being perpetrated by the oppressors of Africa. If peaceful progress to emancipation were possible, or if changed circumstances were to make it possible in the future, we would urge our brothers in the resistance movements to use peaceful methods of struggle even at the cost of some compromise on the timing of change. But while peaceful progress is blocked by actions of those at present in power in the States of Southern Africa, we have no choice but to give to the peoples of those territories all the support of which we are capable in their struggle against their oppressors. This is why the signatory states participate in the movement for the liberation of Africa, under the aegis of the Organization of African Unity. However, the obstacle to change is not the same in all the countries of Southern Africa, and it follows therefore, that the possibility of continuing the struggle through peaceful means varies from one country to another.

13. In *Mozambique* and *Angola*, and in so-called *Portuguese Guinea*, the basic problem is not racialism but a pretence that Portugal exists in Africa. Portugal is situated in Europe; the fact that it is a dictatorship is a matter for the Portuguese to settle. But no decree of the Portuguese dictator, nor legislation passed by any Parliament in Portugal, can make Africa part of Europe. The only thing which could convert a part of Africa into a constituent unit in a union which also includes a European State would be the freely expressed will of the people of that part of Africa. There is no such popular will in the Portuguese colonies. On the contrary, in the absence of any opportunity to negotiate a road to freedom, the peoples of all three territories have taken up arms against the colonial power. They have done this despite the heavy odds against them, and despite the great suffering they know to be involved.

14. Portugal, as a European State, has naturally its own allies in the context of the ideological conflict between West and East. However, in our context, the effect of this is that Portugal is enabled to use her resources to pursue the most heinous war and degradation of man in Africa. The present Manifesto must, therefore, lay bare the fact that the inhuman commitment of Portugal in Africa and her ruthless subjugation of the

people of Mozambique, Angola and the so-called Portuguese Guinea, is not only irrelevant to the ideological conflict of power-politics, but it is also diametrically opposed to the politics, the philosophies and the doctrines practised by her Allies in the conduct of their own affairs at home. The peoples of Mozambique, Angola, and Portuguese Guinea are not interested in Communism or Capitalism; they are interested in their freedom. They are demanding an acceptance of the principles of independence on the basis of majority rule, and for many years they called for discussions on this issue. Only when their demand for talks was continually ignored did they begin to fight. Even now, if Portugal should change her policy and accept the principle of self-determination, we would urge the Liberation Movements to desist from their armed struggle and to co-operate in the mechanics of a peaceful transfer of power from Portugal to the peoples of the African territories.

15. The fact that many Portuguese citizens have immigrated to these African countries does not affect this issue. Future immigration policy will be a matter for the independent Governments when these are established. In the meantime we would urge the Liberation Movements to reiterate their statements that all those Portuguese people who have made their homes in Mozambique, Angola, or Portuguese Guinea, and who are willing to give their future loyalty to those States, will be accepted as citizens. And an independent Mozambique, Angola, or Portuguese Guinea may choose to be as friendly with Portugal as Brazil is. That would be the free choice of a free people.

16. In *Rhodesia* the situation is different in so far as the metropolitan power has acknowledged the colonial status of the territory. Unfortunately, however, it has failed to take adequate measures to reassert its authority against the minority which has seized power with the declared intention of maintaining white domination. The matter cannot rest there. Rhodesia, like the rest of Africa, must be free, and its independence must be on the basis of majority rule. If the colonial power is unwilling or unable to effect such a transfer of power to the people, then the people themselves will have no alternative but to capture it as and when they can. And Africa has no alternative but to support them. The question which remains in Rhodesia is therefore whether Britain will reassert her authority in Rhodesia and then negotiate the peaceful progress to majority rule before independence. In so far as Britain is willing to make this second commitment, Africa will co-operate in her attempts to reassert her authority. This is the method of progress which we would prefer; it would involve less suffering for all the people of Rhodesia, both black and white. But until there is some firm evidence that Britain accepts the principle of

independence on the basis of majority rule and is prepared to take whatever steps are necessary to make it a reality, then Africa has no choice but to support the struggle for the people's freedom by whatever means are open.

17. Just as a settlement of the Rhodesian problem with a minimum of violence is a British responsibility, so a settlement in *South West Africa* with a minimum of violence is a United Nations responsibility. By every canon of international law, and by every precedent, South West Africa should by now have been a sovereign, independent State with a Government based on majority rule. South West Africa was a German colony until 1919, just as Tanganyika, Rwanda and Burundi, Togoland, and Cameroon were German colonies.

It was a matter of European politics that when the Mandatory System was established after Germany had been defeated, the administration of South West Africa was given to the white minority Government of South Africa, while the other ex-German colonies in Africa were put into the hands of the British, Belgian, or French Governments. After the Second World War every mandated territory except South West Africa was converted into a Trusteeship Territory and has subsequently gained independence. South Africa, on the other hand, has persistently refused to honour even the international obligation it accepted in 1919, and has increasingly applied to South West Africa the inhuman doctrines and organization of apartheid.

18. The United Nations General Assembly has ruled against this action and in 1966 terminated the Mandate under which South Africa had a legal basis for its occupation and domination of South West Africa. The General Assembly declared that the territory is now the direct responsibility of the United Nations and set up an *ad hoc* Committee to recommend practical means by which South West Africa would be administered, and the people enabled to exercise self-determination and to achieve independence.

19. Nothing could be clearer than this decision—which no permanent member of the Security Council voted against. Yet, since that time no effective measures have been taken to enforce it. South West Africa remains in the clutches of the most ruthless minority government in Africa. Its people continue to be oppressed and those who advocate even peaceful progress to independence continue to be persecuted. The world has an obligation to use its strength to enforce the decision which all the countries co-operated in making. If they do this there is hope that the change can be effected without great violence. If they fail, then sooner or

later the people of South West Africa will take the law into their own hands. The people have been patient beyond belief, but one day their patience will be exhausted. Africa, at least, will then be unable to deny their call for help.

20. *The Republic of South Africa* is itself an independent Sovereign state and a member of the United Nations. It is more highly developed and richer than any other nation in Africa. On every legal basis its internal affairs are a matter exclusively for the people of South Africa. Yet the purpose of law is people and we assert that the actions of the South African Government are such that the rest of the world has a responsibility to take some action in defence of humanity.

21. There is one thing about South African oppression which distinguishes it from other oppressive regimes. The *apartheid* policy adopted by its Government, and supported to a greater or lesser extent by almost all its white citizens, is based on a rejection of man's humanity. A position of privilege or the experience of oppression in the South African society depends on the one thing which it is beyond the power of any man to change. It depends upon a man's colour, his parentage, and his ancestors. If you are black you cannot escape this categorization; nor can you escape it if you are white. If you are a black millionaire and a brilliant political scientist, you are still subject to the pass laws and still excluded from political activity. If you are white, even protests against the system and an attempt to reject segregation, will lead you only to the segregation and the comparative comfort of a white jail. Beliefs, abilities, and behaviour are all irrelevant to a man's status; everything depends upon race. Manhood is irrelevant. The whole system of government and society in South Africa is based on the denial of human equality. And the system is maintained by a ruthless denial of the human rights of the majority of the population and thus, inevitably of all.

22. These things are known and are regularly condemned in the Councils of the United Nations and elsewhere. But it appears that to many countries international law takes precedence over humanity; therefore no action follows the words. Yet even if international law is held to exclude active assistance to the South African opponents of *apartheid*, it does not demand that the comfort and support of human and commercial intercourse should be given to a government which rejects the manhood of most of humanity. South Africa should be excluded from the United Nations Agencies, and even from the United Nations itself. It should be ostracized by the world community. It should be isolated from world trade patterns and left to be self-sufficient if it can. The South

African Government cannot be allowed both to reject the very concept of mankind's unity, and to benefit by the strength given through friendly international relations. And certainly Africa cannot acquiesce in the maintenance of the present policies against people of African descent.

23. The signatories of this Manifesto assert that the validity of the principles of human equality and dignity extend to the Republic of South Africa just as they extend to the colonial territories of Southern Africa. Before a basis for peaceful development can be established in this continent, these principles must be acknowledged by every nation, and in every State there must be a deliberate attempt to implement them.

24. We re-affirm our commitment to these principles of human equality and human dignity, and to the doctrines of self-determination and non-racialism. We shall work for their extension within our own nations and throughout the continent of Africa.

APPENDIX 2

THE STANLEYVILLE OPERATION: O.A.U. AND CAIRO RESOLUTIONS

THE following items reflect the reaction of the O.A.U. toward the civil strife in the Congo in 1964 following the final withdrawal of U.N. Forces and the appearance of a central government led by Kasavubu and Tshombe backed by American and Belgian aid. On 24 November 1964 U.S. military transport planes landed a unit of Belgian paratroopers at Stanleyville. The object of the operation, which had the sanction of the Tshombe regime, was expressed to be humanitarian. However, the operation was accompanied by atrocities on the part of foreign mercenaries, members of ground forces acting, in co-ordination with the Belgo-American landing, against anti-Tshombe forces in Eastern Congo. For the background see Catherine Hoskyns, *Case Studies in African Diplomacy, I; The Organization of African Unity and the Congo Crisis, 1964–65*, Dar es Salaam, 1969.

(a) O.A.U. Third Extraordinary Session of Council of Ministers, Addis Ababa, 5–10 September 1964: Final Resolution

The Council of Ministers of the Organization of African Unity meeting for its Third Extraordinary session in Addis Ababa from 5 to 10 September 1964, to examine the Congolese problem, its repercussions on the neighbouring states and on the African scene at large;

Having studied the messages addressed to it by several African Heads of State and Government, especially that of President Kasavubu expressing his conviction that the solution to the Congolese problem should be found within the Organization of African Unity;

Having noted the invitations of the Governments of the Democratic Republic of the Congo, the Republic of Congo (Brazzaville) and the Kingdom of Burundi to the OAU to send a fact-finding and goodwill mission to their countries to seek means of restoring normal relations between the Democratic Republic of the Congo and the Republic of Congo (Brazzaville) and between the Democratic Republic of the Congo and the Kingdom of Burundi;

Taking note of the statement by the Prime Minister of the Democratic Republic of the Congo indicating his efforts and desire to bring national reconciliation in his country;

Deeply concerned by the deteriorating situation in the Democratic Republic of the Congo resulting from foreign intervention as well as use

of mercenaries principally recruited from the racist countries of South
Africa and Southern Rhodesia;

Reaffirming the resolutions of the Organization of African Unity
inviting all African states to abstain from any relationship whatsoever with
the Government of South Africa because of its policy of *apartheid*;

Considering that foreign intervention and the use of mercenaries has
unfortunate effects on the neighbouring independent states as well as on
the struggle for national liberation in Angola, Southern Rhodesia,
Mozambique and the other territories in the region which are still under
colonial domination, and constitutes a serious threat to peace in the
African continent;

Convinced that the solution to the Congolese problem although essentially political, depends on the pursuit of national reconciliation and the
restoration of order, so as to permit stability, economic development of
the Congo, as well as the safeguarding of its territorial integrity;

Deeply conscious of the responsibilities and of the competence of the
Organization of African Unity to find a peaceful solution to all the
problems and differences which affect peace and security in the African
continent;

1. *Appeals* to the Government of the Democratic Republic of the
   Congo to stop immediately the recruitment of mercenaries and to
   expel as soon as possible all mercenaries of whatever origin who are
   already in the Congo so as to facilitate an African solution.
2. *Notes* the solemn undertaking of the Prime Minister of the Democratic Republic of the Congo to guarantee the security of combatants
   who lay down their arms.
3. *Requests* especially all those now fighting to cease hostilities so as to
   seek, with the help of the Organization of African Unity, a solution
   that would make possible national reconciliation and the restoration
   of order in the Congo.
4. *Appeals* to all the political leaders of the Democratic Republic of
   the Congo to seek, by all appropriate means, to restore and consolidate national reconciliation.
5. *Decides* to set up and to send immediately to the Democratic Republic
   of the Congo, the Republic of Congo (Brazzaville) and the Kingdom
   of Burundi an *Ad Hoc* Commission consisting of Cameroun,
   Ethiopia, Ghana, Guinea, Nigeria, Somalia, Tunisia, U.A.R., Upper
   Volta and placed under the effective chairmanship of H.E. Jomo
   Kenyatta, Prime Minister of Kenya, which will have the following
   mandate:

(a) to help and encourage the efforts of the Government of the Democratic Republic of the Congo in the restoration of national reconciliation in conformity with paragraphs 2 and 3 above;

(b) to seek by all possible means to bring about normal relations between the Democratic Republic of the Congo and its neighbours, especially the Kingdom of Burundi and the Republic of the Congo (Brazzaville).

6. *Invites* this Commission to submit its report to the Administrative Secretary-General, for immediate distribution to all member states.

7. *Requests* all member states to refrain from any action that might aggravate the situation in the Democratic Republic of the Congo, or worsen the relationship between the Democratic Republic of the Congo and its neighbours.

8. *Appeals* strongly to all powers at present intervening in the internal affairs of the Democratic Republic of the Congo to cease their interference. The member states are further invited to give instructions to their diplomatic missions accredited to these powers with the view of impressing upon them this appeal.

9. *Requests* the Administrative Secretary-General to provide the Commission with all the necessary assistance to accomplish its mission.

(b) *Conference of Non-aligned States, Cairo, 5–10 October 1964: Resolution of 9 October 1964*

Deeply concerned at the rapidly deteriorating situation in the Congo, the participants:

1. support all the efforts being made by the Organization of African Unity to bring peace and harmony speedily to that country;

2. urge the *Ad Hoc* Commission of the Organization of African Unity to shirk no effort in the attempt to achieve national reconciliation in the Congo, and to eliminate the existing tension between that country and the Republic of Congo (Brazzaville) and the Kingdom of Burundi;

3. appeal to the Congolese Government and to all combatants to cease hostilities immediately and to seek, with the help of the Organization of African Unity, a solution permitting of national reconciliation and the restoration of order and peace;

4. urgently appeal to all foreign powers at present interfering in the internal affairs of the Democratic Republic of the Congo, particularly those engaged in military intervention in that country, to cease such interference, which infringes the interests and sovereignty of the Congolese people and constitutes a threat to neighbouring countries;

5. affirm their full support for the efforts being made to this end by the Organization of African Unity's *Ad Hoc* Commission of good offices in the Congo;

6. call upon the Government of the Democratic Republic of the Congo to discontinue the recruitment of mercenaries immediately and to expel all mercenaries, of whatever origin, who are already in the Congo, in order to facilitate an African solution.

(c) Organization of African Unity, Fourth Extraordinary Session of Council of Ministers, New York, 16–20 December 1964: Final Resolution

The Council of Ministers of the Organization of African Unity at its fourth extraordinary session meeting at the United Nations headquarters, New York, from 16 to 21 December 1964;

Having examined the interim report of the *Ad Hoc* Commission established by resolution ECM/Res. 5 (III);

Deeply concerned by the deteriorating situation in the Democratic Republic of the Congo;

Convinced that the Congo problem would find its best solution within the framework of the OAU;

Conscious of the gravity of the recent Belgo-United States military intervention in the Democratic Republic of the Congo,

1. *Takes note* of the interim report of the *Ad Hoc* Commission,

2. *Expresses* gratitude and appreciation to the *Ad Hoc* Commission, and in particular to its Chairman, His Excellency Mr. Jomo Kenyatta, for their efforts in bringing about national reconciliation in the Democratic Republic of the Congo,

3. *Reaffirms* in full resolution ECM/Res. 5 (III) of 10 September 1964, and reiterates in particular paragraphs 1, 2, 3, 4, 7 and 8 of said resolution,

4. *Requests* the *Ad Hoc* Commission to continue its mandate in accordance with paragraph 5 of the said resolution, and to ensure that all the measures recommended by the Council for the settlement of the Congolese problem are carried out,

5. *Appeals* to all Powers who are interfering in the internal affairs of the Democratic Republic of the Congo to cease such interferences in order to enable the Organization of African Unity to work for the achievement of national reconciliation,

6. *Appeals* to all member states, especially to the Democratic Republic of the Congo, the Republic of Congo Brazzaville, and the Kingdom of Burundi to co-operate with the *Ad Hoc* Commission for the successful implementation of its mandate,

7. *Requests* the *Ad Hoc* Commission to submit reports as appropriate,

8. *Disapproves* of the recent foreign military intervention in the Democratic Republic of the Congo, which is disturbing the peace and security of the African continent,

9. *Requests* the Administrative Secretary-General to continue to provide the Commission with all the necessary assistance to accomplish its mission,

10. *Calls* upon the Security Council:

   (*a*) to condemn the recent foreign military interventions which have compromised the efforts being made by OAU to secure national reconciliation in the Congo;

   (*b*) to recommend an African solution to the Congo problem;

   (*c*) to recommend to all the powers concerned that they co-operate with OAU in order to facilitate the solution of the Congolese problem.

APPENDIX 3

ARMS FOR SOUTH AFRICA: THE SIMONSTOWN AGREEMENT

Two documents are set out below. The first consists of an 'exchange of letters constituting an agreement' between Britain and South Africa concerning defence matters. The text is taken from the *United Nations Treaty Series*, vol. 248, p. 190, and is thus the text as registered with the United Nations Secretariat. Apart from the six letters included in this text, there were further letters and enclosures concerning ancillary, administrative, and financial arrangements for the implementation of the Agreement: see Cmnd. 9520 for the full text. Further correspondence between the two governments is contained in a White Paper, Cmnd. 4589.

In 1963 and 1964 the Security Council adopted three major resolutions calling for an embargo on the supply of arms to South Africa (for the text of two of the resolutions see above, pp. 428, 429). The United Kingdom voted as follows on the resolutions. The Resolution of 4 December 1963 was adopted unanimously, the United Kingdom representative voting on the basis that the resolution was not related to Chapter VII of the Charter. The resolution of 9 June 1964 was adopted by 7 votes to none, with 4 abstentions of which the United Kingdom was one. The Resolution of 18 June 1964 was adopted by 8 votes to none with 3 abstentions. The United Kingdom again voted in favour on the basis that Chapter VII was not involved. The United Kingdom votes in favour of the resolutions of 4 December 1963 and 18 June 1964 were also accompanied by and conditional upon a reservation that no arms would be exported to South Africa which would enable the policy of *apartheid* to be enforced. The British abstention on the first resolution on *apartheid*, of 7 August 1963, was explained on similar lines.

The evidence to be found in the debates in the Security Council and in the wording of the resolutions supports the conclusion that the resolutions were not mandatory but had the force of recommendations to member States: in technical terms the resolutions were based upon Chapter VI and not upon Chapter VII of the Charter of the United Nations.

On 20 July 1970 the United Kingdom declared that the Government was ready to consider applications for the export to South Africa of 'certain categories of arms, so long as they are for maritime defence directly related to the security of the sea routes': see statement by Sir Alec Douglas-Home, *Parliamentary Debates, Fifth Series*, vol. 804, col. 49.

This decision created a bitter controversy in Britain and elsewhere. The issue was considered by the Commonwealth Heads of Government Conference in January 1971: Final Communiqué, *The Times*, 23 January 1971; Keesing, 1971, para. 24437A. A critical stand was also taken by the majority of members of the O.A.U.: see the O.A.U. Assembly of Heads of State and Government, September 1970; Keesing, 1969–70, para. 24191A. See further Security Council Resolution 282 (1970), above, p. 435.

Critics of the British policy announced in July 1970 argue that (*a*) the actual delivery of vessels agreed upon occurred in 1963; (*b*) that since 1963 no further deliveries had been made; (*c*) that the Simonstown Agreement does not create obligations to make any further deliveries; (*d*) that there is no viable distinction between arms for use in internal security operations and arms for use against external aggression.

The second item printed below is a letter from the Prime Minister to Lord Brockway and summarizes the Government's position. Two points should be made. First, the letter appears to say that measures may be taken even apart from the obligations of the Simonstown Agreement, as such. Secondly, official explanations of the British position take the view that the supply of arms *for the future* (within the purposes of the Agreement) is in accordance with the intention of the parties to the Agreement. The legal position is discussed in a White Paper: *Legal Obligations of Her Majesty's Government Arising Out of the Simonstown Agreements*, Cmnd. 4589. See also Roy Lewis, *The Times*, 15 January 1971; Charles Rousseau, *Revue Générale de Droit Int. Public*, vol. 75, p. 134. It is the case that a State has a liberty to deliver arms to another, apart from any treaty obligation. This liberty may be restricted by legal considerations in certain situations.

The U.N. resolutions concerned impose a complete arms embargo, but they are not mandatory, as has been pointed out. So far as concerns the supply of arms which could be used for 'internal security', it is very probable that this is illegal whether or not particular resolutions exist, mandatory or otherwise. The reason for this is that a large number of legal authorities of many nationalities, and governments, take the view that there is a standard of (racial) non-discrimination which is a part of general international law binding all States (and this includes the principles or law of the United Nations Charter): see the Judgement of the International Court of Justice in the *Barcelona Traction* case (Second Phase), I.C.J. Reports, 1970, at p. 32. This standard, and also the principle of self-determination, have the status of principles of the U.N. Charter and are rules of a fundamental type (*jus cogens*). The Simonstown Agreement antedated the emergence of these norms as legal principles of this type but its implementation is now illegal in so far as this involves support for the maintenance of *apartheid* and government by a racial minority. Other relevant materials are (*a*) the Declaration on Principles of International Law concerning Friendly Relations and Co-operation Among States in accordance with the Charter of the United Nations (adopted 24 October 1970), which is an authoritative interpretation of the Charter and affirms the legal status of the principle of equal rights and self-determination of peoples; and (*b*) Article 103 of the U.N. Charter which provides: 'In the event of a conflict between the obligations of the Members of the United Nations under the present Charter and their obligations under any other international agreement, their obligations under the present Charter shall prevail.'

TEXT

EXCHANGE OF LETTERS CONSTITUTING AN AGREEMENT[1] ON DEFENCE MATTERS BETWEEN THE GOVERNMENT OF THE UNITED KINGDOM OF GREAT BRITAIN AND NORTHERN IRELAND AND THE GOVERNMENT OF THE UNION OF SOUTH AFRICA. LONDON, 30 JUNE 1955

The Honourable F. C. Erasmus, Minister of Defence of the Union of South Africa, visited the United Kingdom from 15th to 30th June, 1955, for further discussions with Ministers of the United Kingdom Government. These resulted in exchanges of letters embodying agreements and understandings satisfactory to both Governments on the following subjects:

The need for international discussions with regard to regional defence against external aggression.

The defence of the sea routes round Southern Africa.

Transfer of the Simonstown Naval Base and arrangements for its future use.

These exchanges of letters are set out below.

I. *The Need for International Discussions with Regard to Regional Defence against External Aggression*[2]

LETTER 1

MINISTRY OF DEFENCE
LONDON, S.W. 1

30th June, 1955

Dear Mr. Erasmus,

I enclose a Memorandum setting out the terms of our Understanding on the need for international discussions with regard to Regional Defence.

I shall be glad if you will confirm that it represents what was agreed between us.

Yours sincerely,

Selwyn LLOYD

The Honourable F. C. Erasmus, M.P.

---

[1] Came into force on 30 June 1955 by the exchange of the said letters.

[2] The following information is given by the Government of the United Kingdom of Great Britain and Northern Ireland: 'This exchange of letters does not contain any substantive obligations but is registered in order to facilitate understanding of the other two agreements.'

Memorandum on the Need for International Discussions with regard to Regional Defence

1. Southern Africa and the sea routes round Southern Africa must be secured against aggression from without.

2. The internal security of the countries of Southern Africa must, however, remain a matter for each individual country concerned.

3. The defence of Southern Africa against external aggression lies not only in Africa but also in the gateways to Africa, namely in the Middle East. It is therefore the declared policy:

(*a*) of the United Kingdom to contribute forces for the defence of Africa, including Southern Africa, and the Middle East;

(*b*) of the Union Government to contribute forces in order to keep the potential enemy as far as possible from the borders of South Africa, in other words for the defence of Southern Africa, Africa and the Middle East gateways to Africa. While the Union's contribution will depend upon satisfactory arrangements being arrived at between the countries mainly concerned as to the nature and extent of the contribution which each will make, the Union Government is in the meantime building up a task force for use outside South Africa against external aggression.

4. In order to implement the above policies, the lines of communication and logistic support in and around Southern Africa must be adequate and securely defended.

5. In this connection the arrangements set out in a separate agreement for the defence of the sea routes round Southern Africa are of primary importance.

6. The adequacy and security of logistic facilities and communications within Southern Africa, and particularly along the lines of communication to the Middle East are matters which should be further considered.

7. To this end it is agreed that the United Kingdom and South Africa will jointly sponsor a conference to integrate forward and develop the planning already begun at the Nairobi Conference.

8. This would cover the technical adequacy of routes, railways, inland waterways, airfields and seaplane bases, radar facilities for screening, sea transport facilities, tele-communications and mails facilities and arrangements for their defence in the event of external aggression.

9. It would also cover base facilities, e.g., storage and stockpiling arrangements, repair facilities, etc., on the lines of communication through and around Southern Africa.

10. It is agreed that the United Kingdom and the Union will jointly endeavour, at this conference, to secure the setting up of suitable machinery to pursue the aims of the conference on a continuing basis.

LETTER 2

SOUTH AFRICA HOUSE
LONDON, W.C.2

30th June, 1955

Dear Mr. Selwyn Lloyd,

Thank you for your letter of 30th June, 1955, enclosing a Memorandum setting out the terms of our Understanding on the need for international discussions with regard to Regional Defence.

I am glad to confirm that this represents what was agreed between us.

Yours sincerely,

F. C. ERASMUS

The Right Honourable Selwyn Lloyd, C.B.E., T.D., Q.C., M.P.

II. *The Defence of the Sea Routes round Southern Africa*

LETTER 3

MINISTRY OF DEFENCE
LONDON, S.W.1

30th June, 1955

Sir,

I have the honour to refer to our recent discussions in London concerning the defence of the sea routes round Southern Africa and to set out the terms of the agreement which we have reached.

AGREEMENT ON DEFENCE OF THE SEA ROUTES ROUND SOUTHERN AFRICA

1. Recognizing the importance of sea communications to the well-being of their respective countries in peace and to their common security in the event of aggression, the Governments of the Union of South Africa and of the United Kingdom enter into the following Agreement to ensure the safety, by the joint operations of their respective maritime forces, of the sea routes round Southern Africa.

2. The Union Government have approved a programme for the expansion of the South African Navy. The programme will be spread over a

period of eight years from 1955 to 1963, and will involve the purchase of the following vessels, which will be added to the existing fleet:

> 6 Anti-submarine Frigates.
> 10 Coastal Minesweepers.
> 4 Seaward Defence Boats.

3. The Union Government will place firm orders in the United Kingdom for the purchase of these vessels, costing some £18M. The British Admiralty agree to act as agents for the Union Government in this matter.

4. After the control and administration of the Simonstown Naval Base are handed over to the Union Government in accordance with the provisions of the Agreement relating to that subject, the Royal Naval Commander-in-Chief, South Atlantic, will continue to fly the flag to which he is entitled by Royal Naval regulations in the Cape area outside Simonstown and to exercise command over any Royal Naval units in the Union.

5. He will also be designated for purposes of planning and operational command in war as Commander-in-Chief of a maritime strategic zone, the boundaries of which will approximate to those of the Royal Naval South Atlantic Station, and will include the Mozambique Channel. It will, however, exclude waters further north which fall within the responsibility of the Royal Naval Commander-in-Chief, East Indies. These boundaries will be subject to adjustment by agreement in the light of changing strategic considerations.

6. The title of the strategic zone, which the Union Government wish to call the 'Southern Africa Strategic Zone', while the United Kingdom Government wish to retain the title 'South Atlantic', will be decided later.

7. The strategic zone will include an area to be known as the 'South African Area', which will be bounded by the coast of South Africa and a line drawn from the northern boundary of South-West Africa through positions:

	Latitude						Longitude
(a)	20°S	.	.	.	.	.	0°
(b)	50°S	.	.	.	.	.	0°
(c)	50°S	.	.	.	.	.	55°E
(d)	30°S	.	.	.	.	.	55°E

to Cap Sainte Marie (Madagascar), and thence to the boundary between Union territory and Portuguese East Africa. These boundaries will be subject to modification by agreement in the light of changing strategic considerations. The Union Government will appoint the Flag Officer commanding the South African area.

8. As agreed between the two Governments, forces will be earmarked in peacetime for assignment to the Commander-in-Chief and assigned to him in time of war as defined in the Annex[1] or emergency likely to lead to such a war.

9. In peacetime the Commander-in-Chief will be directly responsible only to the United Kingdom Government and will have no executive authority over South African forces, establishments, or services. He will, however, have as one of his primary functions the guiding of maritime war planning in the strategic zone, and will be free to confer on these matters, in consultation with the South African Naval Chief of Staff, with the Union Minister of Defence. The position and method of working of the Commander-in-Chief as the designated supreme naval commander in war will be as described in the Annex, which is based on North Atlantic Treaty Organization practice.

10. A joint maritime war planning committee will be set up, containing representatives of the Royal Navy and the South African Navy, one of whose functions will be to co-ordinate the use of all maritime facilities in British and South African territories in the strategic zone.

11. In a war in which both the United Kingdom and the Union are involved the Commander-in-Chief will be granted operational command as defined in the Annex of all forces assigned to his strategic zone.

12. Since on the transfer of the control of the Simonstown Naval Base in accordance with the provisions of the Agreement relating to that subject, Admiralty House and the adjacent offices and residences will be transferred to the Union Government, the Union Government will in agreement with the United Kingdom Government provide headquarters in the Cape area, but outside Simonstown, with requisite communications and operational facilities, for use by the Commander-in-Chief in peace and war. These headquarters will be at Youngsfield, or at Wingfield or any other suitable place in the Cape area at which the Union Government may decide to establish their maritime headquarters.

13. The command and control of the wireless telegraphy installations known as Slangkop, Klaver, and Cape East will be regulated in accordance with the provisions of the Agreement relating to the transfer of the control and administration of the Simonstown Naval Base.

[1] See p. 546 of this volume.

14. It is agreed in principle that exchanges of officers and ratings between the two navies would be of advantage to both navies and should take place whenever practicable. Such exchanges will be effected by mutual agreement between the two Governments.

15. It is agreed that the South African Navy will introduce a definite programme for the recruitment, as well as the subsequent training in the United Kingdom, of Engineering and Electrical Officers in accordance with existing practice.

16. The arrangement outlined in this Agreement will not preclude the association of other Governments with the defence of the strategic zone, should all the Governments concerned so agree. In that event the Union Government would support the United Kingdom Government in the designation of the Royal Naval Commander-in-Chief, South Atlantic, as Commander-in-Chief of the zone.

17. This Agreement will remain in force until such time as the two Governments decide otherwise by mutual agreement.

ANNEX

Naval Command Structure

Responsibilities and Powers of the Naval Commander-in-Chief Designate of the Strategic Zone

1. It is agreed between the two Governments that the Commander-in-Chief of the strategic zone will in accordance with North Atlantic Treaty Organization practice be accorded the following powers and responsibilities, which he will exercise in consultation with the South African Naval Chief of Staff in so far as Union forces or resources are concerned:

In War

(i.e., war in which the Union and the United Kingdom are co-belligerents)

(a) The Commander-in-Chief will be responsible for the overall direction and conduct of maritime operations within the strategic zone, and will have operational command of all forces assigned to the zone by the United Kingdom Government and the Union Government respectively; that is, he will have authority in relation to those forces to assign missions or tasks to subordinate commanders, to deploy units, both within and between subordinate commands, and to retain or assign operational and/or tactical control as he may deem necessary. It does not, of itself, include administrative command or logistic responsibility, which remains a national responsibility.

(*b*) He will be responsible for the co-ordination of plans and operations with adjacent allied naval authorities.

In Peace

2. The Commander-in-Chief will be responsible for:

(*a*) the development of plans and the necessary preparations for the execution of his wartime tasks

(*b*) the organization for and conduct of combined training of such national units as are assigned or earmarked for assignment to his command in war—and which can be made available—so as to ensure that they can operate as an effective and integrated force

(*c*) the establishment of an efficient organization which will be the nucleus for expansion in war for the control of the strategic zone.

3. To fulfil his peacetime functions the Commander-in-Chief will be authorized:

(*a*) to co-ordinate combined training of national maritime forces of the United Kingdom and of the Union earmarked for assignment to the zone in war

(*b*) to call for reports based on inspections, carried out by national authorities, concerned with the state of readiness and efficiency of forces earmarked for his command, but not under his control in peacetime.

Assignment and Earmarking for Assignment of Forces

4. Forces will be assigned, or earmarked for assignment in war, to the Commander-in-Chief as agreed between Governments.

5. In general, forces designed solely for local operations in coastal waters will not be assigned or earmarked for assignment to the Commander-in-Chief. By agreement, however, such forces may also be re-deployed within the limits of the zone if operational developments so require.

I have the honour to confirm on behalf of the Government of the United Kingdom the terms recorded above and should be glad if you would confirm their acceptance by your Government. This letter and your reply to it would then constitute an agreement between our Governments.

I have the honour to be, Sir,

  Your most obedient servant,

Selwyn LLOYD

The Honourable F. C. Erasmus, M.P.

LETTER 4

30th June, 1955

Sir,

I have the honour to refer to your letter of 30th June, regarding our recent discussions in London concerning the defence of the sea routes round Southern Africa and to confirm that the terms recorded in your letter as set out below are acceptable to my Government.

[*See letter 3*]

I hereby confirm that your letter and this reply of mine to it constitute an agreement between our Governments.

I have the honour to be, Sir,

Your most obedient servant,

F. C. ERASMUS

The Right Honourable Selwyn Lloyd, C.B.E., T.D., Q.C., M.P.

III. *Transfer of the Simonstown Naval Base and Arrangements for its Future Use*

LETTER 5

30th June, 1955

Sir,

I have the honour to refer to our recent discussions in London concerning the transfer of the Simonstown Naval Base and to set out the terms of the agreement which we have reached.

AGREEMENT RELATING TO THE TRANSFER OF THE SIMONSTOWN NAVAL BASE

1. Consequent upon the intention of the Union Government to expand the South African Navy as described in the Agreement on defence of the sea routes round Southern Africa, and in order that the Union Government may be able to provide adequate logistic support for their expanded Navy, the United Kingdom Government agree to hand over to the Union Government the administration and control of the Naval Base at Simonstown in accordance with the provisions which follow and will also transfer the title to certain property to be agreed.

2. It is agreed that the Royal Navy will continue to require the use of facilities at the base in peace and in war. The Union Government agree that the facilities of the base will be available for use by the Royal Navy in peace and by the Royal Navy and ships serving with the Royal Navy and by navies of allies of the United Kingdom in any war in which the United Kingdom is involved.

3. In a war in which the Union is a co-belligerent, priority in the allocation of space and facilities in the base between the two navies will be settled by mutual consultation between the Commander-in-Chief of the strategic zone referred to in the Agreement on the defence of sea routes round Southern Africa and the South African Naval Chief of Staff, as strategic and operational needs may require.

4. The expansion of the South African Navy will necessitate the provision for use in war of naval facilities beyond the capacity of Simonstown, so as to ensure that the facilities of the base will in fact be available, to the extent required, for use by the Royal Navy and its allies in any war in which the United Kingdom, but not the Union, is involved. To this end the Union Government will take, if necessary in peace, any measures required to ensure the availability of additional facilities elsewhere in the Union for use by the South African Navy in a war in which the United Kingdom, but not the Union, is involved.

5. The Union Government will maintain the facilities of the base at Simonstown in a state of efficiency not inferior to that existing at the time of transfer.

6. The Union Government agree to expand the facilities of the base to the extent necessary to ensure the fulfilment of this Agreement, taking into account the expansion of the South African Navy referred to in the Agreement on defence of the sea routes round Southern Africa.

7. It is agreed that the Royal Naval Commander-in-Chief, South Atlantic, will retain his present responsibilities for, and authority over, the wireless telegraphy installations known as Slangkop, Klaver, and Cape East until a date to be decided by mutual agreement, when the South African Navy can provide the officers and senior ratings together with the majority of the remaining communications personnel. After the transfer of the wireless telegraphy installations, the Union Government will continue to fulfil the requirements of the world-wide wireless organization of the Royal Navy, and will provide the Commander-in-Chief with the necessary facilities for that purpose; they will also continue to employ Royal Naval personnel for the maintenance of equipment at the two transmitting stations until, by mutual agreement, the South African Navy

are able to provide all the officers and men required for this purpose. The Union Government will, in the event of a war in which the United Kingdom is involved, place the command and control of the wireless telegraphy installations in the hands of the Commander-in-Chief.

8. It is agreed that the necessary detailed preparations for the transfer of the base will be put in hand immediately upon the signing of this Agreement and will be completed as soon as possible. It is further agreed that transfer of administration and control will take place as soon as all the necessary preparations have been made, but not later than 31st March, 1957. Nevertheless, should it become apparent that all the necessary preparations cannot be completed by that date, the two Governments will consult together on the measures to be taken.

9. This Agreement will remain in force until such time as the two Governments decide otherwise by mutual agreement.

I have the honour to confirm on behalf of the Government of the United Kingdom the terms recorded above and should be glad if you would confirm their acceptance by your Government. This letter and your reply to it would then constitute an agreement between our Governments.

I have the honour to be, Sir,

Your most obedient servant,

Selwyn LLOYD

The Honourable F. C. Erasmus, M.P.

LETTER 6

SOUTH AFRICA HOUSE
LONDON, W.C.2

30th June, 1955

Sir,

I have the honour to refer to your letter of 30th June, regarding our recent discussions in London concerning the transfer of the Simonstown Naval Base, and to confirm that the terms recorded in your letter as set out below are acceptable to my Government.

[See Letter 5]

I hereby confirm that your letter and this reply of mine to it constitute an agreement between our Governments.

I have the honour to be, Sir,

Your most obedient servant,

F. C. ERASMUS

The Right Honourable Selwyn Lloyd, C.B.E., T.D., Q.C., M.P.

Letter from Mr. Heath to Lord Brockway,
November 1970

I am writing in reply to your letter of October 29, which you conveyed to me in your capacity as President of the Movement for Colonial Freedom, opposing the sale of arms to South Africa.

The Security Council Resolutions of 1963, to which you referred in your letter, were not mandatory resolutions, and a specific reservation was made at the time by our Permanent Representative at the United Nations, on behalf of Her Majesty's Government, in relation to Britain's right to export arms for external defence. The Security Council Resolution of July 23 of this year is similarly not a mandatory resolution. It has throughout been made clear by the British Representative that no arms will be exported to South Africa which would assist enforcement of the policy of *apartheid*.

We do not support *apartheid* in any way. It would be to negate totally the stand I and my colleagues took over racial issues in the recent General Election if we were to do so.

On the question of the supply of limited categories of arms for maritime defence, we have had very full consultation with Commonwealth leaders and others on this. It is quite clear from these discussions that it is accepted that the British Government is not racialist and that we are strongly opposed to *apartheid*. It has also been widely accepted that we have the right and duty to assess the threat to Britain's interests and to take what measures we think necessary, even though others may disagree with us. Our position in this respect is the same as that of any other member of the Commonwealth, and there is no cause for any damage to be done to the Commonwealth. Nor is there any threat or harm to the interests of other countries. Our consultations are not yet completed, and our decisions will not be taken until they have been.

EDWARD HEATH

PERIODICALS AND OTHER MAJOR SOURCES

THE serious student will find the following sources useful. The list is not confined to sources used in this book.

Africa, ed. by Forde and Pym (International African Institute, London).

Africa Contemporary Record, ed. by Legum and Drysdale (London).

Africa Digest, ed. by Symonds (London).

Africa Report, ed. by Segal (Washington, D.C.).

African Affairs (Royal African Society, London).

African Abstracts, ed. by Forde and Jones (International African Institute, London).

African Recorder, ed. by Khemchand (New Delhi).

African Review, ed. by Shamuyarira and others (Dar es Salaam).

Afrique contemporaine, ed. by Leygnac (La Documentation française, Paris).

Afrique documents (Dakar, 1966–).

Afrique nouvelle (Dakar).

Annuaire des États d'Afrique Noire (Paris).

Annuaire parlementaire des États d'Afrique Noire (Paris).

British and Foreign State Papers, London.

Chronique politique africaine (Paris).

Documents on International Affairs (Royal Institute of International Affairs, London).

International Affairs (Royal Institute of International Affairs, London).

International Development Review, ed. by Hambridge (Washington, D.C.).

International Legal Materials (American Society of International Law, Washington, D.C.).

International Organization (World Peace Foundation, Boston, Mass.).

Journal of African History, ed. by Oliver and Fage (Cambridge).

Journal of Modern African Studies, ed. by D. and H. Kimble (Cambridge).

Journal of World Trade Law, ed. by Thompson (London).

Keesing's Contemporary Archives (London).

OAU Review (Asmara, 1964–).

Politique étrangère (Paris).

Review (Annually—OECD, Paris).

United Nations:
  Economic Commission for Africa. U.N. Documents. E/CN.14.
    Economic Survey of Africa.
    Economic Bulletin for Africa.
    Annual Report to the Economic and Social Council (Economic and Social Council, Official Records, Supplements).
    Statistical Bulletin for Africa.
    Statistical Yearbook of Africa.
  Economic and Social Council (Official Records, Annexes and Supplements).
West Africa (London).

INDEX